Java
Learning to Program with Robots

Byron Weber Becker, University of Waterloo

THOMSON COURSE TECHNOLOGY

Australia • Canada • Mexico • Singapore • Spain • United Kingdom • United States

THOMSON
COURSE TECHNOLOGY

Java: Learning to Program with Robots
by Byron Weber Becker
is published by Thomson Course Technology

Managing Editor:
Mary Franz

Senior Product Manager:
Alyssa Pratt

Production Editor:
Kelly Robinson

Developmental Editor:
Lisa Ruffolo

Associate Product Manager:
Jennifer Smith

Senior Marketing Manager:
Karen Seitz

Senior Manufacturing Coordinator:
Justin Palmeiro

Marketing Coordinator:
Suelaine Frongello

Cover Artist:
Joel Weber Becker

Cover Designer:
Deborah van Rooyen

Compositor:
GEX Publishing Services

Copyeditor:
Lori Cavanaugh

Proofreader:
Green Pen Quality Assurance

Indexer:
Alexandra Nickerson

Printed in the United States

1 2 3 4 5 6 7 8 9 CW 10 09 08 07 06

Disclaimer
Thomson Course Technology reserves the right to revise this publication and make changes from time to time in its content without notice.

For more information, contact Thomson Course Technology, 25 Thomson Place, Boston, MA 02210; or find us on the World Wide Web at www.course.com.

The Web addresses in this book are subject to change from time to time as necessary without notice.

ISBN 0-619-21724-3

Photo Credits
Figure 1-5: Courtesy of NASA/JPL-Caltech
Figure 1-22: Courtesy of the U.S. Navy
Figure 3-3: Cartoon © 2005 ScienceCartoonsPlus.com. Used with permission.
Cover: Drawing © 2001 by Joel Weber Becker. Used with permission.

Some portions of this work are based on *Karel++: A Gentle Introduction to the Art of Object-Oriented Programming* by Joseph Bergin, Mark Stehlik, Jim Roberts, and Richard Pattis. Copyright © 1997 by John Wiley & Sons, Inc. Used with permission of John Wiley & Sons, Inc.

Contents

Preface

The preface includes:

- Why this book exists
- The approach it takes to teaching object-oriented programming
- The advantages of this approach
- A section for students describing the software they need and the features of this book that they will find particularly helpful
- A section for instructors describing the author's *Use, Then Write* object-oriented pedagogy, the organization and coverage of topics, and supplemental resources
- Who helped the author along the way

How It All Started

As often happens, this book exists because the author was unhappy with the alternatives. When I was first asked to develop a Java version of our introductory programming course for 1,000 students a year, I naturally collected all the relevant Java textbooks I could find. They all left me with a vague sense of uneasiness. Yes, the programming language had changed from Pascal to Java, but the approach had not. A second change was necessary: a change in pedagogy.

The first term of my course did not go well. I had chosen what I considered to be the best textbook available, but the experience of teaching with it only confirmed that the pedagogical paradigm shift had not been made. Shortly thereafter I discovered a small book, *Karel++: A Gentle Introduction to the Art of Object-Oriented Programming* (Wiley, 1997). It was an "Aha!" experience for me. The pedagogy of this book felt right to me. In addition, I knew its metaphor of programming robots would appeal to my students, it had an obvious appeal for visual learners, and I could imagine having lots of fun acting out programs with students. Unfortunately, *Karel++* is a C++ textbook, not Java. Furthermore, at only 175 pages and lacking many language-specific details, it forms the first several weeks of an introductory course. After that, a different textbook is required—a textbook that did not exist.

Discussions with the publisher of *Karel++* led to them granting me permission to translate it to Java for use at the University of Waterloo, Ontario, Canada. After experiencing the joys of teaching with the approach—and the difficulties of changing to an unrelated text after a few weeks—I began to write the textbook I really wanted. *Java: Learning to Program with Robots* combines the wonderful pedagogy of *Karel++* with the full and complete treatment required by an introductory object-oriented programming textbook.

Approach

This text begins with programming virtual robots to teach object-oriented programming in general (dark green in Figure 1). Once students are comfortable with many aspects of objects and classes, the examples shift from robots to a much broader set of examples (white). Each chapter ends with a section on graphics and graphical user interfaces (light green), applying the concepts learned to a different context. Transferring the knowledge gained using robots to another problem (graphics) is an important part of mastering the material. The graphics sections at the end of each chapter should be viewed as an integral part of the curriculum.

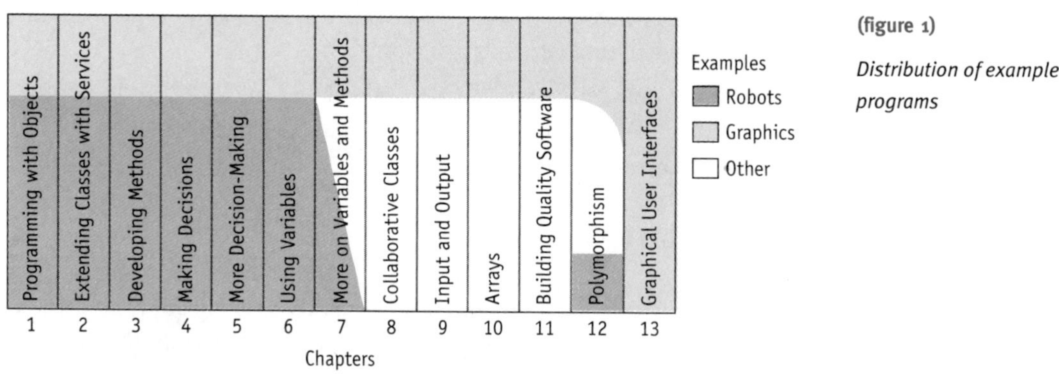

(figure 1)

Distribution of example programs

Starting with Robots

Robots are objects in an object-oriented program that can receive messages telling them to move, turn, pick things up, carry things, and put things down again. We all have a mental image of robots and can easily direct them to perform a task, such as picking up three things in a row and putting them in a pile. This task can be clarified with a pair of diagrams, as shown in Figure 2. The first diagram shows how the task begins: with the robot (an arrowhead) and three things (circles) in front of it. The second diagram shows how the task should end: with the three things all in the same place.

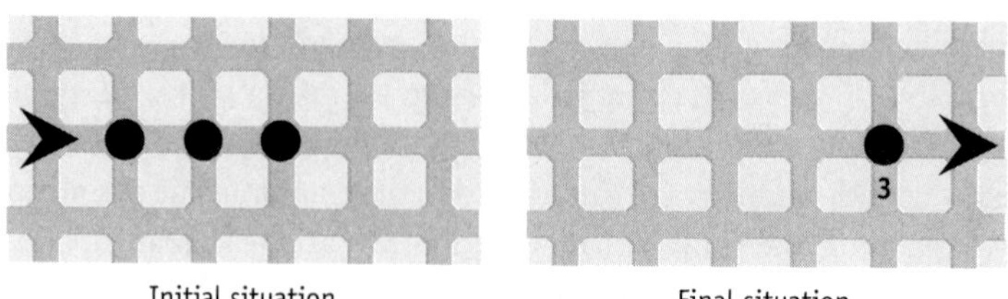

(figure 2)

Robot picking up three things and putting them in a pile

We can easily "program" a student or instructor to complete this task with the following instructions. Assume the person's name is "Karl."

Karl, move
Karl, pick up a thing
Karl, move
Karl, pick up a thing
Karl, move
Karl, pick up a thing
Karl, move
Karl, put down a thing
Karl, put down a thing
Karl, put down a thing
Karl, move

After verbally directing Karl, it is easy to introduce a simple program that does the same thing where karl is the name of a robot object, as follows:

```
karl.move();
karl.pickThing();
karl.move();
karl.pickThing();
karl.move();
karl.pickThing();
karl.move();
karl.putThing();
karl.putThing();
karl.putThing();
karl.move();
```

There are additional details to cover before this Java fragment can be executed as a complete program. However, these details form an easily learned pattern, leaving the focus on using robot objects to accomplish tasks.

Other kinds of objects can be included in robot programs, including walls that can block a robot from moving and lights that can be turned on and off. We can also create new kinds of objects to use.

The fundamental object-oriented concepts learned with robot objects can all be transferred to programs that have nothing to do with robots. Each chapter includes a section focusing on graphics to help with the conceptual transfer. The latter part of the book includes many examples that have nothing to do with robots.

Advantages of Using Robots

Using robots to learn object-oriented programming offers significant advantages. I have used this approach in my classes for half a dozen years, and find that the following qualities are the most important advantages.

Visualization: The visual qualities of robots make it easy to specify a problem using pictures and a few lines of text. They provide visual feedback about the correctness of the program. Watching the robot traverse the screen makes debugging easier. This text makes the most of the human brain's highly optimized processing of visual input.

Ease of Programming: Object-oriented programs are easier to write when programmers can imagine what they would do if they were the objects in the program. Robot objects make this easy. Because moving, turning, picking things up, and putting them down again are activities that we do every day, it is easy for us to give directions to one another or to a robot object. Even though this method is easier to grasp, we still learn important object-oriented programming concepts.

Fun: Robots are fun! I have never had so much fun with a classroom of students as the day we worked with a "paranoid" robot that "looked" to the right and to the left before it moved forward. People who acted it out adopted a hunched, uptight look with shifty eyes that generated much laughter among the students. Later in the same period, we turned this into a paranoid thief that went up the aisle swiping small objects from student desks, all the while looking both ways before it would move. It was fun, but it also taught students about inheritance, one of the three hallmarks of object-oriented programming.

Quick Startup: The robot microworld allows students to begin object-oriented programming immediately using real objects in a real programming environment. Similar approaches often use graphics alone, but robots are more intuitive than graphics and have many more interesting algorithmic aspects.

Pedagogy: Finally, I believe that the largest benefit of using robots is that they lend themselves to a superior pedagogy for teaching object-oriented programming. This ultimate benefit is more fully explained in a later section of this Preface, For Instructors.

For Students

You are about to embark on an exciting journey of learning to program using Java. Before we begin, let's take a few moments to orient ourselves to this textbook and to the software you will need to complete all the exercises in the book.

Textbook Features

This textbook includes a number of features to make your life as a student easier. They include the following:

Objectives: A brief list of objectives appears at the beginning of each chapter to provide an overview of the chapter contents. Knowing your destination helps you make the most of your journey through the chapter.

Program listings: Each chapter contains many examples of working code demonstrating the principles under discussion. The code is often shown as a complete listing that is available for you to download, modify, and run yourself.

Figures: Each chapter provides a rich collection of figures to help illustrate the concepts. Figures include UML diagrams, illustrations of robot programs, flowcharts, screen shots of program output, and many others illustrating program features, object-oriented concepts, and the principles of effective program design.

Key terms and glossary: Every discipline has its own vocabulary, including computer science. When a term is used for the first time, it's highlighted. A complete glossary in Appendix A is a handy reference for those times that you need a reminder.

Margin notes: The margin of each chapter contains four types of notes. *Find the Code* notes direct you to files containing sample code. *Key Idea* notes summarize key ideas discussed on the page and help you review. *Looking Back* notes link current discussions with ideas covered earlier in the book. *Looking Ahead* notes preview concepts or techniques introduced in later chapters.

Pattern icons and discussion: In addition to margin notes, each chapter includes pattern icons to highlight code or to explain common programming patterns. Learning to recognize these patterns is an important part of becoming a good programmer. A section named "Patterns" near the end of each chapter summarizes the patterns and generalizes them so that they're more broadly applicable.

Graphical user interface sections: Each chapter includes a section presenting the chapter's topics in the context of graphical user interfaces, helping you transfer your understanding to new situations. In addition, many of the problems in each chapter have a graphical user interface to make your homework look more like the programs you use every day. In the early chapters, the interface is provided by the robot world. In the middle chapters, graphical user interfaces are often provided to work with the code you write. In the last chapter, you will write the interfaces yourself.

Concept maps and summaries: Each chapter concludes with a brief written summary of the important concepts, followed by a concept map. The concept map gives a visual representation of the ideas discussed and how they are related to each other.

Obtaining and Installing Software

Writing programs requires tools. A minimal set of tools is a text editor and the Java Development Kit (JDK) from Sun Microsystems. The JDK is included in the CD-ROM that accompanies this textbook. Updates can be downloaded from *www.java.sun.com/j2se/*. The software you will be using with this textbook requires Java 5 or higher (also known as JDK 1.5).

Another approach is to use an Integrated Development Environment (IDE). It integrates the text editor and development tools such as the JDK into one environment that is optimized specifically for writing programs. The CD-ROM includes two such IDEs, JCreator and jGrasp. Others include Dr. Java (*www.drjava.org/*), BlueJ (*www.bluej.org/*), and Eclipse (*www.eclipse.org/*). Of these, JCreator and Eclipse are aimed at programmers; the others are developed specifically for students. All of the IDEs listed here have a free version.

In addition to the JDK or an IDE, the introductory programs in this textbook require software implementing the robots. This software and documentation is available on the Robots Web site, *www.learningwithrobots.com*, and on the CD-ROM.

Instructions for installing the software and documentation is available on the CD-ROM (open `InstallationInstructions.html` with your Web browser) and on the Robots Web site (*www.learningwithrobots.com/InstallationInstructions.html*).

For Instructors

Robots uses objects to their fullest extent from day one, but doesn't overwhelm the students. How? It provides a rich set of classes that students use to learn about objects *before* they are asked to write their own classes. Let's explore this *Use, Then Write* pedagogy further by comparing it with the alternatives.

Object-Oriented Pedagogies

The concepts of object and class are intimately related. Each kind of object in a student's program is created from a class that a programmer writes to define the objects' characteristics. Given that students need to master both using objects and writing the classes that define them, a crucial question is how to order these topics. There are three possibilities for *writing* classes and *using* the resulting objects:

Write and use: In this approach students are asked to master the basics of writing a class at the same time they are learning how to use objects. One author, for example, introduces classes and objects by describing how to use a bank account object in only two pages. The author then delves into the details of writing the class to define it. This requires introducing students to the distinction between class and object, declaring objects, object instantiation, invoking methods, the structure of a class, defining methods, declaring parameters and passing arguments, return values, and instance variables. This presents an incredible cognitive load for students. The author chose a wonderful example to convey all these concepts, but it is still difficult to understand all the concepts all at once, even at an introductory level.

Write, then use: When actually writing a program, programmers first write the required classes and then use the objects they define. I am aware of only one textbook that has chosen to follow this same ordering. It includes a light treatment on the idea of an object, but then delves into the details of writing classes with very few examples of how the objects they define would be used. This lessens the cognitive load on the students by focusing on just one of the two aspects, but leaves students wondering how these classes are used. Much of the instruction on writing classes is lost because students don't have practical experience in using the resulting objects.

Use, then write: A third possibility is to first use objects and then learn how to write classes defining new kinds of objects. *Robots* uses this approach. Students make extensive use of robot objects, learning how to declare objects, instantiate objects, and invoke their methods. All the details of writing their own classes come later, after they are comfortable with using objects.

Robots provides a gentle but thorough introduction to object-oriented programming using the *Use, Then Write* pedagogy. It's an approach that helps students write interesting, object-oriented programs right away. It uses objects early and consistently, even with the traditional subjects of selection and repetition. Furthermore, it has been classroom tested with over 6,000 students at the University of Waterloo.

Organization and Coverage

Chapter 1, "Programming with Objects," introduces students to instantiating and using objects.

Chapter 2, "Extending Classes with Services," discusses extending an existing class with new parameterless methods.

Chapter 3, "Developing Methods," continues the theme of writing methods, but with a focus on strategies for writing complex methods—pseudocode and stepwise refinement.

Chapter 4, "Making Decisions," explores how to alter a program's flow with repetition and selection, and includes the basics of the Boolean expressions used in such constructs. Introducing parameters adds even more flexibility to the methods students write.

Chapter 5, "More Decision Making," continues exploring decision-making constructs with a process for writing correct loops, additional control statements, and manipulating Boolean expressions. Temporary (local) variables are introduced to simplify some algorithms.

Chapter 6, "Using Variables," introduces integer instance variables and constants, and expands on using temporary variables and parameter variables.

Chapter 7, "More on Variables and Methods," examines using variables with types other than `int`, including strings. Queries are used to examine the state of an object and to test it using a test harness. This chapter also includes the first large case study that does not involve robots or graphics.

Chapter 8, "Collaborative Classes," presents classes that use references to another class and thoroughly explores the differences between reference types and primitive types. Exceptions are introduced, as well as Java collections to collaborate with many objects.

Chapter 9, "Input and Output," covers reading information from files, writing information to files, and interacting with users via the console.

Chapter 10, "Arrays," explains how to work with arrays. A number of algorithms are discussed, including a careful treatment of Selection Sort. Handling changing numbers of elements and multi-dimensional arrays are also covered.

Chapter 11, "Building Quality Software," identifies characteristics of quality software and explains how to follow a development process that promotes quality.

Chapter 12, "Polymorphism," explores writing polymorphic programs using inheritance and interfaces. It also discusses building an inheritance hierarchy and using the strategy and factory method patterns to make programs more flexible.

Chapter 13, "Graphical User Interfaces," examines how to write a graphical user interface using existing Java components, structure a graphical user interface using the model-view-controller pattern and multiple views, and write new components for use in graphical user interfaces.

Dependencies

This text is, of necessity, printed in a particular order. You may find that a different organization suits you and your students better. The dependency chart shown in Figure 3 serves as a guide to reordering the material. The core material is shown with heavy lines and should be presented in the order shown. Other material can be rearranged around it at your discretion.

Textbook Features

Most of the textbook's features are listed in the section for students. Three features that instructors are more likely than students to appreciate are listed here:

Written exercises: The problem set at the end of each chapter includes written exercises, which provide an opportunity for students to synthesize the ideas and techniques they have learned in the chapter.

Programming exercises: The problem sets also include programming exercises, which prompt students to write, improve, or experiment with smaller programs.

Programming projects: Finally, the problem sets present projects that encourage students to create complete classes or programs.

Supplemental Resources

The following ancillary materials are available when this book is used in a classroom setting. All of the teaching tools available with this book are provided to the instructor on a single CD.

Instructor's Manual: Additional instructional material to assist in class preparation, including suggested syllabi for 14 and 16 week courses, and complete lecture notes.

PowerPoint Presentations®: This book comes with Microsoft PowerPoint slides for each chapter. In addition to reviewing the chapter, they contain examples and case studies illustrating the current topics. The slides are included as a teaching aid for classroom presentation, to make available to students on the network for chapter review, or to be printed for classroom distribution. Instructors can add their own slides for additional topics they may introduce to the class.

Solution Files: Sample solutions to most exercises.

Example Programs: The source code to almost all of the Java programs listed in this book are easily available to you and your students. They are on the CD accompanying each copy of the book, the Instructor Resources CD, the book's Web site (*www.learningwithrobots.com*), and the Thomson Course Technology Web site.

ExamView Test Bank: This assessment tool can help instructors design and administer tests.

Software: JDK 5.0, jGRASP, and JCreator are included with each copy of this book. Also provided are the libraries containing the robot classes. These libraries work with any Java development environment (JDK 5.0 and above) and permit you to write, run, and animate robot programs. Because a regular development environment is used, students do

(figure 3)

Dependency chart

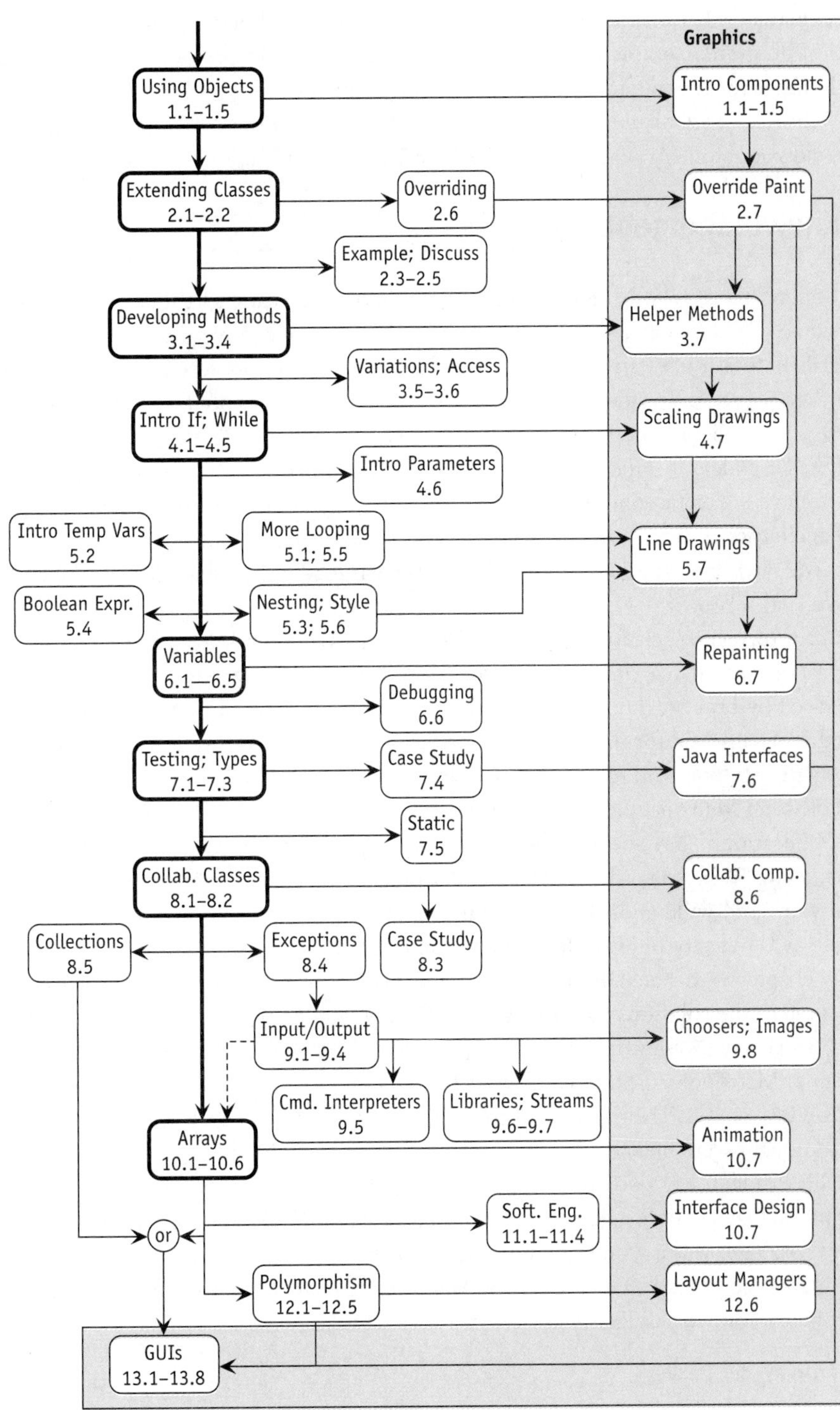

not experience a transition in technology from writing robot programs to any other kind of program. Complete graphical user interfaces are also provided in the supporting libraries for use in a number of homework problems.

Web site: *www.learningwithrobots.com* makes many of these resources available to you and your students wherever you have an Internet connection.

Acknowledgements

In recalling those who have helped this book become a reality, I think of five groups of people.

Originators: Rich Pattis developed the idea of using robots to teach programming in the early 1980s. The idea was later adapted to an object-oriented style by Joe Bergin. These are the giants upon whose shoulders this work stands. Without them, this text and the core ideas it builds on would not exist. Thank you to Rich, in particular, who has been very encouraging of my attempts to adapt his ideas to a full CS1 textbook.

Facilitators: Bruce Spatz, Bill Zobrist, Paul Crockett, and all of John Wiley and Sons were flexible with their intellectual property rights to the original Karel the Robot book. Thank you.

Brainstormers: Jack Rehder, Judene Pretti, and Arnie Dyck are all wonderful colleagues of mine at the University of Waterloo. Much of the text has been shaped and improved by brainstorming sessions with them in the course of teaching this material together. Thank you for the ideas, the clarifications, and the suggestions. A large group of other instructors and tutors also contributed in countless smaller ways.

Polishers: Many people helped put the finishing touches on this book to get it ready for publication. They include the team at Course Technology: Lisa Ruffolo, Alyssa Pratt, Kelly Robinson, Mary Franz, and Mac Mendelsohn. Thank you for all your hard work and willingness to listen to my views on the design. Carrie Howells, a colleague at University of Waterloo, did a wonderful job of proofreading and critiquing many chapters. Michael Diramio, one of our former tutors, rescued my sanity by writing some of the solutions to problem sets. Finally, a huge thank you to the reviewers: John Ridgeway (Wesleyan University), Mary Goodwin (Illinois State University), Noel LeJeune (Metropolitan State College of Denver), and especially Rich Pattis (Carnegie Mellon University). Their insightful comments caused me to rework many sections that I had thought were finished.

Cheerleaders: My two sons, Luke and Joel, who can hardly wait to learn to program with "Dad's robots," cheered me on. Joel's artwork graces the cover. A colleague, Sandy Graham, was a wonderful evangelist for the approach.

Finally, the biggest thank you is to Ann, the most wonderful woman a man could ever marry, for her indulgence as I wrote.

—Byron Weber Becker

Chapter 1 Programming with Objects

Chapter Objectives

After studying this chapter, you should be able to:

- Describe models
- Describe the relationship between objects and classes
- Understand the syntax and semantics of a simple Java program
- Write object-oriented programs that simulate robots
- Understand and fix errors that can occur when constructing a program
- Read documentation for classes
- Apply the concepts learned with robots to display a window as used in a graphical user interface

A computer program usually models something. It might be the ticket sales for a concert, the flow of money in a corporation, or a game set in an imaginary world. Whatever that something is, a computer program abstracts the relevant features into a model, and then uses the model to help make decisions, predict the future, answer questions, or build a picture of an imaginary world.

In this chapter, we create programs that model a world filled with robots, directing them to move, turn, pick up, transport, and put down things. This robot world is simple to model, but quickly reveals key concepts of object-oriented programming: objects, classes, attributes, and services.

1.1 Modeling with Objects

Fifteen years ago I went to the local concert hall and asked the ticket agent for two tickets for the March 21 concert. "Where do you want to sit?" he asked.

"That depends on what's available," I answered.

The agent grabbed a printed map of the concert hall. It was clearly dated "March 21," noted the name of the performer, and showed a map of the auditorium's seats. Seats that had already been sold were marked with a red X. The seats were also color-coded: the most expensive seats were green, the moderately priced seats were black, and the least expensive seats were blue.

Fifteen years ago, the ticket agent showed me the map and stabbed his finger on a pair of seats. "These are the best seats left, but the choice is yours."

I quickly scanned the map and noticed that a pair of less expensive seats with almost the same sightlines was not far away. I chose the cheaper seats, and the agent promptly marked them with a red X.

Fast-forward fifteen years. Today I order tickets from the comfort of my home over the Web. I visit the concert hall's Web site and find the performance I want. I click the "purchase tickets online" button and am shown a color-coded map of the theatre. I click on the seats I want, enter my credit card information, and am assured that the tickets will be mailed to me promptly.

1.1.1 Using Models

A **model** is a simplified description of something. It helps us, for example, make decisions, predict future events, maintain up-to-date information, simulate a process, and so forth. Originally, the local concert hall modeled ticket sales with a simple paper map of the auditorium. Later, a Web-based computerized model performed the same functions—and probably many more.

KEY IDEA

A model is a simplified description of something.

To be useful, a model must be able to answer one or more questions. The paper-based model of ticket sales could be used to answer questions such as:

- What is the date of the concert?
- Who is playing?
- How many tickets have been sold to date?
- How many tickets are still unsold?
- Is the ticket for seat 22H still available?
- What is the price of the ticket for seat 22H?

- Which row has unsold tickets for 10 consecutive seats and is closest to the stage?
- What is the total value of all the tickets sold to date?

Models often change over time. For instance, the ticket sales model was updated with two new red X's when I bought my tickets. Without being updated, the model quickly diverges from the thing it represents and loses its value because the answers it provides are wrong.

We often speak of models or elements of a model as if they were real. When the ticket agent pointed to the map and said, "These are the best seats left," we both knew that what he was pointing at were not seats, but only images that *represented* actual seats. The model provided a correspondence. Anyone could use that model to find those two seats in the concert hall.

We often build models without even being aware of it. For example, you might make a mental list of the errands you want to run before having supper ready for your roommate at 6 o'clock, as shown in Figure 1-1: stopping at the library to pick up a book (10 minutes), checking e-mail on a public terminal at the library (5 minutes), and buying a few groceries (10 minutes). Checking your watch (it's 4:15) and factoring in 45 minutes for the bike ride home and 30 minutes to prepare supper, you estimate that you can do it all, with a little time to spare. It takes longer than expected, however, to find the book, and there's a line at the library checkout counter. The library errand took 20 minutes instead of 10. Now it's 4:35, and you must make some choices based on your updated model: have supper a little late, skip the e-mail, hope that you can cook supper in 25 minutes instead of 30, and so forth. You have been modeling your time usage for the next two hours.

(figure 1-1)

Sample schedule

```
4:15 Pick up library book.
4:25 Check e-mail.
4:30 Buy groceries.
4:40 Bike home.
5:25 Cook supper.
6:00 Supper.
```

KEY IDEA

Models focus on relevant features.

Models form an **abstraction.** Abstractions focus only on the relevant information and organize the remaining details into useful higher-level "chunks" of information. People can only manage about seven pieces of information at a time, so we must carefully choose the information we manage. By using abstraction to eliminate or hide some details and group similar details together into a chunk, we can manage more complex ideas. Abstraction is the key to dealing with complexity.

For example, the ticket sales model gives ticket buyers and agents information about which tickets are available, where the corresponding seats are located, and their price. These were all relevant to my decision of which tickets to purchase. The map did not provide information about the seat's fabric color, and I really didn't care, because that was irrelevant to my decision. Furthermore, the color-coding of the concert hall map conveniently chunked information, which helped me make a decision quickly. It was easier to see all the least expensive seats in blue rather than consulting a long list of seat numbers.

Beyond information, models also provide operations that can be performed on them. In the concert hall model operations include "sell a ticket" and "add a new concert." In the informal time management model for errands, operations include "insert a new errand," "drop an errand from the list," and "recompute the estimated start time for each errand."

1.1.2 Using Software Objects to Create Models

The concert hall's computer program and the paper map it replaced model the ticket-selling problem using different technologies. One uses pre-printed sheets of paper marked with a simple X. The other involves a computer with a detailed set of instructions, called a **program**. If the program is written in an **object-oriented programming language**, such as Java, the computer program uses cooperating **software objects**. A software object usually corresponds to an identifiable entity in the problem. The concert hall program probably has an object modeling the concert hall's physical layout, a collection of objects that each models a seat in the concert hall, and another collection of objects that each models an upcoming concert. A program maintaining student enrollments in courses would likely model each student with an object, and use other objects to model each course.

KEY IDEA

Object-oriented programs use software objects to model the problem at hand.

KEY IDEA

Computer science has a specialized vocabulary to allow precise communication. You must learn this vocabulary.

Each of the software objects can perform tasks such as:

- Maintain information about part of the problem the program models.
- Answer questions about that part of the problem based on the information it maintains.
- Change its information to reflect changes in the real-world entity it models.

The information kept by the object is called its **attributes**. Objects respond to **queries** for information and to **commands** to change their attributes. Queries and commands are collectively referred to as **services**. An object provides these services to other objects, called **clients**. The object providing the service is called, appropriately, the **server**. We will explore these concepts in the coming pages.

KEY IDEA

Server objects provide services—queries and commands—to client objects.

Queries and Attributes

Queries are the questions to which an object can respond. A query is always answered by the object to which it is directed. It might be true or false ("Is the ticket for seat 22H still for sale?"), a number ("How many tickets have been sold?"), a string of characters

("What is the name of the band that is playing?"), or even another object such as a date object ("What is the date of the concert?"). Queries are said to `return` answers to their clients. An object can't respond to just any query, only to those it was designed and programmed to support.

KEY IDEA

Objects have attributes. Answers to queries are based on the values of the attributes.

The answers provided by queries are always based on the object's attributes. If an object must answer the query, "What is the date of the concert?" then it must have an attribute with information about the date. Similarly, if it must answer the question, "How many tickets have been sold to date?" it must have an attribute that has that information directly, or it must have a way to calculate that information, perhaps by counting the number of tickets that have been sold. Information about which tickets have been sold would be kept in an attribute.

The concert hall's program must model ticket sales for many concerts, each represented by its own concert object. If we look at several concert objects, we'll notice they all have the same set of attributes, although the values of those attributes may be different. One way to show the differing attribute values is with an **object diagram**, as shown in Figure 1-2. Each rounded rectangle represents a different concert object. The type of object is shown at the top. Below that is a table with attribute names on the left and attribute values on the right. For example, the attribute "date" has a value of "21-March-2008" for one concert. That same concert has the value "Great Big Sea" for the "performer" attribute.

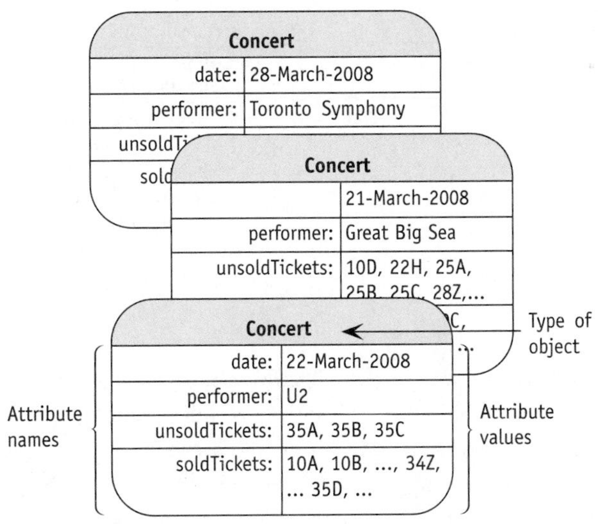

(figure 1-2)

Object diagram showing three concert objects with their attributes

One analogy for objects is that an object is like a form, such as an income tax form. The government prints millions of copies of the form asking for a person's name, address, taxpayer identification number, earned income, and so forth. Each piece of information is provided in a little box, appropriately labeled on the form. Each copy of the form starts like all the others. When filled out, however, each form has unique values in those boxes. It could be that two people have exactly the same income and birthday, with the result that some forms have the same values in the same boxes—but that's only a coincidence.

Just as each copy of that tax form asks for the same information, every concert object has the same set of attributes. Each copy of the form is filled out with information for a specific taxpayer; likewise, each concert object's attributes have values for a specific concert. In general, there may be many objects of a given type. All have the same set of attributes, but probably have different values for those attributes.

KEY IDEA

Every object of a given type has the same set of attributes, but usually has different values for the attributes.

Commands

When a ticket is sold for seat 22H for the March 21 concert, the appropriate concert object must record that fact. This record keeping is done with a command. The object is "commanded" to change its attributes to reflect the new reality. This change can be visualized with a **state change diagram**, as shown in Figure 1-3. A state change diagram shows the state of the object before the command and the state of the object after the command. The **state** is the set of attributes and their values at a given point in time. As time passes, it is normal for the state of an object to change.

KEY IDEA

Commands change the state of the object.

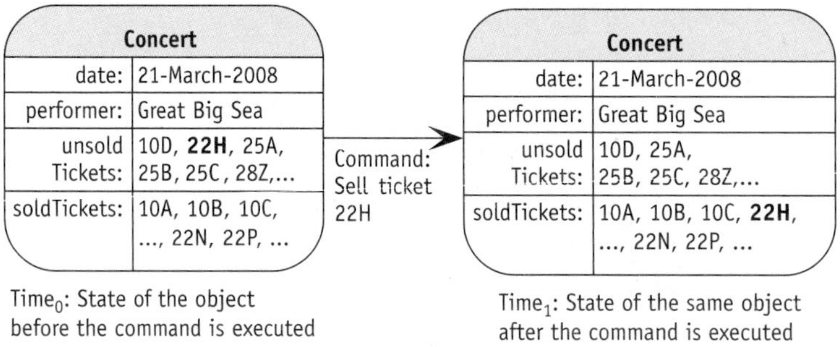

Concert (Time$_0$)

date:	21-March-2008
performer:	Great Big Sea
unsold Tickets:	10D, **22H**, 25A, 25B, 25C, 28Z,...
soldTickets:	10A, 10B, 10C, ..., 22N, 22P, ...

Command: Sell ticket 22H →

Concert (Time$_1$)

date:	21-March-2008
performer:	Great Big Sea
unsold Tickets:	10D, 25A, 25B, 25C, 28Z,...
soldTickets:	10A, 10B, 10C, **22H**, ..., 22N, 22P, ...

Time$_0$: State of the object before the command is executed

Time$_1$: State of the same object after the command is executed

(figure 1-3)

State change diagram showing the change in state after a command to sell seat 22H is given to a concert object

Classes

When we write a Java program, we don't write objects, we write classes. A **class** is a definition for a group of objects that have the same attributes and services. A programmer writing the concert hall program would write a concert class to specify that all concert objects have attributes storing the concert's date, performers, and so on. The class also specifies services that all concert objects have, such as "sell a ticket," and "how many tickets have been sold?"

KEY IDEA

A Java programmer writes a class by specifying the attributes and services the classes' objects will possess.

Once a concert class is defined, the programmer can use it to create as many concert objects as she needs. Each object is an **instance**, or one particular example, of a class. When an object is first brought into existence, we sometimes say it has been **instantiated**.

The distinction between class and object is important. It's the same as the distinction between a factory and the cars made in the factory, or the distinction between a cookie cutter and the cookies it shapes. The pattern used to sew a dress is different from the dress produced from it, just as a blueprint is different from the house it specifies. In each case, one thing (the class, factory, or cookie cutter) specifies what something else (objects, cars, or cookies) will be like. Furthermore, classes, factories, and cookie cutters can all be used to make many instances of the things they specify. One factory makes many cars; one class can make many objects. Finally, just as most of us are not interested in cookie cutters for their own sakes, but in the cookies made from them, our primary interest in classes is to get what we really want: software objects that help model some problem for us.

Class Diagrams

KEY IDEA

A class diagram summarizes all of the objects belonging to that class.

Just as architects and dress designers communicate parts of their designs visually through blueprints and patterns, software professionals use diagrams to design, document, and communicate their programs. We've already seen an object diagram in Figure 1-2 and a state change diagram (consisting of two object diagrams) in Figure 1-3. Another kind of diagram is the **class diagram**. Class diagrams show the attributes and services common to all objects belonging to the class. The class diagram for the concert class summarizes all the possible concert objects by showing the attributes and services each object has in common with all other concert objects.

A class diagram is a rectangle divided into three areas (see Figure 1-4). The top area contains the name of the class. Attributes are named in the middle area, and services are in the bottom area.

(figure 1-4)

Class diagram for the Concert class showing four attributes and six services

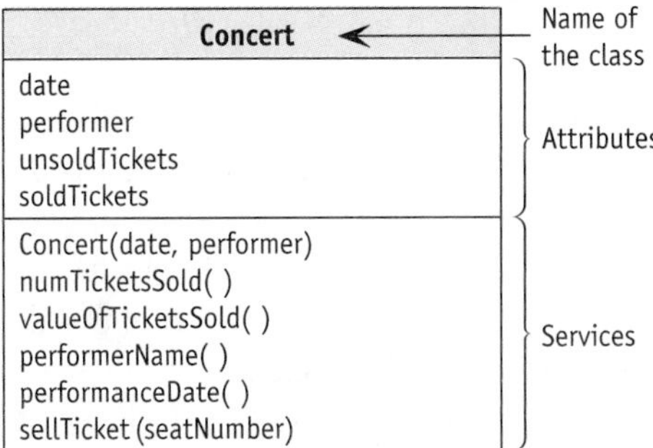

1.1.3 Modeling Robots

Every computer program has a model of a problem. Sometimes the problem is tangible, such as tracking concert ticket sales or the time required to run errands before supper. At other times, the problem may be more abstract: the future earnings of a company under a given set of assumptions or the energy loss of a house. Sometimes the problem is to visualize a figment of someone's imagination, such as a game set on a far-off world at some point in the future.

Many of the programs in this textbook model imaginary robots and the city in which they operate. The programs cause robots to move on the computer screen as they perform various tasks. This model was chosen to be basic enough to grasp easily, yet complex enough to be interesting; simple enough to be easy to program, yet rich enough to show many important object-oriented concepts. The robots and their world are described in Section 1.2. Section 1.3 describes using software objects to model the robots, and Section 1.4 will present the first program.

The robots our programs model are similar to the small robotic explorers NASA landed on Mars. The first, named Sojourner, landed on Mars on July 4, 1997. It could move around the Martian landscape, take photographs, and conduct scientific experiments. Sojourner was about two feet long and could travel at a top speed of two feet per minute. A photo of the explorer is shown in Figure 1-5.

(figure 1-5)

Sojourner, a robotic explorer landed on Mars by NASA

Sojourner was controlled from Earth via radio signals. Because radio signals take approximately 11 minutes to travel from Earth to Mars, Sojourner could not be controlled in real time. (Imagine trying to drive a car with a minimum of 22 minutes elapsing between turning the steering wheel and receiving feedback about the change in direction.) Instead, controllers on Earth carefully mapped out the movements and tasks Sojourner was to do, encoding them as a sequence of messages. These messages were sent to Sojourner, which then attempted to carry them out. Feedback regarding the entire sequence of messages was sent back to Earth, where controllers then worked out the next sequence of messages.

Sojourner had a computer on board to interpret the messages it received from Earth into electrical signals to control its motion and scientific instruments. The computer's processor was an Intel 80C85 processor containing only 6,500 transistors and executing about 100,000 instructions per second. This processor was used almost 15 years earlier in the Radio Shack TRS-80 home computer.

In contrast, a top-of-the-line Pentium processor in 1997 had about 7.5 million transistors and executed about 300,000,000 instructions per second.

Why did Sojourner use such a primitive processor? The 80C85 consumes tiny amounts of power compared with its state-of-the-art cousins and is much more likely to operate correctly in the presence of cosmic rays and extreme temperatures.

1.2 Understanding Karel's World

KEY IDEA

Karel's world is one of the "realities" we will be modeling with software.

The city where `karel`[1] the robot exists is pretty plain. It includes other robots, with a range of capabilities. It also includes intersections connected by avenues and streets on which robots travel, and where there may be several kinds of things. However, the city does not include office buildings, restaurants, traffic lights, newspaper dispensers, or homes. As you learn to program, you may want to change that fact.

1.2.1 Avenues, Streets, and Intersections

What a city does have are **roads**. Some roads, called **streets**, run east and west, while other roads, called **avenues**, run north and south. (A helpful way to remember which is which is that the "A" and "v" in "Avenue" point up and down—or north and south on a map—whereas the cross strokes of the "t"s in "Street" run east and west.)

Streets and avenues are both numbered starting with 0. This convention is unusual among urban planners, but normal among Java programmers. Street 0 is located on the north (top) side, while Avenue 0 runs along the west (left) side. The place where these two roads meet is called the **origin**.

Figure 1-6 shows a small portion of a city with a robot facing east at the origin and another facing south at the intersection of 1st Street and 2nd Avenue. We can use a shorthand notation for specifying intersections. Instead of "1st Street and 2nd Avenue," we can write (1, 2). The first number in the pair gives the street, and the second gives the avenue.

[1] We will often name robots "karel" (pronounced "kär-əl"—the same as "Karl" or "Carl") in recognition of the Czechoslovakian dramatist Karel Capek (1890–1938), who popularized the word *robot* in his 1921 play R.U.R. (Rossum's Universal Robots). The word *robot* is derived from the Czech word *robota*, meaning "forced labor." The name is lowercase, in keeping with Java style.

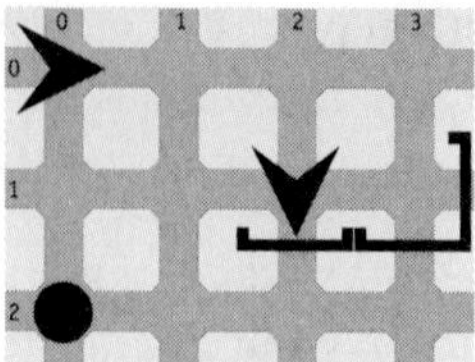

(figure 1-6)

Small city with two robots, one at the origin facing east and one at the intersection of 1st Street and 2nd Avenue facing south

Intersections are unusually wide. Many robots can be on the same intersection at the same time without interfering with each other.

1.2.2 Walls and (other) Things

Intersections may be surrounded by **walls** on one or more sides. A wall stands at an edge of an intersection and blocks robots from entering or leaving the intersection in that direction. Robots can't push walls out of the way. A small extension on the end of each wall extends toward the intersection containing the wall.

The city shown in Figure 1-6 contains three walls, including two at the edges of the intersection at (1, 3). Another wall is immediately in front of the robot at (1, 2) and blocks it from proceeding south. The robot may go around the wall, of course.

Intersections may also have nondescript things. They are purposefully nondescript so we can imagine them to be whatever we want them to be: newspapers, lights, pieces of carpet, or flags. One such thing appears at (2, 0) in Figure 1-6. Robots can usually pick a thing up, put it in a backpack to carry it somewhere else, and then put it down again.

Eventually we will learn how to define classes of things with different appearances and services. Two examples already exist: flashers, like you might find marking a construction site, and streetlights.

1.2.3 Robots

Robots exist to serve their clients. The four services they perform most often are moving, turning, picking things up, and putting things down. Some additional services robots provide include answering queries about their location and direction, and responding to a command controlling their speed.

These are primitive services. Clients using a robot must give many small instructions to tell the robot how to perform a task. Beginning with Chapter 2, we will learn how to create new kinds of robots that provide services tailored to solving the problem at hand.

KEY IDEA

Software objects, such as robots, do things only in response to messages.

Robots don't do anything of their own volition. They respond only to **messages** sent to them from outside themselves. A robot performs a service only when it is invoked by a corresponding message.

In the following sections, we will look at these services in more detail.

Turning

When a robot receives a `turnLeft` message, it responds by turning left 90 degrees. When a robot facing north receives the `turnLeft` message, it turns to face west. A south-facing robot responds to a `turnLeft` message by turning to face east. When a robot turns, it remains on the same intersection.

Robots always start out facing one of the four compass points: north, south, east, or west. Because robots can turn only in 90-degree increments, they always face one of those four directions (except while they are in the act of turning).

LOOKING AHEAD

In Chapter 2, we will create a new kind of robot that responds to a `turnRight` *message.*

Robots do not have a `turnRight` instruction because it is not needed; three `turnLeft` messages accomplish the same task.

Turning is a safe activity. Unlike moving, picking things up, or putting things down, nothing can go wrong when turning.

Moving

When a robot receives a `move` message, it attempts to move from its current intersection to the next intersection in the direction it is facing. It remains facing the same direction. Robots can't stop between intersections; they are either on an intersection or in the process of moving to another one.

Things can go wrong when a robot receives a `move` message. In particular, if there is a wall immediately in front of a robot, moving causes that robot to break. When a robot breaks, it is displayed in three pieces, as shown in Figure 1-7, an error message is printed on the screen, and the program halts. An example of the error message is shown in Figure 1-20.

(figure 1-7)

When a robot facing a wall receives a `move` *command, it crashes into the wall, breaks, and can no longer respond to commands*

Robot facing a wall

Receiving a `move` command and crashing

Handling Things

When a robot receives a `pickThing` message, it attempts to pick up a thing from its current intersection. If there are several things the robot could pick up, it randomly chooses one of them. Robots have a backpack where they carry the things they pick up. Things are small and the backpack is large, so many things fit in it. Robots can also put things down in response to the `putThing` message.

As you might expect, a robot can experience difficulties in handling things. If a robot receives a `pickThing` message when there is nothing to pick up on the current intersection, the robot breaks. Similarly, when a robot receives a `putThing` message and its backpack is empty, the robot breaks. As with moving, after such a malfunction the robot appears damaged, an error message is printed, and the program halts.

LOOKING AHEAD

In Chapter 4 we will learn how to write programs where robots can detect if something can be picked up.

1.3 Modeling Robots with Software Objects

Not surprisingly, the software we will use to model robots mirrors the description in the previous section in many ways. Software objects model intersections, robots, walls, and things.

The software does not actually control real, physical robots that you can touch. Instead, it displays images of robots on the computer screen. The programs we will write cause the images to move about the city (also displayed on the screen) and perform various tasks. These programs are only useful in that they provide an excellent way to learn how to program a computer. You can transfer the knowledge you gain in writing robot programs to writing programs that model the problems that concern you.

As shown earlier in Figure 1-4, we can summarize objects with a class diagram that shows the attributes and services of each object belonging to the class. A class diagram for the `Robot` class is shown in Figure 1-8. The class diagram shows the four services discussed earlier, along with a special service to construct `Robot` objects.

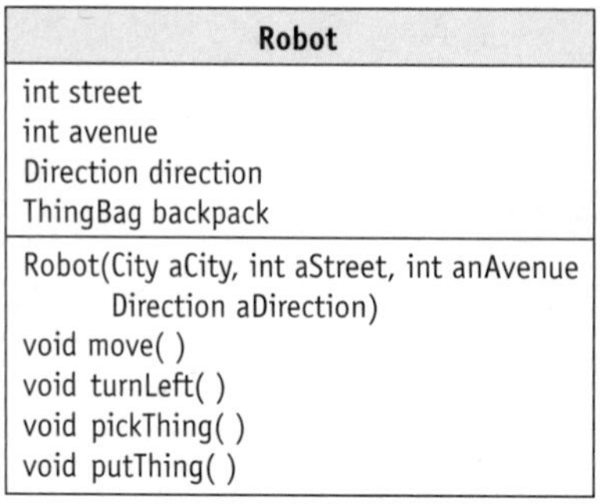

Robot
int street int avenue Direction direction ThingBag backpack
Robot(City aCity, int aStreet, int anAvenue Direction aDirection) void move( ) void turnLeft( ) void pickThing( ) void putThing( )

(figure 1-8)

Incomplete class diagram for the `Robot` *class*

1.3.1 Attributes

Recall that the middle section of the class diagram lists the attributes. From the `Robot` class diagram, we can infer that each `Robot` object has four attributes. We might guess that the two named `street` and `avenue` record the street and avenue the robot currently occupies, and that `direction` records the direction it is facing. Finally, the `backpack` attribute might plausibly be where each robot keeps track of the things it is carrying. We can't know any of these details with absolute certainty, but it makes sense given what we know about the robot world described in Section 1.2, "Understanding Karel's World," and from the names of the attributes themselves.

LOOKING AHEAD

Attributes can have types other than `int`. See Chapter 7.

Preceding the names of the attributes is the type of information to which they refer. The **type** specifies the set of valid values for the attribute. The `street` and `avenue` attributes are preceded by `int`, which is Java shorthand for "integer." This information makes sense because we have been referring to streets and avenues with integers, such as 0, 1, or 5, but never with real numbers, such as 3.14159.

LOOKING AHEAD

The type of an attribute can be the name of a class, like `ThingBag`. See Chapter 8.

The type of `backpack` is a `ThingBag`. `ThingBag`s can store a variable number of `Thing` objects. This attribute illustrates that a robot object makes use of other objects—these objects cooperate to model the problem.

KEY IDEA

Class diagrams are designed to help you understand a class. They may omit low-level details in the interest of clarity.

Sometimes a class diagram does not include all of the attributes. Why? The important part of a class is the services its objects provide—the things they can do. It is appropriate to say that the programmer implementing the class needs to know the attributes, but it's no one else's business how the object works internally. Nevertheless, we will find it helpful in discussing the services to know what attributes they need to maintain. The class diagram shown earlier in Figure 1-8 occupies a middle ground. It shows attributes that contribute to understanding the class, but omits others that don't, even though they are necessary to implement the class.

1.3.2 Constructors

The `Robot` class diagram lists five services: `Robot`, `move`, `turnLeft`, `pickThing`, and `putThing`.

KEY IDEA

Constructors create new objects. Services are performed by an object that already exists.

The first, `Robot`, is actually a constructor rather than a service, but is listed here for convenience. Although constructors have some similarities to services, there are important differences. The key difference is their purposes: services are performed by an object for some client, while constructors are used by a client to construct a new object. (Recall that the client is the object using the services of the `Robot` object.) Constructors always have the same name as the class.

When a new object is constructed, its attributes must be set to the correct initial values. The initial position of the robot is determined by the client. The client communicates the desired initial position to the constructor by providing **arguments**, or specific values, for each of the constructor's **parameters**. The parameters are shown in the class diagram between parentheses: `Robot(City aCity, int aStreet, int anAvenue, Direction aDirection)`. Notice that there is a remarkable similarity between the constructor's parameters and the classes' attributes.

KEY IDEA

The constructor is responsible for correctly initializing the attributes.

1.3.3 Services

Suppose we have a robot that we refer to as `karel`. We can tell `karel` what to do by sending it **messages** such as `move` or `turnLeft`. A message requests that the object perform one of its services for a client, the sender of the message. The services in the `Robot` class diagram tell us which messages we can send to a robot object. A message to `karel` contains the name `karel`, a dot, and the name of a service followed by an argument list and a semicolon, as shown in Figure 1-9.

KEY IDEA

A client requests a service from an object by sending a message to the object.

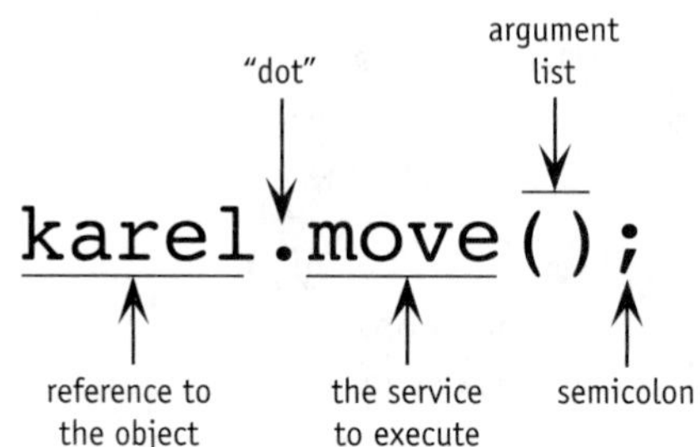

(figure 1-9)

Details of sending a message to an object referred to as `karel`

In this message, `karel` identifies who is supposed to move. We don't want to move any robot (or vehicle or cow or anything else that can move), only the particular robot known as karel. Stating the object first is like having a conversation in a group of people. When you speak to a specific person within the group, you often start by saying his or her name—"Karel, please pass the potatoes." Because a program almost always contains many objects, identifying the recipient of the message is a requirement.

KEY IDEA

A message is always sent to a specific object.

After referring to the object, we place a dot, which connects the object to the message, `move`. The message must be one of the services the object knows how to perform—a service listed in the class diagram. Sending the message "jump" to `karel` would result in an error because `karel` does not have a jumping service.

KEY IDEA

Each message must correspond to one of its recipient's services.

Like the constructor, a service may have a list of parameters to convey information the object needs to carry out the service. Parameter lists always begin and end with parentheses. None of the four `Robot` services listed require additional information, and so all their parameter lists are empty (but the parentheses must still be present). Consequently, when the corresponding messages are sent to a `Robot` object no arguments are needed, although parentheses are still required.

Finally, the message ends with a semicolon.

When a robot receives the `move` message, it moves. It also updates the `street` and `avenue` attributes to reflect its new location. If `karel` is standing at 2nd Street and 1st Avenue facing south, `street` and `avenue` contain 2 and 1, respectively. As the `move` service is executed, `street` is updated to 3, but `avenue` remains 1. The `Robot` object also sends many messages to other objects in the program to make an image move on the computer's screen.

KEY IDEA

Commands are preceded by the word `void` *in class diagrams.*

The `move` service is preceded in the class diagram with the word `void`. This word means that `move` is a command that changes the state of a robot object rather than a query that answers a question. If it were a query, `void` would be replaced with the type of the answer it returns—an integer, a real number, or a string of characters, for example. Using the keyword `void` to mean "returns no answer" can be related to an English meaning of the word: "containing nothing."

PATTERN

Command Invocation

Invoking the remaining services listed in the class diagram (`turnLeft`, `pickThing`, and `putThing`) follows the same pattern as `move`. Start with a reference to a specific robot. Then add a dot, the message you want to send the robot, an empty argument list, and a semicolon. The designated robot responds by turning, picking, or putting, as described earlier. Furthermore, the services of any other class are invoked by following this same pattern. Not only the `Robot`, `Wall`, and `Thing` classes, but also classes modeling students or employees or printers or checkbooks or concerts follow this pattern. *All* objects follow this pattern.

Learning to recognize common patterns is an important part of becoming a good programmer. When this book uses a common pattern, a pattern icon appears in the margin, as shown beside the previous paragraph. A section near the end of each chapter explains the patterns in detail and generalizes them to be more broadly applicable. The first such section is Section 1.7.

1.4 Two Example Programs

It's time to put all this background to use. You know about the program's model, you know about classes and objects, and you know how to send an object a message to invoke one of its services. In this section, we'll take a look at a computer program that uses these concepts to accomplish a task.

1.4.1 Situations

When writing a program (or reading a program someone else has written), you must understand what the program is supposed to do. For our first program, let's imagine that a delivery robot is to pick up a parcel, represented by a `Thing`, at intersection (1, 2) and deliver it to (2, 3). The **initial situation**, shown in Figure 1-10, represents the state of the city before the robot does its task. The **final situation**, also shown in Figure 1-10, is how we want the city to appear after the task is done.

KEY IDEA

Many robot tasks can be specified by showing the way things are at the beginning and how we want things to end up.

This task could be accomplished in many ways. Perhaps the simplest is for the robot to perform the following steps:

move forward until it reaches the parcel
pick up the parcel
move one block farther
turn right
move a block
put the parcel down
move one more block

PATTERN 

Sequential Execution

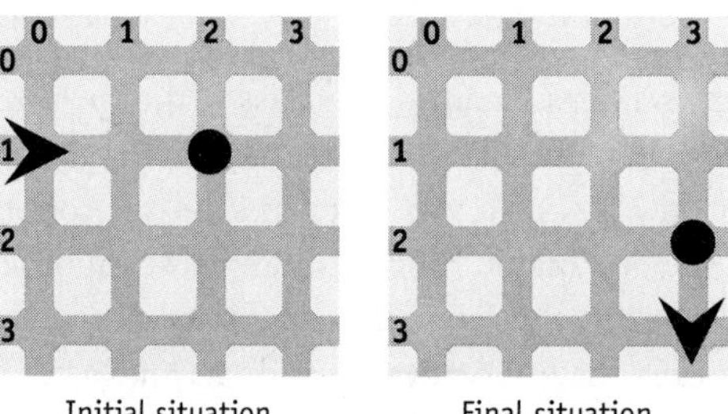

(figure 1-10)

Initial and final situations of a task to pick up and deliver a parcel

This path is illustrated on the left side of Figure 1-11. A more roundabout path is shown on the right. The roundabout path also accomplishes the task but results in a less efficient solution. If the robot were real, which solution would cause the robot to use the least power from its battery pack?

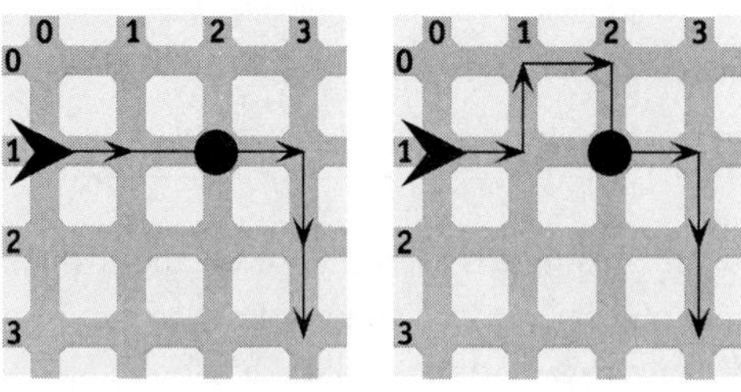

(figure 1-11)

Two approaches for the robot to perform the delivery task

Obviously, the robot could take any one of many possible paths to solve this problem. The following program takes the more efficient approach outlined in Figure 1-11.

1.4.2 Program Listing

LOOKING BACK

Before you can run the program in Listing 1-1, you need to have software installed on your computer. See the Preface for instructions.

Listing 1-1 shows the source code of a program to carry out the task just described. The source code contains the words and other symbols we write to instruct the computer.

Based on the previous discussion, you should be able to read the main body of the program and have a feel for how it works. Of course, you won't understand everything now, but it will all be explained in due course. You may be interested in knowing that much of the code in Listing 1-1 is repeated in every Java program and even more is repeated in every program using robots.

The line numbers on the left are not part of the program. They are included in the listing only so we can easily refer to specific parts of the program.

This program divides naturally into three parts: the code in lines 8–10, which constructs objects to set up the initial situation, the code in lines 13–22, which sends messages directing the robot to the final situation, and the remaining "housekeeping" required by the Java language. This division is reinforced by the comments written by the programmer at lines 7 and 12.

At a lower level of detail, Table 1-1 describes the purpose of each line of code. Use it to get a feel for the kinds of information present in a Java program, but don't expect to understand it all this early in the book. Lines 8–22 are the most important for right now; all will be discussed in detail later in the book.

The source code for the program in Listing 1-1 is available from the Robots Web site. Download the file `examples.zip`. After saving and expanding it, look in the directory `ch01/deliverParcel/`.

FIND THE CODE

ch01/deliverParcel/

Listing 1-1: *A program to move a* `Thing` *from (1, 2) to (2, 3)*

```
1  import becker.robots.*;
2
3  public class DeliverParcel
4  {
5    public static void main(String[] args)
6    {
7      // Set up the initial situation
8      City prague    = new City();
9      Thing parcel   = new Thing(prague, 1, 2);
10     Robot karel    = new Robot(prague, 1, 0, Direction.EAST);
11
12     // Direct the robot to the final situation
13     karel.move();
```

Listing 1-1: *A program to move a* `Thing` *from (1, 2) to (2, 3)* (continued)

```
14        karel.move();
15        karel.pickThing();
16        karel.move();
17        karel.turnLeft();          // start turning right as three turns lefts
18        karel.turnLeft();
19        karel.turnLeft();          // finished turning right
20        karel.move();
21        karel.putThing();
22        karel.move();
23     }
24  }
```

(table 1-1)

An explanation of Listing 1-1

Line	Purpose
1	Makes code written by other programmers, such as the `Robot` class, easily available.
2, 11	Blank lines often add clarity for a person reading the program, but do not affect its execution in any way.
3	Identifies the class being written with the name `DeliverParcel`.
4, 6, 23, 24	Java uses braces to give structure to the program. The braces at lines 4 and 24 contain all the code belonging to the class. The braces at lines 6 and 23 contain all the code belonging to the service named `main`.
5	Identifies where the program will begin execution. Every program must have a line similar to this one.
7, 12	Text between two consecutive slashes and the end of the line is a **comment**. Comments are meant to help human readers and do not affect the execution of the program in any way.
8–10	Construct the objects required by the program.
13–22	Messages telling the robot named `karel` which services it should perform.

We now turn to a detailed discussion of lines 8–22. The remainder of the program will be discussed in Section 1.4.7.

1.4.3 Setting up the Initial Situation

The initial situation, as shown in Figure 1-10, is set up by constructing three objects in lines 8-10. The `City` object corresponds to all the intersections of streets and avenues. The `Robot` and `Thing` objects obviously correspond to the robot and thing shown in the initial situation.

Each of the four statements has a similar structure. Consider line 10 as an example:

PATTERN

Object Instantiation

```
10     Robot karel    = new Robot(prague, 1, 0, Direction.EAST);
```

LOOKING AHEAD

We will see similar declarations in other situations. All have the type first, then the name.

On the left side of the equal sign (=) is a **variable declaration**. A variable declaration first states the type of the object—in this case `Robot`—and then the name of the variable being declared, `karel`. A **variable** uses a name (`karel`) to refer to a value (in this case a `Robot` object), allowing the value to be used easily in many places in the program. The choice of variable name is up to the programmer. A meaningful name helps the understanding of people reading the program, including the programmer.

The object is instantiated on the right side of the equal sign. The keyword `new` signals that a new object will be constructed. After `new`, a constructor is named, in this case, `Robot`. It must be compatible with the type of the variable on the left side of the equal sign. For now, "compatible" means the two are identical. Eventually, we will ease this restriction.

When an object is constructed, the client object may need to provide information for the constructor to do its job. In this case, the client specifies that the new robot is to be created in the city named `prague` at the intersection of Street 1 and Avenue 0, facing east. Recall the values or arguments provided at line 10:

```
10     Robot karel    = new Robot(prague, 1, 0, Direction.EAST);
```

They correspond to the parameters shown in the class diagram:

```
Robot(City aCity, int aStreet, int anAvenue,
      Direction aDirection)
```

The arguments list the city first, then the street, avenue, and direction—in that order. Furthermore, the types of the values provided match the types given in the parameter list. `prague` refers to a `City` object, just as the parameter list specifies what the first value must be. Similarly, the second and third values are integers, just as the types for avenue and street specify.

LOOKING AHEAD

We will learn how to define our own sets of values in Chapter 7.

The type of the `Robot` constructor's last parameter is `Direction` and the value passed to it in line 10 of Listing 1-1 is `Direction.EAST`. `Direction` is a class used to define values with program-specific meanings. `EAST` is one of those special values. It should come as no surprise that `WEST`, `NORTH`, and `SOUTH` are other values defined by the `Direction` class. When one of these values is used in a program, its defining class, `Direction`, must accompany it.

Finally, line 10 ends with a semicolon (`;`), which marks the end of the statement. The function of semicolons in Java is similar to periods marking the end of English sentences.

1.4.4 Sending Messages

Lines 13–22 in Listing 1-1 direct the robot from the initial situation to the final situation. They give a precise sequence of instructions the robot must perform to accomplish the task. If the instructions were performed in a different sequence, the problem is unlikely to be solved correctly.

Each instruction follows the command invocation pattern observed earlier: give the name of the object being addressed, a dot, and then the service desired from that object. For example, `karel.move();` instructs the robot `karel` to execute its `move` service. The result is that the robot moves from one intersection to the next intersection in the direction it is currently facing (unless something blocks its way).

PATTERN
Command Invocation
Sequential Execution

Each of these instructions is one **statement** in the program. Lines 8-10 are another kind of statement, **declaration statements**, because they declare variables and assign initial values to them. In time, we will learn other kinds of statements that allow the program to make decisions, execute other statements repeatedly, and so on. Recall that all statements end with a semicolon.

1.4.5 Tracing a Program

Simulating the execution of a program, also known as **tracing** a program, is one way to understand what it does and verify that the sequence of statements is correct. Tracing a program is like building a state change diagram, such as the one shown in Figure 1-12, for each statement in the program. Notice that the diagram covers two statements and shows the state before each statement and after each statement.

A program almost always involves many objects, so this can involve tracking a lot of information. Also, a formal state change diagram is difficult to draw and maintain. To overcome these problems, it's best to decide at the outset what information is relevant and to organize it in a table. It seems that the relevant information in the `DeliverParcel` program (Listing 1-1) includes the state of the robot and the state of the parcel, represented by a `Thing`. For the state of the robot, we will have four columns, one for each of the four attributes in the class diagram shown in Figure 1-8. For the parcel we will use a column for its street and another for its avenue. These are listed as headings in Table 1-2. If the program contained another robot, we would trace it by adding another group of four columns to the table.

(figure 1-12)

State change diagram tracing the execution of two statements

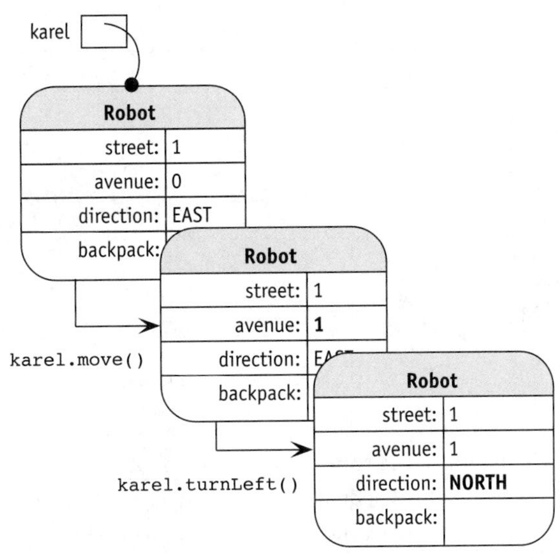

(table 1-2)

A table recording the change of program state while tracing the execution of the `DeliverParcel` *program in Listing 1-1*

Program Statement	karel				parcel	
	street	**avenue**	**direction**	**backpack**	**street**	**avenue**
	1	0	east		1	2
13 `karel.move();`						
	1	1	east		1	2
14 `karel.move();`						
	1	2	east		1	2
15 `karel.pickThing();`						
	1	2	east	parcel	1	2
16 `karel.move();`						
	1	3	east	parcel	1	3
17 `karel.turnLeft();`						
	1	3	north	parcel	1	3
18 `karel.turnLeft();`						
	1	3	west	parcel	1	3
19 `karel.turnLeft();`						
	1	3	south	parcel	1	3

	karel				parcel	
Program Statement	**street**	**avenue**	**direction**	**backpack**	**street**	**avenue**
20 `karel.move();`						
	2	3	south	parcel	2	3
21 `karel.putThing();`						
	2	3	south		2	3
22 `karel.move();`						
	3	3	south		2	3

(table 1-2) ***continued***

A table recording the change of program state while tracing the execution of the `DeliverParcel` *program in Listing 1-1*

Like the state change diagram, the table is organized to show the state of the program both before and after each statement is executed. It does this by inserting the statements between the rows that record the program's state.

The first row of the table gives the initial state as established when the objects are constructed in lines 8–10. This state reflects the initial situation shown in Figure 1-10. As we trace the program, we list the statement executed and then the resulting state. The effect is equivalent to a long series of state change diagrams like the one in Figure 1-12, but considerably easier to manage.

After tracing the program, we see that the robot finishes on intersection (3, 3) as the final situation requires. In addition, it has picked up the thing and deposited it on intersection (2, 3).

Tracing the program helps us understand what it does and increases our confidence in the correctness of the solution. As you trace a program, you must do exactly what the program says. It is tempting to take shortcuts, updating the table with what we intend the program to do. The computer, however, does not understand our intentions. It does exactly what the program says. If we don't do the same while tracing, the value of tracing is lost and we can no longer claim confidence in the correctness of the solution.

KEY IDEA

Computers follow the program exactly. When tracing the execution, we must also be exact.

Having performed a trace, we now understand that the sequence of statements in the program is important. If lines 14 and 15 are reversed, for instance, the robot would try to pick up the thing before it arrives at the thing's intersection. The result would be a broken robot on intersection (1, 1).

Sequential execution is a fundamental pattern in how we solve problems. We often give directions that follow the form "do _____, and then _____": "go to the stoplight and then turn right" or "add the eggs and then beat the batter for two minutes." The *and then* indicates sequential execution.

PATTERN

Sequential Execution

1.4.6 Another Example Program

A second example program is shown in Listing 1-2. Comparing it with the `DeliverParcel` program in Listing 1-1 reveals many common elements—and where the differences are. The initial and final situations are shown in Figure 1-13. In this program, a robot (`mark`) must move around a roadblock to meet a friend (`ann`) on intersection (2, 1). This program is interesting because it uses multiple objects that belong to the same class (two robot objects and two wall objects).

One obvious difference between this program and `DeliverParcel` is the use of `Wall` objects. A wall is instantiated using the same pattern as `Robot` and `City` objects, as shown in the following statement:

```
Wall blockAve0 = new Wall(ny, 0, 2, Direction.WEST);
```

This statement constructs a wall on the western boundary of the intersection at (0, 2). This is the wall that prevents `mark` from proceeding west from its current location. The object is referenced with the name "`blockAve0`," a name chosen by the programmer.

(figure 1-13)

Initial and final situations for two robots, `mark` *and* `ann`

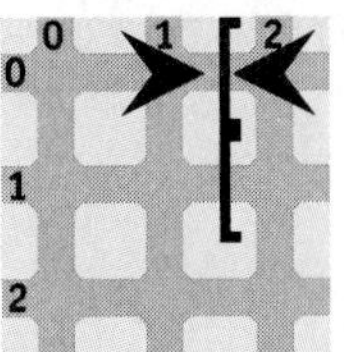

In the initial situation, two robots, `mark` and `ann`, are on opposite sides of a roadblock. They would like to meet on intersection (2, 1).

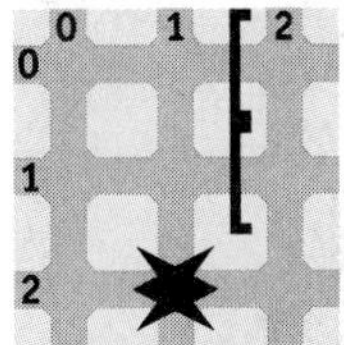

The final situation, where `mark` and `ann` have gone around the roadblock to meet on intersection (2, 1).

You may want to stop here and think about how you would write a program to solve this problem. What changes would you make to the `DeliverParcel` program? Then look at Listing 1-2 and see how much of it makes sense to you.

`GoAroundRoadBlock` and `DeliverParcel` have many features in common. If both programs were written on transparencies and superimposed, they would be identical in a number of places. In particular, the first six lines are nearly identical, with the exception of one name chosen by the programmers. In addition, both programs have two closing braces at the end and the organization of the code in the inner most set of braces is similar—first objects are declared and then messages are sent to them. Both programs have similar patterns of constructing objects, obtaining services from those objects, and requiring statements to be in a particular sequence.

Listing 1-2: *A program where* `mark` *goes around a road block and meets* `ann`

```
import becker.robots.*;

public class GoAroundRoadBlock
{
  public static void main(String[] args)
  {
    // Set up the initial situation
    City  ny          = new City();
    Wall  blockAve0 = new Wall(ny, 0, 2, Direction.WEST);
    Wall  blockAve1 = new Wall(ny, 1, 2, Direction.WEST);
    Robot mark        = new Robot(ny, 0, 2, Direction.WEST);
    Robot ann         = new Robot(ny, 0, 1, Direction.EAST);

    // mark goes around the roadblock
    mark.turnLeft();
    mark.move();
    mark.move();
    mark.turnLeft();          // start turning right as three turns left
    mark.turnLeft();
    mark.turnLeft();          // finished turning right
    mark.move();

    // ann goes to meet mark
    ann.turnLeft();           // start turning right as three turns left
    ann.turnLeft();
    ann.turnLeft();           // finished turning right
    ann.move();
    ann.move();
    ann.turnLeft();
  }
}
```

FIND THE CODE

ch01/roadblock/

PATTERN

Object Instantiation

PATTERN

Command Invocation
Sequential Execution

Multiple Objects

The `GoAroundRoadBlock` program contains two robots, `mark` and `ann`. Each has its own internal state, which is completely independent of the other. `mark` can turn and move without affecting `ann`; `ann` can turn and move without affecting `mark`. The state change diagram in Figure 1-14 shows an object for `mark` and another for `ann`. After `mark` turns, `ann`'s object has not changed (although `mark`'s direction is now different).

(figure 1-14)

State change diagram illustrating the independence of two robot objects

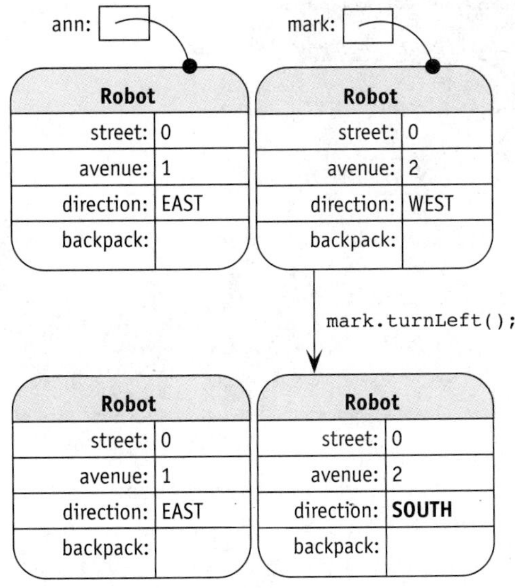

KEY IDEA

The only way to change an object's attributes should be via its services.

In a well-designed object-oriented program, an object's state does not change unless a message has been sent to the object. When `mark` is sent the `turnLeft` message, no message is sent to `ann`, so that object doesn't change. This property of not changing unless an explicit message is received is called **encapsulation**. An object builds a capsule or wall around its attributes so that only the object's services can change them. One strength of object-oriented programming is that it makes encapsulation easy. Earlier programming methodologies did not make encapsulation as easy, with the result that programmers were often left wondering "Now, how did that information get changed?"

It is possible to write Java programs that do not use encapsulation, but it is not recommended.

1.4.7 The Form of a Java Program

Let's turn now to the first six lines and the last two lines of the `DeliverParcel` and `GoAroundRoadBlock` programs. Both programs are almost identical in these areas; we take Listing 1-1 as our example. For programs involving robots, only one of these eight lines vary from program to program. The statements we are interested in are shown in Listing 1-3, with the part that changes shown in a box.

Listing 1-3: *The "housekeeping" statements in a Java program that simulate robots*

```
1  import becker.robots.*;
2
3  public class DeliverParcel
4  {
5    public static void main(String[ ] args)
6    {
       // lines 7-22 omitted
23   }
24 }
```

The programmer chooses this name for each program.

PATTERN

Java Program

Line 1 makes a large body of code written by other people easily available. The 24 lines of code contained in Listing 1-1 are not nearly enough to specify everything that this program does. The program makes use of more than 3,700 lines of code written by the textbook's author. That, in turn, uses many tens or even hundreds of thousands of lines of code written by still other programmers.

All that code is organized into **packages**. The code written by the author is in the package `becker.robots`. It is a group of about 50 classes that work together to enable robot programs. Line 1 makes those classes more easily accessible within the `DeliverParcel` program.

LOOKING AHEAD

In Section 1.6, we will see programs that import packages for manipulating a window on the screen.

The class name on line 3 is simply that—a name by which this class will be known. The name of the file containing the classes' source code must be the same as this name, with "`.java`" added to the end (for example, "`DeliverParcel.java`").

The braces on lines 4 and 24 enclose the statements that are specific to this class.

The special name `main` appears in every Java program. It marks where execution of the program begins. The words surrounding `main` are required and tell Java more about this code. The braces in lines 6 and 23 enclose all of the statements associated with `main`.

1.4.8 Reading Documentation to Learn More

The `Robot` class includes more than 30 services—too many to discuss here. Furthermore, the software accompanying this book contains more than 100 other classes. How can you find out about the other classes and all the services they (including `Robot`) offer?

The creators of Java have included a facility to extract information from the Java source code and put it in a form suitable for the World Wide Web. A sample Web page documenting the `Robot` class is shown in Figure 1-15. You can use a Web browser to find it at *www.learningwithrobots.com* or look in the documentation directory of the CD that accompanies this book.

(figure 1-15)

Web page showing a list of the available packages, classes within the `becker.robots` package, and some of the documentation for the `Robot` class

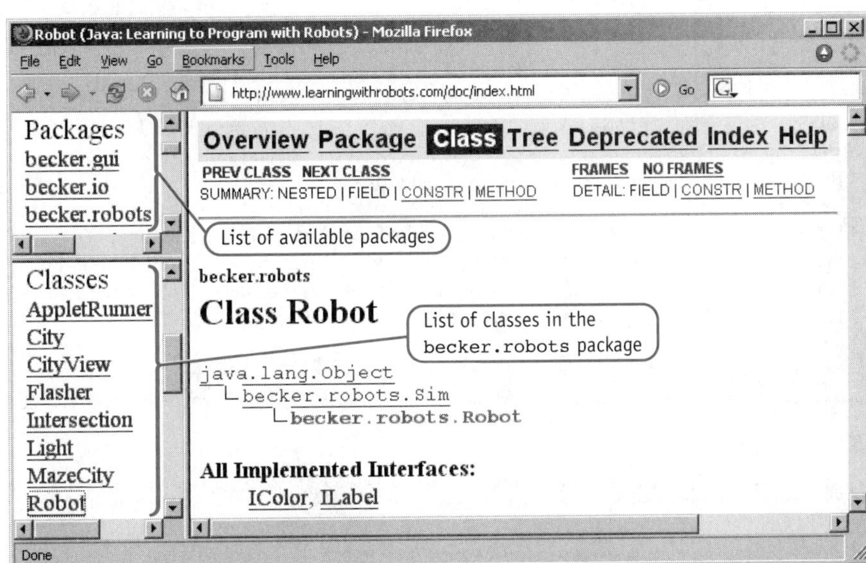

The upper-left panel in the window shows an area labeled "Packages". It contains `becker.robots` and several other packages. Clicking one of these links displays in the lower-left panel a list of the classes contained in that package. For example, if you click `becker.robots`, the lower-left panel displays the classes contained in the `becker.robots` package. The classes used in our programs thus far (`City`, `Robot`, `Wall`, and `Thing`) are listed here.

Clicking one of the class names displays documentation for that class in the main part of the window. For example, if you click the `Robot` class, its documentation appears, the beginning of which is shown in Figure 1-15. It shows the relationship between the `Robot` class and a number of other classes. We'll learn more about these relationships in Chapter 2.

Figure 1-16 shows the documentation's descriptive overview of the `Robot` class. The overview is used to describe the purpose of the class and sometimes includes sample code.

The documentation includes a summary description of each constructor and service (called methods in the documentation). Figure 1-17 shows the summaries for two constructors, one of which hasn't been mentioned in this textbook. Finally, the documentation also contains detailed descriptions of each constructor and service. Figure 1-18 shows the detailed description for the `move` service.

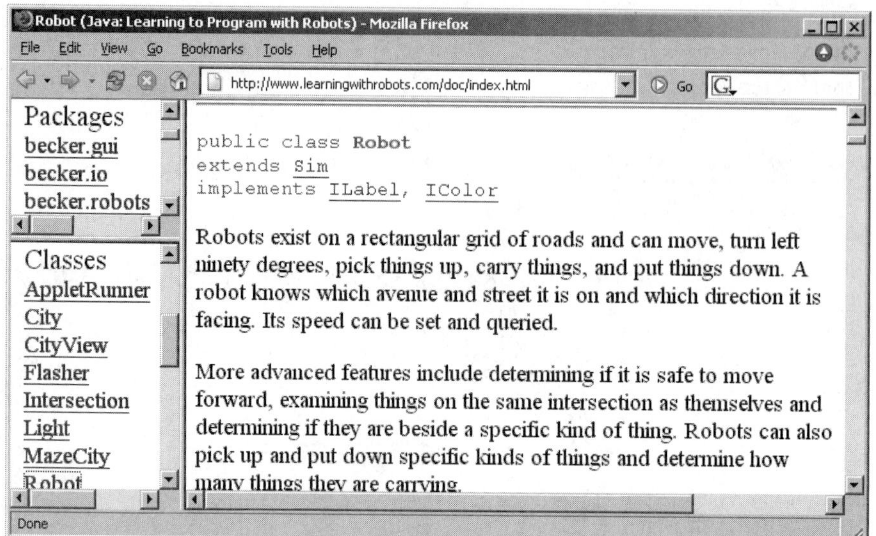

(figure 1-16)

Descriptive overview of the `Robot` *class*

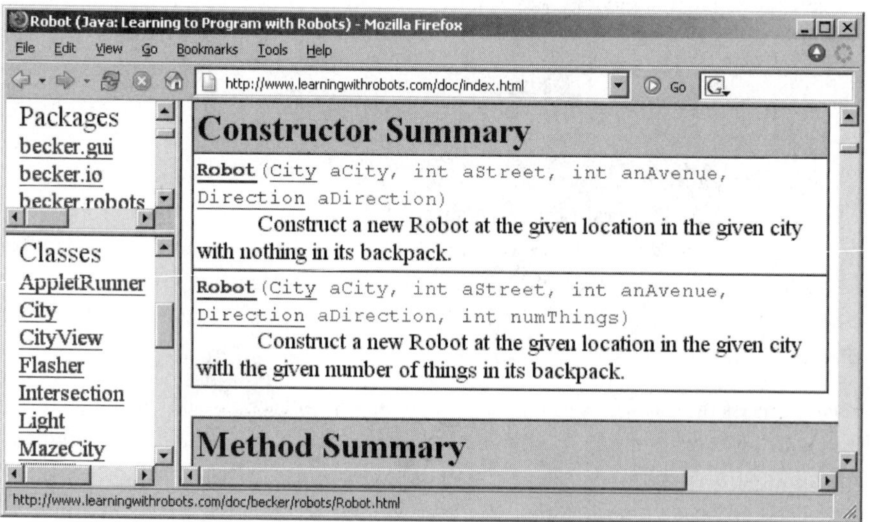

(figure 1-17)

Summary descriptions of `Robot` *constructors; each method has a similar summary*

(figure 1-18)

Detailed description of the `move` *service in the* `Robot` *documentation*

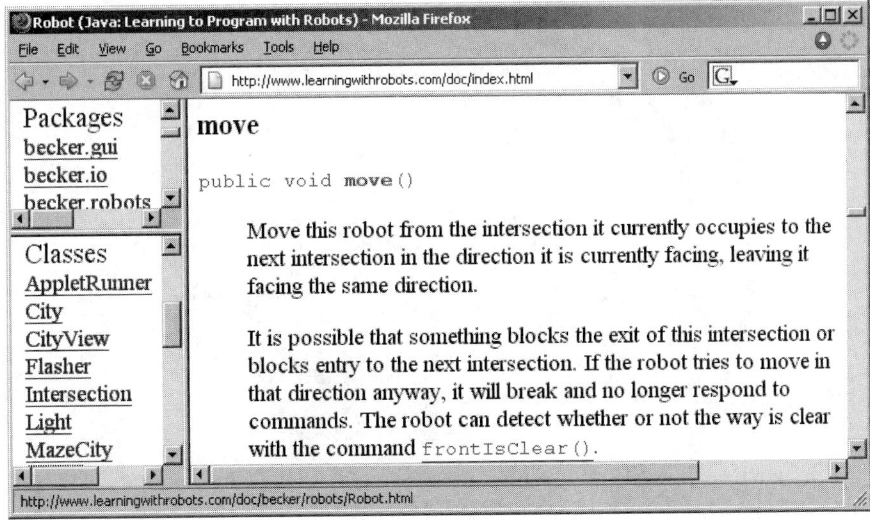

1.5 Compiling and Executing Programs

Now that we have seen two programs and discussed the overall form of a Java program, it is time to discover how to run them on a computer to see them in action. The exact steps to follow vary from computer to computer, depending on the operating system (Unix, Windows, Macintosh OS, and so on), which software is being used, and how that software has been installed. In broad strokes, however, there are three steps:

- Edit the source code in an appropriately named file with a text editor such as `vi` (Unix), `Notepad` (Windows), or `TextEdit` (Macintosh), or an integrated development environment (IDE) such as `JCreator` or `jGrasp`.
- Translate the program from the Java source code into an internal representation called **byte code** which is more easily understood by the computer. This process is called **compiling** and is performed by a program called a **compiler**.
- Run the compiled program.

Errors are often revealed by one of the last two steps. You must then go back to the first step, make changes, and try again. These steps result in a cycle, illustrated in Figure 1-19, of editing, compiling, and running, which is repeated until the program is finished. When things go right, the light path is followed, providing the desired results. When things go wrong, one of the three dark paths is taken and the source code must be edited again to fix the error.

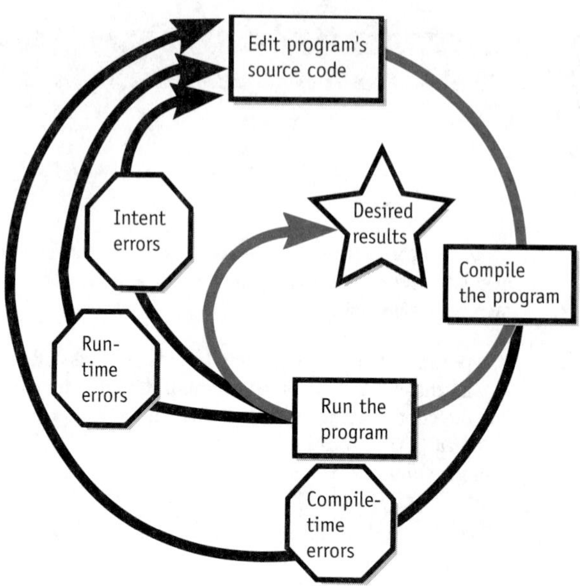

(figure 1-19)

The edit-compile-run cycle

What kinds of things can go wrong? There are three kinds of errors: compile-time errors, run-time errors, and intent errors. **Compile-time errors** are exposed when the compiler translates the program into byte code. **Run-time errors** are discovered when the program runs, but attempts to do something illegal. **Intent errors** are also called **logic errors**. They occur when the program does not carry out the programmer's intentions.

1.5.1 Compile-Time Errors

Compile-time errors occur when the program does not conform to the rules of the Java language. People can easily recognize (or even overlook) errors in written English. Computers cannot. The programmer must obey the rules exactly.

Listing 1-4 contains a program with many compile-time errors. Each is explained by the boxed annotation beside it. You can find the code in `ch01/compileErrors/`.

KEY IDEA

The compiler can help you find compile-time errors.

Every time the compiler finds an error it prints an error message. These messages are helpful in finding the errors—be sure to read them carefully and use them. For example, misplaced semicolons can be a struggle for beginning programmers. The missing semicolon at line 8 results in an error message similar to the following:

```
CompileErrors.java:8: ';' expected
   Robot karel = new Robot(london, 1, 1, Direction.EAST)
                                                        ^
```

This message has three parts. The first is where the error was found. "`CompileErrors.java`" is the name of the file containing the error. It won't be long before our programs are large enough to be organized into several files; you need to know which one contains the error. It is followed by the line number where the error was found, 8.

Second, "`';' expected`" indicates what the compiler identifies as the error.

Third is the line from the program where the compiler found the error. Beneath it is a caret (^) symbol showing where in the line the error was detected.

FIND THE CODE

ch01/compileErrors/

Listing 1-4: *A program with compile-time errors*

```
1  import becker.robots;
2
3  publik class CompileErrors
4  {
5     public static void main(String[] args)
6        karel.move();
7        City london = new Cit y();
8        Robot karel = new Robot(1ondon, 1, 1, Direction.EAST)
9
10       karal.move();
11       karel.mvoe();
12       karel.turnRight();
13       karel.turnleft();
14       move();
15       karel.move;
16    }
17    karel.move();
18 }
```


If you use an integrated development environment (IDE), it may show errors in a different format. It may even move the cursor to the line containing the error. No matter what the format is, however, you should still be able to learn the nature and location of the error.

Sometimes the messages are more cryptic than the one shown in the `CompileErrors` example, and occasionally the location of the error is wrong. For example, the compiler reports many errors if you misspell the variable name at line 8 where it is declared, but spell it correctly everywhere else. Unfortunately, none of the errors are at line 8. In other words, one error can cause many error messages, all pointing to the wrong location.

Because one error can cause many error messages, a reasonable debugging strategy is to perform the following tasks:

- Compile the program to produce a list of errors.
- Fix the most obvious errors, beginning with the first error reported.
- Compile the program again to obtain a revised list of the remaining errors.

Furthermore, do these tasks early in your program's development, and do them often. Waiting too long to compile your program will often result in many cryptic error messages that are hard to understand. Errors are easier to find and fix when you compile early and often.

KEY IDEA

Compiling early and often makes finding compile-time errors easier.

1.5.2 Run-Time Errors

Run-time errors are discovered when the program is actually run or traced. They are the result of instructions executing in an illegal context. For example, the instruction `karel.move();` will compile correctly (as long as a robot named `karel` has been constructed). However, if `karel` is facing a wall when this instruction executes, it will break. The instruction is executed in an illegal context.

The error of crashing a robot into a wall is reported in two different ways. First, the robot's icon is changed to show that the robot is broken. Second, an informative error message is printed. An example is shown in Figure 1-20.

```
1 Exception in thread "main" becker.robots.RobotException: A
  robot at (1, 2) crashed into a wall while moving WEST.
2         at becker.robots.Robot.breakRobot(Robot.java:558)
3         at becker.robots.Robot.move(Robot.java:148)
4         at GoAroundRoadBlock.main(GoAroundRoadBlock.java:17)
```

(figure 1-20)

Error message generated at run-time

This error message results from removing line 17 from Listing 1-2. The result is that `mark` does not move far enough to go around the roadblock and crashes into it.

The first line of the message contains technical information until the colon (`:`) character. A description of what went wrong usually appears after the colon. In this case, we are told that a robot crashed while moving west.

Lines 2-4 say where in the source code the error occurred and how the program came to be executing that code. Line 2 says the error happened while the program was executing line 558 in the source file `Robot.java`. That might be helpful information if we had access to `Robot.java`, but we don't. It is part of the `becker.robots` package imported into our robot programs. Line 3 indicates the error is also related, somehow, to line 148 in that same source file. Finally, line 4 mentions `GoAroundRoadBlock.java`, the file shown in Listing 1-2. At line 17 we find a `move` instruction, the one that caused the robot to crash. This is where our efforts to fix the program should start.

One situation that can be confusing for beginning programmers is when the Java system cannot even begin running your program. Usually, the run-time error message will contain the "word" `NoClassDefFoundError`. This means that the Java system cannot find your program to run, perhaps because it has not been successfully compiled or perhaps because the compiler did not place the compiled version of your program in the expected place.

1.5.3 Intent Errors

An intent error occurs when the program fails to carry out its intended purpose. The program may not have any compile-time or run-time errors, yet still fail to accomplish the job for which it was written. An intent error is also called a logic error.

These errors can be among the hardest to find. The computer can help find compile-time and run-time errors because it knows something is wrong. With an intent error, however, the computer cannot tell that something is wrong, and therefore provides no help other than executing the program. Remember, a computer does what it is told to do, which might be different from what it is meant to do.

For example, consider a program intended to move a thing from (2, 1) to (1, 1). The initial and final situations are shown in Figure 1-21.

(figure 1-21)

Initial and final situations for a task to move a thing

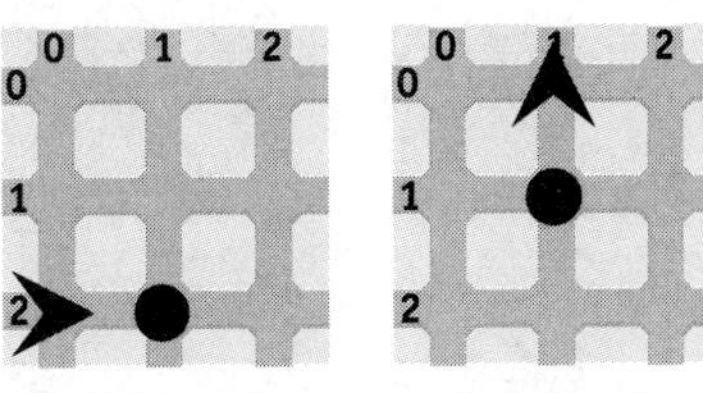

Sequential Execution

Suppose the programmer omitted the `turnLeft` instruction, as in the following program fragment:

```
katrina.move();
katrina.pickThing();
                              // should have turned left here
katrina.move();
katrina.putThing();
katrina.move();
```

As a result, the robot would finish the task at (2, 3) instead of (0, 1), and the thing would be at (2, 2) instead of (1, 1)—not what was intended.

Fortunately, the visual nature of robot programs makes many intent errors easy to find. Debugging intent errors in less visual programs is usually much harder.

1.5.4 A Brief History of Bugs and Debugging

Programming errors of any kind are often called **bugs**. The process of finding and fixing the errors is called **debugging**. The origin of the term is not certain, but it is known that Thomas Edison talked about bugs in electrical circuits in the 1870s. In 1947, an actual bug (a moth) was found in one of the electrical circuits of the Mark II computer at Harvard University, causing errors in its computations (see Figure 1-22). When the moth was found, it was taped into the operator's log book with the notation that it is the "first actual case of a bug being found." Apparently, the term was already in use for non-insect causes of computer malfunctions.

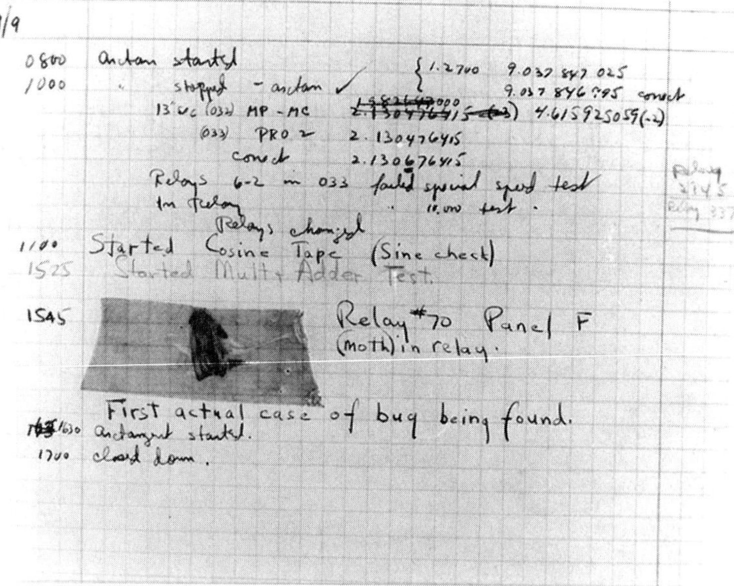

(figure 1-22)

A 1947 entry from a log book for the Mark II computer at Harvard University

1.6 GUI: Creating a Window

We have learned a lot of Java programming in the context of `Robot` objects. These concepts include:

- A class, such as `Robot` or `Thing`, is like a factory for making as many objects as you want. Each class or factory only makes one kind of object.
- A new object is instantiated with the `new` operator, for instance `Robot mark = new Robot(ny, 0, 2, Direction.WEST);`.

- All objects belonging to the same class have the same services, but each has its own attribute values that are independent of all other objects.
- A client can invoke an object's services with the object's name, a dot, and then the name of the desired service.

These concepts are not only for robot programs, but apply to every object-oriented Java program ever written. To illustrate, each chapter of this book includes a section applying the concepts learned using robots to graphical user interfaces, or GUIs (pronounced "gooey"). Applying the concepts to classes supplied with the Java language that have nothing to do with robots shows you how these concepts can be used in many other contexts.

Graphical user interfaces are the part of the program that interacts with the human user. It probably obtains input from the user and displays results to the user. In terms of what the user sees, the GUI consists of the windows, dialog boxes, lists of items to select, and so on.

1.6.1 Displaying a Frame

GUIs add a lot of complexity and development time to a program. Fortunately, Java provides a rich set of resources to help develop interfaces. The beginning point is the window, called a **frame** in Java. The simplest possible frame is shown in Figure 1-23.

(figure 1-23)

Simplest Java frame

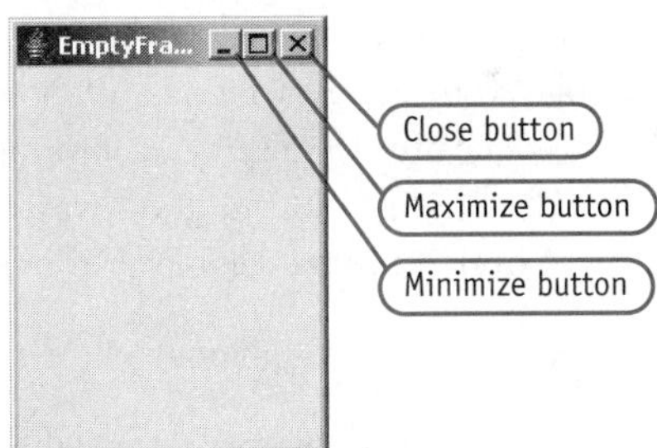

Though it is empty, the frame nevertheless has substantial functionality. If the user clicks the close box, the program quits. If the user clicks the minimize box the frame becomes as small as possible, while clicking the maximize box enlarges the frame to take up the entire screen. The user may also adjust the size of the frame by clicking and dragging an edge of the frame.

The program that displays this frame is even simpler than a robot program and is shown in Listing 1-5. Notice the similarity to Listing 1-1, including the following features:

- Both programs include `import` statements (although the actual packages differ), the declaration of the class at line 3 (although the class name differs), the placement of braces, and the declaration of the special service `main`.

- Both programs instantiate an object.
- Both programs invoke the services of an object.

Listing 1-5 *The* `EmptyFrame` *program displays an empty window*

```
1  import javax.swing.*;        // use JFrame
2
3  public class EmptyFrame
4  {
5    public static void main(String[ ] args)
6    { // declare the object
7      JFrame frame = new JFrame();
8
9      // invoke its services
10     frame.setTitle("EmptyFrame");
11     frame.setDefaultCloseOperation(JFrame.EXIT_ON_CLOSE);
12     frame.setLocation(250, 100);
13     frame.setSize(150, 200);
14     frame.setVisible(true);
15   }
16 }
```

FIND THE CODE

ch01/emptyFrame/

PATTERN

Java Program
Object Instantiation

PATTERN

Command Invocation
Sequential Execution

The `EmptyFrame` program differs from the `DeliverParcel` program in the kinds of objects created and the services demanded of them. A `JFrame` object serves as a container for information displayed to the user. By default, however, the frame has no title, is not visible on the screen, has no area for displaying information, and hides the frame when the close box is clicked (leaving us with no good way to stop the program). The services invoked in lines 10-14 override those defaults to provide the functionality we need.

The `setTitle` service causes its argument to be displayed at the top of the frame.

The `setDefaultCloseOperation` service specifies what the frame object should do when the close box is clicked. `JFrame.EXIT_ON_CLOSE` gives a meaningful name to a particular value; `Direction.EAST` serves a similar function for robot programmers.

The `setLocation` service says where the frame should appear. Its first argument is the distance from the left side of the screen to the left side of the frame. The second argument specifies the distance from the top of the screen to the top of the frame. The `setSize` service specifies the size of the frame. The first argument is the width and the second argument is the height. All of the arguments to these two services are given in **pixels**, an abbreviation for **picture elements**, which are the tiny dots on the screen that make up the image. The meaning of these arguments is illustrated in Figure 1-24.

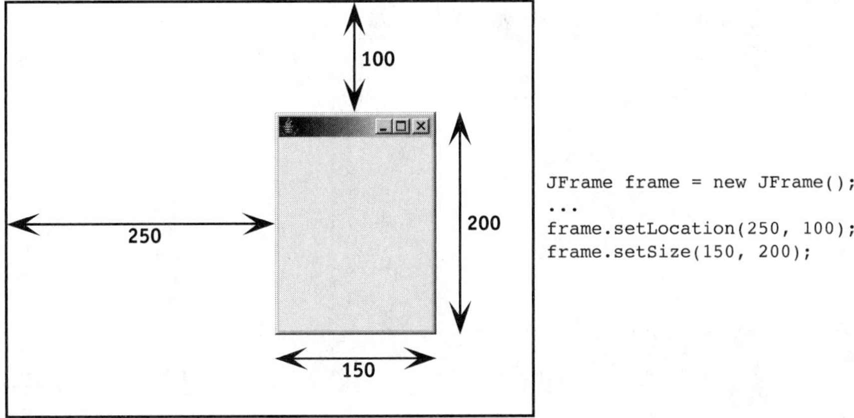

(figure 1-24)

Relationship of the arguments to `setLocation` *and* `setSize` *to the frame's location and size; the outer rectangle represents the computer monitor*

LOOKING AHEAD

`true` *and* `false` *are Boolean values used to represent true or false answers, and are covered in detail in Chapter 4.*

Finally, the `setVisible` service specifies whether the frame is visible on the screen. If the argument is `true`, the frame will be visible, while a value of `false` will hide it.

1.6.2 Adding User Interface Components

A frame with nothing in it is rather boring and useless. We can fix that by setting the **content pane**, the part of a frame designed to display information. We can add to the content pane buttons, textboxes, labels, and other user interface elements familiar to modern computer users. These buttons, labels, and so on are often called **components**. A component is nothing more than an object designed to be part of a graphical user interface.

An early warning, however: The resulting programs may look like they do something useful, but they won't. We are still a long way from writing a graphical user interface that actually accepts input from the user. The following programs emphasize the *graphical* rather than the *interface*.

Figure 1-25 shows a snapshot of a running program that has a button and a text area displayed in a frame. The frame's content pane has been set to hold a `JPanel` object. The `JPanel`, in turn, holds the button and text area. Listing 1-6 shows the source code for the program.

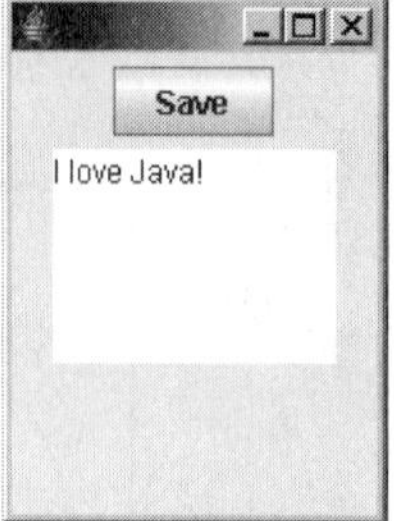

(figure 1-25)

Frame with a content pane containing a button and a text area; the user typed, "I love Java!" while the program was running

Listing 1-6 `FramePlay`, *a program to display a frame containing a button and a text area*

FIND THE CODE

ch01/framePlay/

```
1  import javax.swing.*;      // use JFrame, JPanel, JButton, JTextArea
2
3  public class FramePlay
4  {
5    public static void main(String[ ] args)
6    { // declare the objects to show
7      JFrame frame = new JFrame();
8      JPanel contents = new JPanel();
9      JButton saveButton = new JButton("Save");
10     JTextArea textDisplay = new JTextArea(5, 10);
11
12     // set up the contents
13     contents.add(saveButton);
14     contents.add(textDisplay);
15
16     // set the frame's contents to display the panel
17     frame.setContentPane(contents);
18
19     // set up and show the frame
20     frame.setTitle("FramePlay");
21     frame.setDefaultCloseOperation(JFrame.EXIT_ON_CLOSE);
22     frame.setLocation(250, 100);
23     frame.setSize(150, 200);
24     frame.setVisible(true);
25   }
26 }
```

PATTERN

Display a Frame

In lines 7–10, we declare and instantiate several objects. The `JPanel` instance named `contents` is simply a container. It will hold the things we are really interested in, the button and text area. The button and text area are instances of `JButton` and `JTextArea`, respectively. The `JPanel`'s `add` service in lines 13 and 14 adds them to its list of things to display.

When the button is constructed in line 9, `"Save"` is passed to the constructor's parameter. This text appears on the button when it is displayed. When the text area is constructed in line 10, the number of lines of text it should hold and how many characters wide it should be are passed as arguments. Both measures are approximate.

You can learn much more about these classes by browsing the online documentation at *java.sun.com/j2se/1.5.0/docs/api/.*

If you run the `FramePlay` program, you will find that the objects used have quite a bit of built-in functionality. The frame responds to the close, minimize, and maximize boxes, and resizes when you drag an edge. The save button flashes when clicked, and you can type in the textbox. This amount of functionality is remarkable for a 26-line program. As with the robot programs, much of this functionality is due to the programmers who wrote the classes we are using.

KEY IDEA

The ideas you learn with robots—such as classes, objects, and services—apply to all object-oriented programs.

Again, notice the similarity between the `FramePlay` program and all the other programs in this chapter. The concepts we learned with the robot programs truly are general and can be used in all Java programs. In fact, many of the ideas apply to all programs, whether or not they are written in Java. Some ideas, such as modeling, abstraction, and patterns apply to lots of different problems, whether or not they have a computer solution. You are learning a portable set of skills that can be applied in many circumstances.

1.7 Patterns

Many patterns appear in software—problems that appear repeatedly that have the same solution. A number of these have already been identified for you in the margins of this text. Figure 1-26 shows the icon used to identify a pattern. Expert software developers know many patterns and apply an appropriate one to solve the issue at hand, almost without thinking about it. Much of your work, as you learn to program, will involve learning to recognize which software patterns apply to the issue you are facing.

(figure 1-26)

Icon used to identify an example of a pattern

PATTERN

Software patterns began as a way to capture and discuss big ideas, such as how to structure many classes and objects to model a particular kind of problem. In this book we extend the idea of patterns to smaller ideas that may cover only one or two lines of code. As beginning programmers, our attention will be focused primarily on these elementary patterns.

Our elementary patterns have five elements: name, context, solution, consequences, and related patterns. In the pattern expositions they are clearly shown by name and typography, as shown in Figure 1-27. However, instead of describing an actual pattern, the figure describes what each section of a pattern involves.

Name: The name gives programmers a common vocabulary with which to discuss their work. Soon you will be able to say to a classmate, "I think the Command Invocation pattern applies here," and your classmate will know the kind of issue you think needs solving, your proposed solution, and the consequences of implementing that solution. Naming concepts increases our ability to work with abstractions and communicate them to others.

Context: The context describes the situations in which the pattern is applicable. Obviously, the pattern's context must match the context of your programming issue for the pattern to be useful.

Solution: The solution describes an approach to resolving the programming issue. For many patterns, the most appropriate form for the solution is several lines of code, likely with well-defined places where the code must be customized for the particular issue at hand. The places to customize appear in italics between « *and* ». For other patterns, an appropriate form for the solution is a class diagram that shows how two or more classes work together to resolve the issue.

Consequences: The consequences describe the natural by-products of applying this particular pattern. Sometimes these consequences are good, and sometimes they are bad; sometimes they are some of both. Weighing the consequences is part of deciding whether this pattern is the one to apply to your issue. It may be that another pattern can be applied in the same context with a better result.

Related Patterns: Finally, related patterns name patterns that have a different approach to resolving the issue or are based on the same ideas.

(figure 1-27)

Parts and format of a pattern description

LOOKING AHEAD

Naming is a powerful idea. Here we are naming patterns. In the next chapter, we will name a sequence of instructions. Doing so increases our power to think about complex problems.

Patterns are found or discovered, not invented. They result from sensing that you are repeating something you did earlier, investigating it enough to find the common elements, and then documenting it for yourself and others. Because patterns arise from experience, they are a good way to help inexperienced programmers gain expertise from experienced programmers.

The patterns listed here should feel familiar. You have seen them a number of times already, often accompanied with a margin note like the one shown here. Once the pattern has been formally presented, however, we will no longer call attention to its application with margin notes.

PATTERN

Command Invocation

1.7.1 The Java Program Pattern

Name: Java Program

Context: You want to write a Java program.

Solution: Implement a class that contains a service named main. In particular, customize the following template:

```
import «importedPackage»;              // may have 0 or more import statements

public class «programClassName»
{
  public static void main(String[] args)
  { «list of statements to be executed»
  }
}
```

The import statement makes classes from the named package easier to access. Typical values for *«importedPackage»* include becker.robots.* for robot programs, and java.awt.* and javax.swing.* for programs with graphical user interfaces.

The *«className»* is chosen by the programmer and must match the filename containing the source code.

The *«list of statements to be executed»* may include statements following the Object Instantiation pattern and Command Invocation patterns, among others.

Consequences: A class is defined that can be used to begin execution of the program.

Related Patterns: All of the other patterns in this chapter occur within the context of the Java Program pattern.

1.7.2 The Object Instantiation Pattern

Name: Object Instantiation

Context: A client needs to instantiate or construct an object to carry out various services for it.

Solution: Instantiate the object using the new keyword and a constructor from the appropriate class. Provide arguments for all of the constructor's parameters. Finally, assign the object reference provided by new to a variable. Examples:

```
City manila = new City();
Robot karel = new Robot(manila, 5, 3, Direction.East);
JButton saveButton = new JButton("save");
```

In general, a new object is instantiated with a statement matching the following template:

```
«variableType» «variableName» =
           new «className»(«argumentList»);
```

The «*variableName*» is used in the Command Invocation pattern whenever services must be carried out by the object.

Until we have studied polymorphism in Chapter 12, «*variableType*» and «`className`» will be the same. After that, they will often be different, but related. The «`className`», of course, determines what kind of object is constructed. The «*variableName*» should reveal the purpose or intent of what it names.

LOOKING AHEAD

We will say much more about choosing variable names wisely in Section 2.4.2.

Consequences: A new object is constructed and assigned to the given variable.

Related Patterns: The Command Invocation pattern requires this pattern to construct the objects it uses.

1.7.3 The Command Invocation Pattern

Name: Command Invocation

Context: A client wants an object to perform one of the services it provides.

Solution: Provide a reference to the object, a dot, the name of the desired service, and any arguments. Information about how to use the command, including any arguments it requires, can be found in its documentation. A command invocation is always terminated with a semicolon. Examples:

LOOKING AHEAD

Queries are invoked in a different context than commands. Although they are both services, they have different invocation patterns.

```
karel.move();
collectorRobot.pickThing();
frame.setSize(150, 200);
contents.add(saveButton);
```

In general, a command is invoked with a statement matching the following template:

```
«objectReference».«serviceName»(«argumentList»);
```

where «*objectReference*» is a variable name created using the Object Instantiation pattern.

Consequences: The command is performed by the named object. It is possible to invoke a command in an invalid context, resulting in a run-time error.

Related Patterns:

- The Object Instantiation pattern must always precede this pattern to create the object.
- The Sequential Execution pattern uses this pattern two or more times.

1.7.4 The Sequential Execution Pattern

Name: Sequential Execution

Context: The problem you're working on can be solved by executing a sequence of steps. The order of the steps matters, because later steps depend on earlier steps to establish the correct context for them to execute.

LOOKING AHEAD

Problem 1.4 further explores the idea of "correct order."

Solution: List the steps to be executed in the correct order. A correct order is one where each statement appears after all the statements upon which it depends. Each statement is terminated with a semicolon. An example from the DeliverParcel program (see Listing 1-1) demonstrates the solution:

```
7       // Set up the initial situation
8       City prague = new City();
9       Thing parcel= new Thing(prague, 1, 2);
10      Robot karel = new Robot(prague, 1, 0, Direction.EAST);
11
12      // Direct the robot to the final situation
13      karel.move();
14      karel.move();
15      karel.pickThing();
```

Lines 9 and 10 require a city when they are constructed; they therefore must appear after line 8, where the city is constructed. However, lines 9 and 10 are independent of each other and can appear in either order.

The robot karel cannot pick up a Thing at (2, 1) until it has reached that intersection. Lines 13 and 14 must therefore come before the pickThing command in line 15 to establish the context for it to execute (that is, move the robot to the intersection containing the Thing it picks up).

LOOKING AHEAD

Long sequences of statements are hard to understand. In Chapter 2 we will learn methods to help keep such sequences short.

Consequences: Each statement, except the first one, may depend on statements that come before it. If any of those statements are out of order or wrong, an error or unexpected result may appear later in the program, which can make programming a tedious process.

This model of execution assumes that each statement executes completely before the next one has begun. It is as if each statement were strung on a thread. Follow the thread from the beginning and each statement is reached in order. Follow the thread back through time and you have a complete history of the statements executed prior to the current statement.

Related Patterns: The Command Invocation pattern is used two or more times by this pattern.

1.7.5 The Display a Frame Pattern

Name: Display a Frame

Context: A program must show some visual information to the user.

Solution: Organize the visual information in a `JPanel` which is displayed within a `JFrame`.

```
import javax.swing.*;        // use JFrame, JPanel, JButton, JTextArea

public class «programClassName»
{
  public static void main(String[] args)
  { // declare the objects to show
    JFrame «frame» = new JFrame();
    JPanel «contents» = new JPanel();

    «statements to declare and add components to contents»

    // set the frame's contents to display the panel
    «frame».setContentPane(«contents»);

    // set up and show the frame
    «frame».setTitle("«title»");
    «frame».setDefaultCloseOperation(JFrame.EXIT_ON_CLOSE);
    «frame».setLocation(«xPos», «yPos»);
    «frame».setSize(«width», «height»);
    «frame».setVisible(true);
  }
}
```

Consequences: The frame is displayed along with the contents of the `JPanel`. The `JFrame`'s functionality is automatically available, including resizing, minimizing, and closing the frame.

Related Patterns:

- This pattern is a specialized version of the Java Program pattern.
- The Model-View-Controller pattern (Chapter 13) builds further on this pattern.

1.8 Summary and Concept Map

In this chapter we have learned that programs implement models. Object-oriented programs, such as those written in Java, use software objects to do the modeling. These software objects offer services to either perform a command or answer a query for a client. Documentation helps us learn more about the services an object offers.

Objects are instantiated from classes, a sort of template or definition for objects. Classes in the robot world include `Robot`, `City`, `Wall`, and `Thing`. When instantiating an object, we often assign it to a variable, allowing us to refer to it using the variable's name in many places in the program.

1.8.1 Concept Maps

Each chapter of this textbook includes a **concept map** as part of the summary. A concept map shows the major concepts in the chapter and relates them to each other with short phrases. The short phrases should be read in the direction of the arrow. For example, the following portion of the diagram should be read as "objects are instances of classes."

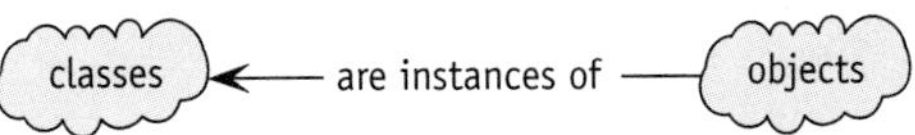

By studying the concept map, you remind yourself of important vocabulary (such as class, object, and instance in the preceding example) and the relationships between concepts.

Three suggested ways to use the concept maps as study tools are:

- After reading the chapter but before you look at the concept map, try drawing your own concept map and then compare it with the one in the chapter. They will undoubtedly be different, but hopefully will include many of the same concepts. The differences will identify places for you to clarify your understanding.
- Try reproducing the concept map but with the arrows running backwards. You will need to adjust the connecting phrase accordingly. Consider the following example:

- The concept maps include the most important concepts, but not all of them. Try to integrate additional concepts into the map. For example, how could you include the concepts of constructors, initial situations, and final situations in the following concept map?

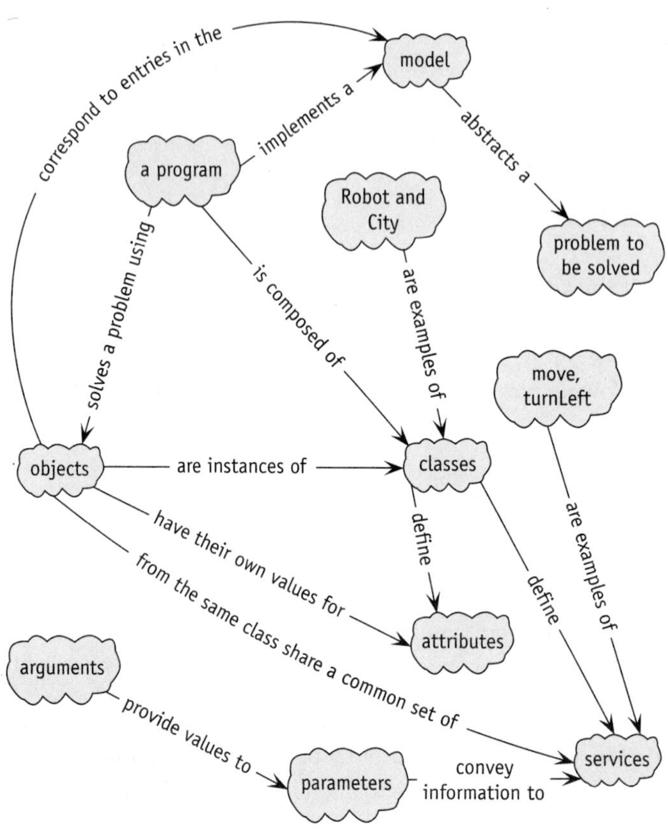

1.9 Problem Set

Problem sets present three types of problems: written exercises, programming exercises, and programming projects. Written exercises do not require programming but may require a computer to read documentation. Programming exercises and projects both require programming, but to a different degree. Exercises are short, such as changes to existing code. Programming projects require considerably more effort.

Written Exercises

1.1 Figure 1-4 shows a class diagram for the `Concert` class. Create a similar class diagram for a `Book` class. It's part of a program at the local public library that loans books to library patrons.

1.2 Trace the following program. In a table similar to Table 1-2, record `karel`'s current street, avenue, direction, and contents of its backpack. If a run-time error occurs, describe what went wrong and at which line. There are no compile-time errors.

```
import becker.robots.*;

public class Trace
{
  public static void main(String[] args)
  { City paris = new City();
    Thing theThing = new Thing(paris, 1, 2);
    Wall w = new Wall(paris, 1, 2, Direction.WEST);
    Robot karel = new Robot(paris, 1, 0, Direction.EAST);

    karel.move();
    karel.turnLeft();
    karel.turnLeft();
    karel.turnLeft();
    karel.move();
    karel.turnLeft();
    karel.move();
    karel.turnLeft();
    karel.move();
    karel.turnLeft();
    karel.pickThing();
    karel.move();
  }
}
```

1.3 Make a table similar to Table 1-2 and trace the program in Listing 1-2. You will need to add extra columns so you can record values for both robots.

1.4 The `DeliverParcel` program in Listing 1-1 makes extensive use of the Sequential Execution pattern. For many pairs of consecutive statements, interchanging the statements causes the program to fail. Give a pair of statements (that are not identical) where changing the order does *not* cause the program to fail.

1.5 In the `DeliverParcel` program in Listing 1-1, change line 8 to read `City prague = new City(5, 10);`. Based on the online documentation for `City`, what effect will this change have?

1.6 The following program contains 12 distinct compile-time errors. List at least nine of them by giving the line number and a short description of the error.

```
1 import becker.robots;
2
3 Public class Errors
4 {
5   public static void main(String[] args)
6   { City 2ny = new City(5, 5);
7     Thing aThing = new Thing(2ny, 2, 1);
8     Wall eastWall = Wall(2, 1, EAST);
9     Robot karel = new Robot(2ny, 0, 1, Direction.EAST);
```

```

        karel.move();
        karel.move(); move();
        karel.pickthing();
        karel..turnLeft(); karel.turnLeft();
        kerel.mve();
        karel.turnLeft(3);
        karel.move;();
        karel.putThing();
    }
}
```

1.7 The `JButton` constructor used in the `FramePlay` program in Listing 1-6 uses a string as a parameter. `JFrame` has a constructor that also has a string as a parameter. What is the effect of replacing line 7 with `JFrame frame = new JFrame("Mystery");`? Which line of the existing program should also change? How? (*Hint*: Consult the online documentation.)

Programming Exercises

1.8 Beginning with the program in Listing 1-1, deliberately introduce one compile-time error at a time. Record the compiler error generated and the cause of the error. If one error causes multiple messages, list only the first two. Find at least six distinct compile-time errors.

1.9 Write a program that creates a robot at (1, 1) that moves north five times, turns around, and returns to its starting point.

a. Run the program and describe what happens to the robot.

b. Describe a way to use the controls of the running program so you can watch the robot the entire time it is moving.

c. Consult the online documentation. Describe a way to change the program so you can watch the robot the entire time it is moving.

1.10 Make a copy of the `FramePlay` program in Listing 1-6. Add a new `JCheckBox` component.

a. Run the program and describe the behavior of the new component.

b. The `JCheckBox` constructor can take a string as a parameter, just like `JButton`. What happens if you use the string "Show All Items"?

1.11 Run the program in Listing 1-2. In your Java development software, choose Save from the File menu, enter a filename, and click the Save button. Find the file that was created.

a. Describe the contents of the file.

b. Search the documentation for the `City` class to find a use for this file. Describe the use.

c. Modify the program to use the file that was created. (*Hint*: You will need to construct the robots yourself within `main`.) Modify the file to place additional walls and things within the city.

Programming Projects

1.12 Write a program that begins with the initial situation shown in Figure 1-28. Instruct the robot to go around the walls counter clockwise and return to its starting position. *Hint:* Setting up the initial situation requires eight walls.

(figure 1-28)

Walking around the walls

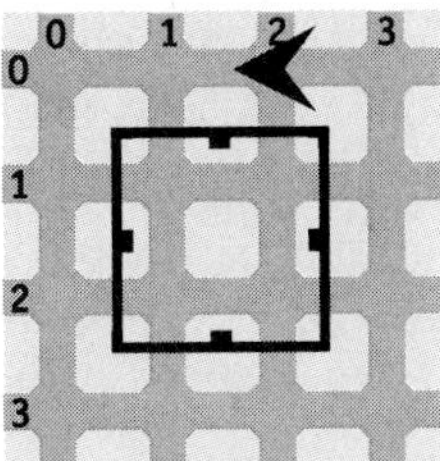

1.13 Every morning `karel` is awakened when the newspaper, represented by a `Thing`, is thrown on the front porch of its house. Instruct `karel` to retrieve the newspaper and return to "bed." The initial situation is as shown in Figure 1-29; in the final situation, `karel` is on its original intersection, facing its original direction, with the newspaper.

(figure 1-29)

Fetching the newspaper

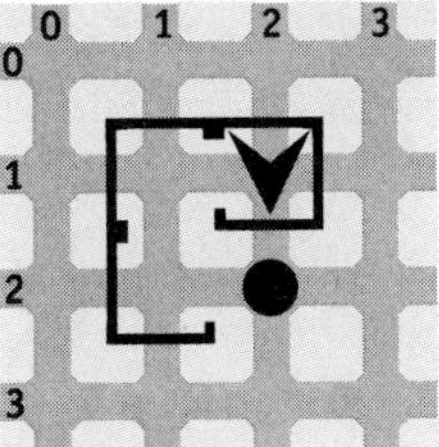

1.14 The wall sections shown in Figure 1-30 represent a mountain (north is up). Write a program that constructs the situation, and then instructs the robot to pick up a flag (a `Thing`), climb the mountain, and plant the flag at the top, descending down the other side. The robot must follow the face of the mountain as closely as possible, as shown by the path shown in the final situation.

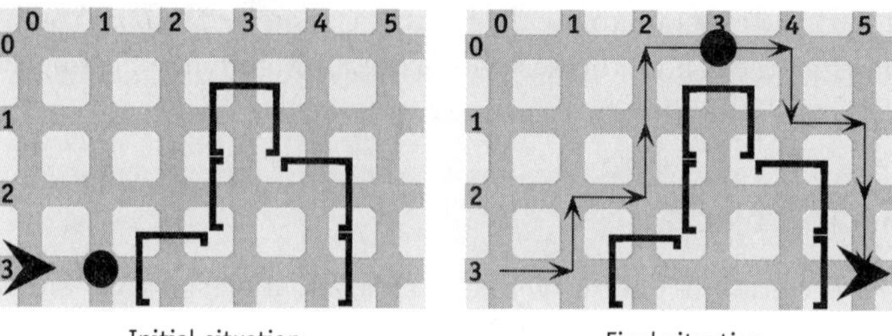

(figure 1-30)

Initial and final situations for a robot that climbs a mountain

1.15 On the way home from the supermarket, `karel`'s bag rips slightly at the bottom, spilling a few expensive items (`Things`) on the ground. Fortunately, `karel`'s neighbor `maria` notices and calls to him as `karel` arrives home. This initial situation is shown on the left in Figure 1-31. Write a program in which `karel` and `maria` both begin picking up the items, meeting as shown in the final situation. Use the `setLabel` service in `Robot` to label each robot.

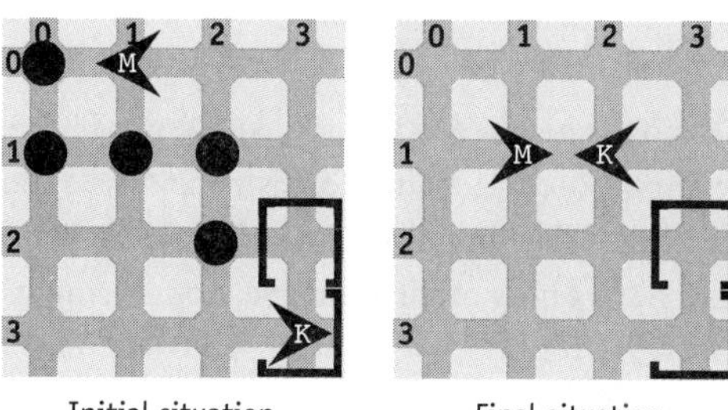

(figure 1-31)

Initial and final situations for robots picking up dropped items

1.16 Write a program that begins with the initial situation and ends with the final situation shown in Figure 1-32. In the final situation, the robot originally at (0, 0) is facing east and the robot originally at (0, 1) is facing west. Alternate the actions of the two robots so they arrive at their destination at approximately the same time.

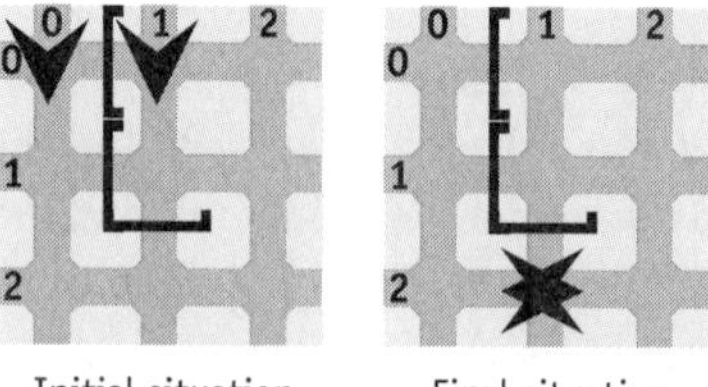

(figure 1-32)

Initial and final situations for two robots moving and meeting each other

1.17 The `JTextArea` class includes the services `setText` and `append`. Read the online documentation to understand what they do and how to use them. The arguments to both might be something like, `"My second point is..."`.

a. Modify the `FramePlay` program from Listing 1-6 so that it displays a short sentence as the program runs; it is *not* typed in by the user as shown in Figure 1-25.

b. Describe what happens if you use a much longer sentence.

c. Research the `JTextArea` class. Find a way to display all the words in your longer sentence.

1.18 Modify the `FramePlay` program from Listing 1-6 to make the frame about three times as wide and twice as tall. Instead of adding a `JButton` and `JTextArea`, add a `JColorChooser` component. Run the program to answer the following questions:

LOOKING AHEAD

This program can be used to choose an appropriate color for Listing 2-6.

a. What color results from a red value of 255, a green value of 255, and a blue value of 200 (255, 255, 200)?

b. How is (255, 255, 0) different from (255, 255, 200)?

c. What color is (255, 193, 0)?

d. The RGB color model specifies the amounts of red, greens and blue that make up a color. There are other models. The HSB model, for example, specifies the hue, saturation, and brightness of a color. Specify RGB and HSB values for a brown color that pleases you. Which model is easiest for you to use? Why?

Chapter 2

Extending Classes with Services

Chapter Objectives

After studying this chapter, you should be able to:

- Extend an existing class with new commands
- Explain how a message sent to an object is resolved to a particular method
- Use inherited services in an extended class
- Override services in the superclass to provide different functionality
- Follow important stylistic conventions for Java programs
- Extend a graphical user interface component to draw a scene
- Add new kinds of `Things` and `Robots` to the robot world

Sometimes an existing class already does almost all of what is needed—but not quite all. For example, in the previous chapter, you may have found it unnatural to write `karel.turnLeft()` three times just to make a robot turn right. By extending a class we can add related services such as `turnRight`, allowing programmers to express themselves using language that better fits the problem.

Other approaches to providing new functionality include modifying the class itself to include the required functionality or writing a completely new class. These two approaches will be considered in later chapters.

2.1 Understanding Programs: An Experiment

Let's try an experiment. Find a watch or a clock that can measure time in seconds. Measure the number of seconds it takes you to understand the program shown in Listing 2-1. In particular, describe the path the robot takes, its final position, and its direction.

FIND THE CODE

ch02/experiment/

Listing 2-1: *An experiment in understanding a longer program*

```
import becker.robots.*;

public class Longer
{
  public static void main(String[] args)
  { City austin = new City();
    Robot lisa = new Robot(austin, 3, 3, Direction.EAST);

    lisa.move();
    lisa.move();
    lisa.move();
    lisa.turnLeft();
    lisa.turnLeft();
    lisa.turnLeft();
    lisa.move();
    lisa.move();
    lisa.move();
    lisa.turnLeft();
    lisa.turnLeft();
    lisa.move();
    lisa.move();
    lisa.move();
    lisa.turnLeft();
    lisa.move();
    lisa.move();
    lisa.move();
    lisa.turnLeft();
    lisa.turnLeft();
  }
}
```

Now, imagine that we had a new kind of robot with commands to turn around, turn right, and move ahead three times. Time yourself again while you try to understand the program in Listing 2-2. The robot in this program does something different. How fast can you accurately figure out what?

FIND THE CODE

ch02/experiment/

Listing 2-2: *An experiment in understanding a shorter program*

```
import becker.robots.*;

public class Shorter
{
  public static void main(String[] args)
  { City austin = new City();
    ExperimentRobot lisa = new ExperimentRobot(
                                   austin, 3, 2, Direction.SOUTH);

    lisa.move3();
    lisa.turnRight();
    lisa.move3();
    lisa.turnAround();
    lisa.move3();
    lisa.turnLeft();
    lisa.move3();
    lisa.turnAround();
  }
}
```

You probably found the second program easier—and faster—to read and understand. The results shown in Table 2-1 are from a group of beginning Java programmers who performed the same experiment.

(table 2-1)

Results of an experiment in understanding programs

Program	Minimum Time (seconds)	Average Time (seconds)	Maximum Time (seconds)
Longer	12	87	360
Shorter	10	46	120

KEY IDEA

Adapt your language to express your ideas clearly and concisely

Why did we comprehend the second program more quickly? We raised the level of abstraction; the language we used (`turnAround`, `turnRight`, `move3`) matches our thinking more closely than the first program. Essentially, we created a more natural programming language for ourselves.

Raising the level of abstraction with language that matches our thinking has a number of benefits.

- Raising the level of abstraction makes it easier to write the program. It's easier for a programmer to think, "And then I want the robot to turn around" than to think, "The robot should turn around so I need to tell it to turn left and then turn left again." We can think of a task such as `turnAround`, deferring the definition of the task until later. Abstraction allows us to concentrate on the big picture instead of getting stuck on low-level details.
- Raising the level of abstraction allows us to understand programs better. An instruction such as `turnAround` allows the programmer to express her intent. Knowing the intent, we can better understand how this part of the program fits with the rest of the program. It's easier to be told that the programmer wants the robot to turn around than to infer it from two consecutive `turnLeft` commands.
- When we know the intent, it is easier to debug the program. Figuring out what went wrong when faced with a long sequence of service invocations is hard. When we know the intent, we can first ask if the programmer is intending to do the correct thing (**validation**), and then we can ask if the intent is implemented correctly (**verification**). This task is much easier than facing the entire program at once and trying to infer the intent from individual service invocations.

LOOKING AHEAD

Quality software is easier to understand, write, debug, reuse, and modify. We will explore this further in Chapter 11.

- We will find that extending the language makes it easier to modify the program. With the intent more clearly communicated, it is easier to find the places in the program that need modification.
- We can create commands that may be useful in other parts of the program, or even in other programs. By reusing old services and creating new services that will be easy to reuse in the future, we can save ourselves effort. We're working smarter rather than harder, as the saying goes.

KEY IDEA

Work smarter by reusing code.

In the next section, we will learn how to extend an existing class such as `Robot` to add new services such as `turnAround`. We'll see that these ideas apply to all Java programs, not just those involving robots.

2.2 Extending the `Robot` Class

Let's see how the new kind of robot used in Listing 2-2 was created. What we want is a robot that can turn around, turn right, and move ahead three times—in addition to all the services provided by ordinary robots, such as turning left, picking things up, and putting them down. In terms of a class diagram, we want a robot class that corresponds to Figure 2-1.

(figure 2-1)

Class diagram for the new robot class, `ExperimentRobot`

ExperimentRobot
int street int avenue Direction direction ThingBag backpack
ExperimentRobot(City aCity, int aStreet, int anAvenue, Direction aDirection) void move( ) void turnLeft( ) void pickThing( ) void putThing( ) void turnAround( ) void turnRight( ) void move3( )

The class shown in Figure 2-1 is almost the same as `Robot`—but not quite. We would like a way to augment the existing functionality in `Robot` rather than implementing it again, similar to the camper shown in Figure 2-2.

(figure 2-2)

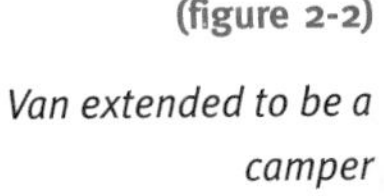

Van extended to be a camper

This vehicle has a number of features for people who enjoy camping: a bed in the pop-up top, a small sink and stove, a table, and so on. Did the camper's manufacturer design and build the entire vehicle just for the relatively few customers who want such a vehicle for camping? No. The manufacturer started with a simple cargo van and then added the special options for camping. The cargo van gave them the vehicle's basic frame, engine, transmission, driver's seat, instrument panel, and so on. Using all this infrastructure from an existing vehicle saved them a lot of work, so they could focus on the unique aspects required by a camper. The same cargo van, by the way, is also extended in different ways to carry more passengers.

Just as the camper manufacturer extended a van with additional features, we will extend `Robot` with additional services. Java actually uses the keyword `extends` for this purpose.

KEY IDEA

Start with something that does most of what you need. Then customize it for your particular use.

Figure 2-3 shows a class diagram in which `ExperimentRobot` extends `Robot`. Notice that the `Robot` class diagram is exactly the same as Figure 1-8. The `ExperimentRobot` class diagram shows only the attributes and services that are added to the `Robot` class. In the case of an `ExperimentRobot`, only services are added; no attributes. The hollow-tipped arrow between the two classes shows the relationship between them: `ExperimentRobot`, at the tail of the arrow, extends `Robot`, at the head of the arrow.

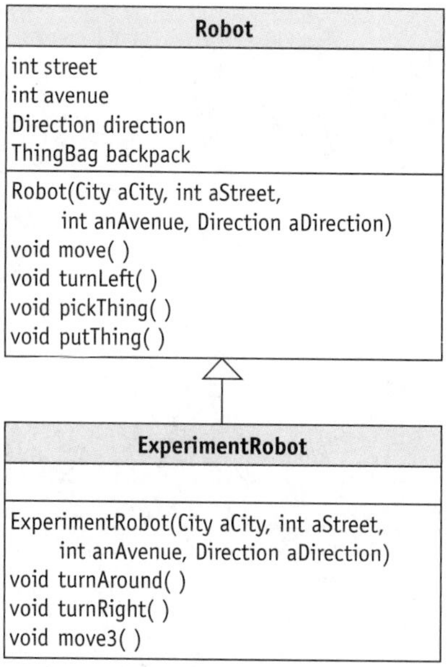

Robot
int street int avenue Direction direction ThingBag backpack
Robot(City aCity, int aStreet, int anAvenue, Direction aDirection) void move( ) void turnLeft( ) void pickThing( ) void putThing( )

ExperimentRobot
ExperimentRobot(City aCity, int aStreet, int anAvenue, Direction aDirection) void turnAround( ) void turnRight( ) void move3( )

(figure 2-3)

Class diagram showing `ExperimentRobot` *extending* `Robot`

2.2.1 The Vocabulary of Extending Classes

When communicating about extending a class, we say that the `Robot` class is the **superclass** and the `ExperimentRobot` class is the **subclass**. Unless you're familiar with the language of mathematical sets or biology, this use of "sub" and "super" may seem backwards. In these settings, "super" means a more inclusive set or category. For example, an `ExperimentRobot` is a special kind of `Robot`. We will also define other special kinds of `Robots`. `Robot` is the more inclusive set, the superclass.

KEY IDEA

The class that is extended is called the "superclass." The new class is called the "subclass."

We might also say that `ExperimentRobot` **inherits** from `Robot` or that `ExperimentRobot` **extends** `Robot`.

If you think of a superclass as the parent of a class, that child class can have a grandparent and even a great-grandparent because the superclass may have its own superclass. It is, therefore, appropriate to talk about a class's superclasses (plural) even though it has only one direct superclass.

In a class diagram such as Figure 2-3, the superclass is generally shown above the subclass, and the arrow always points from the subclass to the superclass.

2.2.2 The Form of an Extended Class

LOOKING AHEAD

When a pattern is used, an icon appears in the margin, as shown here for the Extended Class pattern. The patterns for this chapter are revisited in Section 2.8.

The form of an extended class is as follows:

```
1 import «importedPackage»;
2
3 public class «className» extends «superClass»
4 {
5     «list of attributes used by this class»
6     «list of constructors for this class»
7     «list of services provided by this class»
8 }
```

PATTERN

Extended Class

The `import` statement is the same here as in the Java Program pattern. Line 3 establishes the relationship between this class and its superclass using the keyword `extends`. For an `ExperimentRobot`, for example, this line would read as follows:

```
public class ExperimentRobot extends Robot
```

Lines 5, 6, and 7 of the code template are slots for attributes, constructors, and services. In the next section, we will implement a constructor. In the following sections, we will implement the services `turnAround`, `turnRight`, and `move3`. We will not be adding attributes to our classes until Chapter 6. Until then, we will use only the attributes inherited from the superclass.

2.2.3 Implementing the Constructor

The purpose of the constructor is to initialize each object that is constructed. That is, when the statement `Robot karel = new Robot(austin, 1, 1, Direction.SOUTH)` is executed, the constructor for the `Robot` class ensures that the attributes `street`, `avenue`, `direction`, and `backpack` are all given appropriate values.

We are not adding any attributes to the `ExperimentRobot`. So what is there to initialize? Is a constructor necessary? Yes. Because `ExperimentRobot` extends the `Robot` class, each `ExperimentRobot` object can be visualized as having a `Robot` object inside of it (see Figure 2-4). We need to ensure that the `Robot`-inside-the-`ExperimentRobot` object is correctly initialized with appropriate values for `street`, `avenue`, `direction`, and `backpack`.

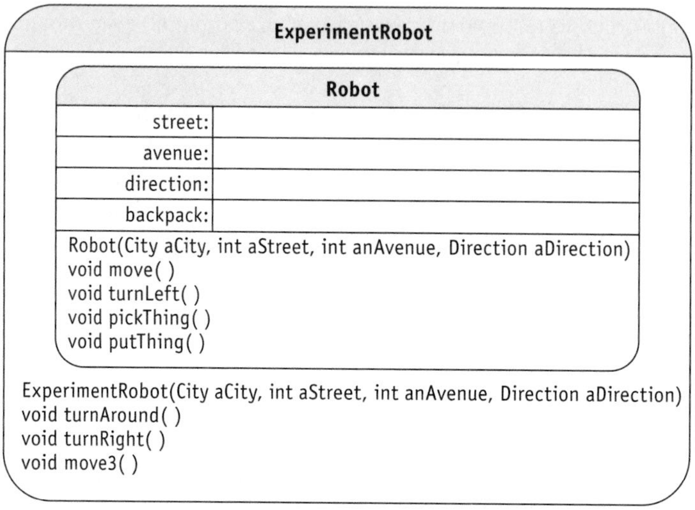

ExperimentRobot

Robot

street:
avenue:
direction:
backpack:

Robot(City aCity, int aStreet, int anAvenue, Direction aDirection)
void move( )
void turnLeft( )
void pickThing( )
void putThing( )

ExperimentRobot(City aCity, int aStreet, int anAvenue, Direction aDirection)
void turnAround( )
void turnRight( )
void move3( )

(figure 2-4)

Visualizing an `ExperimentRobot` *as containing a* `Robot`

The constructor for `ExperimentRobot` is only four lines long—three if all the parameters would fit on the same line:

```
1 public ExperimentRobot(City aCity, int aStreet,
2                        int anAvenue, Direction aDirection)
3 { super(aCity, aStreet, anAvenue, aDirection);
4 }
```

Lines 1 and 2 declare the parameters required to initialize the `Robot`-inside-the-`ExperimentRobot`: a city, the initial street and avenue, and the initial direction. Each parameter is preceded by its type.

Line 3 passes on the information received from the parameters to the `Robot`-inside-the-`ExperimentRobot`. Object initialization is performed by a constructor, so you would think that line 3 would call the constructor of the superclass:

```
Robot(aCity, aStreet, anAvenue, aDirection);        // doesn't work!
```

KEY IDEA

The constructor must ensure the superclass is properly initialized.

However, the designers of Java chose to use a keyword, `super`, instead of the name of the superclass. When `super` is used as shown in line 3, Java looks for a constructor in the superclass with parameters that match the provided arguments, and calls it. The effect is the same as you would expect from using `Robot`, as shown earlier.

LOOKING AHEAD

Section 2.6 explains another use for the keyword `super`.

LOOKING AHEAD

We will explore parameters further in Section 4.6 in the context of writing services with parameters.

When an `ExperimentRobot` is constructed with the following statement, the values passed as arguments (`austin`, `3`, `2`, and `Direction.SOUTH`) are copied into the parameters (`aCity`, `aStreet`, `anAvenue`, and `aDirection`) in the `ExperimentRobot` constructor.

```
ExperimentRobot lisa = new ExperimentRobot(austin,
                                    3, 2, Direction.SOUTH);
```

Then, in line 3, those same values are passed as arguments to the parameters in the superclass's constructor.

Two other details about the constructor are that it must have the same name as the class and it does not have a return type—not even `void`. If a constructor has a name different from the class, the compiler considers it a service without a return type, and issues a compile-time error. If a constructor has a return type, the compiler considers it a service, and may not display an error until a client tries to use the constructor. Then the compiler will complain that it can't find it—because the constructor is being interpreted as a service.

Listing 2-3 contains the first steps in defining the `ExperimentRobot` class. It has a number of the template slots filled in, including imported classes, the class name, and the extended class's name. It also includes a constructor, but none of the new services. Just like the programs we wrote in Chapter 1, this class should be placed in its own file named `ExperimentRobot.java`.

FIND THE CODE

ch02/experiment/

Listing 2-3: *The* `ExperimentRobot` *class with a constructor but no services*

```
import becker.robots.*;

public class ExperimentRobot extends Robot
{
   public ExperimentRobot(City aCity, int aStreet,
                          int anAvenue, Direction aDirection)
   { super(aCity, aStreet, anAvenue, aDirection);
   }

   // The new services offered by an ExperimentRobot will be inserted here.
}
```

With this modest beginning, we can write a program that includes the following statement:

```
ExperimentRobot lisa = new ExperimentRobot(austin,
                                    3, 2, Direction.SOUTH);
```

The robot `lisa` can do all things any normal robot can do. `lisa` can move, turn left, pick things up, and put them down again. An `ExperimentRobot` is a kind of `Robot` object and has inherited all those services from the `Robot` class. In fact, the `Robot` in line 7 of Listing 2-1 could be replaced with an `ExperimentRobot`. Even with no other changes, the program would execute as it does with a `Robot`. However, an `ExperimentRobot` cannot yet respond to the messages `turnAround`, `turnRight`, or `move3`.

KEY IDEA

A class with only a constructor, like Listing 2-3, is complete and can be used in a program. It just doesn't add any new services.

2.2.4 Adding a Service

A service is an idea such as "turn around." To actually implement this idea, we add a **method** to the class, which contains code to carry out the idea. When we want a robot to turn around, we send a message to the robot naming the `turnAround` service. This message causes the code in the corresponding method to be executed.

KEY IDEA

Services are ideas. Methods contain code to implement the idea. Services are invoked with a message. The object responds by executing a method.

An analogy may help distinguish services, messages, and methods. Every child can eat. This is a service provided by the child. It is something the child can do. A message from a parent, "Come and eat your supper" causes the child to perform the service of eating. The particular method the child uses to eat, however, depends on the instructions he or she has received while growing up. The child may use chopsticks, a fork, or a fork and a knife. The idea (eating) is the service. The message ("eat your supper") causes the service to be performed. How the service is performed (chopsticks, fork, and so on) is determined by the instructions in the method.

The service `turnAround` may be added to the `ExperimentRobot` class by inserting the following method between lines 10 and 11 in Listing 2-3:

```
public void turnAround()
{ this.turnLeft();
  this.turnLeft();
}
```

Now the robot `lisa` can respond to the `turnAround` message. When a client says `lisa.turnAround()`, the robot knows that `turnAround` is defined as turning left twice, once for each `turnLeft` command in the body of `turnAround`.

Flow of Control

Recall the Sequential Execution pattern from Chapter 1. It says that each statement is executed, one after another. Each statement finishes before the next one in the sequence begins. When a program uses `lisa.turnAround()` we break out of the Sequential Execution pattern. The **flow of control**, or the sequence in which statements are executed, does not simply go to the next statement (yet). First it goes to the statements contained in `turnAround`, as illustrated in Figure 2-5.

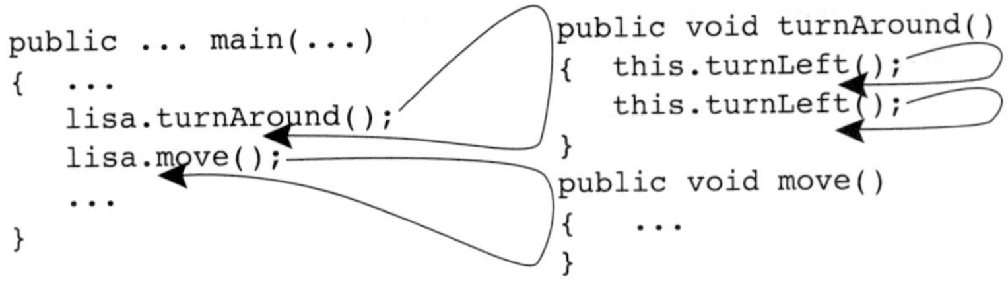

(figure 2.5)

Flow of control when executing methods

```
public ... main(...)              public void turnAround()
{  ...                            {  this.turnLeft();
   lisa.turnAround();                this.turnLeft();
   lisa.move();                   }
   ...                            public void move()
}                                 {  ...
                                  }
```

When main sends the message `lisa.turnAround()`, Java finds the definition of `turnAround` and executes each of the statements it contains. It then returns to the statement following `lisa.turnAround()`. This is an example of a much more general pattern that occurs each time a message is sent to an object:

KEY IDEA

Calling a method temporarily interrupts the Sequential Execution pattern.

- The method implementing the service named in the message is found.
- The statements contained in the method are executed. Unless told otherwise, the statements are executed sequentially according to the Sequential Execution pattern.
- Flow of control returns to the statement following the statement that sent the message.

Look again at Figure 2-5. This same pattern is followed when `lisa` is sent the `move` message, although we don't know what the statements in the `move` method are, so they are not shown in the figure. Similarly, when `turnAround` is executed, each `turnLeft` message it sends follows the same pattern: Java finds the method implementing `turnLeft`, executes the statements it contains, and then it returns, ready to execute the next statement in `turnAround`.

When we are considering only `main`, the Sequential Execution pattern still holds. When we look only at `turnAround`, the Sequential Execution pattern holds there, too. But when we look at a method together with the methods it invokes, we see that the Sequential Execution pattern does *not* hold. The flow of control jumps from one place in the program to another—but always in an orderly and predictable manner.

The Implicit Parameter: this

In previous discussions, we have said that parameters provide information necessary for a method or constructor to do its job. Because `turnAround` has no parameters, we might conclude that it doesn't need any information to do its job. That conclusion is not correct.

One vital piece of information `turnAround` needs is which robot it should turn around. When a client says `lisa.turnAround()`, the method must turn `lisa` around, and if a client says `karel.turnAround()`, the method must turn `karel` around. Clearly the method must know which object it is to act upon.

This piece of information is needed so often and is so vital that the designers of Java made accessing it extremely easy for programmers. Whenever a method is invoked with the pattern *«objectReference».«methodName»(…)*, *«objectReference»* becomes an **implicit parameter** to *«methodName»*. The implicit parameter is the object receiving the message. In the case of `lisa.turnAround()`, the implicit parameter is `lisa`, and for `karel.turnAround()`, the implicit parameter is `karel`.

The implicit parameter is accessed within a method with the keyword `this`. The statement `this.turnLeft()` means that the same robot that called `turnAround` will be instructed to turn left. If the client said `lisa.turnAround()`, then `lisa` will be the implicit parameter and `this.turnLeft()` will instruct `lisa` to turn left.

Sometimes when a person learns a new activity with many steps they will mutter instructions to themselves: "First, *I* turn left. Then *I* turn left again." Executing a method definition is like that, except that "I" is replaced by "this robot." You can think of the `ExperimentRobot` as muttering instructions to itself: "First, *this* robot turns left. Then *this* robot turns left again."

public and void Keywords

The two remaining keywords in the method definition are `public` and `void`. The keyword `public` says that this method is available for any client to use. In Section 3.6, we will learn about situations for which we might want to prevent some clients from using certain methods. In those situations, we will use a different keyword.

The keyword `void` distinguishes a command from a query. Its presence tells us that `turnAround` does not return any information to the client.

2.2.5 Implementing move3

Implementing the `move3` method is similar to `turnAround`, except that we want the robot to move forward three times. The complete method follows. Like `turnAround`, it is placed inside the class, but outside of any constructor or method.

LOOKING AHEAD

Eventually we will learn how to write a method with a parameter so we can say `lisa.move(50)` *— or any other distance.*

```
public void move3()
{ this.move();
  this.move();
  this.move();
}
```

As with `turnAround`, we want the same robot that is executing `move3` to do the moving. We therefore use the keyword `this` to specify which object receives the `move` messages.

2.2.6 Implementing `turnRight`

To tell a robot to turn right, we could say "turn left, turn left, turn left." We could also say "turn around, then turn left." Both work. The first approach results in the following method:

PATTERN

Parameterless Command

```
public void turnRight()
{ this.turnLeft();
  this.turnLeft();
  this.turnLeft();
}
```

KEY IDEA

An object can send messages to itself, invoking its own methods.

The second approach is more interesting, resulting in this method:

```
public void turnRight()
{ this.turnAround();
  this.turnLeft();
}
```

LOOKING AHEAD

Methods calling other methods is a core idea of Stepwise Refinement, the topic of Chapter 3.

The second version works by asking the `ExperimentRobot` object to execute one of its own methods, `turnAround`. The robot finds the definition of `turnAround` and executes it (that is, it turns left twice as the definition of `turnAround` says it should). When it has finished executing `turnAround`, it is told to `turnLeft` one more time. The robot has then turned left three times, as desired.

This flow of control is illustrated in Figure 2-6. Execution begins with `lisa.turnRight()` in the `main` method. It proceeds as shown by the arrows. Each method executes the methods it contains and then returns to its client, continuing with the statement after the method call. Before a method is finished, each of the methods it calls must also be finished.

(figure 2-6)

Flow of control when one method calls another

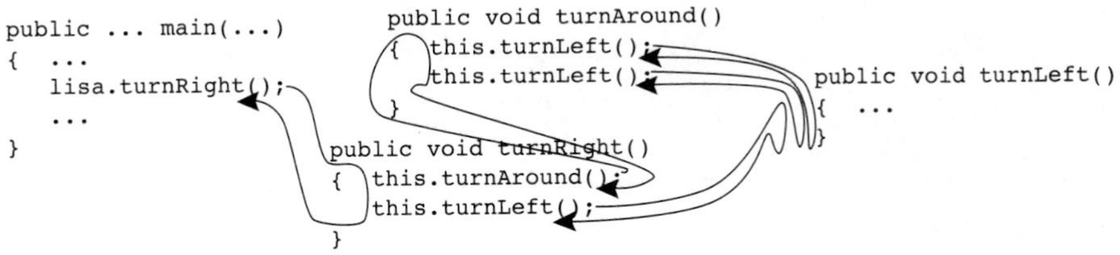

This discussion completes the `ExperimentRobot` class. The entire program is shown in Listing 2-4.

FIND THE CODE

ch02/experiment/

Listing 2-4: *The complete listing for* `ExperimentRobot`

```
import becker.robots.*;

// A new kind of robot that can turn around, turn right, and move forward
// three intersections at a time.
// author: Byron Weber Becker
public class ExperimentRobot extends Robot
{
   // Construct a new ExperimentRobot.
   public ExperimentRobot(City aCity, int aStreet,
                    int anAvenue, Direction aDirection)
   { super(aCity, aStreet, anAvenue, aDirection);
   }

   // Turn this robot around so it faces the opposite direction.
   public void turnAround()
   { this.turnLeft();
     this.turnLeft();
   }

   // Move this robot forward three times.
   public void move3()
   { this.move();
     this.move();
     this.move();
   }

   // Turn this robot 90 degrees to the right by turning around and then left by 90 degrees.
   public void turnRight()
   { this.turnAround();
     this.turnLeft();
   }
}
```

2.2.7 RobotSE

You can probably imagine other programs requiring robots that can turn around and turn right. `DeliverParcel` (Listing 1-1) could have used `turnRight` in one place, while `GoAroundRoadBlock` (Listing 1-2) could have used it twice. Several of the programming projects at the end of Chapter 1 could have used either `turnAround` or `turnRight` or both.

LOOKING AHEAD

You learn how to build your own package of useful classes in Chapter 9.

When we write methods that are applicable to more than one problem, it is a good idea to add that method to a class where it can be easily reused. The `becker` library has a class containing commonly used extensions to `Robot`, including `turnRight` and `turnAround`. It's called `RobotSE`, short for "Robot Special Edition." In the future, you may want to extend `RobotSE` instead of `Robot` so that you can easily use these additional methods.

2.2.8 Extension vs. Modification

LOOKING AHEAD

The `turnRight` method in `RobotSE` actually turns right instead of turning left three times. Section 3.6 explains how.

Another approach to making a robot that can turn around and turn right would be to modify the existing class, `Robot`. Modifying an existing class is not always possible, and this is one of those times. The `Robot` class is provided in a library, without source code. Without the source code, we have nothing to modify. We say that the `Robot` class is **closed for modification.**

There are other reasons to consider a class closed for modification, even when the source code is available. In a complex class, a company may not want to risk introducing errors through modification. Or the class may be used in many different programs, with only a few benefiting from the proposed modifications.

As we've seen, however, the `Robot` class is **open for extension.** It is programmed in such a way that those who want to modify its operation can do so via Java's extension mechanism. When a class is open for extension it can be modified via subclasses without fear of introducing bugs into the original class or introducing features that aren't generally needed.

2.3 Extending the `Thing` Class

KEY IDEA

Classes other than `Robot` can also be extended.

`Robot` is not the only class that can be extended. For example, `City` is extended by `MazeCity`. Instances of `MazeCity` contain a maze for the robots to navigate. At the end of this chapter you will find that graphical user interface components can be extended to do new things as well. In fact, every class can be extended unless its programmer has taken specific steps to prevent extension.

To demonstrate extending a class other than `Robot`, let's extend `Thing` to create a `Lamp` class. Each `Lamp` object will have two services, one to turn it "on" and another to turn it "off." When a lamp is "on" it displays itself with a soft yellow circle and when it is "off" it displays itself with a black circle. Because `Lamp` extends `Thing`, lamps behave like things—robots can pick them up, move them, and put them down again.

2.3.1 Exploring the `Thing` Class

Before attempting to extend the `Thing` class we should become more familiar with it. The beginning of its online documentation is shown in Figure 2-7. Part of the information it provides is the classes `Thing` extends, also called the **inheritance hierarchy**. In this case, `Thing` extends a class named `Sim`, and `Sim` extends `Object`. The `Sim` class defines core methods inherited by everything displayed in a city, including intersections, robots, and things. Below the inheritance hierarchy we are told that `Thing` is extended by at least two classes: `Light` and `Wall`.

LOOKING AHEAD

The `Light` subclass of `Thing` may be useful for defining lamps. We'll explore this idea later, in Section 2.3.6.

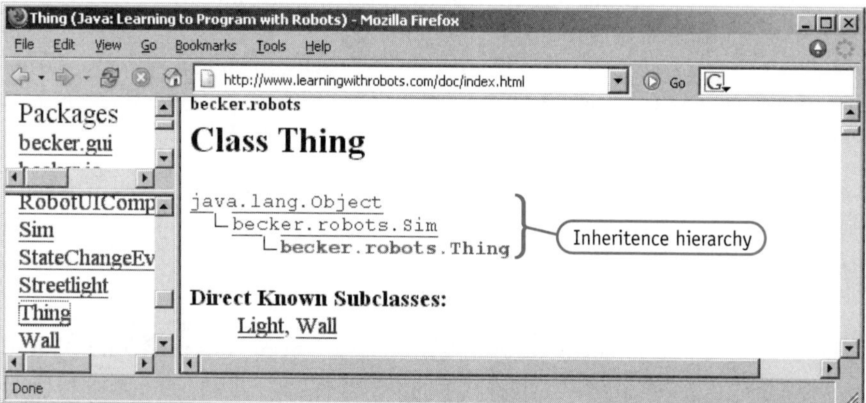

(figure 2-7)

Part of the documentation for the `Thing` class

The summaries for `Thing`'s four constructors are shown in Figure 2-8. The constructor we have used so far provides a "default appearance," which we know from experience is a yellow circle. The second and third constructors tell us that `Thing` objects have other properties such as whether they can be moved (presumably by a robot) and an orientation. The class overview (not shown in Figure 2-8) refers to these properties as well.

The methods listed in the documentation are mostly queries and don't seem helpful for implementing a `lamp` object. They are listed online, of course, and also in Appendix E. However, the `Thing` documentation also includes a section titled "Methods Inherited from Class `becker.robots.Sim`." This section lists a `setIcon` method. Its description says "Set the icon used to display this Sim."

Icons determine how each robot, intersection, or thing object appears within the city. By changing the icon, we can change how something looks. For example, the following few lines of code replace `deceptiveThing`'s icon to make the `Thing` look like a `Wall`:

```
Thing deceptiveThing = new Thing(aCityObject, 3, 4);
WallIcon anIcon = new WallIcon();
deceptiveThing.setIcon(anIcon);
```

LOOKING BACK

The first two lines of code use the Object Instantiation pattern discussed in Section 1.7.2.

(figure 2-8)

Additional documentation for the `Thing` *class*

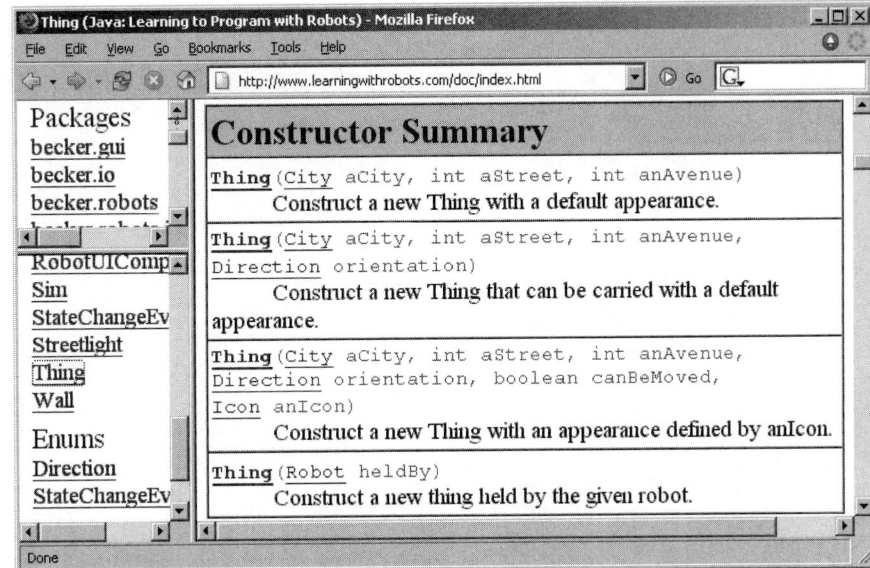

We will do something similar for our `Lamp` class. When the lamp is turned on we will give it a new appearance using `setIcon`, passing it an icon that shows a soft yellow circle. When the lamp is turned off we will pass `setIcon` an icon showing a black circle.

2.3.2 Implementing a Simple `Lamp` Object

We will implement our `Lamp` class by extending `Thing`. Our experience with extending `Robot` tells us that to extend a class we must complete the following tasks:

- Use the `class` and `extends` keywords to specify the class's name and the name of the class it extends. (See Section 2.2.2.)
- Write a constructor that will initialize the superclass appropriately. (See Section 2.2.3.)
- Write methods implementing each of the services offered by the class. (See Section 2.2.4.)

Knowing these three things, we can write the beginnings of our `Lamp` class as shown in Listing 2-5. We still need to replace each ellipsis (...) with additional Java code.

FIND THE CODE

ch02/extendThing/

Listing 2-5: *The beginnings of a* `Lamp` *class*

```
import becker.robots.*;

```

Listing 2-5: *The beginnings of a* `Lamp` *class* (continued)

```
3  public class Lamp extends Thing
4  {
5     // Construct a new lamp object.
6     public Lamp(...)
7     { super(...);
8     }
9
10    // Turn the lamp on.
11    public void turnOn()
12    { ...
13    }
14
15    // Turn the lamp off.
16    public void turnOff()
17    { ...
18    }
19 }
```

PATTERN
Extended Class

Implementing the Constructor

The `Lamp` constructor must ensure that the attributes in its superclass, `Thing`, are completely initialized when a lamp is created. Recall that attributes are initialized by calling one of the constructors in the `Thing` class using the keyword `super`. The arguments passed to `super` must match the parameters of a constructor in the superclass. The documentation in Figure 2-8 confirms that one of the constructors requires a city, initial street, and initial avenue as parameters. As with the `ExperimentRobot` class, this information will come via the constructor's parameters. Putting all this together, lines 6, 7, and 8 in Listing 2-5 should be replaced with the following code:

```
public Lamp(City aCity, int aStreet, int anAvenue)
{ super(aCity, aStreet, anAvenue);
}
```

PATTERN
Constructor

Implementing `turnOn` and `turnOff`

When the `turnOn` service is invoked, the lamp should display itself as a soft yellow circle. As we discovered earlier, the appearance is changed by changing the lamp's icon using the `setIcon` method inherited from a superclass.

LOOKING BACK

Finding robot documentation was discussed in Section 1.4.8.

The robot documentation (in the `becker.robots.icons` package) describes a number of classes that include the word "Icon" such as `RobotIcon`, `ShapeIcon`, `WallIcon`, `FlasherIcon`, and `CircleIcon`. The last one may be able to help display a yellow circle. According to the documentation, constructing a `CircleIcon` requires a `Color` object to pass as an argument. We'll need a `Color` object *before* we construct the `CircleIcon` object.

In summary, to change the appearance of our `Lamp` we must complete the following steps:

create a Color object named "onColor"
create a CircleIcon named "onIcon" using "onColor"
call setIcon to replace this lamp's current icon with "onIcon"

KEY IDEA

Documentation is useful. Bookmark it in your browser to make it easy to access.

We can learn how to construct a `Color` object by consulting the online documentation at *http://java.sun.com/j2se/1.5.0/docs/api/* or, if you have already found the documentation for `CircleIcon`, click on the link to `Color` found in the constructor's parameter list. The documentation describes seven `Color` constructors. The simplest one takes three numbers, each between 0 and 255, that specify the red, green, and blue components of the color. Using 255, 255, and 200 produces a soft yellow color appropriate for a lamp's light. A **color chooser** is a dialog that displays many colors and can help choose these three values. Most drawing programs have a color chooser and Problem 1.18 provides guidance for writing your own color chooser.

We can now convert the preceding steps to Java. Inserting them in the `turnOn` method results in the following five lines of code:

PATTERN

Parameterless Command

```
public void turnOn()
{  Color onColor = new Color(255, 255, 200);
   CircleIcon onIcon = new CircleIcon(onColor);
   this.setIcon(onIcon);
}
```

The `turnOff` method is identical except that `onColor` and `onIcon` should be appropriately named `offColor` and `offIcon`, and `offColor` should be constructed with `new Color(0, 0, 0)`.

Completing the Class and `Main` Method

We have now completed the `Lamp` class. Listing 2-6 shows it in its entirety. Notice that it includes two new import statements in lines 2 and 3. The first one gives easier[1] access to `CircleIcon`; it's in the `becker.robots.icons` package. The second one gives easier access to `Color`.

[1] It is possible to access these classes without the `import` statement. Every time the class is used, include the package name. For example, `java.awt.Color onColor = new java.awt.Color(255, 255, 200);`

FIND THE CODE

ch02/extendThing/

PATTERN

Extended Class

Listing 2-6: *The* Lamp *class*

```
import becker.robots.*;
import becker.robots.icons.*;      // CircleIcon
import java.awt.*;                 // Color

public class Lamp extends Thing
{
  // Construct a new lamp object.
  public Lamp(City aCity, int aStreet, int anAvenue)
  { super(aCity, aStreet, anAvenue);
  }

  // Turn the lamp on.
  public void turnOn()
  { Color onColor = new Color(255, 255, 200);
    CircleIcon onIcon = new CircleIcon(onColor);
    this.setIcon(onIcon);
  }

  // Turn the lamp off.
  public void turnOff()
  { Color offColor = new Color(0, 0, 0);
    CircleIcon offIcon = new CircleIcon(offColor);
    this.setIcon(offIcon);
  }
}
```

PATTERN

Parameterless Command

This example illustrates that many classes can be extended, not just the `Robot` class. To extend a class, we perform the following tasks:

- Create a new class that includes the following line:

  `public class «className» extends «superClass»`

  where *«superClass»* names the class you want to extend. In this example the superclass was `Thing`; in the first example the superclass was `Robot`.
- Create a constructor for the new class that has the same name as the class. Make sure it calls `super` with parameters appropriate for one of the constructors in the superclass.
- Add a method for each of the services the new class should offer.

A short test program that uses the `Lamp` class is shown in Listing 2-7. It instantiates two `Lamp` objects, turning one on and turning the other off. A robot then picks one up and moves it to a new location. The left side of Figure 2-9 shows the initial situation after lines 7–14 have been executed. The right side of Figure 2-9 shows the result after lines 17–21 have been executed to move the lit lamp to another intersection. The actual running program is more colorful than what is shown in Figure 2-9.

(figure 2-9)

Program with two `Lamp` *objects, one "on" at (1, 1) and one "off" at (2, 1) in the initial situation*

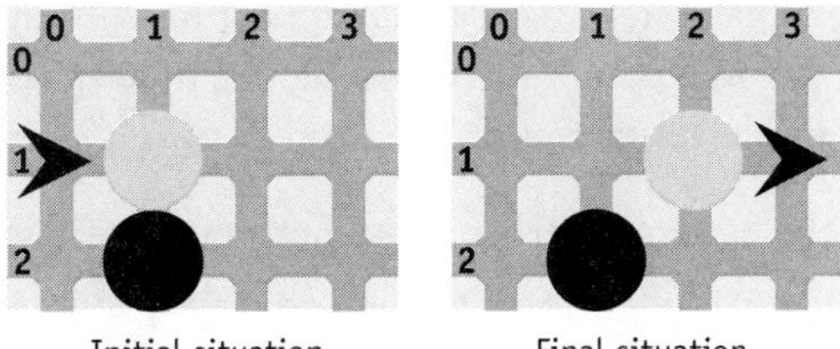

FIND THE CODE

cho2/extendThing/

Listing 2-7: *A* `main` *method for a program that uses the* `Lamp` *class*

```
1  import becker.robots.*;
2
3  public class Main
4  {
5    public static void main(String[] args)
6    { // Construct the initial situation.
7      City paris = new City();
8      Lamp lamp1 = new Lamp(paris, 1, 1);
9      Lamp lamp2 = new Lamp(paris, 2, 1);
10     Robot lampMover = new Robot(paris, 1, 0, Direction.EAST);
11
12     // Turn one lamp on and the other off.
13     lamp1.turnOn();
14     lamp2.turnOff();
15
16     // Use the robot to move one of the lamps.
17     lampMover.move();
18     lampMover.pickThing();
19     lampMover.move();
20     lampMover.putThing();
21     lampMover.move();
22   }
23 }
```

2.3.3 Completely Initializing Lamps

In Listing 2-7, the `main` method instantiates two `Lamp` objects in lines 8 and 9, and then explicitly turns one on and one off in lines 13 and 14. Suppose that lines 13 and 14 were omitted, so that the lamps were turned neither on nor off explicitly. How would they appear? Unfortunately, they would appear just like any other `Thing`—as a medium-sized, bright yellow circle. It seems wrong that a `Lamp` object should appear to be a `Thing` just because the client forgot to explicitly turn it on or off.

The problem is that the `Lamp` constructor did not completely initialize the object. A complete initialization for a lamp not only calls `super` to initialize the superclass, it also sets the icon so the lamp appears to be either on or off.

A constructor can execute statements other than the call to `super`. It could, for example, call `setIcon`. But to follow the Service Invocation pattern of *«objectReference»*`.`*«serviceName»*`(…)`, we need to have an object. The object we want is the object the constructor is now creating.

The methods we have written often use the implicit parameter, `this`, to refer to the object executing the method. The implicit parameter, `this`, is also available within the constructor. It refers to the object being constructed. We can write `this.setIcon(…);` within the constructor. Think of `this` as referring to *this* object, the one being constructed.

LOOKING BACK

The implicit parameter was discussed in more depth in Section 2.2.4.

The new version of the constructor is then as follows. It initializes the superclass with the call to `super`, and then finishes the initialization by replacing the icon with a new one.

```
1 public Lamp(City aCity, int aStreet, int anAvenue)
2 { super(aCity, aStreet, anAvenue);
3   Color offColor = new Color(0, 0, 0);
4   CircleIcon offIcon = new CircleIcon(offColor);
5   this.setIcon(offIcon);
6 }
```

Calling `super` must be the first statement in the constructor. It ensures that the `Thing`-inside-the-`Lamp` is appropriately initialized so it can handle the call to `this.setIcon`.

KEY IDEA

Initializing the superclass is the first thing to do inside a constructor.

You may recognize lines 3–5 as being identical to the body of `turnOff`. Do we really need to type in the code twice, and then fix it twice if we discover a bug or want to change how a `Lamp` looks when it is off? No. Recall that an object can call its own methods. We saw this concept when `ExperimentRobot` called `turnAround` from the `turnRight` method. Similarly, the constructor can call `turnOff` directly, a much better solution.

```
public Lamp(City aCity, int aStreet, int anAvenue)
{ super(aCity, aStreet, anAvenue);
  this.turnOff();
}
```

PATTERN

Constructor

2.3.4 Fine-Tuning the `Lamp` Class (optional)

The `Lamp` class can be fine-tuned in several ways to be more visually pleasing.

Changing the Size of an Icon

A turned-off `Lamp` appears as large as the yellow circle of light cast by a lamp that is on, which is not realistic. It's also unrealistic to represent a lamp with an icon that is as large as an intersection.

To solve this problem, we need a way to make a smaller icon. The documentation for `CircleIcon` includes a method, `setSize`, for this purpose. Its parameter is a number between 0.0 and 1.0. A value of 1.0 makes it full size, 0.001 makes it extremely small, and 0.5 makes it half size. The size must be larger than 0.0.

With this knowledge, let's change `turnOff` to make a smaller icon:

PATTERN

Parameterless Command

```
public void turnOff()
{ Color offColor = new Color(0, 0, 0);
  CircleIcon offIcon = new CircleIcon(offColor);
  offIcon.setSize(0.25);
  this.setIcon(offIcon);
}
```

The only change in this code, compared to Listing 2-6, is to add the extra method call.

Transparency

To make the lamp more realistic, the light from a lamp should be semi transparent to let the intersection show through. With the previous change to `turnOff` and a small change to `turnOn`, the initial situation will look like Figure 2-11 instead of Figure 2-10. Unfortunately, the difference is not as striking in print as it is on-screen in full color.

To obtain a transparent color, we can again use a service `CircleIcon` inherits from its superclass. `setTransparency` takes a number between 0.0 and 1.0 where a value of 0.0 is completely opaque and 1.0 is completely transparent. For the lamp icon a value of about 0.5 works well. The new version of `turnOn` follows:

```
public void turnOn()
{ Color onColor = new Color(255, 255, 200);
  CircleIcon onIcon = new CircleIcon(onColor);
  onIcon.setSize(0.75);
  onIcon.setTransparency(0.5);
  this.setIcon(onIcon);
}
```

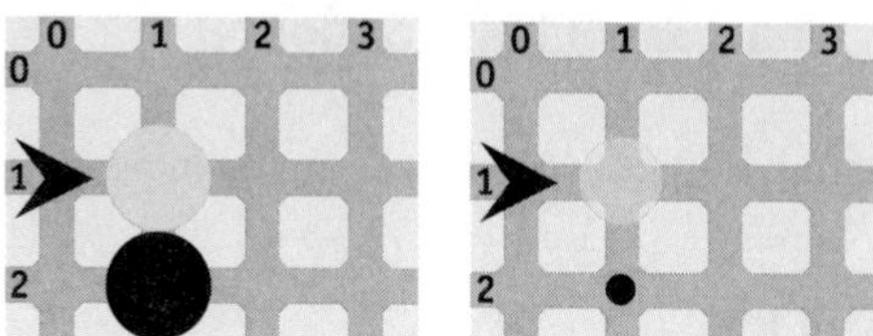

(figure 2-10)

Original initial situation (left)

(figure 2-11)

New initial situation (right)

2.3.5 Other Subclasses of `Thing`

The `becker.robots` package includes several subclasses of `Thing` that have already been defined. They are similar to `Lamp`, except that someone else did the programming, and they have been put into the `becker.robots` package. Interested students may enjoy using them to give additional variety to their programs.

KEY IDEA

The `Thing` class can be extended in many ways.

One subclass of `Thing` is called `Flasher`. It represents the flashing lights used by road maintenance crews to mark hazards. A `Flasher` is like a `Lamp` except that when it is turned on, it flashes. An example is shown in Figure 2-12. The flasher at the origin is turned on. The flasher beside it is turned off.

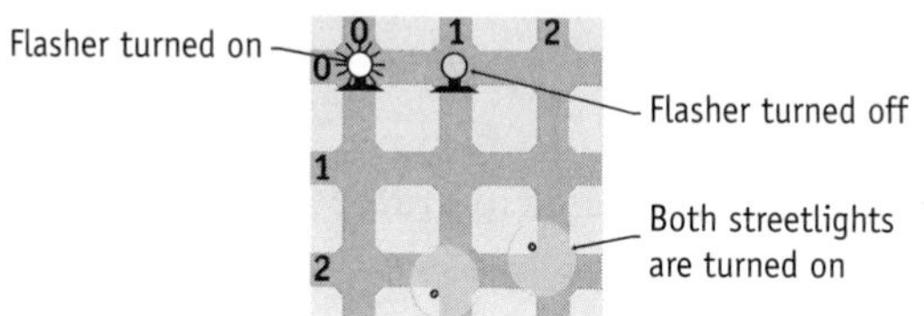

(figure 2-12)

The appearance of `Flashers` and `Streetlights`

Another provided subclass of `Thing` is `Streetlight`. Two instances are shown at (2, 1) and (2, 2). Like walls, streetlights can occupy different positions on an intersection. These streetlights occupy the southwest and northwest corners of their respective intersections. They were created with the following code:

```
Streetlight sLight1 =
      new Streetlight(prague, 2, 1, Direction.SOUTHWEST);
Streetlight sLight2 =
      new Streetlight(prague, 2, 2, Direction.NORTHWEST);
```

Another similarity to walls is that streetlights cannot be picked up and carried by robots. One of the constructors to `Thing` includes a parameter that controls whether robots can pick the thing up; the `Streetlight` constructor makes use of that feature.

The streetlights shown in Figure 2-12 are turned on. Streetlights that are turned off show only the pole in the corner of the intersection. An intersection may have more than one streetlight.

2.3.6 Fun with Lights (optional)

We have already seen how lamps can be turned off and turned on in the `main` method (see Listing 2-7). The same can be done with `Flashers` and `Streetlights`. It is also possible for robots to turn lights on or off, provided the robot and the light are on the same intersection. This requires programming concepts that won't be fully explained until Section 12.1.5, but using them follows a simple pattern and offers more possibilities for creatively using robots.

The key is the `Light` class that we noticed in the documentation shown in Figure 2-7. It has two methods named `turnOn` and `turnOff` and is the superclass for `Flasher` and `Streetlight`. If we extend `Light` when we write the `Lamp` class, all three subclasses are, in some sense, lights that can be turned on and off.

LOOKING AHEAD

This is an example of polymorphism. Learn more in Chapter 12.

In a subclass of `Robot` we can use an inherited method, `examineLights`. It examines the robot's current intersection for a `Light` object. If it finds one, it makes it accessible to the robot. If a light does not exist on the intersection, an error will be printed and the program will stop. Listing 2-8 shows most of a subclass of `Robot` that makes use of `examineLights`. A `SwitchBot`'s `switchLights` method may be used where there are four intersections in a row, each one with a light on it.

FIND THE CODE

ch02/switchLights/

Listing 2-8: *A subclass of* `Robot` *that manipulates lights*

```
import becker.robots.*;

// A robot that switches lights on and off.
public class SwitchBot extends Robot
{
   // Insert a constructor here.

   // Switch every other light off and the remaining lights on.
   public void switchLights()
   { this.move();
     this.examineLights().next().turnOff();
     this.move();
     this.examineLights().next().turnOn();
     this.move();
     this.examineLights().next().turnOff();
     this.move();
     this.examineLights().next().turnOn();
     this.move();
   }
}
```

Notice that lines 11, 13, 15, and 17 have three method calls. This is permitted when a method returns an object. That method call may then be followed with a call to another method. The second method call must be appropriate for the object returned by the first method.

The `Robot` class also has methods named `examineThings` and `examineRobots` that can be used similarly. The `Intersection` and `City` classes have similar methods available.

2.4 Style

As programs become more complex, presenting them clearly to anyone who reads them (including ourselves) becomes vitally important. Attention to presentation, choosing names wisely, indenting, and commenting code all contribute to a program's clarity. In the course of writing and debugging your programs, you will be studying them more thoroughly than anyone else. It's to *your* advantage to make your programs as understandable as possible.

KEY IDEA

Everyone, especially you, benefits from good programming style.

2.4.1 White Space and Indentation

White space is the empty space between the symbols in a program. The Java compiler ignores white space, but its presence (or absence) is important to people reading the program. Consider the program in Listing 2-9. It is identical to the `ExperimentRobot` class in Listing 2-4, except that the white space and comments have been removed. Both classes execute in exactly the same way, but one is considerably easier to read and understand than the other. In particular, Listing 2-9 makes it difficult to see the structure of the class: that there is one constructor and three methods, where each method begins, what the method names are, and so on.

KEY IDEA

Use white space to highlight the logical structure of your program.

Listing 2-9: *A class without white space*

```
import becker.robots.*; public class ExperimentRobot extends
Robot { public ExperimentRobot(City aCity, int aStreet, int
anAvenue, Direction aDirection) { super(aCity, aStreet,
anAvenue, aDirection);} public void turnAround() {
this.turnLeft(); this.turnLeft(); } public void move3(){
this.move(); this.move(); this.move(); } public void
turnRight() { this.turnAround(); this.turnLeft(); }}
```

The following recommendations concerning white space are considered good programming practice:

- Begin each statement on a new line.
- Include at least one blank line between blocks of code with different purposes. For instance, Listing 1-2 includes blank lines between the statements that construct the required objects and the statements that direct the robot `mark` around the road block. There is another blank line between the instructions to `mark` and the instructions to `ann`.
- Line up curly braces so that the closing brace is directly beneath the opening brace.
- Indent everything inside a pair of braces by a consistent number of spaces (this book uses two).

Many conventions govern indenting programs and lining up braces. None of them are right or wrong, but are subject to personal preference. Some people like the preceding style shown through this textbook because it is easy to ensure that braces match.

Nevertheless, your instructor or future employer may have other conventions, complete with reasons to support their preference. As an employee (or student), you will need to accommodate their preferences.

Programs are available that can reformat code to make it adhere to a specific set of conventions. This book's Web site contains references to at least one such program. It is often possible to configure your IDE so that using a code reformatter is as easy as clicking a button.

2.4.2 Identifiers

The symbols that make up a Java program are divided into three groups: special symbols, reserved words, and identifiers. **Special symbols** include the braces `{` and `}`, periods, semicolons, and parentheses. **Reserved words**, also called **keywords**, have a special meaning to the compiler. They include `class`, `package`, `import`, `public`, and `int`. A complete list of reserved words is shown in Table 2-2. Finally, **identifiers** are names: the names of variables (`karel`), the names of classes (`Robot`), the names of services (`move`), and the names of packages (`becker.robots`).

abstract	default	goto	package	this
assert	do	if	private	throw
boolean	double	implements	protected	throws
break	else	import	public	transient
byte	enum	instanceof	return	true
case	extends	int	short	try
catch	false	interface	static	void
char	final	long	strictfp	volatile
class	finally	native	super	while
const	float	new	switch	
continue	for	null	synchronized	

(table 2-2)

Java reserved words. `const` *and* `goto` *are reserved but not currently used*

Programmers have lots of choice in the names they use as identifiers. Wise choices make a program much easier to read and understand, thereby increasing the likelihood that it is correct. Programs with well-chosen identifiers are self-documenting and need fewer explanatory comments.

A well-chosen identifier clearly indicates the purpose of the thing it names. It is better to name a class `Robot` than `R`, for instance. Naming an icon `onIcon` is much better than `on` or `icon` or even just `i`.

KEY IDEA

A name should clearly reveal the purpose of what it names.

Balanced with the need for a clear intent are readability and brevity for the sake of the person who must type the name over and over. Naming a robot `robotThatMovesTheThingFrom2_1To3_2` is clearly overkill.

When naming parts of their program, most Java programmers use conventions established by Java's creators. The name of a class, for example, should be a descriptive, singular noun such as `Robot`, `Wall`, or `Lamp`. Class names begin with an uppercase letter followed by lowercase letters. If the name is composed of two or more words, such as `CircleIcon`, then capitalize each word.

KEY IDEA

Naming conventions make it easier to recognize what an identifier represents.

The name of a variable should be a descriptive noun or noun phrase: `warningLamp`, `westWall`, or a robot named `collectorRobot` in a program where lots of things are collected. The variable name should describe what the variable represents. A variable name begins with a lowercase letter. Names composed of more than one word should have the first letter of each subsequent word capitalized, as in `collectorRobot`. Variable names can also contain digits and underscores after the first letter, but not spaces, tabs, or punctuation.

A method name should be a verb or verb phrase that describes what the method does. Like a variable name, a method name begins with a lowercase letter. In names composed of two or more words, the subsequent words are capitalized. Examples we have seen so far include `move`, `turnLeft`, `turnAround`, and `setLocation`.

Capitalization matters in identifiers. `westWall` is not the same as `westwall`. The Java compiler notices the difference between the uppercase `W` and the lowercase `w`—even if we don't—and treats them as two different identifiers. Table 2-3 summarizes the Java naming conventions.

(table 2-3)

Summary of naming conventions

Identifier	Conventions	Examples

Class	A descriptive singular noun, beginning with an uppercase letter. If the name is composed of several words, each word begins with a capital letter.	`Robot`
		`Lamp`
		`CircleIcon`

Method	A descriptive verb or verb phrase, beginning with a lowercase letter. If the method name is composed of several words, each word, except the first, begins with a capital letter.	`move`
		`pickThing`
		`canPickThing`
		`setSize`

Variable	A descriptive noun or noun phrase, beginning with a lowercase letter. If the name is composed of several words, each word, except the first, begins with a capital letter.	`karel` `newYorkCity`

2.4.3 Comments

KEY IDEA

Comments do not affect the execution of the program.

Comments are annotations inserted by the programmer to help others understand how to use the code she is writing, how it works, or how to modify it. The comments help establish the context of a statement or block of code so that readers can more quickly understand the code. Comments are for people; they do not affect the execution of the program. In this way, they are like white space.

An excellent practice is to first write a comment that states what this section of your program must do. Then write the code to implement your comment. Clearly state in English what you are trying to do, then explain how in Java. This two-part practice helps keep things clear in your mind, minimizing errors and speeding debugging.

Java has three different kinds of comments: single-line comments, multi-line comments, and documentation comments.

Single-Line Comments

A **single-line comment** begins with two consecutive slashes and extends to the end of the line. Single-line comments have already been used in the programs in Chapter 1 to document the purpose of a block of code. The first line in the following block of code is a single-line comment:

```
// Use the robot to move one of the lamps.
lampMover.move();
lampMover.pickThing();
lampMover.move();
lampMover.putThing();
lampMover.move();
```

The comment explains the intent of the code; it does not repeat how the code works. A reader may then consider whether the intent is appropriate at this point in the program, and whether the code correctly carries out the intent.

It is also possible to put a single-line comment at the end of a line of code, as shown in the following line from the `FramePlay` program in Chapter 1:

```
import javax.swing.*;      // use JFrame, JPanel, JButton, JTextArea
```

Multi-Line Comments

If you have more to say than will fit on a single line consider using a multi-line comment. A **multi-line comment** begins with `/*` and extends, possibly over many lines, until the next `*/`. The following example is a multi-line comment extending over three lines.

```
/* Set up the initial situation to match the figure given for problem 5.
   It consists of eight walls positioned to form a 2x2 square.
*/
```

Such a comment should go immediately before the first line of code that implements what is described.

Another use of a multi-line comment is to temporarily remove some lines of code, perhaps so another approach can be tested without losing previous work. For example, in Section 2.2.6, we explored two ways to implement `turnRight`. The programmer could have started with the solution that uses `turnLeft` three times. Perhaps she then thought of the other solution, which turns around first. If she wasn't quite sure the second solution would work, her code might have looked like this:

```
public void turnRight()
{ /*
   this.turnLeft();
   this.turnLeft();
   this.turnLeft();
   */
   this.turnAround();
   this.turnLeft();
}
```

KEY IDEA

Use single-line comments to annotate code and multi-line comments to comment out existing code.

This practice is called **commenting out code**. One of the consequences of using the next `*/` to end a comment is that a multi-line comment can not include another (nested) multi-line comment. That is, you can't comment out multi-line comments. For this reason, some programmers reserve multi-line comments for commenting out code, using single-line comments for actual annotations.

Documentation Comments

Single-line and multi-line comments explain the intent of the code for people reading the code. **Documentation comments** are used to generate Web-based documentation like that shown in Figure 1-15 through Figure 1-18. They describe the purpose of a class, constructor, or method and provide information useful to people who want to use them without understanding how they work internally.

KEY IDEA

Document the purpose of each class, constructor, and method.

Each class, constructor, and method should have a documentation comment. The comment must appear immediately before the class, method, or constructor is declared; that is, immediately before the line containing `public class` *«className»* `extends` *«superClass»* or `public void` *«methodName»*`()`.

A documentation comment is similar to a multi-line comment, except that it begins with `/**` rather than `/*`. Another difference is that a documentation comment may contain **tags** to identify specific information that should be displayed distinctively on a Web page. For example, the documentation comment for a class may contain the `@author` tag to identify the person who wrote the class.

One of the most important tags is `@param`. It allows you to document each parameter's purpose. The `@param` tag is followed by the name of the parameter and a description of that parameter.

Listing 2-10 shows the `ExperimentRobot` listing again, this time with appropriate documentation comments.

Listing 2-10: *A listing of* `ExperimentRobot` *showing appropriate documentation*

```
import becker.robots.*;

/** A new kind of robot that can turn around, turn right, and move forward three intersections
 *  at a time.
 *  @author Byron Weber Becker */
public class ExperimentRobot extends Robot
{
   /** Construct a new ExperimentRobot.
    *  @param aCity          The city in which the robot will be located.
    *  @param aStreet        The robot's initial street.
```

Listing 2-10: *A listing of* `ExperimentRobot` *showing appropriate documentation* (continued)

```
    * @param anAvenue      The robot's initial avenue.
    * @param aDirection    The robot's initial direction. */
   public ExperimentRobot(City aCity, int aStreet,
                          int anAvenue, Direction aDirection)
   { super(aCity, aStreet, anAvenue, aDirection);
   }

   /** Turn the robot around so it faces the opposite direction. */
   public void turnAround()
   { this.turnLeft();
     this.turnLeft();
   }

   /** Move the robot forward three times. */
   public void move3()
   { this.move();
     this.move();
     this.move();
   }

   /** Turn the robot right 90 degrees by turning left. */
   public void turnRight()
   { this.turnAround();
     this.turnLeft();
   }
}
```

2.4.4 External Documentation (advanced)

The tool that extracts the documentation comments and formats them for the Web is known as `javadoc`. Your development environment might have a simpler way to run this tool; if it does not, you can perform the following steps on a computer running Windows (with analogous steps on other computers).

- Open a window for a command-prompt.
- Change directories to the directory containing the Java source code.
- Run `javadoc`, specifying the Java files to process and where the output should be placed.
- View the result with a Web browser.

For example, suppose we want to generate documentation for the three classes used in the experiment at the beginning of the chapter and that the files reside in the directory `E:\experiment`. In the command-prompt window, enter the following commands (the > is called a **prompt** and is displayed by the system to indicate that it is ready to accept your input).

```
> E:
> cd experiment
> javadoc -d doc -classpath e:/robots/becker.jar *.java
```

The first two commands change the focus of the command prompt, first to the correct disk drive (`E:`), and then to the correct directory on that disk (`experiment`). The last command starts the program that produces the Web pages. This `javadoc` command has three sets of parameters:

- `-d doc` specifies that the documentation should be placed in a directory named `doc`.
- `-classpath e:/robots/becker.jar` indicates where to find the `becker` library. It allows `javadoc` to include relevant information about robot classes. You will need to replace the path given here with the location of the library on your computer.
- `*.java` means that `javadoc` should process all the files in the current directory that end with `.java`.

Depending on how your software is installed, the system may not find the `javadoc` program. In that case, you need to find `javadoc`'s location on the disk drive and provide the complete path to it. For example, on my system, I used the search feature of the Windows Explorer program to search for `javadoc`. The results told me that the program was in `C:\java\jdk1.5\bin\javadoc.exe`. I could then modify the last line as follows:

```
> C:\java\jdk1.5\bin\javadoc -d doc -classpath e:/robots/becker.jar *.java
```

Alternatively, you may be able to set your system's `path` variable to include the directory containing `javadoc`.

2.5 Meaning and Correctness

Nothing prevents a programmer from implementing a method called `move3` with 5, 10, or even 100 calls to `move`. In fact, nothing requires a method named `move3` to even contain `move` commands. It could be defined as follows:

PATTERN

Parameterless Command

```
public void move3()
{ this.turnLeft();
  this.pickThing();
  this.turnLeft();
}
```

If we defined the `move3` method this way, someone else reading our program would be confused and surprised. Over time, we could confuse ourselves, introducing errors into the program in spite of defining `move3` ourselves to behave in this manner.

The meaning of a command is the list of commands contained in its body, not its name. When a program is executed, the command does exactly what the commands in the body instruct it to do. There is no room for interpretation.

A good programmer gives each command a meaningful name. Another person should be able to make a reasonable guess about what the command does from its name. There should be no surprises such as the robot picking something up in the middle of a command whose name does not imply picking things up.

KEY IDEA

Use meaningful names.

When we write new programs, it is common to trace the program by hand to verify how it behaves. Because the command name only implies what it does, it is important to trace the actual instructions in each command. The computer cannot and does not interpret the names of commands when it executes a program; we shouldn't either when we trace a program manually.

The correctness of a command is determined by whether it fulfills its **specification**. The specification is a description of what the method is supposed to do. The specification might be included in the method's documentation or in the problem statement given by your instructor. A command may be poorly named, but still correct. For instance, the specification of `ExperimentRobot` at the beginning of the chapter requires a command to turn the robot around. It could have been given the idiotic name of `doIt`. As long as `doIt` does, indeed, turn the robot around (and nothing else) the specification is met and the command is correct.

KEY IDEA

Correct methods meet their specifications.

Because the `move3` command is simple, it is easy to convince ourselves that it is correct. Many other commands are much more complex, however. The correctness of these commands must be verified by writing test programs that execute the command, checking the actual result against the expected result. This practice is not foolproof, however. Conditions in which the command fails may not be tested and go undetected.

A correct command, such as `move3`, can be used incorrectly. For example, a client can place an `ExperimentRobot` facing a wall. Instructing this robot to `move3` will result in an error when the robot attempts to move into the wall. In this case, we say the command's **preconditions** have not been met. Preconditions are conditions that must be true for a command to execute correctly.

2.6 Modifying Inherited Methods

KEY IDEA

A subclass can make limited modifications to inherited methods as well as add new methods.

Besides adding new services to an object, sometimes we want to modify existing services so that they do something different. We might use this facility to make a dancing robot that, when sent a `move` message, first spins around on its current intersection and then moves. We might build a kind of robot that turns very fast even though it continues to move relatively slowly, or (eventually), a robot that checks to see if something is present before attempting to pick it up. In a graphical user interface, we might make a special kind of component that paints a picture on itself. In all of these situations, we replace the definition of a method in a superclass with a new definition. This replacement process is called **overriding**.

2.6.1 Overriding a Method Definition

To override the definition of a method, you create a new method with the same name, return type, and parameters in a subclass. These constitute the method's **signature**. As an example, let's create a new kind of robot that can turn left quickly. That is, we will override the `turnLeft` method with a new method that performs the same service differently.

You may have noticed that the online documentation for `Robot` includes a method named `setSpeed`, which allows a robot's speed to be changed. Our general strategy will be to write a method that increases the robot's speed, turns, and then returns the speed to normal. Turning quickly doesn't seem to be something we would use often, so it has not been added to `RobotSE`. On the other hand, it seems reasonable that fast-turning robots need to turn around and turn right, so our new class will extend `RobotSE`.

As the first step in creating the `FastTurnBot` class, we create the constructor and the shell of the new `turnLeft` method, as shown in Listing 2-11.

FIND THE CODE

ch02/override/

PATTERN

Extended Class

Listing 2-11: *An incomplete class which overrides* `turnLeft`

```
import becker.robots.*;

/** A FastTurnBot turns left very quickly relative to its normal speed.
 *  @author Byron Weber Becker */
public class FastTurnBot extends RobotSE
{
   /** Construct a new FastTurnBot.
   * @param aCity        The city in which the robot appears.
   * @param aStreet      The street on which the robot appears.
   * @param anAvenue     The avenue on which the robot appears.
   * @param aDirection   The direction the robot initially faces. */
```

Listing 2-11: *An incomplete class which overrides* `turnLeft` (continued)

```
   public FastTurnBot(City aCity, int aStreet, int anAvenue,
                      Direction aDirection)
   { super(aCity, aStreet, anAvenue, aDirection);
   }

   /** Turn 90 degrees to the left, but do it more quickly than normal. */
   public void turnLeft()
   {
   }
}
```

PATTERN

Constructor

When this class is instantiated and sent a `turnLeft` message, it does nothing. When the message is received, Java starts with the object's class (`FastTurnBot`) and looks for a method matching the message. It finds one and executes it. Because the body of the method is empty, the robot does nothing.

How can we get it to turn again? We *cannot* write `this.turnLeft();` in the body of `turnLeft`. When a `turnLeft` message is received, Java finds the `turnLeft` method and executes it. The `turnLeft` method then executes `this.turnLeft`, sending *another* `turnLeft` message to the object. Java finds the same `turnLeft` method and executes it. The process of executing it sends *another* `turnLeft` message to the object, so Java finds the `turnLeft` method again, and repeats the sequence. The program continues sending `turnLeft` messages to itself until it runs out of memory and crashes. This problem is called **infinite recursion**.

LOOKING AHEAD

Recursion occurs when a method calls itself. Although recursion causes problems in this case, it is a powerful technique.

What we really want is the `turnLeft` message in the `FastTurnBot` class to execute the `turnLeft` method in a superclass. We want to send a `turnLeft` message in such a way that Java begins searching for the method in the superclass rather than the object's class. We can do so by using the keyword `super` instead of the keyword `this`. That is, the new definition of `turnLeft` should be as follows:

KEY IDEA

Using `super` *instead of* `this` *causes Java to search for a method in the superclass rather than the object's class.*

```
public void turnLeft()
{ super.turnLeft();
}
```

We have returned to where we started. We have a robot that turns left at the normal speed. When a `FastTurnBot` is sent a `turnLeft` message, Java finds this `turnLeft` method and executes it. This method sends a message to the superclass to execute its `turnLeft` method, which occurs at the normal speed.

To make the robot turn faster, we add two calls to `setSpeed`, one before the call to `super.turnLeft()` to increase the speed, and one more after the call to decrease the speed back to normal. The documentation indicates that `setSpeed` requires a single parameter, the number of moves or turns the robot should make in one second.

The default speed of a robot is two moves or turns per second. The following method uses `setSpeed` so the robot turns 10 times as fast as normal, and then returns to the usual speed.

```
public void turnLeft()
{ this.setSpeed(20);
  super.turnLeft();
  this.setSpeed(2);
}
```

The `FastTurnBot` class could be tested with a small program such as the one in Listing 2-12. Running the program shows that `speedy` does, indeed, turn quickly when compared to a `move`.

FIND THE CODE

ch02/override/

Listing 2-12: *A program to test a* `FastTurnBot`

```
import becker.robots.*;

/** A program to test a FastTurnBot.
 *  @author Byron Weber Becker */
public class Main extends Object
{
  public static void main(String[] args)
  { City cairo = new City();
    FastTurnBot speedy = new FastTurnBot(
                cairo, 1, 1, Direction.EAST);

    speedy.turnLeft();
    speedy.move();
    speedy.turnLeft();
    speedy.turnLeft();
    speedy.turnLeft();
    speedy.turnLeft();
    speedy.turnLeft();
    speedy.move();
  }
}
```

2.6.2 Method Resolution

So far, we have glossed over how Java finds the method to execute, a process called **method resolution**. Consider Figure 2-13, which shows the class diagram of a `FastTurnBot`. Details not relevant to the discussion have been omitted, including constructors, attributes, some services, and even some of the `Robot`'s superclasses (represented by an empty rectangle). The class named `Object` is the superclass, either directly or indirectly, of every other class.

When a message is sent to an object, Java always begins with the object's class, looking for a method implementing the message. It keeps going up the hierarchy until it either finds a method or it reaches the ultimate superclass, `Object`. If it reaches `Object` without finding an appropriate method, a compile-time error is given.

Let's look at several different examples. Consider the following code:

```
FastTurnBot speedy = new FastTurnBot(...);
speedy.move();
```

To execute the `move` method, Java begins with `speedy`'s class, `FastTurnBot`, in the search for the method. When Java doesn't find a method named `move` in `FastTurnBot`, it looks in `RobotSE` and then in `Robot`, where a method matching the `move` method is found and executed.

As another example, consider the following code:

```
RobotSE special = new RobotSE(...);
special.move();
```

The search for a `move` method begins with `RobotSE`, the class that instantiated `special`. It doesn't matter that `RobotSE` has been extended by another class; what matters is that when `special` was constructed, the programmer used the constructor for `RobotSE`. Therefore, searches for methods begin with `RobotSE`.

(figure 2-13)

Class diagram of a `FastTurnBot`

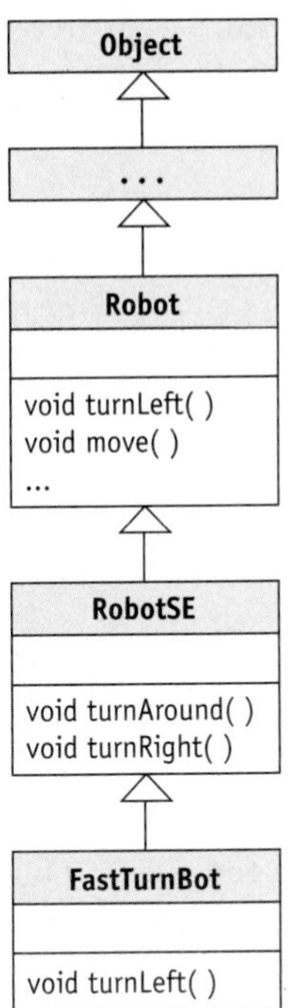

Once again, consider `speedy`. What happens if `speedy` is sent the `turnAround` message? The search for the `turnAround` method begins with `speedy`'s class, `FastTurnBot`. It's found in `RobotSE` and executed. As it is executed, it calls `turnLeft`. Which `turnLeft` method is executed, the one in `FastTurnBot` or the one in `Robot`?

KEY IDEA

Overriding a method can affect other methods that call it, even methods in a superclass.

The `turnLeft` message in `turnAround` is sent to the implicit parameter, `this`. The implicit parameter is the same as the object that was originally sent the message, `speedy`. So Java begins with `speedy`'s class, searching for `turnLeft`. It finds the method that turns quickly and executes it. Therefore, a subclass can affect how methods in a superclass are executed.

LOOKING AHEAD

Written Exercise 2.4 asks you to trace similar examples.

If `turnAround` is written as follows, the result would be different.

```
public void turnAround()
{ super.turnLeft();
  super.turnLeft();
}
```

KEY IDEA

The search for the method matching a message sent to `super` *begins in the method's superclass.*

Now the search for `turnLeft` begins with the superclass of the class containing the method, or `Robot`. `Robot` contains a `turnLeft` method. It is executed, and the robot turns around at the normal pace.

Suppose you occasionally want `speedy` to turn left at its normal speed. Can you somehow skip over the new definition of `turnLeft` and execute the normal one, the one that was overridden? No. If we really want to execute the original `turnLeft`, we should not have overridden it. Instead, we should have simply created a new method, perhaps called `fastTurnLeft`.

2.6.3 Side Effects

`FastTurnBot` has a problem, however. Suppose that Listing 2-12 contained the statement `speedy.setSpeed(20);` just before line 12. This statement would speed `speedy` up dramatically. Presumably, the programmer wanted `speedy` to be speedier than normal all of the time. After its first `turnLeft`, however, `speedy` would return to its normal pace of 2 moves per second.

This phenomenon is called a **side effect**. Invoking `turnLeft` changed something it should not have changed. Our programmer will be very annoyed if she must reset the speed after every command that turns the robot. Ideally, a `FastTurnBot` returns to its previous speed after each turn.

KEY IDEA

Not only are side effects annoying, they can lead to errors. Avoid them where possible; otherwise, document them.

The programmer can use the `getSpeed` query to find out how long the robot currently takes to turn. This information can be used to adjust the speed to its original value after the turn is completed. The new version of `turnLeft` should perform the following steps:

set the speed to 10 times the current speed
turn left
set the speed to one-tenth of the (now faster) speed

The query `this.getSpeed()` obtains the current speed. Multiplying the speed by 10 and using the result as the value to `setSpeed` increases the speed by a factor of 10. After the turn, we can do the reverse to decrease the speed to its previous value, as shown in the following implementation of `turnLeft`:

LOOKING AHEAD

Another approach is to remember the current speed. When the robot is finished turning, set the speed to the remembered value. More in Chapters 5 and 6.

```
public void turnLeft()
{ this.setSpeed(this.getSpeed() * 10);
  super.turnLeft();
  this.setSpeed(this.getSpeed() / 10);
}
```

Using queries and doing arithmetic will be discussed in much more detail in the following chapters.

2.7 GUI: Extending GUI Components

The Java package that implements user interfaces is known as the **Abstract Windowing Toolkit** or **AWT**. A newer addition to the AWT is known as **Swing**. These packages contain classes to display components such as windows, buttons, and textboxes. Other classes work to receive input from the mouse, to define colors, and so on.

The AWT and Swing packages make extensive use of inheritance. Figure 2-14 contains a class diagram showing a simplified version of the inheritance hierarchy. Many classes are omitted, as are many methods and all attributes.

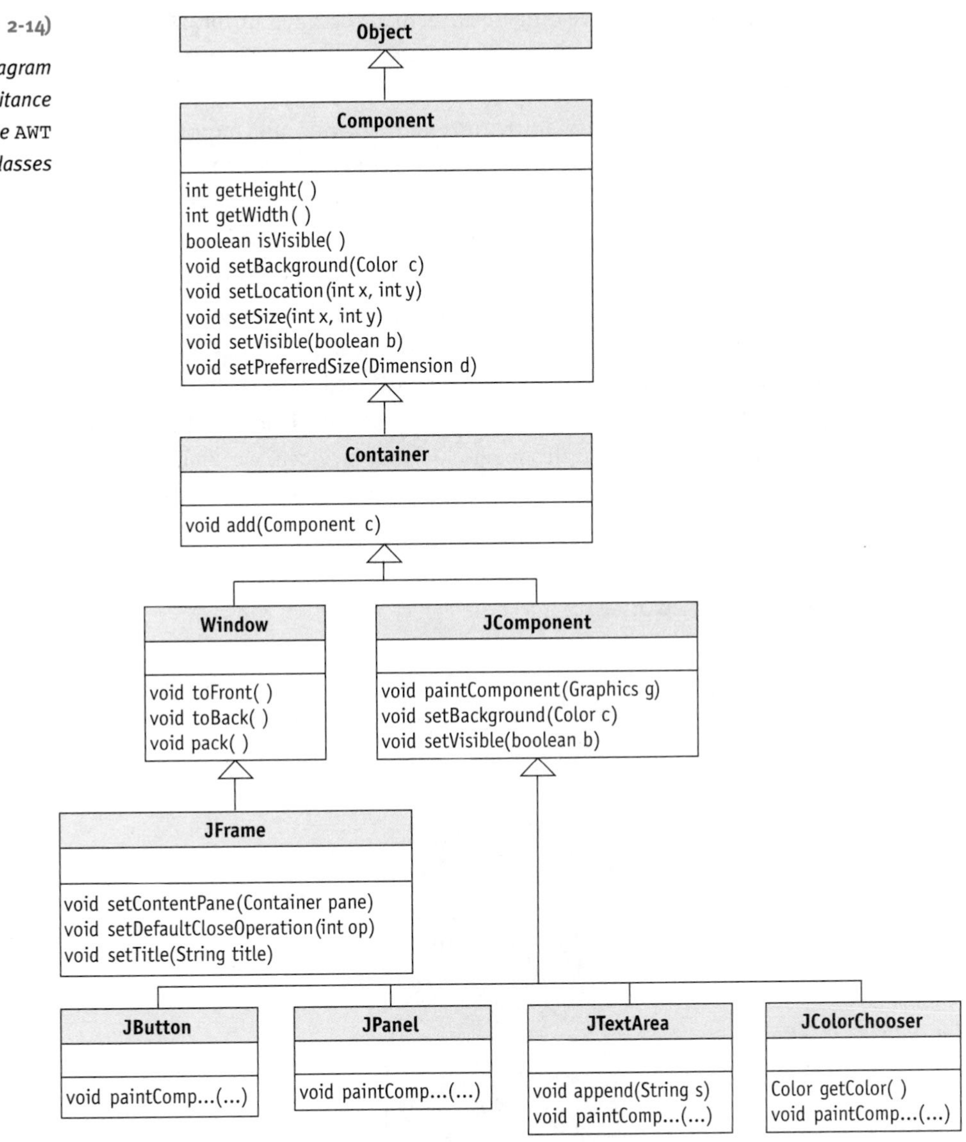

(figure 2-14)

Simplified class diagram showing the inheritance hierarchy for some `AWT` *and* `Swing` *classes*

One new aspect of this class diagram is that some classes have two or more subclasses. For example, `Container` is the superclass for both `Window` and `JComponent`. The effect is that `Window` objects and `JComponent` objects (and their subclasses) have much in common—the set of services they inherit from the `Container` and `Component` classes.

The class diagram reveals several new pieces of information:

- When we implemented the `FramePlay` program in Listing 1-6, we sent six different messages to a `JFrame` object: `setContentPane`, `setTitle`, `setDefaultCloseOperation`, `setLocation`, `setSize`, and `setVisible`. We now realize that only three of these are actually declared by the `JFrame` class. The other three services are offered by `JFrame` because they are inherited from `Component`.
- Because `JFrame`, `JPanel`, `JButton`, and so on, all indirectly extend `Component`, they can all answer queries about their width, height, and visibility, and can all[2] set their background color, position, size, and visibility.
- The `JComponent` class overrides two of the services provided by `Component`. `JComponent` must be doing something extra for each of those services.
- The statement `contents.add(saveButton);` in the `FramePlay` program added a button to an instance of `JPanel`. We now see that `add` is actually a service of the `Container` class, inherited by `JPanel`.
- Each of the classes extending `JComponent` inherits the method `paintComponent`. Perhaps if this method were overridden, we could affect how the component looks. This result would, indeed, be the case and is the topic of the next section.

2.7.1 Extending `JComponent`

In this section we will write a program that paints a picture. Figure 2-15 shows a simple stick figure. When viewed in color, the pants are blue, the shirt is red, and the head is yellow.

(figure 2-15)

Simple stick figure

[2] There is, unfortunately, some fine print. The statements above are true, but in some circumstances you can't see the results. For example, setting the background color of a `JFrame` doesn't appear to have an effect because the content pane completely covers the `JFrame`, and you see the content pane's color.

Our strategy is to create a new class, `StickFigure`, which extends `JComponent`. We choose to extend `JComponent` because it is the simplest of the components shown in the class diagram, and it doesn't already have its own appearance. We will extend it by overriding `paintComponent`, the method responsible for the appearance of the component. As we did with the several components in the `FramePlay` program in Listing 1-6, the stick figure component will be placed in a `JPanel`. The `JPanel` will be set as the content pane in a `JFrame`.

Listing 2-13 shows the beginnings of the `StickFigure` class. It provides a parameterless constructor and nothing more. The constructor doesn't need parameters because `JComponent` has a constructor that does not need parameters. Our constructor calls `JComponent`'s constructor by invoking `super` without parameters.

The constructor performs one important task: in lines 13–14 it specifies a preferred size for the stick figure component. The preferred size says how many pixels wide and high the component should be, if possible. Line 13 creates a `Dimension` object 180 pixels wide and 270 pixels high. The next line uses this object to set the preferred size for the stick figure.

FIND THE CODE

ch02/stickFigure/

PATTERN

Extended Class Constructor

Listing 2-13: *An extended* `JComponent`

```
1  import javax.swing.*;      // JComponent
2  import java.awt.*;         // Dimension
3
4  /** A new kind of component that displays a stick figure.
5   *
6   *  @author Byron Weber Becker */
7  public class StickFigure extends JComponent
8  {
9    public StickFigure()
10   { super();
11
12     // Specify the preferred size for this component
13     Dimension prefSize = new Dimension(180, 270);
14     this.setPreferredSize(prefSize);
15   }
16 }
```

It is also possible to reduce lines 13 and 14 down to a single line:

```
this.setPreferredSize(new Dimension(180, 270));
```

This creates the object and passes it to `setPreferredSize` without declaring a variable. We can avoid declaring the variable if we don't need to refer to the object in the future (as with `Wall` and `Thing` objects), or we can pass it to the only method that requires it as soon as it's created, as we do here.

KEY IDEA

Sometimes we don't need a variable to store object references.

Now would be a good time to implement the `main` method for the program. By compiling and running the program early in the development cycle, we can often catch errors in our thinking that may be much more difficult to change later on. Listing 2-14 shows a program for this purpose. Running it results in an empty frame as shown in Figure 2-16. It follows the Display a Frame pattern and consequently it is similar to the `FramePlay` program in Listing 1-6.

FIND THE CODE

ch02/stickFigure/

Listing 2-14: *A program that uses a class extending* `JComponent`

```
 1 import javax.swing.*;
 2 
 3 /** Create a stick figure and display it in a frame.
 4  *
 5  *  @author Byron Weber Becker */
 6 public class Main extends Object
 7 {
 8    public static void main(String[] args)
 9    {  // Declare the objects to show.
10       JFrame frame = new JFrame();
11       JPanel contents = new JPanel();
12       StickFigure stickFig = new StickFigure();
13 
14       // Add the stick figure to the contents.
15       contents.add(stickFig);
16 
17       // Display the contents in a frame.
18       frame.setContentPane(contents);
19       frame.setTitle("Stick Figure");
20       frame.setDefaultCloseOperation(JFrame.EXIT_ON_CLOSE);
21       frame.setLocation(250, 100);
22       frame.pack();
23       frame.setVisible(true);
24    }
25 }
```

One difference between this program and the `FramePlay` program and the pattern is in how the frame is sized. The previous program explicitly set the size of the frame using the `setSize` method. This version uses the method `pack` in line 22. This method uses the preferred sizes of all the components to calculate the best size for the frame.

The result of running this program is shown in Figure 2-16. It looks exactly like an empty `JFrame` because the `JComponent` is invisible until we override `paintComponent` to change its appearance.

(figure 2-16)

Result of running the program in Listing 2-14 with the incomplete `StickFigure` class from Listing 2-13

2.7.2 Overriding `paintComponent`

To actually draw the stick figure, we need to override `paintComponent` to provide it with additional functionality. We know from both the class diagram in Figure 2-14 and the online documentation that `paintComponent` has a parameter of type `Graphics`. This parameter is often named simply `g`. We will have much more to say about parameters in later chapters. For now, we will just say that `g` is a reference to an object that is used for drawing. It is provided by the client that calls `paintComponent` and may be used by the code contained in the `paintComponent` method.

LOOKING AHEAD

We are practicing incremental development: code a little, test a little, code a little, test a little. For more on development strategies, see Chapter 11.

The superclass's implementation of `paintComponent` may have important work to do, and so it should be called with `super.paintComponent(g)`. It requires a `Graphics` object as an argument, and so we pass it `g`, the `Graphics` object received as a parameter. Doing so results in the following method. The method still has not added any functionality, but adding it to Listing 2-13 between lines 14 and 15 still results in a running program.

```
public void paintComponent(Graphics g)
{ super.paintComponent(g);
}
```

The `Graphics` parameter, `g`, provides services such as `drawRect`, `drawOval`, `drawLine`, and `drawString`, each of which draw the shape described in the service's name. A companion set of services includes `fillRect` and `fillOval`, each of which also draws the described shape and then fills the interior with a color. The color used is determined by the most recent `setColor` message sent to `g`. The color specified is used until the next `setColor` message.

All of the `draw` and `fill` methods require parameters specifying where the shape is to be drawn and how large it should be. Like positioning a frame, measurements are given in relation to an origin in the upper-left corner, and are in pixels.

Figure 2-17 shows the relationship between the parameters and the figure that is drawn. For `drawRect` and `drawOval`, the first two parameters specify the position of the upper left corner of the figure, while the third and fourth parameters specify the width and height. For an oval, the width and height are of the smallest box that can contain the oval. This box is called the **bounding box** and is shown in Figure 2-17 as a dashed line. Of course, the bounding box is not actually drawn on the screen.

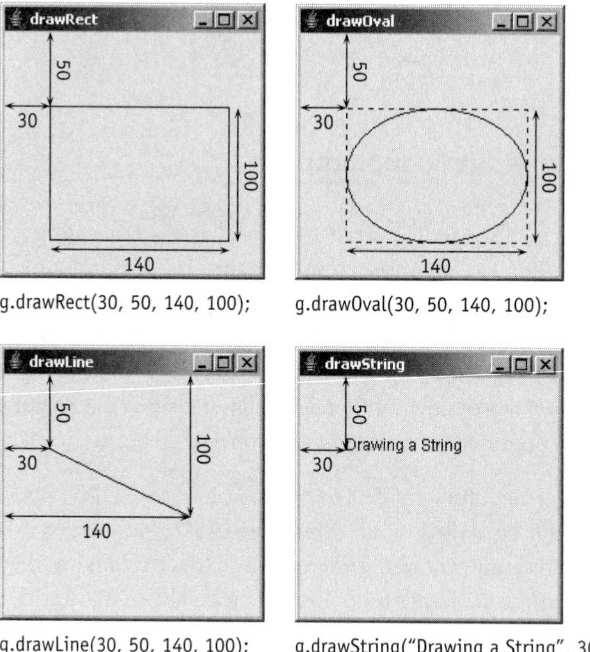

(figure 2-17)

Relationship between the arguments and the effects of four drawing methods

In each of these methods, the order of the arguments is *x* before *y* and *width* before *height*.

The parameters for a line are different from the parameters for rectangles and ovals. The first two parameters specify one end of the line in relation to the origin, while the last two parameters specify the other end of the line in relation to the origin.

The `drawString` method takes a string as the first parameter and the position of the first letter as the second and third parameters.

With this background information, we can finally add the statements to draw the stick figure. The complete code for the `stickFigure` class is given in Listing 2-15. Running it with the `main` method in Listing 2-14 produces the image shown in Figure 2-15.

FIND THE CODE

ch02/stickFigure/

Listing 2-15: *Overriding* `paintComponent` *to draw a stick figure*

PATTERN *Constructor*

PATTERN *Parameterless Command*

```
import javax.swing.*;       // JComponent
import java.awt.*;          // Dimension

/** A new kind of component that displays a stick figure.
 *
 * @author Byron Weber Becker */
public class StickFigure extends JComponent
{
  public StickFigure()
  { super ();
    Dimension prefSize = new Dimension(180, 270);
    this.setPreferredSize(prefSize);
  }

  // Paint a stick figure.
  public void paintComponent(Graphics g)
  { super.paintComponent(g);

    // Paint the head.
    g.setColor(Color.YELLOW);
    g.fillOval(60, 0, 60, 60);

    // Paint the shirt.
    g.setColor(Color.RED);
    g.fillRect(0, 60, 180, 30);
    g.fillRect(60, 60, 60, 90);

    // Paint the pants.
    g.setColor(Color.BLUE);
    g.fillRect(60, 150, 60, 120);
    g.setColor(Color.BLACK);
    g.drawLine(90, 180, 90, 270);
  }
}
```

2.7.3 How `paintComponent` Is Invoked

You may have noticed that the `paintComponent` method is *not* called from anywhere in Listing 2-15 or the client code shown in Listing 2-14. Look all through the code, and you will not find an instance of the Command Invocation pattern `stickFig.paintComponent(g);`. Yet we know it is invoked because it paints the stick figure. How?

In the Sequential Execution pattern in Chapter 1, we described statements as being executed one after another, as if they were strung on a thread of string. A computer program can have two or more of these **threads**, each with their own sequence of statements. The program we just wrote has at least two threads. The first one is in the `main` method. It creates a `JFrame` and invokes a number of its commands such as `setDefaultCloseOperation` and `setVisible`. When it gets to the end of the `main` method, that thread ends.

When a `JFrame` is instantiated, a second thread begins. This is *not* a normal occurrence when an object is instantiated; `JFrame`'s authors deliberately set up the new thread. `JFrame`'s thread monitors the frame and detects when it has been damaged and must be repainted. A frame can be damaged in many ways. It is damaged when the user resizes it by dragging a border or clicking the minimize or maximize buttons. It's damaged when it is first created because it hasn't been drawn yet. It's also damaged if another window is placed on top of it and then moved again. In each of these cases, the second thread of control calls `paintComponent`, providing the `Graphics` object that `paintComponent` should draw upon.

LOOKING AHEAD

We will use this capability in Section 3.5.2 to make two or more robots move simultaneously.

KEY IDEA

`paintComponent` *is called by "the system." We don't call it.*

2.7.4 Extending `Icon`

We learned in Section 2.3.1 that `Icon` is the class used to represent images of things in the robot world—robots, intersections, things, flashers, walls, and so on—all use icons to display themselves. As you might expect, `Icon` has been extended a number of times to provide different icons for different kinds of things. The documentation references classes named `FlasherIcon`, `RobotIcon`, `WallIcon`, and so on.

You, too, can extend the `Icon` class to create your own custom icons. The example shown in Figure 2-18 was produced by the code shown in Listing 2-16.

As with any other subclass, it gives the name of the class it extends (line 5). Before that are the packages it relies on. In this case, it imports the `Icon` class from the `becker.robots.icons` package and the `Graphics` class from `java.awt`.

(figure 2-18)

Custom robot icon

One difference, when compared to extending `JComponent`, is that we must override a method named `paintIcon` instead of `paintComponent`. This fact can be gleaned from reading the documentation for `Icon`. Like `paintComponent`, `paintIcon` has a parameter of type `Graphics` to use for the actual drawing.

An icon is always painted in a standard 100 × 100 pixel space facing north. Lines 14–23 in Listing 2-16 draw the robot in this position. Other parts of the robot system scale and rotate the icons, as necessary.

FIND THE CODE

ch02/extendIcon/

Listing 2-16: *Code for a customized robot icon*

```
 1 import becker.robots.icons.*;          // Icon
 2 import java.awt.*;                     // Graphics, Color
 3
 4 /** Create a robot icon that has arms. */
 5 public class ArmRobotIcon extends Icon
 6 {
 7    /** Create a new icon for a robot. */
 8    public ArmRobotIcon()
 9    { super();
10    }
11
12    /** Paint the icon. */
13    public void paintIcon(Graphics g)
14    { g.setColor(Color.BLACK);
15
16       // body
17       g.fillRoundRect(35, 35, 30, 30, 10, 10);
18       // shoulders
19       g.fillRect(25, 45, 10, 10);
20       g.fillRect(65, 45, 10, 10);
21       // arms
22       g.fillOval(25, 25, 10, 30);
23       g.fillOval(65, 25, 10, 30);
24    }
25 }
```

Use the `setIcon` method to change the icon used to display a robot. One way to call `setIcon` is to create a new class of robots, as shown in Listing 2-17.

Listing 2-17: *An* `ArmRobot` *uses an* `ArmRobotIcon` *to display itself*

FIND THE CODE

ch02/extendIcon/

```
import becker.robots.*;

/** A robot with an icon that shows arms. */
public class ArmRobot extends Robot
{
  /** Construct a new ArmRobot.
   * @param aCity         The City where the robot will reside.
   * @param aStreet       The robot's initial street.
   * @param anAvenue      The robot's initial avenue.
   * @param aDirection    The robot's initial direction. */
  public ArmRobot(City aCity, int aStreet, int anAvenue,
                  Direction aDirection)
  { super(aCity, aStreet, anAvenue, aDirection);
    this.setIcon(new ArmRobotIcon());
  }
}
```

2.8 Patterns

In this chapter we've seen patterns to extend a class, write a constructor, and implement a parameterless command. These are all extremely common patterns; so common, in fact, that many experienced programmers wouldn't even recognize them as patterns. We've also seen a much less common pattern to draw a picture.

2.8.1 The Extended Class Pattern

Name: Extended Class

Context: You need a new kind of object to provide services for a program you are writing. An existing class provides objects with closely related services.

Solution: Extend the existing class to provide the new or different services required. For example, the following listing illustrates a new kind of robot that provides a service to turn around.

```
import becker.robots.*;
public class TurnAroundBot extends Robot
{
```

```
    public TurnAroundBot (City aCity, int aStreet,
                          int anAvenue, Direction aDirection)
    { super(aCity, aStreet, anAvenue, aDirection);
    }

    public void turnAround()
    { this.turnLeft();
      this.turnLeft();
    }
}
```

This listing also makes use of the Constructor and Method patterns. More generally, a Java class uses the following code template:

```
import «importedPackage»;     // may have 0 or more import statements

public class «className» extends «superClass»
{ «list of attributes used by this class»
  «list of constructors for this class»
  «list of services provided by this class»
}
```

The Java Program pattern can be seen as a special version of the Class pattern, which has no constructors or attributes and contains only the specialized service named `main`.

Consequences: Objects instantiated from a subclass respond to the same messages as objects instantiated from the superclass. Instances of the subclass may behave differently from instances of the superclass, depending on whether methods have been overridden. The subclass's objects may also respond to messages not defined by the superclass.

It should make sense for the client using the subclass to also use any of the methods in its superclass. If not, think carefully about the superclass; it may have been chosen incorrectly. If there is no class to serve as the superclass, use `Object`, a class that contains the minimal set of methods required of every Java class.

Related Patterns:

- The Constructor pattern is always applied within an instance of the Extended Class pattern.
- The Parameterless Command pattern is always applied within an instance of the Extended Class pattern.

2.8.2 The Constructor Pattern

Name: Constructor

Context: Instances of a class must be initialized when they are constructed.

Solution: Add a constructor to the class. A constructor has the same name as the class and is usually preceded by the keyword `public`. It often has parameters so that the client constructing the object can provide initialization details at run time. The constructor must also ensure that the object's superclass is appropriately initialized, using the keyword `super`. The types of the parameters passed to `super` should match the types required by one of the constructors in the superclass. Constructors and their parameters should always have a documentation comment.

Following is an example of a constructor that simply initializes its superclass with values received via its parameters:

```
/** Construct a new special edition robot.
 *  @param aCity     The city containing the robot.
 *  @param str       The robot's initial street.
 *  @param ave       The robot's initial avenue.
 *  @param dir       The robot's initial direction. */
public RobotSE(City aCity, int str, int ave, Direction dir)
{ super(aCity, str, ave, dir);
}
```

More generally, a constructor makes a call to super and may then execute other Java statements to initialize itself.

```
/**«Description of what this constructor does.»
 * @param «parameterName» «Description of parameter»
 */
public «className»(«parameter list»)
{ super(«arguments»);
  «list of Java statements»
}
```

If the parameter list is empty, the documentation comment does not contain any `@param` tags. Otherwise, the documentation comment contains one `@param` tag for each parameter.

Consequences: A constructor should ensure that each object it creates is completely and consistently initialized to appropriate values. Doing so leads to higher quality software.

In some circumstances the compiler supplies a missing constructor, but don't rely on the compiler to do so. If you always supply a constructor, you increase your chances of remembering to initialize everything correctly. You also minimize the possibility that future changes will break your software.

Related Patterns: The Constructor pattern always occurs within a pattern for a class. The Extended Class pattern is one such pattern.

2.8.3 The Parameterless Command Pattern

Name: Parameterless Command

Context: You are writing or extending a class and need to provide a new service to clients. The service does not require any information other than the object to act upon (the implicit parameter) and does not return any information.

Solution: Use a parameterless command with the following form:

```
/** «Description of the command.»
*/
public void «commandName»()
{ «list of statements»
}
```

One example that implements this pattern is the `turnAround` method:

```
/** Turn the robot around to face the opposite direction. */
public void turnAround()
{ this.turnLeft();
  this.turnLeft();
}
```

Consequences: The new service is available to any client of objects instantiated from this class. In future chapters we will see replacements for the `public` keyword that make the command's use more restricted.

Related Patterns: The Parameterless Command pattern always occurs within a pattern for a class. The Extended Class pattern is one such pattern.

2.8.4 The Draw a Picture Pattern

Name: Draw a Picture

Context: You want to show an image to the user that is constructed from ovals, rectangles, lines, and strings.

Solution: Extend `JComponent` and override the `paintComponent` method to draw the image. Display the new component inside a frame using the Display a Frame pattern.

In general, the code for the extension of `JComponent` will be as follows:

```
import java.awt.*;
import javax.swing.*;

public class «className» extends JComponent
{
```

```
    public «className»()
    { super ();
      this.setPreferredSize(
           new Dimension(«prefWidth», «prefHeight»));
    }

    // Draw the image.
    public void paintComponent(Graphics g)
    { super.paintComponent(g);

      «statements using g to draw the image»
    }
}
```

Consequences: The component will display the image drawn in `paintComponent`, but it is not very smart about the image size and may give some strange results if the frame is resized. These issues will be addressed in Section 4.7.1.

Related Patterns:

- The extended component can be displayed using the Display a Frame pattern.
- The Draw a Picture pattern is a specialization of the Extended Class pattern and contains an example of the Constructor pattern.

2.9 Summary and Concept Map

Extending an existing class is one way to customize a class with new or modified services. Instances of the resulting class (subclass) can be visualized as having an instance of the existing class (superclass) inside it. The subclass's constructor must ensure that the superclass is initialized by calling `super` with appropriate arguments.

The subclass inherits all of the methods from the superclass. New methods added to the subclass may call methods in the superclass or other methods in the subclass. When a message is sent to an object, the process of determining which method to execute is called method resolution. Method resolution always starts with the class used to instantiate the object, unless the method is called using `super` in which case method resolution begins with the superclass of the class making the call.

A method in the subclass overrides an existing method when it has the same name and parameter types as a method in one of the superclasses. The overridden method may be called using the keyword `super`.

The components used to display graphical user interfaces make extensive use of inheritance and overriding. For example, one overrides the `paintComponent` method to alter the appearance of a component.

Style is an important part of writing understandable programs. White space, indentation, and choice of identifiers all make a significant contribution to the overall clarity of the program.

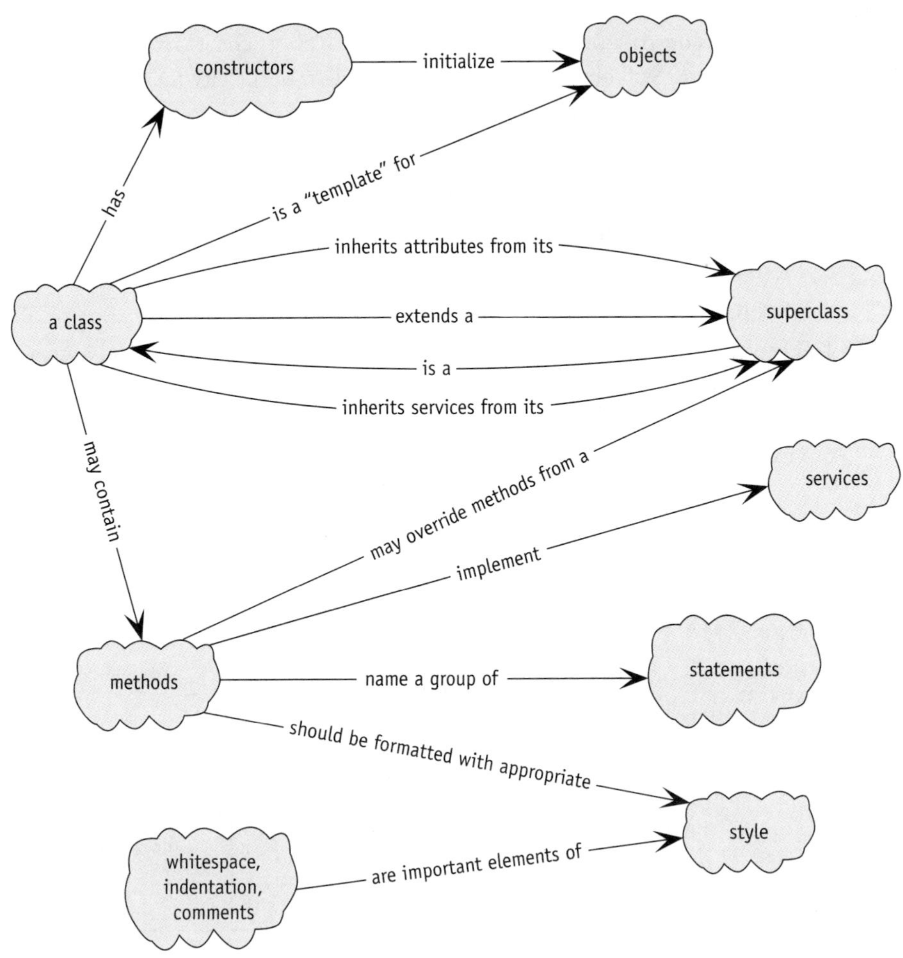

2.10 Problem Set

Written Exercises

2.1 Based on what you now know about the `getSpeed` and `setSpeed` services from Section 2.6.1, revise the `Robot` class diagram shown in Figure 1-8.

2.2 Consider a robot that implements `turnRight` as shown in Listing 2-4 and implements `turnAround` by calling `turnRight` twice.

a. Describe what a robot executing this version of `turnAround` does.

b. How much time does this version of `turnAround` require compared to the version in Listing 2-4?

2.3 Write a new constructor for the `RobotSE` class. Robots constructed with this new constructor will always be placed at the origin of the city facing `EAST`.

2.4 Add arrows to Figure 2-19, which is similar to Figure 2-6, showing the following method calls:

a. Method calls resulting from `bob.turnLeft()`

b. Method calls resulting from `lisa.turnLeft()`

c. Method calls resulting from `lisa.turnAround1()`

d. Method calls resulting from `lisa.turnAround2()`

To keep the diagrams uncluttered, answer each part of the question on a separate copy of the diagram and omit arrows the second time a method is called from the same place (for example, do not draw arrows for the second call to `turnLeft` in `turnAround1`).

```
… class Main
… main(…)
{ …
  RobotSE bob = …
  FastTurnBot lisa =
  …
  bob.turnLeft();
  lisa.turnLeft();
  lisa.turnAround1();
  lisa.turnAround2();
}
```

```
… FastTurnBot …
        extends RobotSE
{
  … void turnLeft()
  { this.setSpeed(20);
    super.turnLeft();
    this.setSpeed(2);
  }
}
```

```
… class RobotSE
        extends RobotSE
{
  … void turnAround1
  { this.turnLeft();
    this.turnLeft();
  }

  … void turnAround2
  { super.turnLeft();
    super.turnLeft();
  }
}
```

```
… class Robot …
{
  … void move()
  { …
  }

  … void turnLeft()
  { …
  }

  … void setSpeed()
  { …
  }

  … int getSpeed()
  {
  }
}
```

(figure 2-19)

Illustrating method calls and method resolution

2.5 The change from the initial situation to the final situation shown in Figure 2-20 is accomplished by sending the robot exactly one `move` message. Ordinarily such a stunt would cause the robot to crash. There are at least three fundamentally different approaches to solving this seemingly impossible problem. Explain two of them.

(figure 2-20)

A seemingly impossible situation

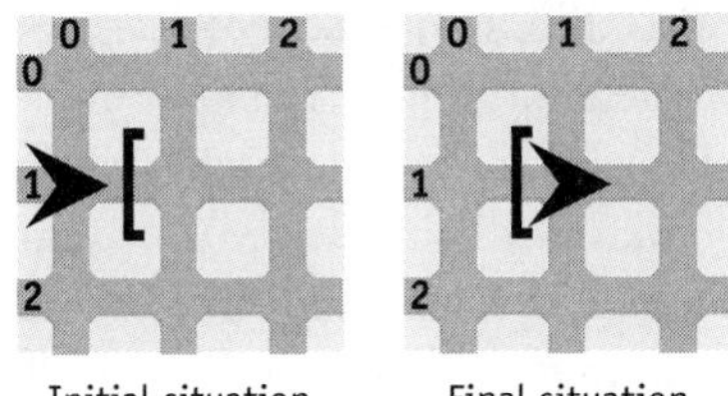

Programming Exercises

2.6 Write a new class, `MileMover`, that includes two methods: `moveMile` moves a robot forward 10 intersections, and `move1000Miles` which moves the robot forward 1,000 miles. Your solution should be *much* shorter than 1,000 lines of code.

2.7 Instances of the `BackupBot` class can respond to the `backup` message by moving to the intersection immediately behind it, facing their original direction.

a. Create the `BackupBot` class by extending `Robot`.

b. Arrange for the `backup` method to take the same amount of time as the `move` method.

c. Create the `BackupBot` class by extending `RobotSE` and taking advantage of the methods it contains.

2.8 Extend `RobotSE` to create a `LeftDancer` class. A `LeftDancer`, when sent a `move` message, ends up at the same place and facing the same direction as a normal robot. But it gets there more "gracefully." A `LeftDancer` first moves to the left, then forward, and then to the right.

2.9 Extend `RobotSE` to create a `TrailBot` class. A `TrailBot` leaves behind a trail of "crumbs" (`Thing` objects) whenever it moves. Arrange for instances of `TrailBot` to always start with 100 `Things` in its backpack. (*Hint*: Check out the `Robot` constructors in the documentation.)

a. Add a `trailMove` method. When called, it leaves a "crumb" on the current intersection and moves forward to the next intersection. `move` still behaves as usual.

b. Arrange for a `TrailBot` to always leave a "crumb" behind when it moves.

2.10 Extend `Robot` to make a new class, `PokeyBot`. `PokeyBots` ordinarily make one move or turn every two seconds (that is, 0.5 moves per second). However, the statement `pokey.setSpeed(3)` makes a robot named `pokey` go faster until a subsequent `setSpeed` command is given. Write a program that instantiates a `PokeyBot` and verifies that it moves more slowly than a standard `Robot`. Also verify that `setSpeed` works as described. *Hint*: You do not need to override `move` or `turnLeft`.

2.11 Implement `turnLeft` as discussed in Section 2.6.1 but using `this.turnLeft()` instead of `super.turnLeft()`. Run a test program and describe what happens, using a diagram similar to Figure 2-5 to illustrate what happened. (*Hint*: You may not be able to read the first line of the resulting error message. It probably says something about "Stack Overflow," which means the computer ran out of memory. A little bit of memory is used each time a method is called until that method is finished executing.)

Programming Projects

2.12 `karel` the robot has taken up diving. Write a program that sets up the following situation with `karel` at the top of the diving board. The single message `dive` should cause it to do a triple front flip (turn completely around three times) at the location shown while it dives into the pool (see Figure 2-21). `karel` is an instance of the `Diver` class.

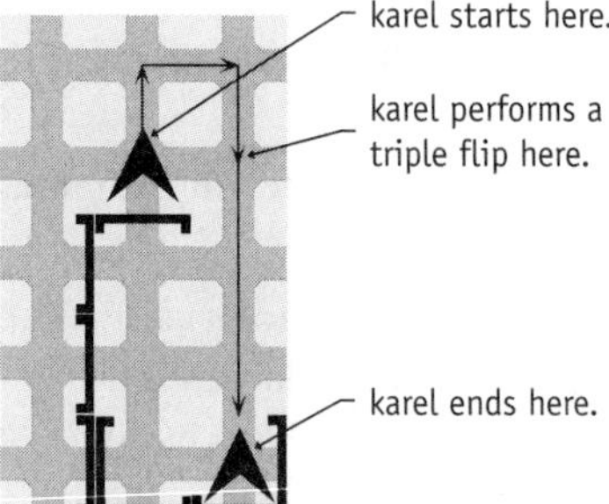

(figure 2-21)

Diving into a pool

2.13 You would like to send a greeting to astronauts in the International Space Station orbiting Earth. Create a `WriterBot` class that can be used to "write" the message "Hello" by lighting bonfires (`Things`). The final situation is shown in Figure 2-22. The `WriterBot` class will contain a method to write each letter.

a. Write a `main` method that uses a single `WriterBot` to write the entire message. Instantiate the robot with at least 48 `Things` in its backpack. (Check the documentation for the `Robot` or `RobotSE` class for an alternate constructor.)

b. Write a `main` method that uses five `WriterBots`, one for each letter. Instantiate each robot with enough `Things` to write its assigned letter.

(figure 2-22)

Friendly message

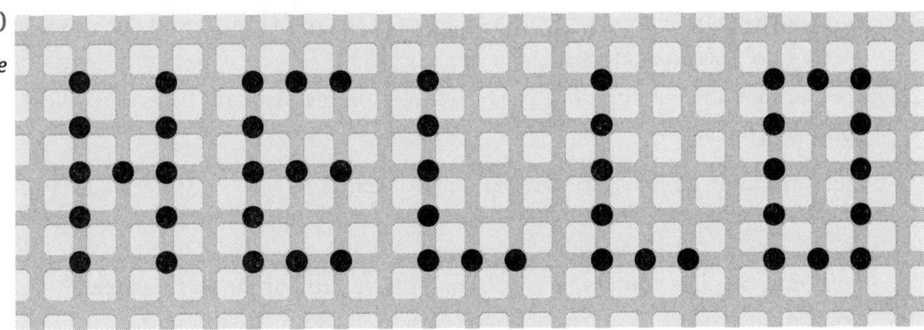

2.14 Write a program where robots practice playing soccer, as shown in Figure 2-23. Your program will have four `SoccerBot` robots. Each has methods to `advance`, `advanceLeft`, and `advanceRight`. Each of these methods begins with picking up the "ball" (a `Thing`), moving it in the pattern shown, and then dropping it.

a. Write a `main` method that sets up the city as shown and directs the four players to move the ball along the path shown by the arrows.

b. Write a subclass of `City`, `SoccerField`, that arranges the "goals" as shown. Add the ball and soccer players in the `main` method, as usual. (*Hint*: The `Wall` constructor requires a `City`. Which city? "this" city.)

(figure 2-23)

Soccer field with practicing robots

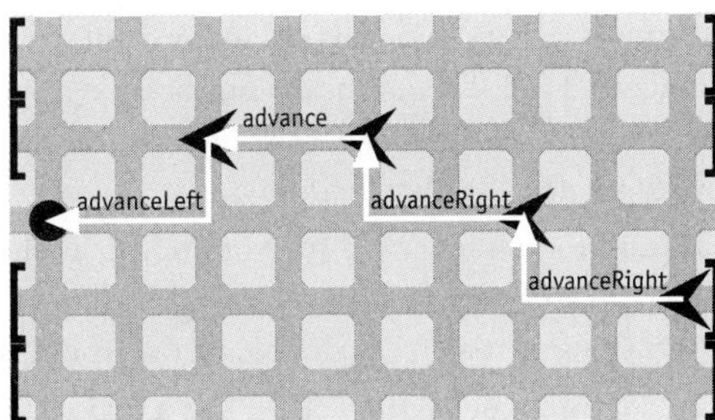

2.15 When a `Lamp` is on all that is visible is a soft yellow circle representing the "light." The "lamp" itself doesn't show unless it is off. Read the documentation for `CompositeIcon`. Then modify Listing 2-6 to make `Lamp` objects show both the "lamp" and the "light" when they are on.

2.16 In Section 2.3.2, we extended the `Thing` class, and in Section 2.2.4, we saw that `this` can be used to invoke methods inherited from the superclass.

a. Use these techniques to extend `JFrame` to obtain `CloseableJFrame`, which sets its default close operation, automatically opens to a default position and size of your choice, and is visible. Write a test program to ensure your new class works.

b. Modify your solution so the client creating the frame can specify its position and size via parameters.

2.17 Extend the functionality of `JFrame` so that a simple program containing the following code:

```
public static void main(String[] args)
{ ColorChooserFrame ccf = new ColorChooserFrame();
}
```

will cause a frame containing a `JColorChooser` to appear on the screen, appropriately sized. See Programming Project 1.18 for background.

2.18 Sketch a scene on graph paper that uses a combination of several rectangles, ovals, lines, and perhaps strings (text). Write a program that displays your scene.

2.19 Extend the `Icon` class as shown in Figure 2-24. The grid is to aid you in painting; it is not intended to be displayed by your icons.

a. Choose one of the icons shown in Figure 2-24 to implement. Instantiate a `Thing` and use its `setIcon` method to display your icon.

b. Introduce a `Car` class to the robot world. A `Car` is really a `Robot`, but uses a `CarIcon`, as shown in Figure 2-24.

c. Write a `TreeIcon` class that appears approximately as shown in Figure 2-24, using at least three shades of green. Extend `Thing` to make a `Tree` class and construct a city with several trees in it. Robots should not be able to pick up and move trees.

d. Create a `Lake` class that extends `Thing` and is displayed with a `LakeIcon` as shown in Figure 2-24. Robots should not be able to pick up and move lakes, and if they try to enter a lake, they break. Research the `Thing` class to discover how to implement these features.

e. Write an `R10Icon` for an advanced type of `Robot`, as shown in Figure 2-24. Research the `setFont` method in the `Graphics` class and the `Font` class to label the robot. Construct a city with at least one robot that uses your icon.

f. Extend `Wall` to create a `Building` class. Use a `BuildingIcon`, as shown in Figure 2-24, to display your buildings. Robots should not be able to pass through or over your buildings.

g. Write a `DetourIcon`. Use it in `DetourSign`, an extension of `Thing`. You will need to research the `Polygon` class and then use the `fillPolygon` method in the `Graphics` class. Research the `Thing` class to learn how to make your sign block robots from entering or exiting the intersection on the `NORTH` side. You may assume that the sign will always be placed on the north side of the intersection.

(figure 2-24)

Patterns for icons

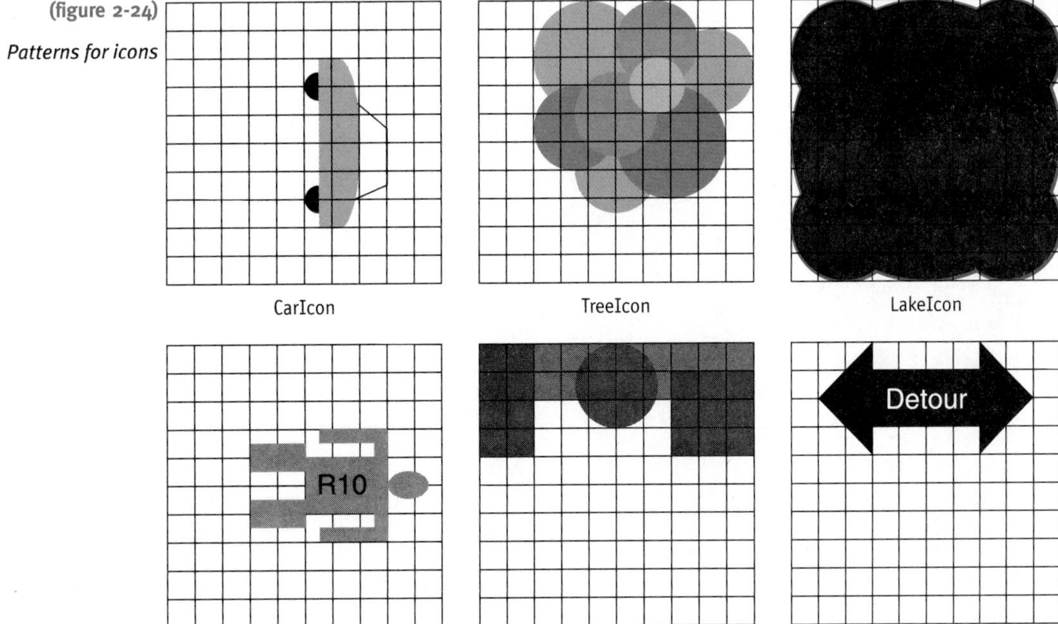

Chapter 3

Developing Methods

Chapter Objectives

After studying this chapter, you should be able to:

- Use stepwise refinement to implement long or complex methods
- Explain the advantages to using stepwise refinement
- Use pseudocode to help design and reason about methods before code is written
- Use multiple objects to solve a problem
- Use inheritance to reduce duplication of code and increase flexibility
- Explain why some methods should not be available to all clients and how to appropriately hide them

In Chapter 2, we wrote new services such as `turnRight` and `turnAround`. These services were very simple, consisting of only a few steps to accomplish the task.

In this chapter, we will examine techniques for implementing much more complex services that require many steps to accomplish the task.

3.1 Solving Problems

Writing programs involves solving problems. One model[1] describes problem solving as a process that has four activities: defining the problem, planning the solution, implementing the plan, and analyzing the solution.

When programming, the solution is called an **algorithm**. An algorithm is a finite set of step-by-step instructions that specifies a process of moving from the initial situation to the final situation. That is, an algorithm is the "solution" spelled out in a step-by-step manner.

We find many algorithms in our lives. A recipe for lasagna is an algorithm, as are the directions for assembling a child's wagon. Even bottles of shampoo have algorithms printed on them:

wet hair with warm water
gently work in the first application of shampoo
rinse thoroughly and repeat

While people may have no trouble interpreting this algorithm, it is not precise enough for computers. How much warm water? How much shampoo? What does it mean to "gently work in?" How many times should it be repeated? Once? A hundred times? Indefinitely? Is it necessary to wet the hair (again) for the repeated applications?

Not all algorithms are equally effective. Good algorithms share five qualities. Good algorithms are:

- correct
- easy to read and understand
- easy to debug
- easy to modify to solve variations of the original task
- efficient[2]

This chapter is about designing algorithms, particularly algorithms that can be encoded as computer programs and executed by a computer. This concept is not new—from the very beginning of this text, we have been writing algorithms and turning them into programs. Now we will focus more deliberately on the process.

[1] G. Polya, *How to Solve It,* Princeton University Press, 1945, 1973.

[2] Meaning that the algorithm does not require performing more steps than necessary. Efficiency should never compromise the first guideline, and only rarely should it compromise the other three.

3.2 Stepwise Refinement

Stepwise refinement is a method of constructing algorithms. An algorithm to solve a complex problem may be written by decomposing the problem into smaller, simpler subproblems, each with its own algorithm. Each sub-problem solves a logical step in the larger problem. The problem as a whole is solved by solving all of the subproblems.

When algorithms are expressed as computer programs, algorithms are encoded in methods. Stepwise refinement encourages us to write each method in terms of other methods that implement one logical step in solving the problem. In this way, we can write programs that are more likely to be correct, simple to read, and easy to understand.

It may appear natural to define all the new classes and services needed for a task first, and then write the program using these services. But how can we know what robots and which new services are needed before we write the program? Stepwise refinement tells us to first write the program using any robots and service names we desire, and then define these robots and their services. That is, we write the `main` method first, and then we write the definitions of the new services we used. Finally, we assemble the class containing `main` and any new classes we wrote into a complete program.

We will explore this process more concretely by writing a program for the task shown in Figure 3-1. The initial situation represents a harvesting task that requires one or more robots to pick up a rectangular field of `Things`. The robot(s) may start and finish wherever is most convenient.

(figure 3-1)

Harvesting task

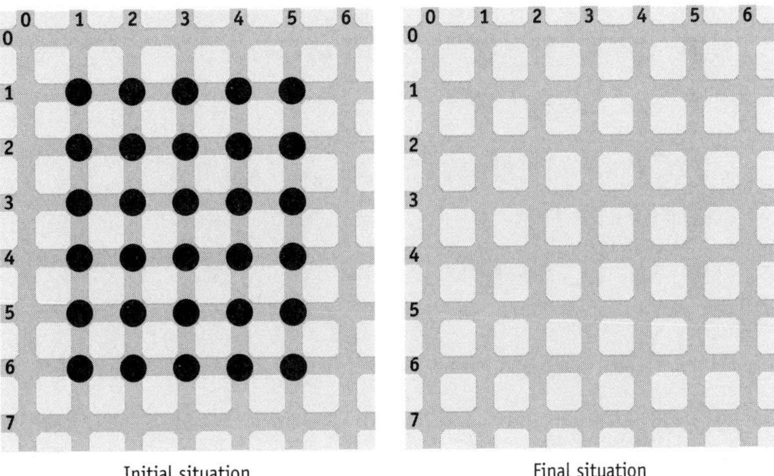

The first step is to develop an overall plan to guide us in writing a robot program to perform the given task. Planning is often best done as a group activity. Sharing ideas in a group allows members to present different plans that can be thoughtfully examined for strengths and weaknesses. Even if we are working alone, we can think in a question-and-answer pattern, such as the following:

Question How many robots do we need to perform this task?

Answer We could do it with one robot that walks back and forth over all of the rows to be harvested, or we could do it with a team of robots, where each robot picks some of the rows.

Question How many shall we use?

Answer Let's try it with just one robot, named `mark`, for now. That seems simpler than using several robots.

LOOKING AHEAD

In Section 3.5, we'll find that these are not well-founded assumptions.

Question Where should `mark` start?

Answer Probably at one of the corners. Then it doesn't need to go back to harvest rows behind it. Let's pick intersection (1, 0), facing the first row it will pick.

With these decisions made about how many robots to use and where to start, we can be more definite about the initial situation. The revised version appears in Figure 3-2.

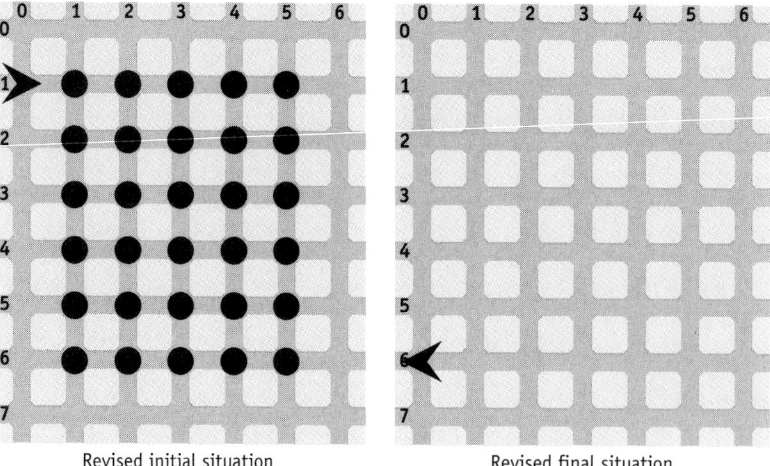

(figure 3-2)

Revised situations

3.2.1 Identifying the Required Services

Now that the initial situation is complete, we turn our attention to identifying the services `mark` must offer.

Question What do we want mark to do?

Answer Harvest all the things in the field.

Question So it sounds like we need a new service, perhaps called harvestField. Does mark need to have any other services?

Answer Well, the initial situation doesn't actually put mark in the field. We could either adjust the initial situation so it starts at (1, 1) or simply call move before it harvests the field. Other than that, harvestField seems to be the only service required.

Once the services required have been identified, we can make use of them in writing the main method. At this point, we won't worry about the fact that they don't exist yet.

We briefly move from planning to implementing our plan. We will call the new class of robots Harvester and implement the main method in a class named HarvestTask.

Defining a city with 30 Things would clutter Listing 3-1 significantly. To avoid this, the City class has a constructor, used in line 10, that can read a file to determine where Things are positioned. The requirements for such a file are described in the online documentation for the City class.

FIND THE CODE

ch03/harvest/

Listing 3-1: *The main method for harvesting a field of things*

```
1  import becker.robots.*;
2
3  /** A program to harvest a field of things 5 columns wide and 6 rows high.
4   *
5   * @author Byron Weber Becker */
6  public class HarvestTask
7  {
8    public static void main (String[] args)
9    {
10     City stLouis = new City("Field.txt");
11     Harvester mark = new Harvester(
12                          stLouis, 1, 0, Direction.EAST);
13
14     mark.move ();
15     mark.harvestField();
16     mark.move ();
17   }
18 }
```

3.2.2 Refining harvestField

We now know that the Harvester class must offer a service named harvestField that harvests a field of things. As we develop this service, we will follow the same pattern as before—asking ourselves questions about what it must do and what services we want to use to implement the harvestField service.

Using other services to implement harvestField builds on the observation we made in Section 2.2.4 when we implemented turnRight: methods may use other methods within the same class. Recall the declaration of turnRight:

```
public void turnRight()
{ this.turnAround();
  this.turnLeft();
}
```

When we implemented turnRight, we noticed that turnAround, a method we had already written, would be useful. However, to implement harvestField, we are turning that process around. We need to write a method, harvestField, and begin by asking which methods we need to help make writing harvestField easier. These methods are called **helper methods**. We will write harvestField as if those methods already existed. Helper methods are used frequently enough to qualify as a pattern.

KEY IDEA

Write a long or complex method using helper methods.

Eventually, of course, we will have to write each of the helper methods. It may be that we will have to follow the same technique for them as well: defining the helper methods in terms of other services that we wish we had. Each time we do so, the helper methods should be simpler than the method we are writing. Eventually, they will be simple enough to be written without helper methods.

PATTERN

Helper Method

We must be realistic when imagining which helper methods would be useful to implement harvestField. Step 2 in Figure 3-3—"then a miracle occurs"—would *not* be an appropriate helper method.

(figure 3-3)

A rather vague step

First Refinement Attempt

If you are working in a group to develop a program, a conversation between a Java expert and a novice to define the helper methods might proceed as follows. Even if you are working alone, it is still helpful to hold a "conversation" like this with yourself.

Expert So, what does a `Harvester` robot need to do to pick a field of things?

Novice Harvest all the things in each of the rows of the field.

Expert How could a `Harvester` robot harvest just one row?

Novice It could move west to east across the northern-most unharvested row of things, picking each thing as it moves.

Expert How could it harvest the entire field?

KEY IDEA

Use a helper method when doing the same thing several times.

Novice At the end of each row, the robot could turn around and move back to the western side of the field, move south one block, face east, and repeat the actions listed earlier. It could do so for each row of things in the field. Since the field has six rows, the robot needs to repeat the actions six times.

Expert If you were to write this down in an abbreviated form, what would it look like?

Novice *pick all the things in one row*
return to the start of the row
move south one block

pick all the things in one row
return to the start of the row
move south one block

pick all the things in one row
return to the start of the row
move south one block

Performing the actions in these nine lines would harvest the first three rows of the field. They need to be repeated to harvest the last three rows.

Analysis of the First Refinement Attempt

Before we continue with this plan, we should analyze it, looking at its strengths and weaknesses. Are we asking for the right helper methods? Are there other ways of solving the problem that might work better? Our analysis might proceed as follows:

Expert What are the strengths of this plan?

Novice The plan simplifies the `harvestField` method by defining three simpler methods, using each one several times.

Expert What are the weaknesses of the plan?

Novice The same three lines are repeated over and over. Maybe we should have `harvestField` defined as

harvest one row
harvest one row
harvest one row

and so on. The method to harvest one row could be defined using the helper methods mentioned earlier.

Expert That's easy enough to do. Any other weaknesses in this plan?

Novice The `Harvester` robot makes some "empty trips."

Expert What do you mean by "empty trips?"

Novice The robot returns to the starting point on the row that was just harvested.

Expert Why is this bad?

Novice It seems like a better solution to have the robot doing productive work (as opposed to just moving) in both directions. I know that if I were picking that field personally, I'd look for every efficiency I could find!

Instead of harvesting only one row and then turning around and returning to the start, the `Harvester` robot could pick all the things in one row, move south one row, and come back to the west, harvesting a second row. It could then move one row south to begin the entire process over for the next two rows. If `mark` repeats these steps one more time, the entire field of things will be harvested, as shown in Figure 3-4.

(figure 3-4)

Harvesting the field in two directions

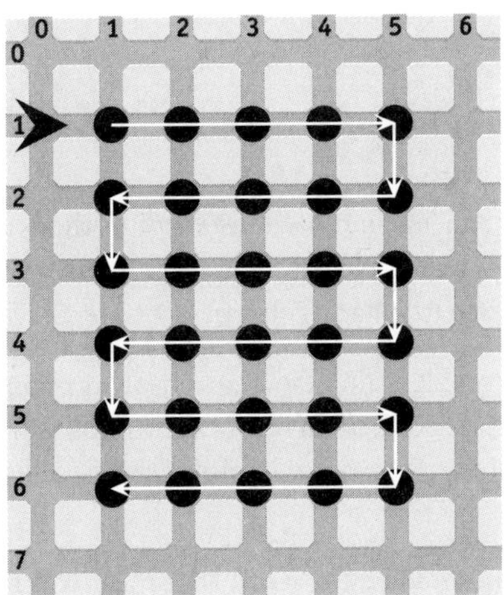

Expert How would you write that in an abbreviated form?

Novice Well, `harvestField` would be defined as follows:

harvest two rows
position for next harvest
harvest two rows
position for next harvest
harvest two rows

Again we analyze this new plan for its strengths and weaknesses.

Expert What advantage does this offer over the first plan?

Novice Now the robot makes only six trips across the field instead of 12. There are no empty trips.

Expert What are the weaknesses of this new plan?

Novice The robot harvests two rows at a time. If the field had an odd number of rows, we would have to think of something else.

When we are planning solutions, we should be very critical and not just accept the first plan as the best. We now have two different plans, and you can probably think of several more. Let's avoid the empty trips and implement the second plan.

Implementing `harvestField`

Recall the brief form of the idea:

harvest two rows
position for next harvest
harvest two rows
position for next harvest
harvest two rows

LOOKING AHEAD

This brief form is called pseudocode. We'll learn more about it in Section 3.4.

Let's turn each of these statements into invocations of methods named `harvestTwoRows` and `positionForNextHarvest`. We can then begin implementation of the `Harvester` class and `harvestField` in particular, as shown in Listing 3-2.

PATTERN

Helper Method

The listing includes the complete implementation of `harvestField` as well as stubs for `harvestTwoRows` and `positionForNextHarvest`. A method that has just enough code to compile, but not to actually do its job is called a **stub**. Stubs are useful for at least three reasons:

- Stubs serve as placeholders for work that must still be completed. The associated documentation records our ideas for what the methods should do, helping to jog our memory when we come back to actually implement the methods. In large programs with many methods, a span of days or even months might elapse before you have a chance to complete the method. If you are part of a team, perhaps someone else can implement the method based on the stub and its documentation.
- A stub allows the program to be compiled even though it is not finished. When we compile the program, the compiler may catch errors that are easier to find and fix now rather than later. Waiting to compile until the entire program is written may result in so many interrelated errors that debugging becomes very difficult.
- A compiled program can be run, which may allow some early testing to be performed that validates our ideas (or uncovers bugs that are easier to fix now rather than later). We might run the program to verify that the initial situation is correctly set up, for instance.

FIND THE CODE

ch03/harvest/

Listing 3-2: *An incomplete implementation of the* `Harvester` *class*

```
import becker.robots.*;

/** A class of robot that can harvest a field of things. The field must be 5 things wide
 *  and 6 rows high.
 *
 *  @author Byron Weber Becker */
public class Harvester extends RobotSE
{
   /** Construct a new Harvester robot.
    *  @param aCity The city where the robot will be created.
    *  @param str    The robot's initial street.
    *  @param ave    The robot's initial avenue.
    *  @param dir    The initial direction, one of Direction.{NORTH, SOUTH, EAST, WEST}. */
   public Harvester(City aCity,
                    int str, int ave, Direction dir)
   { super(aCity, str, ave, dir);
   }

   /** Harvest a field of things. The robot is on the northwest corner of the field. */
   public void harvestField()
   { this.harvestTwoRows();
     this.positionForNextHarvest();
     this.harvestTwoRows();
     this.positionForNextHarvest();
     this.harvestTwoRows();
   }

   /** Harvest two rows of the field, returning to the same avenue but one street
    *  farther south. The robot must be facing east. */
   public void harvestTwoRows()
   { // Incomplete.
   }

   /** Go one row south and face east. The robot must be facing west. */
   public void positionForNextHarvest()
   { // Incomplete.
   }
}
```

PATTERN

Helper Method

We must now begin to think about planning the instructions `harvestTwoRows` and `positionForNextHarvest`.

3.2.3 Refining `harvestTwoRows`

Our plan contains two subtasks: one harvests two rows and the other positions the robot to harvest two more rows. The planning of these two subtasks must be just as thorough as the planning was for the overall task. Let's begin with `harvestTwoRows`.

Expert What does `harvestTwoRows` do?

Novice `harvestTwoRows` must harvest two rows of things. One is harvested as the `Harvester` robot travels east and the second is harvested as it returns to the west.

Expert What does the robot have to do?

Novice It must pick things and move as it travels east. At the end of the row of things, it must move south one block, face west, and return to the western edge of the field, picking things as it travels west. In an abbreviated form, it must complete the following tasks:

harvest one row while moving east
go south to the next row
harvest one row while moving west

We analyze this plan as before, looking for strengths and weaknesses.

Expert What are the strengths of this plan?

Novice It seems to solve the problem.

Expert What are the weaknesses of this plan?

Novice Possibly one—we have two different instructions that harvest a single row of things.

Expert Do we really need two different harvesting instructions?

Novice We need one for going east and one for going west.

Expert Do we really need a separate method for each direction?

Novice Harvesting is just a series of `pickThings` and `moves`. The direction the robot is moving does not matter. If we plan `goToNextRow` carefully, we can use one instruction to harvest a row of things when going east and the same instruction for going west.

By reusing a method, we make the program smaller and potentially easier to understand. The new plan is as follows:

harvest one row
go to the next row
harvest one row

Translating this idea to Java, we arrive at the following method and stubs, which should be added to the code in Listing 3-2.

```
/** Harvest two rows of the field, returning to the same avenue but one street
 * farther south. The robot must be facing east. */
public void harvestTwoRows()
{ this.harvestOneRow();
  this.goToNextRow();
  this.harvestOneRow();
}

/** Harvest one row of five things. */
public void harvestOneRow()
{ // incomplete
}

/** Go one row south and face west. The robot must be facing east. */
public void goToNextRow()
{ // incomplete
}
```

PATTERN
Helper Method

This doesn't look good! Every time we implement a method, we end up with even more methods to implement. We now have three outstanding methods, `positionForNextHarvest`, `harvestOneRow`, and `goToNextRow`, all needing to be finished. Rest assured, however, that these methods are getting more and more specific. Eventually, they will be implemented only in terms of already existing methods such as `move`, `turnLeft`, and `pickThing`. Then the number of methods left to implement will begin to decrease until we have completed the entire program.

KEY IDEA
Implement the methods in execution order.

We have a choice of which of the three methods to refine next. One good strategy is to choose the first uncompleted method we enter while tracing the program. This strategy allows us to run the program to verify that the work done thus far is correct. Applying this strategy indicates that we should work on `harvestOneRow` next.

3.2.4 Refining `harvestOneRow`

We now focus our efforts on `harvestOneRow`.

Expert What does `harvestOneRow` do?

Novice Starting on the first thing and facing the correct direction, the robot must harvest each of the intersections that it encounters, stopping on the location of the last thing in the row.

Expert What does the `Harvester` robot have to do?

Novice It must harvest the intersection it's on and then move to the next intersection. It needs to do that five times, once for each thing in the row.

harvest an intersection
move
harvest an intersection
move
harvest an intersection
move
harvest an intersection
move
harvest an intersection
move

Expert Are you sure? It seems to me that it moves right out of the field.

Novice Right! The last time it doesn't need to move to the next intersection. It can just go to the next row of the field.

We can implement `harvestOneRow` and `harvestIntersection` as follows.

```
/** Harvest one row of five things. */
public void harvestOneRow()
{ this.harvestIntersection();
  this.move();
  this.harvestIntersection();
  this.move();
  this.harvestIntersection();
  this.move();
  this.harvestIntersection();
  this.move();
  this.harvestIntersection();
}

/** Harvest one intersection. */
public void harvestIntersection()
{ this.pickThing();
}
```

PATTERN

Helper Method

It may seem silly to define a method such as `harvestIntersection` that contains only one method. There are two reasons why it is a good idea:

- The language of the problem has been about "harvesting," not "picking." This method carries that language throughout the program, making the program easier to understand.

- What it means to harvest an intersection may change. By isolating the concept of harvesting an intersection in this method, we provide a natural place to make future changes. For example, suppose a future field requires harvesting two things on each intersection. With the helper method, we need to add just one `pickThing` to the `harvestIntersection` method. Without the helper method, we would need to change the program at five places in the `harvestOneRow` method.

3.2.5 Refining goToNextRow

Let's now plan `goToNextRow`.

Expert What does `goToNextRow` do?

Novice It moves the `Harvester` robot south one block to the next row and faces it in the opposite direction. I think we can implement this one without creating any new helper methods, like this:

turn right
move
turn right

3.2.6 Refining positionForNextHarvest

At last, we have only one stub to complete, `positionForNextHarvest`.

Expert What does `positionForNextHarvest` do?

Novice It moves the `Harvester` robot south one block to the next row.

Expert Didn't we do that already? Why can't we use the instruction `goToNextRow`?

Novice The robot isn't in the correct situation. When executing `goToNextRow`, the robot is on the eastern edge of the field facing east. When it executes `positionForNextHarvest`, it has just finished harvesting two rows and is on the western edge of the field facing west.

Take a moment to simulate the `goToNextRow` instruction on paper. Start with a `Harvester` robot facing west and see where the robot is when you finish simulating the instruction.

Expert What does the robot have to do?

Novice It must turn left, not right, to face south, move one block, and turn left again to face east.

The implementation of this new method follows:

```
/** Position the robot for the next harvest by moving one street south and facing west. */
public void positionForNextHarvest()
{ this.turnLeft();
  this.move();
  this.turnLeft();
}
```

All of the method stubs have now been completed.

3.2.7 The Complete Program

Because we have spread this class out over several pages, the complete program is printed in Listing 3-3 so that you will find it easier to read and study.

FIND THE CODE

ch03/harvest/

Listing 3-3: *The complete* `Harvester` *class*

```
import becker.robots.*;

/** A class of robot that can harvest a field of things. The field must be 5 things wide
 *  and 6 rows high.
 *
 *  @author Byron Weber Becker */
public class Harvester extends RobotSE
{
  /** Construct a new Harvester robot.
   *  @param aCity The city where the robot will be created.
   *  @param str    The robot's initial street.
   *  @param ave    The robot's initial avenue.
   *  @param dir    The initial direction, one of Direction.{NORTH, SOUTH, EAST, WEST}. */
  public Harvester(City aCity,
                   int str, int ave, Direction dir)
  { super(aCity, str, ave, dir);
  }

  /** Harvest a field of things. The robot is on the northwest corner of the field. */
  public void harvestField()
  { this.harvestTwoRows();
    this.positionForNextHarvest();
    this.harvestTwoRows();
    this.positionForNextHarvest();
    this.harvestTwoRows();
  }
```

Listing 3-3: *The complete* `Harvester` *class* (continued)

```

   /** Harvest two rows of the field, returning to the same avenue but one
    * street farther south. The robot must be facing east. */
   public void harvestTwoRows()
   { this.harvestOneRow();
     this.goToNextRow();
     this.harvestOneRow();
   }

   /** Harvest one row of five things. */
   public void harvestOneRow()
   { this.harvestIntersekction();
     this.move();
     this.harvestIntersection();
     this.move();
     this.harvestIntersection();
     this.move();
     this.harvestIntersection();
     this.move();
     this.harvestIntersection();
   }

   /** Go one row south and face west. The robot must be facing east. */
   public void goToNextRow()
   { this.turnRight();
     this.move();
     this.turnRight();
   }

   /** Go one row south and face east. The robot must be facing west. */
   public void positionForNextHarvest()
   { this.turnLeft();
     this.move();
     this.turnLeft();
   }

   /** Harvest one intersection. */
   public void harvestIntersection()
   { this.pickThing();
   }
}
```

3.2.8 Summary of Stepwise Refinement

Stepwise refinement can be viewed as an approach to bridging the gap between the method we need (`harvestField`) and the methods we already have (`move`, `pickThing`, and so on). The methods we already have available are sometimes called the **primitives**. For drawing a picture, the primitives include `drawRect` and `drawLine`.

Figure 3-5 shows the situation near the beginning of the design process. We know we want a method to harvest a field and we know that robots can move, pick things up, turn left, and so on. The question is, how do we bridge the gap between them? Stepwise refinement helps fill in intermediate methods, as shown in Figure 3-6, in an orderly manner to help solve the problem.

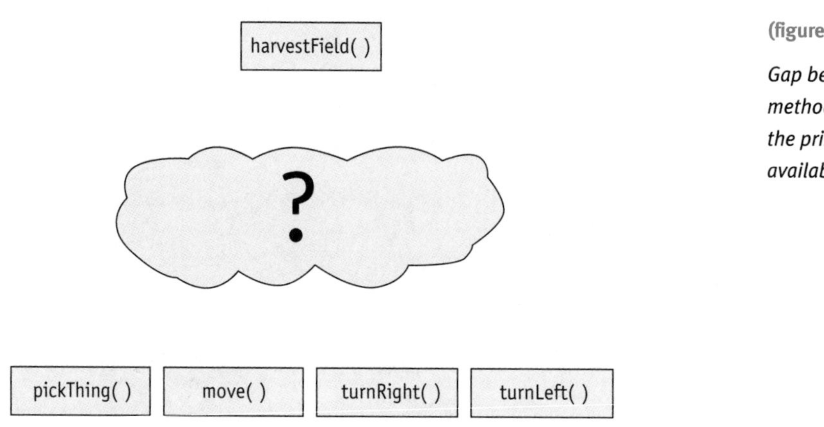

(figure 3-5)

Gap between the method we need and the primitives we have available

Design is best performed starting at the top of the diagram and working down. This approach is often called **top-down design**. Stepwise refinement is simply another name for top-down design.

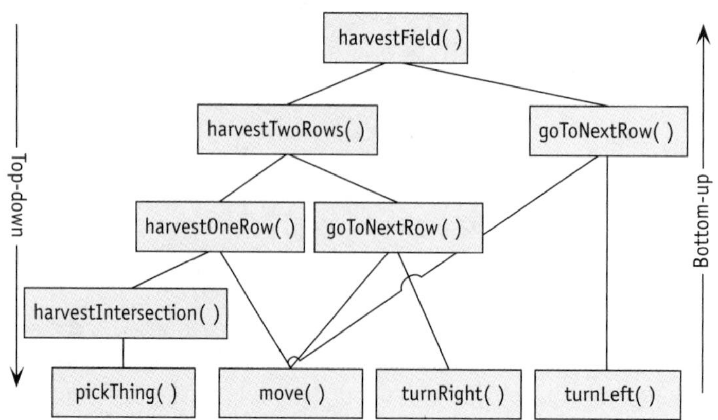

(figure 3-6)

Bridging the gap between the method we need and the primitives we have available

Sometimes we may have a flash of intuition and realize that harvesting one row would be a useful step in harvesting a field and that such a method could be easily constructed with the `move` and `pickThing` methods. When such an insight occurs before being derived in a top-down design, it's called **bottom-up design**. Bottom-up design happens within the context of top-down design.

It is also useful to make a distinction between top-down and **bottom-up implementation**. A top-down design may be done only on paper using pseudocode or even a diagram such as Figure 3-6. When actually writing the methods, we can start at the top and work down (as we did in this section of the book) or we can start at the bottom and work up. One advantage of the top-down approach is that it matches the design process. A significant advantage of the bottom-up approach is that methods can be implemented and tested before the entire program is complete. Testing methods as they are written almost always improves the correctness of the overall program.

3.3 Advantages of Stepwise Refinement

Developing programs using stepwise refinement has a number of advantages. The programs we create are more likely to be:

- Easy to understand
- Free of programming errors
- Easy to test and debug
- Easy to modify

All of these advantages follow from a few simple facts. First, as we noted in Section 1.1.1, most people can only manage about seven pieces of information at once. By breaking each problem into a small number of subproblems, the stepwise refinement technique helps us avoid information overload.

Furthermore, stepwise refinement imposes a structure on the problem. Related parts are kept together in methods; unrelated parts will be in different methods.

Finally, by identifying each of these related parts (methods) with well-chosen names, we can think at a higher level of abstraction; we can think about what the part does rather than how it does it.

We now investigate each of the four advantages of stepwise refinement.

3.3.1 Understandable Programs

Writing understandable programs is as important as writing correct ones; some say that it is even more important, since most programs initially have a few errors, and understandable programs are easier to debug. Successful programmers are distinguished from ineffective ones by their ability to write clear and concise programs that someone else can read and quickly understand. What makes a program easy to understand? We present three criteria.

- Each method, including the `main` method, is composed of a few easily understood statements, including method calls.
- Each method has a single, well-defined purpose, which is succinctly described by the method's name.
- Each method can be understood by examining the statements it contains and understanding the purpose of the methods it calls. Understanding the method should not depend on knowing how other methods work. It should only depend upon the methods' purposes.

Each of these criteria help limit the number of details a person must keep in mind at one time.

If a method cannot correctly accomplish its purpose unless it begins in a certain situation, that fact should be documented. For example, an instruction directing a robot to always pick something up should indicate in a comment where that thing must appear:

```
public class Collector extends Robot
{
  /** Collects one thing from the next intersection. Breaks the robot if nothing is present. */
  public void collectOneThing()
  { this.move();
    this.pickThing();
  }
}
```

3.3.2 Avoiding Errors

Many novices think that all of the planning, analyzing, tracing, and simulating of programs shown in the `Harvester` example take too much time. They would rather start typing their programs into a computer immediately, without planning first.

What really takes time is correcting mistakes. These mistakes fall into two broad categories.

KEY IDEA

A T-shirt slogan: Days of programming can save you hours of planning.

The first category is planning mistakes. They result in execution and intent errors and happen when we write a program without an adequate plan. Planning mistakes can waste a lot of programming time. They are usually difficult to fix because large segments of the program may have to be modified or discarded. Careful planning and thorough analysis of the plan can help avoid planning mistakes.

The second category is programming mistakes. They result in compile-time errors and happen when we actually write the program. Programming mistakes can be spelling, punctuation, or other similar errors. Compiling the program each time we complete a method helps find such errors so that they can be fixed. If we write the entire program before compiling it, we will undoubtedly have many errors to correct, some of which may be multiple instances of the same error. By using stubs and compiling often, we can both reduce the overall number of errors introduced at any one time and help prevent multiple occurrences of the same mistake.

Stepwise refinement is a tool that allows us to plan, analyze, and implement our plans in a way that should lead to a program containing a minimum of errors.

3.3.3 Testing and Debugging

Removing programming errors is easier in a program that has been developed using stepwise refinement. Removing errors has two components: identifying errors, and fixing the errors. Stepwise refinement helps in both steps.

LOOKING AHEAD

In Section 7.1.1, we will learn to write small programs designed to test single methods.

First, each method can be independently tested to identify errors that may be present. When writing a program, we should trace each method immediately after it is written until we are convinced that it is correct. Then we can forget how the method works and just remember what it does. Remembering should be easy if we name the method accurately, which is easiest if the method does only one thing.

Errors that are found by examining a method independently are the easiest ones to fix because the errors cannot have been caused by some other part of the program. When testing an entire program at once, this assumption cannot be made. If methods have not been tested independently, it is often the case that one has an error that does not become obvious until other methods have executed—that is, the signs of an error can first appear far from where the error actually occurs, making debugging difficult.

Second, stepwise refinement imposes a structure on our programs, and we can use this structure to help us find bugs in a completed program. When debugging a program, we should first determine which of the methods is malfunctioning. Then we can concentrate on debugging that method, while ignoring the other parts of the program, which are irrelevant to the bug. For example, suppose our robot makes a wrong turn and tries to pick up a thing from the wrong place. Where is the error? If we use helper methods to write our program, and each helper method performs one specific task (such as `positionForNextHarvest`) or controls a set of related tasks (such as `harvestTwoRows`), then we can usually determine the probable location of the error easily and quickly.

3.3.4 Future Modifications

Programs are often modified because the task to perform has changed in some way or there is an additional, related task to perform. Programs that have been developed using stepwise refinement are easier to modify than those that are not for the following reasons:

- The structure imposed on the program by stepwise refinement makes it easier to find the appropriate places to make modifications.
- Methods that have a single purpose and minimal, well-defined interactions with the rest of the program can be modified with less chance of creating a bug elsewhere in the program.
- Single-purpose methods can be overridden in subclasses to do something slightly different.

We can illustrate these points with an example modifying the `Harvester` class. Figure 3-7 shows two situations that differ somewhat from the original harvesting task. In the first one, each row has six things to harvest instead of just five. In the second, there are eight rows instead of six.

Obviously, this problem is very similar to the original harvesting problem. It would be much simpler to modify the `Harvester` program than to write a completely new program.

LOOKING AHEAD

Repetition and parameters (Chapters 4 and 5) will help our code adapt to variations of the same problem.

How difficult would it be to modify the `Harvester` class to accomplish the new harvesting tasks? We have two different situations to consider.

The first situation is one in which the original task has really changed, and it therefore makes sense to change the `Harvester` class itself. In this case, harvesting longer rows can be easily accommodated by adding the following statements to the `harvestOneRow` method:

```
this.move();
this.harvestIntersection();
```

A similar change to the `harvestField` method would solve the problem of harvesting additional rows.

(figure 3-7)

Two variations of the harvesting task

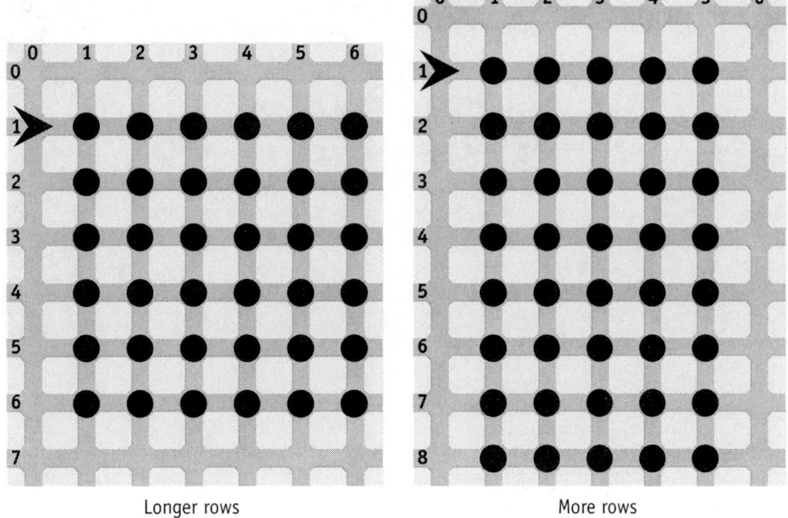

Our use of stepwise refinement in developing the original program aids this change tremendously. Stepwise refinement led us to logical subproblems. By naming them appropriately, it was easy to find where to change the program and how to change it. Furthermore, because the interactions between the methods were few and well defined, we could make the changes without creating a bug elsewhere in the program.

A second situation to consider is where we still need to solve the original problem—that is, it is inappropriate to change the original `Harvester` class, because it is still needed. We can then use inheritance to solve the new problem. By overriding `harvestOneRow`, we can make modifications to harvest longer rows, and by overriding `harvestField`, we can harvest more (or fewer) rows. A new robot class to harvest longer rows is shown in Listing 3-4.

FIND THE CODE

ch03/harvestLongRow/

Listing 3-4: *An extended version of* `Harvester` *that harvests longer rows*

```
import becker.robots.*;

/** A kind of Harvester robot that harvests fields with 6 things per row rather than just 5.
 *
 *  @author Byron Weber Becker */
public class LongRowHarvester extends Harvester
{ /** Construct the harvester. */
  public LongRowHarvester(City acity,
                                     int str, int ave, Direction dir)
  { super(acity, str, ave, dir);
  }
```

Listing 3-4: *An extended version of* `Harvester` *that harvests longer rows* (continued)

```
   /** Override the harvestOneRow method to harvest the longer row. */
   public void harvestOneRow()
   { super.harvestOneRow();              // harvest first 5 intersections
     this.move();                        // harvest one more
     this.harvestIntersection();
   }
}
```

3.4 Pseudocode

Sometimes it is useful to focus more on the algorithm than on the program implementing it. When we focus on the program, we also need to worry about many distracting details, such as placing semicolons appropriately, using consistent spelling, and even coming up with the names of methods. Those details can consume significant mental energy—energy that we would rather put into thinking about how to solve the problem.

Pseudocode is a technique that allows us to focus on the algorithms. Pseudocode is a blending of the naturalness of our native language with the structure of a programming language. It allows us to think about an algorithm much more carefully and accurately than we would with only **natural language**, the language we use in everyday speech, but without all the details of a full programming language such as Java. Think of it as your own personal programming language.

KEY IDEA

Pseudocode is a blend of natural and programming languages.

We've been using pseudocode for a long time without saying much about it. When planning our first program in Chapter 1, we presented the pseudocode for the algorithm before we wrote the program:

move forward until it reaches the thing,
pick up the thing
move one block farther
turn right
move a block
put the thing down
move one more block

Looking back for text set in this distinctive font, you'll also see that we used pseudocode in Chapter 2 when we developed the `Lamp` class and overrode `turnLeft` to make a faster-turning robot. We've also used it extensively in this chapter.

There are several advantages to using pseudocode:

- Pseudocode helps us think more abstractly. As we discussed briefly in Section 1.1.1, abstractions allow us to "chunk" information together into higher level pieces so that we don't need to remember as much. In this case, pseudocode enables us to chunk together many lower-level steps into a single higher-level step, such as `pick all the things in one row`. Such higher-level thinking, however, comes at a cost: less precision. This lack of precision may allow us to accidentally slip in a "miracle" (see the cartoon in Figure 3-3), but overall, the benefits of using pseudocode outweigh the costs.
- Pseudocode allows us to simulate, or trace, our program very early in its development. We can trace the program after only scratching out a few lines on paper. If we find a bug, it is much easier to change and fix it than if we had invested all the time and energy into obeying the many details of the Java language.
- If we are working with other people, even nontechnical users, pseudocode can provide a common language. With it, we can describe the algorithm to others. They might see a special case we missed or a more efficient approach, or even help implement it in a programming language.
- Algorithms expressed with pseudocode can be converted into any computer programming language, not just Java.

Pseudocode's usefulness increases as the complexity of the algorithm you are designing increases. In the next chapter, we will introduce Java constructs that allow us to choose whether to execute some statements. Other constructs allow us to repeat statements. These constructs are very powerful and vital to writing interesting programs—but they also add complexity, a complexity that pseudocode can help manage in the early stages of programming.

3.5 Variations on the Theme

Consider again the field harvesting task discussed in Section 3.2. There are many variations. Perhaps several robots are available to perform the task, or instead of harvesting things, the robot needs to plant things. This section explores these variations. In the process, we will see that early in the development of the `Harvester` class we made a key assumption that we should use a single robot. This assumption needlessly complicated the program; we should have explored more alternatives. We will also see how to make the computer appear to do several things at once, such as six robots all harvesting a row of things simultaneously.

3.5.1 Using Multiple Robots

One approach to solving the harvesting problem is to use several robots, which we briefly considered early in the process. In this approach, each robot harvests only a part of the field. For example, our `main` method could be modified to instantiate three robots, each of which harvests two rows. The initial situation is shown in Figure 3-8 and in the program in Listing 3-5. `mark` will harvest the first two rows; `lucy` the middle two rows; and `greg` the last two rows. Of course, the work does not need to be divided evenly. If there were only two robots, one could harvest two rows, and the other could harvest four rows.

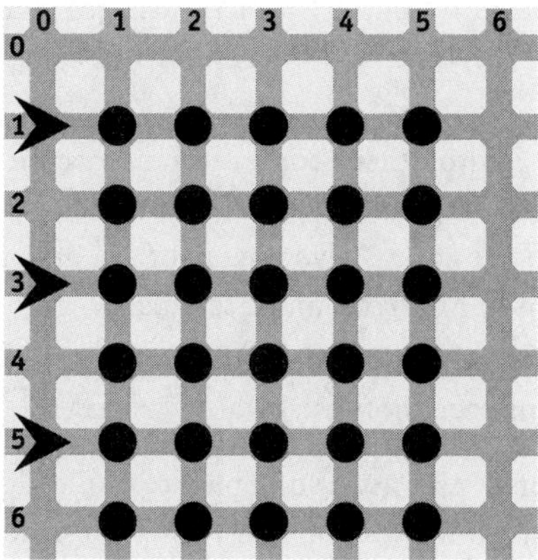

(figure 3-8)

Harvesting a field with three robots each harvesting two rows

FIND THE CODE

ch03/harvestWithThree/

Listing 3-5: *The* `main` *method for harvesting a field with three robots*

```
import becker.robots.*;

/** Harvest a field of things using three robots.
 *
 * @author Byron Weber Becker */
public class HarvestTask extends Object
{
  public static void main(String[] args)
  {
    City stLouis = new City("Field.txt");
    Harvester mark = new Harvester(
                        stLouis, 1, 0, Direction.EAST);
    Harvester lucy = new Harvester(
                        stLouis, 3, 0, Direction.EAST);
    Harvester greg = new Harvester(
                        stLouis, 5, 0, Direction.EAST);
```

Listing 3-5: *The* `main` *method for harvesting a field with three robots* (continued)

```

      mark.move();
      mark.harvestTwoRows();
      mark.move();

      lucy.move();
      lucy.harvestTwoRows();
      lucy.move();

      greg.move();
      greg.harvestTwoRows();
      greg.move();
   }
}
```

FIND THE CODE

ch03/harvestWithSix/

In fact, the original problem does not specify the number of robots to use, where they start, or where they finish. Perhaps the simplest solution is to have six robots each harvesting one row, and ending on the opposite side of the field. The initial and final situations are shown in Figure 3-9. If we had chosen this solution, the `Harvester` class would have consisted of only `harvestOneRow` and `harvestIntersection`—much simpler than what we actually implemented.

(figure 3-9)

Harvesting with six robots

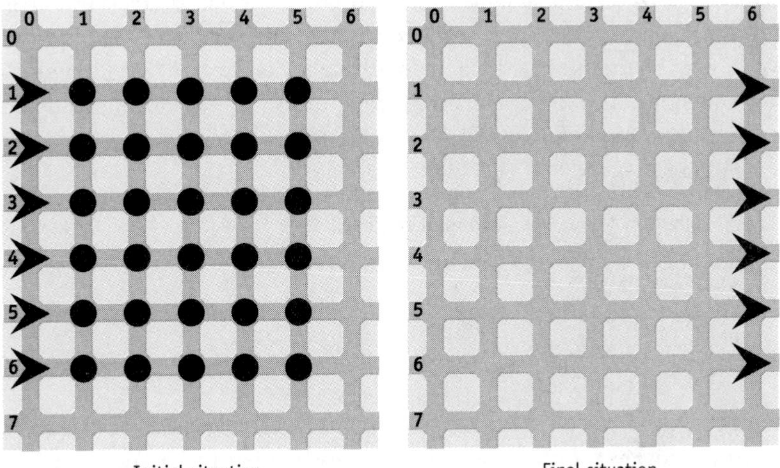

3.5.2 Multiple Robots with Threads (advanced)

In the previous example, which uses six robots, one robot finishes its entire row before the next one begins to harvest its row. The entire task takes about six times as long as harvesting a single row, even though we have six robots.

If we were paying a group of people an hourly wage to perform this task, we would be pretty upset with this strategy. We would want them working simultaneously so that the entire job is done in about the same amount of time it takes one person to harvest one row.

In this section, we'll explore how to make the robots (appear to) do their work simultaneously. This material is normally considered advanced, but robots provide a clear introduction to these ideas, and it's a fun way to stimulate your thinking about other ways to do things. Check with your instructor to find out if he or she expects you to know this material.

Example: ThreadedRowHarvester

When you have several robots working simultaneously, each robot must be self-contained. The `main` method will start each robot, after which your robots will perform their tasks independently. This approach implies that each robot must be instantiated from a subclass of `Robot`, which "knows" what to do without further input from the program. We'll call this subclass `ThreadedRowHarvester`.

The instructions each robot should execute after it's started are placed in a specially designated method named `run` in the `ThreadedRowHarvester`. The `run` method is free to call other methods to get the job done. In our case, we call the `HarvestOneRow` and `move` methods, as shown in the following method. The `run` method should be inserted in the `ThreadedRowHarvester` class. `harvestOneRow` is defined as in the `Harvester` class.

KEY IDEA

The `run` method contains the instructions the thread will execute.

```
/** What the robot does after its thread is started. */
public void run()
{ this.move();
  this.harvestOneRow();
  this.move();
}
```

In the `main` method, we need to construct six `ThreadedRowHarvester` robots, one for each row. However, instead of instructing each robot to harvest a row, we start each robot's thread. The `run` method defined earlier then instructs the robot what to

PATTERN

Multiple Threads

do. A thread is started with two statements, one to create a `Thread` object and one to call its `start` method. For a robot named `karel`, use the following statements:

FIND THE CODE

ch03/ harvestWithSix Threads/

```
ThreadedRowHarvester karel = new ThreadedRowHarvester(...);
...
Thread karelThread = new Thread(karel);
karelThread.start();
```

The `start` method in the last statement invokes the `run` method, which contains the instructions for the robot. For this strategy to work, the `Thread` class must be assured that the `ThreadedRowHarvester` class actually has a `run` method. You do so by adding `implements Runnable` to the line defining the class:

```
public class ThreadedRowHarvester extends Robot
                                  implements Runnable
```

This statement is your promise to the compiler that `ThreadedRowHarvester` will include all of the methods listed in the `Runnable` interface. The `run` method is the only method listed in the documentation for `Runnable`.

In summary, three things need to be completed to start a thread:

- Include the instructions for the robot in a specially designated method called `run`.
- Implement the interface `Runnable` to tell Java that your class is set up to run in a thread.
- Start the thread.

In this example, each thread performs identical tasks, which need not be the case. We could, for instance, set up two threads with robots harvesting two rows each, and two more threads with robots harvesting one row each.

About Threads

A thread starts a new flow of control. We learned in the Sequential Execution pattern that each flow of control is a sequence of statements, one after the other, where each statement finishes before the next one begins.

The `main` method begins execution in its own thread. As long as we don't start any new threads, execution proceeds one statement after another, as shown in Figure 3-10. This figure supposes that we have two robots named `mark` and `lucy`. The `main` method first calls `mark.harvestOneRow();` and then `lucy.harvestOneRow();`. Between these calls, many other statements are executed, one after the other.

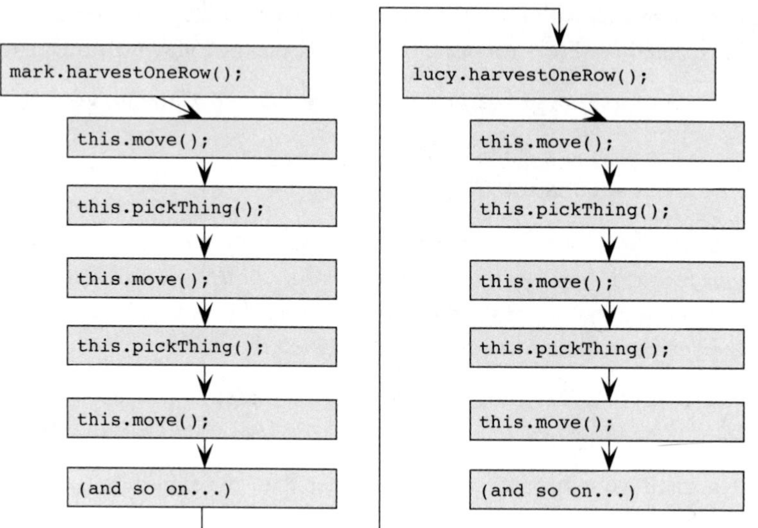

(figure 3-10)

Flow of control with only one thread

When we have two or more flows of control, execution switches among them. The statements *within* each flow of control still execute in order with respect to each other, but statements from a different thread might execute between them. This concept is illustrated in Figure 3-11.

The `main` method's flow of control starts a thread for `mark` and then for `lucy`, represented by the light arrow between the two left-most boxes.

But now that we have three threads of control (one for `main`, one for `mark`, and one for `lucy`), the execution switches between all three threads, as represented by the heavier arrows. Execution switches among the threads so quickly that it *appears* that all the robots are moving simultaneously, though they are not (unless you are fortunate enough to have a computer with at least as many processors as the program has threads). The computer's operating system ensures that each thread runs at least a little bit before stopping it and starting another thread. It also ensures that every thread is eventually run.

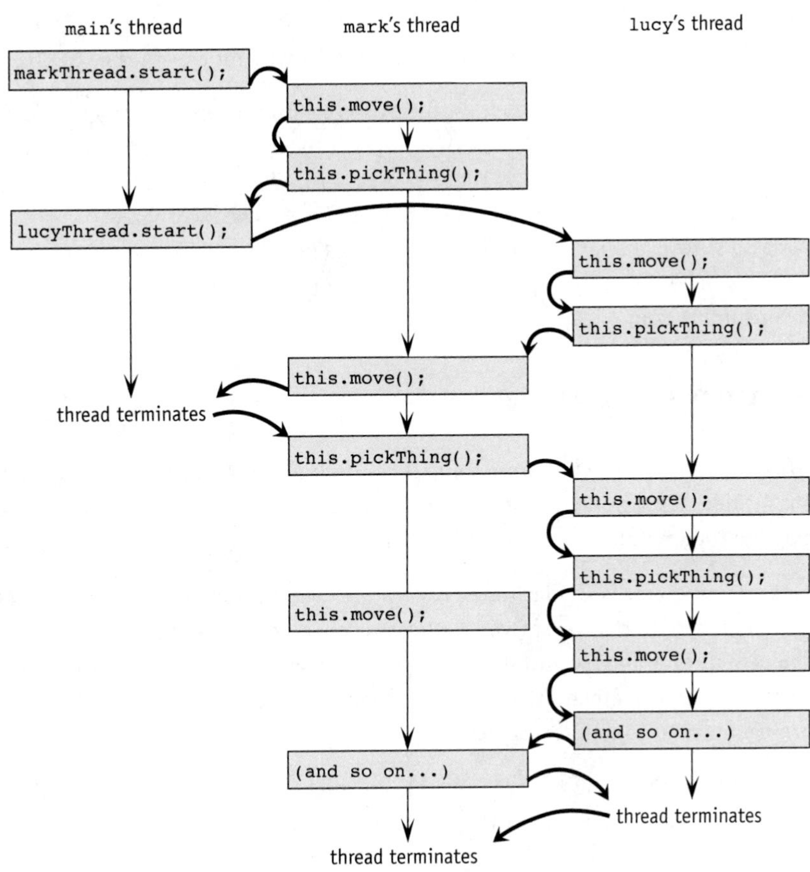

(figure 3-11)

One possible flow of control with three threads

Notice that although execution switches among the threads, the statements within each thread are still executed in the same order as before. The only difference is that statements from another thread might be executed between the statements.

Complexities

This simple example glosses over some complexities. For instance, each robot's task in these examples is independent of the tasks performed by the other robots. If a seventh robot collected all the things harvested by the first six robots, it would need a way to wait for those robots to finish their task before starting.

In the next chapter, we will explore ways that programs can make decisions. For example, a robot can check if a `Thing` is present on the intersection. Suppose `mark` is programmed to check for a `Thing` on the current intersection. If there is one, `mark` picks it up; otherwise, `mark` goes on to the next intersection. But the check is in one program statement and the call to `pickThing` is in another. `lucy`, running in another thread, might come along and snatch the thing between those two statements. So the thing mark thought was there disappears, and mark breaks when it executes pickThing.

In spite of these and other complexities, threads are a useful tool in many applications. For example, animations run in their own threads. Many word processors figure out page breaks in a separate thread so that the user can continue typing at the same time. Printing usually has a separate thread so that the user can do other work instead of waiting for a slow printer. Graphical user interfaces usually run in one or more threads so that they can continue to respond to the user even while the program is carrying out a time-consuming command.

LOOKING AHEAD

In Section 10.7, we'll learn how to use a thread to perform animation in a user interface.

3.5.3 Factoring Out Differences

Suppose that instead of picking one thing from each intersection in the field, we want to plant a thing at each intersection. Other alternatives include picking two things or counting the total number of things in the field.

Each of these programs is similar to the harvesting task. In particular, the part that controls the movement of the robot over the field is the same for all of these problems; it is only the task at each intersection that differs. The original task of harvesting things is only one example of a much more general problem: traversing a rectangular area and performing a task at each intersection.

KEY IDEA

Think about variations of the problem early in the design.

If we started with this view of the problem, we might design the program differently. Instead of solving the harvesting problem directly, we could design a TraverseAreaRobot that traverses a rectangular area. At each intersection, it calls a method named visitIntersection that is defined to do nothing, as follows:

```
public void visitIntersection()
{
}
```

By overriding this method in different subclasses, we can create robots that harvest each intersection or plant each intersection, and so on. A class diagram illustrating this approach is shown in Figure 3-12.

It may seem strange to include a method like visitIntersection that does nothing. However, this method must be present in TraverseAreaRobot because other methods in that class call it. On the other hand, we don't know what to put in the method because we don't know if the task is harvesting or planting the field, and so we simply leave it empty, ready to be overridden to perform the appropriate action.

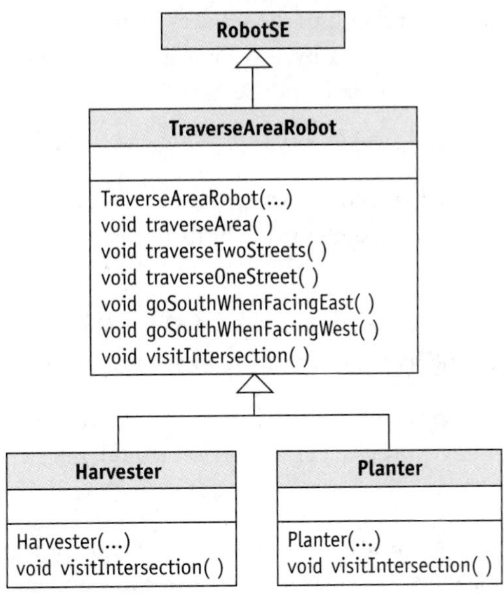

(figure 3-12)

Class diagram for a group of classes for working with fields

Of course, we could have solved the planting problem by extending the `Harvester` class and overriding `harvestIntersection`. The approach shown in Figure 3-12 differs from that in two ways. The first difference is that we planned for various tasks to occur at each intersection and named the methods accordingly. It is confusing to override a method named `harvestIntersection` so that it plants something instead of harvesting.

PATTERN
Template Method

The second difference is that the `TraverseAreaRobot` class deliberately does nothing when it visits an intersection. Instead, `visitIntersection` serves as an intentional point where subclasses can modify the behavior of `traverseArea`. In fact, the documentation for `visitIntersection` and `traverseArea` should explicitly describe the possibilities of overriding the method. In a sense, `traverseArea` is a template for a common activity, which is modified by overriding `visitIntersection`.

3.6 Private and Protected Methods

The `TraverseAreaRobot` class makes available six new services: `traverseArea`, `traverseTwoStreets`, `traverseOneStreet`, `goSouthWhenFacingEast`, `goSouthWhenFacingWest`, and `visitIntersection`. Should these all be available to all clients? For example, should a client such as `main` be able to invoke the `goSouthWhenFacingEast` method? After all, it was developed as a helper method, not as a service to be offered by a `TraverseAreaRobot`. Perhaps a client should not be allowed to invoke it.

Recall that a client is an object that uses the services of another object, called the server. The client uses the server's services by invoking its corresponding method with the Command Invocation pattern described in Section 1.7.3:

```
«objectReference».«methodName»(«parameterList»);
```

The client is the class that contains code, such as `karel.move()`, `joe.traverseArea()`, or even `this.goSouthWhenFacingEast()`. In these cases, `karel`, `joe`, and `this` are the *«objectReference»*s.

Java has a set of **access modifiers** that control which clients are allowed to invoke a method. The access modifier is placed as the first keyword before the method signature.

So far, we have used the access modifier `public`, as in `public void traverseArea()`. The keyword `public` allows any client to access the method. Like a public telephone, anyone who comes by can use it.

KEY IDEA

Public methods may be invoked by any client.

The access modifier `private` is at the other end of the scale. It says that no one except clients who belong to the same class, may invoke the method, and that the method may not be overridden. Staying private is what we want for many helper methods. `goSouthWhenFacingEast`, for example, was designed to help `traverseTwoStreets` do its work; it should not be called from outside of the class where it was declared. It should therefore be declared as follows:

KEY IDEA

Private methods can only be invoked by methods defined in the same class.

```
private void goSouthWhenFacingEast()
```

A middle ground is to use the `protected` access modifier. Protected methods may be invoked from clients that are also subclasses. Like all methods, protected methods can also be invoked from within the class defining them.

KEY IDEA

Protected methods can be used from subclasses.

Using `protected` on the `traverseOneStreet` and `visitIntersection` methods would be appropriate. It would allow us to override and use those methods in a subclass to traverse longer streets. We also did this in Section 3.3.4 when we overrode `harvestOneRow` to harvest a longer row. This approach is shown in Listing 3-6 and Listing 3-7. Listing 3-8 shows code that does *not* compile because it attempts to use `protected` and `private` methods.

Listing 3-6: *Using* `protected` *and* `private` *access modifiers in* `TraverseAreaRobot`

```
public class TraverseAreaRobot extends RobotSE
{ public TraverseAreaRobot(...)          {    ...    }

  public void traverseArea()             {    ...    }

  private void traverseTwoStreets()      {    ...    }

```

Listing 3-6: *Using* `protected` *and* `private` *access modifiers in* `TraverseAreaRobot` (continued)

```
  protected void traverseOneStreet()      {     ...     }
  private void goSouthWhenFacingEast()    {     ...     }
  private void goSouthWhenFacingWest()    {     ...     }
  protected void visitIntersection()      {     ...     }
}
```

Listing 3-7: *Using* `protected` *methods in a subclass of* `TraverseAreaRobot`

```
public class TraverseWiderAreaRobot extends TraverseAreaRobot
{ public TraverseWiderAreaRobot(...)      {     ...     }
  protected void traverseOneStreet()
  { super.traverseOneStreet();          // traverse first 5 intersections
    this.move();                        // traverse one more
    this.visitIntersection();
  }
}
```

Listing 3-8: *A program that fails to compile because it attempts to use* `private` *and* `protected` *methods*

```
public class DoesNotWork
{ public static void main(String[] args)
  { ...
    TraverseAreaRobot karel = new TraverseAreaRobot(...);
    ...
    karel.traverseArea();               // works—method is public
    karel.traverseTwoStreets();         // compile error
                                        // traverseTwoStreets is private
    karel.visitIntersection();          // compile error
                                        // visitIntersection is protected
  }
}
```

It is also possible to omit the access modifier. The result is called "package" access. It restricts the use of the method to classes in the same package. The `becker.robots` package sometimes uses package access to make services available within all classes in the package that should not be available to students. For example, `Robot` actually has a `turnRight` method (contrary to what you read in Section 1.2.3), but it has package access, so most clients can't use it. `RobotSE`, however, is in the same package and thus has access to it. It makes `turnRight` publicly available with the following method, which overrides `turnRight` with a less restrictive access modifier.

```
public void turnRight()
{ super.turnRight();
}
```

Students should not need to use package access.

As a rule of thumb, beginning programmers should declare methods as `private` except in the following cases:

- The method is specifically designed to be a public service. In this case, you should declare it as `public`.
- The method is used only by a subclass. In this case, you should declare it as `protected`.

KEY IDEA

Declare methods to be `private` unless you have a specific reason to do otherwise.

Access modifiers are often shown in class diagrams with the symbols +, #, and –. They stand for `public`, `protected`, and `private` access, respectively. Figure 3-13 shows a class diagram for the `Harvester` class that includes these symbols.

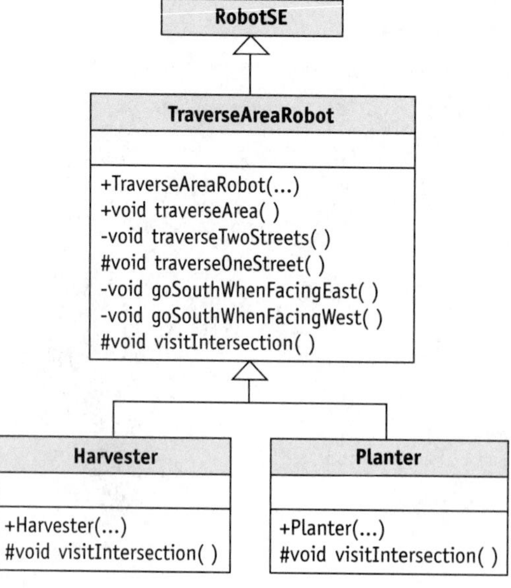

(figure 3-13)

Showing the accessibility of the helper methods in the `TraverseAreaRobot` class

3.7 GUI: Using Helper Methods

KEY IDEA

Helper methods are a powerful way to help organize a class.

Stepwise refinement and helper methods are useful in graphics programs, too. For example, consider the pair of stick figures in Figure 3-14. They are based on the stick figure program written in Section 2.7. The `paintComponent` method from that program is reproduced in Listing 3-9, but lines 17 to 29 need to somehow be executed twice to draw both figures. Simply executing the same code twice isn't enough—that would just draw one figure on top of the other. We also need to offset the second figure so that they stand side-by-side.

(figure 3-14)

Pair of stick figures

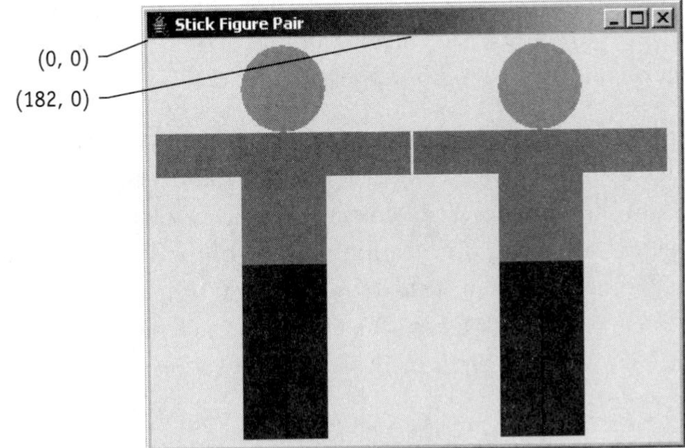

FIND THE CODE

ch02/stickFigure/

Listing 3-9: *The code to draw a single stick figure at a predetermined location*

```
12 // Paint a stick figure.
13 public void paintComponent(Graphics g)
14 { super.paintComponent(g);
15
16    // Paint the head.
17    g.setColor(Color.YELLOW);
18    g.fillOval(60, 0, 60, 60);
19
20    // Paint the shirt.
21    g.setColor(Color.RED);
22    g.fillRect(0, 60, 180, 30);
23    g.fillRect(60, 60, 60, 90);
24
25    // Paint the pants.
26    g.setColor(Color.BLUE);
27    g.fillRect(60, 150, 60, 120);
```

Listing 3-9: *The code to draw a single stick figure at a predetermined location* (continued)

```
28     g.setColor(Color.BLACK);
29     g.drawLine(90, 180, 90, 270);
30  }
```

One approach is to duplicate lines 17 to 29 inside the `paintComponent` method and adjust the arguments to offset the second figure. A much better approach is to place lines 17 to 29 inside a helper method. The `paintComponent` method calls the method twice to draw the two figures—except that we once again have the problem of offsetting the second figure to stand beside the first one. We could make two helper methods, one for each figure, but they would be almost identical.

The best solution is one helper method that uses parameters to specify the location of the figure. We have already made extensive use of parameters. For example, consider the method calls in lines 17 to 29 of Listing 3-9. They each pass arguments to the method's parameters indicating the location and size of the shape to draw. We will use the same strategy except that instead of drawing a simple oval or rectangle, our method will draw an entire stick figure. We will use parameters only for the location of the stick figure. Using such a helper method, the `paintComponent` method is simplified to the following:

```
1  /** Paint two stick figures
2   *   @param g The graphics context to do the painting. */
3  public void paintComponent(Graphics g)
4  { super.paintComponent(g);
5    this.paintStickFig(g, 0, 0);
6    this.paintStickFig(g, 182, 0);
7  }
```

Line 5 causes a stick figure to be drawn with its upper-left corner placed at (0, 0)—that is, the upper-left corner of the component. Figure 3-14 is annotated with this location. Line 6 causes the second figure to be painted at (182, 0), or 182 pixels from the left and 0 pixels down from the top. This location is also noted in Figure 3-14. The value of 182 was picked because each stick figure is 180 pixels wide, plus two pixels for a tiny gap between them.

Lines 5 and 6 also pass `g`, the `Graphics` object used for painting, as an argument because `paintStickFig` will need it to draw the required shapes.

3.7.1 Declaring Parameters

PATTERN
Parameterized Method

To use arguments such as `g`, `182`, and `0` inside our helper method, we need to declare corresponding parameters. These should look familiar because we have been declaring parameters in `Robot` constructors since the beginning of Chapter 2. The first line of the `paintStickFig` method should be:

```
private void paintStickFig(Graphics g2, int x, int y)
```

The first part of this line, `private void paintStickFig`, is the same as our Parameterless Command and Helper Method patterns.

LOOKING BACK
***Type** was defined in Section 1.3.1 as specifying a valid set of values for an attribute. Here it specifies the set of values for the parameter.*

Next come the three parameters. Each specifies a type and a name, and is separated from the next parameter with a comma. `Graphics` is the name of a class and specifies that the first argument to `paintStickFig` must be a reference to a `Graphics` object. This is similar to our `Robot` constructors. There, the first parameter has a type of `City`; consequently, we always pass a `City` object as the first argument. The next two parameters must always be passed integer arguments because they are declared with `int`.

Inside the method, the values passed as arguments will be given the name of the corresponding parameter. If the method is called with `this.paintStickFig(g, 182, 0)`, then inside `paintStickFig`, every time we use the name `x` it will be interpreted as `182`—the value passed to it.

3.7.2 Using Parameters

With this background, we can rewrite the method to use the parameters to specify the stick figure's position. Each time we refer to an *x* or a *y* location in drawing the stick figure, we add the appropriate `x` or `y` parameter. This action offsets the figure, as shown in Figure 3-15. Adding two numbers together uses the plus sign, and if one of the "numbers" happens to be a parameter, Java will use the number it represents (in this case, the number passed to it as an argument). The revised code for `paintStickFig` appears in Listing 3-10.

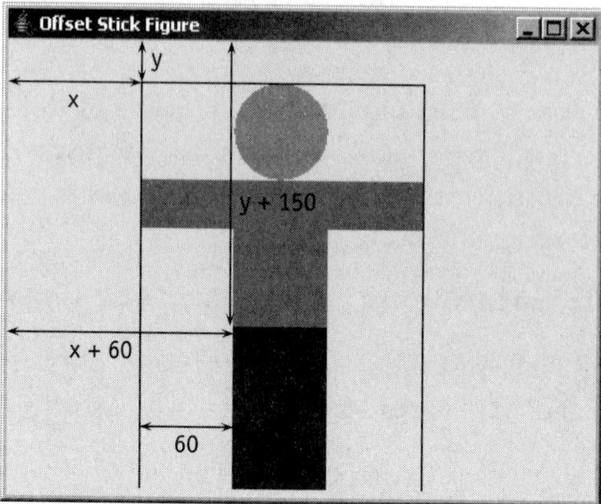

(figure 3-15)

Offsetting the location of the stick figure with the `x` *and* `y` *parameters*

Consider line 36 to paint the rectangle used for the pants. In the original code, we wrote `g.fillRect(60, 150, 60, 120)` to draw a rectangle 60 pixels from the left side and 150 pixels down from the top. The last two arguments specify that it should be 60 pixels wide and 120 pixels high. In line 36, this is changed to `g2.fillRect(x+60, y+150, 60, 120)`. Now the rectangle starts 60 pixels to the right of `x`. If `x` is passed 0, the pants are painted 60 pixels from the left side of the panel. If `x` is passed 182, the pants are painted 242 (182 + 60) pixels from the left side.

FIND THE CODE

ch03/stickFigure/

Listing 3-10: *A component that paints two stick figures, one beside the other*

```
1  import java.awt.*;                    // Graphics, Dimension, Color
2  import javax.swing.*;                 // JComponent
3
4  public class StickFigurePair extends JComponent
5  {
6     public StickFigurePair()
7     { super ();
8        Dimension prefSize = new Dimension(2*180+5, 270);
9        this.setPreferredSize(prefSize);
10    }
11
12    /** Paint two stick figures
13     * @param g The graphics context to do the painting. */
14    public void paintComponent(Graphics g)
15    { super.paintComponent(g);
16       this.paintStickFig(g, 0, 0);
17       this.paintStickFig(g, 182, 0);
18    }
19
20    /** Paint one stick figure at the given location.
```

Listing 3-10: *A component that paints two stick figures, one beside the other* (continued)

```
    * @param g2  The graphics context to do the painting.
    * @param x   The x coordinate of the upper-left corner of the figure.
    * @param y   The y coordinate of the upper-left corner of the figure. */
   private void paintStickFig(Graphics g2, int x, int y)
   { // Paint the head.
     g2.setColor(Color.YELLOW);
     g2.fillOval(x+60, y+0, 60, 60);

     // Paint the shirt.
     g2.setColor(Color.RED);
     g2.fillRect(x+0, y+60, 180, 30);
     g2.fillRect(x+60, y+60, 60, 90);

     // Paint the pants.
     g2.setColor(Color.BLUE);
     g2.fillRect(x+60, y+150, 60, 120);
     g2.setColor(Color.BLACK);
     g2.drawLine(x+90, y+180, x+90, y+270);
   }
}
```

Using a helper method helps keep the `paintComponent` method to a reasonable size. By adding parameters to the helper method, we allow the method to be used more flexibly with the result that we only need one helper method instead of two.

3.8 Patterns

This chapter introduced four patterns: Helper Method, Multiple Threads, Template Method, and Parameterized Method.

3.8.1 The Helper Method Pattern

Name: Helper Method

Context: You have a long or complex method to implement. You want your code to be easy to develop, test, and modify.

Solution: Look for logical steps in the solution of the method. Put the code to solve this step in a well-named helper method. For example, if the problem is for a robot to travel in a square pattern, the problem could be decomposed like this:

```
public void squareMove()
{ this.sideMove();
  this.sideMove();
  this.sideMove();
  this.sideMove();
}
```

where `sideMove` is defined as follows:

```
private void sideMove()
{ this.move();
  this.move();
  this.move();
  this.turnLeft();
}
```

Of course, the problem may involve writing several different helper methods. Because helper methods are usually not services the class provides, they should generally be declared `private` or at least `protected`, depending on whether subclasses need to access or override them.

Consequences: Long or complex methods are easier to read, develop, test, and modify when you break them into smaller steps and use helper methods.

Related Patterns: This pattern is almost identical to the Parameterless Command pattern and other method-related patterns we will see in future chapters. The difference is in the intent: helper methods designate methods that exist to perform a piece of a larger operation whereas the Parameterless Command, for example, does not have that connotation.

3.8.2 The Multiple Threads Pattern

Name: Multiple Threads

Context: You have multiple objects such as robots that should appear to carry out their tasks simultaneously.

Solution: Start each of the tasks in its own thread of control. This requires three tasks:

- Write a method named `run`. It contains code to execute in a thread.
- Implement the `Runnable` interface so that Java knows your class is set up to run as a thread.
- Start the thread.

The first two steps are expressed in code according to the following template:

```
public class «className» extends «superclassName»
                          implements Runnable
{ ...
  public void run()
  { «statements to execute inside a separate thread»
  }
}
```

The third step is often included in an instance of the Java Program pattern but can also be used in other contexts.

```
public class «programClassName»
{ public static void main(String[] args)
  {  ...
     «className» «runnableObject» = new «className»(...);
     Thread «threadName» = new Thread(«runnableObject»);
     «threadName».start();
     ...
  }
}
```

The three lines to create the object, create the thread, and start the thread are repeated as many times as there are threads.

Consequences: A separate thread of control is started whose execution is interleaved with the execution of other threads. This is relatively easy as long as the threads cannot interfere with each other. If interference is a possibility, many problems can arise.

Related Patterns: This pattern makes use of common patterns, such as the following:

- Java Program
- Extended Class
- Object Instantiation
- Method Invocation
- Sequential Execution

3.8.3 The Template Method Pattern

Name: Template Method

Context: You have a set of similar classes. Each has a method that does almost the same thing as a corresponding method in the other classes, but not quite. You would like to avoid duplicating the common code so that you only need to write it, debug it, and maintain it once.

Solution: The method that shares the similar code among classes is called the **template method**. Write it using helper methods for the parts that are different from one version to another. However, instead of putting these helper methods in the same class as the template method, put them in subclasses. The subclasses provide the variations in the code that are used to solve the different problems.

LOOKING AHEAD

Methods can be declared `abstract` *instead. We'll learn more in Section 12.1.5.*

To compile the template method, you need to include empty methods with the same names as the helper methods.

For an example, see Section 3.5.3.

Consequences: Writing the common code once helps reduce the effort to write, debug, and maintain it. By explicitly identifying where the differences occur and writing methods for them, it's easier to add a new class that solves another variation of the same problem.

On the other hand, needing to look in a different class for part of the solution to the problem can be confusing.

Related Pattern: This pattern is a specialization of the Extended Class pattern where specific methods are provided for the express purpose of being overridden.

3.8.4 The Parameterized Method Pattern

Name: Parameterized Method

Context: A method might do many variations of its task if it only had some information from its client to say which variation to perform. The different variations are often quantified—how many pixels over to paint a figure, how many times to turn a robot, or how much money to deposit in a bank account.

Solution: Use one or more parameters to communicate information from the client to the method. Use this information to control which of many possible variations of the task to perform.

In general, the method will declare one or more parameters, each having a type and a name. Consecutive pairs are separated with commas, as shown in the following template:

```
public void «methodName»(«paramType1» «paramName1»,
                         «paramType2» «paramName2»,
                         ...
                         «paramTypeN» «paramNameN»)
{ «list of statements, at least some of which use paramName»
}
```

The method is used with a method invocation matching the following template:

```
«objectReference».«methodName»(«arg1», «arg2», ..., «argN»);
```

where the type of each argument is compatible with the type of the corresponding parameter.

A concrete example of this pattern is illustrated in Listing 3-10.

Consequences: The method is much more flexible than a similar method written without parameters. Parameters give opportunities to the client to influence how the method carries out its task.

LOOKING AHEAD

This pattern will be discussed more fully in Chapters 4 and 6.

Related Patterns: The Parameterized Method pattern is a variation of the other following patterns:

- Parameterless Command
- Helper Method

3.9 Summary and Concept Map

Stepwise refinement is a process of breaking a problem down into smaller and simpler steps until, ultimately, the problems are constrained enough to be directly solved with the primitives at hand. The advantages of using stepwise refinement include code that is easier to understand, test, debug, and modify, precisely because the solution is expressed in terms of logical subproblems discovered by the stepwise refinement process.

Stepwise refinement naturally results in helper methods: methods that exist to help another method by solving a subproblem. Helper methods are often `private`, but may also be `protected`. When they are protected, subclasses can often be used to easily solve variations of the same problem using the Template Method pattern.

Pseudocode is another tool for designing methods. It is a mixture of a natural language, such as English, and a programming language. It allows us to express our algorithms at a high level and reason about them without investing the time and overhead of coding them in a language such as Java.

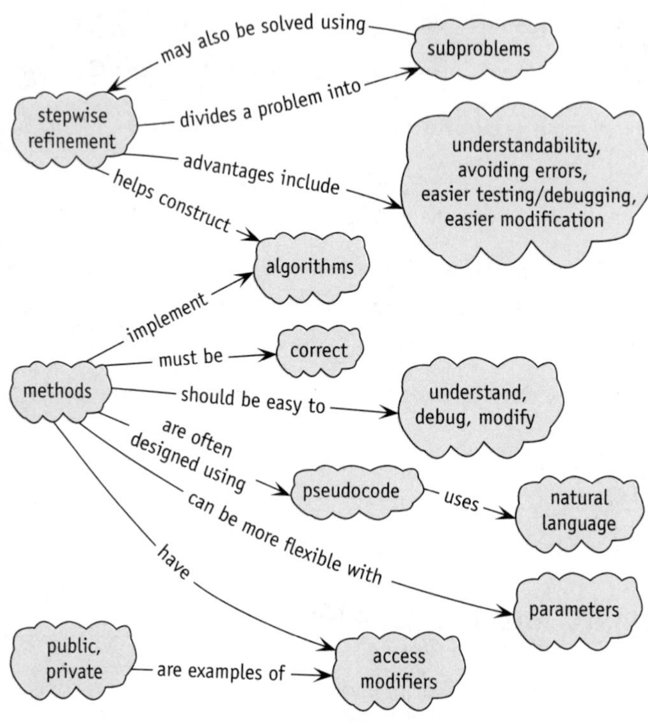

3.10 Problem Set

Written Exercises

3.1 In Listing 3-3, all of the methods have public access. Is this appropriate? Should any of them have a different access modifier? If so, which ones?

3.2 Examine problem 2.13 again, in which `karel` wrote the message "Hello" using `Things`. What helper methods would you suggest?

3.3 Suppose the `TraverseAreaRobot` class is extended to create the `Harvester` class, as described in Section 3.5.3. What happens if the method in `Harvester` is misspelled vistIntersection?

3.4 Consider the choice of access modifiers for `TraverseAreaRobot` suggested in Listing 3-6. Explain their effects on the creation of a subclass to harvest every other row of the field.

Programming Exercises

3.5 If necessary, download the source code for the examples and find `ch03/debugging/`. It contains two kinds of robots, both of which perform the same task. However, `MonolithicBot` contains a single method named `doit`.

`StepRefineBot` also contains a method named `doit`, but it was developed using stepwise refinement. Run the program once to see what it is supposed to do.

Work with a partner for the remainder of this problem. Assign `MonolithicBot` to one partner and `StepRefineBot` to the other. Each of you makes one small, secret change to the other's robot. "One small change" is defined as deleting a statement, adding a statement, or substituting a new statement for an existing statement. Run each program and time how long it takes each person to find the mistake in their assigned robot. Repeat five times. Summarize your results.

Programming Projects

3.6 Rewrite the `harvestField` method using a different stepwise refinement. In particular, move the robot over the field in a spiral pattern, as shown in Figure 3-16.

a. Write pseudocode to solve the problem using this idea.

b. Analyze the solution for strengths and weaknesses.

c. Write a program implementing your solution.

(figure 3-16)

Harvesting in a spiral

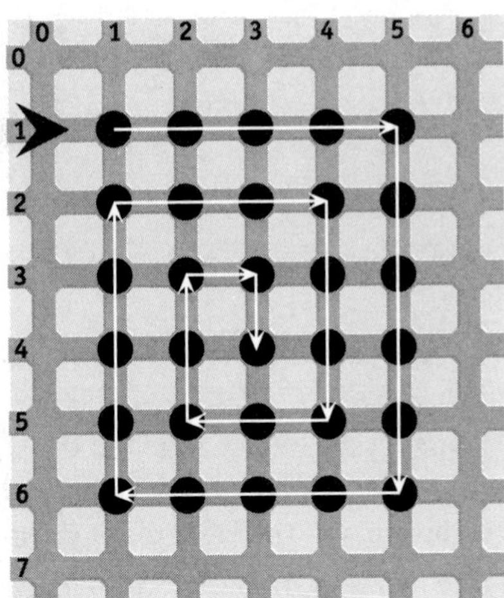

3.7 Program a robotic synchronized swimming team. The team has four members that begin their routine as shown in Figure 3-17 in the middle of the pool. Each swimmer goes through the same motions: a small counter-clockwise square, a large counter-clockwise square, turn around, a small clockwise square, and finally a large counter-clockwise square. Each square leaves the swimmer in the same position as when it started the square. Small squares involve moving once on each side; for large squares, the swimmers move twice. Start each swimmer in its own thread (see Section 3.5.2).

(figure 3-17)

Initial situation for a team of synchronized swimmers

3.8 `karel` sometimes works as a pinsetter in a bowling alley. Examine the initial and final situations shown in Figure 3-18, and then complete the following tasks:

a. Develop pseudocode for two different refinements of a method named `setPins`.

b. Analyze both solutions for strengths and weaknesses.

c. Write a program that implements one of your solutions.

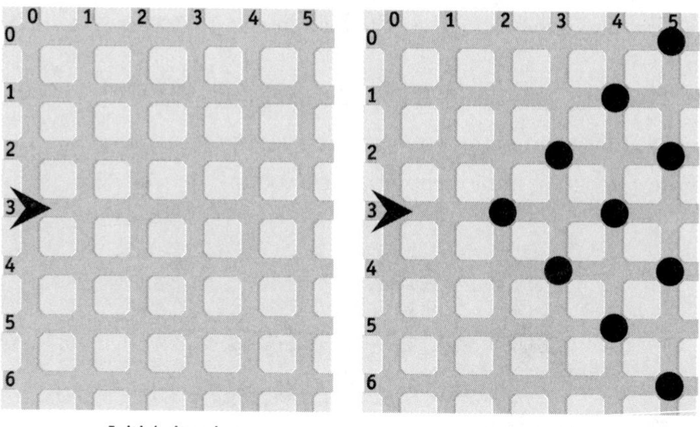

(figure 3-18)

Initial and final situations for `setPins`

3.9 The CEO of a highly successful local software company has a plus-shaped wall in her garden, as shown in Figure 3-19. She would like to use robots to plant one and only one `Thing` at each location around the wall. Robots will always start with enough `Things` to finish their task (look in the documentation for a constructor to specify how many `Things` a robot starts with).

a. Use a single robot to do the planting. It begins and ends at (0, 0).

b. Use a team of four robots. You may choose their beginning and ending positions.

c. Use a team of eight robots. You may choose their beginning and ending positions.

d. Use threads so that a team of robots plants the garden simultaneously.

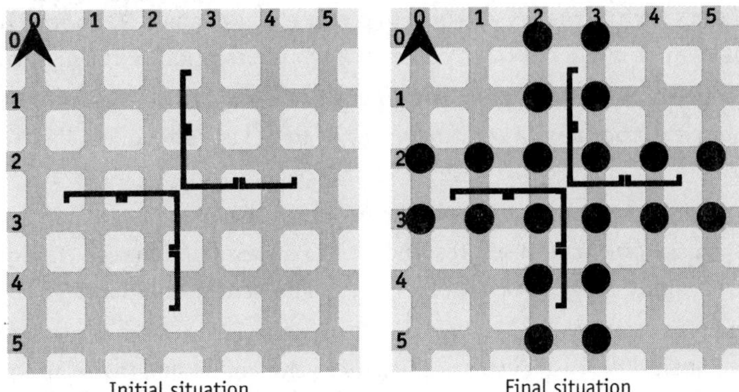

(figure 3-19)
Planting things in a garden

3.10 Spiderman has a new superhero rival: Spiderbot. Just like Spiderman, Spiderbot can climb tall buildings, as shown in Figure 3-20. However, Spiderbot must stay as close to a building as possible as it climbs, and it can't jump between buildings.

a. Write a `SpiderBot` class that has a `climbBuilding` method. Use it to instruct Spiderbot to climb over the three buildings. Use a file to place the walls of the buildings. Consult the online documentation for the `City` constructors for the file format.

b. Extend the `City` class to make `CityBuilder`. The `CityBuilder` class has a method named `placeBuilding` that takes one parameter: the avenue where the building should be placed. Use it to build the city.

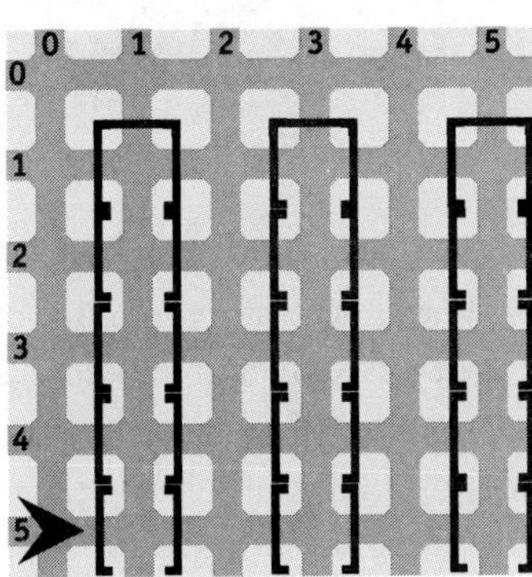

(figure 3-20)
Series of skyscrapers for Spiderbot to climb

3.11 Section 3.5.3 describes how to use `TraverseAreaRobot` as a template for classes that do variations of the same task. Implement the `TraverseAreaRobot` class.

a. Extend `TraverseAreaRobot` to create a class named `Harvester`. Instances of `Harvester` will pick one `Thing` from each intersection of the area traversed.

b. Extend `TraverseAreaRobot` to create a class named `Planter`. Instances of `Planter` will put one `Thing` on each intersection of the area traversed.

c. Extend `TraverseAreaRobot` to create a class named `BumperCropHarvester`. Instances of this class will collect five `Things` from each intersection of the area traversed.

d. Extend `TraverseAreaRobot` to create a class named `SparseRowHarvester`. Instances of this class will harvest `Things` from every other row of the area traversed. The field should have 12 rows.

3.12 King Java's castle, shown in Figure 3-21, needs to be guarded. Write a `GuardBot` class to patrol the castle walls in the pattern shown. Be sure to use appropriate stepwise refinements. Choose an appropriate place for the guard to begin its duties.

a. Write a `main` method that uses a single `GuardBot` to guard the castle.

b. Write a `main` method that uses four `GuardBots` to patrol the castle, one on each side.

c. Modify your solution so that all the guards patrol their wall simultaneously.

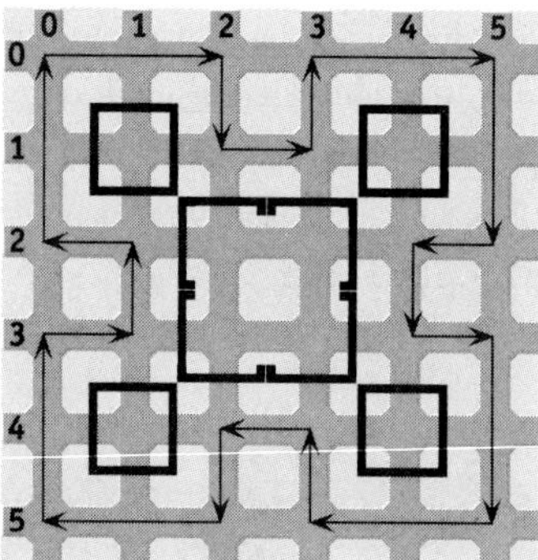

(figure 3-21)

King Java's castle

3.13 King Java's neighbor, King Caffeine, is impressed with the `GuardBots` developed in Problem 3.12. He wants to hire four `GuardBots` to patrol his castle. However, his castle is larger, as shown in Figure 3-22.

a. Refer to the class diagram in Figure 3-12, which discusses the Template Method pattern. Adapt it to this problem, showing the relationships and methods needed for three classes: `GuardBotTemplate`, `LongWallGuard`, and `ShortWallGuard`.

b. Using the Template Method pattern, develop three classes named `GuardBotTemplate`, `LongWallGuard`, and `ShortWallGuard`. Write a `main` method that creates castles for both King Caffeine and King Java and then uses four `LongWallGuards` to patrol King Caffeine's castle and four `ShortWallGuards` to patrol King Java's castle.

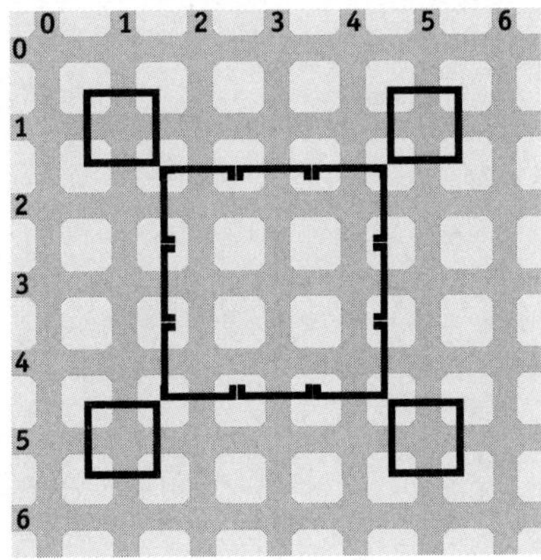

(figure 3-22)

King Caffeine's castle

3.14 Create a program that draws four copies of the Olympic rings, one in each corner of the component. The colors of the five rings, from left to right, are blue, yellow, black, green, and red. The rings may simply overlap rather than interlock, as in the official symbol.

Chapter 4 Making Decisions

Chapter Objectives

After studying this chapter, you should be able to:

- Use an `if` statement to perform an action once or not at all.
- Use a `while` statement to perform an action zero or more times.
- Use an `if-else` statement to perform either one action or another action.
- Describe what conditions can be tested and how to write new tests.
- Write a method, called a predicate, that can be used in the test of an `if` or `while` statement.
- Use parameters to communicate values from the client to be used in the execution of a method.
- Use a `while` statement to perform an action a specified number of times.

In the preceding chapters, a robot's exact initial situation was known at the start of a task. When we wrote our programs, this information allowed robots to find things and avoid running into walls. However, these programs worked only in their specific initial situations. If a robot tried to execute one of these programs in a slightly different initial situation, the robot would almost certainly fail to perform the task.

To address this situation, a robot must make decisions about what to do next. Should it move or should it pick something up? In this chapter we will learn about programming language statements that test the program's current state and choose the next statement to execute based on what they find. One form of this capability is the `if` statement: *If* something is true, then execute a group of statements. *If* it is not true, then skip the group of statements. Another form of this capability is the `while` statement: *while* something is true, execute a group of statements.

4.1 Understanding Two Kinds of Decisions

So far, our programs have been composed of a sequence of statements executed in order. These statements have included creating new objects (the Object Instantiation pattern) and invoking their services (the Command Invocation pattern). The only deviation we've seen from this sequential order is in defining our own commands or methods. In that case, whenever one method includes a statement invoking another method, all the statements in the called method are executed in order before execution moves on to the next statement in the calling method.

The `if` and `while` statements are different. As the program is running, they can ask a question. Based on the answer, they choose the next statement or group of statements to execute. In a robot program, the question asked might be, "Is the robot's front blocked by a wall?" or "Is there something on this intersection the robot can pick up?" In the concert hall program from Chapter 1, questions asked by an `if` or `while` statement might include "Is the ticket for seat 22H still available?" or "Have all of the sold tickets been processed yet?"

KEY IDEA

`if` and `while` statements choose the next statement to execute by asking a yes/no question.

All of these questions have "yes" or "no" answers. In fact, `if` and `while` statements can only ask yes/no questions. Java uses the keyword `true` for "yes" and `false` for "no." These keywords represent Boolean values, just like the numbers `0` and `23` represent integer values.

KEY IDEA

`true` means "yes" and `false` means "no."

When the simplest form of an `if` statement asks a question and the answer is `true`, it executes a group of statements once and then continues with the rest of the program. If the answer to the question is `false`, that group of statements is not executed.

When a `while` statement asks a question and the answer is `true`, it executes a group of statements (just like the `if` statement). However, instead of continuing with the rest of the program, the `while` statement asks the question again. If the answer is still `true`, that same group of statements is executed again. This continues until the answer to the question is `false`.

The `if` statement's question is "Should I execute this group of statements *once*?" The `while` statement's question is "Should I execute this group of statements *again*?" This ability to ask a question and to respond differently based on the answer liberates our programs from always executing the same sequence of statements in exactly the order given. For example, these two statements will allow us to generalize the `Harvester` class shown in Listing 3-3 in the following ways:

KEY IDEA

`if` statements execute code once or not at all. `while` statements might execute the statements repeatedly.

- Harvest any number of things from the intersection.
- Have a single `goToNextRow` method that works at both ends of the row. The current solution has one method for the east end of the row and another method for the west end.
- Harvest fields of varying sizes.

4.1.1 Flowcharts for `if` and `while` Statements

One way to illustrate the flow of control through the `if` and `while` statements is with a flowchart, as shown in Figure 4-1. The diamond represents the question that is asked. The box represents the statements that are optionally executed. The arrows show what the computer does next.

By tracing the arrows in the flowchart for `if`, you can easily verify that the statements in the box are executed once or not at all. Tracing the arrows for the `while` statement, however, shows that you can reach the statements in the box over and over again—or that they might not be executed at all.

(figure 4-1)

Flowcharts for the `if` and `while` statements

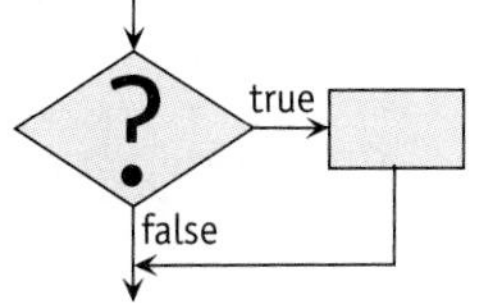

Flowchart for the `if` statement

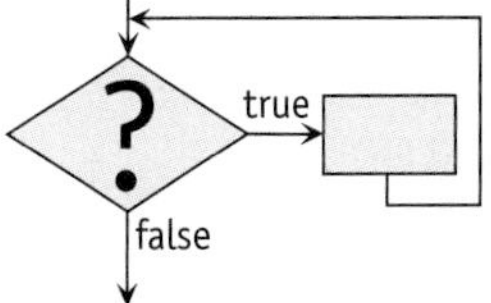

Flowchart for the `while` statement

KEY IDEA

Decide between `if` and `while` by asking how many times the code should execute.

The key question you should ask when deciding whether to use an `if` statement or a `while` statement is "How many times should this code execute?" If the answer is once or not at all, choose the `if` statement. If the answer is zero or more times, then choose the `while` statement.

4.1.2 Examining an `if` Statement

Suppose that a robot, `karel`, is in a city that has walls. If `karel`'s path is clear, it should move and then turn left. Otherwise, `karel` should just turn left.

You can use an `if` statement to have `karel` make this decision. The `if` statement's question is "Is `karel`'s front clear of obstructions?" If the answer is `true` (yes), `karel` should move forward and then turn left. If the answer is `false` (no), `karel` should skip the move instruction and just turn left. This program fragment[1] is written like this:

PATTERN

Once or Not at All

```
if (karel.frontIsClear())
{ karel.move();
}
karel.turnLeft();
```

[1] To conserve space, we will often demonstrate a programming idea without writing a complete program or even a complete method. Instead, we will write only the necessary statements, which are called a **program fragment**.

Consider two different initial situations. In Figure 4-2, the answer to the `if` statement's question is "Yes, `karel`'s front is clear of obstructions." As a result, `karel` performs the test, moves, and then turns left. These three actions are shown in the figure, where the heavy arrows show the statements that are executed to produce the situation shown on the right.

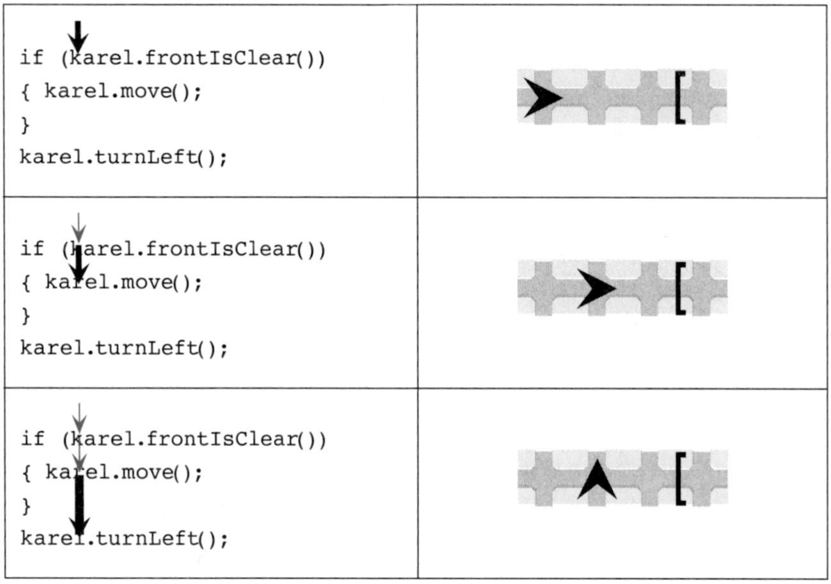

```
if (karel.frontIsClear())
{ karel.move();
}
karel.turnLeft();
```

```
if (karel.frontIsClear())
{ karel.move();
}
karel.turnLeft();
```

```
if (karel.frontIsClear())
{ karel.move();
}
karel.turnLeft();
```

(figure 4-2)

Execution of an `if` *statement when the robot's front is initially clear of obstructions*

Suppose `karel` starts in the situation shown in Figure 4-3. Then the answer to the `if` statement's question is "No, `karel`'s front is *not* clear of obstructions" and the statement instructing `karel` to move is *not* executed. `karel` does not move, although it does turn left because the `turnLeft` command is outside the group of statements controlled by the `if` statement.

KEY IDEA

The `if` *statement causes the robot to behave differently, depending on its situation.*

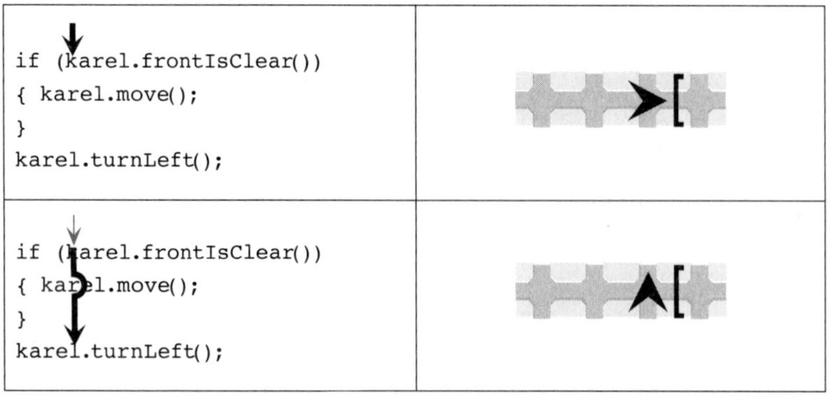

```
if (karel.frontIsClear())
{ karel.move();
}
karel.turnLeft();
```

```
if (karel.frontIsClear())
{ karel.move();
}
karel.turnLeft();
```

(figure 4-3)

Execution of an `if` *statement when the robot's front is initially obstructed*

Consider the code without the `if` statement:

```
karel.move();
karel.turnLeft();
```

In the first situation (shown in Figure 4-2), the result would be the same. However in the second situation, `karel` would crash into the wall and break.

Use an `if` statement when you want statements to execute once or not at all.

4.1.3 Examining a `while` Statement

Let's now consider a similar situation but control the `move` instruction with a `while` statement:

PATTERN

Zero or More Times

```
while (karel.frontIsClear())
{ karel.move();
}
karel.turnLeft();
```

KEY IDEA

The `while` statement repeatedly asks a question and performs an action until the answer is "no."

Recall that a `while` statement also asks a question. If the answer is `true`, the statements inside the braces are executed and then the question is asked again. This continues until the answer to the question is `false`. In the preceding code fragment, the question is "Is `karel`'s front clear of obstructions?"

Let's again consider `karel` in different initial situations. In Figure 4-4, `karel`'s front is clear and the answer to the `while` statement's question is "it is `true`, `karel`'s front is clear." `karel` moves and asks the question again—until the answer to the question is finally `false`. The heavy arrows in the code show the statements that are executed to reach the situation shown to the right of the code.

In this example, `karel` moves as many times as necessary to reach the wall. Then it turns. In the situation shown in Figure 4-4, the wall happens to be only two intersections away. It could be 20 or 2 million intersections away—`karel` would still move to the wall and then turn left with those same four lines of code.

If `karel` starts in a situation where its front is blocked, the answer to the question is immediately `false` and the move does not occur. Execution continues with the `turnLeft` instruction after the `while` statement. This situation is illustrated in Figure 4-5. Notice the similarities to the last two illustrations in Figure 4-4.

The `while` statement's test is always `false` after the statement finishes executing because the loop continues until the test becomes `false`. In fact, if nothing inside the `while` statement can make the test `false`, the statement will execute indefinitely.

```
while (karel.frontIsClear())
{ karel.move();
}
karel.turnLeft();
```

```
while (karel.frontIsClear())
{ karel.move();
}
karel.turnLeft();
```

```
while (karel.frontIsClear())
{ karel.move();
}
karel.turnLeft();
```

```
while (karel.frontIsClear())
{ karel.move();
}
karel.turnLeft();
```

(figure 4-4)

Illustrating the execution of a `while` *statement when the robot's front is initially clear of obstructions*

(figure 4-5)

Illustrating the execution of a `while` *statement when the robot's front is initially obstructed*

The ability to go to a wall might be generally useful. The following method, inserted into a class extending Robot, provides such a service:

```
public void gotoWall()
{ while (this.frontIsClear())
  { this.move();
  }
}
```

4.1.4 The General Forms of the if and while Statements

The general form of a statement marks the parts that can change, depending on the needs of the situation, leaving the parts that are always the same clearly identified.

The General Form of an if Statement

The if statement has the following general form:

```
if («test»)
{ «list of statements»
}
```

The reserved word if signals the reader of the program that an if statement is present. The braces ({ and }) enclose a list of one or more statements, *«list of statements»*. These statements are known as the **then-clause**. The statements in the then-clause are indented to emphasize that *«list of statements»* is a component of the if statement. Note that we do not follow the right brace of an if statement with a semicolon.

KEY IDEA

Boolean expressions ask true/false questions.

The *«test»* is a **Boolean expression** such as a query that controls whether the statements in the then-clause are executed. A Boolean expression always asks a question that has either true or false as an answer.

The General Form of a while Statement

The general form of the while statement is:

```
while («test»)
{ «list of statements»
}
```

The reserved word while starts this statement. Like the if statement, the *«test»* is enclosed by parentheses and the *«list of statements»* is enclosed by braces[2]. The

[2] If the list of statements has only one statement, the braces can be omitted. More about this in Section 5.6.3.

list of statements is called the **body** of the statement. The Boolean expressions that can replace «`test`» are the same ones used in the `if` statements.

A statement that repeats an action, like a `while` statement, is often called a **loop**.

The `if` and `while` statements have similar **syntax**. That is, their structure, or the way they look, is similar. On the other hand, they have different **semantics**. That is, the way they behave is different. The `if` statement decides whether to execute a list of statements or to skip over them. The `while` statement decides how many times to execute a list of statements.

4.2 Questions Robots Can Ask

The `if` and `while` statements both ask a question to discover something about the current state of the program. In the previous section the question was whether the front of the robot was clear of obstructions. In this section we'll learn about other questions a robot can ask. The answers, of course, can be used to control the robot's behavior.

4.2.1 Built-In Queries

In Chapter 1, we briefly mentioned that one kind of service objects can provide is a query—a service that answers a question. Robots offer queries that answer questions such as "Which avenue are you on?", "Which direction are you facing?", "Can you pick up a `Thing` from the intersection you are currently on?", and "Is your front clear of obstructions?" The following class diagram, displayed in Figure 4-6, shows many of the queries robots can answer.

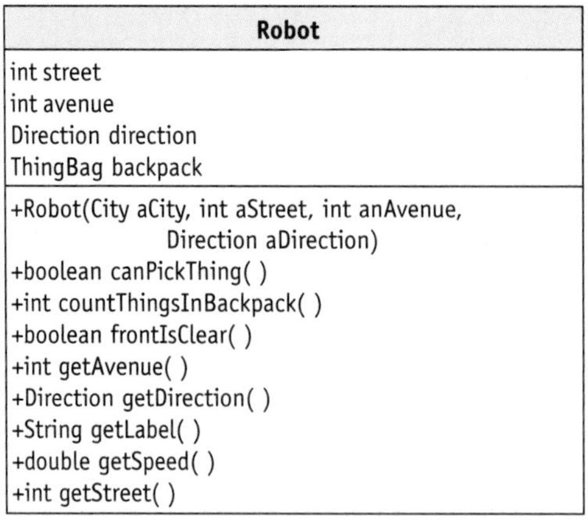

Robot
int street int avenue Direction direction ThingBag backpack
+Robot(City aCity, int aStreet, int anAvenue, Direction aDirection) +boolean canPickThing( ) +int countThingsInBackpack( ) +boolean frontIsClear( ) +int getAvenue( ) +Direction getDirection( ) +String getLabel( ) +double getSpeed( ) +int getStreet( )

(figure 4-6)

Class diagram showing many of the queries a robot can answer

KEY IDEA

Predicates are methods that return either `true` *or* `false`.

Each of the queries indicates what kind of answer it returns. `getAvenue`, for example, returns an integer value (abbreviated `int`) such as `1` for 1st Avenue or `9` for 9th Avenue. `canPickThing`, on the other hand, returns a `boolean`[3] value. If the robot is on the same intersection as a `Thing` it can pick up, `canPickThing` returns `true`; otherwise, it returns `false`. Queries that return a `boolean` answer are called **predicates**. The `frontIsClear` service described in the previous section is a predicate.

None of these queries change the state of the robot. The robot doesn't change in any way; it merely reports a piece of information about itself or its environment. This information is used in **expressions**. Expressions may be used in many ways, such as controlling `if` and `while` statements, passed as a parameter to a method, or saved in a variable. In this chapter, we will focus almost exclusively on expressions used to control `if` and `while` statements.

4.2.2 Negating Predicates

Sometimes we want a robot to do something when a test is *not* true, as in the following pseudocode:

```
if (karel cannot pick up a thing)
{ put a thing down
}
```

The `Robot` class does not provide a predicate for testing if the robot *cannot* pick up a `Thing`, only if it *can*.

KEY IDEA

Give a boolean expression the opposite value with `"!"`

Fortunately, any Boolean expression may be **negated**, or given the opposite value, by using the **logical negation operator**, "`!`". In English, this is usually written and pronounced as "not". The negation operator is placed immediately before the Boolean expression that is to be negated. Thus, the previous pseudocode could be coded as follows:

PATTERN

Once or Not at All

```
if (!karel.canPickThing())
{ karel.putThing();
}
```

Negation is our first exploration of **evaluating** expressions. You already have experience evaluating expressions from studying arithmetic. When you figure out that $5 + 3 * 2$ is the same as $5 + 6$ or 11, you are evaluating an arithmetic expression. The expression often includes an unknown, such as $5 + x * 2$. When you know the value of x, you can substitute it into the expression before evaluating it. For example, if x has the value 4, then the expression $5 + x * 2$ is the same as $5 + 4 * 2$ or 13.

[3] Boolean values are named after George Boole, one of the early developers of logic.

Evaluating a Boolean expression, an expression that uses values of `true` and `false`, is similar to evaluating arithmetic expressions. The expression `!karel.canPickThing()` involves an unknown (`karel.canPickThing()`), similar to x in the arithmetic expression. Suppose the unknown has the value `true` (that is, `karel` is on the same intersection as a `Thing` it can pick up). Then the expression evaluates to `!true` ("not `true`") which is the same as `false`.

LOOKING AHEAD

In Section 5.4.1, we will look at combining expressions with "and" and "or", much like "+" and "" combine arithmetic expressions.*

4.2.3 Testing Integer Queries

The `if` and `while` statements always ask true-or-false questions. "Should I execute this code, `true` or `false`?" This approach works well for queries that return a `boolean` value, but how can we use queries that return integers? The solution is to compare the query's answer to another integer. For example, we could use the following code to ask if the robot is on 1st Street:

```
if (karel.getStreet() == 1)
{  // what to do if karel is on 1st street
}
```

PATTERN

Once or Not at All

We could also use the following loop to make sure `karel` has at least eight things in its backpack:

```
while (karel.countThingsInBackpack() < 8)
{ karel.pickThing();
}
```

PATTERN

Zero or More Times

A total of six **comparison operators** can be used to compare integers. They are shown in Table 4-1.

(table 4-1)

Java comparison operators

Operator	Name	Example	Meaning
<	less than	`karel.getAvenue() < 5`	Evaluates to `true` if `karel`'s current avenue is strictly less than 5; otherwise, evaluates to `false`.
<=	less than or equal	`karel.getStreet() <= 3`	Evaluates to `true` if `karel`'s current street is less than or equal to 3; otherwise, evaluates to `false`.
==	equal	`karel.getStreet() == 1`	Evaluates to `true` if `karel` is currently on 1st Street; otherwise, evaluates to `false`.
!=	not equal	`karel.getStreet() != 1`	Evaluates to `true` if `karel` is not currently on 1st Street; if the robot *is* on 1st Street, evaluates to `false`.

(table 4-1) *continued*

Java comparison operators

Operator	Name	Example	Meaning
>=	greater than or equal	`5 >= karel.getAvenue()`	Evaluates to `true` if 5 is greater than or equal to `karel`'s current avenue. Most people find this easier to understand when written as `karel.getAvenue() <= 5`.
>	greater than	`karel.getAvenue() > 5`	Evaluates to `true` if `karel`'s current street is strictly greater than 5; otherwise, evaluates to `false`.

The examples in Table 4-1 always show an integer on only one side of the comparison operator. Java is much more flexible than this, however. For example, it can have a query on both sides of the operator, as in the following statements:

```
if (karel.getAvenue() == karel.getStreet())
{ ...
}
```

This test determines whether `karel` is on the diagonal line of intersections (0, 0), (1, 1), (2, 2), and so on. It also includes intersections with negative numbers such as (-3, -3).

Java also allows a more complex arithmetic expression on either side. The following code tests whether the robot's avenue is five more than the street. Locations where this test returns `true` include (0, 5) and (1, 6).

```
if (karel.getAvenue() == karel.getStreet() + 5)
{ ...
}
```

KEY IDEA

Assignment (=) is not *the same as equality (==).*

One common error is writing = instead of ==. The assignment statement, such as `Robot karel = new Robot(...)` uses a single equal sign. Comparing integers, on the other hand, uses two equal signs. Fortunately, Java usually catches this error and issues a compile-time error. Some other languages, such as C and C++, do not.

4.3 Reexamining Harvesting a Field

Let's return to the primary example from Chapter 3, traversing a field of `Thing` objects. In the following examples we use `if` and `while` statements to solve variations of that problem. The original program is in Listing 3-3.

We again use the dialogue format introduced in Chapter 3 to reveal the thinking that leads to the final solution.

4.3.1 Putting a Missing Thing

Instead of harvesting a field, consider planting a field. Such a robot class, `PlanterBot`, is the same as Listing 3-3 except for renaming the methods to use "plant" instead of "harvest" and, in the `plantIntersection` method, using `putThing` instead of `pickThing`.

Now, consider a minor variation: someone has already planted some intersections, but not all. Our `PlanterBot`, `karel`, must go through the field and put a `Thing` on only those intersections that don't already have one. The initial and final situations are shown in Figure 4-7. Of course, `karel` must either be created with a supply of `Thing` objects in its backpack (see the documentation for an alternate constructor) or pick up a supply before it starts.

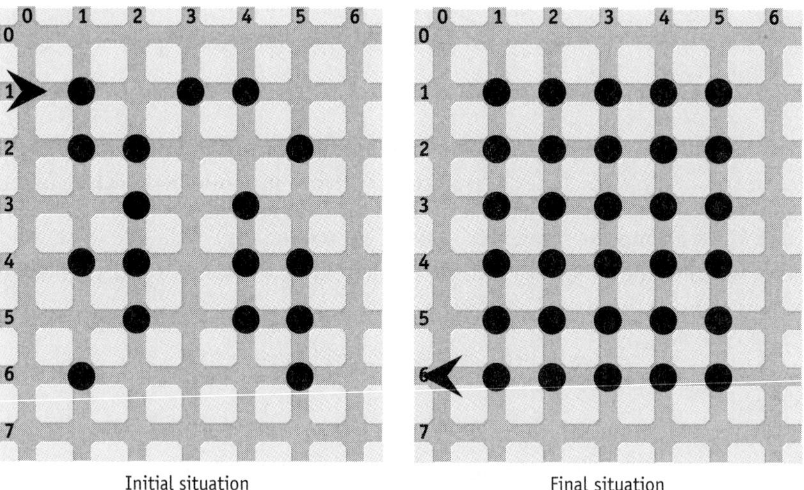

(figure 4-7)

Initial and final situations for planting intersections that don't have a `Thing`

Expert What does `karel` have to do?

Novice It must traverse the entire field, as before. Each time it comes to an intersection it must ensure that the intersection has a `Thing` before the `PlanterBot` leaves.

Expert Does it always perform the same action at each intersection?

Novice No. Its actions depend on whether a `Thing` is already there.

Expert Does the `PlanterBot` perform its actions once or not at all? Or does it perform them zero or more times?

Novice It either puts a `Thing` down or it doesn't, depending on whether a `Thing` is already present on the intersection. So it does an action, putting a `Thing`, once or not at all.

Expert Can you write that in pseudocode?

Novice I had a feeling that was coming.... Performing an action once or not at all uses an `if` statement, as follows:

```
if (there isn't a thing on this intersection)
{ put a thing on this intersection
}
```

Expert How can you express the test for the `if` statement in Java?

Novice We haven't seen a test for the absence of a `Thing` on an intersection. The closest test we've studied is `canPickThing`—can the robot pick up a thing from this intersection. If it can, there must be a `Thing` present. If it can't, there isn't a `Thing` present.

I think the test we want is `if` (*not a thing that can be picked up*). "Not", in Java, is written with an exclamation point. Therefore, we want `!this.canPickThing`.

The definition of `PlantThing` follows the pseudocode closely and is shown in Listing 4-1.

Listing 4-1: *The* `plantIntersection` *method*

```
/** Ensure that there is one thing on this intersection. */
public void plantIntersection()
{ if (!this.canPickThing())
  { this.putThing();
  }
}
```

4.3.2 Picking Up a Pile of Things

Suppose that instead of a single `Thing`, each of the field's intersections may have many `Things`. The original program in Listing 3-3 has a method, `harvestIntersection`, declared as follows:

```
/** Harvest one intersection. */
public void harvestIntersection()
{ this.pickThing();
}
```

In the revised version of the program, we want this method to pick up all of the `Things` on the intersection.

Expert What does `karel` have to do?

Novice Pick up all the `Thing` objects that are on the same intersection as itself.

Expert Can it pick them all up with a single instruction?

Novice The `pickThing` instruction picks up one `Thing` at a time.

Expert Does the robot always perform the same actions to pick up all the `Things`?

Novice No. Its actions depend on how many `Things` are on the intersection. It must use a test to decide what to do.

Expert Is the decision to do the action once or not at all? Or is the decision to repeat the action zero or more times?

Novice The robot should repeat an action (picking up a `Thing`) zero or more times—until there is nothing left to pick up.

Expert Can you express this idea in pseudocode?

Novice Sure:

```
while (this robot can pick up a Thing object)
{  pick up the Thing object
}
```

Expert How can you express the test in Java?

Novice With `this.canPickThing()`.

This pseudocode can be expressed in Java and placed in a revised version of the `harvestIntersection` method as shown in Listing 4-2.

Listing 4-2: *A version of* `harvestIntersection` *that harvests all the* `Things` *there*

ch04/harvest/

```
/** Harvest one intersection. */
public void harvestIntersection()
{ while (this.canPickThing())
  { this.pickThing();
  }
}
```

The `while` statement will continue to ask the question "Can this robot pick up a `Thing`?" until the answer is "no" or `false`. As long as the answer is "yes" or `true`, it will pick up a `Thing`. This method also works if some of the intersections don't have any `Things` on them. In that case, the first time the question is asked, the answer is "no, there is nothing here that can be picked up" and the body of the loop is not executed. In either case, when the loop is finished executing there will be nothing on the intersection that the robot can pick up.

4.3.3 Improving goToNextRow

The original `Harvester` class has two methods moving the robot one street south. One, `goToNextRow`, is used on the east side of the field. The other, `positionForNextHarvest`, is used on the west side of the field. The existing definitions of these two methods are as follows:

```
/** Go one row south and face west. */
public void goToNextRow()
{ this.turnRight();
  this.move();
  this.turnRight();
}

/** Go one row south and face east. */
public void positionForNextHarvest()
{ this.turnLeft();
  this.move();
  this.turnLeft();
}
```

It would be preferable to have a single method that will work correctly at either end of the row. Now, the distinction between `goToNextRow` and `positionForNextHarvest` is not clear from the names of the methods. It would be easier for people reading and writing the code to have only one descriptive name like `goToNextRow`.

Expert What does the robot have to do?

Novice When it is at the east end of the row, it must turn right to move to the next row. When it is at the west end it must turn left.

Expert So the robot must decide if it is at the east end of the row or the west end and the action it carries out is to turn. Is the action performed once or not at all, or is it performed zero or more times?

Novice The method is called many times—once at the end of each row. So in that sense the action is performed many times.

Expert Hmm.... That's not what I had in mind. Let's focus on only one invocation of `goToNextRow`. The robot is at the end of one particular row and needs to perform an action. Is that action performed once or not at all or is it performed zero or more times?

Novice It's once or not at all. It performs a group of actions (turn right, move, turn right) once if it is at the east end of the row and not at all if it isn't. Similarly, it performs a group of actions once if it is at the west end and not at all if it isn't.

Expert What statement can we use to control the robot's actions?

Novice It's the `if` statement that performs an action once or not at all. But I'm confused, because it isn't a single test. We need one test for the east end of the row and another test for the west end of the row.

Expert Perhaps it's not only two tests we need, but two complete `if` statements.

Novice So using pseudocode, it would be as follows:

```
if (this robot is at the east end of the row)
{ turn right, move, and turn right again
}
if (this robot is at the west end of the row)
{ turn left, move, and turn left again
}
```

Expert Exactly. Now, how can you determine if the robot is at the east end of the row?

Novice Looking at Figure 3-2, the east end of the row is on Avenue 5 and the west end of the row is on Avenue 1. In the first `if` statement, we can compare `this.getAvenue` to 5 and in the second `if` statement we can compare `this.getAvenue` to 1.

This pseudocode and the insight into the tests can be turned into the required Java method, as shown in Listing 4-3.

FIND THE CODE

ch04/harvest/

LOOKING AHEAD

Written Exercise 4.3 focuses on this method.

Listing 4-3: *A revised version of `goToNextRow` that will work at either end of the row.*

```
/** Go one row south. The robot must be on either Avenue 1 or Avenue 5. */
public void goToNextRow()
{ if (this.getAvenue() == 5)      // at the east end of the row
  { this.turnRight();
    this.move();
    this.turnRight();
  }
  if (this.getAvenue() == 1)      // at the west end of the row
```

Listing 4-3: *A revised version of* `goToNextRow` *that will work at either end of the row.* (continued)

```
   { this.turnLeft();
     this.move();
     this.turnLeft();
   }
 }
```

4.4 Using the `if-else` Statement

The `if` statement performs an action once or not at all. Another version of the `if` statement, the `if-else` statement, chooses between two groups of actions. It performs one or it performs the other based on a test. Unlike the `if` statement, the `if-else` statement always performs an action. The question is, which action?

The general form of the `if-else` is as follows:

PATTERN
Either This or That

```
if («test»)
{ «statementList1»
} else
{ «statementList2»
}
```

The form of the `if-else` statement is similar to the `if` statement, except that it includes the keyword `else`, *«statementList2»* and another set of braces. Note the absence of a semicolon before the word `else` and at the end.

An `if-else` is executed in much the same manner as an `if`. First, the *«test»* is evaluated to determine whether it is `true` or `false` in the current situation. If the *«test»* is `true`, *«statementList1»* is executed; if the test is `false`, *«statementList2»* is executed. Thus, depending on the current situation, either *«statementList1»* or *«statementList2»* is executed, but not both. The first statement list is called the **then-clause**, just like an `if` statement. The second statement list is called the **else-clause**.

When the else-clause is empty, the `if-else` statement behaves just like the `if` statement. In fact, the `if` statement is just a special case of the `if-else` statement.

The flowchart for an `if-else` statement is shown in Figure 4-8.

(figure 4-8)
Flowchart for an `if-else` *statement*

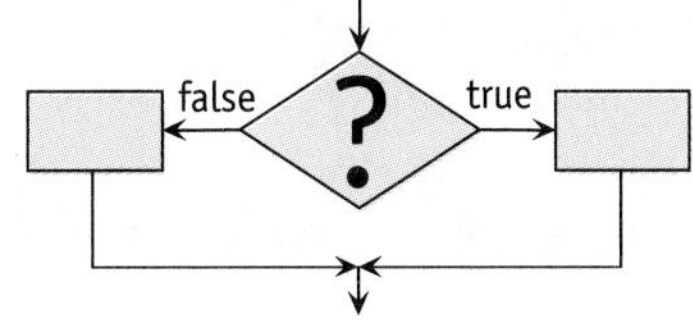

4.4.1 An Example Using `if-else`

Let's look at an example that uses the `if-else` statement. Suppose that we want to program a `Racer` robot to run a hurdle race, where vertical wall sections represent hurdles. The hurdles are only one block high and are randomly placed between any two intersections in the race course. The finish line is marked with a `Thing`. One of the many possible race courses for this task is illustrated in Figure 4-9. Figure 4-10 shows the final situation and the path the robot should take for this particular race course.

Here we think of the city as being vertical, with down being south. To run the fastest race possible, we require the robot to jump if, and only if, it is faced with a hurdle.

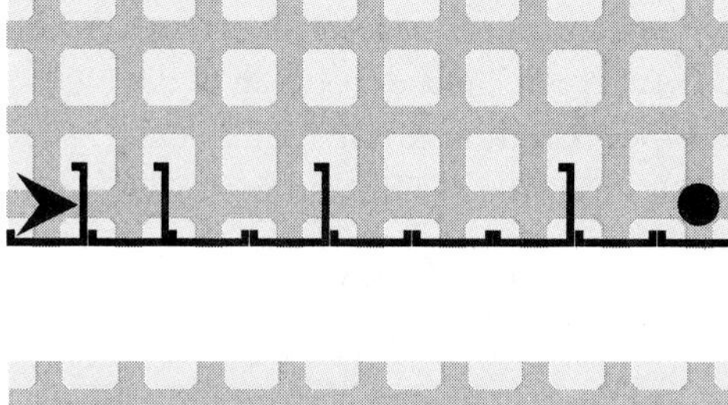

(figure 4-9)

Hurdle-jumping robot's initial situation

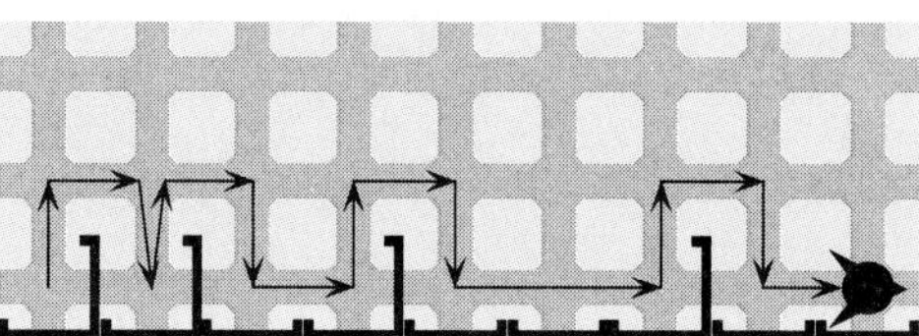

(figure 4-10)

Hurdle-jumping robot's final situation and the path it took

We will assume that a stepwise refinement process is being used and that the `Racer` class is partially developed, as shown in Listing 4-4. We need to continue the process by developing the `raceStride` method. It should move the robot forward by one intersection.

Listing 4-4: *A partially developed implementation of* `Racer`

```
import becker.robots.*;

/** A class of robots that runs a hurdles race (steeplechase).
 *
 *  @author Byron Weber Becker */
public class Racer extends RobotSE
{
   /** Construct a new hurdle-racing robot. */
   public Racer(City aCity, int str, int ave, Direction aDir)
   { super(aCity, aStreet, anAvenue, aDir);
   }
```

Listing 4-4: *A partially developed implementation of* `Racer` (continued)

```
   /** Run the race by repeatedly taking a raceStride until the finish line is crossed. */
   public void runRace()
   { while (!this.canPickThing())
     { this.raceStride();
     }
   }
}
```

We could easily develop a class of robots that run this race by jumping between every pair of intersections. Although this strategy is simple to program, it doesn't meet the requirements of running the fastest race possible. Instead, we must program the robot to move straight ahead when it can, and jump over hurdles only when it must.

Expert So, assume the `Racer` is on an intersection of the racetrack and ready to take its next stride. What should it do?

Novice It needs to move forward to the next intersection.

Expert Does the robot always perform the same actions?

Novice No, they depend on the situation. If there is a hurdle, it needs to be jumped. If there isn't a hurdle, the `Racer` can just move.

Expert Can you express these thoughts using pseudocode?

Novice

```
if (facing a hurdle)
{ jump the hurdle
}
move
```

Expert You seem to be thinking that the robot should always move. The only question is whether it jumps a hurdle first. Have you considered what would happen if there are two consecutive hurdles? The first pair of hurdles in Figure 4-9 shows that kind of a situation.

Novice Well, it would jump the first hurdle, landing right before the second one. Then it would move... and crash into the hurdle. I guess we need a different plan.

Expert So, what does the robot need to do?

Novice It should either jump the hurdle or move (but not both), depending on whether it is facing a hurdle. In pseudocode,

```
if (facing a hurdle)
{ jump the hurdle
} else
{ move
}
```

Putting these ideas into a method results in the following code. It should be added to Listing 4-4. The `jumpHurdle` method can be developed using the stepwise refinement techniques found in Section 3.2.

```
public void raceStride()
{ if (!this.frontIsClear())
  { this.jumpHurdle();
  } else
  { this.move();
  }
}
```

PATTERN

Either This or That

4.5 Writing Predicates

In Section 4.2.1, we learned about eight queries that are built in to the `Robot` class and examples of how to use them. But what if we frequently need to check if a robot's front is *not* clear? We could write the following code, which includes a negation:

```
if (!this.frontIsClear())
{ // what to do if this robot's front is blocked
}
```

PATTERN

Simple Predicate

However, the following positive statement is easier to understand:

```
if (this.frontIsBlocked())
{ // what to do if this robot's front is blocked
}
```

Fortunately, Java allows us to define our own predicates. Recall that a predicate is a method that returns one of the Boolean values, either `true` or `false`. Returning a value has two requirements:

- The method's return type must be indicated in its declaration. The type `boolean` is appropriate for predicates. It replaces the keyword `void` we have used so far.

KEY IDEA

A return statement always causes a method to stop immediately and return to its caller.

- The new predicate must indicate what value to return. To do so, we need a new kind of statement: the `return` statement. The form of the `return` statement is the reserved word `return`, followed by an expression. Because our method's return type is `boolean`, the expression must evaluate to a Boolean value, either `true` or `false`. Executing a `return` statement immediately terminates the execution of the method.

4.5.1 Writing `frontIsBlocked`

A Boolean expression that can be used as a test in an `if` or `while` statement can be easily turned into a predicate by inserting it into the following template:

PATTERN

Simple Predicate

```
«accessModifier» boolean «predicateName»(«optParameters»)
{ return «booleanExpression»;
}
```

where

- *«accessModifier»* is `public`, `protected`, or `private`.
- *«predicateName»* is the name of the predicate. Valid names are the same as for any other method.
- *«optParameters»* provide additional information from the client. Parameters are optional; many predicates do not have them.
- *«booleanExpression»* evaluates to either `true` or `false` and is the expression that could be placed in the test of an `if` or `while` statement.

The Java method for the `frontIsBlocked` predicate is as follows:

```
public boolean frontIsBlocked()
{ return !this.frontIsClear();
}
```

PATTERN

Simple Predicate

When this method is called, it evaluates the Boolean expression `!this.frontIsClear()`. In the situation shown on the left side of Figure 4-11, `frontIsClear` evaluates to `false` and, because of the `!`, the expression as a whole evaluates to `true`. This value is returned. It is `true` that the robot's front is blocked.

On the other hand, consider the situation shown on the right side of Figure 4-11. `frontIsClear` evaluates to `true`, but is negated by the `!`, resulting in the entire expression evaluating to `false`—the robot's front is *not* blocked.

(figure 4-11)

Evaluating `frontIsBlocked` *in two different situations*

Robot's front is blocked

Robot's front is not blocked

4.5.2 Predicates Using Non-Boolean Queries

When developing the `goToNextRow` method (see Listing 4-3) we included the following `if` statement and comment:

```
3 { if (this.getAvenue() == 5)        // at the east end of the row
4   { this.turnRight();
5     this.move();
6     this.turnRight();
7   }
```

With an appropriate predicate, line 3 could be rewritten as follows:

```
3 { if (this.atRowsEastEnd())
```

Predicates such as `atRowsEastEnd` can help us produce self-documenting code. The goal of **self-documenting code** is to make the code so readable that internal comments explaining the code are not needed. In this case, `atRowsEastEnd` tells us the intention of the test nearly as well as the comment, enabling us to remove the comment. It's a good idea to replace comments with self-documenting code because comments are often overlooked as the code changes. When this happens comments can become incomplete, misleading, or wrong.

KEY IDEA

Appropriately named predicates lead to self-documenting code.

Having a predicate such as `atRowsEastEnd` is also an advantage if the test must be done at many places in the program. With a predicate, when the problem changes to have rows that end at a different place or a bug is discovered, there is only one easily identified place to change.

Coding this predicate follows the same procedure as before: take the Boolean expression that would be included in the `if` or `while` statement and place it inside a method. The method is as follows:

```
protected boolean atRowsEastEnd()
{ return this.getAvenue() == 5;
}
```

PATTERN

Simple Predicate

The query `getDirection` is similar to `getAvenue` except that it returns one of the special values such as `Direction.NORTH` or `Direction.EAST`. These values can be compared using == and `!=`, but not <, >, and so on.

KEY IDEA

Enumerated types such as `Direction` can be tested for equality only.

This fact can be used to create the predicate `isFacingSouth` as follows:

```
protected boolean isFacingSouth()
{ return this.getDirection() == Direction.SOUTH;
}
```

This predicate, along with `isFacingNorth`, `isFacingEast`, and `isFacingWest`, are used often enough that they have been added to the `RobotSE` class.

4.6 Using Parameters

The ability to make decisions with `if` and `while` statements gives our methods a tremendous amount of flexibility. They can have even more flexibility when we use parameters. We have already used parameters by passing them arguments to specify where to place robots when they are created, how large to draw a rectangle, and which icon a `Thing` should use to display itself.

We have declared parameters every time we extended the `Robot` class and wrote a constructor, as well as in Section 3.7.1 where we used parameters to place a stick figure at a precise location. From these contexts, we know that each parameter declaration has a type, such as `int`, and a name. Parameter declarations are placed between the parentheses following the method's name. If there is more than one declaration, consecutive pairs are separated with commas. These points are illustrated in Figure 4-12.

(figure 4-12)

Declaring parameters

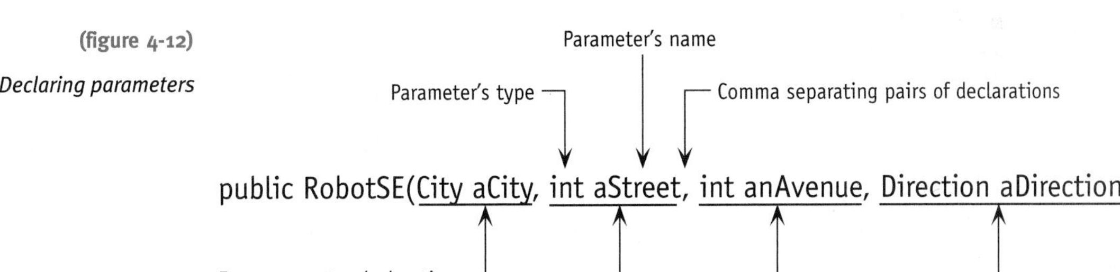

The type of the parameter determines what kind of values can be used as arguments. If the parameter's type is `int`, the arguments must be integers such as 15 or -23. Similarly, only an object of type `City` can be passed as an argument to a parameter of type `City`.

Inside the constructor or method, the name of the parameter can be used to reference the value passed to it as an argument. Let's use an example to understand how this works.

Suppose we want a subclass of `Robot` that can easily tell us if it has gone past a particular avenue, say Avenue 50. We could use the `getAvenue` method and compare it to 50, but our code is more self-documenting with a predicate, as follows:

```
if (this.isPastAvenue(50))
{ // what to do when the robot has strayed too far
```

The `isPastAvenue` method is written as follows:

PATTERN

Simple Predicate

```
private boolean isPastAvenue(int anAvenue)
{ return this.getAvenue() > anAvenue;
}
```

Inside the `isPastAvenue` method, `anAvenue` refers to the value passed as an argument. In the preceding example, that value is 50 and the Boolean expression is evaluated as `this.getAvenue() > 50`. However, if the argument is 100, as in `if (this.isPastAvenue(100))`, then inside `isPastAvenue` the parameter `anAvenue` will refer to the value 100. This one method can be used with any avenue—a tremendous amount of flexibility compared to methods without parameters.

KEY IDEA

The parameter refers to the value passed as an argument.

4.6.1 Using a `while` Statement with a Parameter

A parameter can also be used in the test controlling a `while` or `if` statement—and can make the method more flexible, as well. For example, the following method moves a robot east to Avenue 50:

```
/** Move the robot east to Avenue 50. The robot must already be facing east and
 *  must be on an avenue that is less than 50. */
public void moveToAvenue50()
{ while (this.getAvenue() < 50)
  { this.move();
  }
}
```

This method is extremely limited—it is only useful to move the robot to Avenue 50. With a parameter, however, it can be used to move the robot to any avenue east of its current location. The following method includes a parameter with an appropriate documentation comment:

```
/** Move the robot east to destAve. The robot must already be facing east and
 *  must be on an avenue that is less than destAve.
 *  @param destAve       The destination avenue to move to. */
public void moveToAvenue(int destAve)
{ while (this.getAvenue() < destAve)
  { this.move();
  }
}
```

The statement `karel.moveToAvenue(50)` moves `karel` to Avenue 50 while `karel.moveToAvenue(5000)` moves `karel` much farther. In both cases the argument, 50 or 5000, is referred to inside the method as `destAve`.

4.6.2 Using an Assignment Statement with a Loop

Consider the following ill-advised method:

```
public void step(int howFar)
{ while (howFar > 0)
  { this.move();
  }
}
```

KEY IDEA

Something in the body of the loop must change how the test is evaluated.

Why is it ill advised? Consider telling karel to step four times with karel.step(4). The while statement evaluates the expression howFar > 0, concluding that it is true—four is larger than zero. The statement executes the move method and evaluates howFar > 0 again. howFar is still four, four is still greater than zero, and so the move method is executed again. The value of howFar does not change in the body of the loop, the test will always be true, and the loop will execute "forever."

Suppose, however, that we could decrease the value of howFar in the body of the loop, as indicated by the following pseudocode:

PATTERN

Count-Down Loop

```
public void step(int howFar)
{ while (howFar > 0)
  { this.move();
    make howFar one less than it is now
  }
}
```

That is, howFar starts with the value 4, then has the value 3, then 2, and so on—assuming that step was called with an argument of 4, as in the preceding code. Now we have a useful method, as illustrated in Figure 4-13. When howFar reaches the value 0, the loop stops and the robot has traveled four intersections. If we want karel to take four steps, we write karel.step(4). If we want karel to take 400 steps, it's as easy as writing karel.step(400).

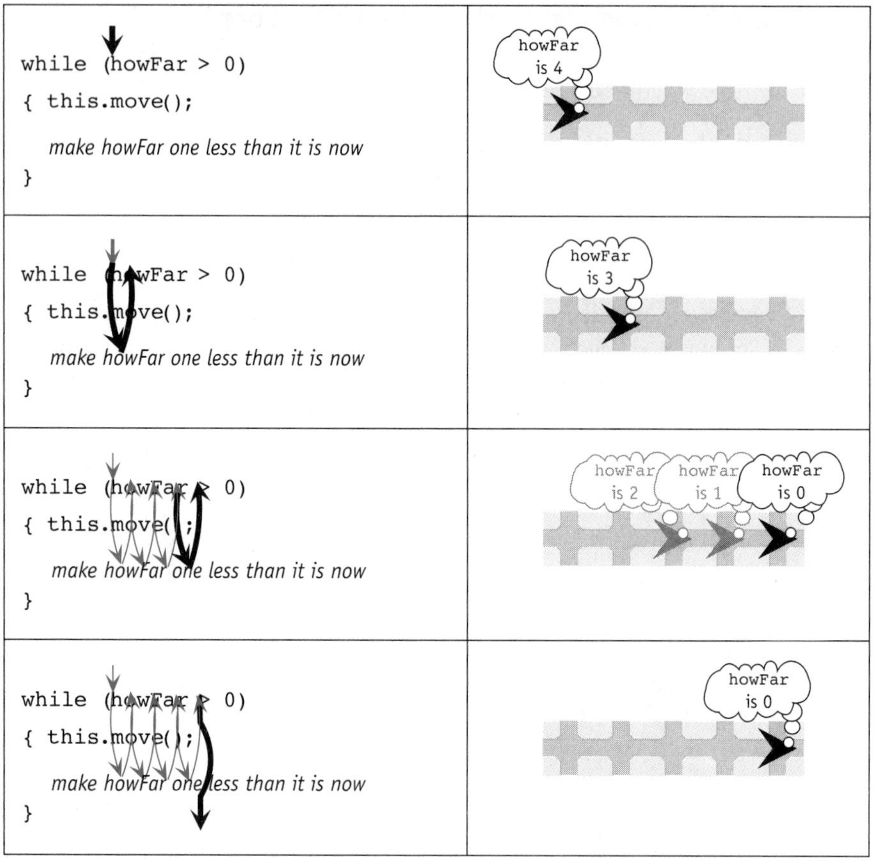

`while (howFar > 0)`
`{ this.move();`
make howFar one less than it is now
`}`
	howFar is 4

`while (howFar > 0)`
`{ this.move();`
make howFar one less than it is now
`}`
	howFar is 3

`while (howFar > 0)`
`{ this.move();`
make howFar one less than it is now
`}`
	howFar is 2 / howFar is 1 / howFar is 0

`while (howFar > 0)`
`{ this.move();`
make howFar one less than it is now
`}`
	howFar is 0

(figure 4-13)

Illustrating the execution of a count-down loop

A `while` statement that counts from a number down to zero is called a **count-down loop**.

We still need to explain, of course, how to make `howFar` be one less than it is now. This change is accomplished with an **assignment statement**. An assignment statement evaluates an expression and assigns the resulting value to a variable. A parameter is one kind of variable.

The following is an assignment statement that decreases `howFar`'s value by one:

```
howFar = howFar - 1;
```

LOOKING AHEAD

Other kinds of variables will be discussed in Chapters 5 and 6.

When this assignment statement is executed, it evaluates the expression on the right side of the equal sign by subtracting one from the current value of `howFar`. When `howFar` refers to the value 4, `howFar - 1` is the value 3. The value 3 is then assigned to `howFar`. The parameter will refer to this new value until we change it with another assignment statement or the method ends. Parameters are destroyed when the method declaring them completes its execution.

KEY IDEA

A count-down loop performs actions a specified number of times.

A count-down loop, like the one used in `step`, can be used to do many different activities a specified number of times: picking up a specified number of things; turning a specified number of times; and, with a more complicated loop body, harvesting a specified number of rows from a field.

4.6.3 Revisiting Stepwise Refinement

A count-down loop can have a body that is more complex than a single `move`. The body could contain more statements, or preferably, a call to a helper method. Furthermore, a method can have more than one parameter and parameters can be passed as arguments to helper methods. In this section we will develop a class of robots that illustrate all of these principles. Our robots will plant `Things` in the shape of a hollow rectangle. The width and height of the rectangle is specified with parameters when the `plantRect` method is invoked. A sample initial and final situation is shown in Figure 4-14.

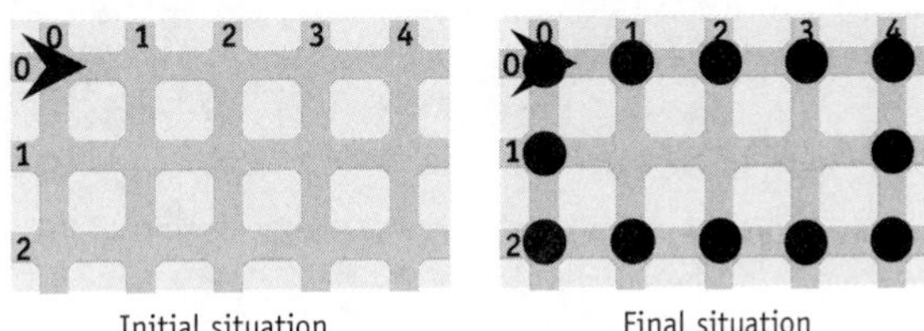

(figure 4-14)

One pair of many possible initial and final situations for planting a rectangle

Our class is called `RectanglePlanter` and has a single service, `plantRect`. We want the robot to be able to plant many different sizes of rectangles, a kind of flexibility that is well-suited for using parameters. Two parameters are needed—one for the rectangle's width and one for the height. This usage follows the `setSize` command for a `JFrame` and the `drawRect` command in the `Graphics` class. The following code fragment instructs `karel` to plant a rectangle five `Things` wide and three `Things` high, as shown in Figure 4-14. One notable feature is that the constructor allows specifying the number of things initially in the robot's backpack. Here it is set to 50.

```
RectanglePlanter karel = new RectanglePlanter(
                              garden, 0, 0, Direction.EAST, 50);
...
karel.plantRect(5, 3);
```

Implementing `plantRect`

The `plantRect` method requires two integer parameters, one for the width and one for the height, corresponding to the arguments `5` and the `3` in the previous code fragment. The beginning of the class, including a stub for `plantRect` and the constructor allowing the initial number of `Things` in the backpack to be set, is as shown in Listing 4-5.

Listing 4-5: *Beginning the* `RectanglePlanter` *class*

```
import becker.robots.*;

/** A class of robots that plants Things in the form of a hollow rectangle.
 *
 * @author Byron Weber Becker */
public class RectanglePlanterextendsRobotSE
{
   /** Create a new rectangle planter.
    *  @param aCity        The robot's city.
    *  @param aStreet      The robot's initial street.
    *  @param anAvenue     The robot's initial avenue.
    *  @param aDir         The robot's initial direction.
    *  @param numThings    The number of things initially in the robot's backpack. */
   public RectanglePlanter(City aCity, int aStreet,
            int anAvenue, Direction aDir, int numThings)
   { super(aCity, aStreet, anAvenue, aDir, numThings);
   }

   /** Plant a hollow rectangle of Things. The robot must be positioned in the
    *  rectangle's upper-left corner facing east.
    *  @param width       The number of avenues wide.
    *  @param height      The number of streets high. */
   public void plantRect(int width, int height)
   {
   }
}
```

FIND THE CODE

cho4/rectanglePlanter/

To implement `plantRect` we need a strategy. Assuming we don't want two `Things` on each corner, one strategy is to plant a side of the rectangle by planting one less than the length of the side. This strategy is illustrated in Figure 4-15. To make a side of length five, for example, the robot will plant four things beginning with the next intersection and then turn right. In general, the number of `Things` it plants is one less than the length of the side.

Planting a side four times, with the appropriate lengths for each side, results in the desired rectangle.

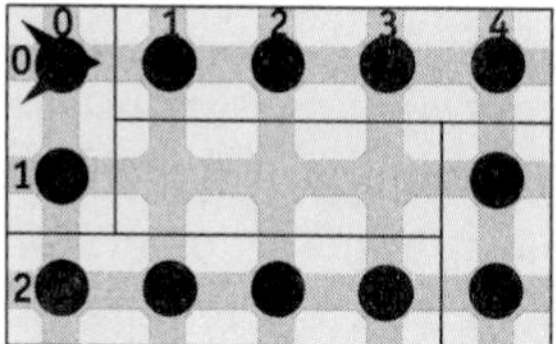

(figure 4-15)

Strategy for planting a rectangle

To carry this out, we can create a helper method, `plantSide`, that takes a parameter specifying how long that side of the rectangle should be. Assuming that we can write this helper method, the `plantRect` method can be completed as follows:

```
public void plantRect(int width, int height)
{ this.plantSide(width);
  this.plantSide(height);
  this.plantSide(width);
  this.plantSide(height);
}
```

Note that the parameters, `width` and `height`, are passed as arguments to the helper method. However, the `plantSide` method only requires one parameter because it is only concerned with the length of a side and not the overall dimensions of the rectangle.

Implementing `plantSide`

The strategy for `plantSide` was already determined when outlining the overall strategy. We already know, from the way it was used in `plantRect`, that it has a single, integer parameter. The parameter can have any name, but we will call it `length` because it determines the length of the side.

`plantSide` plants a line that is one less than the length of the side and then turns right. In pseudocode, this is as follows:

length = length - 1
plant a line of Things that is length Things long
turn right

The Java translation of this pseudocode uses of an assignment statement to decrease the value passed to the parameter by one and a helper method to plant a line of things. The completed method follows:

```
/** Plant one side of the rectangle with Things, beginning with the next intersection.
 *  @param length       The length of the line. */
protected void plantSide(int length)
{ length = length - 1;
  this.plantLine(length);
  this.turnRight();
}
```

Implementing `plantLine`

Planting a line of `Things` requires repeating actions zero or more times (a `while` statement). It's not a question of performing actions once or not at all (an `if` statement) or performing either this action or that action (an `if-else` statement).

What are the actions we must repeat? To plant a line of three things beginning with the next intersection, for example, we must perform the following actions:

move
plant a thing
move
plant a thing
move
plant a thing

The actions that are repeated are moving and planting a thing. They form the body of the `while` statement. We want them to be performed a specific number of times, as specified by the parameter. This is an ideal application for a count-down loop. This method is, in fact, identical to the `step` method developed earlier except that we also need to plant a `Thing` on the intersection. The code for the method follows:

PATTERN

Count-Down Loop

```
/** Plant a line of Things beginning with the intersection in front of the robot.
 *  @param length      The length of the line. */
protected void plantLine(int length)
{ while (length > 0)
  { this.move();
    this.plantIntersection();
    length = length - 1;
  }
}
```

Finally, `plantIntersection` is a method to make future change easy. It contains a single call to `putThing`, as shown in the following code:

```
/** Plant one intersection. */
protected void plantIntersection()
{ this.putThing();
}
```

This completes the implementation of the `RectanglePlanter` class. In the course of its development we have demonstrated:

- A method with more than one parameter
- Passing parameters as arguments to helper methods
- A count-down loop with a more complex set of actions

4.7 GUI: Scaling Images

The graphical user interface section of Chapter 2 introduced us to drawing pictures similar to the one shown in Figure 4-16. In this section, we'll see how to use queries in the `JComponent` class to make our image adapt to different sizes.

(figure 4-16)

Stick figure and a grid used to design it

The code for the main method is shown in Listing 2-13. `StickFigure` is the class that does the actual drawing. It was originally shown in Chapter 2 and is reproduced in Listing 4-6. Notable points are that it sets the preferred size for the component in the constructor at lines 8 and 9, and overrides `paintComponent` to draw the actual image.

FIND THE CODE

ch02/stickFigure/

Listing 4-6: *A class to draw a stick figure*

```
1  import java.awt.*;
2  import javax.swing.*;
3
4  public class StickFigure extends JComponent
5  {
6    public StickFigure()
7    { super();
8      Dimension prefSize = new Dimension(180, 270);
9      this.setPreferredSize(prefSize);
10   }
11
12   // Draw a stick figure.
13   public void paintComponent(Graphics g)
14   { super.paintComponent(g);
15
16     // head
17     g.setColor(Color.YELLOW);
18     g.fillOval(60, 0, 60, 60);
19
20     // shirt
21     g.setColor(Color.RED);
22     g.fillRect(0, 60, 180, 30);
23     g.fillRect(60, 60, 60, 90);
```

Listing 4-6: *A class to draw a stick figure* (continued)

```

      // pants
      g.setColor(Color.BLUE);
      g.fillRect(60, 150, 60, 120);
      g.setColor(Color.BLACK);
      g.drawLine(90, 180, 90, 270);
   }
}
```

Now, suppose that we wanted the image to be a different size. The preferred size set in the `StickFigure` constructor could be replaced with, for example, `new Dimension(90, 135)` to make the image half as big in each dimension.

There is a problem, however. Making only this one change results in an image similar to the one shown in Figure 4-17. Unfortunately, all of the calculations to draw the stick figure were based on the old size of 180 pixels wide and 270 pixels high.

(figure 4-17)

Naively changing the size of the stick figure

4.7.1 Using Size Queries

We can make the image less sensitive to changes in size by drawing it relative to the current size of the component. We can obtain the current size of the component, in pixels, with the `getWidth` and `getHeight` queries. To paint a shape that covers a fraction of the component, multiply the results of these queries by a fraction. For example, to specify an oval that is two-sixths of the width of the component and two-ninths of the height, we can use the following statement:

```
g.fillOval(0, 0, this.getWidth()*2/6, this.getHeight()*2/9);
```

The first two parameters will place the oval at the upper-left corner of the component.

The original stick figure was designed on a grid six units wide and nine units high. Figure 4-16 shows this grid explicitly and makes it easy to figure out which fractions to multiply by the width or the height. For example, the head can be painted with

```
g.fillOval(this.getWidth()*2/6, this.getHeight()*0/9,
           this.getWidth()*2/6, this.getHeight()*2/9);
```

The first pair of parameters says the head's bounding box should start $2/6^{\text{th}}$ of the component's width from the left edge and $0/9^{\text{th}}$ of the component's height from the top. The second parameter could be replaced by 0.

Converting the remaining method calls to use the `getWidth` and `getHeight` queries follows a similar pattern. It is tedious, however. Fortunately, there is a better approach.

4.7.2 Scaling an Image

Using `getWidth` and `getHeight` to scale an image follows a very predictable pattern, as shown in the last section. Fortunately, the designers of Java have provided a way for us to exploit that pattern with much less work on our part. They have provided a way for the computer to automatically multiply by the width or the height of the component and divide by the number of units on our grid. All we need to do is supply the numerator of the fraction that places the image or says how big it is. For example, in the previous section we wrote the following statements:

```
g.fillOval(this.getWidth()*2/6, this.getHeight()*0/9,
           this.getWidth()*2/6, this.getHeight()*2/9);
```

Java's drawing methods can be set up so that this method call is replaced with the following statement:

```
g.fillOval(2, 0, 2, 2);
```

Using this approach requires three things: Using a more capable version of the `Graphics` object, setting the scale to be used in drawing, and scaling the width of the lines to use in drawing. All are easy and follow a pattern consisting of the following four lines inserted at the beginning of `paintComponent`:

PATTERN

Scale an Image

```
// Standard stuff to scale the image
Graphics2D g2 = (Graphics2D)g;
g2.scale(this.getWidth()/6, this.getHeight()/9);
g2.setStroke(new BasicStroke(1.0F/this.getWidth()));
```

Explaining this code in more detail requires advanced concepts; however, the overview is as follows:

- Line 2 makes a larger set of capabilities in `g` available. More about this in Chapter 12.
- Line 3 tells the `Graphics` object how to multiply values to scale our paintings appropriately.
- Line 4 makes the width of a line, also called a **stroke**, proportional to the scaling performed in line 3.

Whether or not we understand exactly what these lines of code do, using them is easy:

- Import the package `java.awt.*`.
- Copy these four lines to the beginning of your `paintComponent` method.
- Decide on the size of your grid, and change the "6" and "9" in the call to `scale` accordingly. For a 50 x 100 grid, change the 6 to 50 and the 9 to 100.
- Use `g2` instead of `g` to do the painting.

The resulting `paintComponent` method is shown in Listing 4-7.

FIND THE CODE

ch04/stickFigure/

Listing 4-7: *Painting a stick figure by scaling the image*

```
public void paintComponent(Graphics g)
{ super.paintComponent(g);

   // Standard stuff to scale the image
   Graphics2D g2 = (Graphics2D)g;
   g2.scale(this.getWidth()/6, this.getHeight()/9);
   g2.setStroke(new BasicStroke(1.0F/this.getWidth()));

   // head
   g2.setColor(Color.YELLOW);
   g2.fillOval(2, 0, 2, 2);

   // shirt
   g2.setColor(Color.RED);
   g2.fillRect(0, 2, 6, 1);
   g2.fillRect(2, 2, 2, 3);

   // pants
   g2.setColor(Color.BLUE);
   g2.fillRect(2, 5, 2, 4);
   g2.setColor(Color.BLACK);
   g2.drawLine(3, 6, 3, 9);
}
```

4.8 Patterns

4.8.1 The Once or Not at All Pattern

Name: Once or Not at All

Context: You are in a situation where executing a group of one or more statements may or may not be appropriate, depending on the value of a Boolean expression. If the expression is true, the statements are executed once. If the expression is false, they are not executed at all.

Solution: Use the `if` statement, as in the following two examples:

```
if (this.canPickThing())
{ this.pickThing();
}

if (this.numStudentsInCourse() < 100)
{ this.addStudentToCourse();
}
```

In general, use the following template:

```
if («test»)
{ «list of statements»
}
```

If possible, state the test positively. Easily understood predicate names contribute to easily understood code. For example, if the statement `if (this.numStudentsInCourse() < this.maxEnrollment())` is really checking if there is room in the course for one more student to be added, then using a predicate such as `if (this.roomInCourse())` makes the code easier to understand.

Consequences: Programs are able to respond differently, depending on the situation. In particular, an action is executed either once or not at all.

Related Patterns:

- The Either This or That pattern executes one of two actions. This pattern is a special case of that one.
- The Zero or More Times pattern is useful if an action is to be executed repeatedly rather than once or not at all.
- The Simple Predicate pattern is often used to create more easily understood *«test»*s.

4.8.2 The Zero or More Times Pattern

Name: Zero or More Times

Context: You are in a situation where a group of one or more statements must be executed a (usually) unknown number of times. It might be as few as zero times, or possibly many times. Whether to repeat the statements again can be determined with a Boolean expression.

Solution: Use a `while` statement to control the execution of the statements. When the test evaluates to `true`, the statements are executed and the test is performed again. This continues until the test evaluates to `false`. The following example is an example of the pattern:

```
while (this.frontIsClear())
{ this.turnLeft();
}
```

This loop turns the robot until it is facing a wall. If there is no wall blocking one of the four directions, it will turn forever.

In general, use the following template:

```
while («test»)
{ «list of statements»
}
```

As with the `if` statement, a `while` statement is easiest to read and understand if the test is stated positively.

Consequences: The list of statements may be executed as few as zero times or they may execute forever. Such infinite loops are not desirable and should be guarded against.

Related Patterns:

- The Count-down Loop pattern is a special case of Zero or More Times.
- The Once or Not at All pattern executes an action either zero or one times rather than zero or more times.
- The Simple Predicate pattern is often used to create more easily understood *«test»*s.

4.8.3 The Either This or That Pattern

Name: Either This or That

Context: You have two groups of statements. Only one group should be executed and which one depends on the result of a Boolean expression.

Solution: Use an `if-else` statement to perform the test and govern which group of statements is executed, as in the following example:

```
if (this.frontIsClear())
{ this.move();
} else
{ this.turnLeft();
}
```

Following is the general form of an `if-else` statement:

```
if («test»)
{ «statementGroup1»
} else
{ «statementGroup2»
}
```

If *«test»* evaluates to `true`, *«statementGroup1»* is executed and *«statement-Group2»* is not executed. If *«test»* evaluates to `false`, *«statementGroup2»* is executed and *«statementGroup1»* is not.

Consequences: The pattern allows programs to choose between two courses of action by evaluating a Boolean expression.

Related Patterns:

- The Once or Not at All pattern is a special case of this pattern useful for when there is only one action that may or may not be executed.
- If there are more than two actions, only one of which is executed, consider the Cascading-If pattern, described in Section 5.8.6.
- The Simple Predicate pattern is often used to create more easily understood *«test»*s.

4.8.4 The Simple Predicate Pattern

Name: Simple Predicate

Context: You are using a Boolean expression that is not as easy to read or understand as is desirable. Perhaps it is a complicated expression or perhaps the names of the queries don't match the problem.

Solution: Define a new method that performs the processing to find the required result, returning `true` or `false` to its client. Such methods are called predicates. For example, the following code defines a predicate named `frontIsBlocked`:

```
public boolean frontIsBlocked()
{ return !this.frontIsClear();
}
```

With this predicate, we could write `while (this.frontIsBlocked())` instead of `while (!this.frontIsClear())`.

Following is a template for such a predicate:

```
public boolean «predicateName»()
{ return «a boolean expression»;
}
```

Consequences: Statements that use a predicate, such as `this.frontIsBlocked()`, are easier to understand than those that use the equivalent test, such as `!this.frontIsClear()`. A predicate can be easily used many times, reducing the total time to code, test, and debug the program.

Related Patterns:

- The Predicate pattern is often used to define predicates used in the Once or Not at All, Zero or More Times, and Either This or That patterns, among others.
- The Simple Predicate pattern is a specialization of the more general Predicate pattern discussed in Section 5.8.5.

4.8.5 The Count-Down Loop Pattern

Name: Count-Down Loop

Context: You must perform an action a specified number of times. The number is often given via a parameter.

Solution: Write a `while` statement that uses a variable, often a parameter variable, to count down to zero. When the value reaches zero, the loop ends. The general form of the count-down loop is as follows:

```
while («variable» > 0)
{ «list of statements»
  «variable» = «variable» - 1;
}
```

A concrete example of the count-down loop is the `plantLine` method which puts a row of `Things`, the length of which is determined by the parameter.

```
public void plantLine(int length)
{ while (length > 0)
  { this.move();
    this.putThing();
    length = length - 1;
  }
}
```

Consequences: The Count-Down Loop pattern gives programmers the ability to perform an action a specified number of times, even if the number is large. Putting the count-down loop inside a method and using a parameter provides even more flexibility.

Related Patterns: The Count-Down Loop pattern is a special case of the Zero or More Times pattern.

4.8.6 The Scale an Image Pattern

Name: Scale an Image

Context: An image drawn by the `paintComponent` method in a subclass of `JComponent` needs to scale to different component sizes.

Solution: Draw the image based on a predefined grid for the coordinates. Then use the following code template to use that coordinate grid while drawing.

```
public void paintComponent(Graphics g)
{ super.paintComponent(g);

  // Standard stuff to scale the image
  Graphics2D g2 = (Graphics2D)g;
  g2.scale(this.getWidth()/«gridWidth»,
           this.getHeight()/«gridHeight»);
  g2.setStroke(new BasicStroke(1.0F/this.getWidth()));

  «statements using g2 to draw the image»
}
```

Consequences: The parameters provided to methods in `Graphics2D` such as `drawRect` are multiplied by either `this.getWidth()/«gridWidth»` or `this.getHeight/«gridHeight»`, as appropriate. The changes made to `g2` will persist even if it is passed to a helper method.

Related Patterns: This pattern is a specialization of the Draw a Picture pattern.

4.9 Summary and Concept Map

Programs that always execute the same set of statements, one after another, are fairly limited. Introducing Boolean expressions that can be evaluated—such as whether a robot is facing north or is on Avenue 8—makes programs much more flexible. They can execute statements once or not at all with an `if` statement or execute statements zero or more times with a `while` statement. An `if-else` statement uses the test to determine which of two actions to execute and a count-down loop can execute an action a specified number of times.

Using predicates in the tests used by `if` and `while` statements can make them easier to understand, debug, test, and maintain, all of which increases the quality of programs.

Boolean expressions used in `if` and `while` statements allow a program to respond to varying situations. Using parameters can make a program even more flexible. A parameter receives a value passed as an argument from the client code. That value can then be used inside the method to control its execution.

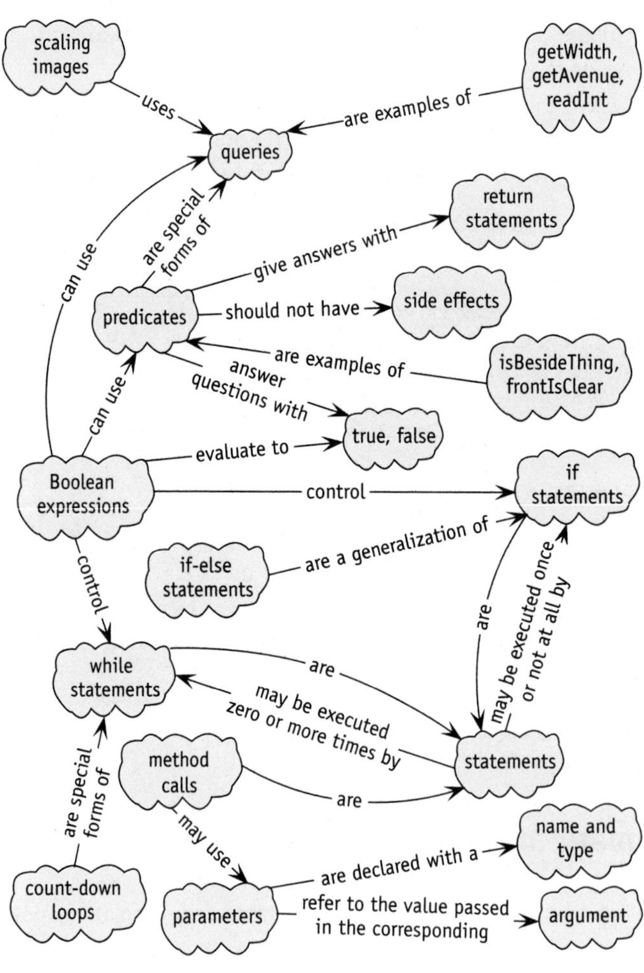

4.10 Problem Set

Written Exercises

4.1 Evaluate the following Boolean expressions for a `Robot`. Assume the robot is on intersection (1, 5) facing north. There is a `Wall` immediately in front of it.

a. `this.getAvenue() > 0`

b. `this.getAvenue() <= 5`

c. `this.getStreet() != 1`

d. `!(this.getStreet() == 1)`

e. `this.frontIsClear()`

f. `!this.frontIsClear()`

g. `!!this.frontIsClear()`

h. `this.frontIsClear() == false`

4.2 Consider the following `if-else` statements. Do they behave the same way or differently? Justify your answer.

```
if (this.canPickThing())
{ this.turnRight();
} else
{ this.turnLeft();
}
```

```
if (!this.canPickThing())
{ this.turnLeft();
} else
{ this.turnRight();
}
```

4.3 Consider the `goToNextRow` method developed in Section 4.3.3 and shown in Listing 4-3.

a. In a table similar to Table 1-2, trace the method when the robot is on (1, 1) facing west, again when it is on (1, 3) facing west, and once again when the robot is on (1, 5) facing east.

b. Describe what happens if the method is modified for rows of length 1. That is, the west end of the row is on Avenue 1 and the east end is also on Avenue 1.

c. Rewrite the method using an `if-else` statement.

d. The current method requires the rows to start and end on specified avenues. Rewrite the method using a different test to remove this restriction. The new method will allow the method to be used in any size field without modification.

4.4 Figure 4-13 illustrates the execution of a `while` loop. Trace the loop using a table similar to Table 1-2. Include columns for the robot's street, avenue, direction, and the parameter `howFar`. Assume the robot begins on (2, 5) facing east and that the `step` method was called with an argument of `4`.

Programming Exercises

4.5 Write methods named `turnLeft`, `pickThing`, and `putThing` that allow the client to specify how many times the robot turns, picks, and puts, respectively.

4.6 Write a pair of methods, as follows:

a. `carryExactlyEight` ensures a robot is carrying exactly eight things in its backpack. Assume the robot is on an intersection with at least eight things that can be picked up

b. Generalize `carryExactlyEight` to `carryExactly`. The new method will take a parameter specifying how many `Things` the robot should carry.

4.7 Write a new robot method, `faceNorth`. A robot that executes `faceNorth` will turn so that `getDirection` returns `Direction.NORTH`.

a. Write `faceNorth` so that the robot turns left until it faces north. Use several `if` statements.

b. Write `faceNorth` so that the robot turns left until it faces north. Use a `while` statement.

c. Write `faceNorth` so that the robot turns either left or right, depending on which direction requires the fewest turns to face north.

4.8 Write a robot method named `face`. It takes a single direction as a parameter and turns the robot to face in that direction. The robot does *not* need to use the minimal number of turns.

4.9 Code and run brief examples of the following errors and report how your compiler handles them.

a. A method with a return type of `void` that includes the statement `return !this.canPickThing();`.

b. A method with a return type of `boolean` that does not include a `return` statement.

c. A method named `experiment` that takes a single integer argument. Call it without an argument, with two arguments, and with `Direction.NORTH`.

Programming Projects

4.10 Finish the implementation of the `Racer` class shown in Listing 4-4. Demonstrate your class with at least two different race courses.

4.11 Listing 3-3 is the complete implementation of the `Harvester` class, a class of robots designed to harvest a field of things. Implement the class again using your knowledge of `if` and `while` statements. Your new class of robots should be able to harvest a rectangular field of any size provided that things cover the field completely and the field is bordered by intersections that do not have any things on it (in particular, there are no walls bordering the field). Note that the original solution required the field to have an even number of rows. Your solution should not have that restriction. Assume the upper-left corner of the field is at (1, 1). Demonstrate your robot harvesting at least two fields with different sizes.

4.12 `karel` and `tina`, instances of `ShovelBot`, are in business together as snow shovelers. `karel` shovels the snow (`Things`) from the driveways, placing them on the sidewalk. Then, while `karel` rests, `tina` moves all the snow left on the sidewalk to the end of the sidewalk.

An initial situation with its corresponding final situation is shown in Figure 4-18. It is known that `karel` and `tina` always start at one end of the sidewalk. The sidewalk always extends beyond the first and last driveways, but it is not known how many driveways there are, the width of the driveways, or the length of the driveways.

(figure 4-18)

Neighborhood that requires snow to be shoveled

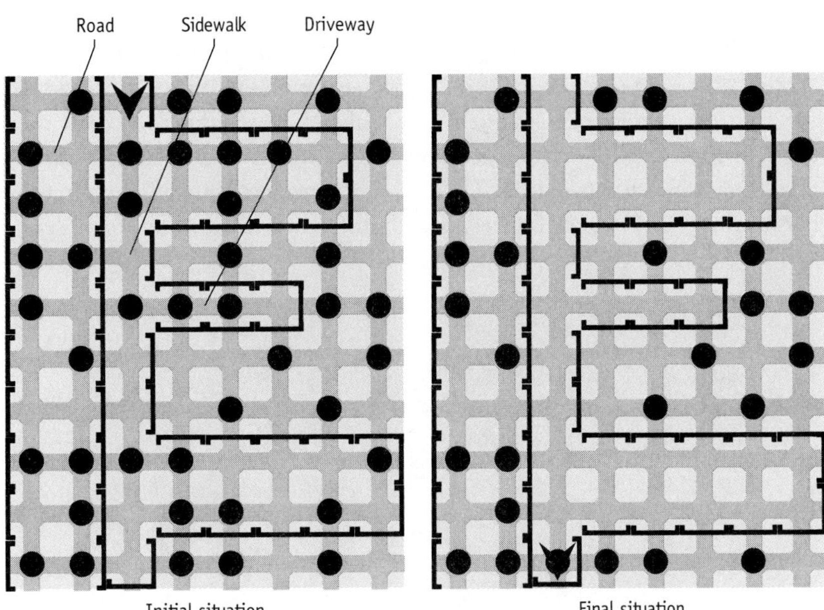

4.13 Implement a `Guard` class of robots that can guard either King Java's castle or King Caffeine's castle, plus other castles with similar layouts but different sizes. See Programming Projects 3.12 and 3.13 for descriptions of these castles. You may assume that the corner turrets are each one wall square and that the central courtyard of the castle has at least one wall on each side. Create several files specifying different sizes of castles to use in testing your program.

4.14 A method named `goToOrigin` could use the following algorithm to move a robot to intersection (0, 0):

face avenue 0
move to avenue 0
face street 0
move to street 0

Assume the city has no obstructions such as `Walls`.

a. Implement `goToOrigin` using the given algorithm.
b. Write a method named `goTo` that allows the programmer to specify the intersection the robot is to go to.

4.15. Suppose that data from a poll is represented by `Thing` objects. There is one `Thing` object on intersection (1, 1) for each person who selected response “a”. Two people selected response “b” in the poll, resulting in two `Thing` objects on intersection (1, 2). Similarly, the number of objects on the remaining intersections represents the number of people selecting particular responses.

Write `HistogramBot` to create a histogram (commonly called a bar chart) for the data. An instance of `HistogramBot` will pick up the things on each intersection and spread them out (one per intersection) to form a bar. Sample initial and final situations are shown in Figure 4-19. Test your program with different numbers of things on each pile as well as with different numbers of piles.

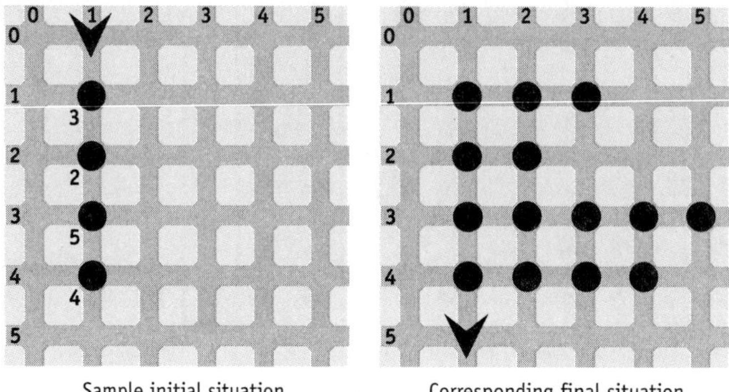

(figure 4-19)

Sample pair of initial and final situations for a `HistogramBot`

16. Sketch a scene on graph paper that uses a combination of ovals, rectangles, lines, and perhaps strings (text). Write a program that paints your scene, using the scaling techniques in Section 4.7.

Chapter 5 More Decision Making

Chapter Objectives

After studying this chapter, you should be able to:

- Follow a process for constructing `while` loops with fewer errors
- Avoid common errors encountered with `while` loops
- Use temporary variables to remember information within methods
- Nest statements inside other statements
- Manipulate Boolean expressions
- Perform an action a predetermined number of times using a `for` statement
- Write `if` and `while` statements with appropriate style

The `if` and `while` statements studied in Chapter 4 form the basis for making decisions in programs. Any program you care to write can be written with using only the `if` and `while` statements to change the flow of control. This chapter continues the discussion with variations of the `if` statement and other ways to repeatedly execute statements that can simplify our code even though they are not strictly required. It explores a process for constructing `while` statements and points out errors to avoid. In short, this chapter summarizes the accumulated wisdom of programming with `if` and `while` statements.

Sometimes decisions are made based on what has happened in the past. Such decisions are facilitated by temporary variables that can remember information for later use in the same method.

5.1 Constructing while Loops

In Chapter 4, we learned how to affect the sequence in which program statements are executed with the `if` and `while` statements. In this section, we will examine some common errors and a more rigorous process for constructing `while` loops that can help you avoid those errors.

5.1.1 Avoiding Common Errors

The `while` statement provides a powerful programming tool. By using it wisely, we can solve complex problems. However, the sharper the ax, the deeper it can cut, as they say. With the power of the `while` statement comes the potential for making some significant mistakes. This section will examine several typical errors beginning programmers make when using the `while` statement. If we are aware of these errors, we have a better chance of avoiding them and an easier time identifying them for correction when they do occur.

The Fence-Post Problem

If we want to build three fence sections, how many fence posts will we need? The obvious answer is three, but that is wrong. Look at Figure 5-1. The figure should help us to understand why the correct answer is four.

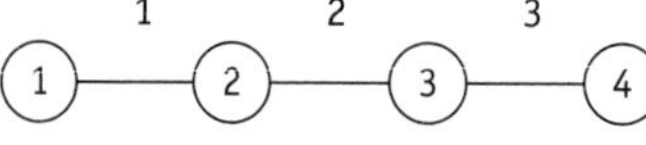

(figure 5-1)

Fence-post problem

We can encounter the fence-post problem when using the `while` loop. For example, consider the problem of clearing all the `Things` between a robot and a wall. The robot's starting intersection also contains a `Thing`, as shown in Figure 5-2.

(figure 5-2)

Initial situation for an example of the fence-post problem

It might seem that a natural way to solve this problem is with the following method:

```
public void clearThingsToWall()
{ while (this.frontIsClear())
  { this.pickThing();
    this.move();
  }
}
```

If we trace the method's execution carefully, we discover that the loop finishes and the robot does not crash into the wall. However, the easternmost `Thing` is not picked up, as shown in Figure 5-3.

(figure 5-3)

After executing `clearThingsToWall`

In this example, the `Thing`s are the fence posts and the `move`s are the fence sections. The `while` loop executes the same number of `pickThing` and `move` statements. Consequently, one `Thing` will be left when the loop finishes. We can handle this situation by adding an extra `pickThing` command after the `while` loop finishes executing, as shown in the following code fragment:

PATTERN

Loop-and-a-Half

```
public void clearThingsToWall()
{ while (this.frontIsClear())
  { this.pickThing();
    this.move();
  }
  this.pickThing();
}
```

LOOKING AHEAD

The `while-true` *loop is an elegant solution to the loop-and-a-half problem. See Section 5.5.3.*

It is surprising how often the fence-post problem occurs in computer science. It is also known as the **loop-and-a-half** problem because, in one sense, the loop executes an extra half iteration when the last thing is picked.

Infinite Loops

You may have experienced a computer program that **hangs**. It appears to be running fine and then mysteriously fails to respond to your commands. The entire program appears "frozen." Such a program is probably caught in an **infinite loop**. An infinite loop is one that has no way of ending because the programmer has forgotten to include a statement (or sequence of statements) whose execution allows the loop's test to become `false`. Here is an example:

```
while (this.isFacingNorth())
{ this.pickThing();
  this.move();
}
```

KEY IDEA

Every loop must have a statement that can affect the test.

Nothing within this loop will change the robot's direction. As a result, the loop will iterate zero times if the robot is initially facing any direction other than north. Unfortunately, if it is facing north, we condemn the robot to walk forever (unless, of course, it breaks because there is no `Thing` to pick up or it runs into a wall; it will also stop if the computer itself crashes or the computer's power supply is disrupted).[1] We must be very careful when we plan the body of the `while` loop to avoid the possibility of an infinite loop.

5.1.2 A Four-Step Process for Constructing `while` Loops

The common errors discussed in the previous section, plus difficulties you probably experienced constructing loops in the previous chapter, should motivate you to study a formal process to construct `while` loops. The goal is to structure our thinking so that our loops are more likely to be written correctly.

There are four steps. We first outline them briefly and then illustrate them with two examples.

Step 1: Identify the actions that must be repeated to solve the problem.

Step 2: Identify the Boolean expression that must be true when the `while` statement has completed executing. Negate it.

Step 3: Assemble the `while` loop with the actions from Step 1 as the body and the Boolean expression from Step 2 as the test.

Step 4: Add additional actions before or after the loop to complete the solution.

We will now apply this four-step process to two examples. The first is the `clearThingsToWall` problem discussed in Section 5.1.1. The second is a more complicated problem.

Applying the Four-Step Process to Clearing Things

Consider again the problem of clearing all the `Things` between (and including) the robot's intersection and a `Wall`, as shown in Figure 5-2. We don't know how far away the `Wall` is.

Step 1 is to identify the actions that must be repeated. One way to do this is to solve a small example of the problem without a loop. The four `Things` in Figure 5-2 already qualifies as a small problem (much smaller than, say, 400!). To solve it, we need to perform the following actions:

[1] Of course, if we have overridden `pickThing` or `move`, then anything is possible. One of the new versions could change the direction, and then the robot would exit the `while loop`.

pick a thing
move
pick a thing
move
pick a thing
move
pick a thing

Clearly, two actions are repeated, ***pick a thing*** and **move**. In particular, note that the two actions appear in groups—as shown by the brackets on the right—and that one of the actions doesn't appear in any of the groups. Because of that extra action, there are actually two ways to group the repeated actions. The other grouping results in an extra *pick a thing* at the beginning of the sequence.

Step 2 is to identify the Boolean expression that must be true when the loop finishes. The robot should stop collecting things when it is blocked by a wall; that is, the loop should stop when the test `this.frontIsBlocked` is true. But the test for a `while` statement isn't whether the loop should stop; the test is whether the loop should continue. Therefore, the test to use is the negation of `this.frontIsBlocked()`: `!this.frontIsBlocked()` or `this.frontIsClear()`.

Step 3 assembles the `while` loop using a group of repeated actions from Step 1 and the Boolean expression from Step 2. This yields the following code:

```
while (this.frontIsClear())
{ this.pickThing();
  this.move();
}
```

Finally, Step 4 cleans things up. Recall, for example, that there was one action in Step 1 that wasn't included in any of the groups. This is the extra fence post from the loop-and-a-half problem. The extra action was at the end of the preceding sequence and so it is placed after the loop. The final solution is as follows:

PATTERN
Loop-and-a-Half

```
while (this.frontIsClear())
{ this.pickThing();
  this.move();
}
this.pickThing();
```

Applying the Four-Step Process to Shifting `Things`

A more difficult looping problem is a robot shifting a pile of `Things` from one intersection to the next, as shown in Figure 5-4.

(figure 5-4)

Shifting a pile of `Thing` *objects to the next intersection*

There are four requirements:

- The pile will always have at least one `Thing`.
- The robot can only move one `Thing` at a time.
- The robot must finish on the intersection to which it has moved the pile.
- The robot must not move unnecessarily. Specifically, it must not go back to the original intersection when that intersection is empty.

This problem clearly requires actions to be performed zero or more times rather than once or not at all. Therefore a `while` loop is required, and we can apply the four-step process.

KEY IDEA

Identify the repeating steps with a loopless solution.

Step 1 is to identify the steps that must be repeated. As before, we assume a typical initial situation and solve the problem without a loop. In this case, assume the pile has four `Things` on it. (Remember, our final solution must handle a pile of any size. We are assuming four things only while we find the steps that repeat.) To move all four `Things` to the next intersection, the robot must perform the following steps:

pick up one thing
shift it to the next intersection
go back to the original intersection
pick up one thing
shift it to the next intersection
go back to the original intersection
pick up one thing
shift it to the next intersection
go back to the original intersection
pick up one thing
shift it to the next intersection

This sequence of actions has three actions that must be repeated: *pick up one thing*, *shift it to the next intersection*, and *go back to the original intersection*. As before, we group them with brackets, as shown in the preceding pseudocode. With two actions left over in the sequence, however, determining what comes before and after the loop will be trickier than in the previous example.

Step 2 identifies the test that must be true when the loop has finished executing. We can consider several possible tests:

- *the robot is on the next intersection*—This can't be the correct test to end the loop because the robot is on the next intersection many times while moving the `Things`.

- *the original intersection has no things on it*—This is the test that must be true when the loop is finished executing. If it's not true, the task obviously isn't finished. If it is true, we might have a little cleanup to do, but the repetitious work is over.

In Java, this test can be expressed with the Boolean expression `!this.canPickThing()`. That is, the loop stops when the robot can't pick up any more `Things` from the original intersection. The test that determines when the `while` loop should continue is the negation of this, or `this.canPickThing()`.

Step 3 assembles the loop. The test was identified in Step 2, giving us the following structure:

```
while (this.canPickThing())
{ ...
}
```

The question is how to arrange the repeated action inside the loop. There are actually three possibilities, as follows. In each case, Step 4 is anticipated and the leftover actions are placed either before or after the loop, depending on how they appear in the loopless solution from Step 1.

```
while (this.canP...)
{ pick up one thing
  shift it
  go back
}
pick up one thing
shift it
```

```
pick up one thing
while (this.canP...)
{ shift it
  go back
  pick up one thing
}
shift it
```

```
pick up one thing
shift it
while (this.canP...)
{ go back
  pick up one thing
  shift it
}
```

Barring a flash of insight, the way to choose one of these options is to trace them. An excellent situation to use for your first trace is the smallest possible problem: one `Thing` on the original intersection. Try tracing the left-most loop for yourself. You should convince yourself that it fails for two reasons. First, it tries to pick a `Thing` from an empty intersection. Second, the problem specification says it can't return to the intersection after it is empty, which it does.

The right-most loop also has problems. On any sized problem it picks up a `Thing` and shifts it to the next intersection. But then it determines if it can pick up the `Thing` it, just shifted. It's performing the test on the wrong intersection.

The middle loop executes correctly. It picks up a `Thing` from the intersection and then asks if there is another `Thing` for the *next* trip. When the pile has just one `Thing` in it, there is nothing left for another trip, and so it skips the loop body and shifts the `Thing` it just picked up to the next intersection.

This is *not* an obvious solution. It takes a deep insight to realize that the test for picking up a `Thing` should be performed *after* picking one up and not before. There is no algorithm for solving such a problem, but the four-step process provides significant guidance in finding a solution.

Reasoning about the `while` Statement

We just demonstrated that, at least in pseudocode, our solution works for one particular instance of the problem. But what about all the other sizes of piles? We cannot test all possible initial situations (there are infinitely many of them), but we can test several and do a reasonable job of convincing ourselves that the solution is correct.

One method of informally reasoning about the statement has two steps. First, we must show that the statement works correctly when the initial situation results in the `while` statement's test being `false`. That is, in fact, the situation we just traced where the pile contained only one `Thing`. It picked that `Thing` up and then performed the test, which evaluated to `false`.

KEY IDEA

Trace a situation where the loop body does not execute.

Second, we must show that each time the loop body is executed, the new situation is a smaller but similar version of the old situation. By smaller, we mean there is less work to do before finishing the loop. By similar, we mean that the situation has not radically changed while executing the loop body. (In this example, a non-similar change could be that the robot is facing a different direction.)

KEY IDEA

Demonstrate that executing the loop body results in a smaller but similar version of the problem.

By tracing a few iterations of the loop, we see that after each iteration, the size of the pile decreases by one. This gives us confidence that the situation will eventually reach the case where the `while` loop becomes `false`, which we already checked for correctness.

5.2 Temporary Variables

The `Robot` class has a method to count the number of `Things` in its backpack, but there is no corresponding method to count the number of `Things` on an intersection. One can imagine, for example, a `Robot` that is following a trail left behind by another `Robot`. Finding zero `Things` on the intersection means to go forward, finding one `Thing` means to go left, and finding two `Things` means to go right. With the knowledge we have now, such a problem would be very difficult to solve.

A **temporary variable**, also called a **local variable**, is the core of one solution. A temporary variable stores a value for later use within the same method. We have already used temporary variables, starting with Chapter 1. `sanDiego` and `karel` are both temporary variables in the following code fragment:

KEY IDEA

A temporary variable stores a value for later use in the method.

```
City sanDiego = new City();
Robot karel = new Robot(sanDiego, 1, 2, Direction.EAST);
...
karel.move();
```

Both of them are storing a value, a reference to an object, for later use within the same method (`main`).

To count the number of `Things` on an intersection, we'll use a temporary variable, but one storing an integer rather than a reference to a `Robot` or `City`.

A temporary variable used to count something would typically be declared like this:

```
int counter = 0;
```

PATTERN
Temporary Variable

Like the `City` and `Robot` declarations shown earlier, this declaration has a type and a name followed by its initial value. The type is `int` and the name is `counter`. The type of `int` specifies that this variable will only store a particular kind of value, integers. The **initial value** is zero, the first value assigned to the variable.

We have already worked with one kind of integer variable when we used parameters in Section 4.6.1. In that case, we decremented the parameter `howFar` with the statement `howFar = howFar - 1`. Similarly, `counter` can be decremented with the statement `counter = counter - 1`. It's not surprising that `counter = counter + 1` increments the value in `counter` by one.

5.2.1 Counting the `Things` on an Intersection

With this background, let's count the `Things` on an intersection with the idea that a robot may be used to follow a trail, as described earlier. In pseudocode, we use the following:

```
count the number of things here
if (number of things here == 0)
{ move
}
if (number of things here == 1)
{ turn left
}
if (number of things here == 2)
{ turn right
}
```

We begin by declaring a temporary variable to use in determining the number of `Things` on the intersection. We can also update the pseudocode to use it in appropriate places, as follows:

PATTERN
Temporary Variable

```
int numThingsHere = 0;

update numThingsHere with the number of things on this intersection

if (numThingsHere == 0)
{ this.move();
}
```

```
if (numThingsHere == 1)
{ this.turnLeft();
}
if (numThingsHere == 2)
{ this.turnRight();
}
```

We can now focus on the remaining pseudocode to update `numThingsHere`. Our strategy will be to pick up all of the `Things` on the intersection, increasing `numThingsHere` by one each time a thing is picked up. There may be many things, so a `while` loop is appropriate. In terms of the four-step process for writing a loop, the actions to repeat (Step 1) are picking a `Thing` and incrementing the variable. The test for stopping (Step 2) is when there is nothing left on the intersection. Therefore, the loop should continue while `canPickThing` returns `true`. Assembling the loop (Step 3) yields the following code:

```
while (this.canPickThing())
{ this.pickThing();
  numThingsHere = numThingsHere + 1;
}
```

For this problem, there is nothing to do before or after the loop (Step 4).

The completed code fragment for counting the number of `Things` on an intersection and turning in the appropriate direction is shown in Listing 5-1.

Listing 5-1: *A code fragment to count the number of* `Things` *on an intersection and move appropriately*

```
int numThingsHere = 0;
while (this.canPickThing())
{ this.pickThing();
  numThingsHere = numThingsHere + 1;
}

if (numThingsHere == 0)
{ this.move();
}
if (numThingsHere == 1)
{ this.turnLeft();
}
if (numThingsHere == 2)
{ this.turnRight();
}
```

PATTERN

Counting

5.2.2 Tracing with a Temporary Variable

We can increase our understanding of the code in Listing 5-1 by tracing it. Doing so will also increase our confidence in its correctness. As usual, we shall employ a table to record the statements executed and the state of the program. To adequately trace the state for this fragment, we need to record the `Robot`'s street, avenue, and direction; the value of `numThingsHere`; and the number of `Things` on the intersection. It is also useful to record the results of the tests performed by the `if` and `while` statements. A single column will do for both tests, and we will only record the result in the line where it is executed. We don't need to record the number of `Things` in the robot's backpack because that information is not used in the code fragment.

(table 5-1)

Tracing the execution of the code fragment in Listing 5-1

Table 5-1 traces the situation in which the `Robot` is facing north on (3, 5). That intersection has two `Thing` objects. The code should cause the `Robot` to turn right to face east—which it does.

Program Statement	test	(str, ave)	Direction	numThingsHere	Number on Intersection
		(3, 5)	north	???	2
1 `int numThingsHere = 0;`					
		(3, 5)	north	0	2
2 `while (this.canPickThing())`					
	true	(3, 5)	north	0	2
3 `{ this.pickThing();`					
		(3, 5)	north	0	1
4 `numThingsHere = numThingsHere + 1;`					
		(3, 5)	north	1	1
2 `while (this.canPickThing())`					
	true	(3, 5)	north	1	1
3 `{ this.pickThing();`					
		(3, 5)	north	1	0
4 `numThingsHere = numThingsHere + 1;`					
		(3, 5)	north	2	0
2 `while (this.canPickThing())`					
	false	(3, 5)	north	2	0

Program Statement	test	(str, ave)	Direction	numThingsHere	Number on Intersection
`7 if (numThingsHere == 0)`					
	false	(3, 5)	north	2	0
`10 if (numThingsHere == 1)`					
	false	(3, 5)	north	2	0
`13 if (numThingsHere == 2)`					
	true	(3, 5)	north	2	0
`14 { this.turnRight();`					
		(3, 5)	east	2	0

(table 5-1) *continued*

Tracing the execution of the code fragment in Listing 5-1

5.2.3 Storing the Result of a Query

In Listing 5-1 we turned a `Robot` based on how many `Things` it found on the intersection. We could perform a similar task based on how many `Things` are in its backpack. One way to do this is shown in the following code fragment:

```
if (this.countThingsInBackpack() == 0)
{ this.move();
}
if (this.countThingsInBackpack() == 1)
{ this.turnLeft();
}
if (this.countThingsInBackpack() == 2)
{ this.turnRight();
}
```

Suppose you had your own backpack and performed this same task. You probably wouldn't count the number of things in the backpack three times—you would count them once and then remember the answer long enough to decide whether to turn or move. Using a temporary variable, a `Robot` can do the same thing. Instead of assigning a value of `0` to the temporary variable when we declare it, we will assign whatever value `countThingsInBackpack` returns, as shown in the following fragment:

```
int numThings = this.countThingsInBackpack();
if (numThings == 0)
{ this.move();
}
if (numThings == 1)
{ this.turnLeft();
}
```

```
 8 if (numThings == 2)
 9 { this.turnRight();
10 }
```

Suppose that the robot has one thing in its backpack. Then `countThingsInBackpack` will return the value 1. The variable `numThings` will refer to that value until it is changed or the method ends. In line 2, the value that `numThings` refers to (1) is compared to 0. They are different, and so line 3 is not executed. In line 5, the value that `numThings` refers to (1) is again compared, this time to the value 1. They are equal, and so the robot turns left. In line 8, `numThings` is again compared, but the values are not equal and so the turn in line 9 is not completed.

5.2.4 Writing a Query

Assigning the result of `countThingsInBackpack` to a temporary variable seems valuable. Can we write similar queries that return a value, such as the number of `Things` on an intersection? Yes. In fact, we have already written queries that return a value—predicates such as `frontIsBlocked`.

KEY IDEA

The value returned must match the query's return type.

Like predicates, a query such as `countThingsHere` (on the robot's intersection) will have a return type and a `return` statement. The return type in this case will be `int` because we expect this query to return an integer value. The `return` statement returns a value whose type must match the query's return type. In this particular query, the `return` statement will return the value stored in the temporary variable at the end of the method. See line 11 of Listing 5-2.

PATTERN

Query
Temporary Variable

Listing 5-2: *A method to count and return the number of* `Things` *on an intersection*

```
 1 /** Count and return the number of things on this robot's current intersection. Replace the
 2  * things after counting them.
 3  * @return the number of things on this robot's current intersection. */
 4 public int countThingsHere()
 5 { int numThingsHere = 0;
 6   while (this.canPickThing())
 7   { this.pickThing();
 8     numThingsHere = numThingsHere + 1;
 9   }
10   this.putThing(numThingsHere);
11   return numThingsHere;
12 }
```

It's a good idea for a query to return information without changing the situation in which it was called. If it needs to make changes to the program's state—such as picking `Things` up—the query should undo those changes before returning the answer. This query does so in line 10 where it calls a helper method to put down a specific number of `Things`. This helper method could be implemented using the Count-Down Loop pattern. A query that changes the program's state is said to have **side effects**.

5.2.5 Using a `boolean` Temporary Variable

Temporary variables, as well as parameters and other types of variables, can have one of many different types. `int` is just one of the possibilities. Besides references to objects like `City` and `Robot`, another possibility is the `boolean` type.

To illustrate, consider a predicate to determine whether the right side of a `Robot` is blocked. To answer this, the robot must turn to the right, determine if its path in that direction is blocked, and then somehow remember that answer while it turns back to its original direction and returns the answer. Remembering a value for use later in the method is a perfect application for a temporary variable. In this case, it just happens to be a `boolean` and will store either `true` (the right side is blocked) or `false` (no, it isn't). See Listing 5-3.

Listing 5-3: *The* `rightIsBlocked` *predicate*

PATTERN

Temporary Variable Predicate

```
1 /** Determine whether the right side of this robot is blocked. The robot's state doesn't change.
2  *  @return true if this robot's right side is blocked; false otherwise. */
3 public boolean rightIsBlocked()
4 { this.turnRight();
5   boolean blocked = this.frontIsBlocked();
6   this.turnLeft();
7   return blocked;
8 }
```

This predicate uses a helper method to determine if its front is blocked. Line 5 could also be written `boolean blocked = !this.frontIsClear()`. The value is stored in the temporary variable `blocked` until it is returned in line 7.

5.2.6 Scope

Temporary variables are always declared within a pair of braces. It may be the pair of braces defining the body of a method or the pair of braces used to define the body of a loop or a clause in an `if` statement. Each of these pairs of braces defines a **block**.

The region of the program in which a variable may be used is called its scope. The scope of a variable extends from its declaration to the end of the smallest enclosing block. Four examples are shown in Figure 5-5, where the scope of `tempVar` is shaded. Statements outside of the shaded areas may not use `tempVar`.

(figure 5-5)

Examples of the scope of a temporary variable

```
public void method()
{ int tempVar = 0;
  «statements»
}
```

```
public void method()
{ «statements»
  int tempVar = 0;
  «statements»
}
```

```
public void method()
{ if («booleanExpression»)
  { «statements»
    int tempVar = 0;
    «statements»
  }
  «statements»
}
```

```
public void method()
{ «statements»
  int tempVar = 0;
  while («booleanExpression»)
  { «statements»
  }
  «statements»
}
```

5.3 Nesting Statements

Recall that the general form of the `while` statement is as follows:

```
while («test»)
{ «list of statements»
}
```

The general form of the `if` and `if-else` statements are similar. So far all of our examples have used only method calls and assignment statements in *«list of statements»*. That need not be the case. `if` and `while` statements are also statements and can be included in *«list of statements»*.

5.3.1 Examples Using `if` and `while`

For example, consider the situation shown in Figure 5-6. A robot is an unknown distance from a wall. Between it and the wall are a number of `Thing` objects placed randomly on the intersections. The robot is to pick up one thing from each intersection (if there is one) and stop at the last intersection before the wall.

(figure 5-6)

Task requiring both `if` and `while` statements

The robot needs to move zero or more times, indicating that a `while` loop is needed. In addition, at each intersection, the robot must execute `pickThing` either once or not at all, depending on whether or not a thing is present. An `if` statement solves this kind of problem.

These two ideas can be combined in a single method, as shown in Listing 5-4. The `if` statement is said to be **nested** within the `while` statement, just as toys such as blocks or dolls are sometimes nested, one inside another.

Listing 5-4: *An `if` statement nested inside a `while` statement*

```
/** Pick up one thing (if there is a thing) from each intersection between this robot and the
 *  nearest wall it is facing. */
public void pickThingsToWall()
{ while (this.frontIsClear())
  { this.move();
    if (this.canPickThing())
    {  this.pickThing();
    }
  }
}
```

In `pickThingsToWall`, the `while` loop executes zero or more times to move the robot to the wall. The test ensures the robot will stop when it reaches the wall. Inside the loop, two things happen. First, the robot moves to the next intersection. Once it is there, it asks if it can pick up a `Thing`. If the answer is yes, the robot picks that thing up.

It is also possible to nest `if` or `while` statements within an `if` statement. For example, suppose that when a `Robot` comes to an intersection with a `Thing`, it should turn. However, which way it turns is determined by whether it has `Things` in its backpack. If it does, it turns right; if it doesn't, it turns left. The following nested `if` statements implement these actions:

```
if (this.canPickThing())
{ // There's a thing here, so this robot will turn
  if (this.countThingsInBackpack() > 0)
  { this.turnRight();
  } else
  { this.turnLeft();
  }
}
```

Any kind of statement can be nested within an `if` or `while` statement—including other `if` and `while` statements.

5.3.2 Nesting with Helper Methods

KEY IDEA

Use helper methods to simplify nested statements.

Nesting statements sometimes makes a method hard to understand, particularly if we use several levels of nesting or many steps within the `if` or `while` statement. When a method becomes too complicated, the appropriate approach is to use helper methods. For example, the `pickThingsToWall` method could have been written using helper methods, as shown in Listing 5-5.

Listing 5-5: *Using a helper method to simplify a method*

```
/** Pick up one thing (if there is a thing) from each intersection between this robot
 *  and the nearest wall it is facing. */
public void pickThingsToWall()
{ while (this.frontIsClear())
  { this.move();
    this.pickThingIfPresent();
  }
}

/** Pick up one thing (if there is a thing) from the robot's intersection. */
private void pickThingIfPresent()
{ if (this.canPickThing())
  { this.pickThing();
  }
}
```

This solution has more lines in total, but each method can be understood more easily than the larger version of `pickThingsToWall` in Listing 5-4.

5.3.3 Cascading-`if` Statements

Another useful form of nesting involves nesting `if-else` statements within `if-else` statements. If the nesting is always done in the else-clause, the effect is to choose at most one of a list of alternatives. For example, suppose that a robot should do exactly one of the actions shown in Table 5-2.

(table 5-2)

Actions a robot performs in certain situations

Situation	Action
Front is blocked	Turn around
Can pick a `Thing`	Turn right
Left is blocked	Turn left
Anything else	Move

It could be that more than one of these situations is true. For example, it could be that the robot's front and left are blocked. We still want the robot to perform only one action. We'll assume that the first matching situation listed in the table should be performed.

This could be coded in Java using a nested **if-else** construct, as follows:

```
 1 if (this.frontIsBlocked())
 2 { this.turnAround();
 3 } else
 4 { if (this.canPickThing())
 5   { this.turnRight();
 6   } else
 7   { if (this.leftIsBlocked())
 8     { this.turnLeft();
 9     } else
10     { this.move();
11     }
12   }
13 }
```

You should trace this code to convince yourself that only one of the actions listed in the table is executed. That is, only one of lines 2, 5, 8, or 10 is executed, no matter what situation the robot is in. Furthermore, when this code is read from top to bottom, the first test that returns `true` determines which statement is executed.

Figure 5-7 illustrates this code graphically using a flowchart.

Each of the else-clauses in this code fragment contain a single statement—another `if-else` statement. In this case, Java allows us to omit the braces. We can then rearrange the line breaks slightly to emphasize that only one of the actions is performed:

PATTERN

Cascading-`if`

```
if (this.frontIsBlocked())
{ this.turnAround();
} else if (this.canPickThing())
{ this.turnRight();
} else if (this.leftIsBlocked())
{ this.turnLeft();
} else
{ this.move();
}
```

KEY IDEA

Use a cascading-`if` to choose one of several groups of statements.

When an `if-else` statement is structured in this way, it is called a **cascading-`if`**. This structure is a clear signal to the reader that only one of the expressions evaluated will cause an action to be taken. To be more specific, the action taken will be associated with the *first* expression that evaluates to `true`.

(figure 5-7)

Flowchart illustrating a nested `if` statement

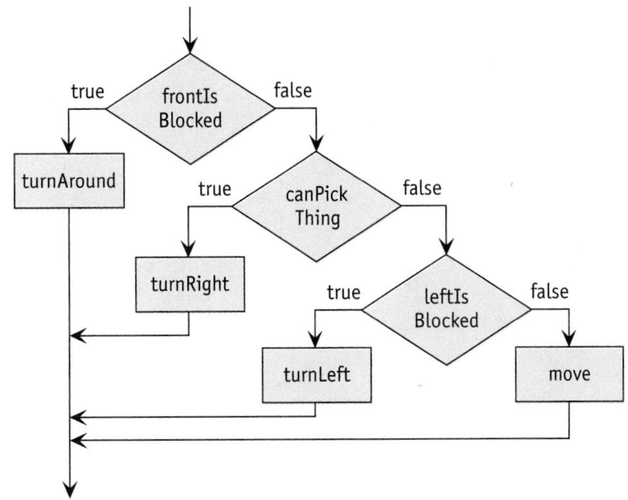

Using the `switch` Statement (optional)

The `switch` statement is similar to the cascading-`if` statement in that both are designed to choose one of several alternatives. The `switch` statement is more restrictive in its use, however, because it uses a single value to choose the alternative to execute. The cascading-`if` can use any expressions desired. This restriction is also the `switch` statement's strength: the reader knows that the decision is based on a single value.

In Section 5.2.1, we used a series of `if` statements to direct a `Robot` based on the number of things on the intersection. Either a cascading-`if` or a `switch` statement would be a better choice because it makes clear that the `Robot` should perform only one of the actions.

The two code fragments shown in Figure 5-8 both implement a variant of the problem just described and behave exactly the same way when executed.

```
int numHere =
  this.countThingsHere();
if (numHere == 0)
{ this.move();

} else if (numHere == 1)
{ this.turnRight();

} else if (numHere == 2)
{ this.turnLeft();

} else
{ this.turnAround();

}
```

```
int numHere =
  this.countThingsHere();
switch (numHere)
{ case 0:
    this.move();
    break;

  case 1:
    this.turnRight();
    break;

  case 2:
    this.turnLeft();
    break;

  default:
    this.turnAround();
}
```

(figure 5-8)

Comparing a cascading-`if` *statement and a* `switch` *statement*

The `break` statement causes execution to continue after the end of the `switch` statement. If the `break` statement is not included, execution "falls through" to the next case of the `switch`. For example, in the following code, the `break` is omitted from the first case. The result is that a `Robot` on an intersection with zero `Things` will move and turn right because it "falls through" to the second case. However, a `Robot` on an avenue with one thing will only turn right.

```
switch (this.countThingsHere())
{ case 0:
    this.move(); // Fall though

  case 1:
    this.turnRight();
    break;
}
```

This behavior is sometimes useful if the robot should do exactly the same thing for two or more cases, but this is rare. In reality, the `break` is often forgotten and is a source of bugs. If you choose to use the `switch` statement, it is a good idea to use a compiler setting to warn you if you omit a `break` statement. If you deliberately omit a `break` statement, be sure to document why.

The `default` keyword may be used instead of `case` to indicate the group of actions that occurs if none of the cases match. It is equivalent to the last `else` in the cascaded-`if` statement.

The value used in a `switch` statement must be countable. Integers, as shown in Figure 5-8, fit this description. In later chapters, we will learn about characters and enumerations that also work in a `switch` statement.

5.4 Boolean Expressions

The test in `if` and `while` statements are Boolean expressions that give a yes or no, `true` or `false`, answer to a question. So far, our questions have been simple. As our programming skills grow, however, we will want to ask more complex questions, which will need more complex Boolean expressions to answer.

5.4.1 Combining Boolean Expressions

Consider a situation in which `karel` is facing east. It is known that in the distance are things and walls. We want `karel` to travel forward, stopping at the first thing or wall it comes to. Figure 5-9 shows two such situations.

(figure 5-9)

Two situations where `karel` *should stop at the first* `Thing` *or* `Wall` *found*

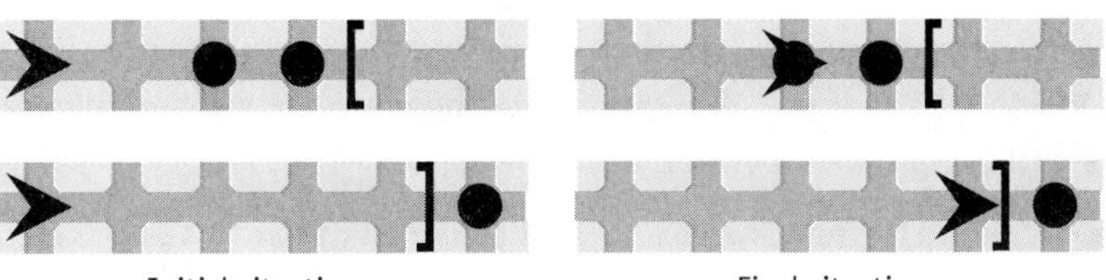

The robot might need to move zero or more times to reach the first thing or wall, so a `while` statement is appropriate. To construct it, we follow the four-step process discussed earlier. The first step is already apparent: the body of the loop should contain a `move` statement.

The second step in the process requires some thought. We want the robot to stop when it reaches a thing or a wall. We have a predicate, `canPickThing`, to determine if it is beside a thing. Another predicate, `frontIsClear`, will determine when a wall is reached. But we do not have a predicate that combines these two tests.

Fortunately, programming languages have **operators** that can combine Boolean expressions into more complex expressions. You are already familiar with operators from the mathematics you have studied: plus, minus, multiply, and divide are all operators that combine two arithmetic expressions to create a more complex expression. The equivalents for Boolean expressions are the **and** and **or** operators.

KEY IDEA

Both sides of an "and" must be true to do the action.

We often use Boolean operators in our everyday language. You might say, "I will go swimming if the weather is hot and sunny." From this statement, I know that if the weather is cloudy, you will not go swimming. Similarly, if the weather is cool, you will not go swimming. In order to go swimming, both expressions joined by "and" must be true.

On the other hand, if you say "I will go swimming if it is hot or sunny," we might question your sanity. With this statement, you might go swimming in a thunderstorm (if it happens to be hot that day) or you might go swimming in a frozen pond (if it happens to be a sunny winter day). The "or" operator requires a minimum of one of the two tests to be true. Of course, if it happens to be both hot and sunny, you would still go swimming.

KEY IDEA

Only one side of an "or" is required to be true to do the action.

Java's logical operators work in the same way except that instead of writing "and," we write `&&`, and instead of writing "or," we write `||`. Like English, an expression including `&&` is true only if both expressions it joins are true. For an expression including `||` to be true, one or both of the expressions it joins must be true.

KEY IDEA

In Java, write "and" as `&&` and write "or" as `||`.

In the earlier problem, we want `karel` to stop when it's beside a thing or its front is blocked. This can be written in Java as follows:

```
karel.canPickThing() || karel.frontIsBlocked()
```

Step 2 of the four-step process says that we should negate this expression to find out when the loop should continue. We can negate the entire expression by wrapping it in parentheses and using the `!` operator, as follows:

```
while (!(karel.canPickThing() || karel.frontIsBlocked()))
{ karel.move();
}
```

The Form of Legal Expressions

The informal descriptions of `&&` and `||` given previously mention the "expressions it joins." Let's be more precise about what constitutes a legal expression. There are four rules:

1. Literal values such as `true`, `false`, and `50` are legal expressions. The type of the expression is the type of the literal. For example, `boolean` and `int` in these examples.
2. A variable is a legal expression. The type of the expression is the type of the variable.
3. A method call whose arguments are legal expressions with the appropriate types is a legal expression. The type of the expression is the return type of the method.
4. An operator whose operands are legal expressions with the appropriate types is a legal expression. The type of the expression is given by the return type of the operator. Operators include `&&`, `||`, `!`, the comparison operators, and the arithmetic operators. Their **operands** are the expressions they operate on.

The first two rules just set the groundwork. The power is all in the last two rules, which let us combine expressions to any level of complexity. For example, within the `Robot` class, `this.canPickThing()` and `this.frontIsClear()` are both expressions (by rule 3). These two expressions can be joined with an operator such as `&&` to make a more complex expression (rule 4):

```
this.canPickThing() && this.frontIsClear()
```

Two other expressions are `this.getAvenue()` and `0` (rules 3 and 1). They can be joined by the operator > to form a new expression (by rule 4). This expression has type `boolean` and can be combined with the previous expression by rule 4. For example, using || gives the following expression:

```
this.canPickThing() && this.frontIsClear() ||
this.getAvenue() > 0
```

This expression can also be combined with other expressions in ever-increasing complexity.

Evaluating Boolean Expressions

Suppose we have a complex expression. How can we evaluate it to find its value? We can use a technique we'll call **evaluation diagrams** to annotate the expression.

To construct an evaluation diagram, begin by drawing an oval around each literal, variable, and parameterless method call. Write the expression's type above the oval and value below the oval.

The second step is to repeatedly draw an oval around an operator with its operands or a method with its arguments until the entire expression is enclosed in a single oval. For each oval drawn:

- Verify that all operands and arguments enclosed in the new oval already have ovals around them, from either the first step or a previous iteration of the second step.
- Verify that the type of each operand or argument is appropriate for the operator or method call being enclosed in the new oval. For example, you may not draw an oval around the `&&` operator if one of its operands has type `int`. If such a situation occurs, it means that the expression as a whole is not well-formed and will be rejected by the Java compiler. Some operators, such as negation (`!`), use only one operand. In that case, the oval will include only the operator and one operand.
- Write the type returned by the operator or method above the oval and the value returned below the oval.

Figure 5-10 shows the process of constructing an evaluation diagram. The top cell of the diagram shows the robot's situation. The bottom four cells of the diagram illustrate the series of steps required to construct the diagram. From the last step we conclude that in the given situation, the expression returns `true`.

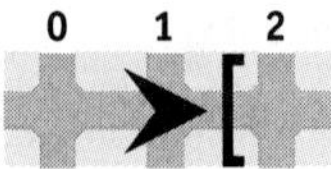

Robot's situation

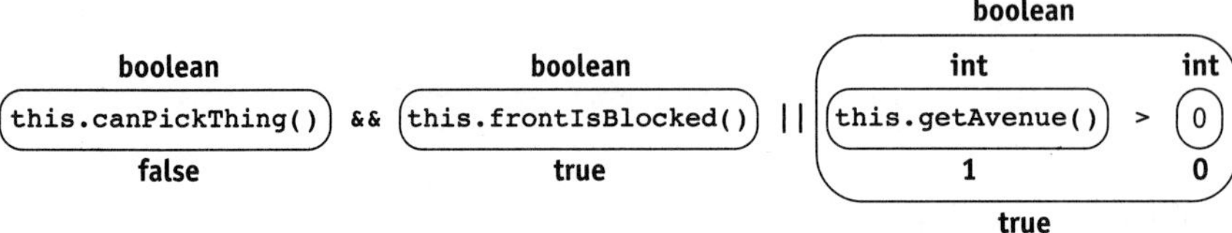

Step one in constructing the evaluation diagram

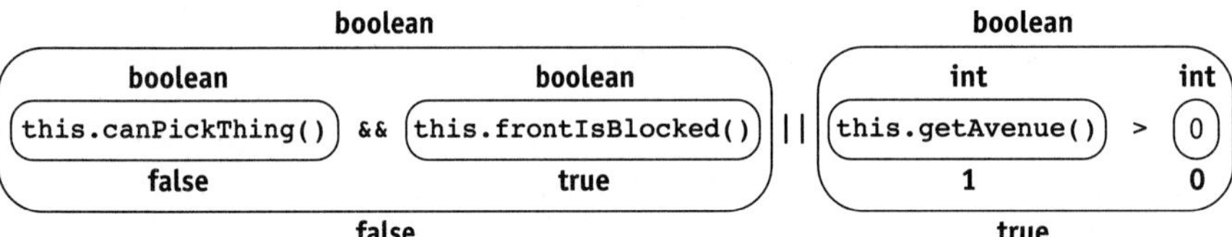

First iteration of step two in constructing the evaluation diagram

Second iteration of step two in constructing the evaluation diagram

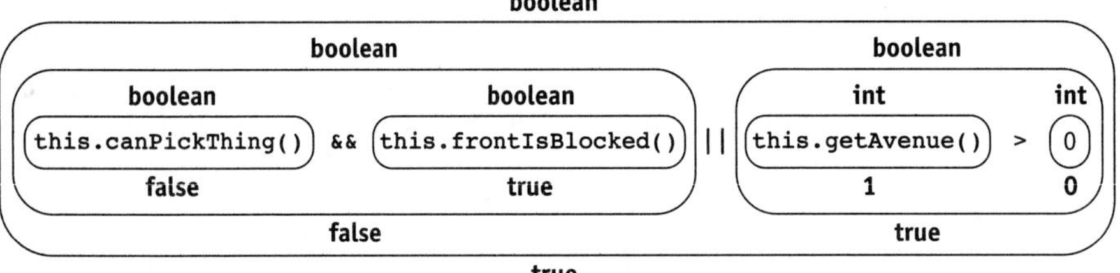

Last iteration of step two in constructing the evaluation diagram

(figure 5-10)

Evaluating a Boolean expression using an evaluation diagram

Operator Precedence

You may have noticed that some discretion was involved in choosing which operator to include in an oval. For example, in the second iteration of step two in Figure 5-10, we could have drawn the oval around the `||` operator instead of the `&&` operator. The resulting evaluation diagram is shown in Figure 5-11. Notice that the value of the expression as a whole is `false` rather than `true`.

(figure 5-11)

Alternative (and incorrect) evaluation diagram

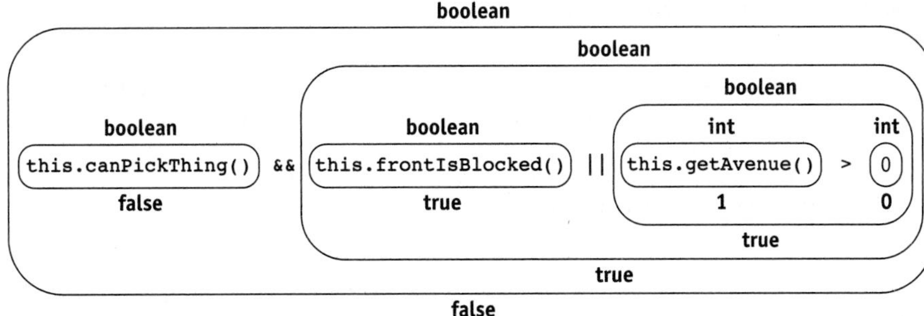

The operators are chosen in order of their precedence. **Precedence** denotes the priority they are given when evaluating the expression. The operators we have encountered, from the highest precedence to the lowest, are listed in Table 5-3. We see that `&&` is listed before `||`. Therefore, the expression diagram in Figure 5-11 is incorrect because it drew an oval around `||` when `&&` should have been chosen.

(table 5-3)

Operator precedence, from highest to lowest, of the operators encountered so far

Operator	Precedence
methodName(parameters)	15
`!`	14
`* / %`	12
`+ -`	11
`< > <= >=`	9
`== !=`	8
`&&`	4
`||`	3

It may be that the normal precedence rules are not what you want. For example, you really do want the answer shown in Figure 5-11. In that case, override the precedence rules with parentheses—just like you would in an arithmetic expression. The following example has an expression diagram as shown in Figure 5-11:

```
this.canPickThing() &&
      (this.frontIsBlocked() || this.getAvenue() > 0)
```

LOOKING AHEAD

These rules are not yet complete. We will expand them in Chapter 7.

If an expression has two or more operators with equal precedence, circle them in order from left to right.

A Common Error in Combining Expressions

Perhaps we want `karel` to turn around if the number of things in its backpack is either 1 or 2. A direct translation of this English statement into Java might be as follows:

```
if (karel.countThingsInBackpack() == 1 || 2)
{ karel.turnAround();
}
```

If we attempt to diagram this expression, however, we will encounter the problem shown in Figure 5-12. The next iteration of the algorithm calls for drawing an oval around the `||` operator, which requires two Boolean operands. However, the evaluation diagram has one Boolean operand and one integer operand. This situation tells us that the expression is incorrectly formed and will be rejected by the Java compiler. Notice that we were able to determine this without knowing how many things are in `karel`'s backpack. The analysis of the expression types, as recorded on top of the ovals, was sufficient.

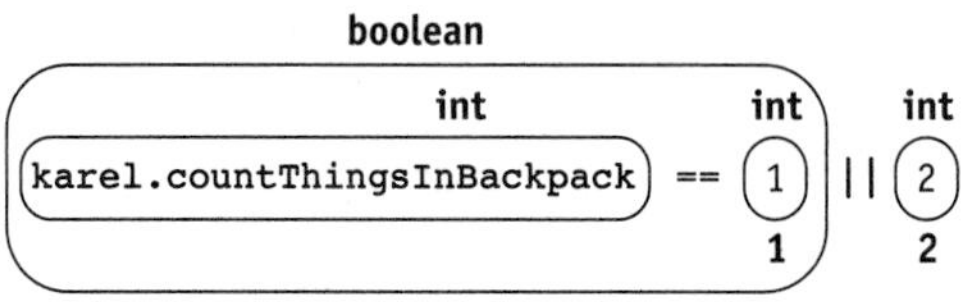

(figure 5-12)

Evaluation diagram for an incorrectly formed expression

A correct expression for determining if `karel` has one or two things in its backpack is as follows:

```
if (karel.countThingsInBackpack() == 1 ||
    karel.countThingsInBackpack() == 2)
{ karel.turnAround();
}
```

5.4.2 Simplifying Boolean Expressions

Sometimes Boolean expressions can become quite complicated as they are combined and negated. Simplifying them can be a real service, both to yourself as the programmer and to others who need to understand your code.

Simplifying Negations

Many simplifications are common sense—for example, double negatives. `!!karel.frontIsClear()` is the same as `karel.frontIsClear()`. Other such equivalencies are shown by example in Table 5-4.

(table 5-4)

Examples of equivalent, simplified expressions

Expression	Simplification
`!!karel.frontIsClear()`	`karel.frontIsClear()`
`!karel.frontIsBlocked()`	`karel.frontIsClear()`
`!(this.getAvenue() == 0)`	`this.getAvenue() != 0`
`!(this.getAvenue() != 0)`	`this.getAvenue() == 0`

De Morgan's Laws

When negations involve more complex expressions, it's easy to get mixed up. Faced with this problem, Augustus De Morgan (1806–1871) introduced what have become known as De Morgan's Laws, which formalize the process of finding the opposite form of a complex test. De Morgan's Laws state the following equivalencies (≡ means that the expression on the left is equivalent to the expression on the right):

```
!(b1 && b2) ≡ !b1 || !b2   (1st law)
!(b1 || b2) ≡ !b1 && !b2   (2nd law)
```

where `b1` and `b2` are arbitrary Boolean expressions.

These laws can be used to simplify the following expression:

```
!(karel.canPickThing() ||
      (karel.leftIsBlocked() && karel.rightIsBlocked()))
```

This code is equivalent to the following by De Morgan's second law:

```
!karel.canPickThing() &&
      !(karel.leftIsBlocked() && karel.rightIsBlocked())
```

This can be further simplified by applying the first law:

```
!karel.canPickThing() &&
      (!karel.leftIsBlocked() || !karel.rightIsBlocked())
```

This can be simplified again by restating each negated predicate, using new predicates if necessary:

```
!karel.canPickThing() &&
      (karel.leftIsClear() || karel.rightIsClear())
```

5.4.3 Short-Circuit Evaluation

Suppose you have a robot in the situation shown in Figure 5-13 that is about to execute the following code fragment:

```
if (this.frontIsClear() && this.thingOnSixthAvenue())
{ this.putAllThings();
}
```

(figure 5-13)

Time-consuming test

We can observe two things. First, the robot can find out quickly if its front is clear. On the other hand, it will take a relatively long time to move all the way to Sixth Avenue to find out if a `Thing` is there. Second, when the robot is in a situation like this, it doesn't need to waste its time checking Sixth Avenue. The definition of "and" says that if the first part of the test is false (the robot's front is *not* clear), then the entire test will be false. It doesn't matter whether the second part of the test is true or false.

With these two observations, we can conclude that the following is a more efficient way to write the previous code fragment:

```
if (this.frontIsClear())
{ if (this.thingOnSixthAvenue())
  { this.putAllThings();
  }
}
```

This fragment will only cause the robot to check Sixth Avenue if that test will really make a difference to the robot's behavior.

KEY IDEA

Java only performs a test if it needs to.

However, running these two code fragments in the situation shown in Figure 5-13 results in exactly the same behavior. In neither case does the robot check Sixth Avenue. This is because Java uses **short-circuit evaluation**. When evaluating a Boolean expression `test1 && test2`, Java will only execute `test2` if `test1` is true. If `test1` is false, Java knows that executing `test2` is a waste of time and doesn't do it.

Similarly, in the expression `test1 || test2`, `test2` will only be executed if `test1` is false. If `test1` is true, the entire expression will be true regardless of whether `test2` is true or false.

5.5 Exploring Loop Variations

The `while` loop is only one of several ways that Java can execute a code fragment repeatedly. In this section, we will explore the `for` statement and two variations of the `while` statement.

5.5.1 Using a `for` Statement

Sometimes we know before a loop begins exactly how many times we want it to execute. For example, consider a problem in which a robot named `suzie` must move clockwise around a square defined by walls, as shown in Figure 5-14.

(figure 5-14)

Moving around a square

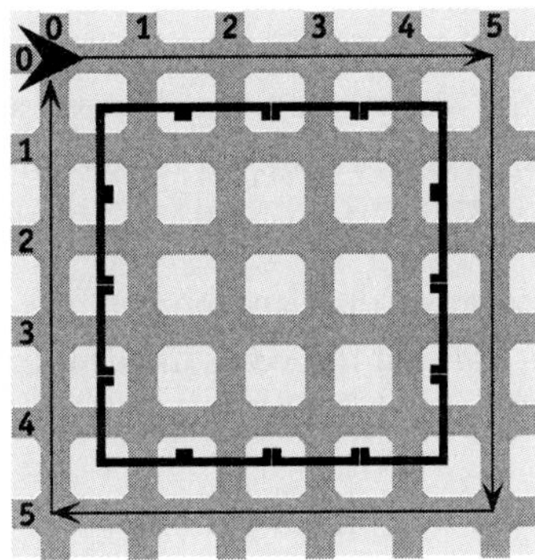

To solve the problem, `suzie` must traverse exactly four sides of the square—no more, no less. For each side, `suzie` must move exactly five times. At each corner, `suzie` must turn left exactly three times.

KEY IDEA

Use `while` when the number of iterations is unknown. Use `for` when the number is known.

A `while` loop works well when statements must be repeated an unknown number of times—while some condition is true. However, `suzie`'s situation is different. Here, we know exactly how many times the statements must be executed even before the loop begins. Java includes the `for` statement just for such situations.

The Form of the `for` Statement

The form of the `for` statement used to repeat statements a fixed number of times is as follows:

```
for (int «counter» = 0; «counter» < «limit»;
                                «counter» = «counter» + 1)
{ «statements to repeat»
}
```

where

- *«statements to repeat»* are the instructions to be executed each time through the loop. They are called the body of the loop, the same term used for the statements in the `while` loop.
- *«counter»* is an identifier or name, such as `numTurns` or `sideCount`.
- «limit» is the number of times *«statements to repeat»* should be executed.

Here is an example of `turnRight` implemented with a `for` loop:

```
public void turnRight()
{ for (int turns = 0; turns < 3; turns = turns + 1)
  { this.turnLeft();
  }
}
```

PATTERN

Counted Loop

In the `for` loop, `turns` is the «counter» that keeps track of how many times the `turnLeft` method has been executed. The «limit», or total number of times we want `turnLeft` to execute, is 3.

The `for` statement is nothing more than an abbreviation of a particular form of the `while` loop. The component parts of the `for` statement can be rearranged to create a `while` loop that behaves in exactly the same way.

KEY IDEA

A `for` statement is a shortcut for a common form of the `while` loop.

```
{
  int «counter» = 0;
  while («counter» < «limit»)
  { «statements to repeat»
    «counter» = «counter» + 1;
  }
} // Note: «counter» is not available beyond this closing brace
```

Examples of the `for` Statement

To gain further comfort with the `for` statement, let's solve the problem illustrated in Figure 5-14. We will extend `Robot` to create the class `SquareMover`. We can use stepwise refinement and pseudocode to solve the problem. To move around the square, the robot needs to move along four sides:

```
To move around a square:
 for (4 times)
 { move along one side
 }
```

To move along one side, the robot needs to move five times:

```
To move along one side:
 for (5 times)
```

```
{ move
}
turn right
```

Finally, to turn right, it needs to turn left three times:

```
To turn right:
  for (3 times)
  { turn left
  }
```

In each of these refinements, the robot must perform an action a number of times—and that number is known before the loop begins executing. Such circumstances are ideal for using a `for` statement. The class definition corresponding to this pseudocode is shown in Listing 5-6.

FIND THE CODE

ch05/squareMover/

PATTERN

Counted Loop

Listing 5-6: *A class of robot that moves around squares*

```
import becker.robots.*;

/** A class of robot that goes around squares.
 *
 *    @author Byron Weber Becker */
public class SquareMover extends Robot
{
  public SquareMover(City c, int str, int ave, Direction dir)
  { super(c, str, ave, dir);
  }

  /** Move around a square by traversing each of its four sides. */
  public void moveAroundSquare()
  { for (int side = 0; side < 4; side = side + 1)
    { this.moveAlongSide();
    }
  }

  /** Move along one side of the square by moving 5 times. */
  private void moveAlongSide()
  { for (int moves = 0; moves < 5; moves = moves + 1)
    { this.move();
    }
    this.turnRight();
  }

  /** Turn right by turning left three times. */
  private void turnRight()
```

Listing 5-6: *A class of robot that moves around squares* (continued)

```
  { for (int turns = 0; turns < 3; turns = turns + 1)
    { this.turnLeft();
    }
  }
}
```

Java provides a shortcut for `«counter» = «counter» + 1`. This statement occurs so frequently that Java allows the abbreviation `«counter»++`, which means "add 1 to the value stored in `«counter»`." Another abbreviation is `«counter» += «expression»`. It means to add the value on the right side to the variable on the left.

LOOKING AHEAD

This, and other shortcuts, are discussed in Section 7.2.5.

Finally, it should be noted that the `for` statement is more flexible than implied by these examples. The `«counter»` need not start at 0; any Boolean expression can be used for the test; and `«counter» = «counter» + 1` can be replaced by a more general statement. In particular, the `for` statement's template can be generalized as follows:

```
for («initialization»; «test»; «update»)
{ «statements to repeat»
}
```

For example, the `turnRight` method could also be written as

```
private void turnRight()
{ for (int turns = 3; turns > 0; turns = turns - 1)
  { this.turnLeft();
  }
}
```

5.5.2 Using a `do-while` Loop (optional)

The `while` loop always performs its test before the body of the loop is executed. If the test happens to be false right away, the loop's body may not be executed at all. Another loop, the `do-while` loop, performs its test after the loop body executes. This means that it will always execute at least once.

KEY IDEA

A `do-while` loop always executes at least once.

The general form of the `do-while` loop can be expressed as follows:

```
do
{ «statements to repeat»
} while («test»);
```

The loop begins by executing «*statements to repeat*». After each execution, the «*test*» is evaluated. If it is `true`, execution resumes at the `do` keyword and the body of the loop is executed again. If the test is false, execution resumes with the statement after the `while` keyword.

It is unusual to have a loop that *always* executes at least once, and so the `do-while` loop itself is unusual. A search of three projects[2] totaling more than 20,000 lines of code revealed not even one `do-while` loop.

5.5.3 Using a `while-true` Loop (optional)

The `while-true` loop is the most flexible loop available in Java. The other looping forms, including the `for` loop, test either at the beginning of the loop's body or at the end. The `while-true` can test any place you want—and can even test several times during the body's execution.

A Brief History Lesson on Structured Programming

A word of warning: All modern programmers advocate some form of **structured programming** whereby a control structure such as a loop, `if`, or a method restricts the program to entering at only a single point and often also restricts how it exits. This is in stark contrast to early programming languages that did not have such restrictions and permitted programmers to write **spaghetti code**, which was as hard to untangle as a bowl of spaghetti.

Why is this history lesson relevant? The `while-true` loop is less structured than the other loops because it allows multiple exits from the loop. Your instructor may feel uncomfortable with that and not want you to use such loops. On the other hand, many programmers believe that it strikes an excellent balance between the rigor of one-entry/one-exit structured programming and the flexibility to solve problems easily. One such person is Eric Roberts, a noted computer science educator who wrote a paper[3] on the topic. Another is the designer of the Turing programming language, in which `while-true` is used for all forms of looping except the `for` loop.

[2] The `becker` library (10,500 lines), a testing tool named `junit3.8.1` (5,000 lines), and an implementation of a marine biology simulation (5,000 lines).

[3] "Loop exits and structured programming: reopening the debate," pages 268–272 in *Proceedings of the Twenty-sixth SIGCSE Technical Symposium on Computer Science Education*, ACM Press, March 1995.

The Form of a `while-true` Loop

At first glance, a `while-true` loop looks like it will execute forever. That's because the test is the value `true`—which can never be `false` and cause the loop to end. That observation tells us there *must* be another way out of the loop.

The loop uses an `if` statement combined with a `break` statement to end the loop. It's common for the `break` to be the only statement in the `if`, so it can all be put on a single line. It uses the following form:

```
1  while (true)        // use a break statement to exit!
2  { «optional statements1»
3    if («test»)    {     break;   }
4    «optional statements2»
5  }
```

The test in line 1 is always `true` and so the program always enters the loop. When execution reaches the `if` statement in line 3, it performs its test. If the test is `false`, execution resumes with the optional statements in line 4. If the test is `true`, the `break` instruction causes execution to resume after the end of the loop.

This flow of control is summarized in Figure 5-15. All the statements in the loop are executed until the *«test»* is `true`. At that point, the `break` statement causes the loop to end.

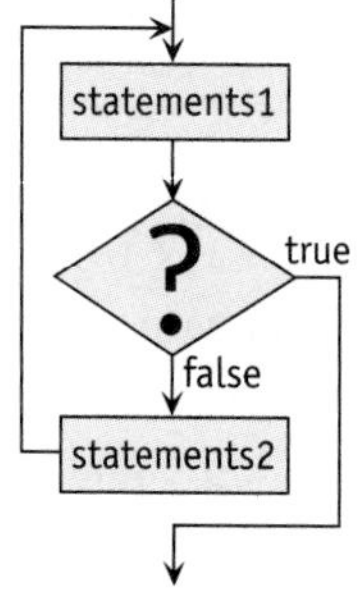

(figure 5-15)

Flowchart for the `while-true` *loop*

The statements before the test (line 2 in the preceding code) might be omitted, in which case the loop is like a standard `while` loop but with the test negated. On the other hand, if the statements after the test (line 4 in the preceding code) are omitted, the loop is like a `do-while` loop.

The loop can also have several tests. This may make the loop easier to understand than an equivalent `while` loop with a compound Boolean expression for the test.

LOOKING AHEAD

See Programming Exercise 5.7.

An Example

Consider again the fence-post problem shown in Figure 5-2. We wanted a robot to pick up all of the things between its current location and a wall. We solved it with the following method, noting that we needed an extra call to pickThing after the loop.

PATTERN
Loop-and-a-Half

```
public void clearThingsToWall()
{ while (this.frontIsClear())
  { this.pickThing();
    this.move();
  }
  this.pickThing();
}
```

The extra call to pickThing is needed because we need the robot to pick up four things but move only three times.

Here is the same problem solved with a while-true loop:

PATTERN
Loop-and-a-Half

```
public void clearThingsToWall()
{ while (true)
  { this.pickThing();
    if (this.frontIsBlocked())     {     break; }
    this.move();
  }
}
```

When only two things remain to be picked up, this code executes as illustrated in Figure 5-16.

(figure 5-16)
Illustrating the execution of a while-true *loop*

```
while (true)
{  this.pickThing();
   if (this.frontIsBlocked())  {  break;  }
   this.move();
}

while (true)
{  this.pickThing();
   if (this.frontIsBlocked())  {  break;  }
   this.move();
}

while (true)
{  this.pickThing();
   if (this.frontIsBlocked())  {  break;  }
   this.move();
}

while (true)
{  this.pickThing();
   if (this.frontIsBlocked())  {  break;  }
   this.move();
}
```

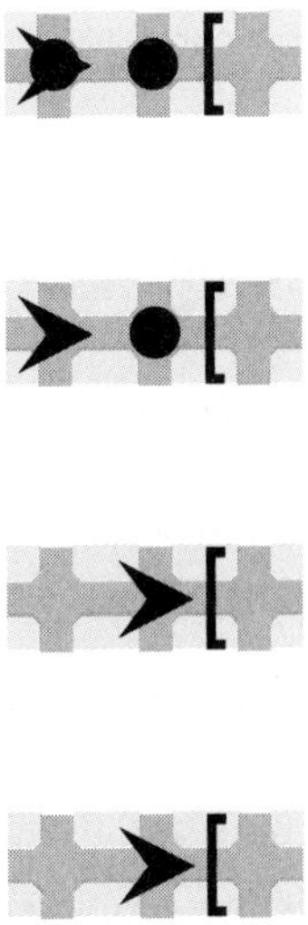

The `while-true` loop provides a general solution to the fence-post problem, also known as the **loop-and-a-half** problem. Solving these kinds of problems with a traditional `while` statement requires repeating some of the code, because the loop must execute an extra "half" iteration to perform the last action. In this case, the repeated code is the call to `pickThing`. By putting the test inside the body of the loop, the repeated code is no longer needed.

5.5.4 Choosing an Appropriate Looping Statement

We have studied a number of different kinds of looping statements. Table 5-5 provides guidelines on when to use each kind.

(table 5-5)

Guidelines for choosing a looping statement

If...	Then...
a parameter refers to the number of times the loop will execute and the value is not needed for other purposes...	use a count-down loop or a `for` statement.
the number of times the loop will execute is known before the loop is entered...	use a `for` statement.
the loop might execute zero times...	use a `while` statement.
the loop has a relatively simple test that appears at the top of the loop...	use a `while` statement.
the loop always executes at least once...	use a `do-while` statement.
the loop executes an extra "half" time for a fence-post problem...	use a `while-true` loop.
the loop has multiple exit tests or a complex test that can be more easily understood as separate tests...	use a `while-true` loop.

5.6 Coding with Style

As we have seen in previous sections, the style of our code makes a difference in how easily it can be understood. Selection and repetition statements such as `if`, `while`, and `for` are no different in this sense—we must consider the style of these statements to make sure they are easy to interpret.

The most important elements of style, stated briefly, are:

- Use stepwise refinement to avoid having deeply nested statements or long sequences of statements.
- Use positively stated, simple Boolean expressions.
- Indent your code so the visual structure reflects the logical structure.

The following subsections explore these ideas more carefully.

5.6.1 Use Stepwise Refinement

A long list of statements inside the body of a loop or `if` statement can cause the reader to lose track of the loop or `if` statement as a whole. It should be easy for the reader to remember when a loop terminates or what case is being handled by an `if` statement. Long bodies in either structure make doing so difficult.

Using stepwise refinement naturally breaks long bodies into smaller steps. Some programmers put the entire body into a helper method so that the loop or `if` statement contains only one line—the invocation of the helper method.

5.6.2 Use Positively Stated Simple Expressions

One of the most crucial aspects of good style is to keep tests easy to understand. First, avoid negations if you can because people usually find them harder to understand than positive statements. It is easier to understand `while (this.frontIsBlocked())` than `while (!this.frontIsClear())`, for example. This style may mean that you need to define your own predicate to put the test in a positive form.

A second way to keep tests easy to understand is to use predicates with descriptive names. For example, `if (this.isFacingSouth())` is easier to understand than `if (this.getDirection() == Direction.SOUTH)`.

If you will be using the same test several times in the program, writing the predicate is particularly worthwhile.

A third possibility, applicable to `if-else` statements, is to rewrite them with the goal of making them simpler and easier to understand. Rewriting an `if` statement should not change the execution of the program, only the way in which it is written. These techniques are explored in the following subsections.

Test Reversal

Consider the following code:

```
if (!this.frontIsClear())
{ this.turnLeft();
} else
{ this.move();
}
```

When the robot's front is not clear, it turns left. Otherwise it moves forward. This can be rewritten to use the opposite test if we interchange the then-clause and the else-clause:

KEY IDEA

An `if` statement executes the same way if you negate the test and swap the then-clause with the else-clause.

```
if (this.frontIsClear())
{ this.move();
} else
{ this.turnLeft();
}
```

This code is easier to read and understand, primarily because we eliminated the negation in the test. Another way to make this code easier to read is to replace `!this.frontIsClear()` with a new predicate, `this.frontIsBlocked()`.

Occasionally, we may write an `if-else` statement with an empty then-clause:

```
if (this.canPickThing())
{ // do nothing
} else
{ this.turnLeft();
}
```

Test reversal allows us to rewrite this code fragment as follows:

```
if (!this.canPickThing())
{ this.turnLeft();
} else
{ // do nothing
}
```

When written this way, it's easy to see that we can drop the else-clause and use only the Once or Not At All pattern.

```
if (!this.canPickThing())
{ this.turnLeft();
}
```

Bottom Factoring

Compare the following two fragments of code.

```
if (this.canPickThing())
{ this.pickThing();

  this.turnAround();
} else

{ this.putThing();
  this.turnAround();
}
```

```
if (this.canPickThing())
{ this.pickThing();

} else
{ this.putThing();

}
this.turnAround();
```

Both code fragments result in the same final situation. In both fragments, the robot finishes by turning around. The code on the right, however, makes this more obvious by moving `this.turnAround()` outside of the `if-else` statement. Only the actions that actually depend on the test are left inside the `if-else` statement.

Moving identical lines of code that appear at the end of both the then-clause and the else-clause to just after the `if-else` statement is called **bottom factoring**.

Top Factoring

When identical code appears at the beginning of the then-clause and the else-clause, we may be able to **top factor**. Top factoring means moving identical code from the beginning of the then- and else-clauses to just before the `if-else` statement. For example:

```
if (this.canPickThing())
{ this.turnAround();
  this.pickThing();
} else
{ this.turnAround();
  this.putThing();
}
```

```
this.turnAround();
if (this.canPickThing())
{
  this.pickThing();
} else
{
  this.putThing();
}
```

Both versions of this code will always result in the same final situation. In both versions, the robot always turns around, regardless of the test's result.

Top factoring is not as simple as bottom factoring, however. If the identical lines of code affect the outcome of the test, they *cannot* simply be moved. Consider the following example:

```
if (this.isFacingNorth())
{ this.turnAround();
  this.pickThing();
} else
{ this.turnAround();
  this.putThing();
}
```

```
this.turnAround();
if (this.isFacingNorth())
{
  this.pickThing();
} else
{
  this.putThing();
}
```

KEY IDEA

Top factor only if the code moved outside the `if` statement has no effect on the test.

Suppose the robot's initial situation is facing north on an intersection with a thing. Executing the code on the left leaves the robot facing south and having picked up one thing. Executing the code on the right also leaves the robot facing south, but this time the robot has put a thing down rather than picking a thing up.

5.6.3 Visually Structure Code

Another important stylistic rule is to line up braces vertically and indent the bodies of loops. This rule is the same as appropriately indenting methods.

If you read code written by someone else, you may notice that sometimes braces are omitted in an `if` or `while` statement. When the body consists of a single statement, the braces surrounding it are optional. For example, both of the following statements are legal:

```
if (this.frontIsClear())
  this.move();
else
  this.turnRight();
```

```
while (this.frontIsClear())
  this.move();
```

There are, however, dangers in leaving out the braces. The first comes from adding code. Suppose that after executing the `if` statement we realize that if the front is not clear, the robot should turn right and move. We might add an extra statement, as in the following example:

```
if (this.frontIsClear())
  this.turnLeft();
else
  this.turnRight();
  this.move();
```

In spite of the indentation, the `move` will occur whether the front is clear or not, which is not what was desired. Why? Braces should group the new line with the instruction to turn right. Without the braces, a compiler interprets the preceding code as follows:

```
if (this.frontIsClear())
{ this.turnLeft();
} else
{ this.turnRight();
}
this.move();
```

The compiler is interpreting the code correctly. The mistake is the programmer's in using white space to imply an incorrect program structure.

The second danger is called a **dangling else**. If braces are not included, where the `else` goes can be confusing. For example, consider the following fragment:

```
if (this.frontIsClear())
  if (this.canPickThing())
    this.pickThing();
else
  this.turnLeft();
}
```

The question is, which `if` goes with the `else`? The indentation seems to say the `else` should go with the first `if` statement. In fact, an `else` goes with the closest unmatched `if`. That is, the code is equivalent to the following:

```
if (this.frontIsClear())
{ if (this.canPickThing())
    this.pickThing();
  else
    this.turnLeft();
}
```

If we want to write code that does what the indentation implies, we are forced to add braces so that the `if` without an `else` is clearly identified, as follows:

```
if (this.frontIsClear())
{ if (this.canPickThing())
    this.pickThing();
} else
    this.turnLeft();
```

5.7 GUI: Using Loops to Draw

LOOKING BACK

See Sections 2.7.1 (a `main` *method), 2.7.2 (overriding* `paintComponent`*), and 4.7.2 (scaling images).*

In previous chapters, we learned how to draw a figure, such as a line, by writing a class extending `JComponent` and overriding the `paintComponent` method. An instance of this class is set as the content pane of a `JFrame`. The following simple class overrides `paintComponent` to scale the image and the stroke, and then draws a single line from the upper-left to the lower-right (see Listing 5-7).

FIND THE CODE

ch05/lineArt/

Listing 5-7: *Drawing a single diagonal line*

```
import javax.swing.*;
import java.awt.*;

/** Create a component that paints our "art."
 *  @author Byron Weber Becker */
public class ArtComponent extends JComponent
{
  public ArtComponent()
  { super();
    this.setPreferredSize(new Dimension(300,300));
  }

  /** Paint the component with our "art." */
  public void paintComponent(Graphics g)
  { super.paintComponent(g);
```

Listing 5-7: *Drawing a single diagonal line* (continued)

```
16
17         // Standard stuff to scale the image.
18         Graphics2D g2 = (Graphics2D) g;
19         g2.scale(this.getWidth()/11, this.getHeight()/11);
20         g2.setStroke(new BasicStroke(1.0F/this.getWidth()));
21
22         // draw our "art"
23         g2.drawLine(1, 1, 10, 10);
24     }
25 }
```

With a `for` loop, we can draw a shape over and over again. But if we replace line 23 with the following loop, we draw the same line repeatedly in the same place, having no visible effect.

```
for (int line = 1; line <= 10; line = line + 1)
{ g2.drawLine(1, 1, 10, 10);
}
```

What we need is a way to change the position of the line in each iteration of the loop.

LOOKING AHEAD

The number `10` has a special significance in this code. In Chapter 6 we will see a better way to handle it using named constants.

5.7.1 Using the Loop Counter

One way to change the position of the line with each iteration of the loop is to use `line`, the loop counter, as a parameter to `drawLine`. The parameters to `drawLine` are integers, and `line` holds integers. The value of this integer changes from 1 to 10 as the loop executes. With each iteration of the loop, a different value is passed to `drawLine`, changing the position of each of the 10 lines.

For example, we can replace line 23 in Listing 5-7 with the following loop:

```
for (int line = 1; line <= 10; line = line + 1)
{ g2.drawLine(1, 1, 10, line);
}
```

PATTERN

Counted Loop

This loop yields the image shown in Figure 5-17. Each of the 10 iterations of the loop draws a line. The location of the left end-point is fixed, but the right end-point's location varies according to the current value stored in `line`, the loop's counter variable.

The loop counter can be used for more than one of drawLine's parameters. What would be the effect of the following code fragment?

```
for (int line = 1; line <= 10; line = line + 1)
{ g2.drawLine(1, line, 10, line);
}
```

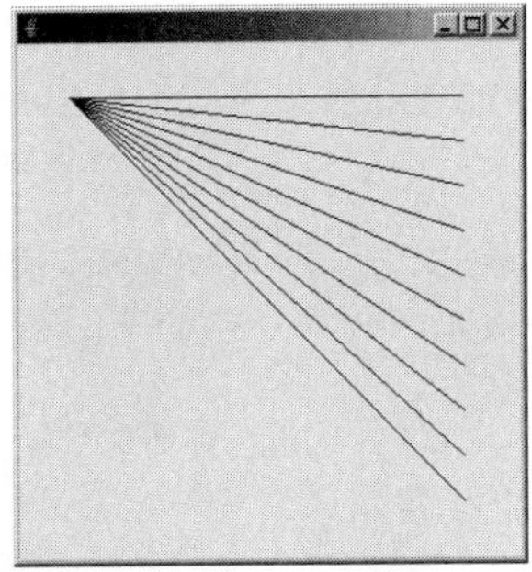

(figure 5-17)

Image resulting from using a loop to control drawing lines

5.7.2 Nesting Selection and Repetition

In Section 5.3 we saw that if statements and while statements can be nested—that is, one can be placed inside the other. for statements control any number of if, while, and for statements. As such, for statements may be nested, just like if and while. We could, for example, replace the single drawLine command at line 23 in Listing 5-7 with the following **nested loop**.

PATTERN

Counted Loop

```
for (int left = 1; left <= 5; left = left + 1)
{  for (int right = 1; right <= 10; right = right + 1)
   { g.drawLine(1, left, 10, right);
   }
}
```

These five lines cause a total of 50 lines to be drawn. The outer loop executes five times. In each of the five iterations of the outer loop, the inner loop executes completely, performing 10 iterations each time.

The image drawn after one iteration of the outer loop looks like Figure 5-18a. After two iterations of the outer loop, it looks like Figure 5-18b, and so on. Each iteration of the outer loop draws one more spray of lines (see Figures 5-18c and d). Each spray is drawn by the inner loop. In each iteration through the outer loop, the variable left has a value one larger than the previous iteration. When passed as an argument to drawLine, the coordinates of the left end of the line change.

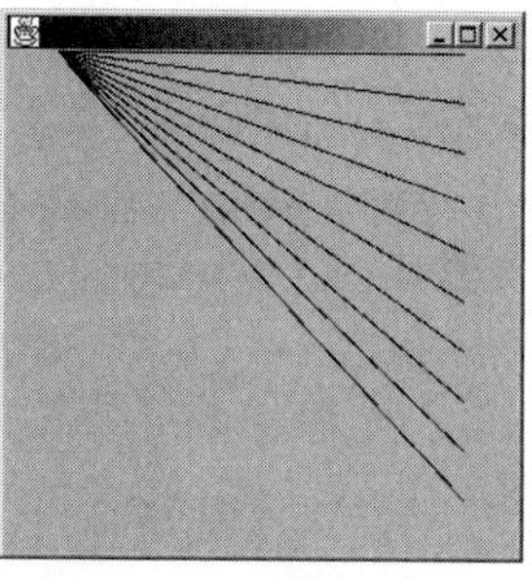

a. Image after one loop

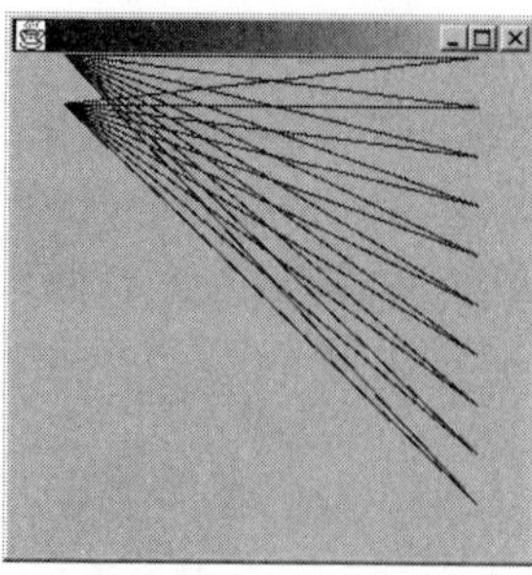

b. Image after two loops

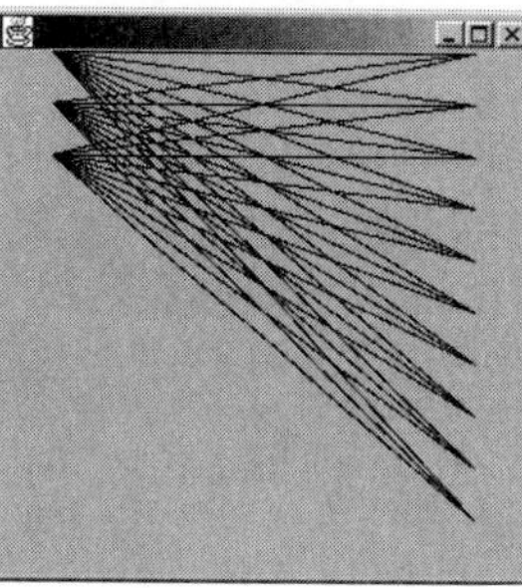

c. Image after three loops

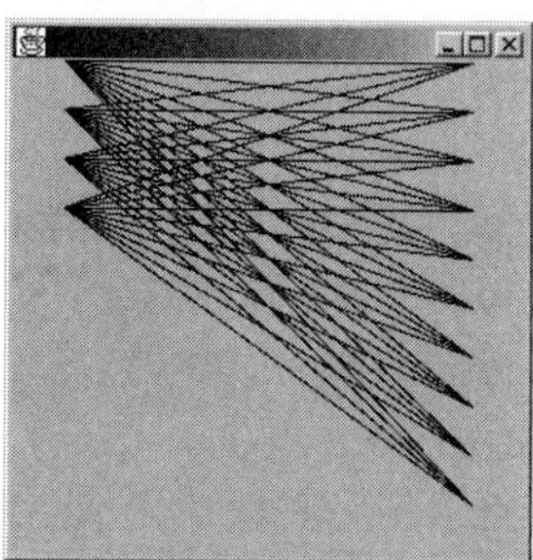

d. Image after four loops

(figure 5-18)

Images produced by a nested loop after 1, 2, 3, and 4 iterations of the outer loop

The initial value in a `for` loop need not be 0. For example, the following nested loop starts the outer loop at 3 instead of 0. The result is shown in Figure 5-19.

```
for (int left = 3; left <= 7; left = left + 1)
{ for (int right = 1; right <= 10; right = right + 1)
  { g.drawLine(1, left, 10, right);
  }
}
```

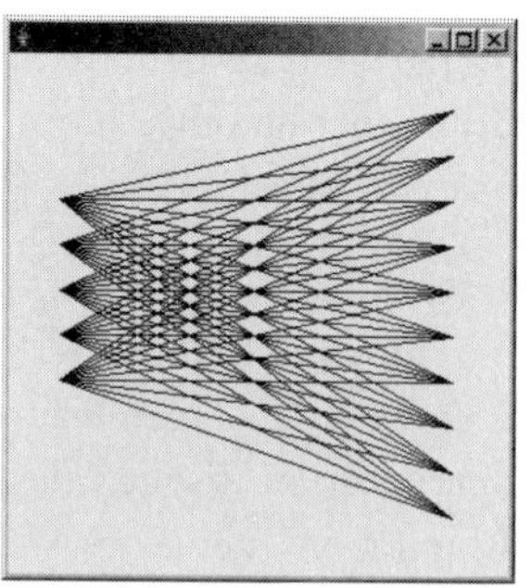

(figure 5-19)

Starting the outer loop at 3

The control variable from the outer loop can also be used as a starting value or a limiting value in the inner loop. Here, the test for the inner loop is `right <= left`:

```
for (int left = 1; left <= 10; left = left + 1)
{ for (int right = 1; right <= left; right = right + 1)
  { g.drawLine(1, left, 10, right);
  }
}
```

The first time the outer loop executes, the variable `left` has a value of 1. This value limits the inner loop to executing 1 time. The second time through the outer loop, `left` has a value of 2. The inner loop draws a spray consisting of two lines. The third time through the outer loop, `left` has a value of 3 and so the inner loop draws a spray of 3 lines. See Figure 5-20.

(figure 5-20)

Limiting the inner loop with the outer loop's control variable

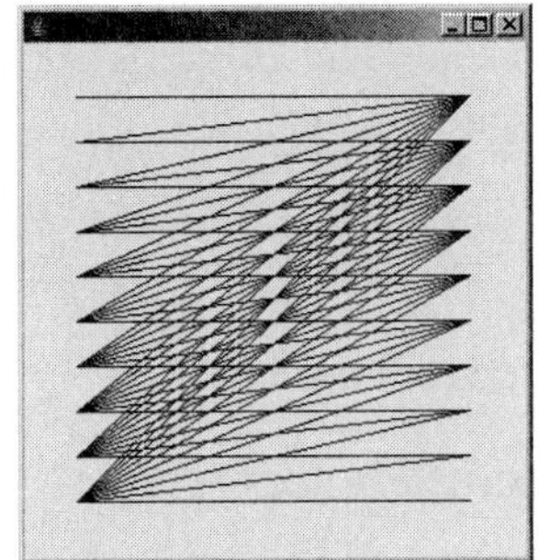

We can also add `if` statements inside a loop. Consider this program fragment:

```
for (int left = 1; left <= 10; left = left + 1)
{ if (left <= 5)
  { g2.setColor(Color.WHITE);
  } else
  { g2.setColor(Color.BLACK);
  }

  for (int right = 1; right <= 10; right = right + 1)
  { g.drawLine(1, left, 10, right);
  }
}
```

The `if` statements test the loop control variable against an integer, just as we tested the result of an integer query such as `getAvenue()` against an integer. The drawing color is set based on the test's outcome. The result is shown in Figure 5-21a, in which the first five sprays are white and the last five are black. The background is set to a darker shade of gray to show the white lines more effectively.

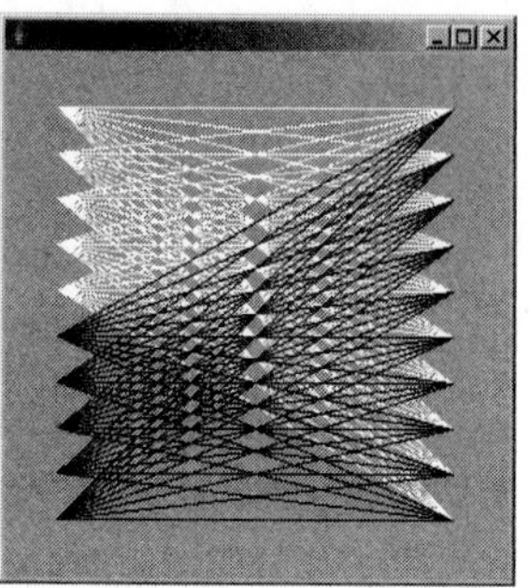

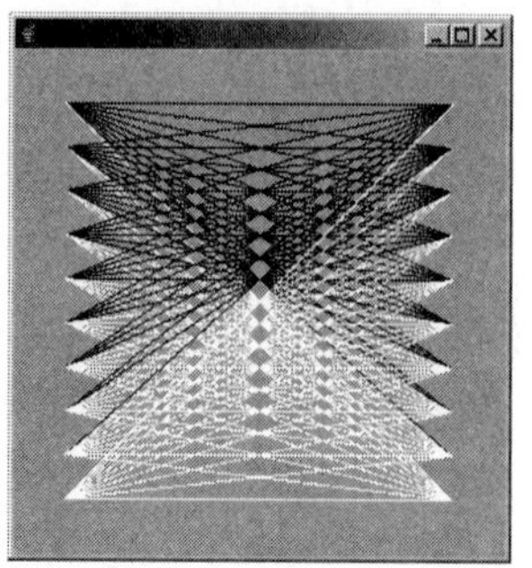

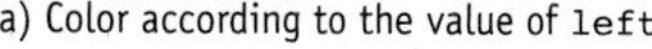

a) Color according to the value of `left`

b) Color according to the value of `left + right`

(figure 5-21)

Sprays of lines with varying colors, colored according to the sum of `inner` *and* `outer`

One more possibility is to perform a slightly more complex test for the color. It is possible to compare two integer expressions in the `if` statement's test. In the following example, the `if` statement is moved into the inner loop. It makes the line white if the sum of the values contained in `left` and `right` is greater than 10, and black otherwise. The result is shown in Figure 5-21b.

```
for (int left = 1; left <= 10; left = left + 1)
{ for (int right = 1; right <= 10; right = right + 1)
  { if (left + right > 10)
    { g2.setColor(Color.WHITE);
    } else
    { g2.setColor(Color.BLACK);
    }

    g.drawLine(1, left, 10, right);
  }
}
```

We can also use Java's **remainder operator** (`%`) in the test. The remainder operator gives the remainder when one number is divided into another. For example, `4 % 2` is 0 because 2 goes into 4 an even number of times. On the other hand, `5 % 2` is 1 because when 5 is divided by 2, 1 is left over. This mathematical relationship gives us an easy test for whether a number is even or odd. For example, if `left % 2` is 0, then the value contained in `left` is even. If `left % 2` is 1, then the value contained in `left` is odd. In the following program fragment, this fact is used to color alternating sprays differently. The result is shown in Figure 5-22.

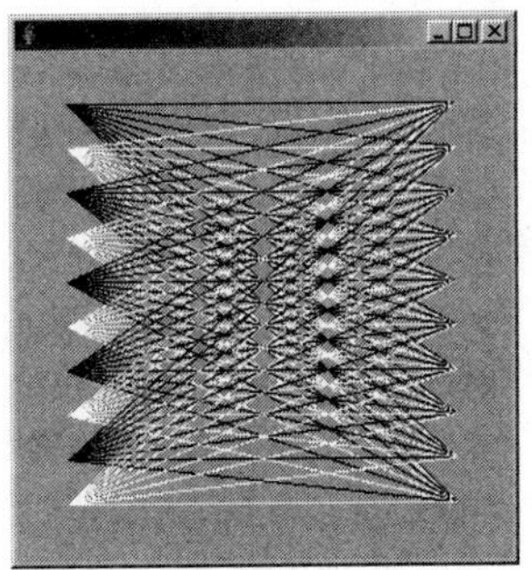

(figure 5-22)

Alternating the color of each spray

```
for (int left = 1; left <= 10; left = left + 1)
{ if (left % 2 == 0)
  { g2.setColor(Color.WHITE);
  } else
  { g2.setColor(Color.BLACK);
  }

  for (int right = 1; right <= 10; right = right + 1)
  { g.drawLine(1, left, 10, right);
  }
}
```

As you can see, selection and repetition statements such as `if`, `while`, and `for` can be combined in many ways.

5.8 Patterns

5.8.1 The Loop-and-a-Half Pattern

Name: Loop-and-a-Half

Context: A loop is used for a variation of the fence-post problem; that is, some of the repeated actions (the "fence-post actions") must be performed one more time than the other repeated actions (the "fence-section actions").

Solution: There are two standard solutions. The first repeats part of the code either before or after the loop, as appropriate. Templates for two variants follow:

```
«fencePost actions»
while («booleanExpression»)
{ «fenceSection actions»
  «fencePost actions»
}
```

```
while («booleanExpression»)
{ «fencePost actions»
  «fenceSection actions»
}
«fencePost actions»
```

The second solution avoids the repeated code with a `while-true` loop, as shown in the following template:

```
while (true)
{ «fencePost actions»
  if («booleanExpression»)  {  break;  }
  «fenceSection actions»
}
```

Consequences: The *«fencePost actions»* are executed one more time than the *«fenceSection actions»*. The *«fencePost actions»* are always executed at least once.

Related Pattern: This pattern is a variation of the Zero or More Times pattern. That pattern is used when all of the repeated steps are executed an equal number of times.

5.8.2 The Temporary Variable Pattern

Name: Temporary Variable

Context: You need to store a value that is used in the task being performed rather than as an attribute of the object. The value is only used in one method and perhaps in the methods it invokes—for example, a variable to control a loop, to store a temporary result for use in later calculations, or to accumulate a value to return to a client.

Solution: Use a temporary variable. For example, a `Robot` might be extended with the following method, which uses a temporary variable, `numWalls`:

```
public int numBlockedDirections()
{ int numWalls = 0;
  for(int turns = 0; turns < 4; turns = turns + 1)
  { if (!this.frontIsClear())
    { numWalls = numWalls + 1;
    }
    this.turnLeft();
  }
  return numWalls;
}
```

The general form for declaring a temporary variable is:

```
«type» «name» = «initialValue»;
```

where *«type»* is the type of value stored, such as `int`, `double`, or even the name of a class; *«name»* is the name used for the variable; and *«initialValue»* is the first value used for the variable. The initial value is optional; however, it must be assigned before the variable is first used, and it is good practice to initialize the variable when it is declared.

Consequences: A variable is declared that may only be used within the smallest enclosing block of code. Because it is only used locally, the reader's burden of remembering the name and purpose of the variable is significantly reduced, speeding the comprehension of the program and reducing errors.

Related Patterns: This pattern always occurs within an instance of a method pattern, such as the Helper Method, Query, or Parameterized Method patterns.

5.8.3 The Counting Pattern

Name: Counting

Context: You need to count a number of events, such as the number of times a `Thing` is picked up, the number of moves a robot makes, or the number of times a test returns `true`.

Solution: Increment a temporary variable each time the event occurs. Initialize the variable to zero before counting begins.

```
int «counter» = 0;
while («booleanExpression»)
{ «statements»
  «counter» = «counter» + 1;
}
```

Variations of this template may increment *«counter»* only if a certain test is met or may use a different looping strategy.

Consequences: *«counter»* will record the number of events that have occurred since it was initialized.

Related Patterns:

- This pattern uses a loop, typically the Zero or More Times pattern and the Temporary Variable pattern.
- This pattern is often placed in an instance of the Query pattern.

5.8.4 The Query Pattern

Name: Query

Context: A calculation that yields a single value is required. This pattern is particularly applicable if:

- the calculation involves a number of steps
- the calculation is complicated
- program readability is improved by giving the calculation a name
- the calcualtion is used more than once in the program

Solution: Write a method with a return value of the required type that uses a `return` statement to identify the calculation's answer. In general:

```
«accessModifier» «returnType» «queryName»(«optParameters»)
{ «optionalStatements»
  «returnType» answer = «expression»;
  «optionalStatements»
  return answer;
}
```

An example is `countThingsHere`, shown in Listing 5-2. Another example is to calculate the distance from a given street, as follows:

```
private int distanceFromStreet(int targetStr)
{ int answer;
  if (this.getStreet() > targetStr)
  { answer = this.getStreet() - targetStr;
  } else
  { answer = targetStr - this.getStreet();
  }
  return answer;
}
```

Queries should avoid side effects.

Consequences: Queries make code easier to understand because they name a calculation. They also make the calculation easier to reuse.

Related Patterns:

- The Query pattern is a specialization of the method creation patterns, such as the Parameterless Command, Helper Method, and Parameterized Method patterns.
- The Simple Predicate and Predicate patterns are specializations of this pattern.

5.8.5 The Predicate Pattern

Name: Predicate

Context: You are using a Boolean expression that is not as easy to read or understand as is desired, or a test is needed that can't be written as a Boolean expression because it requires extra processing.

Solution: Use the Query pattern where the *«returnType»* is `boolean`. Such a query is called a predicate. The predicate may have parameters to make it more flexible.

Consequences: The processing required for the test is encapsulated in a reusable method. With appropriate naming, the code using the predicate is more readable.

Related Patterns:

- The Predicate pattern is a specialization of the Query pattern.
- The Predicate pattern is often used to define predicates used in the Once or Not At All, Zero or More Times, and Either This or That patterns, among others.
- The Simple Predicate pattern is a simplified version of this pattern that does not use a temporary variable or the optional statements.

5.8.6 The Cascading-`if` Pattern

Name: Cascading-`if`

Context: You have a situation in which exactly one of several groups of statements should be executed based on a sequence of tests.

Solution: Order the tests from the most specific test to the most general test, pairing each test with the appropriate group of actions. Format the tests and actions to emphasize the pairings:

```
if («test1»)
{ «statementGroup1»
} else if («test2»)
{ «statementGroup2»
...
} else if («testN»)
{ «statementGroupN»
} else
{ «defaultStatements»
}
```

Consequences: The tests are executed in order from 1 to N. The first one that returns `true` will cause the associated statement group to be executed once. The final `else` and *«defaultStatements»* are optional. They will be executed if none of the tests return `true`.

Related Patterns:

- If there is only one test and one group of statements, this pattern becomes the Once or Not At All pattern. Similarly, if there is only one test but two groups of statements, this pattern becomes the Either This or That pattern.
- The `switch` statement, while not included as a pattern, solves similar kinds of problems when the decision of which group of statements to execute is based on a single value.

5.8.7 The Counted Loop Pattern

Name: Counted Loop

Context: You have a group of statements that must be executed a specific number of times, a number that is known when the loop begins execution.

Solution: Use a `for` statement, as in the following example:

```
// move to avenue 0; assumes the robot is on an avenue west of 0 and is facing West
int howFar = this.getAvenue();
for (int i=0; i<howFar; i = i + 1)
{ this.move();
}
```

The general form for this pattern is shown in Section 5.5.1. There is an equivalent form of the `while` statement, also shown in that section.

Consequences: The body of the `for` statement is executed zero or more times, depending on the specifics of the loop.

Related Pattern: The Counted Loop pattern is a specialization of the Zero or More Times pattern.

5.9 Summary and Concept Map

A `while` statement is used to execute a group of statements zero or more times. Writing such a loop correctly can be made easier by following a formal four-step process. There are also specialized forms of the `while` loop. For example, when it should execute a known number of times, a `for` statement is the preferred alternative. Loops that always execute at least once may use the `do-while` statement while the `while-true` variation is particularly useful for solving fence-post problems using the Loop-and-a-Half pattern.

Statements may be nested, for example, by putting an `if` statement within a `while` or `for` statement. When only one of several groups of statements should be executed, a particular pattern of nesting `if` statements called a cascading-`if` is useful. Complicated nesting structures should be avoided by using helper methods.

Temporary or local variables are used to remember a value for later use in the same method. They can simplify many methods and enable techniques such as the Counting pattern. Temporary variables are also useful to remember a value to be returned from a query. The value a temporary variable refers to can be changed with an assignment statement in which the expression on the right side is evaluated and the resulting value is assigned to the variable on the left side.

Boolean expressions may be combined using "and" (&&) and "or" (||). As such expressions become complicated, encapsulating them in a predicate and simplifying them, perhaps with De Morgan's Laws, can make the program easier to understand.

The statements discussed in this chapter and the previous chapter can significantly increase the complexity of our programs, making appropriate style important. Writing helper methods identified with stepwise refinement, using positively stated tests, and visually structuring the code are all important techniques.

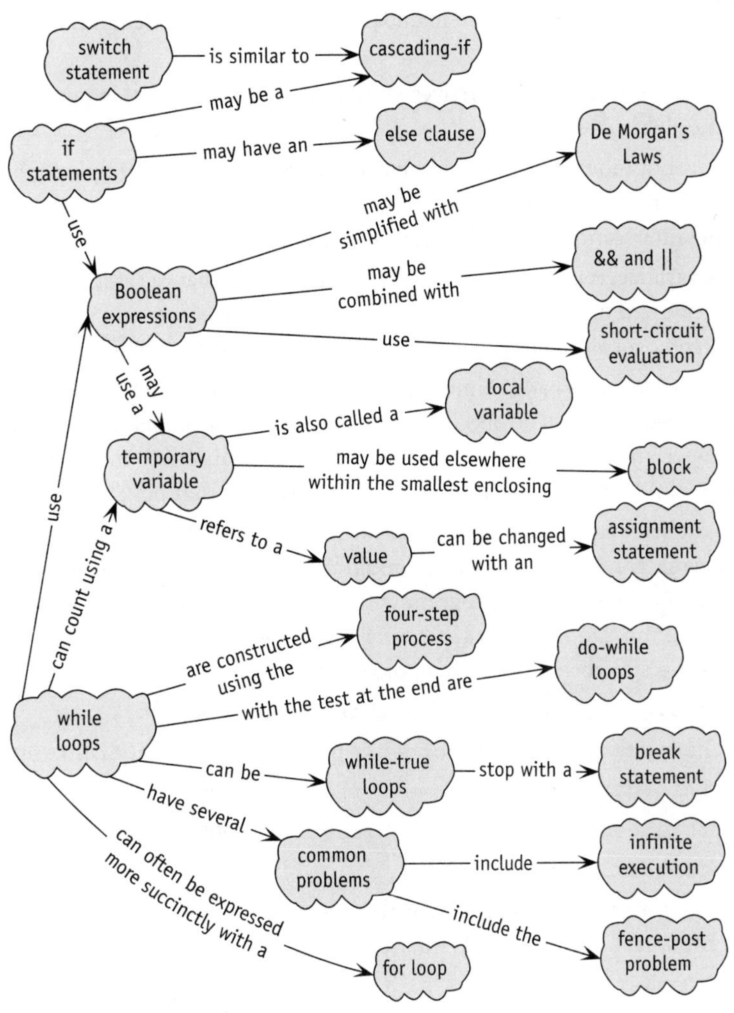

5.10 Problem Set

Written Exercises

5.1 Show the four steps used to derive a `while` loop for the following situations:

a. A robot must pick up all the things on the intersection it occupies.

b. A robot must pick up the same number of things as it has in its backpack.

c. A robot facing east must move until it is on the nearest street that is divisible by eight. (*Hint*: Use the remainder operator (`%`) discussed in the code used for Figure 5-22.)

d. A robot moves until it arrives at an intersection with a thing and a wall on the right edge.

e. A robot moves between consecutive intersections picking up one thing from each intersection, beginning with the one it is on. If there is still a thing on the intersection after it has picked one up, the robot stops.

f. A variable, `maxToPick`, holds the maximum number of things a robot should pick up. It picks up that many things from its current intersection unless there aren't enough things present. In that case, it picks up as many as it can.

5.2 The `pickThingsToWall` method, shown in Listing 5-4 and illustrated in Figure 5-6, instructs a robot to move to a wall, picking one `Thing` from each intersection that has one. Describe the changes required to make the robot pick up an entire pile of things from those intersections that have them.

5.3 For each subproblem, write a predicate that returns the same value as the given Boolean expression. That is, you could use your predicate instead of the Boolean expression in a program with no difference in the overall behavior of the program. Do not use `&&`, `||`, or `!` inside the predicate. (*Hint*: Use `if` and `if-else` statements with a temporary variable and possibly helper methods.)

a. `this.getAvenue() > 5 && this.getAvenue() < 10`

b. `this.countThingsInBackpack() > 10 && !this.frontIsClear()`

c.
```
(this.getDirection() == Direction.NORTH ||
 this.getDirection() == Direction.SOUTH) &&
 this.frontIsClear()
```

5.4 For each subproblem, draw an oval diagram for the given expression, assuming the robot is in the described situation.

a. `this.getAvenue() > 5 && this.getAvenue() < 10`
(the robot is on avenue 5)

b. `this.countThingsInBackpack() > 10 && !this.frontIsClear()`
(the robot has 12 things in its backpack and is facing a wall)

c. `(this.getDirection() == Direction.NORTH || this.getDirection() == Direction.SOUTH) && this.frontIsClear()`
(the robot is facing north and its front is clear)

Programming Exercises

5.5 Use the cascading-`if` statement to write a method named `faceNorth` that always turns a robot to face north.

5.6 A `HomingRobot`'s "home" is at 4th Street and 3rd Avenue in a city that has no obstructions, such as walls. `HomingRobot` contains a method named `goHome`, which returns the robot to (4, 3) no matter where the robot is in the city. `goHome` is written as follows:

```
public void goHome()
{ while (!this.atHome())
  { this.faceHome();
    this.move();
  }
}
```

a. Write the predicate `atHome`.

b. Use a cascading-`if` to write `faceHome`.

5.7 Consider again the situation shown in Figure 5-9 in which a robot should stop at a thing or a wall, whichever comes first.

a. Solve the problem using a `while-true` loop with one `break` statement.

b. Solve the problem using a `while-true` loop with two `break` statements.

5.8 Consider again the problem of shifting things from one intersection to another, as illustrated in Figure 5-4. Solve the problem using a `while-true` loop.

5.9 Use techniques presented in Section 5.6.2 to improve the following code fragments. If they can't be improved, explain why.

a.

```
if (this.isFacingNorth())
{ this.turnAround();
  this.pickThing();
} else
{ this.turnAround();
  this.putThing();
}
```

b.

```
if (this.getStreet() != 5)
{ this.turnleft();
} else
{ this.turnRight();

}
```

c.

```
if (this.canPickThing())
{ this.move();
  this.turnLeft();
} else
{ this.move();
  this.turnRight();
}
```

d.

```
if (count != 5 &&
      !this.frontIsClear())
{ this.turnRight();
  count = count + 1;
} else
{ this.turnLeft();
  count = count + 1;
}
```

e.

```
int n = this.thingsHere();
if (n == 0)
{ this.turnLeft();
  this.move();
} else if (n == 1)
{ this.turnRight();
  this.move();
} else if (n == 2)
{ this.turnAround();
  this.move();
} else
{ this.move();
}
```

f.

```
if (this.frontIsClear())
{ if (this.canPickThing())
  { this.pickThing();
    this.move();
  } else
  { this.move();
  }
} else
{ this.turnLeft();
  this.move();
}
```

5.10 Assume that a `Prospector` robot is on an intersection with either one or two things. Write a new method named `followTrail` that commands the robot to face north if it is on an intersection with one thing and to face south if it is on an intersection with two things. The robot must leave the same number of things on the intersection as it found originally.

5.11 Write a predicate that returns `true` if and only if a robot is completely surrounded by walls and unable to move in any direction. Of course, the predicate should not have side effects.

5.12 Implement the pile-shifting robot described in Section 5.1.2.

Programming Projects

5.13 `karel` is in a completely enclosed rectangular room that has, unfortunately, litter strewn all over it (see Figure 5-23). Create a new class of robot that can pick up the litter. The size of the room is unknown and the amount of litter on each intersection is also unknown. However, its top-left corner is always on intersection (1, 1), and `karel` always starts there, facing east. `karel` should return to its starting position when its task is complete. Make use of stepwise refinement and helper methods. Create files representing different rooms to test your program.

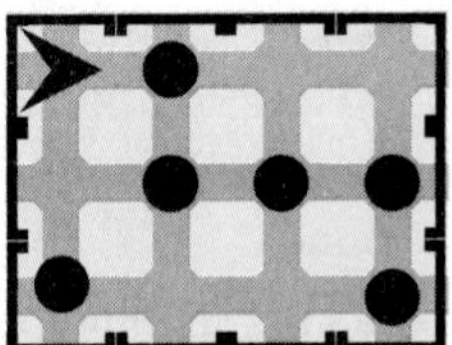

(figure 5-23)

Littered room

5.14 Write a new `Robot` class, `Houdini`, that includes a method named `escapeRoom`. It will cause the robot to search for an exit to a rectangular room—a break in the wall. Such an exit always exists and is never in a corner. The robot may start anywhere in the room, but it will not be facing the exit. When the exit is found, the robot will move through the exit and then stop. See Figure 5-24 for two of many possible initial situations.

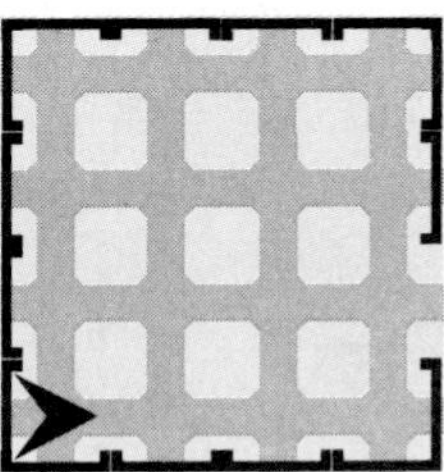

(figure 5-24)

Two possible rooms to escape

5.15 Program a robot to run a mile-long steeplechase. The steeplechase course is similar to the hurdle race (see Section 4.4.1), but here, the barriers can be one, two, or three walls high. One sample situation is shown in Figure 5-25. The robot begins the race on the lower-left corner facing east and follows the path shown. Call the class of this new robot `SteepleChaser`. It should have `Racer` as a parent class (see Section 4.4.1). Override appropriate statements of `Racer` to implement the new behavior.

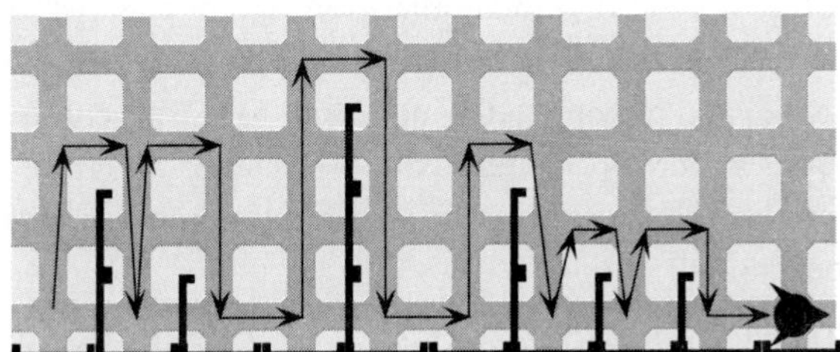

(figure 5-25)

One possible steeplechase situation

5.16 Extend the `RobotSE` class to create a `MazeWalker`. `MazeWalker` has a single public method, `followWallRight`. Assume that when it executes, the robot has a wall directly to its right. By calling this method repeatedly, the robot will eventually find its way out of a maze.

Study the online documentation for the `MazeCity` class to learn how to construct a city with a maze in it. Place your `MazeWalker` at (0, 0) facing south and a `Thing` someplace within the city for it to find. Call `followWallRight` repeatedly until the thing is found.

a. One strategy for `followWallRight` involves four different position changes, as shown in Figure 5-26. The dark robot signifies the initial position and the light robot signifies its position after `followWallRight` is invoked.

b. Another strategy for `followWallRight` is for the robot to make exactly one move each time the method is called.

c. Develop a solution that minimizes the number of "useless" turns the robot makes to determine if its right or left side is blocked.

Comments: Option (a) is easy because there are hints in Figure 5-26, but it's hard to get the robot to stop at the right place. Option (b) is hard because it has no hints, but it's easy to get the robot to stop at the right place.

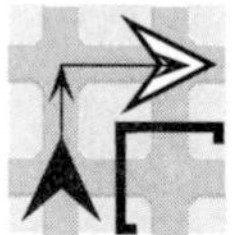

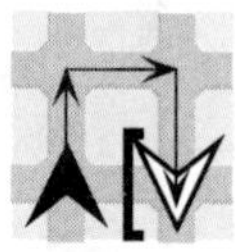

(figure 5-26)

Movements of a `MazeWalker` *robot*

5.17 Implement a class named `TrailBot` that extends `RobotSE` and contains a single public method, `followTrail`. A `TrailBot` follows a trail to a destination. Trails begin at (0, 0) with the robot facing south. Trails consist of various signs that indicate how to continue following the trail. The robot must leave the trail signs as they were found. One way to test this is to have two robots follow the same trail. The robots may or may not start with `Things` in their backpacks.

a. The trail signs consist of piles of one or more things. The number of `Things` in the pile instruct the robot how far to move forward. After moving that distance, the robot may find another trail sign (a pile of `Things`). If so, the number present instructs the robot how far to go to find the next trail sign. Finding a pile and moving a distance equal to its size continues until the robot arrives at an empty intersection (the end of the trail). There may be things between the piles that instruct the robot how far to go. If so, they should be ignored.

b. The trail signs are as follows:

- A `Wall` and one `Thing`: end of the trail
- One `Thing`: move one intersection to the right
- A `Wall`: move one intersection to the left
- Empty intersection: move one intersection forward.

c. Design your own set of trail signs and create a robot to follow it.

5.18 karel is an instance of DeliveryBot and has a unique delivery task. It starts with some number of Things in its backpack. When its deliverThings method is called, it begins to place Things on consecutive intersections. On the first intersection it places one thing. On the next intersection it places two things, and on the next intersection, three things. Each intersection receives one more thing than the previous intersection. Each intersection receives its full allotment of things or none at all. Figure 5-27 shows several pairs of sample initial and final situations.

(figure 5-27)

Pairs of initial and final situations for a DeliveryBot

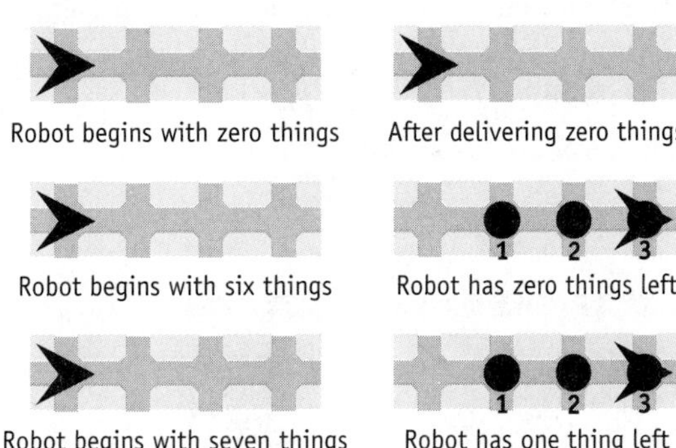

5.19 An instance of ClearTunnelBot is facing a tunnel that has at least one Thing on each intersection. When given the clearTunnel command, the robot should remove all of the Things, placing them as shown in the final situation. The robot may carry at most one Thing at a time and may not make any trips back to the tunnel once all the Things have been removed. Figure 5-28 shows two typical situations and their corresponding final situations. The robot will always start with a wall behind it, marking where the things should be placed. The distance to the tunnel and the length of the tunnel may vary.

(figure 5-28)

Tunnel-clearing situation and its corresponding final situation

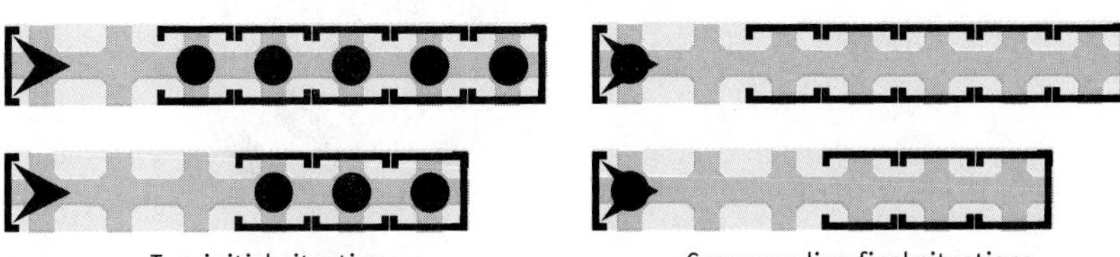

5.20 Modify the program in Listing 5-7 as follows:

a. Draw sprays of lines, starting at the top of the image and extending down, as shown in Figure 5-29a.

b. Draw lines from the upper-left corner to evenly spaced points on the bottom and right edges, as shown in Figure 5-29b. *Hint*: You only need one loop, but each iteration draws two lines.

c. Draw a line of circles that alternate in color, as shown in Figure 5-29c.

d. Draw a bull's eye, as shown in Figure 5-29d. You will need a single loop. Use the loop counter to specify the top left corner of the circles and a second variable for the size of the circles.

e. Fill the entire component with circles, as shown in Figure 5-29e.

f. Fill the entire component with circles, as shown in Figure 5-29f. Define a predicate returning `true` if the given row and column are part of the cross, and false otherwise.

g. Fill the entire component with circles, as shown in Figure 5-29g. Define a predicate returning true if the given row and column are part of the cross, and false otherwise.

h. Create a checkerboard, as shown in Figure 5-29h.

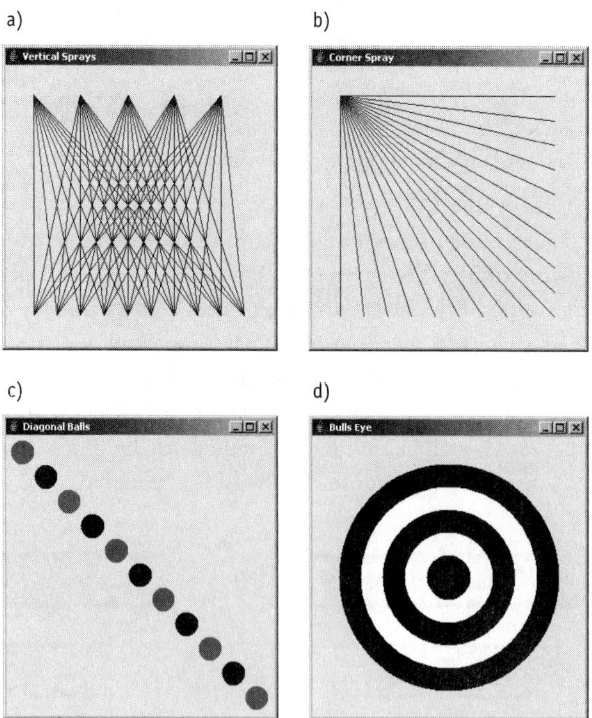

(figure 5-29)

Various fine pieces of art

(figure 5-29) *continued*

Various fine pieces of art

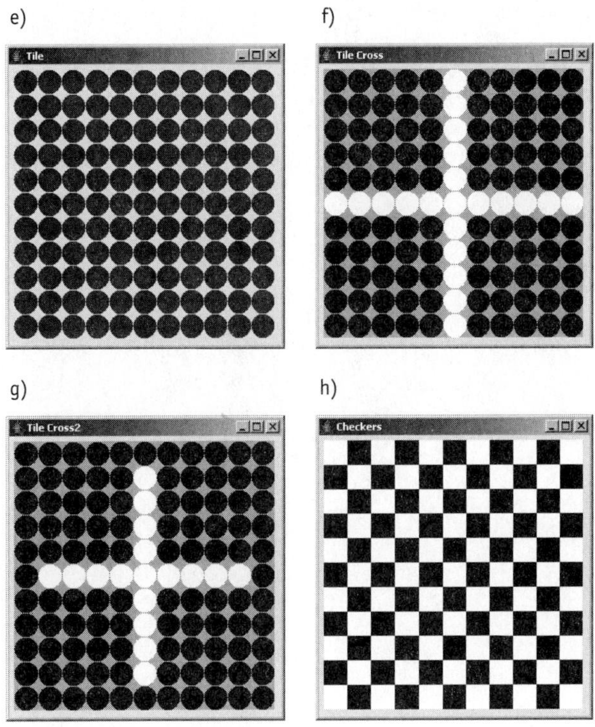

Chapter 6

Using Variables

Chapter Objectives

After studying this chapter, you should be able to:

- Add new instance variables to a simple version of the `Robot` class
- Store the results of calculations in temporary variables and use those results later in the method
- Write methods using parameter variables
- Use constants to write more understandable code
- Explain the differences between instance variables, temporary variables, parameter variables, and constants
- Extend an existing class with new instance variables

Every computer program stores and updates information. When we tell a robot to move, it updates its current street and avenue information. When a robot picks up a thing from an intersection, the intersection updates its list of things, removing the thing the robot picked up. The robot also updates its list of things to include the new thing it picked up.

A variable is a place in the computer's memory where information can be stored. When stored in a variable, the information can be changed, copied, or used in an expression. Programming languages offer several kinds of variables. The best one to use depends on factors such as how long the information must be stored and the source of the first value to store.

6.1 Instance Variables in the Robot Class

If we could look inside the Robot class, what would we find? We would certainly find methods implementing the move and turnLeft services. We would find that it extends another class that provides basic functionality on which robots depend. We would also find several varieties of **variables**. Some of these variables specify the street and avenue currently occupied by the robot. A variable is like a box that can hold one piece of information. We can ask for a copy of the information in the box anytime we like. We can also replace the information in the box with new information.

KEY IDEA

Variables store information for later use.

In this chapter, we will write a simplified version of the Robot class, named SimpleBot, to see its variables in action. It will also use a simplified version of City, named SimpleCity. By the end of this chapter, you will be able to understand all of the classes used except for three that are intimately involved with displaying the robots on the screen. By the end of Chapter 13, you will be able to understand those three as well.

You are strongly encouraged to download these classes from the software downloads section of the Robots Web site (*www.learningwithrobots.com/software/downloads.html*). You will increase your understanding if you write and run the programs as we develop the SimpleBot class.

FIND THE CODE

ch06/simpleBots/

We will spend most of our time developing the SimpleBot class, but you need a brief introduction to the SimpleCity class for everything to make sense. The SimpleCity class is a container for all the things that are "in" the city and need to be displayed by the city. In our simple version, the city only contains intersections and robots.

The intersections and robots in the city are displayed by calling their paint method. In the SimpleBot class, the paint method paints a robot; in the SimpleIntersection class, the paint method paints a street and an avenue. We will guarantee to the SimpleCity object that the objects we ask it to display have a paint method by requiring these paintable objects to extend a class named Paintable. This class is very simple: It extends Object and has a single method that does nothing—the paint method. Classes that should display themselves override this method. The Paintable class is shown, in its entirety, in Listing 6-1.

LOOKING AHEAD

In Section 7.6, we will see how the presence of particular methods can be assured with Java interfaces.

Listing 6-1: *The complete source code for the* Paintable *class*

```
import java.awt.Graphics2D;

/** Subclasses of Paintable can be displayed in the city. Each subclass should
 *   override the paint method to paint an image of itself.
 *   @author Byron Weber Becker */
public class Paintable extends Object
{
```

FIND THE CODE

ch06/simpleBots/ Paintable.java

Listing 6-1: *The complete source code for the* `Paintable` *class* (continued)

```
   public Paintable()
   { super();
   }

   /** Each subclass should override paint to paint an image of itself. */
   public void paint(Graphics2D g)
   {
   }
}
```

The city displays the intersections and the robots by calling `paint` about twenty times each second, first for the intersections and then for the robots. If a robot has moved since the last time the city was displayed, painting the intersections will erase the old robot image, and painting the robot will position it in its new location.

The following sections concentrate on the `SimpleBot` class and, in particular, how it uses variables to store and manipulate the information a robot needs. The robots in this section are simple—they only move and turn left. Eventually you will be able to increase their capabilities substantially.

KEY IDEA

Start simply. Add functionality in small increments.

Our approach is to start simply, adding functionality in small increments. First, we'll display a round "robot" on intersection (4, 2). Then we'll make it move and turn left—except that we won't be able to tell which way it faces (because it is displayed as a circle) until it moves again. We will then improve its appearance so that it shows which direction it's facing, and enhance its functionality in other ways.

6.1.1 Implementing Attributes with Instance Variables

We know from our previous experience with robots that they have attributes that specify the street and avenue they currently occupy. In Figure 1-8, reproduced in Figure 6-1, we were introduced to a `Robot` class diagram showing these attributes. The instances of the class, as shown on the right side of Figure 6-1, have specific values for these attributes. Recall that each instance has its own copies of the attributes defined by the class. Each individual robot has its own street and avenue, for example.

Robot
int street int avenue Direction direction ThingBag backpack
Robot(City aCity, int aStreet, int anAvenue, Direction aDirection) void move( ) void turnLeft( ) void pickThing( ) void putThing( )

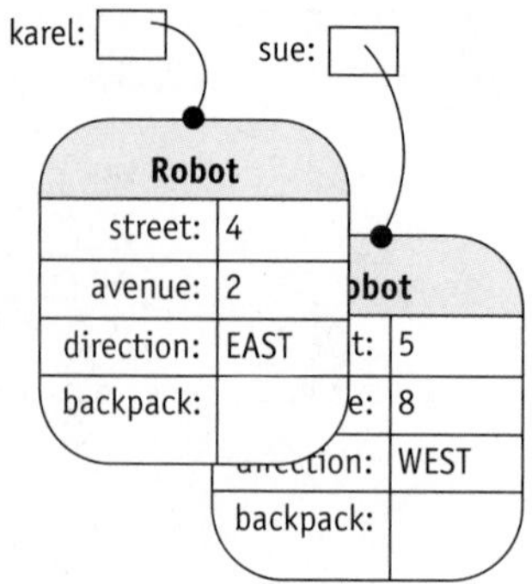

(figure 6-1)

A `Robot` *class diagram, reproduced from Chapter 1, and two object diagrams corresponding to two possible instances*

When a `Robot` object paints itself on the city, it evidently looks at the street and avenue attributes to determine where to paint the image. If the attributes hold the values `4` and `2`, respectively, then the robot image is painted on the intersection of 4th Street and 2nd Avenue.

The idea of an attribute is implemented in Java with an **instance variable**. You can imagine an instance variable as a box that has a name. Inside the box can be one, and only one, value. When the name of the box is used in the code, a copy of the value currently inside the box is retrieved and used. An instance variable also allows us to change the value inside the box.

KEY IDEA

An instance variable stores a value, such as 10 or –15, for later use.

Instance variables have the following important properties:

- Each object has its own set of instance variables. Each robot, for example, has its own street and avenue variables to remember its location.
- The scope of an instance variable extends throughout the entire class. An instance variable can be used within any method.
- The **lifetime** of an instance variable—the length of time its values are retained—is the same as the lifetime of the object to which it belongs.

KEY IDEA

Each object has its own set of instance variables.

6.1.2 Declaring Instance Variables

We create and name an instance variable—a named "box" that holds a value—with a **variable declaration**. The declaration is often combined with an assignment statement to specify the variable's initial value. Instance variables are declared inside the classes' first and last braces but outside of any methods. The beginnings of the `SimpleBot` class, including two instance variables to hold the street and avenue, are shown in Listing 6-2.

KEY IDEA

A variable declaration sets aside space in memory to store a value and associates a name with that space.

PATTERN

Instance Variable

Listing 6-2: *The beginnings of the* `SimpleBot` *class with two instance variables declared*

```
public class SimpleBot extends Paintable
{
  private int street = 4;   // Create space to store the robot's current street.
  private int avenue = 2;   // Create space to store the robot's current avenue.

  public SimpleBot()
  { super();
  }

  // An incomplete class!
}
```

These instance variable declarations have four key parts that occur in the following order:

- Declarations start with an access modifier. For reasons we will explore in Chapter 11, the keyword `private` should be used almost exclusively. Like using `private` before a helper method, this keyword identifies this part of the class as "for internal use only."
- Declarations specify the type of values stored. The `int` says that these "boxes" hold integers—values such as 1, 33, or -15. Later, we'll study other possibilities, such as `double` (values such as 3.14159) and `String` (values such as `"I love Java"`).
- Declarations name the variable. In these examples, the names are `street` and `avenue`. Instance variables are generally named like methods, using one or more descriptive words, with the first letter of the entire name being lowercase and the first letter of subsequent words being uppercase. Examples include `avenue`, `direction`, and `nextLocation`.
- Declarations may include an initial value, placed after an equal sign. In these examples, `street` and `avenue` are given initial values of `4` and `2`, respectively. If the initial value is not explicitly assigned, Java will provide a default initial value appropriate to the type. The default for integers is `0` and for `boolean` variables is `false`. However, your code is more understandable if you explicitly initialize your variables.

These declarations are very similar to declaring temporary variables, as studied in Section 5.2, with two exceptions. First, instance variable declarations always occur outside of methods, whereas temporary variable declarations always occur inside of methods. Second, instance variable declarations should have an access modifier, whereas temporary variables never do.

6.1.3 Accessing Instance Variables

Two major tasks remain in writing the `SimpleBot` class. First, we need to display the robot within the city. To do this, we will access the values stored in the instance variables. Second, we need to make the robot move. We will do this by updating the values stored in the instance variables. Then, when the robot is painted again, it will appear at a different place in the city.

As we learned in the introduction to Section 6.1, objects to be displayed by a city must extend `Paintable` and override the `paint` method. Our first version of `paint` displays the robot as a black circle on the intersection of 4th Street and 2nd Avenue. Figure 6-2 shows the robot on a background of streets and avenues with annotations for drawing it. We will assume that each intersection is 50 pixels square. Therefore, 4th Street starts at pixel 200 (4 × 50) and 2nd Avenue starts at pixel 100 (2 × 50). The following code paints the robot and should be inserted between lines 10 and 11 of Listing 6-2.

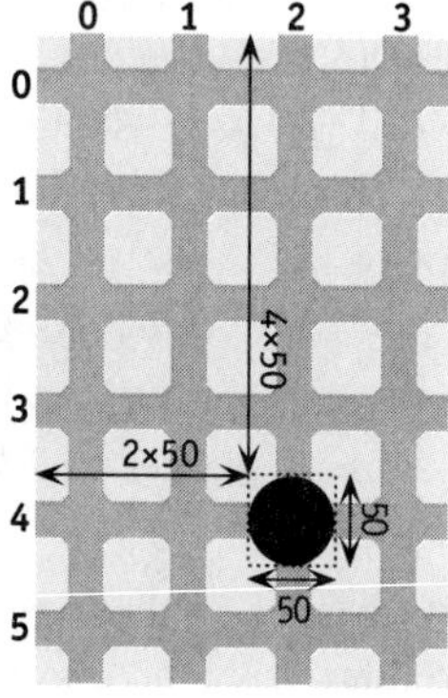

(figure 6-2)

Simple robot and its location

```
1 public void paint(Graphics2D g)
2 { g.setColor(Color.BLACK);
3   g.fillOval(100, 200, 50, 50);
4 }
```

This method takes a parameter, `g`, which is an object used to paint on the screen. Line 2 says to use the color black in subsequent painting operations. Line 3 says to paint a solid oval. Recall that the first argument to `fillOval` is the *x* (horizontal) coordinate, the second argument is the *y* (vertical) coordinate, and the last two arguments are the height and width, respectively.

LOOKING AHEAD

We will discuss parameters in depth in Section 6.2.2.

There is no need for us to perform the multiplications to calculate the coordinates of the upper-left corner. Computers are very good at multiplication, and we should let them do that for us. Line 3 may be replaced by the following:

```
3 g.fillOval(2 * 50, 4 * 50, 50, 50);
```

Java uses `*` to indicate multiplication.

However, we don't *always* want to draw the robot at intersection (4, 2). We want to access the street and avenue attributes—implemented as instance variables—to determine where the robot is drawn. To do so, we use the names of the instance variables in place of the 4 and 2 in the new lines of code. That is, the following `paint` method will display the robot at the street and avenue specified in the instance variables.

PATTERN

Instance Variable

```
1 public void paint(Graphics2D g)
2 { g.setColor(Color.BLACK);
3   g.fillOval(this.avenue * 50, this.street * 50, 50, 50);
4 }
```

We will use the keyword `this` to access the instance variables in our code. Using `this` to access an instance variable is like using `this` to access a helper method: It reinforces that the variable belongs to *this* object, the one that contains the currently executing code.[1]

Line 3 of the preceding code can be better understood with the help of an evaluation diagram, like the one we used in Section 5.4. Recall that we begin by drawing ovals around literals (like `50`) and variables (like `this.avenue`), and writing their type above and their value below the ovals. We then repeatedly circle method calls and operators, together with their arguments and operands, in order of their precedence. This process is shown in Figure 6-3, where we assume that the robot is on (4, 2).

Notice that the arguments to `fillOval` are circled before `fillOval` is circled. This means that the arguments are evaluated before the method is called. Also note that the type of the oval around `fillOval` is `void` because `fillOval` has a return type of `void`. It doesn't return a value to place below the oval. Instead, the side effect of the method is written.

[1] The keyword `this` is actually optional much of the time. Students are strongly encouraged to use it, however, to reinforce that they are accessing an instance variable that belongs to a particular object. There is also the practical reason that many modern programming environments display a list of instance variables and methods when "this." is typed, reducing the burden on the programmer's memory and eliminating many spelling mistakes.

(figure 6-3)

Evaluation diagram for line 3 in `SimpleBot`'s `paint` method, assuming the robot is on intersection (4, 2)

```
          int           int        int          int   int   int
g.fillOval( this.avenue * 50 , this.street * 50 , 50 , 50 ) ;
          2             50         4            50    50    50
```

After the first step in drawing an evaluation diagram

```
              int                    int
          int           int        int          int   int   int
g.fillOval( this.avenue * 50 , this.street * 50 , 50 , 50 ) ;
          2             50         4            50    50    50
              100                    200
```

After two iterations of step two in drawing an evaluation diagram

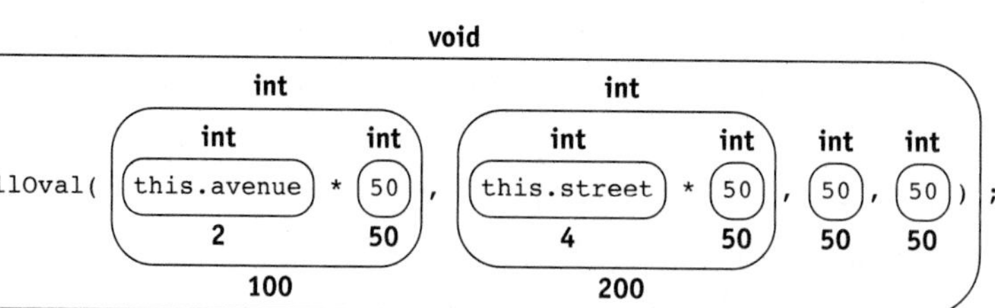

(the oval is drawn)

After the last iteration of step two in drawing an evaluation diagram

The code for the `paint` method needs one last detail: The classes `Graphics2D` and `Color` must be imported before we can use them in lines 1 and 2, respectively. To do so, add the following two lines at the beginning of the file:

```
import java.awt.Graphics2D;
import java.awt.Color;
```

6.1.4 Modifying Instance Variables

Our robot needs a `move` method. When it is invoked, the robot should move to another intersection. From previous experience, we know that invoking `move` changed a robot's attributes. Because attributes are implemented with instance variables, we now know that `move` must change either `street` or `avenue` by 1, depending on the direction.

LOOKING BACK

Take a look at the state change diagram in Figure 1-12 to better understand the effect of `move` on the avenue and street attributes.

We already discussed incrementing and decrementing parameters and temporary variables in Chapters 4 and 5. Changing an instance variable by 1 is similar and is shown in the following partially implemented `move` method:

```
// Move the robot one intersection east, assuming it is facing east and nothing blocks it.
public void move()
{ this.avenue = this.avenue + 1;      // incomplete
}
```

PATTERN

Instance Variable

Because we are accessing an instance variable, a variable that belongs to an object, we use `this.` before the variable name.

Recall that an assignment statement works in two steps. First, it calculates the value of the expression to the right of the equal sign. Second, it forces the variable on the left of the equal sign to store whatever value was calculated. The variable continues to store that value until it is changed with another assignment statement. The assignment statements used with parameter and temporary variables in Chapters 4 and 5 behaved the same way.

How does this process move the robot? The entire city is repainted about 20 times per second with a loop such as the following:

```
while (true)
{ paint everything in layer 0 (the intersections)
  paint everything in layer 1 (the things)
  paint everything in layer 2 (the robots)
}
```

When `move` is called, the entire city is repainted within about 50 milliseconds. Repainting the intersections has the effect of erasing the robot's old image at its old location. Shortly thereafter, the robot's `paint` method is called. It paints the robot's image in its new location, as determined by the current values of `street` and `avenue`. The effect is that the robot appears to move on the screen.

But there is a problem. Executing the `move` method takes far less than 50 milliseconds. If several consecutive `move` instructions are executed, we won't see most of them because they occur in the time between repainting the screen. To solve this problem, we need to ensure that `move` takes at least 50 milliseconds to execute. This is done by instructing the `move` method to sleep, or do nothing, for a while. The `becker` library contains a method to sleep for a specified number of milliseconds. To use it, import `becker.util.Utilities` and add `Utilities.sleep(400)` to the `move` method. The robot will then stop for 0.400 seconds each time it moves.

The code for the `SimpleBot` class, as developed so far, is shown in Listing 6-3. Robots instantiated from this class will always start out on intersection (4, 2) and can only travel east. We will remove these restrictions soon.

FIND THE CODE

ch06/simpleBots/SimpleBot.java

Listing 6-3: *The `SimpleBot` class, as developed so far*

```
import java.awt.Graphics2D;
import java.awt.Color;
import becker.util.Utilities;

```

Listing 6-3: *The* `SimpleBot` *class, as developed so far* (continued)

```
/** A first try at the SimpleBot class. These robots are always constructed on street 4,
 *  avenue 2. There is no way to tell which way they are facing and they can only move east.
 *
 *  @author Byron Weber Becker */
public class SimpleBot extends Paintable
{
  private int street = 4;
  private int avenue = 2;

  /** Construct a new Robot at (4, 2). */
  public SimpleBot()
  { super();
  }

  /** Paint the robot at its current location. */
  public void paint(Graphics2D g)
  { g.setColor(Color.BLACK);
    g.fillOval(this.avenue * 50, this.street * 50, 50, 50);
  }

  /** Move the robot one intersection east. */
  public void move()
  { this.avenue = this.avenue + 1;
    Utilities.sleep(400);
  }

  /** Turn the robot 90 degrees to the left. */
  public void turnLeft()
  {
  }
}
```

6.1.5 Testing the `SimpleBot` Class

The `main` method to test this class is slightly different from the ones we've written in previous chapters, in which we passed the city to the robot's constructor. The constructor then added the robot to the city. The constructor in Listing 6-3 isn't that sophisticated (yet). Therefore, we must add the robot to the city in the `main` method, specifying that it appears in layer 2 so that it is painted after the intersections (layer 0) and things (layer 1). A second change is to explicitly wait for the user to press the Start button before moving the robots. These two details are at lines 11-14 of Listing 6-4.

The `SimpleBot` classes we are discussing are *not* part of the `becker` library. Therefore, to compile the program, you will not be importing classes from the library. Instead, you need to have the source code for `SimpleBot`, `SimpleCity`, and several others in the same directory as the `TestSimpleBot` class shown in Listing 6-4. Recall that all of this source code is available from the Robots Web site (*www.learningwithrobots.com/software/downloads.html*). However, you will need to implement much of the code for the `SimpleBot` class yourself.

FIND THE CODE

ch06/simpleBots/Main.java

Listing 6-4: *A* `main` *method to test the* `SimpleBot` *class*

```
/** A main method to test the SimpleBot and related classes.
 *
 * @author Byron Weber Becker */
public class Main extends Object
{
   public static void main(String[] args)
   { SimpleCity newYork = new SimpleCity();
     SimpleBot karel = new SimpleBot();
     SimpleBot sue = new SimpleBot();

     newYork.add(karel, 2);
     newYork.add(sue, 2);

     newYork.waitForStart();      // Wait for the user to press the Start button.

     for(int i=0; i<4; i = i+1)
     { karel.move();
       karel.move();
       karel.turnLeft();
     }

     sue.move();
   }
}
```

6.1.6 Adding Another Instance Variable: `direction`

LOOKING AHEAD

In Section 7.4, we will look at a detailed example that has nothing to do with robots.

So far we've seen how to declare, initialize, access, and modify instance variables to implement the street and avenue attributes for a robot. Keep in mind that instance variables are also used to implement classes that have nothing to do with robots: bank accounts, employees, properties for a Monopoly game, and so on.

Right now, however, let's implement another attribute of robots: direction. When we're done, the robots will be able to turn left and move in the direction they are facing.

Representing Directions

Our basic plan is to use a new instance variable, `direction`, to store the direction the robot is facing. `direction` will be an integer. When it has a value of 0, the robot is facing east; 1 means the robot is facing south, 2 is west, and 3 is north. Turning left is as easy as subtracting 1 from `direction`—unless the robot is facing east (0). Then we need to wrap around and set `direction` to north (3). As with the `move` method, forcing the robot to sleep after turning allows us to see what has happened.

Listing 6-5 shows the addition of the `direction` instance variable and the `turnLeft` method in a skeleton of the `SimpleBot` class.

Listing 6-5: *Changes to the `SimpleBot` class to add the `turnLeft` service*

```
public class SimpleBot extends Paintable
{ ...
  private int direction = 0;    // Begin facing east.
  ...

  /** Turn the robot left 1/4 turn. */
  public void turnLeft()
  { if (direction == 0)                  // If facing east...
    { this.direction = 3;                // face north.
    } else
    { this.direction = this.direction - 1;
    }
    Utilities.sleep(400);
  }
}
```

Using the `final` Keyword with Instance Variables

Remembering that `0` means east and `3` means north makes `turnLeft` difficult to understand. Listing 6-5 compensates with comments, but we can do better. One approach is to declare four new instance variables, as follows:

```
private int east = 0;
private int south = 1;
private int west = 2;
private int north = 3;
```

Now we can rewrite lines 8 and 9 as follows:

```
8 { if (direction == this.east)
9   { this.direction = this.north;
```

However, these "variables" seem different from instance variables such as avenue and direction because they should not change while the program executes. We should always use 0 to mean east, and it would be a programming error if east ever had a different value.

KEY IDEA

Use the final keyword when a variable should never be assigned a new value.

Java uses the keyword final to indicate that the first value a variable receives should also be the final value it ever receives. If we try to change the variable's value, Java will issue a compile-time error. Such variables are often called **constants**. It is traditional to use all uppercase characters to name constants to emphasize that they are unchanging, as follows:

```
private final int EAST = 0;
```

PATTERN

Named Constant

Another useful constant would be INTERSECTION_SIZE, to be used in the paint method in place of 50. Notice the underscore character separating the individual words that make up the name.

In addition to making the code easier to read, constants are useful because they provide one place to change when assumptions change. For example, we assumed that intersections are 50 pixels square. If we ever need to display larger cities, we may want to change it to 40 pixels. Finding and changing one constant is much easier than finding and changing every place the value 50 is used in the program.

Using the static Keyword with final Instance Variables

LOOKING AHEAD

Using static with non-final instance variables is discussed in Section 7.5.1.

A second keyword, static, is often used with final instance variables. It allows programmers to access the variable using the class name rather than an object reference. For example, suppose EAST were declared as follows:

```
public static final int EAST = 0;
```

Programmers could then use it like this:

```
if (this.direction == SimpleBot.EAST)
```

PATTERN

Named Constant

This may not seem like much of an improvement, but if the variable is public, then it can be used from any class without using an object. We have, in fact, done this already in the main method of graphics programs when we use JFrame.EXIT_ON_CLOSE to set the frame's default close operation.

Sometimes constants are used in many different classes. In such cases, it can make sense to have a class named something like Constants that contains nothing but public constants.

Finishing the move Method

Now that we can easily represent directions using `final` instance variables and can change a robot's direction with the `turnLeft` method, we must reimplement the `move` method so that it actually moves in the correct direction.

Each time the robot moves, we will adjust both the street and the avenue by the values shown in Table 6-1.

Direction	Change street by	Change avenue by
EAST	0	1
WEST	0	-1
NORTH	-1	0
SOUTH	1	0

(table 6-1)

Adjustments to `street` *and* `avenue` *when moving in each direction*

This is a perfect job for two helper methods, `strOffset` and `aveOffset`. They use a cascading-`if` statement to set a temporary variable to the appropriate offset, based on testing the value stored in the `direction` instance variable. They then return that value using a `return` statement, just like the queries written in Section 5.2.4.

The new `direction` instance variable, the new `turnLeft` method, the modified `move` method, and the two helper methods are all shown in Listing 6-6. The class assumes that appropriate constants have been declared in a class named `Constants`. The `turnLeft` method uses two additional constants to clarify why they constitute a special case. They are declared in `Constants` as follows:

```
public static final int FIRST_DIR = EAST;
public static final int LAST_DIR = NORTH;
```

6.1.7 Providing Accessor Methods

Methods that provide access to private instance variables are called **accessor methods**. An accessor method is a query that answers the question "What value does attribute *X* currently hold?" That is, it makes the value stored in an instance variable accessible to code outside of the class.

You can use the following pattern to write an accessor method:

```
public «typeReturned» get«Name»()
{ return this.«instanceVariable»;
}
```

PATTERN

Accessor Method

«*typeReturned*» specifies what kind of value the method returns. It should be the same type as the instance variable itself. The variables `avenue`, `street`, and `direction` are all integers, so their accessor methods will have `int` as a return type.

«*Name*» is usually the name of the instance variable. It should be a name that is meaningful to users of the class.

Finally, «*instanceVariable*» is the name of the appropriate instance variable to access.

Three examples of accessor methods, one each for `street`, `avenue`, and `direction`, are shown in Listing 6-6.

Listing 6-6: *A `SimpleBot` class that includes the ability to turn left*

```
import java.awt.Graphics2D;
import java.awt.Color;
import becker.util.Utilities;


/** A second try at the SimpleBot class. These robots are always constructed at (4, 2) facing
 *  east. Robots can move forward and turn left, although the user cannot determine which
 *  way the robot is facing until it moves.
 *
 *  @author Byron Weber Becker */
public class SimpleBot extends Paintable
{
  private int street = 4;
  private int avenue = 2;
  private int direction = 0;

  /** Construct a new robot at (4, 2) facing east. */
  public SimpleBot()
  { super();
  }

  /** Paint the robot at its current location. */
  public void paint(Graphics2D g)
  { g.setColor(Color.BLACK);
    g.fillOval(this.avenue * Constants.INTERSECTION_SIZE,
               this.street * Constants.INTERSECTION_SIZE,
               Constants.INTERSECTION_SIZE,
               Constants.INTERSECTION_SIZE);
  }

```

Listing 6-6: *A* `SimpleBot` *class that includes the ability to turn left* (continued)

```
/** Move the robot forward 1 intersection. */
public void move()
{ this.street = this.street + this.strOffset();
  this.avenue = this.avenue + this.aveOffset();
  Utilities.sleep(400);
}

/** Turn the robot left 1/4 turn. */
public void turnLeft()
{ if (direction == Constants.FIRST_DIR)
  { this.direction = Constants.LAST_DIR;
  } else
  { this.direction = this.direction - 1;
  }
  Utilities.sleep(400);
}

/** Get this robot's street.
 * @return The street this robot is currently on. */
public int getStreet()
{ return this.street;
}

/** Get this robot's avenue.
 * @return The avenue this robot is currently on. */
public int getAvenue()
{ return this.avenue;
}

/** Get this robot's direction.
 * @return The direction this robot is facing. */
public int getDirection()
{ return this.direction;
}

/** Calculate how far the robot should move along the avenue.
 * @return {-1, 0, or 1} */
private int aveOffset()
{ int offset = 0;
  if (this.direction == Constants.EAST)
  { offset = 1;
  } else if (this.direction == Constants.WEST)
  { offset = -1;
```

Listing 6-6: *A `SimpleBot` class that includes the ability to turn left* (continued)

```
      }
      return offset;
   }

   /** Calculate how far the robot should move along the street.
    * @return {-1, 0, or 1} */
   private int strOffset()
   { int offset = 0;
      if (this.direction == Constants.NORTH)
      { offset = -1;
      } else if (this.direction == Constants.SOUTH)
      { offset = 1;
      }
      return offset;
   }
}
```

6.1.8 Instance Variables versus Parameter and Temporary Variables

Like parameter and temporary variables, instance variables store a value. They are also different in important ways. We will have more to say about these similarities and differences in Section 6.5, but for now, remember the following:

- Instance variables are declared inside a class but outside of all methods. Parameter and temporary variables are declared inside a method.
- Instance variables have a larger scope. They may be used within any of the methods in the class. Parameter and temporary variables can be used only within the method in which they are declared.
- Instance variables have a longer lifetime. They retain their value until changed by an assignment statement or until the object is no longer in use. Parameter and temporary variables disappear when their method finishes executing and are reinitialized each time the method executes again.

6.2 Temporary and Parameter Variables

Temporary and parameter variables were introduced in Chapters 4 and 5, respectively. In this section, they are used extensively to improve the `SimpleBot`. We will also use them with more complex expressions and apply the `final` keyword to them.

6.2.1 Reviewing Temporary Variables

Right now our robots are displayed with a black oval that covers the entire intersection. We can't tell which direction the robot is facing unless it moves. In this section, we will upgrade our robot to correct these problems. Our new, improved robot will appear as shown in Figure 6-4.

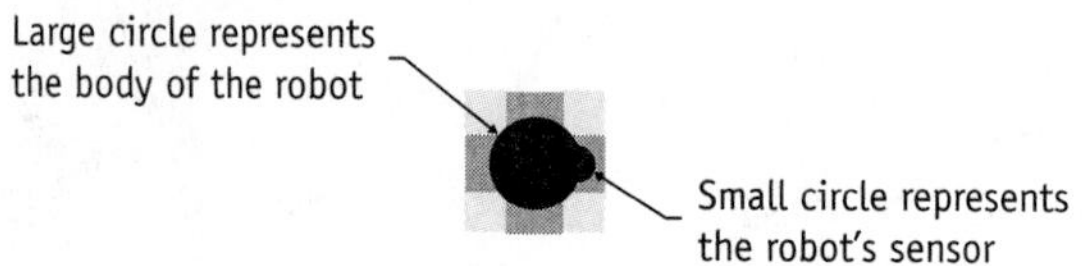

(figure 6-4)

Robot showing its direction

The large circle, representing the body of the robot, is centered on the middle of the intersection and has a radius of 15 pixels. The smaller circle, representing the robot's sensor, is centered on the perimeter of the larger circle with a radius of 6 pixels.

Because the size of the circle no longer matches the size of the intersection, more work will be required to paint the robot. Figure 6-5 shows relevant values that we will need to calculate. They depend heavily on the center of the robot's body and the center of the sensor. We will find it useful to calculate and store these values in temporary variables.

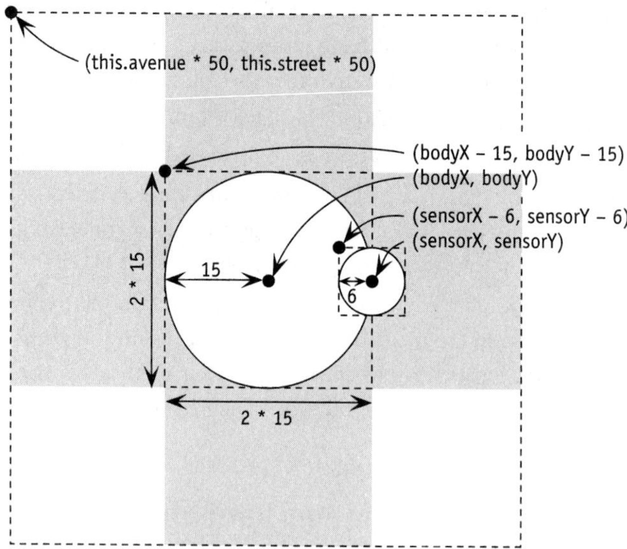

(figure 6-5)

Drawing a circle, given its center and radius

LOOKING BACK

Temporary variables were introduced in Section 5.2.

LOOKING BACK

Scope and block were defined in Section 5.2.6.

Before we proceed, let's recall what we know about temporary variables:

- They are declared inside a method.
- Declarations have a type, a name, and usually an initial value. For example, `int numThingsHere = 0`. Declarations do not include an access modifier.
- The value stored by the variable is accessed with just the variable's name; it is not prefixed with `this`.
- The scope of a temporary variable—the region in which it can be used—extends from its point of declaration to the end of the smallest enclosing block.
- Each time the variable's block is executed, the variable is created and reinitialized; each time execution exits the block, the variable disappears.

Listing 6-7 provides a skeleton for the `paint` method. It declares four temporary variables to store the center coordinates of the body and the sensor in lines 5-8. Their initialization is shown in pseudocode.

Listing 6-7: *A skeleton of the* `paint` *method*

```
1  /** Paint the robot at its current location. */
2  public void paint(Graphics2D g)
3  { g.setColor(Color.BLACK);
4
5     int bodyX = x coordinate of robot body's center
6     int bodyY = y coordinate of robot body's center
7     int sensorX = x coordinate of robot sensor's center
8     int sensorY = y coordinate of robot sensor's center
9
10    // Draw the robot's body.
11    g.fillOval(bodyX - 15, bodyY - 15, 2 * 15, 2 * 15);
12
13    // Draw the robot's sensor.
14    g.fillOval(sensorX - 5, sensorY - 5, 2 * 6, 2 * 6);
15 }
```

The values in these four variables are used in lines 11 and 14 to paint the two circles representing the robot's body and sensor. Recall that `fillOval`'s first two arguments represent the upper-left corner of the smallest rectangle that will include the oval, shown with dotted lines in Figure 6-5. The expression `bodyX - 15` in line 11 uses the center of the circle to calculate the left edge of the body's enclosing rectangle. `bodyY - 15` calculates the top edge of the body's enclosing rectangle.

Calculating the Body's Center

The center of the robot's body is the same as the center of the intersection. To calculate it, we can calculate the intersection's upper-left corner and then add one half of the intersection's width and height. Recall that the intersection's size is stored in `Constants.INTERSECTION_SIZE`. This name is unwieldy to use repeatedly in a method, so we first assign it to a temporary variable with a shorter name.

```
int iSize = Constants.INTERSECTION_SIZE;
int bodyX = this.avenue * iSize + iSize / 2;
int bodyY = this.street * iSize + iSize / 2;
```

We can increase our confidence that these calculations are correct by producing an evaluation diagram with some sample values for the robot's location and intersection size. For example, see Figure 6-6.

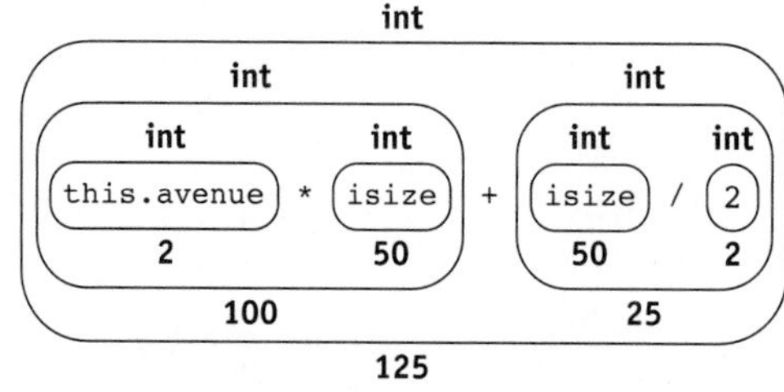

(figure 6-6)

Evaluation diagram for `bodyX` *when the robot is at (4, 2) on intersections of size 50*

One question that arises is what happens when two numbers do not divide evenly. For example, what would the preceding expression produce if the intersection size was 51 instead of 50? One might expect an answer of 125.5 because 51/2 is 25.5—but that answer is wrong.

Java performs **integer division** when both operands are integers. Integer division is like the long division you learned in grade school, but with the remainder thrown away. That is, 51 divided by 2 is 25 with a remainder of 1. The remainder is thrown away, and the answer is 25. Java has a second kind of division that preserves the decimal portion. We will study it in Section 7.2.2.

KEY IDEA

Dividing two integers results in an integer. The decimal portion, if any, is lost.

If the divisor (the second number) happens to be 0, an exception will be thrown to indicate that the division can't be performed.

A related operator is `%`, the **remainder operator**. It returns the remainder of the long division. For example, `51 % 2` returns `1` because 51 divided by 2 is 25 with a remainder of 1. If the first operand happens to be negative, the answer will be negative as well.

KEY IDEA

`n % d` *gives the remainder of dividing* `n` *by* `d`.

The remainder operator has four common uses in programming:

- The remainder operator can be used to determine if a number is even or odd, as in the following example:

```
if (n % 2 == 0)
{ // n is even...
```

- The remainder operator can be used to process every n^{th} item. For example, consider a robot traveling east until it finds a wall. The following code will place a `Thing` on every 5th intersection.

```
while (karel.frontIsClear())
{ if (this.getAvenue() % 5 == 0)
  { this.putThing();
  }
}
```

- The remainder operator can be used together with the / operator to find the individual digits of a number. For example, `123 % 10` gives the right-most digit, `3`. Dividing by 10 gives the number without the right-most digit. For example, `123 / 10` gives `12`. Taking the remainder of this number gives the next digit, `2`, and so on.
- The remainder operator can be used to perform "wrap around" or "clock" arithmetic. We've already seen an example of this kind of arithmetic when we implemented `turnLeft`. We subtracted one from `direction`, unless the direction was `EAST` (`0`); then we wrapped around back to `NORTH` (`3`). The more common case is incrementing by one until an upper limit is reached, then starting over at 0. This calculation can be implemented as follows:

```
var = (var + 1) % upperLimit;
```

Calculating the Sensor's Center

We now turn to calculating the sensor's center, as required by lines 7 and 8 in Listing 6-7. Once again, we turn to Figure 6-5 for guidance. It appears that `sensorY` is the same as `bodyY` and that `sensorX` is the same as `bodyX + 15`, the body's radius.

Unfortunately, it isn't that simple. These calculations only work if the robot is facing east. Figure 6-7 shows the robot in all four positions with the associated calculations.

(figure 6-7)

Drawing the robot in each of the four directions

```
sensorX = bodyX+15
sensorY = bodyY
```

```
sensorX = bodyX-15
sensorY = bodyY
```

```
sensorX = bodyX
sensorY = bodyY-15
```

```
sensorX = bodyX
sensorY = bodyY+15
```

We could solve this problem with a cascading-if statement, but there is an easier way. This situation is similar to moving the robot. There, we wanted to add -1, 0, or 1 to the street or avenue, depending on the direction the robot is facing. Here we want to add -15, 0, or 15. For the move method, we used two helper methods—strOffset and aveOffset. For this problem, we just need to multiply their results by 15.

Lines 7 and 8 in Listing 6-7 can be replaced by the following two lines:

```
int sensorX = bodyX + this.aveOffset() * 15;
int sensorY = bodyY + this.strOffset() * 15;
```

Using the final Keyword with Temporary Variables

The final keyword can be used with any kind of variable, not just instance variables. It always means that the first value assigned to the variable should also be the final value assigned.

In the paint method, we assigned the constant INTERSECTION_SIZE to a temporary variable, iSize, for convenience. However, it would be a bug if iSize were mistakenly changed. For this reason, using final would be an excellent idea, as follows:

```
final int iSize = Constants.INTERSECTION_SIZE;
```

It's also worth noting that none of the temporary variables change after they are initialized. (They may, however, have a different value the next time the paint method is called and the variables are initialized again.) It wouldn't hurt to make the fact that they don't change while paint is executing explicit by using final for all of the temporary variables.

Delaying Initialization

It is possible to separate a temporary variable's declaration and initialization. This is useful, for example, if we use a cascading-if statement to calculate sensorX, as follows:

```
int sensorX;
if (this.direction == Constants.EAST)
{ sensorX = bodyX + 15;
} else if (this.direction == Constants.NORTH)
{ sensorX = bodyX;
...
```

When initialization is delayed, the temporary variable holds an unknown value between the time it is declared and when it is initialized. It would be an error to try to use it. Fortunately, the Java compiler actively tries to prevent this error. For example,

KEY IDEA

An uninitialized temporary variable holds an unknown value.

the following program fragment produces an error message saying "variable bodyX may not have been initialized."

```
int bodyX;
int sensorX = bodyX + 15;
```

Occasionally, the compiler will issue this error even though the variable is initialized in an `if` statement. In that case, simply initialize the variable when it is declared even though you know it will have a new value assigned before it is used.

Temporary Variable Summary

This `paint` method could have been written without temporary variables (see Listing 6-8). However, temporary variables allow us to break the calculation into smaller pieces. The pieces can be individually named and documented, making them easier to understand than one large calculation.

Another use of temporary variables is to reuse a calculation in several places in the same method. By performing the calculation once and storing the result, we save time and effort in programming and debugging.

Listing 6-8: *The `paint` method without temporary variables*

```
/** Paint the robot at its current location. */
public void paint(Graphics2D g)
{ g.setColor(Color.BLACK);

   // Draw the robot's body.
   g.fillOval(this.avenue * 50 + 50/2 - 15,
              this.street * 50 + 50/2 - 15,
              2*15, 2*15);

   // Draw the robot's sensor.
   g.fillOval(
         this.avenue * 50 + 50/2 + this.aveOffset() * 15 - 5,
         this.street * 50 + 50/2 + this.strOffset() * 15 - 5,
         2*5, 2*5);
}
```

KEY IDEA

Use temporary variables when you can; instance variables only if you must.

Temporary variables and instance variables are similar in that they both store a value that can be used later. Their major differences are in how long the value is stored and in where the value can be used. Because instance variables have a longer lifetime and a larger scope, they can often be used in place of temporary variables. This can lead to mistakes. The shorter lifetimes of temporary variables and their much smaller scope (a method rather than the entire class) result in a much smaller opportunity for misuse. Instance variables are vitally important in object-oriented programming, but should only be used when other kinds of variables cannot be used.

6.2.2 Reviewing Parameter Variables

We were introduced to parameter variables in Section 4.6, where we wrote a method that took an argument specifying how far the robot should move. In this section, we will show how parameter variables are closely related to temporary variables, explore using parameters with constructors, and discuss overloading.

Parameter Variables versus Temporary Variables

Consider the following modification of the `move` method in the `SimpleBot` class. It causes the robot to move two intersections in the direction it is currently facing.

```
1 public void moveFar()
2 { int howFar = 2;
3   this.street = this.street + this.strOffset() * howFar;
4   this.avenue = this.avenue + this.aveOffset() * howFar;
5   Utilities.sleep(400);
6 }
```

A method to move the robot three intersections can be developed by copying `moveFar` to a new method, `moveReallyFar`, and changing the `2` in line 2 to `3`. Another method, `moveReallyReallyFar`, could be identical to `moveFar` except for setting `howFar` to `4`.

The methods are all identical except for that one number. This seems silly, for a number of reasons:

- What if we discover a bug in the first one—for example, if line 3 used `aveOffset()` instead of `strOffset()`? Chances are good that the same bug has been cut and pasted into the other methods.
- What if we want to move 7 intersections? We must define a new method, with a new name—and that still wouldn't help us move 25 intersections in another part of the program.
- What if we want to calculate the distance to move, storing it in a variable? We need to resort to a messy cascading-`if` or `switch` statement to choose the specific method to execute.

Instead of initializing `howFar` when we *write* the method, we want to initialize it when we *call* the method. Using parameter variables, we can accomplish this goal. Parameters allow us to replace `karel.moveFar()` with `karel.move(2)` and to replace `karel.moveReallyReallyFar()` with `karel.move(4)`. The argument—the number in the parentheses—specifies how far we want the robot to move. If we want the robot to move five intersections, we can write `karel.move(5)`.

KEY IDEA

The argument, provided when the method is called, is used to initialize the parameter variable.

The argument is used to initialize a parameter variable defined inside the `move` method. The parameter variable is similar to a temporary variable except that it is declared differently and is initialized by the argument.

Consider the temporary variable `howFar` from the `moveFar` method:

```
int howFar = 2;
```

To transform it into a parameter, think of its two distinct parts: the declaration and the initialization. The declaration, `int howFar`, stays inside the method, where it becomes the parameter variable. The value it is initialized with, `2`, becomes the argument. It is provided when the method is called. (The equal sign is discarded in the process.)

The left side of Figure 6-8 shows relevant portions of a program that uses `moveFar`. On the top is a `main` method that calls `moveFar`, and on the bottom is the definition of `moveFar`. The right side of the figure shows the program after transforming it to use a parameter variable.

(figure 6-8)

Transforming a temporary variable into a parameter variable

```
public class TestRobot...          public class TestRobot...
{ public static void               { public static void
      main(String[] args)                main(String[] args)
  {                                  {
   ...                                ...
   karel.moveFar();                   karel.move(2);
   ...                                ...
  }                                  }
}                                  }
--------------------------         --------------------------
public class SimpleBot...          public class SimpleBot...
{ ...                              { ...
  public void moveFar()              public void move(int howFar)
  { int howFar = 2;                  {
    this.avenue = this...             this.avenue = this...
    this.street = this...             this.street = this...
  }                                  }
```

Inside the method, the parameter variable behaves like any other temporary variable. It can be used in expressions, passed as an argument to another method, and assigned a new value. Its scope is the entire method. Like a temporary variable, it has a short lifetime, disappearing when the method finishes executing. It is re-created and reinitialized each time the method is executed. The difference is in how it is initialized.

As we've seen in previous chapters, a method may have more than one parameter. For example, the following method is called with two arguments, `karel.move(5, Constants.EAST)`. It turns `karel` to face the specified direction and then move the specified distance. Each pair of declarations is separated with a comma.

```
public void move(int howFar, int aDir)
{ this.face(aDir);
  this.move(howFar);
}
```

Overloading Methods

We now have three methods named move, the usual one without a parameter, one with a single parameter, and one with two parameters. Fortunately, this does not usually cause a problem as long as every method in the class has a different **signature**. A method's signature is its name together with an ordered list of its parameter types.

The signature of the usual move method is simply `move()`. It has no parameters and hence its ordered list of parameter types is empty. The signature of the move method shown in the right side of Figure 6-8 is `move(int)`. Notice that the parameter name is not included in the signature. The last version of move has the signature `move(int, int)`.

Assuming `karel` is an instance of a `SimpleBot` class that has these three methods defined, `karel.move()`, `karel.move(3)`, and `karel.move(3, Constants.NORTH)` are all legal method calls. In each case, Java executes the method with the matching signature.

Methods and constructors that have the same name but different signatures are said to be **overloaded**. Note that we now have two terms incorporating the word "over":

- **Overload**—A method overloads another method in either a superclass or the same class when they have the same name but different signatures. Any of the methods may be executed, depending on the arguments provided when it is called.
- **Override**—A method in a subclass overrides a method in a superclass if they have the same signatures. The overriding method is executed and the overridden method is not (unless it is called by the overriding method).

Constructors may also be overloaded. The same principles apply to them.

Using Parameters to Initialize Instance Variables

Parameters are also useful for writing constructors. Our current implementation of `SimpleBot` always begins on 4th Street and 2nd Avenue facing east. We can use parameters in the constructor to make it more flexible.

Listing 6-9 shows a constructor with four parameters to construct a robot in a specified city at a specified location. Three of the parameters are used to provide the initial values to the instance variables `street`, `avenue`, and `direction`. Because the initial

KEY IDEA

Initialize each instance variable either where it is declared or in the constructor.

values are provided in the constructor, initial values are no longer needed on lines 2–4 where the variables are declared; there is no need to initialize them in both places.

Listing 6-9: *A version of the* `SimpleBot` *class that uses parameters to initialize its location*

```
 1 public class SimpleBot extends Paintable
 2 { private int street;
 3   private int avenue;
 4   private int direction;
 5
 6   /** Construct a new robot in the given city at the given location.
 7    *   @param aCity              The city in which this robot appears.
 8    *   @param aStreet            This robot's initial street.
 9    *   @param anAvenue           This robot's initial avenue.
10    *   @param aDirection         This robot's initial direction. */
11   public SimpleBot(SimpleCity aCity,
12                    int aStreet, int anAvenue, int aDirection)
13   { super();
14     this.street = aStreet;
15     this.avenue = anAvenue;
16     this.direction = aDirection;
17     aCity.add(this, 2);      // Add this robot to the given city in the top level.
18   }
19   // Remainder of the class omitted.
20 }
```

One of the constructor's parameters—the city—is *not* used to initialize an instance variable. Recall that the robot must be added to the city, which keeps a list of all the objects to be painted. So far the robot has been added to the city in the `main` method. The following lines show how it was done in Listing 6-4.

```
 7 SimpleCity newYork = new SimpleCity();
 8 SimpleBot karel = new SimpleBot();
   ...
11 newYork.add(karel, 2);
```

With this new constructor, line 8 is changed as follows to place the robot in the city named `newYork` on 4th Street and 2nd Avenue, facing east:

```
 8 SimpleBot karel = new SimpleBot(newYork, 4, 2, Constants.EAST);
```

Line 11 is omitted from the `main` method because that task is now performed in the `SimpleBot` constructor. When the constructor is called as shown in the preceding code, the value stored in `newYork` is assigned to the parameter variable `aCity`. The reference to the newly created object is assigned to the implicit parameter variable this. Both variables are used in line 17 of Listing 6-9 to add *this* robot to the city known within the constructor as aCity. The effect is the same as our previous approach, newYork.add(karel, 2).

KEY IDEA

A reference to this object can be passed as a parameter using this.

Name Conflicts

It is often the case that the natural name for a parameter is the same as the name of an instance variable. For example, some people find the parameter names in lines 11 and 12 of Listing 6-9 awkward and would rather use names like street and avenue. In fact, the names of the parameters can be the same as the names of the instance variables. Using this removes the ambiguity that would otherwise be present. For example, lines 11–14 could be reimplemented as follows:

```
11 public SimpleBot(City city,
12                      int street, int avenue, Direction direction)
13 { super();
14   this.street = street;
...
```

A temporary variable may also have the same name as an instance variable, but temporary and parameter variables within the same method must have unique names.

There is, however, a danger in using the same names. As noted briefly earlier, this is actually optional in most circumstances, and many programmers, unfortunately, habitually omit it. Omitting this when the parameter name and instance variable name are different poses no danger. But suppose this was omitted from line 14 of the preceding code, as follows:

```
14 street = street;
```

The compiler would interpret this as assigning the value in the parameter to itself—a useless but perfectly valid action. The instance variable would remain uninitialized.

Using the final Keyword with Parameter Variables

Like other kinds of variables, parameter variables can use the keyword final. As elsewhere, it means that the variable's value may not be changed. As with other kinds of parameters, use final to emphasize and enforce that intention.

6.3 Extending a Class with Variables

In Section 6.1, we saw how instance variables can be used inside a class such as SimpleBot. It is also possible to extend an existing class with new instance variables,

KEY IDEA

Instance variables in a subclass add to the information maintained by the superclass.

just as we extended an existing class with new methods in Chapter 2. In defining the new class, we will specify only the new instance variables. The Java compiler will automatically include them with the instance variables already defined in the superclass.

In the following example, we will extend `Robot` (*not* the `SimpleBot` class used earlier in this chapter) to create a new class, `LimitedBot`. Our goal is to create a kind of robot that can carry only a limited number of things; if it attempts to carry more, it will break. Each of these limited robots will need to know two pieces of information: How many things it can hold before breaking, and how many things it is currently holding. We'll call one `maxHold` (the maximum the robot can hold at one time) and call the other `numHeld` (the number held right now).

These two pieces of information will be stored as instance variables. Why use instance variables and not some other kind of variable? A temporary variable won't work because the robot needs to remember this information even when a method is not being executed. A parameter variable isn't what we need because we don't want to rely on the client to tell the robot how much it can carry every time a method is called.

In Chapter 1, we illustrated the attributes of a robot with an object diagram similar to the one shown on the left side of Figure 6-9. It represents a robot on the corner of (1, 0) facing east.

We can imagine an instance of `LimitedBot` as having a `Robot` object inside itself, along with the new instance variables it defines. This is illustrated on the right side of Figure 6-9. In this case, the robot is limited to holding five things at a time; it is currently holding none.

(figure 6-9)

Visualizing instance variables in a `Robot` *object and a* `LimitedBot` *object*

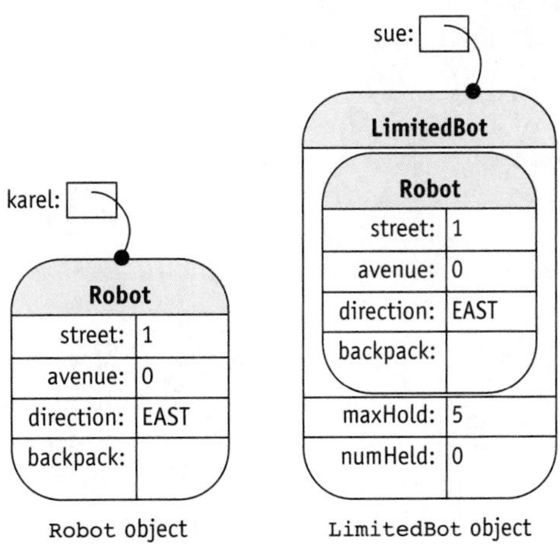

6.3.1 Declaring and Initializing the Variables

Listing 6-10 shows the beginning of our new kind of robot, `LimitedBot`. It includes the two new instance variables and the constructor, but nothing else. `LimitedBot` objects are identical to normal `Robot` objects except for the (currently unused) instance variables.

Listing 6-10: *A* `LimitedBot` *is like a normal Robot, but has two additional (yet to be used) instance variables*

```
1  import becker.robots.*;
2
3  /** A LimitedBot can carry or hold only a limited number of things. The
4   *  actual limit set when the robot is constructed.
5   *
6   *  @author Byron Weber Becker */
7  public class LimitedBot extends Robot
8  {
9    private int maxHold;            // Maximum # of things this robot can hold.
10   private int numHeld = 0;        // Number of things currently held by this robot.
11
12   /** Construct a new LimitedBot.
13    *  @param aCity           This robot's city.
14    *  @param aStr            This robot's initial street.
15    *  @param anAve           This robot's initial avenue.
16    *  @param aDir            This robot's initial direction.
17    *  @param maxCanHold      The maximum number of things this robot can carry/hold. */
18   public LimitedBot(City aCity, int aStr, int anAve,
19                     Direction aDir, int maxCanHold)
20   { super(aCity, aStr, anAve, aDir);
21     this.maxHold = maxCanHold;
22   }
23 }
```

The number of things held by the robot will always be zero when the robot is constructed, and so the `numHeld` instance variable is initialized to `0` when it is declared in line 10. The initial value of `maxHold`, however, isn't known when the class is written. It is initialized in the constructor with the value passed to the `maxCanHold` parameter, allowing its initial value to be determined when the `LimitedBot` is constructed.

Invoking `super` in line 20 calls a constructor in the superclass. Parameters such as `aStr` and `anAve` are passed as arguments to `super`, where they are likely used to initialize instance variables in the superclass.

This example illustrates two guidelines that are seldom broken:

- Every instance variable is initialized either where it is declared or in the constructor, with information passed via a parameter.
- Parameters to a constructor are used to initialize an instance variable in the same class via an assignment statement or an instance variable in a superclass via the call to `super`.

6.3.2 Maintaining and Using Instance Variables

Having the `maxHold` and `numHeld` instance variables is not enough. We need to maintain and use the information they store.

First, we need to monitor how many things are currently held by the robot, and call `breakRobot` if this number exceeds the number stored in `maxHold`. The number of things held by the robot changes whenever it picks a thing up or puts a thing down. Thus, we will need to override the definitions of `pickThing` and `putThing`.

Let's focus on `pickThing` first. In pseudocode, we want it to perform the following tasks:

```
if (already holding the maximum number of things)
{ break the robot
} else
{ pick up a thing
  increment the count of the number of things being held
}
```

The pseudocode for putting a thing down is similar except that there is no need to check if the maximum has been exceeded:

```
put down a thing
decrement the count of the number of things being held
```

These two methods are shown in lines 24–33 and 35–39 of Listing 6-11.

FIND THE CODE

ch06/limitedBot/

Listing 6-11: *Source code for a kind of robot that can pick up only a limited number of things*

```
1 import becker.robots.*;
2
3 /** A LimitedBot can carry or hold only a limited number of things. The
4  * actual limit set when the robot is constructed.
5  *
6  * @author Byron Weber Becker */
7 public class LimitedBot extends Robot
```

Listing 6-11: *Source code for a kind of robot that can pick up only a limited number of things* (continued)

```
 8 {
 9    private int maxHold;               // Maximum # of things this robot can hold.
10    private int numHeld = 0;           // Number of things currently held by this robot.
11 
12    /** Construct a new LimitedBot.
13     * @param aCity          This robot's city
14     * @param aStr           This robot's initial street.
15     * @param anAve          This robot's initial avenue.
16     * @param aDir           This robot's initial direction.
17     * @param maxCanHold     The maximum number of things this robot can carry/hold. */
18    public LimitedBot(City aCity, int aStr, int anAve,
19                           Direction aDir, int maxCanHold)
20    { super(aCity, aStr, anAve, aDir);
21      this.maxHold = maxCanHold;
22    }
23 
24    /** Pick up a thing. If the robot is already holding the maximum number
25     * of things, it breaks. */
26    public void pickThing()
27    { if (this.numHeld == this.maxHold)
28      { this.breakRobot("Tried to pick up too many things.");
29      } else
30      { super.pickThing();
31        this.numHeld = this.numHeld + 1;
32      }
33    }
34 
35    /** Put down one thing. */
36    public void putThing()
37    { super.putThing();
38      this.numHeld = this.numHeld - 1;
39    }
40 }
```

In `pickThing`, we call `super.pickThing()` at line 30. This statement calls the unmodified version of `pickThing` provided by the `LimitedBot`'s superclass. The code surrounding this call details the additional steps that should be taken when a `LimitedBot`'s version of `pickThing` is called. `super.putThing()` is called at line 37 for similar reasons.

LOOKING BACK

Overriding methods was discussed in Section 2.6.1.

6.3.3 Blank Final Instance Variables

In Listing 6-11, `maxHold` is given a value when the object is initialized, but thereafter the value is unchanged. This suggests that `maxHold` is really a kind of constant even though we don't know its value until the object is instantiated.

The constructor may assign a value to a final instance variable as long as the variable hasn't been used already. This suggests that line 9 of Listing 6-11 should be rewritten as follows:

```
9  private final int MAX_HOLD;     // Maximum # of things this robot can hold.
```

Appropriate changes in the variable name should also be made in lines 21 and 27. A final variable that is not initialized until later is called a **blank final**. The compiler must be able to verify that a blank final is not used before it is assigned a value.

6.4 Modifying vs. Extending Classes

We now have two distinct approaches to modifying a class to do something new:

- Extending the class with additional methods and instance variables.
- Adding additional functionality within the class itself. In fact, the problem set for this chapter asks for many modifications to `SimpleBot`.

So, which is preferable: to extend a class with new functionality or modify the class itself?

As usual, the answer depends on the context. If the source code is not available (as is the case with `Robot`), you can't modify the class directly. The question becomes more interesting when the source code is available. The decision is usually made based on two criteria:

- How extensively has the class already been used, including subclasses? Modifying a class that is extensively used carries a significant risk of breaking code that already works. It also carries the burden of significant testing. In these cases, extending the class is usually the better idea.
- Are the proposed changes useful in many circumstances? If they are, modifying the class may be a good idea. However, if the changes are of limited use, the class becomes cluttered with features that are not typically used. Extending the class is often the wiser course in this situation as well.

These observations are represented in Table 6-2.

	Modifications are useful almost everywhere.	Modifications are useful in many settings.	Modifications are useful in only a few settings.
Class is already used extensively.	Modify the class.	Extend the class.	Extend the class.
Class is not used extensively.	Modify the class.	Modify the class.	Extend the class.

(table 6-2)

Factors in deciding whether to modify or extend a class

A third option is to create a new class that makes substantial use of an existing class to do its job. That's the topic of Chapter 8.

6.5 Comparing Kinds of Variables

We have examined three kinds of variables: instance variables, temporary variables, and parameter variables. How do you choose which kind of variable to use? This section compares and contrasts them, and provides some guidelines on selecting an appropriate kind of variable.

6.5.1 Similarities and Differences

Table 6-3 compares and contrasts the different kinds of variables.

	Instance Variables...	Temporary Variables...	Parameter Variables...
are declared...	inside a class but outside of the methods.	inside a method.	inside a method's parameter list.
are declared...	with an access modifier; beginning programmers should always use `private`.	without an access modifier.	without an access modifier.
use the `final` keyword when...	the value stored should not be changed.	the value stored should not be changed.	the value stored should not be changed.
are named (by convention)...	like methods: the first "word" is lowercase; subsequent "words" have an initial capital. If the `final` keyword is used, names should be all uppercase.	like methods: the first "word" is lowercase; subsequent "words" have an initial capital.	like methods: the first "word" is lowercase; subsequent "words" have an initial capital.
can be used...	in any method in the class.	in the smallest block enclosing the declaration.	in the method where they are declared.

(table 6-3)

Comparing the different kinds of variables

(table 6-3) *continued*

Comparing the different kinds of variables

	Instance Variables...	Temporary Variables...	Parameter Variables...
are initialized...	where they are declared or in the constructors.	where they are declared.	where the method is called.
store their value until...	it is changed or the object is no longer used.	it is changed or the smallest enclosing block has finished executing.	it is changed or the method has finished executing.
are referenced...	with the keyword `this`, a dot, and the variable's name; may be accessed with the class name when modifiers permit and they have the `static` keyword.	with only the variable's name.	with only the variable's name.

6.5.2 Rules of Thumb for Selecting a Variable

Table 6-4 can help you decide when each kind of variable is an appropriate choice based on your program's needs. The solutions are ordered from the most preferred to the least preferred; therefore, read the table from the top and use the first solution that meets your needs.

(table 6-4)

Rules of thumb for choosing which kind of variable to use

If you...	Then...
need a value that never changes while the program is running	use a `final` instance variable (constant). Valid exceptions are for the values 0, 1, and -1, unless the special value could be something else but just happens to be one of these.
need to store a value that will be used in a calculation later in the same method but then discarded	use a temporary variable.
have a method that could do things slightly differently based on a value known by the client	use a parameter.
find yourself writing almost identical code several times	look for a way to put the code in a method, accounting for the differences with parameters.
need a value in many methods within a class	consider using an instance variable.
need to implement an attribute of an object	use an instance variable or calculate the value based on existing instance variables.
have an object that must store a value even when none of its services are being used	use an instance variable.

6.5.3 Temporary versus Instance Variables

One of the hardest choices for many beginning programmers is deciding whether to use an instance variable or a temporary variable. This choice is difficult because nearly anything that can be done with a temporary variable can also be done with an instance variable. This situation often leads beginning programmers to overuse instance variables and underuse temporary variables.

Suppose that you need a query, `numIntersectionsWithThings`, that counts the number of intersections containing `Things` between the robot's current location and a wall that is somewhere in front of it. Invoking `numIntersectionsWithThings` on the robot shown in Figure 6-10 would move the robot to just before the wall and return the value 3.

(figure 6-10)

Initial situation for counting the number of things before a wall

We could solve this problem using an instance variable, as shown in Listing 6-12. This approach is not appropriate for an instance variable, however, because it stores temporary information, not an attribute of the robot.

FIND THE CODE

ch06/counter/

LOOKING AHEAD

This code can give an incorrect answer. See Written Exercise 6.3.

Listing 6-12: *An inappropriate use of an instance variable*

```
import becker.robots.*;

public class CounterBot1 extends RobotSE
{ private int intersections = 0;

  public CounterBot1(City c, int str, int ave, Direction d)
  { super(c, str, ave, d);
  }

  public int numIntersectionsWithThings()
  {  while(true)
     {  if (this.canPickThing())
        {  this.intersections = this.intersections + 1;
        }
        if (!this.frontIsClear())   {  break; }
        this.move();
     }
     return this.intersections;
   }
}
```

A better solution is to use a temporary variable. Rewriting the class in Listing 6-12 to use a temporary variable results in the class shown in Listing 6-13. The differences are shown in bold in both listings.

FIND THE CODE

ch06/counter/

Listing 6-13: *A robot using a temporary variable in* `numIntersectionsWithThings`

```
import becker.robots.*;

public class CounterBot2 extends RobotSE
{
  public CounterBot2(City c, int str, int ave, Direction d)
  { super(c, str, ave, d);
  }

  public int numIntersectionsWithThings()
  { int intersections = 0;
    while(true)
    { if (this.canPickThing())
      { intersections = intersections + 1;
      }
      if (!this.frontIsClear())   { break; }
      this.move();
    }
    return intersections;
  }
}
```

Does it matter whether you choose an instance variable or a temporary variable? Yes, for the following reasons:

- Reading a program is easiest if variables are declared close to their use. Temporary variables keep declarations as close to their use as possible. That way the reader doesn't have to remember as many details for as long a time.
- The class as a whole is easier to understand if it isn't cluttered by extraneous instance variables. Readers assume that each instance variable has a meaning to the class as a whole and to several methods. If that's not true, it can take longer to understand the class.
- The longer lifetimes and larger scope of instance variables give programmers more opportunity to misuse them. Don't provide such opportunities unless you must.
- Extra instance variables increase the amount of memory required to run the program. For large programs, this can become an issue because it may limit the amount of data it can handle.

Temporary variables should be used when the value is not an attribute of the object and is primarily local to a method, or when storing a temporary value. Prime candidates include loop counters, a temporary variable to store an intermediate calculation, an accumulator such as `intersections` in Listing 6-13, or the temporary storage of the answer to a query before it's used in further calculations.

KEY IDEA

Use parameter and temporary variables when you can; instance variables only when you must.

For each instance variable, you should think carefully about whether it must be an instance variable. Is the data relevant to more than one public method? Does the data represent an attribute of the class? If so, make it an instance variable. If not, consider other options.

6.6 Printing Expressions

When debugging programs that use variables and expressions, it is often useful to print their values as the program is running. There are two approaches: inserting temporary code in the class to print the values out, and using a tool called a debugger.

6.6.1 Using `System.out`

`System.out` is an object that is automatically made available throughout every Java program. It has two methods, `print` and `println`, that are used to print values in the **console** window. The console is usually a separate window used specifically for default textual input and output. This is also where Java prints its error messages.

For example, the `pickThing` method in `LimitedBot` (see Listing 6-11) can be modified to print out useful debugging information by adding lines 2 and 3 in the following code:

```
 1 public void pickThing()
 2 { System.out.print("PickThing: numHeld=");          // debug
 3   System.out.println(this.numHeld);                 // debug
 4   if (this.numHeld == this.maxHold)
 5   { this.breakRobot("Tried to pick up too many things.");
 6   } else
 7   { super.pickThing();
 8     this.numHeld = this.numHeld + 1;
 9   }
10 }
```

The result of picking up three things using the modified class is shown in Figure 6-11. The black window in front of the usual robot window is the console.

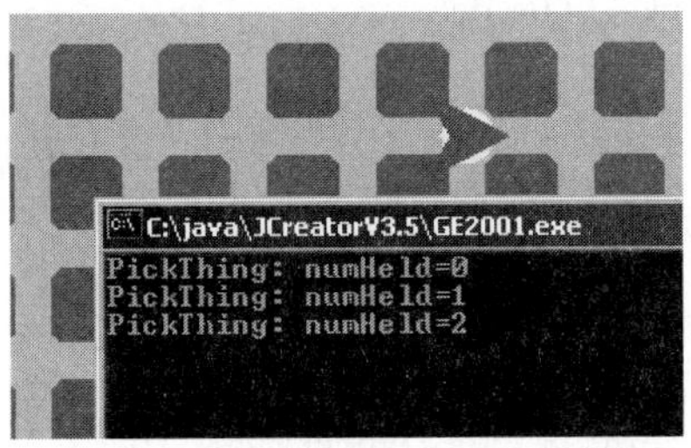

(figure 6-11)

Information printed in the console window using `System.out`

The `print` and `println` methods are overloaded to take all of Java's types as arguments. In line 2, the `print` method is used to print the given string literal. In the next line, the `println` method is used to print the value stored in an integer variable.

Most programmers would combine lines 2 and 3 as follows:

```
System.out.println("PickThing: numHeld=" + this.numHeld);
```

When the plus operator (+) is used with a string, the result is a single string composed of the first operand textually followed by the second operand. The resulting string is then printed.

The difference between `print` and `println` is in where text will go the *next* time one of these methods is called. Using `print` causes subsequent text to be printed on the same line; using `println` causes subsequent text to be printed on the next line. The "ln" in `println` stands for "line."

6.6.2 Using a Debugger

A **debugger** is a tool that can be used to view values while the program is running. It does not require you to add temporary code to your program. An example of one debugger is shown in Figure 6-12. It is part of the Eclipse project, a freely available integrated development environment. Three areas of the debugger are shown under the robot's window:

- The source code that is currently being executed is shown in the bottom left of the figure. It helps remind the programmer which variables are currently relevant. It is possible to set **breakpoints** before running the program. A breakpoint is associated with a program statement and causes the debugger to stop executing the program each time the statement is reached, giving the user an opportunity to examine the values held by variables.
- The variables that are currently in scope are shown in the upper-right corner of Figure 6-12. In this example, all the variables happen to be instance variables, but parameter and temporary variables can also appear in this area. The current value held by each variable is also shown. If the variable happens to refer to an object, a plus sign appears to the left, allowing its instance variables

to be shown as well. The debugger even shows private instance variables in `LimitedBot`'s superclasses.

➤ After a program stops at a breakpoint, the toolbar shown in the upper-left corner of Figure 6-12 is used to continue execution. For example, the arrow on the far left continues execution until the next breakpoint is reached. Some of the other tools allow the programmer to step to the next statement. One tool treats a method call as one statement to execute while another steps into a method to execute the next statement.

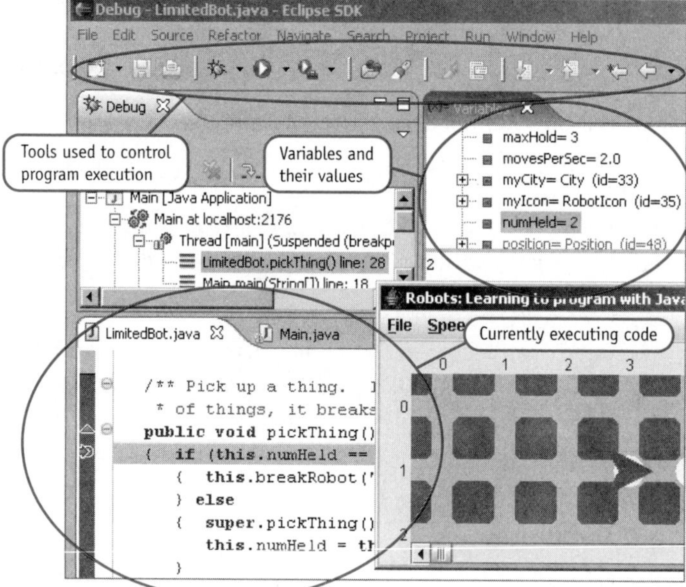

(figure 6-12)

Eclipse debugger in use

Debuggers are powerful tools that are worth learning. However, they are also complex and may distract beginning programmers from more important learning tasks.

6.7 GUI: Repainting

In this section, we'll create a new kind of graphical user interface component, a `Thermometer`. The major difference between a `Thermometer` and the `StickFigure` component created in Chapter 2 is that the `Thermometer` has an instance variable that controls its appearance. As Figure 6-13 shows, each thermometer can be set to show a different temperature.

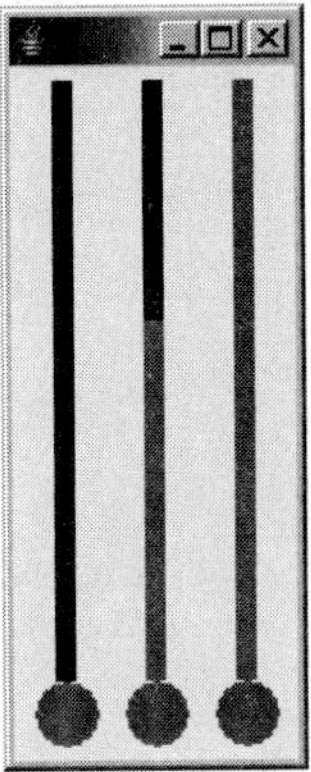

(figure 6-13)

Three `Thermometer` *components, each with a different temperature setting*

The program in Listing 6-14 was used to create this image and may be used as a test harness during the development process. It creates three instances of the `Thermometer` class, displays them, and sets each to show a different temperature.

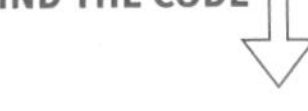

FIND THE CODE

ch06/thermometer/

Listing 6-14: *A test harness for the* `Thermometer` *class*

```
import javax.swing.*;

/** Test a thermometer component.
 *
 *  @author Byron Weber Becker */
public class Main extends Object
{
  public static void main(String[] args)
  { // Create three thermometer components.
    Thermometer t0 = new Thermometer();
    Thermometer t1 = new Thermometer();
    Thermometer t2 = new Thermometer();

    // Create a panel to hold the thermometers.
    JPanel contents = new JPanel();
    contents.add(t0);
    contents.add(t1);
    contents.add(t2);

    // Set up the frame.
    JFrame f = new JFrame();
    f.setDefaultCloseOperation(JFrame.EXIT_ON_CLOSE);
    f.setContentPane(contents);
    f.pack();
    f.setVisible(true);

```

Listing 6-14: *A test harness for the* `Thermometer` *class* (continued)

```
      // Set the temperature of each thermometer.
      t0.setTemperature(0);
      t1.setTemperature(30);
      t2.setTemperature(50);
   }
}
```

6.7.1 Instance Variables in Components

In Section 2.7.3, we learned that the `paintComponent` method can be called by the Java system at any time. The user can resize a frame or expose a previously hidden frame. In either case, `paintComponent` will be called to repaint the contents of the frame. Therefore, the `paintComponent` method must be able to determine what the component should look like. For a `Thermometer`, this includes determining how high the alcohol (the modern replacement for mercury) should be drawn. It does so by consulting an instance variable. A client can set the instance variable to a given temperature with a small method called `setTemperature`.

Listing 6-15 shows the beginnings of the `Thermometer` class, complete with the instance variable used to store the current temperature. Most of the code in `paintComponent` must still be developed.

FIND THE CODE

cho6/thermometer/

Listing 6-15: *The beginnings of the* `Thermometer` *class*

```
import javax.swing.*;
import java.awt.*;

/** A thermometer component to use in graphical user interfaces. It can
 *  display temperatures from MIN_TEMP to MAX_TEMP, inclusive.
 *
 *  @author Byron Weber Becker */
public class Thermometer extends JComponent
{
   public final int MIN_TEMP = 0;
   public final int MAX_TEMP = 50;
   private int temp = MIN_TEMP;

```

Listing 6-15: *The beginnings of the* `Thermometer` *class* (continued)

```
14     /** Construct a new thermometer. */
15     public Thermometer()
16     { super();
17       this.setPreferredSize(new Dimension(50, 250));
18     }
19
20     /** Paint the thermometer to show the current temperature. */
21     public void paintComponent(Graphics g)
22     { super.paintComponent(g);
23
24       // paint the thermometer
25     }
26
27      /** Set the thermometer's temperature.
28       * @param newTemp the new temperature. */
29      public void setTemperature(int newTemp)
30      { this.temp = newTemp;
31      }
32  }
```

Recall that the preferred size, set in line 17, is used by the frame to determine how large the thermometer should be. Forgetting to set the preferred size will make the component so small that it is almost invisible.

LOOKING AHEAD

Programming Project 6.15 asks you to improve upon the hard-coded minimum and maximum.

This version of the class fixes the minimum and maximum temperature the thermometer can display with two named constants.

Working out the actual code for `paintComponent` is somewhat tedious. It helps to declare temporary variables initialized with significant values. The diagram in Figure 6-14 illustrates the meaning of those used in Listing 6-16.

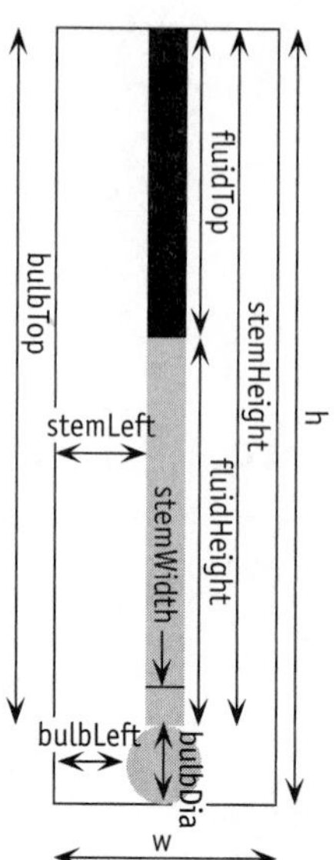

(figure 6-14)

`Thermometer` *calculations*

The height and width of the component are found first in lines 5 and 6 and stored in variables to make using them more convenient. All the calculations should ultimately depend on the height and width so that the thermometer is drawn appropriately as the component is resized.

The variables with names ending in `Left` and `Top` hold values specifying the location of a shape. Variables with names ending in `Height`, `Width`, and `Dia` (short for "diameter") hold values specifying the size of a shape.

FIND THE CODE

ch06/thermometer/

Listing 6-16: *The finished implementation of* `paintComponent`

```
1  /** Paint the thermometer to show the current temperature. */
2  public void paintComponent(Graphics g)
3  { super.paintComponent(g);
4
5    final int w = this.getWidth();
6    final int h = this.getHeight();
7
8    final int bulbDia = h/10;
9    final int bulbLeft = w/2 - bulbDia/2;
10   final int bulbTop = h - bulbDia;
11
12   final int stemWidth = bulbDia/3;
13   final int stemLeft = w/2 - stemWidth/2;
```

Listing 6-16: *The finished implementation of* `paintComponent` (continued)

```
    final int stemHeight = h - bulbDia;

    final int fluidHeight = stemHeight *
          (this.temp - MIN_TEMP) / (MAX_TEMP - MIN_TEMP);
    final int fluidTop = stemHeight - fluidHeight;

    // paint the fluid
    g.setColor(Color.RED);
    g.fillOval(bulbLeft, bulbTop, bulbDia, bulbDia);
    g.fillRect(stemLeft, fluidTop, stemWidth, fluidHeight);

    // paint the stem above the fluid
    g.setColor(Color.BLACK);
    g.fillRect(stemLeft, 0, stemWidth, fluidTop);
  }
```

6.7.2 Triggering a Repaint

If you run the test harness with the current version of `Thermometer`, you will notice that the thermometers are painted as though the temperature is 0 rather than the temperatures set in the test harness. However, if you resize the frame, forcing the thermometers to be repainted, then they will be drawn with the correct temperatures. In other words, the thermometers display a temperature change only when they are repainted.

KEY IDEA

Call `repaint` *when instance variables affecting the image change.*

Somehow we need to be able to trigger the repainting of the component whenever the temperature changes. We do so with an inherited method, `repaint`. Calling `repaint` after we have reset the instance variable informs the Java system that it should call `paintComponent` as soon as possible. The revised version of `setTemperature` is:

```
public void setTemperature(int newTemp)
{ this.temp = newTemp;
  this.repaint();
}
```

6.7.3 Animating the `Thermometer`

Adding the following code to the end of the test harness will cause the thermometer to show a steadily increasing temperature—just like the temperature climbing on a hot summer's morning.

```
for(int temp = t0.MIN_TEMP; temp <= t0.MAX_TEMP; temp = temp
+ 1)
{  t0.setTemperature(temp);
   Utilities.sleep(50);
}
```

The call to `Utilities.sleep` causes the current thread to pause for 50 milliseconds, or 0.050 seconds, to give the Java system a chance to repaint the screen—and so you have time to see the change in the thermometer.

The `sleep` method should *not* be called inside the `paintComponent` method. `paintComponent` is called by the Java system; it has many important things to do and should not be forced to wait for anything.

6.8 Patterns

Every time you are writing an expression, you need values. These values could come from any of the constructs discussed in this chapter. In almost every situation, one of the constructs is a better choice than the others. Carefully consider which of the following patterns best describes your situation and is best suited to solve your problem.

6.8.1 The Named Constant Pattern

Name: Named Constant

Context: You have a literal value used one or more times in your program. The value is known when you write the program and does not change while the program is running.

Solution: Use a named constant, as suggested by the following examples:

```
private static final int DAYS_IN_WEEK = 7;
private static final int COST_PER_MOVE = 25;
```

In general, a named constant has the following form:

```
«accessModifier» static final «type» «name» = «value»;
```

where *«accessModifier»* is `public`, `protected`, or `private`. Use `private` if the value is used only within the class where it is defined. Use `public` if other classes might need it—for example, as an actual parameter to a method defined within the class.

«type» is the type of the value stored in the constant. So far, we have discussed only integers, but any type (including a class name) is possible. *«name»* is the name of the variable, and *«value»* is the first (and last) value assigned to it.

Graphics programs often use many constants in the course of drawing a picture. (See `paintComponent` in Section 2.7.3 for an example.) Having a named constant for each can become tedious, and it is common practice to use literals instead. An excellent middle ground is to look for relationships between the numbers. It is often possible to define a few well-chosen constants that can be used in expressions to calculate the remaining values.

Consequences: Programs become more self-documenting when special values are given meaningful names. Reading, debugging, and maintaining a program become easier and faster when the program uses meaningful names.

Related Patterns:

- This pattern is a specialization of the Instance Variable pattern.
- When constants are used to distinguish a set of values, such as the four directions or `MALE` and `FEMALE`, the Enumeration pattern (see Section 7.7.3) is often a better choice.

6.8.2 The Instance Variable Pattern

Name: Instance Variable

Context: An object needs to maintain a value. The value must be remembered for longer than one method call (when a temporary variable would be appropriate). The value is usually needed in more than one method.

Solution: Use an instance variable. Instance variables are declared within the class but outside of all the methods. Following are examples of instance variables:

```
private int numMoves = 0;
private int currentAve;
```

An instance variable is declared with one of two general forms:

```
«accessModifier» «type» «name» = «initialValue»;
«accessModifier» «type» «name»;
```

where *«accessModifier»* is usually `private` and *«type»* is the type of the variable. Examples include `int`, `double`, `boolean`, and names of classes such as `Robot`. *«name»* is the name used to refer to the value stored. The variable's initial value should either be established in the declaration, as shown in the first form, or assigned in the constructor. Assign the initial value in the declaration if all instances of the class start with the same value. Assign it in the constructor if each instance will have its initial value supplied by parameters to a constructor.

An instance variable may be accessed within methods or constructors with the implicit parameter, `this`, followed by a dot and the name of the variable. It may also be accessed by giving the name of the variable if the name is not the same as a parameter or temporary variable.

An instance variable that is not explicitly initialized will be given a default value appropriate for its type, such as `0` for integer types and `false` for `boolean`.

Consequences: An instance variable stores a value for the lifetime of the object. It can be explicitly changed by an assignment statement.

Related Patterns:

- The Instance Variable pattern is inappropriate for storing values used within a single method for intermediate calculations, counting events, or loop indices. Use the Temporary Variable pattern instead.
- The Instance Variable pattern is inappropriate for communicating a value from client code to a method. Use the Parameterized Method pattern instead.
- The Instance Variable pattern always occurs within an instance of the Class pattern.

6.8.3 The Accessor Method Pattern

Name: Accessor Method

Context: You have a class with instance variables that are private to prevent misuse by clients. However, clients have a legitimate need to know the values of the instance variables even though they should not be allowed to directly change them.

Solution: Provide public accessor methods using the following template:

```
public «typeReturned» get«Name»()
{ return this.«instanceVariable»;
}
```

An example is an accessor for the `street` in the `SimpleBot` class, as follows:

```
public class SimpleBot
{ private int street;
  ...
  public int getStreet()
  { return this.street;
  }
}
```

Consequences: Restricted access is provided to an instance variable.

Related Patterns: The Accessor Method pattern is a specialization of the Query pattern.

6.9 Summary and Concept Map

Variables are used to store information that will be useful at a later point in the program. The three fundamental kinds of variables are instance variables, temporary variables, and parameter variables. They differ in their scope, lifetime, and initialization.

Instance variables belong to an object. Each instance of a class has its own set of instance variables that implement that object's attributes. The lifetime is the same as the lifetime of the object. The scope is the entire class.

Temporary variables belong to the method or the block within a method in which they are declared, which also limits their scope. Of the three kinds of variables, temporary variables have the most limited scope. They are used for tasks such as storing intermediate calculations and counting events, such as loop iterations, within the method.

Parameter variables are temporary variables that are initialized when the method is called. Their scope is the entire method where they are declared, and their lifetime is for as long as the method executes. Both temporary and parameter variables disappear when the method in which they are declared finishes execution. If the method is executed again, space for the variable is reallocated and the variable is reinitialized.

Classes may be extended with additional instance variables, much as they can be extended with additional methods.

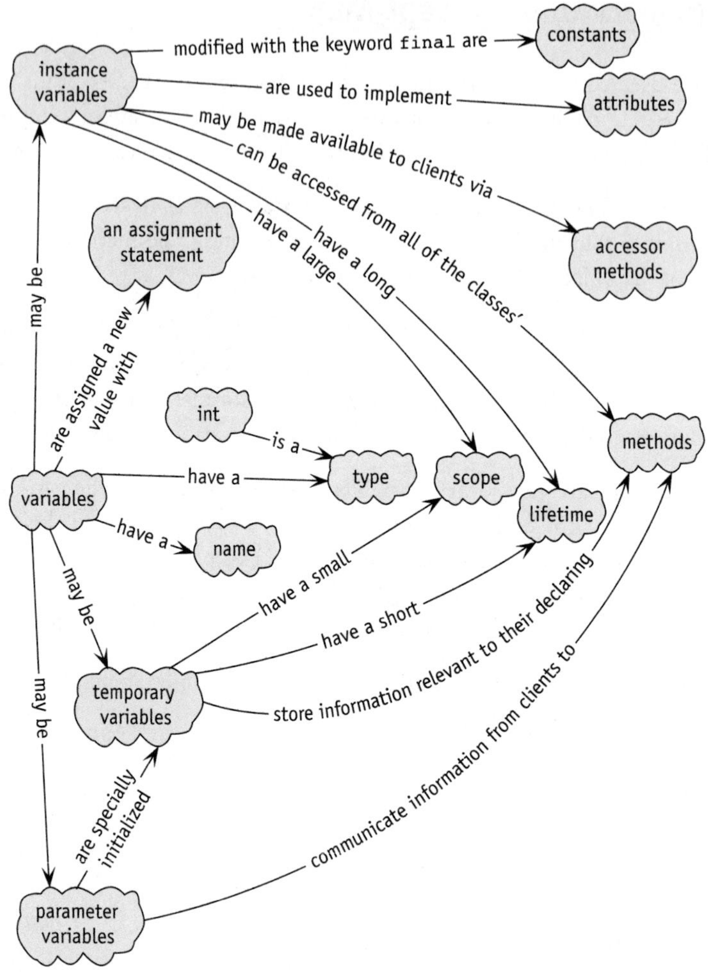

6.10 Problem Set

Written Exercises

6.1 What kind of variable does not occur in a class diagram?

6.2 The `Account` class models a bank account. Identify which type of variable (temporary, parameter, or instance) should be used in each of the following values. Justify your answers using Table 6-4.

a. The bank account's balance.

b. The amount to deposit in the account.

c. The account's current interest rate.

d. The amount of interest earned in the last month.

6.3 Listing 6-12 and Listing 6-13 contain code for `CounterBot1` and `CounterBot2`, both of which purport to count the number of intersections with things between the robot's current location and a wall. Consider executing the following `main` method in the initial situation shown in Figure 6-15. Execute it again, but using `CounterBot2` in line 3. The two solutions display different values for `side1` and `side2`.

a. What are the four values printed (two for `CounterBot1` and two for `CounterBot2`)?

b. Explain why they differ.

```
1  public static void main(String[] args)
2  { City testCity = new City("testCity.txt");
3    CounterBot1 karel = new CounterBot1(...);
4
5    int side1 = karel.numIntersectionsWithThings();
6    karel.turnLeft();
7    int side2 = karel.numIntersectionsWithThings();
8
9    System.out.println("side1 =" + side1);
10   System.out.println("side2 =" + side2);
11 }
```

(figure 6-15)

Count the number of things

6.4 Draw an evaluation diagram for the expression assigned to `fluidHeight` in lines 16 and 17 of Listing 6-16. Assume the value of `stemHeight` is `225`, `this.temp` is `35`, `MIN_TEMP` is `-30`, and `MAX_TEMP` is `110`.

6.5 Section 6.2.1 noted that the remainder operator can be used to implement "wrap around" arithmetic and gave the example of `var = (var + 1) % upperLimit`.

a. Assume `upperLimit` has a value of `4`. Calculate the new value for `var` assuming that `var` is `0, 1, 2, ..., 9`.

b. Implementing `turnLeft` with the following expression seems like it should work, but it doesn't. Explain why.

```
this.direction = (this.direction - 1) % 4
```

6.6 In Section 6.2.1 we saw the following code to place a `Thing` on every 5th intersection:

```
while (...)
{ if (this.getAvenue() % 5 == 0)
  { this.putThing();
  ...
```

What difference would it make if the `if` statement's Boolean expression was changed to `this.getAvenue() % 5 == 2`?

Programming Exercises

6.7 Finish the following code to sum, and print the individual digits stored in `digits`. For example, the sum, of the digits of `312` is `6` because 3 + 1 + 2 = 6. (*Hint*: Review the integer division and remainder operations and apply the four-step process to construct a loop.)

```
public static void main(String[] args)
{ int digits = 312;
  int sum ...

  System.out.println(sum);
}
```

6.8 Write a class named `FixedDistanceBot` that can only travel a specified number of intersections. The exact limit should be specified when the robot is constructed. If the limit is reached, the robot should break. Write a `main` method to test your class.

6.9 Extend the harvester robot from Section 3.2.7 to pick up all the things on each intersection (there may be 0, 1, or many), and count the total number of things it collects. Make the total available to the robot's client with a query. The robot is not guaranteed to start with an empty backpack.

6.10 Write a class named `DistanceBot` that extends `Robot`. It will have a query named `totalDistance` that returns the total distance traveled by the robot so far. A second query, `tripDistance`, returns the distance traveled since the "trip" was started by a call to `resetTrip`.

6.11 Create a component similar to the stick figure shown in Figure 2-15. Add methods named `setShirtColor` and `setPantsColor` that each take a single parameter of type `Color`. Invoking these methods should change the color of the corresponding article of clothing. (*Hint*: You will need variables of type `Color`; import `java.awt.Color`.)

6.12 Create a subclass of `JFrame` named `JClosableFrame`. Its constructor takes a `JPanel` as a parameter and does everything necessary to display it. Rewrite the `main` method in Listing 6-14 to test your class. (*Hint*: Your class will have a constructor but no methods of its own.)

6.13 Modify the `Thermometer` class as follows:

a. Allow different minimum and maximum temperatures for each instance of `Thermometer`. For example, a candy thermometer might show 100 to 400 degrees Fahrenheit, whereas a fever thermometer might show 37 to 42 degrees Celsius. Don't forget to test the class with negative numbers. The Fahrenheit or Celsius isn't relevant, only the numeric range.

b. Modify the `Thermometer` class so that it prints the minimum and maximum temperatures beside the fluid to form a scale. Also, print the current temperature beside the top of the fluid.

Programming Projects

Robot problems in this section use the simplified `Robot` classes. Get them from your instructor or download them from the Examples section of *www.learningwithrobots.com/software/downloads.html*.

6.14 Download the `SimpleBot` classes from the Robots Web site. Make the following enhancements to the `SimpleBot` class. In all cases, write a `main` method to test your work.

a. Complete the `SimpleBot` class as described in this chapter, including the `move`, `turnLeft`, and `paint` methods as well as the `SimpleBot` constructor.

b. Add a `turnRight` method.

c. Add a method named `goToOrigin`. The effect of calling `karel.goToOrigin()` is to have the robot named `karel` appear at the origin, facing east, the next time its `paint` method is called.

d. Add a method named `teleport`. The effect of calling `karel.teleport(5, 3)` is to have `karel` appear on the intersection of 5th Street and 3rd Avenue the next time `paint` is called. The direction it faces should not change. Of course, your method should work with values other than 5 and 3.

e. Implement a suite of three methods in the `SimpleBot` class that modify the robot's speed. `ben.goFaster()` causes the robot named `ben` to move 10% faster. `ben.goSlower()` causes `ben` to move 10% slower. Finally, `ben.setMoveTime(400)` causes `ben` to wait 400 milliseconds each time it moves. Also accommodate values other than 400.

f. Modify the `SimpleBot` class so that its color can be specified. This change will require a new instance variable, a change to the `paint` method, and a new method named `setColor` that takes a parameter variable of type `Color`.

g. Modify the `SimpleBot` class so that the size of each robot can be specified. `puffer.setSize(30)` causes the robot named `puffer` to have a body with a radius of 30 pixels. Other features, such as the sensor, should change size accordingly. Note that the size of the intersection should *not* change and that your method should work with many different values, not just 30.

h. Rewrite the `paint` method in `SimpleBot` so that robots have two "eyes" set on short antennae, as shown in Figure 6-16. Choose different colors for the eyes and the body.

(figure 6-16)

Robot with two eyes

i. A color can be created with three integers that specify the red, green, and blue components of the color. There is a constructor for the `Color` class that takes these three values as parameters. Each color component must be in the range of 0 to 255.

   Modify the `SimpleBot` class so that the robot will change color slightly every time it is painted. (*Hint*: Use the remainder operator (`%`).)

j. Modify the `SimpleBot` class so that the robot will move in four steps from one intersection to the next—that is, instead of moving instantly to the next intersection, move one step, wait a moment, move another step, wait a moment, step again, wait, and then complete the move and wait again.

   (*Hint*: This requires changes to both the `move` and the `paint` methods. One approach is to add a new instance variable that represents which step the robot is taking. This instance variable is set in `move` and used in `paint`.)

6.15 Write a class named `HomingBot`. A `HomingBot`'s home is the intersection where it is constructed. Add a method named `goHome` that moves the robot to its home facing east. Assume there are no obstacles. Write a `main` method to test your class.

6.16 Write a class named `FuelBot`. A `FuelBot` has a "fuel tank" that can hold "fuel." The maximum number of units of fuel it can hold is specified when the robot is created. Each move consumes one unit of fuel. If there is no fuel, the robot won't move. Each time the robot encounters an intersection with a `Thing` on it, the fuel tank is refilled.

Extend the `RobotRC` (Remote Controlled) class and read the documentation to learn to direct the robot's actions from the keyboard. Set up a game to see if you can choose a path to move between two points—with appropriate refueling stops—without running out of fuel.

6.17 Write a new class named `RobotME` (My Edition) that extends `Robot` and includes a method named `clearArea`. This method takes four parameters. The first two are an avenue and street that specify the upper-left corner of a rectangular area. The third and fourth specify the width and height of the area. Calling `clearArea` causes the robot to pick up everything in the given rectangular area and then move to the area's upper-left corner and face east.

The robot may start anywhere in the city. Once it has reached the area, it should not leave it.

6.18 Create a component similar to the stick figure shown in Section 4.7.

a. Modify the stick figure component so that a stick figure may be constructed as either a child or an adult. An adult's preferred size is 180 by 270 pixels. A child has a preferred size that is half as large. Modify the test harness shown in Listing 6-14 to show two child stick figures and 1 adult.

(*Hints*: First, each stick figure will be similar to the `Thermometer` class. Use a test harness similar to Listing 6-14 to test your class. Second, define two constants, `CHILD` and `ADULT`. Pass one of them as a parameter to the stick figure's constructor. Third, assuming the `JPanel` containing the stick figures is named `contents`, include the statement `contents.setLayout (new RowLayout())` in your `main` method; it will align the stick figures appropriately. You will need to import `becker.gui.RowLayout`.)

b. Modify the stick figure constructor so that it takes three parameters. One, as in Part a, specifies whether the stick figure is an adult or a child. The other two parameters specify whether the left and right arms should be up, down, or straight out. Modify the test harness to construct six stick figures that are holding hands, as shown in Figure 6-17.

c. Modify the stick figure from Part b to add methods allowing the client to specify while the program is running whether an arm is up, down, or straight out. Modify the test harness to make the stick figures at each end of the line wave their free arm.

(figure 6-17)

Stick figures holding hands

Chapter 7 More on Variables and Methods

After studying this chapter, you should be able to:

- Write queries to reflect the state of an object
- Use queries to write a test harness that tests your class
- Write classes that use types other than integer, including floating-point types, `booleans`, characters, and strings
- Write and use an enumerated type
- Write a class modeling a simple problem
- Describe the difference between a class variable and an instance variable
- Write classes that implement an interface and can be used with provided graphical user interfaces from the `becker` library

We now have the intellectual tools to start writing object-oriented programs that have nothing to do with robots. In this chapter, we'll learn about additional kinds of information we can store (such as dollar values, individual characters, or strings of characters). We'll use that knowledge to build a class that could be used as part of a gas pump at your local gas station.

One problem, however, is that such programs are not nearly as easy to debug as robot programs because they are not as visual. We'll start by learning some techniques for testing and debugging our programs and finish by learning techniques for coupling a class with a graphical user interface.

7.1 Using Queries to Test Classes

Writing a class that functions correctly is difficult; many things can go wrong. Having a set of tests that demonstrates that a class is functioning correctly makes the job easier. Tests are also useful to students before handing in an assignment and to customers before they buy software. We'll begin by learning how to test the `SimpleBot` class used in Chapter 6. Later in this chapter, we'll apply these same techniques to a non-robot class.

KEY IDEA

A good set of tests makes a programmer's life much easier.

7.1.1 Testing a Command

It is tempting to test the `SimpleBot` class by writing and running a short program that creates a robot and moves it several times, and then looking at the screen to verify that the robot did, indeed, move correctly. The problem with this approach is that a person must remember what should happen and verify that it actually did happen. Relying on people for such tedious details is a risky proposition.

Remembering and verifying tedious details is something that computers do well, however. Our goal is to completely automate as much of the testing as possible by writing a program called a **test harness**. A test harness is used to test a class, and usually contains many individual tests.

KEY IDEA

Testing involves many tedious details—something computers are good at. Use them as much as possible in the testing process.

Writing a test involves five steps.

1. Decide which method you want to test.
2. Set up a known situation.
3. Determine the expected result of executing the method.
4. Execute the method.
5. Verify the results.

For example, we may want to test the `move` method in the `SimpleBot` class (Step 1). To set up a known situation (Step 2), we create a robot named `karel` at (4, 2) facing east in an empty city. This is shown in lines 7 and 8 of Listing 7-1. The choice of (4, 2) facing east is not critical. We could just as easily use a different intersection. However, we need to know which intersection is chosen so we can determine the expected result (Step 3). In this case, moving from (4, 2) should result in the robot being on intersection (4, 3), still facing east.

Line 11 in Listing 7-1 executes the code we want to test (Step 4).

Finally, we verify the results (Step 5) in lines 14–18. Before explaining these lines, let's take a look at the result of running the program, as shown in Figure 7-1, and note the following:

- This program prints results of the tests in the console window.
- One line is printed for each invocation of `ckEquals` in lines 15–18. It prints "`Passed`" if the last two arguments have equal values. If they do not, it prints "`***Failed`". In either case, `ckEquals` also prints the values of both arguments.
- The `ckEquals` method also prints the string given as the first argument. This serves simply to identify the test.

PATTERN

Test Harness

Listing 7-1: *A program to test the* `SimpleBot`*'s* `move` *method*

```
1  import becker.util.Test;
2
3  public class TestHarness
4  {
5    public static void main(String[ ] args)
6    { // Set up a known situation (an empty city; a robot on (4, 2) facing east).
7      SimpleCity c = new SimpleCity();
8      SimpleBot karel = new SimpleBot(c, 4, 2, Constants.EAST);
9
10     // Execute the move method.
11     karel.move();
12
13     // Verify the results -- robot on intersection (4, 3).
14     Test tester = new Test();        // This line isn't needed. See Section 7.5.2.
15     tester.ckEquals("new ave", 3, karel.getAvenue());
16     tester.ckEquals("same str", 4, karel.getStreet());
17     tester.ckEquals("same dir", Constants.EAST,
18                                 karel.getDirection());
19   }
20 }
```

KEY IDEA

Testing a method usually requires repeating Steps 2–5 several times.

We should not be under the illusion that Listing 7-1 is sufficient to test the `move` method. At a minimum, it should test moving in each of the four directions. If programs using `SimpleBots` can include walls or similar obstructions, more tests are required to verify that `move` behaves correctly when a robot is blocked. This observation implies that Steps 2–5 for testing a method should be repeated as many times as necessary.

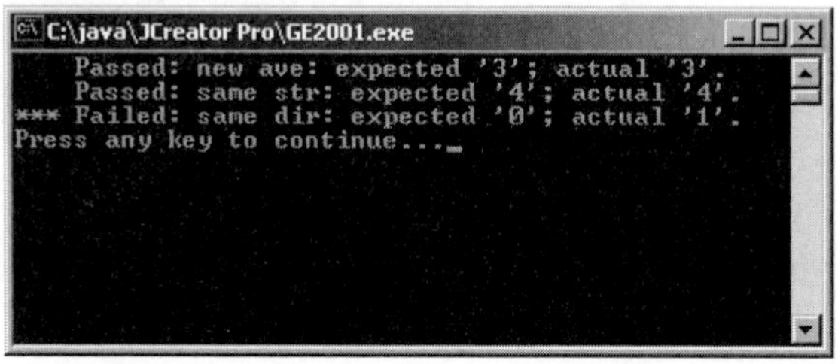

```
C:\java\JCreator Pro\GE2001.exe
    Passed: new ave: expected '3'; actual '3'.
    Passed: same str: expected '4'; actual '4'.
*** Failed: same dir: expected '0'; actual '1'.
Press any key to continue...
```

(figure 7-1)

Running the test in Listing 7-1, with a deliberate bug

What does `ckEquals` do? It compares the expected value (the second argument) with the actual value (the third argument) and prints an appropriate message. It is implemented approximately as shown in Listing 7-2. Overloaded versions for non-integer types have a few minor variations.

KEY IDEA

`ckEquals` compares the expected value with the actual value and prints an appropriate message.

Listing 7-2: *A possible implementation of the `ckEquals` method for integers*

```
public void ckEquals(String msg, int expected, int actual)
{ String result;
  if (expected == actual)
  { result = "  Passed: " + msg;
  } else
  { result = "*** Failed: " + msg;
  }
  result += ": expected '" + expected + "'; actual '" + actual + "'.";
  System.out.println(result);
}
```

7.1.2 Testing a Query

Testing a query is actually easier than testing a command. To test a command, we need some way to verify what the command did. In the previous example, we used accessor methods to get the current values of the critical instance variables. To test a query, we only need to compare the query's actual result with the expected result.

To further illustrate testing, let's define a new `SimpleBot` query that answers the question "How far is this robot from the origin?" Remember that the origin is the intersection (0, 0). Let's assume that the distance we want is "as the robot moves" (the legs of a triangle) rather than "as the crow flies" (the hypotenuse of a triangle). If the robot is on Street 4, Avenue 2, the answer is 4 + 2 = 6.

A first attempt at our query is as follows:

```
public int distanceToOrigin()                    // Contains a bug.
{ return this.street + this.avenue;
}
```

To begin writing a test harness, we can perform the five steps mentioned previously. The code to test (Step 1) is `distanceToOrigin`. Our first known situation (Step 2) will be to create a robot at the origin facing east (testing easy cases first is a good strategy). In this situation, the distance to the origin should be 0 (Step 3). Executing the code (Step 4) and verifying the result (Step 5) is shown in the following code in lines 7 and 10, respectively:

PATTERN

Test Harness

```
 1 public static void main(String[] args)
 2 { // Create a robot in an empty city at the origin facing east.
 3   SimpleCity c = new SimpleCity();
 4   SimpleBot k = new SimpleBot(c, 0, 0, Constants.EAST);
 5
 6   // Execute the code to test.
 7   int d = k.distanceToOrigin();
 8
 9   // Verify the result.
10   Test tester = new Test();          // This line isn't needed. See Section 7.5.2.
11   tester.ckEquals("at origin", 0, d);
12 }
```

This is a very incomplete test, however. The `distanceToOrigin` query could be written as follows and still pass this test:

```
public int distanceToOrigin()
{ return 0;
}
```

We can add more tests to this test harness that build from the original known situation. For example, it's not hard to see that after the previous test the robot should still be at the origin. So let's add another test immediately after it that moves the robot from the origin and then checks the distance again.

```
public static void main(String[] args)
{ // Create a robot in an empty city at the origin facing east.
  SimpleCity c = new SimpleCity();
  SimpleBot k = new SimpleBot(c, 0, 0, 0);

  // Execute the code to test.
  int d = k.distanceToOrigin();

  // Verify the result.
```

```
10    Test tester = new Test();          // This line isn't needed. See Section 7.5.2.
11    tester.ckEquals("at origin", 0, d);
12
13    // Move east 2 intersections and verify.
14    k.move();
15    k.move();
16    d = k.distanceToOrigin();
17    tester.ckEquals("east 2", 2, d);
18 }
```

So far we have only tested the robot on streets and avenues that are numbered zero or larger. What if the robot turned left (facing north) and moved to Street -1, as shown in Figure 7-2? Let's test it to make sure `distanceToOrigin` works correctly.

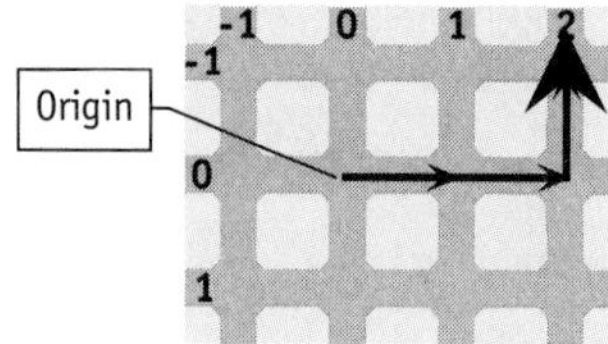

(figure 7-2)

Robot at (-1, 2), three moves from the origin

We could add the new test to our test harness by continuing to move the robot to (-1, 2). The following code uses a simpler approach. It constructs a robot on intersection (-1, 2) and then tests the result of the `distanceToOrigin` method. In this case, moving the robot isn't necessary. This code should be added after line 17 of the test harness.

```
SimpleBot k2 = new SimpleBot(c, -1, 2, 0);
d = k2.distanceToOrigin();
tester.ckEquals("neg str", 3, d);
```

Running the test harness says that the test fails. The expected value is 3, but the actual value is 1.

Reviewing the `distanceToOrigin` method shows why: we add the current street to the current avenue. When both are positive values, that works fine. But in this situation, it gives -1 + 2, or 1—a wrong answer.

The problem is that we want to add the *distance* between the origin and the robot's street. Distances are always positive. When the street (or avenue) is negative, we need to convert it to a positive number. We can do this with the helper method `abs`, short for "absolute value."

The following implementation of `distanceToOrigin` will fix this problem.

```
public int distanceToOrigin()
{ return this.abs(this.street) + this.abs(this.avenue);
}

private int abs(int x)
{ int answer = x;
  if (x < 0)
  { answer = -x;
  }
  return answer;
}
```

LOOKING AHEAD

In Section 7.5.2 we will learn about using a library of math functions. It already has `abs`.

With this change, all of the tests shown earlier will pass.

7.1.3 Using Multiple Main Methods

One fact that is implicit in the previous discussion is that Java allows multiple `main` methods. You can have only one `main` method in any given class, but as many classes as you want may each have their own `main` method. This is a good thing. If only one `main` method were allowed, we would need to choose between writing a test harness and writing a `main` method to run the program to perform its task.

KEY IDEA

Each class can have its own `main` *method.*

One common way to exploit the ability for each class to have a `main` method is to write one class that has nothing but `main`—the way we have been doing. This class is used to run the program to perform the desired task. However, every *other* class also has a `main` method to act as a test harness for that class. For example, the test harness shown in Listing 7-1 is in its own class. Instead, this could be written as part of the `SimpleBot` class. An outline of this approach is shown in Listing 7-3. Lines 1–14 show representative parts of the `SimpleBot` class. The test harness is in lines 16–28.

PATTERN

Test Harness

Listing 7-3: *An outline of how to include a test harness in the* `SimpleBot` *class*

```
1  import java.awt.*;
2  import becker.util.Test;
3  ...
4
5  public class SimpleBot extends Paintable
6  {
7    private int street;
8    private int avenue;
9    private int direction;
10   ...
11   public SimpleBot(...) { ... }
```

Listing 7-3: *An outline of how to include a test harness in the* `SimpleBot` *class* (continued)

```
12     public void move() { ... }
13     ...
14
15     // A test harness to test a SimpleBot.
16     public static void main(String[] args)
17     { // Set up a known situation -- a robot on intersection (4, 2)
18       SimpleCity c = new SimpleCity();
19       SimpleBot karel = new SimpleBot(c, 4, 2, EAST);
20
21       // Execute the code we want to test.
22       karel.move();
23
24       // Verify the results -- robot on intersection (4, 3).
25       Test tester = new Test();      // This line isn't needed. See Section 7.5.2.
26       tester.ckEquals("new ave", 3, karel.getAvenue());
27       ...
28     }
29   }
```

One issue that may be initially confusing is that even though `main` is within the `SimpleBot` class, we don't use the keyword `this`. Inside the test harness, we construct a specific `SimpleBot` object, `karel`. Throughout the `main` method, we invoke `karel`'s methods to test what has happened to that specific object.

KEY IDEA

The `main` *method can't use* `this`.

One advantage of placing a `main` method inside the class it tests is that we have access to the classes' private instance variables. For example, line 26 of Listing 7-3 can be replaced with the following:

```
tester.ckEquals("new ave", 3, karel.avenue);
```

We should use an accessor method such as `getAvenue` when it is available. However, we can access the instance variables directly when their values are needed for testing but should not be provided to others via an accessor method.

Many programmers take testing even further with a tool named JUnit. It provides a graphical user interface, shown in Figure 7-3, and does a better job of isolating individual tests from each other. More information, and the tool itself, is available at *www.junit.org*.

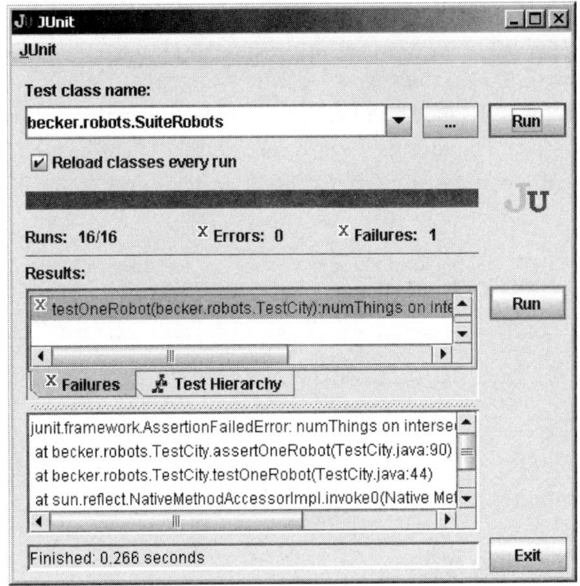

(figure 7-3)
A popular testing tool named `JUnit`

7.2 Using Numeric Types

KEY IDEA
Java's primitive types store values such as `159` *and* `'d'`.

Not everything in Java is an object like a `Robot` or a `Thing`. Integers and the type `int` are the most prominent examples we've seen of a **primitive type**. Primitive types store values such as integers (`159`) and characters (`'d'`), and correspond to how information is represented in the computer's hardware. Primitive types can't be extended and they don't have methods that can be called. In this sense, primitive types distort the design of the language. However, the designers of Java felt it necessary to use primitive types for integers and similar values to increase the execution speed of programs.

Java includes eight primitive types. Six of these store numbers, one stores the Boolean values `true` and `false`, and the last one stores characters.

7.2.1 Integer Types

KEY IDEA
An `int` *can only store values in a certain range.*

Why would Java have six different types to store numbers? Because they differ in the size and precision of the values they store. An `int`, for example, can only store values between `-2,147,483,648` and `2,147,483,647`. This range is large enough to store the net worth of most individuals, but not that of Bill Gates. It's more than enough to store the population of any city on earth, but not the population of the earth as a whole.

To address these issues, Java offers several kinds of integers, each with a different **range**, or number of different values it can store. The ranges of the four integer types are shown in Table 7-1. Variables with a greater range require more memory to store. For programs with many small numbers to store, it makes sense to use a type with a smaller range. Because beginning programmers rarely encounter such programs, we won't need to use `byte` and `short` in this book and will use `long` only rarely.

KEY IDEA

Different types can store different ranges of values.

Type	Smallest Value	Largest Value	Precision
`byte`	`-128`	`127`	exact
`short`	`-32,768`	`32,767`	exact
`int`	`-2,147,483,648`	`2,147,483,647`	exact
`long`	`-9,223,372,036,854,775,808`	`9,223,372,036,854,775,807`	exact

(table 7-1)

Integer types and their ranges

7.2.2 Floating-Point Types

Two other primitive types, `float` and `double`, store numbers with decimal places, such as 125.25, 3.14259, or -134.0. They are called **floating-point** types because of the way they are stored in the computer hardware.

Floating-point types can be so large or small that they are sometimes written in **scientific notation**. The number 6.022E23 has two parts, the **mantissa** (6.022) and the **exponent** (23). To convert 6.022E23 to a normal number, write down the mantissa and then add enough zeros to slide the decimal point 23 places to the right. If the exponent is negative, you must add enough zeros to slide the decimal point that many places to the left. For example, 6.022E23 is the same number as 602,200,000,000,000,000,000,000, while 5.89E-4 is the same as 0.000589. Their ranges and precisions are listed in Table 7-2.

KEY IDEA

Scientific notation can be used to express very large or very small numbers.

Type	Smallest Magnitude	Largest Magnitude	Precision
`float`	`±1.40239846E-45`	`±3.40282347E+38`	About 7 significant digits
`double`	`±4.94065645841246544E-324`	`±1.79769313486231570E+308`	About 16 significant digits

(table 7-2)

The ranges and precisions of the various floating-point types

How big are these numbers? Scientists believe the diameter of the universe is about 1.0E28 centimeters, or 1.0E61 plank units—the smallest unit we can measure. The universe contains approximately 1.0E80 elementary particles such as quarks, the component parts of atoms. So the range of type `double` will certainly be sufficient for most applications.

Floating-point numbers don't behave exactly like real numbers. Consider, for a moment, 1/3 written in decimal: 0.33333.... No matter how many threes you add, 0.33333 won't be exactly equal to 1/3. The situation is similar with 1/10 in binary, the number system computers use. It's impossible to represent 1/10 exactly; the best we can do is to approximate it. The closeness of the approximation is given by the **precision**. `float`s have about 7 digits of precision, while `double`s have about 16 digits. This means, for example, that a `float` can't distinguish between `1.00000001` and `1.00000002`. As far as a `float` is concerned, both numbers are indistinguishable from `1.0`. Another effect is that assigning `0.1` to a `float` and then adding that number to itself 10 times does *not* yield `1.0` but `1.0000001`.

KEY IDEA

Comparing floating-point numbers for equality is usually a bad idea.

The fact that floating-point numbers are only approximations can cause programmers headaches if their programs require a high degree of precision. For beginning programmers, however, this is rarely a concern. One exception, however, is when comparing a `float` or a `double` for equality, the approximate nature of these types may cause an error. For example, the following code fragment appears to print a table of numbers between `0.0` and `10.0`, increasing by `0.1`, along with the squares of those numbers.

```
double d = 0.0;

while (d != 10.0)
{ System.out.println(d + "  " + d*d);
  d = d + 0.1;
}
```

The first few lines of the table would be:

```
0.0 0.0
0.1 0.010000000000000002
0.2 0.04000000000000001
0.30000000000000004 0.09000000000000002
0.4 0.16000000000000003
```

Already we can see the problem: `d`, the first number on each line, is not increasing by exactly `0.1` each time as expected. In the fourth line the number printed is only approximately `0.3`.

By the time d gets close to 10.0, the errors have built up. The result is that d skips from 9.99999999999998 to 10.09999999999998 and is never exactly equal to 10.0, as our stopping condition requires. Consequently, the loop keeps printing for a very long time.

The correct way to code this loop is to use an inequality, as in the following code:

```
while (d <= 10.0)
{ ...
}
```

7.2.3 Converting Between Numeric Types

Sometimes we need to convert between different numeric types. In many situations, information is not lost and Java makes the conversion automatically. For example, consider the following statement:

```
double d = 159;
```

Java will implicitly convert the integer 159 to a double value (159.0) and then assign it to d.

The reverse is not true. If assigning a value to another type risks losing information, a cast is required. A cast is our assurance to the compiler that we either know from the nature of the problem that information will not be lost, or know that information will be lost and accept or even prefer that result.

KEY IDEA

Casting converts values from one type to another. Sometimes it loses information.

For example, consider the following statements:

```
double d = 3.999;
int i = d;
```

Java will display an error message regarding the second assignment because an integer can't store the decimal part of 3.999, only the 3. If we want to perform this assignment anyway and lose the .999, leaving only 3 in the variable i, we need to write it as follows:

LOOKING AHEAD

Section 7.5.2 discusses a method to round a number rather than truncate it.

```
double d = 3.999;
int i = (int)d;
```

The new part, (int), is the cast. The form of a cast is the destination type placed in parentheses. It can also apply to an entire expression, as in the following statement:

```
int i = (int)(d * d / 2.5);
```

Casting has a high precedence, so you will usually need to use parentheses around expressions.

Assigning from a `double` to an `int` is not the only place information can be lost and a cast required. Information can also be lost assigning values from a `double` to a `float` or from a bigger integer type such as `long` to a smaller type such as `int`.

7.2.4 Formatting Numbers

Java automatically converts a primitive type to a string before concatenating it to another string. This capability allows us to easily print out a mixture of strings and numbers, such as `System.out.println("Age = " + age);` where `age` is an integer.

Automatic conversion to a string does not work as well for `double` values, where we often want to control how many significant digits are printed. For example, the following code might be used in calculating the price of a used car:

```
double carPrice = 12225.00;
double taxRate = 0.15;

System.out.println("Car: " + carPrice);
System.out.println("Tax: " + carPrice * taxRate);
System.out.println("Total: " + carPrice * (1.0 + taxRate));
```

This code gives the following output:

```
Car: 12225.0
Tax: 1833.75
Total: 14058.749999999998
```

These results are far from ideal. We want to see a currency symbol such as $ or £ printed. All of the amounts should have exactly two decimal places, rounding as necessary. The thousands should also be grouped with commas or spaces, depending on local conventions. It's difficult to implement all these details correctly.

Using a `NumberFormat` Object

Fortunately, Java provides a set of classes for formatting numbers, including currencies. These classes all include a method named `format` that takes a number as an argument and returns a string formatted appropriately. Listing 7-4 shows how to use a currency formatting object named `money`. These statements produce formatted output such as the following:

```
Car: $12,225.00
Tax: $1,833.75
Total: $14,058.75
```

Listing 7-4: *Using a currency formatting object*

FIND THE CODE

ch07/formatNumbers/

```
1 double carPrice = 12225.00;
2 double taxRate = 0.15;
3
4 System.out.println("Car: " + money.format(carPrice));
5 System.out.println("Tax: " +
6                     money.format(carPrice * taxRate));
7 System.out.println("Total: " +
8                     money.format(carPrice * (1.0 + taxRate)));
```

A formatting object is not normally obtained by using a constructor. Instead, a **factory method** in the `NumberFormat` class is called. A factory method returns an object reference, as a constructor does. Unlike a constructor, a factory method has the option of returning a subclass of `NumberFormat` that is specialized for a specific task. In this case, the factory method tries to determine the country where the computer is located and returns an object customized for the local currency.

LOOKING AHEAD

Implementing factory methods will be discussed in Chapter 12.

The `NumberFormat` class contains the `getCurrencyInstance`, `getNumberInstance`, and `getPercentInstance` factory methods, along with several others. The `getCurrencyInstance` factory method can be used by importing `java.text.NumberFormat` and including the following statement before line 4 in Listing 7-4.

KEY IDEA

Factory methods help you obtain an object already set up for a specific situation.

```
NumberFormat money = NumberFormat.getCurrencyInstance();
```

A formatter for general numbers can be obtained with the `getNumberInstance` factory method. It can be customized to format numbers with a certain number of decimal places and to print grouping characters. Consider the following example:

```
NumberFormat f = NumberFormat.getNumberInstance();
f.setMaximumFractionDigits(4);
f.setGroupingUsed(true);
System.out.println(f.format(3141.59265359));
```

These statements will print the value `3,141.5927`—the value rounded to four decimal places with an appropriate character (in this case, a comma) used to group the digits.

Columnar Output

Programs often produce lots of numbers that are most naturally formatted in columns. Even with the program to calculate the tax for a car purchase, aligning the labels and numbers vertically makes the information easier to read.

One of the easiest approaches uses the `printf` method in the `System.out` object. It was added in Java 1.5, and is not available in earlier versions of Java.

KEY IDEA

`printf`'s format string says how to format the other arguments.

The `printf` method is unusual in that it takes a variable number of arguments. It always takes at least one, called the **format string**, that includes embedded codes describing how the other arguments should be printed.

Here's an example where `printf` has three arguments.

FIND THE CODE

ch07/formatNumbers/

```
System.out.printf("%-10s%10s", "Car:", money.format(carPrice));
```

The first argument is the format string. It includes two **format specifiers**, each one beginning with a percent (`%`) sign and ending with a character indicating what kind of data to print. The first format specifier is for the second argument; the second specifier is for the third argument. Additional specifiers and arguments could easily be added.

In each case, the `s` indicates that the argument to print should be a string. The `10` instructs `printf` to print the string in a field that is 10 characters wide. The minus sign (`-`) in one says to print that string **left justified** (starting on the left side of the column). The specifier without the minus sign will print the string **right justified** (on the right side of the column).

This line, as specified, does not print a newline character at the end; thus, any subsequent output would be on the same line. We could call `println()` to end the line, or we could add another format specifier. The specifier `%n` is often added to the format string to begin a new line. It does *not* correspond to one of the arguments.

Table 7-3 gives several examples of the most common format specifiers and the results they produce. A `d` is used to print a decimal number, such as an `int`. An `f` is used to print a floating-point number, such as a `double`. In addition to the total field width, it specifies how many decimal places to print. More examples and a complete description are available in the online documentation for the `java.util.Formatter` class.

(table 7-3)

Examples of common format specifiers; dots signify spaces

Format Specifier and Argument	Result
`"%-10s", "Car:"`	`Car:······`
`"%10s", "Car:"`	`······Car:`
`"%10d", 314`	`·······314`
`"%10.4f", 3.1415926`	`3.1416····`
`"%-10.4f", 3.1415926`	`····3.1416`

The `printf` method has many other options that are documented in the `Formatter` class. Discussing them further, however, is beyond the scope of this book.

7.2.5 Taking Advantage of Shortcuts

Java includes a number of shortcuts for some of the most common operations performed with numeric types. For example, one of the most common is to add 1 to a variable. Rather than writing `ave = ave + 1`, Java permits the shortcut of writing `ave++`. A similar shortcut is writing `ave--` in place of `ave = ave - 1`.

KEY IDEA

`i++` is a shortcut for `i = i + 1`.

It is also common to add the result of an expression to a variable. For example, the following is `SimpleBot`'s `move` method as written in Listing 6-6:

```
public void move()
{ this.street = this.street + this.strOffset();
  this.avenue = this.avenue + this.aveOffset();
  Utilities.sleep(400);
}
```

Instead of repeating the variable on the right side of the equal sign, we can use the `+=` operator, which means to add the right side to the value of the variable on the left, and then store the result in the variable on the left. More precisely, *«var»* `+=` *«expression»* means *«var»* `=` *«var»* `+ (`*«expression»*`)`. The parentheses are important in determining what happens if *«expression»* contains more than a single value. The following example is equivalent to the previous code:

```
public void move()
{ this.street += this.strOffset();
  this.avenue += this.aveOffset();
  Utilities.sleep(400);
}
```

There are also `-=`, `*=`, and `/=` operators. They are used much less frequently but behave the same as `+=` except for the change in numeric operation.

7.3 Using Non-Numeric Types

Variables can also store information that is not numeric, using the types `boolean`, `char`, and `String`.

7.3.1 The `boolean` Type

The `boolean` type is used for `true` and `false` values. We have already seen Boolean expressions used to control `if` and `while` statements, and as a temporary variable and the return type in predicates (see, for example, Listing 5-3). We have also explored using `boolean` values in expressions (see Section 5.4).

Instance variables, named constants, and parameter variables can also be of type boolean. For example, a Boolean instance variable can store information about whether a robot is broken. The robot might consult that variable each time it is asked to move, and only move if it has not been previously broken.

```
public class SimpleBot extends Paintable
{ private int avenue;
  private int street;
  private boolean isBroken = false;
  ...

  public void breakRobot()
  { this.isBroken = true;
  }

  public void move()
  { if (!this.isBroken)
    { this.avenue = ...
      this.street = ...
    }
  }
  ...
}
```

7.3.2 The Character Type

A single character such as a, Z, ?, or 5 can be stored in a variable of type char. These include the characters you type at the keyboard—and many more that you can't type directly. Like the other primitive types, the char type may be used for instance variables, temporary variables, parameter variables, and named constants, and may be returned from queries.

One use for characters is to control a robot from the keyboard. Sim, a superclass of Robot, has a protected method named keyTyped that is called each time a key is typed, yet it does nothing. The method has a char parameter containing the character that was typed. By overriding the method, we can tell a robot to move when 'm' is typed, turn right when 'r' is typed, and so on. The KeyBot class in Listing 7-5 defines such a robot. The same technique can be used in subclasses of Intersection and Thing because they all descend from Sim—the class implementing keyTyped. (When running a program using this feature, you must click on the image of the city before it will accept keystrokes. The image will have a black outline when it is ready to accept keystrokes.)

Listing 7-5: *A robot that responds to keystrokes*

```
1  import becker.robots.*;
2
3  public class KeyBot extends RobotSE
4  {
5     public KeyBot(City c, int str, int ave, Direction dir)
6     { super(c, str, ave, dir);
7     }
8
9     protected void keyTyped(char key)
10    { if (key == 'm' || key == 'M')
11      { this.move();
12      } else if (key == 'r' || key == 'R')
13      { this.turnRight();
14      } else if (key == 'l' || key == 'L')
15 { this.turnLeft();         // Watch out. The above test uses
16                            // a lowercase 'L', not a "one".
17    }
18 }
```

FIND THE CODE

ch07/keyBot/

The parameter, `key`, is compared to the letters '`m`', '`r`', and '`l`' in lines 10, 12, and 14. In each case, if the comparison is true (that is, the parameter contains an '`m`', '`r`', or '`l`'), an action is taken. If a different key is pressed, the robot does nothing. A slightly enhanced version of this method is implemented in the `RobotRC` class. You can extend `RobotRC` anytime you want to use the keyboard as a remote control (RC) for a robot.

KEY IDEA

Override `keyTyped` to make a robot that can be controlled from the keyboard.

The `'m'`, `'r'`, and `'l'` are character literals. To write a specific character value, place the character between two single quotes. What if you want to compare a value to a single quote? Placing it between two other single quotes (`'''`) confuses the compiler, causing an error message. The solution is to use an **escape sequence**. An escape sequence is an alternative way to write characters that are used in the code for other purposes. The escape sequence for a single quote is `\'` (a backslash followed by a single quote). All escape sequences begin with a backslash. The escape sequence is placed in single quotes, just like any other character literal. Table 7-4 shows some common escape sequences, many of which have their origins in controlling printers.

KEY IDEA

Some characters have special meaning to Java. They have to be written with an escape sequence.

The last escape sequence, `\u`*dddd*, is used for representing characters from a wide range of languages, and includes everything from accented characters to Bengali characters to Chinese ideograms. You can find more information online at *www.unicode.org*. Unfortunately, actually using these characters requires corresponding fonts on your computer.

(table 7-4)

Character escape sequences

Sequence	Meaning
`\'`	Single quote
`\"`	Double quote
`\\`	Backslash
`\n`	Newline—used to start a new line of text when printing at the console
`\t`	Tab—inserts space so that the next character is placed at the next **tab stop**. Each tab stop is a predefined distance from the previous tab stop.
`\b`	Backspace—moves the cursor backwards over the previously printed character
`\r`	Return—moves the cursor to the beginning of the current line
`\f`	Form feed—moves the cursor to the top of the next page in a printer
`\u`*dddd*	A Unicode character, each *d* being a hexadecimal digit (0–9, a–f, A–F)

7.3.3 Using Strings

Strings of characters such as "Hello, karel!" are used frequently in Java programs. Strings are stored, appropriately, in variables of type `String`. A string can hold thousands of characters or no characters at all (the empty string). These characters can be the familiar ones found on the keyboard or those specified with escape characters, as shown in Table 7-4.

`String` is *not* a primitive type. In fact, it is a class just as `Robot` is a class. On the other hand, strings are used so often that Java's designers included special support for them that other classes do not have—so much special support that it sometimes feels like strings are primitive types.

Special Java Support for Strings

KEY IDEA

Java provides special support for the `String` *class.*

The special support the `String` class enjoys from the Java compiler falls into three categories:

- Java will automatically construct a `String` object for each sequence of characters between double quotes; that is, Java has literal values for strings just like it has literal values for integers (`5`, `-259`), doubles (`3.14159`), and Booleans (`true`).
- Java will "add" two strings together with the plus operator to create a new string consisting of one string followed by the other. This is called **concatenation**.
- Java will automatically convert primitive values and objects to strings before concatenating them with a string.

Listing 7-6 shows several examples of this special support. The program uses `System.out.println` to print the strings, as we did in Section 6.6.1. The difference here is the manipulations of the strings before they are printed.

FIND THE CODE

ch07/stringDemo/

Listing 7-6: *A simple program demonstrating built-in Java support for the* `String` *class*

```
1  import becker.robots.*;
2
3  public class Main
4  {
5    public static void main(String[] args)
6    { String greeting = "Hello";
7      String name = "karel";
8
9
10     System.out.println(greeting + "," + name + "!");
11
12
13
14     System.out.println("Did you know that 2*PI = " + 2*Math.PI + "?");
15
16     City c = new City();
17     Robot karel = new Robot(c, 1, 2, Direction.SOUTH);
18     System.out.println("c=" + c);
19   }
20 }
```

A `String` object is created automatically from the string literal "Hello"

Four strings are concatenated using the "+" operator to produce a single string, "Hello, karel!"

The primitive value resulting from this expression is automatically converted to a string and concatenated using the plus operator

The object referenced by `c` is automatically converted to a string by calling its `toString` method

Program output:

```
Hello, karel!
Did you know that 2*PI = 6.283185307179586?
c=becker.robots.City[SimBag[robots=[becker.robots.Robot
[street=1, avenue=2, direction=SOUTH, isBroken=false, numThings
InBackpack=0]], things=[]]]
```

In lines 6 and 7, two `String` objects are created using the special support the Java language provides for strings. These lines would look more familiar if they used a normal constructor, which works as expected:

```
String greeting = new String("Hello");
String name = new String("karel");
```

Line 14 contains an expression that is evaluated before it is passed as an argument to `println`. The normal rules of evaluation are used: multiplication has a higher precedence than addition, so `2*Math.PI` is evaluated first. Then, two string additions, or concatenations, are performed left to right. Because the left and right sides of the first addition operator do not have the same type, the less general one (the result of `2*Math.PI`) is converted to a string before being "added" to the other operand.

Finally, when Java converts an object to a string, as it does in line 18, it calls the method named `toString`, which every class inherits from `Object`.

Overriding `toString`

KEY IDEA

Every class should override `toString` to provide meaningful information.

Java depends on the fact that every object has a `toString` method that can be called to provide a representation of the object as a string. The default implementation, inherited from the `Object` class, only prints the name of the class and a number identifying the particular object. To be useful, the method should be overridden in classes you write. The information it presents is often oriented to debugging, but it doesn't have to be.

The standard format for such information is the name of the object's class followed by an open bracket, "`[`". Information relevant to the object follows, and then ends with a closing bracket, "`]`". This format allows objects to be nested. For example, when the `City` object is printed, we see that it prints the `Robot` and `Thing` objects it references. Each of these, in turn, print relevant information about themselves, such as their location.

Listing 7-7 shows a `toString` method that could be added to the `SimpleBot` class shown in Listing 6-6.

PATTERN

toString

Listing 7-7: *A sample `toString` method*

```
public class SimpleBot extends Paintable
{ private int street;
  private int avenue;
  private int direction;

  // Constructor and methods are omitted.

 /** Represent a SimpleBot as a string. */
 public String toString()
 { return "SimpleBot" +
       " [street=" + this.street +
       ", avenue=" + this.avenue +
       ", direction=" + this.direction +
       "]";
 }
}
```

Querying a String

The `String` class provides many methods to query a `String` object. These include finding out how long a string is, whether two strings start the same way, the first location of a particular character, and so on. The most important of these queries are shown in Table 7-5.

(table 7-5)

Methods that query a string

Method	Description
`char charAt(int index)`	Returns the character at the location specified by the **index**. The index is the position of the character—an integer between 0 (the first character) and one less than the length of the string (the last character).
`int compareTo(String aString)`	Compares this string to `aString`, returning a negative integer if this string is lexicographically smaller than `aString`, 0 if the two strings are equal, and a positive integer if this string is lexicographically greater than `aString`.
`boolean equals(Object anObject)`	Compares this string to another object (usually a string). Returns `true` if `anObject` is a string containing exactly the same characters in the same order as this string.
`int indexOf(char ch)`	Returns the index within this string of the first occurrence of the specified character. If the character is not contained within the string, `-1` is returned.
`int indexOf(char ch, int fromIndex)`	Returns the index within this string of the first occurrence of the specified character, starting the search at `fromIndex`. If no such character exists, `-1` is returned.
`int indexOf(String substring)`	Returns the index of the first character of the first occurrence of the given substring within this string. If the given substring is not contained within this string, `-1` is returned.
`int lastIndexOf(char ch)`	Returns the index of the last occurrence of the given character within this string. If the given character is not contained within this string, `-1` is returned.
`int length()`	Returns the number of characters contained in this string.
`boolean startsWith(String prefix)`	Returns `true` if this string starts with the specified prefix.

KEY IDEA

Characters in strings are numbered starting at position 0.

The `charAt` and `indexOf` methods in Table 7-5 refer to a character's index, or position within the string. In the string "Hello", 'H' is at index 0, 'e' is at index 1, and 'o' is at index 4. For example, if the variable `greeting` refers to "Hello", then `greeting.charAt(1)` returns the character 'e'.

It may seem strange for strings to begin indexing at zero, but this is common in computer science. We have already seen it in the robot cities, where streets and avenues begin with zero. We'll see it again in upcoming chapters, where collections of values are indexed beginning with zero.

KEY IDEA

>, >=, <, and <= don't work for strings.

When `a` and `b` are primitive types, we can compare them with operators such as `a == b`, `a < b`, and `a >= b`. For reference types such as `String`, only the `==` and `!=` operators work—and they do something different than you might expect.

KEY IDEA

Use the `equals` method to compare strings for equality.

Instead of `==`, compare two strings for equality with the `equals` method. It returns true if every position in both strings has exactly the same character.

```
if (oneString.equals(anotherString))
{ System.out.println("The strings are equal.");
}
```

Instead of `!=`, use a Boolean expression, as follows:

```
!oneString.equals(anotherString)
```

KEY IDEA

Use `compareTo` to compare strings for order.

The string equivalent to less than and greater than is the `compareTo` method. It can be used as shown in the following code fragment:

```
String a = ...
String b = ...
if (a.compareTo(b) < 0)
{ // a comes before b in the dictionary
} else if (a.compareTo(b) > 0)
{ // a comes after b in the dictionary
} else // if (a.compareTo(b) == 0)
{ // a and b are equal
}
```

The `compareTo` method determines the **lexicographic order** of two strings—essentially, the order they would have in the dictionary. To determine which of two strings comes first, compare the characters in each string, character by character, from left to right. Stop when you reach the end of one string or a pair of characters that differ. If you stop because one string is shorter than the other, as is the case with "`hope`" and "`hopeful`" in Figure 7-4, the shorter string precedes the longer string. If you stop because characters do not match, as is the case with "`f`" and "`l`" in "`hopeful`" and "`hopeless`", then compare the mismatched characters. In this case "`f`" comes before "`l`", and so "`hopeful`" precedes "`hopeless`" in lexicographic order.

```
hope
hopeful
hopeless
```

(figure 7-4)

Lexicographic ordering

If the strings have non-alphabetic characters, you may consult Appendix D to determine their ordering. For example, a fragment of the ordering is as follows:

```
! " # ... 0 1 2 ... 9 : ; < ... A B C ... Z [ \ ... a b c ... z { | }
```

This implies that "`hope!`" comes before "`hopeful`" because `!` appears before `f` in the previous ordering. Similarly, "`Hope`" comes before "`hope`".

Transforming Strings

Other methods in the `String` class do not answer questions about a given string, but rather return a copy of the string that has been transformed in some way. For example, the following code fragment prints "`Warning WARNING`"; `message2` is a copy of `message1` that has been transformed by replacing all of the lowercase characters with uppercase characters.

```
String message1 = "Warning";
String message2 = message1.toUpperCase();
System.out.println(message1 + " " + message2);
```

The designers of the `String` class had two options for the `toUppercase` method. They could have provided a command that changes all of the characters in the given string to their uppercase equivalents. The alternative is a method that makes a copy of the string, changing each lowercase letter in the original string to an uppercase letter in the copy.

The designers of the `String` class consistently chose the second option. This makes the `String` class immutable. After a string is created, it cannot be changed. The methods given in Table 7-6, however, make it easy to create copies of a string with specific transformations. The `StringBuffer` class is similar to `String`, but includes methods that allow you to modify the string instead of creating a new one.

KEY IDEA

An immutable class is one that does not provide methods to change its instance variables.

The `substring` method is slightly different. Its transformation is to extract a piece of the string, returning it as a new string. For example, if `name` refers to the string "`Karel`", then `name.substring(1,4)` returns "`are`". Recall that strings are indexed beginning with 0, so the character at index 1 is `a`. The second index to `substring`, 4 in this example, is the index of the first character *not* included in the substring.

(table 7-6)

Methods that return a transformed copy of a string

Method	Description
`String replace(char oldChar, char newChar)`	Returns a copy of this string that has all occurrences of `oldChar` replaced with `newChar`.
`String substring(int beginIndex, int endIndex)`	Returns a new string containing all the characters between `beginIndex` and `endIndex-1`, inclusive. The character at `endIndex` is the first character not included in the new string.
`String toLowerCase()`	Returns a copy of this string that has all the uppercase characters replaced with their lowercase equivalents.
`String toUpperCase()`	Returns a copy of this string that has all the lowercase characters replaced with their uppercase equivalents.
`String trim()`	Returns a copy of this string that has all white space (such as space, tab, and newline characters) removed from the beginning and end of the string.

Example: Counting Vowels

As an illustration of what you can do with strings, let's write a program that counts the number of vowels (a, e, i, o, u) in a string. As a test, we'll use the famous quotation from Hamlet, "To be, or not to be: that is the question." The expected answer is 13.

To begin solving this problem, let's think about how to solve it without a computer. One straightforward method is to look at each letter, proceeding from left to right. If the letter is a vowel, we can put a tick mark on a piece of paper. When we get to the end, the number of ticks corresponds to the number of vowels. Our program can adopt a similar strategy by using a variable to record the number of vowels.

This illustration will require us to examine individual letters in a string and compare letters to other letters. We don't have experience solving these kinds of problems, so let's proceed by solving a series of simpler problems. First, let's print the individual letters in the quotation. This shows that we can process the letters one at a time. After mastering that, let's count the number of times a single vowel, such as 'o', occurs. Finally, after solving these subproblems, we'll count all the vowels.

To print all the letters in the quotation, we must access each individual letter. According to Table 7-5, the `charAt` method will return an individual character from a string. However, it needs an index, a number between 0 and one less than the length of the string. Evidently, the `length` method will also be useful. To obtain the numbers between 0 and the length, we could use a `for` loop. We'll start a variable named `index` at 0 and increment it by 1 each time the loop is executed until `index` is just less than the length. These ideas are included in the following Java program that prints each character in the quotation, one character per line.

```
public static void main(String[] args)
{ String quotation = "To be, or not to be: that is the question.";

  // Loop over each letter in the quotation.
  for (int index = 0; index < quotation.length(); index++)
  { // Examine one letter in the quotation.
    char ch = quotation.charAt(index);
    System.out.println(ch);
  }
}
```

Notice that the `for` loop starts the index at `0`, the first position in the string. The loop continues executing as long as the index is *less* than the length of the string. As soon as it equals the length of the string, it's time to stop. For example, Figure 7-5 illustrates a string of length 5, but its largest index is only 4. Therefore, the appropriate test to include in the `for` loop is `index < quotation.length()`.

KEY IDEA

A string of length 5 *has indices numbered* 0 *to* 4.

Index:	*0*	*1*	*2*	*3*	*4*
Characters:	T	o		b	e

(figure 7-5)

A string with its index positions marked

To modify this program to count the number of times 'o' appears, we can replace the `println` with an `if` statement and add a counter. The call to `println` in line 14 concatenates the value of our `counter` variable with two strings to make a complete sentence reporting the results. The modifications are shown in bold in the following code:

```
 1 public static void main(String[] args)
 2 { String quotation = "To be, or not to be: that is the question.";
 3
 4   int counter = 0;          // Count number of os.
 5   // Loop over each letter in the quotation.
 6   for (int index = 0; index < quotation.length(); index++)
 7   { // Examine one letter in the quotation.
 8     char ch = quotation.charAt(index);
 9     if (ch == 'o')
10     { counter += 1;
11     }
12   }
13
14   System.out.println("There are " + counter + " occurrences of 'o'.");
15 }
```

The last step is to count *all* the vowels instead of only the os. A straightforward approach is to add four more `if` statements, all similar to the one in lines 9–11. However, when we consider that other quotations might include uppercase vowels (totaling 10 `if` statements), looking for an alternative becomes attractive.

We can reduce the number of tests if we first transform the quote using `toLowerCase`, as shown in line 3 of Listing 7-8. This assures us that all vowels will be lowercase.

KEY IDEA

`indexOf` searches a string for a particular character.

The `indexOf` method shown in Table 7-5 offers an interesting possibility. It will search a string and return the index of the first occurrence of a given character. If the character isn't there, `indexOf` returns -1. Suppose we take a letter from our quotation and search for it in a string that has only vowels. If the letter from the quotation is a vowel, it will be found and `indexOf` will return a 0 or larger. If it's not there, `indexOf` will return -1. This idea is implemented in Listing 7-8. The changes from the previous version are again shown in bold.

FIND THE CODE

ch07/countVowels/

Listing 7-8: *Searching a string to count the number of vowels*

```
 1 public static void main(String[] args)
 2 { String quotation = "To be, or not to be: that is the question";
 3   String lowerQuote = quotation.toLowerCase();
 4   String vowels = "aeiou";
 5
 6   int counter = 0;          // Count the number of vowels.
 7   // Loop over each letter in the quotation.
 8   for (int index = 0; index < lowerQuote.length(); index++)
 9   { // Examine one letter in the quotation.
10     char ch = lowerQuote.charAt(index);
11     if (vowels.indexOf(ch) >= 0)
12     { counter += 1;
13     }
14   }
15
16   System.out.println("There are" + counter + "vowels.");
17 }
```

7.3.4 Understanding Enumerations

KEY IDEA

Java version 1.5 or higher is required to use this feature.

Programmers often need a variable that holds a limited set of values. For example, we may you need to store a person's gender—either male or female. For this we need only two values.

We could define some constants, using `m` for male and `f` for female, as follows:

```
public class Person extends Object
{ public static final char MALE = 'm';
  public static final char FEMALE = 'f';

  private String name;
  private char gender;

  public Person(String aName, char aGender)
  { super();
    this.name = aName;
    this.gender = aGender;
  }
  ...
}
```

But still, someone could create a `Person` object like this, either by mistake or maliciously:

```
Person juan = new Person("Juan", 'z');
```

Is Juan male or female? Neither. This mistake might create a severe problem later in the program. It might crash, or it could just cause embarrassment if Juan happened to be male and was assigned to a sports team with the following `if` statement:

```
if (juan.getGender() == MALE)
{ add to the boy's team
} else
{ add to the girl's team
}
```

A better solution is to define an **enumeration**, also called an **enumerated type**. An enumeration lists all of the possible values for that type. Those values can be used as literals in the program, and the compiler will allow only those literals to be used. This makes it impossible to assign Juan the gender of 'z'. `Direction`, used extensively in robot programs, is an example of an enumeration.

KEY IDEA

An enumeration has an explicitly listed set of values.

An enumeration for gender can be defined as shown in Listing 7-9. Like a class, the code is placed in a file matching the type name, `Gender.java`.

FIND THE CODE

ch07/enums/

PATTERN

Enumeration

Listing 7-9: *Defining an enumeration*

```
/** An enumeration of the genders used in the Person class.
 *
 * @author Byron Weber Becker */
public enum Gender
{ MALE, FEMALE
}
```

This is similar to a class definition except that the keyword `class` replaces the keyword `enum` and the enumeration does not include a clause to extend another class. Inside the braces, we list the different values for variables of type `Gender`, separating each with a comma.

KEY IDEA

The compiler guarantees that only valid values are assigned to enumerations.

The `Person` class shown earlier can be rewritten using this enumeration, as shown in Listing 7-10. Notice that `Gender` is used as a type, just like `int` or `Robot`, when the instance variable `gender` is declared in line 9. Similarly, it's used to declare a parameter variable in line 12 and a return type in line 19. In each of these cases, the Java compiler will guarantee that the value is `Gender.MALE`, `Gender.FEMALE`, or `null`—and nothing else. `null` is a special value that means "no value"; we will learn more about `null` in Section 8.1.2.

The `main` method in lines 24–29 uses the value `Gender.MALE` twice, once to construct a new `Person` object and once to test that the `getGender` method returns the expected value.

FIND THE CODE

ch07/enums/

PATTERN

Enumeration

Test Harness

Listing 7-10: *Using the* `Gender` *enumerated type*

```
1  import becker.util.Test;
2
3  /** Represent a person.
4   *
5   *  @author Byron Weber Becker */
6  public class Person extends Object
7  {
8    private String name;
9    private Gender gender;
10
11   /** Construct a person. */
12   public Person(String aName, Gender aGender)
13   { super();
14     this.name = aName;
15     this.gender = aGender;
16   }
17
18   /** Get this person's gender. */
19   public Gender getGender()
20   { return this.gender;
21   }
22
23   // Test the Person class
24   public static void main(String[ ] args)
25   { Person juan = new Person("Juan", Gender.MALE);
26     Test tester = new Test();     // This line isn't needed. See Section 7.5.2.
```

Listing 7-10: *Using the* `Gender` *enumerated type* (continued)

```
      tester.ckEquals("gender", Gender.MALE, juan.getGender());
   }
}
```

7.4 Example: Writing a Gas Pump Class

We now have all the pieces needed to write a class that has nothing to do with robots. It could be a part of a drawing program, a payroll package, or a word processor.

For our first example, we'll start small and write a class that could be used as part of a gas pump. Every gas pump must have a meter to measure the gas that is delivered to the customer. Of course, measuring the gas is not enough. We must also be able to get the measurement so that we can display it on the gas pump. Our meter can also provide the following information:

- The price of one unit of gas (the price per liter or price per gallon)
- The octane level of the gas (a performance measure, typically between 87 and 93)
- A marketing name for that kind of gas (for example, "silver" or "ultra")
- The total cost of the gas delivered to the customer

LOOKING AHEAD

In this chapter's GUI section, we'll learn how to add a prepared user interface to this class.

In addition, when one customer is finished and another one arrives, we must be able to reset the measurements.

We'll call this class a `Meter`. To develop it, we'll build on the testing strategies outlined in Section 7.1.1 and include a `main` method for testing. An initial skeleton is shown in Listing 7-11. It extends `Object` because a meter doesn't seem to be based on any of the classes we've seen so far. It includes a constructor with no parameters (so far), and a `main` method for testing purposes. The `main` method creates a new `Meter` object, but there is nothing to test (yet).

Listing 7-11: *Beginning the* `Meter` *class*

```
public class Meter extends Object
{
  public Meter()
  { super();
  }

  // Test the class.
  public static void main(String[] args)
```

Listing 7-11: *Beginning the* `Meter` *class* (continued)

```
    { Meter m = new Meter();
    }
}
```

KEY IDEA

Write tests as you write the class.

We'll proceed by repeating the following steps until we think we're finished with the class:

- Choose one part of the description that we don't have working and decide what method is required to implement it.
- Understand what the method is to do and give it a name.
- Write one or more tests to determine if the method is working correctly.
- Write code so that the method passes the test(s).

7.4.1 Implementing Accessor Methods

Once again, we'll use a question-and-answer style to get started.

Expert What is one part of the description that isn't working?

Novice Well, nothing is working, so we're really just looking for something to implement. I think the first bullet in the description, to provide the price of one unit of gas, would be a good place to start.

Expert What is this method supposed to do?

Novice Return the price of one unit of gas. I guess that would be, for example, \$1.109/liter or \$2.85/gallon. I think a good name for the method would be `getUnitCost`.

Expert How can we test if `getUnitCost` is working correctly?

Novice We can add a statement in `main` that calls `ckEquals`:

```
tester.ckEquals("unit cost", 1.109, m.getUnitCost());
```

Expert So, you're assuming that gas costs \$1.109 per liter?

Novice Yes.

Expert How would you implement `getUnitCost` so that it passes this test?

Novice It's easy. Just return the value. I'll even throw in the documentation:

```
/** Get the cost per unit of fuel.
 * @return cost per unit of fuel */
public double getUnitCost()
{ return 1.109;
}
```

A number with a decimal point like `1.109` can be stored in a variable of type `double`, so that will be the return type of the method.

Expert Aren't you assuming that gas is always $1.109 per liter? What if the price goes up or down? Or what if the gas pump can deliver three different grades of gasoline? Surely they wouldn't all have the same price.

Novice I see your point. Somehow each `Meter` object should have its own price for the gas it measures, just like each `Robot` object must have its own street and avenue. To test that, we want to have two `Meter` objects, each with a different price:[1]

```
tester.ckEquals("Cost 1", 1.109, m1.getUnitCost());
tester.ckEquals("Cost 2", 1.159, m2.getUnitCost());
```

It sounds like we need to have an instance variable to store the unit price.

Expert Suppose you had an instance variable. How would you initialize it?

Novice Well, it couldn't be where the instance variable is declared because then we're right back where we started—each `Meter` object would always have the same price for its gas. I guess we'll have to initialize it in the constructor. I think that means the constructor requires a parameter so that the price can be specified when the `Meter` object is created.

Putting these observations together results in the class shown in Listing 7-12. It adds an instance variable, `unitCost`, at line 5 to remember the unit cost of the gas for each `Meter` object. The instance variable is initialized at line 11 using the parameter variable declared in line 9. In line 22, the value `1.109` is passed to the `Meter` constructor. This value is copied into the parameter variable `unitCost` declared in line 9. The value in `unitCost` is then copied into the instance variable in line 11. The value is stored in `unitCost` for as long as the object exists (or it is changed with an assignment statement).

Finally, the contents of `unitCost` are returned at line 17 each time `getUnitCost` is called.

[1] `ckEquals` verifies that two `double` values differ by less than 0.000001.

Listing 7-12: *A partially completed* `Meter` *class*

```
import becker.util.Test;

public class Meter extends Object
{
  private double unitCost;

  /** Construct a new Meter object.
   * @param unitCost The cost for one unit (liter or gallon) of gas */
  puhlic Meter(double unitCost)
  { super();
    this.unitCost = unitCost;
  }

  /** Get the cost per unit of fuel.
   * @return cost per unit of fuel */
  public double getUnitCost()
  { return this.unitCost;
  }

  // Test the class.
  public static void main(String[] args)
  { Meter m1 = new Meter(1.109);
    Test tester = new Test(); // This line isn't needed. See Section 7.5.2.
    tester.ckEquals("unit cost", 1.109, m1.getUnitCost());
    Meter m2 = new Meter(1.149);
    tester.ckEquals("unit cost", 1.149, m2.getUnitCost());
  }
}
```

Two other parts of the requirements—getting the octane level and getting the marketing name—follow a similar strategy. The difference is that they will use an integer and a `String`, respectively. See Listing 7-13 for their implementations.

7.4.2 Implementing a Command/Query Pair

Expert So, how are you going to implement the actual measurement of the gas? Wasn't the point of the `Meter` class to measure how much gas is delivered to a customer?

Novice Yes. Somehow, it seems we need to find out when the pump is actually pumping gas—and how much. You know, when the handle is only squeezed a little way, only a little gas flows from the pump into the car. But when you squeeze the handle all the way, a lot of gas flows.

Expert It sounds like the pump—the code that is going to be using your `Meter` class—needs to call a method every time a little bit of gas is pumped. Does it get called repeatedly?

Novice Yes, and it needs to tell how much gas was pumped in that time. The job of the `Meter` object is to keep track of the units of gas that are pumped.

Expert I'm getting confused. Can you explain it another way?

Novice Sure. Think of a real pump. It has a motor to pump the gas. Every time the motor goes around, some gas is pumped. How much depends on the speed of the motor.

In our system, it's as if the motor called a method in the `Meter` class every time it turns. Furthermore, it will tell that method how much gas it pumped. If the motor is turning slowly, it pumps only a small amount of gas; but if the motor is turning fast, it pumps more. We'll add up all the units of gas that are pumped to calculate the total amount delivered to the customer.

Expert What do you want to call this method that is called by the motor?

Novice How about calling it `pump`? It will need a parameter, so the full signature will be

```
public void pump(double howMuch)
```

It's a command, not a query, so the return type is `void`.

Expert How would you test this method? How will you know if it's working correctly?

Novice It's like the `move` method in the `Robot` class. To test it, we had to have some queries: `getAvenue` and `getStreet`. For the `Meter` class, we'll need a query—something like `getVolumeSold`.

Expert How will that help you?

Novice First, we'll call pump to "pump" some gas. Maybe we'll call it several times, just like the real pump would. Then we'll call getVolumeSold and make sure that the value it returns matches the amount we "pumped." We could put the following in the test harness:

```
Meter m = new Meter(1.109);
tester.ckEquals("vol. sold", 0.0, m.getVolumeSold());
m.pump(0.02);
m.pump(0.03);
m.pump(0.01);
tester.ckEquals("vol. sold", 0.06, m.getVolumeSold());
```

Expert How will you implement these methods?

Novice Well, somehow we need to add up all the units of gas that get passed as an argument to the pump command. I'm thinking of using a temporary variable inside the pump command.

Expert Are you sure about that? Doesn't a temporary variable disappear each time the method is finished, only to be re-created the next time the method is called? Besides, how would getVolumeSold get access to a temporary variable?

Novice You're right. We should use an instance variable instead. It maintains a value even when a method is not being executed—and every method, including getVolumeSold—can access an instance variable.

Expert Please recap the plan for me.

Novice We'll have an instance variable called volumeSold. It will be initialized to 0.0 when the Meter object is created. Every time pump is called, it will add the value passed in the parameter variable to volumeSold. Each time getVolumeSold is called, we'll just return the current contents of the volumeSold instance variable.

Expert Sounds good. What about resetting when a new customer comes? That was another one of the requirements. I think we're also supposed to return the cost of the gas sold.

Novice We'll create a reset method that will assign 0.0 to the volumeSold instance variable. A method named calcTotalCost can simply return the volume sold times the cost per unit. Both of those values will be stored in instance variables.

Expert And your plan for testing?

Novice Much like the others. We'll set up a `Meter` object with a known unit price for the gas. We'll "pump" some gas and then call `getVolumeSold` and `calcTotalCost`. Then we can reset the pump and verify that the volume sold is back to 0.

This plan is a good one and is implemented in Listing 7-13.

FIND THE CODE

ch07/gasPump/Meter3.java

Listing 7-13: *The completed code for the* `Meter3` *class*

```
import becker.util.Test;

/** Measure the volume of fuel sold and calculate the amount owed by the
 *  customer, given the current fuel cost.
 *
 *  @author Byron Weber Becker */
public class Meter3 extends Object
{
  private double unitCost;             // unit cost
  private double volumeSold = 0.0;     // volume sold
  private int octane;                  // octane rating
  private String label;                // marketing label

  /** Construct a new Meter object.
   *  @param unitCost The cost for one unit (liter or gallon) of gas
   *  @param octaneRating An integer related to the "performance" of
   *  the fuel;  usually between 87 and 93.
   *  @param theLabel A label for the fuel, such as "Gold" or "Ultra". */
  public Meter3(double unitCost, int octaneRating,
                          String theLabel)
  { super();
    this.unitCost = unitCost;
    this.octane = octaneRating;
    this.label = theLabel;
  }

  /** Get the cost per unit of fuel.
   *  @return cost per unit of fuel */
  public double getUnitCost()
  { return this.unitCost;
  }

  /** Get the octane rating of the fuel.
   *  @return octane rating (typically between 87 and 93) */
  public int getOctane()
  { return this.octane;
```

Listing 7-13: *The completed code for the* `Meter3` *class* (continued)

```
   }

   /** Get the label for this meter's fuel. For example, "Gold" or "Ultra".
   *  @return this meter's fuel label */
   public String getLabel()
   { return this.label;
   }

   /** Pump some fuel into a tank. This method is called
   *  repeatedly while the "handle" on the pump is pressed.
   *  @param howMuch How much fuel was pumped since the last time
   *  this method was called. */
   public void pump(double howMuch)
   { this.volumeSold = this.volumeSold + howMuch;
   }

   /** Get the volume of fuel sold to this customer.
   *  @return volume of fuel sold */
   public double getVolumeSold()
   { return this.volumeSold;
   }

   /** Calculate the total cost of fuel sold to this customer.
   *  @return price/unit * number of units sold */
   public double calcTotalCost()
   { double tCost = this.unitCost * this.volumeSold;
     return tCost;
   }

   /** Reset the meter for a new customer. */
   public void reset()
   { this.volumeSold = 0.0;
   }

   // Test the class.
   public static void main(String[] args)
   { Test tester = new Test();
     Meter3 m1 = new Meter3(1.109, 87, "Regular");
     tester.ckEquals("unit cost", 1.109, m1.getUnitCost());
     tester.ckEquals("octane", 87, m1.getOctane());
     tester.ckEquals("label", "Regular", m1.getLabel());

     Meter3 m2 = new Meter3(1.149, 89, "Ultra");
```

PATTERN

Test Harness

Listing 7-13: *The completed code for the* `Meter3` *class* (continued)

```
        tester.ckEquals("unit cost", 1.149, m2.getUnitCost());
        tester.ckEquals("octane", 89, m2.getOctane());
        tester.ckEquals("label", "Ultra", m2.getLabel());

        tester.ckEquals("volSold", 0.0, m2.getVolumeSold());
        m2.pump(0.02);
        m2.pump(0.03);
        m2.pump(0.01);
        tester.ckEquals("volSold", 0.06, m2.getVolumeSold());
        tester.ckEquals("totCost", 0.06*1.149, m2.calcTotalCost());
        m2.reset();
        tester.ckEquals("after reset", 0.0, m2.getVolumeSold());
        tester.ckEquals("after reset", 0.0, m2.calcTotalCost());
    }
}
```

7.5 Understanding Class Variables and Methods

So far we have studied instance variables, temporary variables, parameter variables, constants, and methods. We now need to look at variables and methods that use the `static` keyword. Such variables and methods apply to the entire class rather than to a single object.

KEY IDEA

Variables and methods declared with `static` *apply to the entire class.*

7.5.1 Using Class Variables

Instance variables are always associated with a specific object. Each `Robot` object knows which avenue and street it is on. Each `Meter` object knows the price of the gas it is measuring.

A **class variable** (also called a **static variable**) relates to the class as a whole rather than to an individual object. A class variable is declared using the `static` keyword and is used to store information common to *all* the instances of the class.

Consider an analogy: suppose that `people` are objects and that all `people` live in the same town. Some information is specific to each individual—their name, age, birth date, and so on. This information is stored in instance variables. But other information is known by everyone—the current year, the name of the town, the name of the mayor, whether the sun is up, and so on. In this situation, it doesn't make sense for each `person` object to have its own instance variable to store the year. Using a class variable, the year is stored only once but is still accessible to each person object. Using an instance variable, there are as many copies of the year as there are person objects.

A class variable is declared like an instance variable but includes the static keyword:

```
public class Person extends Object
{ ...
  private int birthYear;
  private static int year;              // a class variable
  ...
}
```

Inside the class, a class variable can be accessed using the name of the class, the name only, or this. For example, here are three different implementations of the method getAge:

```
public int getAge()
{ return Person.year - this.birthYear;
}

public int getAge()
{ return year - this.birthYear;
}

public int getAge()
{ return this.year - this.birthYear;
}
```

KEY IDEA

Access a class variable with the name of the class containing it.

Of these three, the first is preferred because it is clear that year is a class variable. The second example is probably the most common because it saves a few keystrokes (this could also be omitted for birthYear). Accessing the year with this.year strongly implies that year is an instance variable and is discouraged.

A method may also change a class variable. For example, the following method could be used on January 1:

```
public void incrementYear()
{ Person.year = Person.year + 1;
}
```

The effect of this is to change the year for every Person object—and it's accomplished with only *one* method call.

Class variables are created and initialized before a class is first used. They are set up even before the first object is created for that class.

Assigning Unique ID Numbers

One use of class variables is to assign individual objects identification numbers. For example, suppose that we want each person to have a unique identification number. Obviously, if each person has a unique number, we need to store it in an instance variable. We can use a class variable to make it unique, as follows:

- Declare a class variable to store the ID number to assign to the next `Person` object created.
- In the `Person` constructor:
  - Assign the ID number using the class variable.
  - Increment the class variable in preparation for assigning the next number.

PATTERN

Assign a Unique ID

```
public class Person extends Object
{ ...
  private int id;
  private static int nextID = 1000000;     // first id is 1000000
  ...

  public Person(String name)
  { super();
    this.id = Person.nextID;
    Person.nextID++;
    ...
  }
}
```

With this scheme, every time a `Person` object is created, it is assigned an ID number. Because `nextID` is a class variable and is incremented as soon as it has been assigned, the next `Person` object constructed will receive the next higher number.

A Guideline for Class Variables

KEY IDEA

Class variables are relatively rare in object-oriented code.

Class variables are quite rare in object-oriented code. If you find yourself declaring a class variable, you should be able to clearly explain why *every* instance of the class should access the same value or why there won't be any instances of the class at all.

7.5.2 Using Class Methods

KEY IDEA

Class methods cannot use instance variables or nonstatic methods.

The `static` keyword can also be applied to methods; doing so, however, involves a trade-off. On the one hand, such a method cannot access any instance variables and are limited to calling methods that are also declared `static`. On the other hand, class methods can be called using only the name of the class. Because no object is needed, this makes them easier to use in some circumstances.

We can use two methods in the previous section as examples. The method `getAge` *cannot* be a class method because it accesses an instance variable. However, `incrementYear` is a perfect candidate because it accesses only a class variable. To make it into a class method, add the `static` keyword as shown in the following code fragment:

```
public static void incrementYear()
{ Person.year = Person.year + 1;
}
```

KEY IDEA

Class methods can be called without using an object.

With this change, the year can be incremented as follows:

```
Person.incrementYear();
```

This works even if no `Person` objects have been created yet. Using a specific object such as `john.incrementYear()` also works but using the class name is preferred because it tells the reader that `incrementYear` applies to the entire class.

Class Methods in the `Math` Class

One of Java's provided classes, `java.lang.Math`, contains *only* class methods. For example, consider a method to calculate the maximum of two numbers:

```
public static int max(int a, int b)
{ int answer = a;
  if (b > a)
  { answer = b;
  }
  return answer;
}
```

This method does not use any instance variables. In fact, all of the methods in the `Math` class are like this. Because the `Math` class does not have any instance variables, all of the methods are static. Thus, all of the methods are called using the class name, `Math`, as a prefix, as shown in the following example:

```
int m = Math.max(0, this.getStreet());
```

Most of the functions in the `Math` class are listed in Table 7-7. Some of them are overloaded with different numeric types for their parameters.

(table 7-7)

Many of the mathematical functions included in `java.lang.Math`

Method	Returned Value
`int abs(int x)` `double abs(double x)`	absolute value of *x*; also overloaded for `long` and `float`
`double acos(double x)`	arccosine of *x*, $0.0 \leq x \leq \pi$
`double asin(double x)`	arcsine of *x*, $-\pi/2 \leq x \leq \pi/2$
`double atan(double x)`	arctangent of *x*, $-\pi/2 \leq x \leq \pi/2$
`double cos(double x)`	cosine of the angle *x*, where *x* is in radians
`double exp(double x)`	*e*, the base of natural logarithms, raised to the power of *x*
`double log(double x)`	natural logarithm (base *e*) of *x*
`int max(int x, int y)` `double max(double x, double y)`	larger of *x* and *y*; also overloaded for `long` and `float`
`int min(int x, int y)` `double min(double x, double y)`	the smaller of *x* and *y*; also overloaded for `long` and `float`
`double pow(double x, double y)`	*x* raised to the power of *y*
`double random()`	random number greater than or equal to 0.0 and less than 1.0
`long round(double x)`	integer nearest *x*
`double sin(double x)`	sine of the angle *x*, where *x* is in radians
`double sqrt(double x)`	square root of *x*
`double tan(double x)`	tangent of the angle *x*, where *x* is in radians
`double toDegrees(double x)`	converts an angle, *x*, measured in radians to degrees
`double toRadians(double x)`	converts an angle, *x*, measured in degrees to radians

In addition to these functions, `java.lang.Math` also includes two public constants: `PI` (3.14159...) and `E` (2.71828...).

In Section 7.1.2, we wrote our own version of the absolute value function to use in the `distanceToOrigin` query. We now know that we could have used the `Math` class, as follows:

```
public int distanceToOrigin()
{ return Math.abs(this.street) + Math.abs(this.avenue);
}
```

The absolute value function is overloaded for both `int` and `double`. Because `street` and `avenue` are integers, Java selects the method with `int` parameters (which happens to have an `int` return type).

Our version of `distanceToOrigin` was the "as the robot moves" interpretation. If we wanted the "as the crow flies" interpretation, we could use the Pythagorean theorem ($a^2 + b^2 = c^2$) and the square root function, as follows:

```
public double distanceToOrigin()
{ double a2 = this.street * this.street;    // one way to square a #
  double b2 = Math.pow(this.avenue, 2.0); // another way to square a #
  return Math.sqrt(a2 + b2);
}
```

In Section 7.2.3 we discussed casting. For example, when the variable `d` holds `3.999`, the statement `int i = (int)d` assigns the value `3` to the variable `i`. In many cases, however, we want the nearest integer, not just the integer portion. For example, we want to round `3.999` to `4`.

The `Math` class has a `round` method that will do just that. However, when the method is passed a `double` as an argument it returns a `long` integer. This implies that we often cast the result when working with integers. For example,

```
int i = (int)Math.round(d);
```

KEY IDEA

`random` *returns a pseudorandom number, x, such that* $0 \leq x < 1$.

One of the most fun methods in the `Math` class is `random`. Each time it is called, it returns a number greater than or equal to 0 and less than 1. When called repeatedly, the sequence of numbers appears to be random.[2] The first 10 numbers returned in one experiment are shown in Figure 7-6. The first number in the sequence depends on the date and time the program begins running.

(figure 7-6)

Sequence of 10 pseudorandom numbers

```
0.425585145743809
0.49629326982879207
0.4467070769009338
0.23377387885697887
0.33762066427975934
0.25442482711460535
0.9986103921074468
0.9822012645708958
0.420499613228824
0.22309030308848088
```

[2] These numbers appear to be random but are not. If the numbers were really random, the next number could not be predicted. Since the next number in these sequences can be predicted, they are called "pseudorandom."

A computer implementation of a game with dice will often use `random` to simulate the dice. In this case, we need to map a `double` between 0 and 1 to an integer between 1 and 6. The following method will do so:

```
public int rollDie()
{ return (int)(Math.random() * 6 + 1);
}
```

We can understand how this works with a slight variation of an evaluation diagram, as shown in Figure 7-7. The fact that the `random` method returns a value greater than or equal to 0 and less than 1 is reflected below its oval with the notation [0, 0.9999...]. After the multiplication by 6, the expression has a value in the range [0, 5.9999...], a number greater than or equal to 0 and less than 6. After the other operations are carried out, we see that the result is an integer between one and six—exactly what is needed to simulate rolling a die.

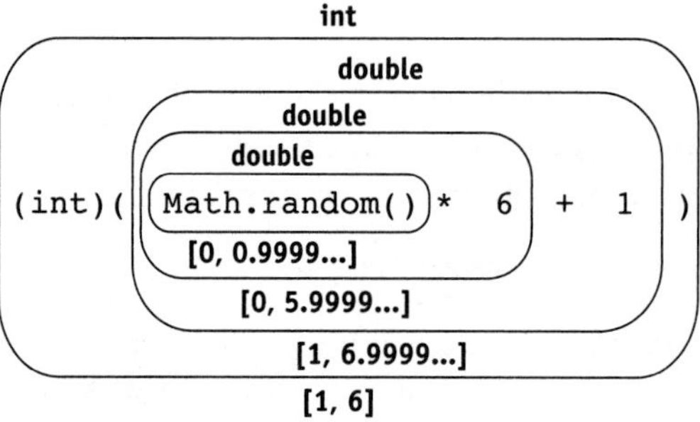

(figure 7-7)

Evaluating an expression used in simulating dice

Class Methods in the `Character` Class

The `Character` class is automatically imported into every Java class and includes a number of methods for classifying characters. A selection of these methods is shown in Table 7-8. They are all declared `static` and can be called using the `Character` class name, as shown in the following example:

```
if (Character.isDigit(ch))...
```

(table 7-8)

A selection of useful methods in the `Character` *class*

Method	Returned value
`boolean isDigit(char ch)`	`true` if the specified character is a digit; `false` otherwise
`boolean isLetter(char ch)`	`true` if the specified character is a letter; `false` otherwise
`boolean isLowerCase(char ch)`	`true` if the specified character is a lowercase character; `false` otherwise
`boolean isUpperCase(char ch)`	`true` if the specified character is an uppercase character; `false` otherwise
`boolean isWhitespace(char ch)`	`true` if the specified character is white space (space, tab, new line, etc.) ; `false` otherwise

Class Methods in the `Test` Class

The methods in the `Test` class are other examples of class methods. The code for `ckEquals`, as shown in Listing 7-2, does not use any instance variables or nonstatic methods and can therefore be declared with the `static` keyword. Indeed, all the methods in the class are like this.

Because the methods are static, a typical test harness will not instantiate a `Test` object. For example, the test harness in Listing 7-1 could be rewritten by removing line 14 and replacing `tester` with `test` in lines 15–17, as follows:

```
1  import becker.util.Test;
2
3  public class TestHarness extends Object
4  {
5    public static void main(String[] args)
6    { // Set up a known situation (an empty city; a robot on (4, 2) facing east).
7      SimpleCity c = new SimpleCity();
8      SimpleBot karel = new SimpleBot(c, 4, 2, Constants.EAST);
9
10     // Execute the move method.
11     karel.move();
12
13     // Verify the results -- robot on intersection (4, 3).
14     ~~Test tester = new Test();~~
15     ~~tester~~Test.ckEquals("new ave", 3, karel.getAvenue());
16     ~~tester~~Test.ckEquals("same str", 4, karel.getStreet());
17     ~~tester~~Test.ckEquals("same dir", Constants.EAST,
18                                  karel.getDirection());
19   }
20 }
```

The `City` class in the `becker` library automatically displays the city which is usually not desirable in a test harness. This behavior can be controlled with another class method, `showFrame`. The following code fragment shows how to use this method to avoid having the city show.

```
public static void main(String[] args)
{ City.showFrame(false);
  City c = new City();
  ...
}
```

The `main` Method

We also write a class method for every program—`main`. Java requires `main` to be static so that the Java system can call it using only the name of the class containing it. The name of the class is passed to the Java system when the program is run.

7.6 GUI: Using Java Interfaces

The `becker.xtras` package contains a number of graphical user interfaces that can be used to make programs that look and feel more professional than we can write with the skills learned so far. The `GasPumpGUI` class in the `becker.xtras.gasPump` package is an example; it can be used with the `Meter` class we developed earlier in this chapter to create a program with the graphical user interface shown in Figure 7-8.

LOOKING AHEAD

The skills to write a graphical user interface like `GasPumpGUI` *are covered in Chapter 13.*

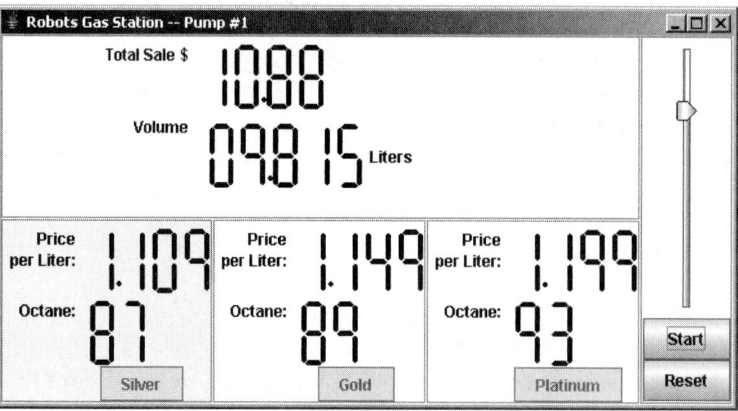

(figure 7-8)

Image of the graphical user interface provided by the `gasPump` *package*

The problem set refers to several such GUIs in the `becker.xtras` package. A problem will often begin by directing you to explore the documentation for a particular package. You may want to do that now for the `gasPump` package. Go to *www.learningwithrobots.com*.

Navigate to "Software" and then "Documentation." In the large panel on the right, click `becker.xtras.gasPump`. You'll see a brief description of each of the classes included in the package. Scroll down and you'll find an image of the graphical user interface and a sample `main` method that you can use to run the program (see Listing 7-14).

This gas pump user interface is set up for a program that uses three instances of the `Meter` class—one for each of three different octane levels. Of course, each octane level has its own price.

FIND THE CODE

ch07/gasPump/

Listing 7-14: *A sample `main` method to run our class (`Meter`) with the provided graphical user interface*

```
1  import becker.xtras.gasPump.*;
2
3  /** Run a gas pump with a graphical user interface.
4   *
5   * @author Byron Weber Becker */
6  public class Main extends Object
7  {
8    public static void main(String[] args)
9    { // Create three meters for the pump.
10     Meter silver = new Meter(1.109, 87, "Silver");
11     Meter gold = new Meter(1.149, 89, "Gold");
12     Meter platinum = new Meter(1.199, 93, "Platinum");
13
14     // Create the graphical user interface.
15     GasPumpGUI gui = new GasPumpGUI(
16                          silver, gold, platinum, "Liter");
17   }
18 }
```

7.6.1 Specifying Methods with Interfaces

The graphical user interface class `GasPumpGUI` will not work with just any class. It must somehow be assured that the `Meter` objects passed in lines 15 and 16 have methods to get the price of the gasoline, the octane level, how much gas has been pumped to the current customer, and how much that gasoline is worth so that it can display this information to the user. Furthermore, just having methods that perform these functions is not enough. The methods must be named exactly as `GasPumpGUI` expects, return the expected types of values, and take the expected arguments; otherwise, it won't be able to call them.

This is a common problem: Two classes need to work together, but they are written by different people at different times and places. This problem was also faced by the programmers who wrote the classes used in graphical user interfaces, such as JComponent, JButton, and JFrame. To fully exploit their functionality, classes written several years ago must be assured that objects we give them possess methods with specified signatures.

Fortunately, Java provides a solution. The person who writes the first class also provides a list of the methods it requires to be in the second class. The list written by the author of GasPumpGUI includes the following methods:

```
public double getUnitCost();
public double getVolumeSold();
public int getOctane();
public String getLabel();
public void reset();
public void pump(double howMuch);
public double calcTotalCost();
```

This list, together with documentation, is put into a Java **interface**. Unfortunately, the word *interface* has two meanings in this section. One meaning is "graphical user interface," like the one shown in Figure 7-8. The other meaning—the one intended here—is a Java file used to guarantee that a class contains a specified set of methods.

KEY IDEA

A Java interface is used to guarantee the presence of specified methods.

Listing 7-15 shows a complete interface except for the documentation, and is similar to a class. It has a name (IMeter) and must be in a file with the same name as the interface (IMeter.java). The list of methods is enclosed in curly braces. Interfaces may also have constants, defined as they would be defined in a class. An interface should be documented like a class.

The differences between an interface and a class are as follows:

- An interface uses the keyword interface instead of class.
- An interface cannot extend a class.[3]
- Method bodies are omitted. Each method lists its return type and signature. If an access modifier is present, it must be public (all methods in an interface are assumed to be public).

[3] It is possible, however, for an interface to extend another interface. In fact, it can extend several interfaces, but that's beyond the scope of this textbook.

Listing 7-15: *An interface for* `IMeter` *(documentation is omitted to better show the essential structure)*

```
public interface IMeter
{
  public double getUnitCost();
  public int getOctane();
  public String getLabel();
  public double getVolumeSold();
  public void reset();
  public void pump(double howMuch);
  public double calcTotalCost();
}
```

7.6.2 Implementing an Interface

KEY IDEA

An interface name can be used as the type in variable declarations.

So, how is the `IMeter` interface used? The author of `GasPumpGUI` used it in at least one place—defining the type of object required by the constructor. From the online documentation, we know that the constructor's signature is as follows:

```
public GasPumpGUI(IMeter lowOctane, IMeter medOctane,
                  IMeter highOctane, String volumeUnit)
```

KEY IDEA

An interface name can be used to declare the type of a variable.

As this example shows, an interface can be used as the type in a variable declaration, including parameter variables, temporary variables, and instance variables.

The way we use `IMeter` is in the line that begins the definition of the `Meter` class:

```
public class Meter extends Object implements IMeter
```

KEY IDEA

An interface name is used in a class declaration.

It's the last part—`implements IMeter`—that tells the Java compiler that our class must be sure to implement each method listed in `IMeter` and that the signatures must match exactly. This phrase is also the part that allows a `Meter` object to be passed to a `GasPumpGUI` constructor even though the constructor's signature says the argument should be an `IMeter` object.

There is no required relationship between the names `IMeter` and `Meter`, although they are often similar. Both names are chosen by programmers, but should follow conventions. In the `becker` library, the convention is for interface names to begin with `I`. What follows the `I` should give an indication of the interface's purpose. The person implementing the `Meter` class can choose any name he wants, but should of course follow the usual conventions for naming a class.

A class can implement as many interfaces as required, although implementing only one is the usual case. To implement more than one, list all the interfaces after the `implements` keyword, separating each one from the next with a comma.

What happens if the `Meter` class omits one of the methods specified by `IMeter`, say `calcTotalCost`? The Java compiler will print an error message and refuse to compile the class. The error message might refer to a missing method or might say that the class "does not override the abstract method `calcTotalCost`."

7.6.3 Developing Classes to a Specified Interface

In a sense, we developed the `Meter` class in a backwards fashion. We first wrote the class and then found out that it just happened to match the `IMeter` interface. A more usual situation is one where we know, at the beginning, that we will be implementing a particular interface. Suppose, for example, that our instructions were to develop a class to use with the graphical user interface in the `becker.xtras.gasPump` package. As soon as we investigated the package, we would know that we need to write a class implementing the `IMeter` interface.

How should we proceed?

Begin by creating a class with your chosen name and a `main` method to be used for testing. Add the `implements` keyword followed by the name of the interface. Add the methods specified by the interface and a constructor that is implied by the `main` method shown in the documentation. For each method with a non-`void` return type, add a `return` statement—it doesn't matter what value is returned—so that the method will compile. Such a method is called a stub. Following these clues results in the skeleton shown in Listing 7-16. Some development environments will do this much for you almost automatically.

LOOKING BACK

A stub is a method with just enough code to compile. Stubs were first discussed in Section 3.2.2.

Finally, write tests and develop the methods, as we did earlier in this chapter.

FIND THE CODE

ch07/gasPump/

Listing 7-16: *Beginning the* `Meter` *class with methods required to implement* `IMeter`

```
import becker.xtras.gasPump.IMeter;
import becker.util.Test;

public class Meter extends Object implements IMeter
{
  public Meter(double unitCost, int octaneRating,
             · String theLabel)
  { super();
  }

```

Listing 7-16: *Beginning the `Meter` class with methods required to implement `IMeter`* (continued)

```
   public double getUnitCost()
   { return 0.0;
   }

   public int getOctane()
   { return 0;
   }

   public String getLabel()
   { return "dummy";
   }

   public void pump(double howMuch)
   {
   }

      ...

   /** To use for testing. */
   public static void main(String[] args)
   { Meter m = new Meter(1.109, 87, "Regular");
   }
}
```

7.6.4 Informing the User Interface of Changes

Graphical user interfaces often use a pattern known as Model-View-Controller. We will study this pattern in depth in Chapter 13, which is devoted to writing graphical user interfaces.

KEY IDEA

The model must inform the user interface when changes have been made.

The `Meter` class is the "model" part of this pattern. It keeps track of the information that the user interface—the "view" and "controller" parts—displays. The model must inform the user interface each time information on the screen needs updating. In practice, this means calling a method named `updateAllViews` at the end of each method in `Meter` that changes an instance variable. This can always be done in the same way, as shown in Listing 7-17. The changes from the previous version of `Meter` (Listing 7-13) are shown in bold.

FIND THE CODE

ch07/gasPump/

Listing 7-17: *Code required in the* `Meter` *class to inform the view of changes*

```
 1 import becker.gasPump.IMeter;
 2 import becker.util.*;
 3 
 4 public class Meter extends Object implements IMeter
 5 { // Instance variables...
 6   private ViewList views = new ViewList();
 7 
 8   // Methods that do not change instance variables...
 9 
10   // Methods that do change instance variables...
11   public void reset()
12   { this.volumeSold = 0;
13     this.views.updateAllViews();
14   }
15 
16   public void pump(double howMuch)
17   { this.volumeSold += howMuch;
18     this.views.updateAllViews();
19   }
20 
21   public void addView(IView aView)
22   { this.views.addView(aView);
23   }
24 }
```

`views`, declared in line 6, is an object that maintains a list of graphical user interface parts (the views) that need to be updated when this model changes. The class, `ViewList`, is imported from the package `becker.util` in line 2.

The graphical user interface adds views to this list by calling the method `addView`, which is declared in lines 21–23. It receives a parameter that implements the `IView` interface. By using an interface, we don't need to know exactly what kind of object is passed as an argument—only that it includes the methods named in `IView`. The `addView` method doesn't actually do anything with the view except tell the list of views to add it.

With this infrastructure in place, the last step is to call the `updateAllViews` method in the `views` object at the appropriate times. It should be called at the end of each method in the model that changes an instance variable. What happens if you forget to call `updateAllViews`? The user interface will not change when you expect it to.

Finally, `addView` is in the `IMeter` interface even though it was omitted from Listing 7-15.

7.7 Patterns

7.7.1 The Test Harness Pattern

Name: Test Harness

Context: You want to increase the reliability of your code and make the development process easier with testing.

Solution: Write a `main` method in each class. The following template applies:

```
import becker.util.Test;
public class «className» ...
{ // Instance variables and methods
  ...
  public static void main(String[] args)
  { // Create a known situation.
    «className» «instance» = new «className»(...);

    // Execute the code being tested.
    «instance».«methodToTest»(...);

    // Verify the results.
    Test.ckEquals(«idString», «expectedValue»,
                              «actualValue»);

    ...
  }
}
```

Verifying the results will often require multiple lines of code. A typical test harness will include many tests, all of which set up a known situation, execute some code, and then verify the results.

Consequences: Writing tests before writing code helps you focus on the code you need to write. Being able to test as you write usually speeds up the development process and results in higher quality code.

Related Pattern: The Test Harness pattern is a specialization of the Java Program pattern.

7.7.2 The `toString` Pattern

Name: `toString`

Context: You would like to be able to easily print information about an object, usually for debugging purposes.

Solution: Override the `toString` method in the `Object` class. The usual format lists the class name with values of relevant instance variables between brackets, as shown in the following template:

```
public String toString()
{  return "«className»[" +
          "«instanceVarName1»=" + this.«instanceVarName1» +
          ", «instanceVarName2»=" + this.«instanceVarName2»
+
          ...
          ", «instanceVarNameN»=" + this.«instanceVarNameN»
+
          "]";
}
```

Consequences: The `toString` method is called automatically when an object is concatenated with a string or passed to the `print` or `println` method in `System.out`, making it easy to use a textual representation of the object.

Related Patterns: This pattern is a specialization of the Query pattern.

7.7.3 The Enumeration Pattern

Name: Enumeration

Context: You would like to have a variable with a specific set of values such as `MALE` and `FEMALE` or the four compass directions.

Solution: Define an enumeration type listing the desired values. A template follows:

```
public enum «typeName»
{ «valueName1», «valueName2», ..., «valueNameN»
}
```

For example, a set of values identifying styles of jeans for a clothing store inventory system could be defined as follows:

```
public enum JeanStyle
{  CLASSIC, RELAXED, BOOT_CUT, LOW_RISE, STRAIGHT
}
```

Use the name of the enumeration to declare variables and return types, such as the following:

```
public class DenimJeans
{ private JeanStyle style;

  public DenimJeans(JeanStyle aStyle)
  { this.style = aStyle;
  }

  public JeanStyle getStyle()
  { return this.style;
  }
}
```

Consequences: Variables using an enumeration type are prevented from having any value other than those defined by the enumeration and the special value `null`, helping to avoid programming errors. Well-chosen names help make programs more understandable. Enumerations cannot be used with versions of Java prior to 1.5.

Related Pattern: Prior to Java 1.5, programmers often used the Named Constant pattern to define a set of values. The Enumeration pattern is a better choice.

7.7.4 The Assign a Unique ID Pattern

Name: Assign a Unique ID

Context: Each instance of a specified class needs a unique identifier. The class should not depend on something external to itself to establish and maintain the uniqueness of the identifiers.

Solution: Store the unique identifier in an instance variable. Use a class variable to maintain the next unique identifier to assign. For example:

```
public class «className»
{ private int «uniqueID»;
  private static final int «nextUniqueID» = «firstID»;

  public «className»()
  { super();
    this.«uniqueID» = «nextUniqueID»;
    «nextUniqueID»++;
  }
}
```

Consequences: Unique identifiers are assigned to each instance of the class for each execution of the program. If objects are stored in a file and then read again (see Section 9.4), care must be taken to save and restore *«nextUniqueID»* appropriately.

Related Patterns: This pattern makes use of the Instance Variable pattern.

7.8 Summary and Concept Map

Variables can have one of many types, such as `int`, `double`, `boolean`, and `String`. Incrementally testing variables and the methods that use them is a vital part of demonstrating that a program is correct. Developing tests before writing the code is a sound development practice that can help programmers develop correct code faster. Class variables and methods don't depend on an instance of a class for their operation.

Methods and variables provide the essential tools needed to write classes that address many different kinds of problems; the gas pump meter class is just one example.

Interfaces include a list of methods that implementing classes are required to define. Interfaces allow classes to work together in situations where it isn't possible or desirable to specify a class name. One example of this is when two programmers work on a project, one writing the graphical user interface and the other writing the model.

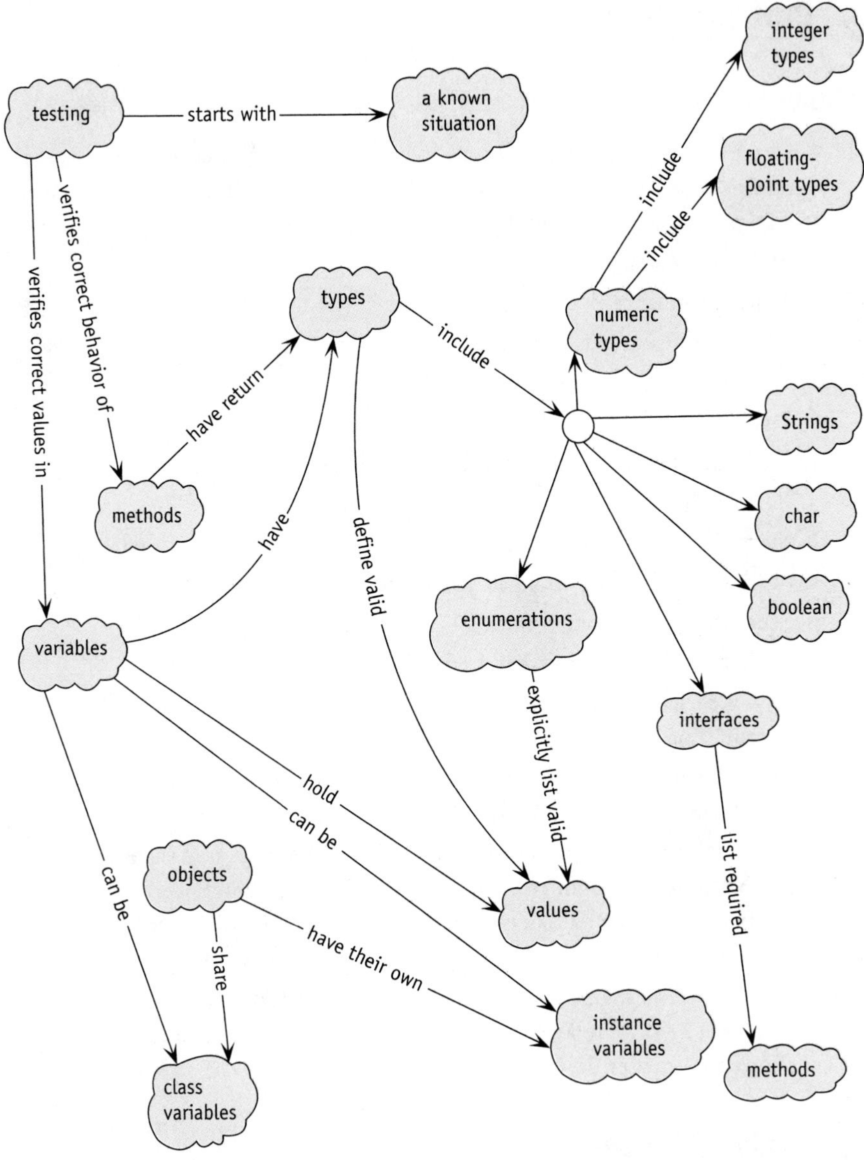
testing
starts with
a known situation
verifies correct behavior of
verifies correct values in
types
have return
methods
have
define valid
include
numeric types
include
include
integer types
floating-point types
Strings
char
boolean
enumerations
explicitly list valid
interfaces
list required
methods
variables
hold
can be
values
can be
objects
share
have their own
class variables
instance variables

7.9 Problem Set

Written Exercises

7.1 For each of the following situations, what would be the best choice(s) for the variable's type? Answer with one or more of `int`, `double`, `char`, `boolean`, `String`, or an enumeration defined by a programmer.

a. Store the current temperature.

b. Store the most recent key typed on the keyboard.

c. Store a compass heading such as "north" or "southeast."

d. Store the height of your best friend.

e. Pass the Dewey decimal number of a book to a method.

f. Store whether a recording is on cassette, CD, or a vinyl record.

g. Return the name of a company from a method.

h. Store the month of the year.

i. Store the number of books in your school's library.

j. Store the area of your room.

k. Store the title of your favorite novel.

l. Pass a person's admission category for the local museum (one of "Child," "Adult," or "Senior") to a method.

7.2 Place the following strings in increasing lexicographic order: `grated`, `grate!`, `grate`, `grateful`, `grate99`, `grace`, `grate[]`, `gratitude`, `grate(grace)`.

7.3 Recall that a `SimpleBot` must extend `Paintable` to guarantee to the compiler that it has a `paint` method. Could `Paintable` be an interface instead of a class? If so, explain what changes to `Paintable` and `SimpleBot` are required. If not, explain why.

7.4 Draw evaluation diagrams for the expressions `(double)3/4` and `(double)(3/4)`. Pay attention to the effects of precedence, automatic conversion, and integer division.

Programming Exercises

7.5 Run the following `main` method. Describe what happens. Based on what you know about the range of the type `byte`, why do you think this occurs?

```
public static void main(String[] args)
{ for (byte b = 0; b <= 128; b += 1)
  { System.out.println(b);
    Utilities.sleep(30);
  }
}
```

7.6 Write the following methods in the class `Name`. They all have a single `String` parameter and return a string. The argument is a full name such as "Frank Herbert," "Orson Scott Card," "Laura Elizabeth Ingalls Wilder," or "William Arthur Philip Louis Mountbatten-Windsor."

a. `firstName` returns the first name (e.g., "Laura").

b. `lastName` returns the last name (e.g., "Mountbatten-Windsor").

c. `initials` returns the first letter of each name (e.g., "WAPLM").

d. `shortName` returns the first initial and the last name (e.g., "O. Card").

e. `name` returns all of the initials except the last plus the last name (e.g., "L. E. I. Wilder").

7.7 Write a `main` method that outputs a multiplication table as shown on the left side of Figure 7-9. Then modify it to print a neater table as shown on the right side of the figure.

(figure 7-9)

Multiplication tables

```
1 2 3 4 5 6 7 8 9 10
2 4 6 8 10 12 14 16 18 20
3 6 9 12 15 18 21 24 27 30
4 8 12 16 20 24 28 32 36 40
5 10 15 20 25 30 35 40 45 50
6 12 18 24 30 36 42 48 54 60
7 14 21 28 35 42 49 56 63 70
8 16 24 32 40 48 56 64 72 80
9 18 27 36 45 54 63 72 81 90
10 20 30 40 50 60 70 80 90 100
```

```
  1   2   3   4   5   6   7   8   9  10
  2   4   6   8  10  12  14  16  18  20
  3   6   9  12  15  18  21  24  27  30
  4   8  12  16  20  24  28  32  36  40
  5  10  15  20  25  30  35  40  45  50
  6  12  18  24  30  36  42  48  54  60
  7  14  21  28  35  42  49  56  63  70
  8  16  24  32  40  48  56  64  72  80
  9  18  27  36  45  54  63  72  81  90
 10  20  30  40  50  60  70  80  90 100
```

7.8 Rewrite the `SimpleBot` class to use an enumeration for the directions.

7.9 Write a class that implements `IMeter` but contains no methods whatsoever. Compile the class. What error message or messages does your compiler give you concerning the missing methods?

7.10 Write a class named `BustedBot` that extends `RobotSE`. A `BustedBot` is unreliable, occasionally turning either right or left (apparently at random) before moving. The probabilities of turning are given as two values (the probability of turning left and the probability of turning right) when the `BustedBot` is constructed. Write a `main` method that demonstrates your class.

Programming Projects

7.11 Explore the documentation for `becker.xtras.comboLock`. Write a class named `CombinationLock` that implements the `IComboLock` interface. Run it with the graphical user interface provided in `becker.xtras.comboLock.ComboLockGUI`. The result should be as shown in Figure 7-10. (*Hint*: This project is easier than the gas pump example.)

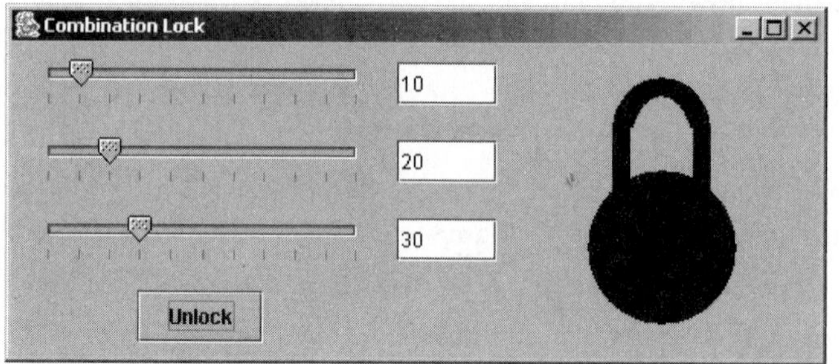

(figure 7-10)

Virtual combination lock

7.12 Implement a `Counter` class that could be used as part of the admission program for a carnival. A `Counter` object will keep track of how many people have entered the carnival so far. Each time a person enters, the `increment` method will be called. A query, `getCount`, will return the number of people who entered so far. A command, `reset`, will reset the counter back to zero to begin counting the next day. Write a main method to test your class.

7.13 Implement a class, `FuelUse`, to track the fuel use in an automobile. The `fillTank` method is called each time fuel is added to the automobile. It requires two arguments: the amount of fuel added and the distance driven since the last time the tank was filled. Provide two queries. One, `getMileage`, returns the miles per gallon or liters per 100 km (depending on your local convention) since record keeping began. The other query, `getTripMileage`, returns the miles per gallon or liters per 100 km since the most recent invocation of the command `resetTrip`. Return `-1` if mileage is requested when no miles have actually been traveled. Write a `main` method to test your class.

7.14 Explore the documentation for `becker.xtras.grapher`. The provided graphical user interface, `GrapherGUI`, will display the graph of a mathematical function when given a class that implements one of the interfaces `IFunction`, `IQuadraticFunction`, or `IPolynomialFunction` (see Figure 7-11).

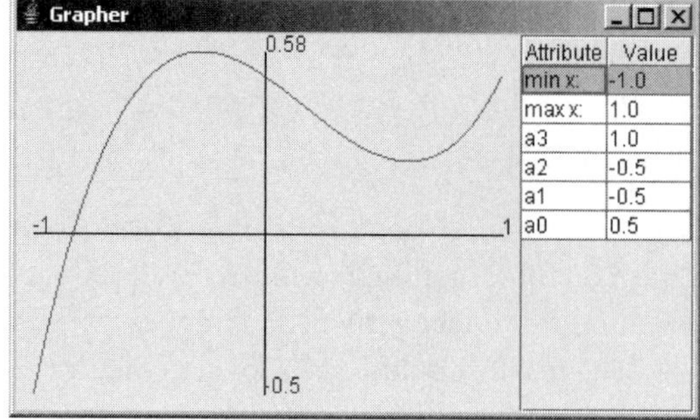

(figure 7-11)

Graphing a mathematical function

a. Write a class named `FuncA` that extends `Object`, implements `IFunction`, and evaluates sin(x) + cos(x).

b. Write a class named `FuncB` that extends `Object`, implements `QuadraticFunction`, and evaluates $ax^2 + bx + c$.

7.15 Write a class named `Time` that represents the time of day in hours and minutes. It should provide a constructor that can initialize the object to a specific time of day, and accessor methods `getHour`, `getMinute` as well as `toString`. Write four additional commands: `addHour()` and `addMinute()` to add a single hour and minute, respectively; and `addHours(int n)` and `addMinutes(int n)` to add the specified number of hours or minutes. Thoroughly test your class.

a. Write the `Time` class assuming a 24-hour clock. `toString` should return strings such as "00:15" and "23:09."

b. Write the `Time` class assuming a 12-hour clock—that is, `getHour` will always return a number between 0 and 12. Add an additional accessor method, `getPeriodDesignator`. The last accessor method returns a value for "AM" if the time is between midnight and noon and "PM" if the time is between noon and 1 minute before midnight. Use an enumerated type if you can; otherwise, use a `String`. `toString` should return values such as "00:15AM," "12:00PM" (noon), and "11:59PM" (1 minute to midnight).

7.16 Write a class named `Account`. Each `Account` object has an account owner such as "Suelyn Wang" and an account balance such as $349.12. Add an appropriate constructor and methods with the following signatures:

```
public int getBalance()
public String getOwner()
public void deposit(double howMuch)
public void withdraw(double howMuch)
public void payInterest(double rate)
```

The last method adds one month's interest by multiplying the `rate` divided by 12 times the current balance and adding the result to the current balance. Write a test harness.

7.17 Explore the documentation for `becker.xtras.radio`. Write two classes, one named `RadioTuner` that extends `Radio` and implements the `ITuner` interface, and another named `Main` that runs the program. The result should be similar to Figure 7-12. The graphical user interface will use `RadioTuner` to keep track of the current frequency, to search up and down for the next available frequency, and to remember up to five preset frequencies.

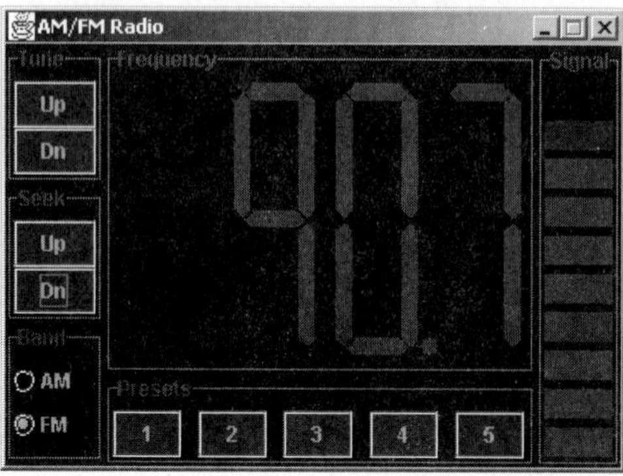

figure 7-12

Graphical user interface for an AM/FM radio

7.18 Explore the documentation for `becker.xtras.hangman`. Write two classes, one named `Hangman` that implements the `IHangman` interface and another named `HangmanMain` that includes a `main` method to run the program. The result should be similar to Figure 7-13. Your `Hangman` class will use a `String` to store the phrase the player is trying to guess and a second `String` to store the letters the player has guessed so far. You could use a `String` to store the phrase as the player has guessed it, but an instance of `StringBuffer` would be easier. `StringBuffer` is very similar to `String` but allows you to change individual characters.

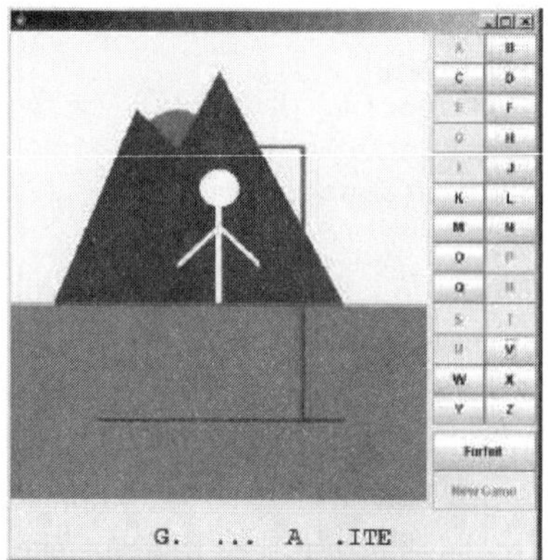

(figure 7-13)

Graphical user interface for a game of Hangman

Chapter 8 Collaborative Classes

After studying this chapter, you should be able to:

- Write a class that uses references to an object by storing them in instance variables, passing them to parameter variables, and using them with temporary variables
- Draw class diagrams depicting collaborating classes
- Explain how reference variables are different from primitive variables
- Explain what an alias is and what dangers arise from aliasing
- Write code that compares two objects for equivalence
- Throw and catch exceptions
- Use a Java collection object to collaborate with many objects, all having the same type

So far, our programs have usually required writing only a single class plus the `main` method. Almost any program of consequence, however, involves at least several classes that work together—or collaborate—to solve the problem. In fact, most of our programs already have this property of collaboration. For example, the `Robot` class collaborates with `City` and `Intersection` objects, and the `Meter` class collaborates with the `GasPumpGUI` that displays it. However, the mechanics of these collaborations have usually been hidden.

In this chapter, we become more intentional about a particular kind of collaboration: when one object has a reference to another object as an instance variable or is passed a reference to another object via a parameter variable. We will also begin to investigate exceptions, and how a class can collaborate with many instances of another class.

Now that we have many programming tools at our disposal, we will move away from the robot examples. The rest of the book uses examples involving a `Person` class, a program for a charitable organization, games, and others.

8.1 Example: Modeling a Person

A `Person` class might be useful in many kinds of programs. Payroll systems, student information systems, airline reservation systems, tax preparation programs, and programs to track genealogies all maintain information about people and might use a `Person` class.

In this section, we will develop a simple `Person` class, first as a single class using the techniques we've seen so far, but then using collaborating classes. Complex concepts can be modeled more easily using collaborating classes because they can divide the work.

Our simple `Person` class will be oriented toward registering births and deaths, perhaps within a government, an insurance company, or a genealogical program. It will model a person's name, mother, father, birth date, and death date. Of course, it will need a constructor and some accessor methods. We'll also be interested in a `daysLived` method. If the person has died, `daysLived` returns the number of days between his birth and death dates. If the person is still alive, it returns the number of days between his birth and the current date.

8.1.1 Using a Single Class

Building on what we have already learned, it's not hard to imagine how a `Person` class could be constructed. A suggested class diagram is shown in Figure 8-1, and an initial test harness is shown in Listing 8-1.

Listing 8-1: *The beginnings of a test harness for the `Person` class*

```
import becker.util.Test;

public class Person extends Object
{
   // instance variables and methods omitted

   // Test the class.
   public static void main(String[ ] args)
   { Person p = new Person("Joseph Becker",
                  "Jacob B. Becker", "Elizabeth Unruh", 1900, 6, 14);

      p.setDeathDate(1901, 6, 14);
      Test.ckEquals("exactly 1 year", 365, p.daysLived());
      p.setDeathDate(1901, 6, 13);
      Test.ckEquals("1 year less a day", 364, p.daysLived());
```

Listing 8-1: *The beginnings of a test harness for the* `Person` *class* (continued)

```
      p.setDeathDate(1902, 6, 15);
      Test.ckEquals("2 years plus a day", 365*2+1, p.daysLived());
   }
}
```

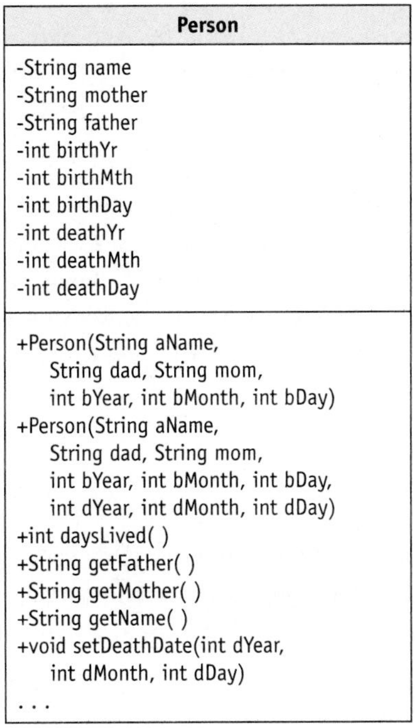

(figure 8-1)

Suggested class diagram for the `Person` *class*

```
Person
-------------------------------------
-String name
-String mother
-String father
-int birthYr
-int birthMth
-int birthDay
-int deathYr
-int deathMth
-int deathDay
-------------------------------------
+Person(String aName,
    String dad, String mom,
    int bYear, int bMonth, int bDay)
+Person(String aName,
    String dad, String mom,
    int bYear, int bMonth, int bDay,
    int dYear, int dMonth, int dDay)
+int daysLived( )
+String getFather( )
+String getMother( )
+String getName( )
+void setDeathDate(int dYear,
    int dMonth, int dDay)
...
```

All of the methods shown in the class diagram should be easy to write and test with the exception of `daysLived`. The test harness chooses several easy ages to calculate—exactly one year old, a year less one day, and two years plus a day. Many other combinations would be worth testing, but these three make a good start.

After considerable thought, we might come up with pseudocode for `daysLived` that appears to solve the problem:

```
declare variables for end date
if (not dead)
{ set end date to today's date
} else
{ set end date to death date
```

```
}

days = 0
for each full year lived
{ days = days + days in the year (remember leap years!)
}

daysLivedInFirstYear = # days between birth date and Dec 31
daysLivedInLastYear = # days between Jan 1 and end date
return days + daysLivedInFirstYear + daysLivedInLastYear
```

This is a complicated algorithm and some problems haven't been solved yet (finding the number of days between January 1 and a given date, getting today's date, and determining if a year is a leap year). Furthermore, these details are not part of the main purpose of the class: maintaining information about a person. The `Person` class would be easier to write and maintain if the details related to dates were in a separate class.

KEY IDEA

Delegate peripheral details to a separate class.

Using a separate class for dates is also a good idea because working with dates is a common activity. Having a separate class allows us to write and debug the class once but use it in many classes. For these reasons, we should either write our own `Date` class or find one that has already been written. For both of these scenerios, we need to learn to write the `Person` class to make effective use of a date class; this is the primary focus of this chapter.

8.1.2 Using Multiple Classes

In fact, Java provides classes to deal with dates. One is `GregorianCalendar` in the package `java.util`. It is rather complex to use, however. A simpler class is found in `becker.util` and is called `DateTime`. We'll use this class to simplify our implementation of `Person`.

The `DateTime` Class

One possible class diagram for `DateTime` is shown in Figure 8-2. The diagram is abbreviated because, as the name implies, the class also handles time. This aspect has been omitted from the class diagram.

The first constructor in this class creates an object corresponding to the current date, the second constructor allows you to create an object for a specific date, and the third creates a copy of the specified `DateTime` object. The `add` methods allow the date to be adjusted, either forward or backward in time. The `daysUntil` method calculates the number of days between two dates.

(figure 8-2)

Class diagram for `DateTime` *(methods related to time are not shown)*

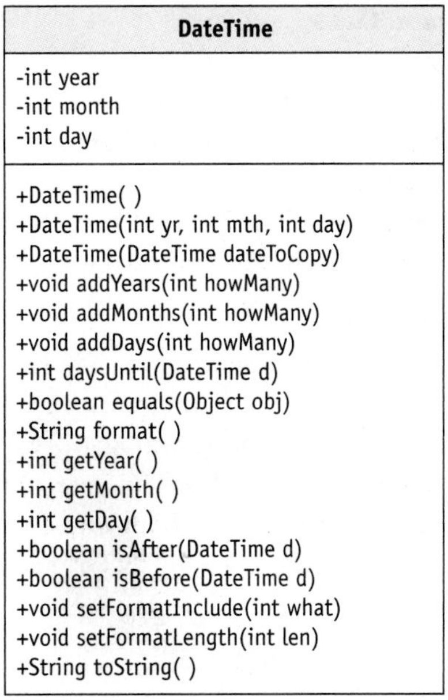

DateTime
-int year -int month -int day
+DateTime( ) +DateTime(int yr, int mth, int day) +DateTime(DateTime dateToCopy) +void addYears(int howMany) +void addMonths(int howMany) +void addDays(int howMany) +int daysUntil(DateTime d) +boolean equals(Object obj) +String format( ) +int getYear( ) +int getMonth( ) +int getDay( ) +boolean isAfter(DateTime d) +boolean isBefore(DateTime d) +void setFormatInclude(int what) +void setFormatLength(int len) +String toString( )

Listing 8-2 shows a simple program to calculate and print Luke's age, in days. It uses two of the constructors and the query `daysUntil` to calculate the number of days from Luke's birthday until the current date.

Running this program on the day this paragraph was written gives an answer of 5,009 days.

FIND THE CODE

ch08/lukesAge/

Listing 8-2: *A simple program to calculate and print someone's age, in days*

```
import becker.util.DateTime;

public class Main extends Object
{ public static void main(String[] args)
  {
    DateTime lukesBD = new DateTime(1990, 10, 1);
    DateTime today = new DateTime();

    int daysOld = lukesBD.daysUntil(today);
    System.out.println("Luke is " + daysOld + " days old.");
  }
}
```

Reimplementing the `Person` Class

Using the `DateTime` class, we can replace six instance variables in our original class with only two—one to represent the birth date and another to represent the death date. Besides eliminating instance variables, some of the code from the `Person` class can now be delegated to the `DateTime` class. This is like a high-level manager delegating work to one of her employees. Delegation can make more effective use of the resources available.

In Listing 8-3, this delegation of work occurs at line 45. The `daysLived` method uses the `daysUntil` method in `DateTime` by calling `this.birth.daysUntil`, which is just like calling `lukesBD.daysUntil` (line 9, Listing 8-2) except that `luke` was a temporary variable within the `main` method. Here, we use `this` to access the instance variable referring to the `DateTime` object. In both cases, we are asking a `DateTime` object to perform a service on our behalf—and if `DateTime` can do it for us, we don't have to do it ourselves.

KEY IDEA

Collaborative classes are all about getting someone else to do the work.

But we're getting ahead of ourselves. Lines 12 and 13 of Listing 8-3 show the declaration of the two `DateTime` objects to store the birth and death dates. These declarations are like other instance variable declarations except that instead of a primitive type such as `int`, they use the name of a class or interface.

FIND THE CODE

ch08/collabPerson/

Listing 8-3: *An implementation of* `Person` *that collaborates with the* `DateTime` *class*

```
 1  import becker.util.Test;
 2  import becker.util.DateTime;
 3
 4  /** Represent a person.
 5   *
 6   *  @author Byron Weber Becker */
 7  public class Person extends Object
 8  {
 9    private String name;                  // person's name
10    private String mother;                // person's mother's name
11    private String father;                // person's father's name
12    private DateTime birth;               // birth date
13    private DateTime death = null;        // death date (null if still alive)
14
15    /** Represent a person who is still alive. */
16    public Person(String aName, String mom, String dad,
17                  int bYear, int bMonth, int bDay)
18    { this(aName, mom, dad, bYear, bMonth, bDay, 0, 0, 0);
19    }
20
```

PATTERN

Has-a (Composition)

Listing 8-3: *An implementation of* `Person` *that collaborates with the* `DateTime` *class* (continued)

```
21    /** Represent a person who has died. */
22    public Person(String aName, String mom, String dad,
23                  int bYear, int bMonth, int bDay,
24                  int dYear, int dMonth, int dDay)
25    { super();
26      this.name = aName;
27      this.mother = mom;
28      this.father = dad;
29
30      this.birth = new DateTime(bYear, bMonth, bDay);
31      if (dYear > 0)
32      { this.death = new DateTime(dYear, dMonth, dDay);
33      }
34    }
35
36    /** Return the number of days this person has lived. */
37    public int daysLived()
38    { DateTime endDate = this.death;
39      if (this.death == null)
40      { endDate = new DateTime();
41      }
42      return this.birth.daysUntil(endDate);
43    }
44
45    /** Set the death date to a new value. */
46    public void setDeathDate(int dYear, int dMonth, int dDay)
47    { this.death = new DateTime(dYear, dMonth, dDay);
48    }
49
50    // Accessor methods omitted.
51    // main method omitted. It's the same as Listing 8-1 but with a few additional tests.
52  }
```

The instance variable `birth` is initialized in line 30 to refer to a new `DateTime` object. The form of its initialization is like all the objects we've constructed except that we use `this` to access the instance variable assigned the new value. The birth date is always dependent on information passed to the constructor's parameters and is therefore always performed in the constructor.

KEY IDEA

Variables refer to objects rather than containing them.

We say `birth` "refers" to an object rather than "contains" an object. This is a subtlety that we'll explore in detail in Section 8.2. Until then, we'll use the appropriate language for accuracy even though it hasn't been fully explained.

null Values

Unlike birth, death may or may not refer to an object, depending on whether the person has already died. Lines 13 and 32 address the issue of what to do with a person who hasn't died. The declaration in line 13 assumes that the person has not died and initializes death to the special value **null**. null can be assigned to any reference variable and means that the variable does not refer to any object at all. If it turns out that the person has died, the variable is reinitialized in line 32 with a DateTime object.

KEY IDEA

Use null when there is no object to which the variable can refer.

This example represents a common situation: A reference variable is needed but sometimes no object is appropriate to store there. At those times, use null. In this case, storing null means that the person has not yet died. We can determine if the person has died by comparing death with null using the == and != operators. This is shown in line 39. If the death date is null, the person is still alive and the temporary variable endDate is assigned the current date. Otherwise, endDate is assigned the date the person died.

Null values can lead to trouble for beginning and experienced programmers alike. The problem stems from assuming the variable refers to an object when it does not. For example, suppose you want to know how many days have passed since a person died. A natural approach is to add the following method to Person:

```
public int daysSinceDeath()
{ DateTime today = new DateTime();
  return this.death.daysUntil(today);
}
```

If death refers to a DateTime object, this works as desired. However, if death contains null, executing this code will result in a NullPointerException. An exception stops the program and prints a message that contains helpful information for finding the problem. Adding a line that calls daysSinceDeath to the main method in Listing 8-3 results in the following error message:

KEY IDEA

Variables containing null can't be used to call methods.

```
Exception in thread "main" java.lang.NullPointerException
        at Person.daysSinceDeath(Person.java:53)
        at Person.main(Person.java:75)
```

This message says that the problem was a NullPointerException (which means we tried to use a null value as if it referred to an object). Furthermore, it tells us that it occurred in the method we added (daysSinceDeath), which would appear in Listing 8-3 at line 53. Note that the error message tells us the filename and line number. If we're curious about why the program was executing daysSinceDeath in the first place, the subsequent line(s) trace the execution all the way back to the main method.

KEY IDEA

Exceptions give useful information to help find the error.

8.1.3 Diagramming Collaborating Classes

KEY IDEA

Class diagrams show the relationships between collaborating classes.

We have used class diagrams regularly to give an overview of an individual class. These diagrams can also be used to show the relationships between collaborating classes. In fact, we've already seen class diagrams showing such collaborating classes: when we extended one class to form a new one with additional capabilities (see Sections 2.2 and 3.5.3). In that situation, we generally place the superclass above the subclass and connect the two with a closed arrow pointing to the superclass. A generic example is shown in Figure 8-3.

(figure 8-3)

Class diagram showing two classes collaborating via inheritance

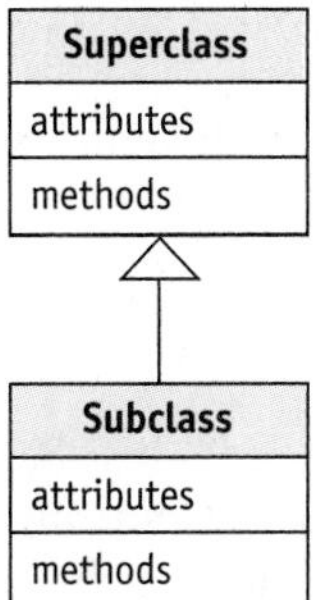

However, the `Person` class does not extend `DateTime` (nor is the reverse true), and so we use a different diagramming convention. This convention uses an open-headed arrow from one class to the other. The tail of the arrow is the class containing the instance variable and the head of the arrow is the class representing the variable's type. Usually the classes are drawn side by side, if possible. A class diagram for the `Person` class in Figure 8-4 serves as an example.

(figure 8-4)

Class diagram for the `Person` *class showing its collaboration with* `DateTime`

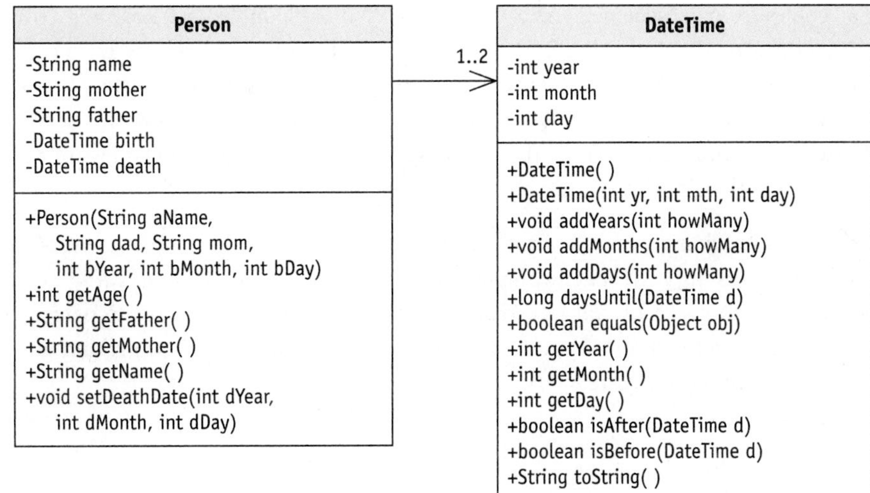

Another feature of the diagram is the **multiplicity** near the arrowhead. The `1..2` in the diagram shows that each `Person` object uses at least one but no more than two `DateTime` objects. A class diagram will show each class only once, no matter how many objects are actually created using the classes. In general, the first number is the minimum number of objects that will be used, and the second number is the maximum number that will be used in the running program.

PATTERN

Has-a (Composition)

Other multiplicities are common. `1` is an abbreviation for `1..1` and means that exactly one object is used. An asterisk (`*`) is used to mean "many." An asterisk by itself is an abbreviation for `0..*` meaning "anywhere from none to many." If there will always be at least one but possibly many, use `1..*`. An arrow without an explicit multiplicity is assumed to be `1`.

The inheritance relationship, as shown in Figure 8-3, never includes a multiplicity.

Clients and Servers

In Section 1.1.2, we briefly discussed the terms **client** and **server**. Here we see those roles depicted graphically. The arrow goes from the client to the server. The client, `Person`, requests a service such as finding the days until another date. The server, `DateTime`, is the class or object that performs the service.

"Is-a" versus "Has-a"

How do you know which diagramming convention to use? If you already have the Java code, you examine the code. If the code says `public class X extends Y`, use the "**is-a**" relationship shown in Figure 8-3. If the class has an instance variable referring to an object, use the "**has-a**" relationship shown in Figure 8-4.

"Is-a" comes from the sentence "An `X` is a kind of `Y`." For example, "a `Harvester` robot is a kind of `Robot`" (see Listing 3-3) or "a `Lamp` is a kind of `Thing`" (see Listing 2-6). Other examples include "a `Circle` is a kind of `Shape`," "an `Employee` is a kind of `Person`," and "an `Automobile` is a kind of `Vehicle`." Given two classes, if a sentence like any one of these makes sense, then using `extends` and a diagram like Figure 8-3 is often the right thing to do.

LOOKING AHEAD

We'll examine is-a relationships more carefully in Chapter 12.

On the other hand, it's more often the case that "an `X` has a `Y`." In that case, we use the "has-a" relationship, also called **composition**. "A `Person` has a `birth date`" or "a `GasPump` has a `Meter`" or "an `Automobile` has an `Engine`." Has-a relationships are implemented by adding an instance variable in the class that "has" something and is diagrammed similar to Figure 8-4.

8.1.4 Passing Arguments

LOOKING BACK

Overloading involves two or more methods with the same name but different signatures. See Section 6.2.2.

Passing object references as arguments is like passing an integer: declare a parameter variable in the method's declaration and pass a reference to an object when the method is called. For example, the `setDeathDate` method (lines 46–48 in Listing 8-3) could be overloaded with another version of `setDeathDate` that takes an object reference as an argument:

```
public void setDeathDate(DateTime deathDate)
{ this.death = deathDate;
}
```

Both this method and the original accomplish the same purpose: assigning a new `DateTime` object to the `death` instance variable. The difference is in where the object is constructed. In the original version, the method received the year, month, and day, and then constructed the object itself. In this version, the client constructs the object.

8.1.5 Temporary Variables

We have been using temporary variables to refer to objects since our first program. In our first program, we wrote the following lines:

```
City prague = new City();
Thing parcel = new Thing(prague, 1, 2);
Robot karel = new Robot(prague, 1, 0, Direction.EAST);
```

We didn't mention that `prague`, `karel`, and `parcel` are all temporary variables referring to objects, but they are. They can be similarly used in any method, not just `main`. However, remember that temporary variables only exist while the method containing them is executing. As soon as the method is finished, so are the temporary variables.

8.1.6 Returning Object References

Finally, a query may return an object reference as easily as it can return an integer. For example, we could add a query to our `Person` class to get the person's birth date. Listing 8-4 shows an abbreviated version of the class.

Listing 8-4: *An abbreviated version of the* `Person` *class showing* `getBirthDate`

```
public class Person extends Object
{ ... // instance variables omitted
  private DateTime birth;                          // birth date
  private DateTime death;                          // death date (null if still alive)
  ...

  public DateTime getBirthDate()
  { return this.birth;
  }
}
```

A client could use this query to compare the ages of two persons, as in the following example. Assume that `luke` and `caleb` both refer to `Person` objects.

```
1 DateTime lukesBD = luke.getBirthDate();
2 if (lukesBD.isBefore(caleb.getBirthDate())
3 { System.out.println("Luke is older.");
4 } else if (caleb.getBirthDate().isBefore(lukesBD))
5 { System.out.println("Caleb is older.");
6 } else
7 { System.out.println("Luke and Caleb are the same age.");
8 }
```

In line 1, the `getBirthDate` query is used to assign a value to the temporary variable `lukesBD`.

The `isBefore` query is used in line 2 to compare two dates—Luke's birth date and Caleb's birth date. In this case, Luke's birth date is held in a temporary variable, but the value to use for Caleb's birth date is obtained directly from the relevant `Person` object via our new query.

Line 4 shows that the object reference returned by `getBirthDate` does not even have to be saved in a variable before it can be used to call a method. Read the statement left to right. The first part, `caleb`, is a reference to a `Person` object. Any such reference can be used to call the methods in the object, including `getBirthDate`. This call returns a reference to a `DateTime` object. Any such reference, whether it is stored in a variable or returned by a query, can be used to call methods in the `DateTime` class, including `isBefore`. This query returns a Boolean value, so no further method calls can be chained to the end of this expression.

KEY IDEA

Methods that return references can be chained together, eliminating the need for some temporary variables.

8.1.7 Section Summary

In this section, we've seen how to implement a class, `Person`, that collaborates with another class, `DateTime`. This particular relationship is sometimes called the "has-a" relationship because a person has a birth date and a death date. This relationship is also called composition.

We have also seen that references to objects such as the birth date and death date can be used much like integers and other primitive types. They can be used as instance variables, temporary variables, and parameter variables, and can be returned by queries.

8.2 Reference Variables

Throughout the previous section, we used phrases like "references to objects" and "object references." What do those phrases really mean?

Consider again the program to calculate Luke's age in days, which appeared in Listing 8-2 and is reproduced in Listing 8-5. We'll focus on two variables, `lukesBD` and `daysOld`. We know that a variable stores a value; this was one of the basic concepts introduced in Chapter 6, where variables were described as being like a box that has a name. Inside the box is a value, such as 5009, that can be retrieved by giving the name of the variable.

Listing 8-5: *A simple program reproduced from Listing 8-2*

```
import becker.util.DateTime;

public class Main extends Object
{ public static void main(String[] args)
  {
    DateTime lukesBD = new DateTime(1990, 10, 1);
    DateTime today = new DateTime();

    int daysOld = lukesBD.daysUntil(today);
    System.out.println("Luke is " + daysOld + " days old.");
  }
}
```

At this point you might imagine `daysOld` and `lukesBD` as something like the illustrations in Figure 8-5. The "box" for `daysOld` holds the value `5009` and the "box" for `lukesBD` holds an object, represented with an object diagram.

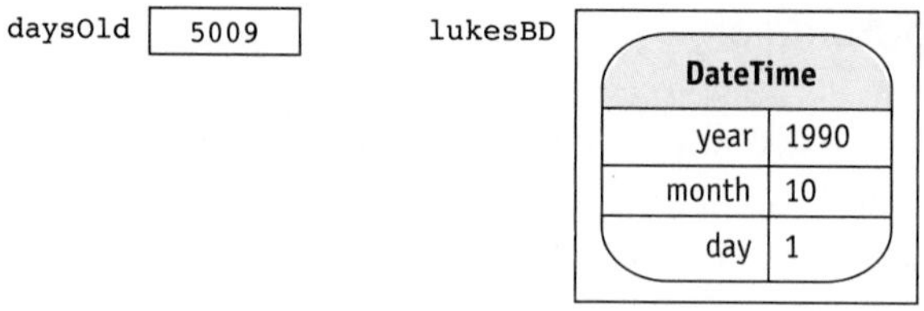

daysOld | 5009 | lukesBD

DateTime	
year	1990
month	10
day	1

(figure 8-5)

Simplistic visualization of two variables

This is an accurate enough description for `daysOld`, but not for `lukesBD`. `lukesBD` is a reference variable, a variable that refers to an object rather than actually holding the object. To understand what this means, we need to better understand the computer's memory.

8.2.1 Memory

Every computer has memory, where it stores information. This information includes values stored in variables such as `daysOld` and `lukesBD`, objects, text, images, and audio clips. Even the programs themselves constitute information stored in the computer's memory.

Memory is composed of many storage locations; these are the "boxes" we've described that hold the information. Each location has its own address, numbered consecutively beginning with 0. The address is how the computer program identifies which memory location it should access. Each variable name in the program is associated by the Java compiler with a specific memory address, as shown in Figure 8-6a. It shows the variable `daysOld` associated with the memory address 5104. The current value of `daysOld`, 5009, is in that location. Notice that every location has a value, even if it's 0.

The point of this discussion is that objects are handled differently from primitive types, such as integers. The variable `lukesBD`, for example, is associated with an address, and its value is stored in a memory location just like `daysOld`. However, that memory location does not store the object itself but the address of the object; that is, it *refers* to the object, as shown in Figure 8-6b. Notice that the object takes up several memory locations—one for each of the three instance variables.[1]

[1] We are glossing over the fact that one location is only big enough to store a value between –128 and 127. A larger number, such as occupied by an `int` or an address, requires four locations. Every `int` requires four locations, even if the actual value is between –128 and 127.

(figure 8-6)

Illustrating a variable storing a primitive type and a reference variable

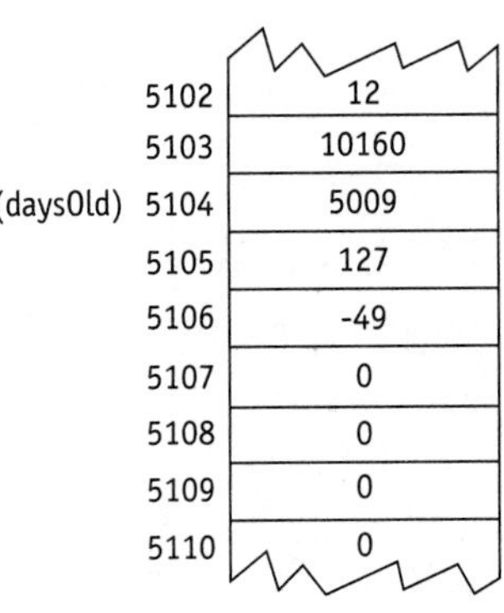

a. Variable storing a primitive type

b. Reference variable

Why not store the object at the address associated with `lukesBD`, as illustrated in Figure 8-5? Why do we store the address of the object in `lukesBD` instead? The answer involves efficiency—making the program run faster. If you need to pass an object as an argument, for example, it is faster to pass a reference than to pass the entire object. A reference is always the same size and does not occupy very much memory. Objects, on the other hand, vary in length and can occupy a large amount of memory.

Fortunately, we can usually ignore addresses and memory locations, and let the computer manage them. We only need to keep in mind that reference variables refer to an object instead of hold the object directly. A simplified diagram, as shown in Figure 8-7 will be sufficient to do this.

(figure 8-7)

Simplified diagram showing a reference variable

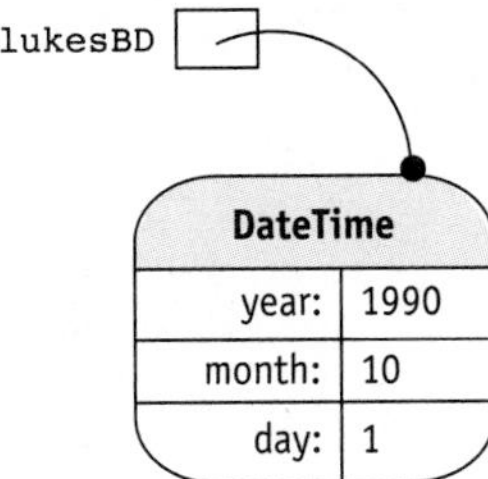

References are often held in an object, as with the birth and death dates in a `Person` object. In these cases, we can diagram the objects as shown in Figure 8-8.

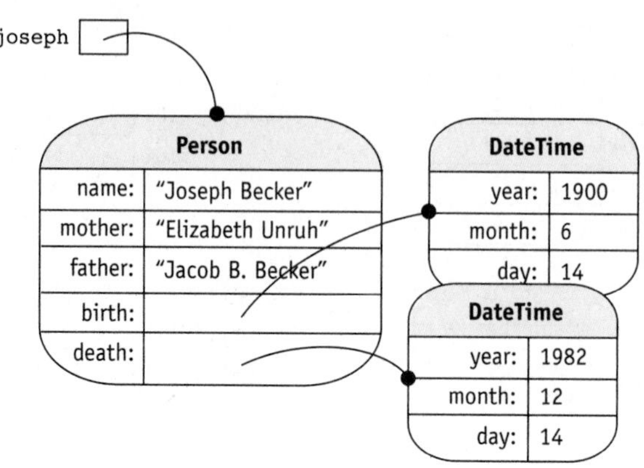

(figure 8-8)

Object with two instance variables referring to other objects

8.2.2 Aliases

One way that reference variables are different from primitive variables is that it is possible to have several variables refer to the same object. For example, consider the following statements:

```
DateTime lukesBD = new DateTime(1990, 10, 1);
DateTime annasBD = lukesBD;
```

KEY IDEA

Assigning reference variables copies the address from one to the other. The object itself is not copied.

The results of these statements are shown in Figure 8-9. In the second line, it's the address of the date object that is copied from `lukesBD` to `annasBD`. Now both variables refer to the same object.

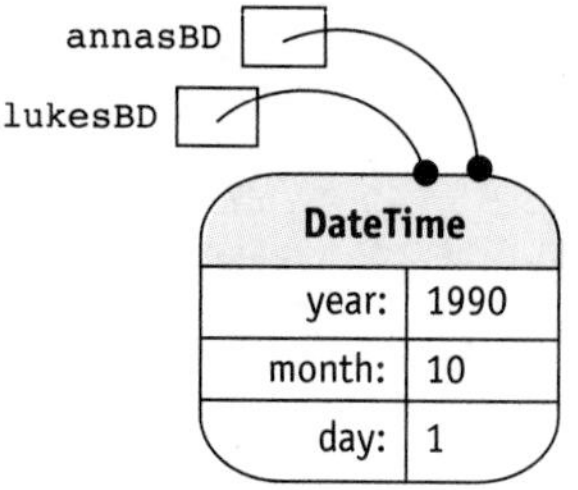

(figure 8-9)

Assigning one reference variable to another

We can use either reference variable to invoke the object's methods, as in the following statements:

```
lukesBD.addYear(1);
annasBD.addYear(2);
```

Executing these statements changes the date for this object from 1990 to 1993.

Having two or more variables refer to the same object is called **aliasing** and is similar to people with aliases. For example, the Beatles drummer would presumably answer to either Ringo Starr or the name his parents gave him, Richard Starkey.

The question is, why would you want two variables that refer to the same object? The example involving Luke's and Anna's birthdays is clear but rarely used. A closely related example, however, occurs frequently. That is when a reference variable is passed as an argument to a method. Consider the following method:

```
public void adjustDate(DateTime d)
{ d.addYear(2);
}
```

This method could be called as follows:

```
DateTime lukesBD = new DateTime(1990, 10, 1);

lukesBD.addYear(1);
this.adjustDate(lukesBD);
```

While the method `adjustDate` is executing, both `lukesBD` and the parameter variable `d` refer to the same object. When `adjustDate` is called, the value in the argument, `lukesBD`, is copied into the parameter variable, `d`. Once again, two variables contain the address of the same object. Either one can be used to invoke the object's methods, and the net result of this three-line fragment is that the object's year, 1990, is changed to 1993.

The Dangers of Aliases (advanced)

Aliases can lead to dangerous situations. Consider the following code, where `joseph` and `esther` are both instances of `Person`. They died eight years apart.

```
1 DateTime death = new DateTime(1974, 1, 11);
2 esther.setDeathDate(death);
3 death.addYears(8);
4 joseph.setDeathDate(death);
```

KEY IDEA

Aliases can be used to change objects unintentionally or maliciously.

Here, the programmer avoids constructing a new `DateTime` object. What is the effect of this code? Because both `esther` and `joseph` refer to the same `DateTime` object, one of their death dates will be wrong. In lines 1 and 2, `esther`'s death date is set correctly. However, when `death` is changed in line 3, `esther`'s death date inadvertently changes as well because they both refer to the same object. Finally, the date is set for `joseph`, resulting in the situation shown in Figure 8-10—a single `DateTime` object that has three references to it and is shared by both `esther` and `joseph`.

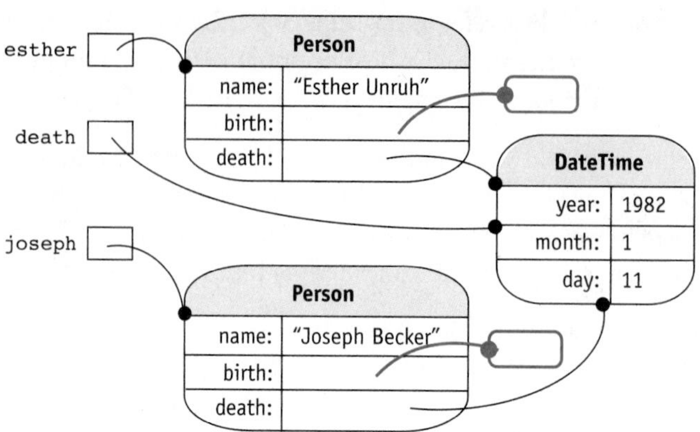

(figure 8-10)

Two `Person` *objects inadvertently sharing the same* `DateTime` *object*

A similar danger can result from an accessor method that returns a reference. The `getBirthDate` method (Section 8.1.6) returns a reference to the relevant `DateTime` object. Once the client has that reference, it could use it to reset the birth date—perhaps to a year that has not yet occurred.

```
DateTime birth = joseph.getBirthDate();
birth.addYears(291);
```

A two-line example makes the error obvious, but such an error can also be separated by many lines of code and be much more difficult to identify.

There are measures you can take to protect your code from aliasing errors. First, you could verify that the referenced object is immutable, meaning it has no methods to change its state. If the state can't change, it doesn't matter if the object is shared. Unfortunately, `DateTime` is not immutable, so this approach won't work here. `String`, a commonly used class, is immutable.

LOOKING BACK

Immutable classes were discussed in Section 7.3.3.

Second, the methods could avoid accepting or returning references in the first place. The first version of `setDeathDate`, which takes integer values for the year, month, and day, avoids this problem. Instead of having `getBirthDate` return a reference, determine why the client wants the reference. For example, if the purpose is to change the birth date, provide an `updateBirthDate` method that performs integrity checks to ensure the new date is reasonable.

LOOKING AHEAD

Listing 11-4 shows how to use `DateTime` *to make an immutable* `Date` *class.*

A third approach, and probably the most common, is to hope that the object's clients won't cause problems with the references. This is good enough in many situations, particularly if the program is well tested. However, in safety-critical applications or an application that may be the target of fraud, this approach is not sufficient.

The fourth, and safest, approach when using a mutable class is to make a object. For example, `setDeathDate` could be implemented as follows:

```
public void setDeathDate(DateTime deathDate)
{ DateTime copy = new DateTime(deathDate.getYear(),
                     deathDate.getMonth(), deathDate.getDay());
  this.death = copy;
}
```

Another `DateTime` constructor returns a copy of a `DateTime` object it is passed. The following `getBirthDate` method uses it to return a copy of the birth date.

```
public DateTime getBirthDate()
{ DateTime copy = new DateTime(this.birth);
  return copy;
}
```

8.2.3 Garbage Collection

Not only can an object have several variables referencing it, but it might have none. Consider the following situation, illustrated in Figure 8-11. An object is created, but then its reference is assigned a new value. The result is that the first object is **garbage**; there is no way to access the object because there are no references to it.

```
DateTime lukesBD = new DateTime(1990, 10, 1);
...
lukesBD = new DateTime(1994, 1, 28);
```

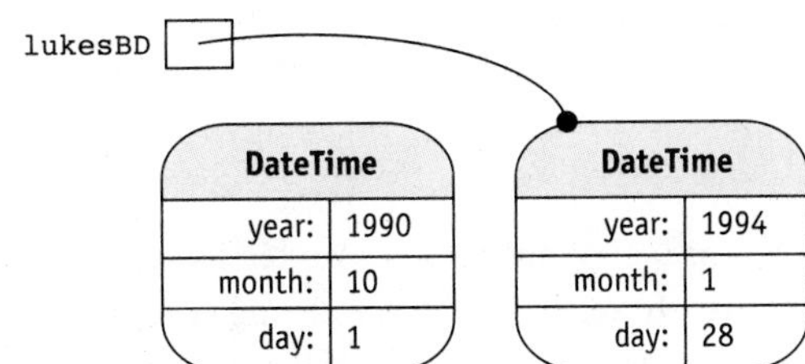

(figure 8-11)
Object with no references

As in the rest of life, garbage is undesirable. It consumes computer memory but cannot affect the running of the program because there is no way to access it. To address this situation, the Java system periodically performs **garbage collection**. It scans the computer's memory for unreferenced objects, enabling the memory they consume to be reused again when new objects are allocated. Because the memory can be reused, "memory recycling" might be a better name than "garbage collection."

8.2.4 Testing for Equality

Testing two objects for equality is a bit tricky. Suppose you have the situation shown in Figure 8-12a.

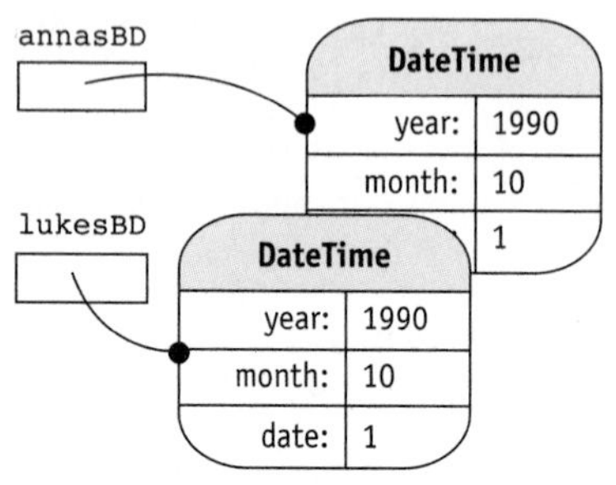

a. `annasBD == lukesBD` returns `false`

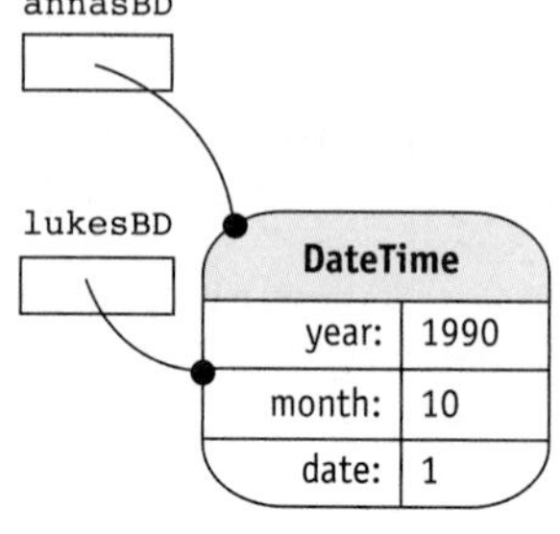

b. `annasBD == lukesBD` returns `true`

(figure 8-12)

Testing to determine if Anna and Luke have the same birthday

If you want to check whether Anna and Luke were born on the same day, you might write the following statement:

```
if (annasBD == lukesBD)
{   // what to do if they have the same birthday
```

This is, after all, what you would write to compare two integer variables. For example, if `annasAge` and `lukesAge` are two integer variables containing the ages of Anna and Luke, then the following code tests whether both variables contain the same value.

```
if (annasAge == lukesAge)
{   // what to do if they are the same age
```

If they both contain 18, for example, the == operator returns `true`.

KEY IDEA

Comparing object references with == returns `true` if they refer to exactly the same object.

The statement `if (annasBD == lukesBD)` also tests whether both variables contain the same value. In this case, however, the values being compared are object references, not the objects themselves. In other words, the test will be true if `annasBD` and `lukesBD` both contain the same address in memory and thus refer to exactly the same object. A situation where this is `true` is shown in Figure 8-12b.

Sometimes this behavior is exactly what is needed. For example, in Chapter 10, we will search lists of objects. We may want to know if a specific object is in the list or not, and a test containing == is the tool to use. This approach to equality is called **object identity**.

A Method to Test Equivalence

In the case of comparing birth dates, what we really need is **object equality**, or **equivalence**. We want to compare two date objects and determine if they have the same meaning. In the case of DateTime objects, they are equivalent if both objects have the same values for year, month, and day.

Testing for equivalence is done with a method such as the following in the DateTime class:

PATTERN

Equivalence Test

```
public boolean isEquivalent(DateTime other)
{ return other != null &&     // Make sure other actually refers to an object!
         this.year == other.getYear() &&
         this.month == other.getMonth() &&
         this.day == other.getDay();
}
```

The test for null protects against a NullPointerException occurring later in the method.

After the test for null comes a series of tests to ensure that all the relevant fields in the two objects are equivalent. If the relevant fields are primitive types, as shown here, use == for the test. If they are reference fields, use either an isEquivalent method that you've written or equals for provided classes.

This method could be used to test whether annasBD and lukesBD refer to objects with equivalent dates by writing one of the following statements:

```
if (annasBD.isEquivalent(lukesBD)) ...
```

or

```
if (lukesBD.isEquivalent(annasBD)) ...
```

KEY IDEA

Code in a given class can use the private instance variables of any instance of that class.

This version of isEquivalent is more verbose than necessary. So far we have only accessed private instance variables using this. However, Java allows us to access the private members of any object belonging to the same class. That is, inside the DateTime class, we can also access the instance variables for other—the DateTime object passed as an argument. Using this fact, the method can be rewritten as follows:

```
public boolean isEquivalent(DateTime other)
{ return other != null &&     // make sure other actually refers to an object!
         this.year == other.year &&
         this.month == other.month &&
         this.day == other.day;
}
```

Overriding equals

LOOKING AHEAD

equals is discussed again in Section 12.4.2.

The Object class has a method named equals that is meant to test for equivalence. Most classes should provide a method named equals that overrides the one in Object. Unfortunately, technicalities in doing so are difficult to explain without knowing about polymorphism, the topic of Chapter 12.

8.3 Case Study: An Alarm Clock

Suppose you are one of those people who lose all track of time when you're working at your computer. What you need is a computer-based alarm clock that rings an alarm to remind you when it's time to take a break, call a friend, attend a meeting, or quit for the day. You set the alarms for the day when you begin work and let the program run. When one of the alarms is due, it will print a message on the console and play a sound to get your attention. Our first version will be limited to four alarms.

Now that our problems are getting more complex and will often involve several classes, it may not be obvious which classes we need and how they work together. A design methodology is helpful. The methodology shown in Figure 8-13 is a set of steps to help us get started.

KEY IDEA

A design methodology can help us figure out how to get started on a complex problem.

1. Read the description of what the program is supposed to do, highlighting the nouns and noun phrases. These are the objects your program must declare. If there are any objects that cannot be directly represented using existing types, define classes to represent such objects.
2. Highlight the verbs and verb phrases in the description. These are the services. If a service is not predefined:
   a. Define a method to perform the service.
   b. Place it in the class responsible for providing the service.
3. Apply the services from Step 2 to the objects from Step 1 in a way that solves the problem.

(figure 8-13)

Object-based design methodology

Program design is as much art as science. The methodology leaves room for interpretation, and programming experience helps with recognizing and implementing common design patterns. Nevertheless, these basic steps have proven helpful to object-oriented programmers of all experience levels and on all sizes of projects. In fact, the larger the project, the more help these steps are in getting started.

The opening paragraph of Section 8.3 is our description of what the program is supposed to do.

8.3.1 Step 1: Identifying Objects and Classes

The first step in the methodology is to use nouns and noun phrases to identify the relevant classes to solve the problem. A noun is a person, a place, a thing, or an idea. The most important nouns in the description are *alarm clock*, *alarm*, and *time*. Other nouns include *program*, *message*, *console*, and *sound*.

KEY IDEA

Nouns in the specification often identify classes needed in the program.

Some of these can be represented with objects from existing classes. For example, time can be represented with the `DateTime` class, and a message with the `String` class; the console is where strings are printed by `System.out.println`. Exploring the online *Java Tutorial*[2] reveals the `AudioClip` class as one way to work with sound.

This leaves only the nouns *alarm clock* and *alarm* to develop into classes. We'll call them, appropriately, `AlarmClock` and `Alarm`.

Class Relationships

KEY IDEA

Sometimes a noun represents an attribute, not a class.

Sometimes the less important nouns go with another noun. For example, *message* and *sound* go with `Alarm` ("when an alarm is due, it will print a message...and play a sound"). They will appear as instance variables in the `Alarm` class. The "has-a" test from Section 8.1.3 also applies here: "An `Alarm` has-a message to display" and "an `Alarm` has-a sound to play."

The noun *time* applies in two ways. First, time is linked to `Alarm` in the statement "rings an alarm...when it's time," and "when one of the alarms is due" implies time. The "has-a" test makes sense, too: "An `Alarm` has-a time when it rings."

KEY IDEA

A solid arrow in a class diagram indicates an instance variable. A dotted line indicates a temporary variable or parameter.

Second, *time* is used by the `AlarmClock` class to keep track of the current time. The instance of `DateTime` will be a temporary variable, not an instance variable.

In addition, the alarm clock has up to four alarms. Again, the appearance of the word *has* indicates the presence of instance variables in the `AlarmClock` class.

Putting these observations together results in the classes, attributes, and class relationships shown in Figure 8-14. The class diagram also includes a class holding the `main` method where execution begins.

(figure 8-14)

First class diagram of the alarm clock program

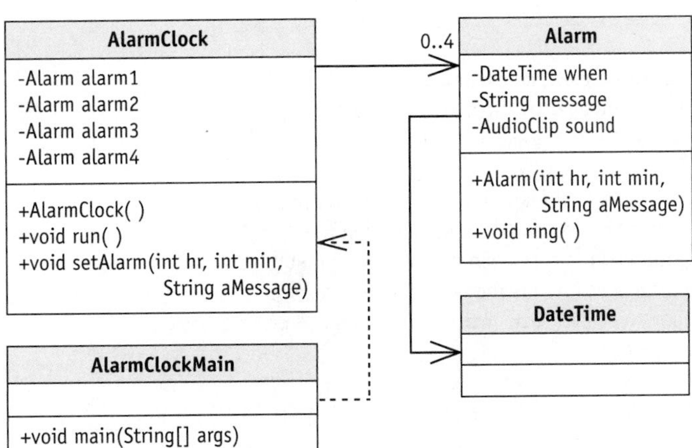

[2] See *http://java.sun.com/docs/books/tutorial/sound/index.html*

8.3.2 Step 2: Identifying Services

Step 2 in the object-based design methodology is to identify the services required in the classes by analyzing the verbs and verb phrases. Verbs are action words such as *ring*, *run*, *set*, and *print*. Verbs are used in the program description as "ring an alarm," "remind you when," "set the alarm," "run (the program)," "print a message," and "play a sound."

KEY IDEA

Verbs in the specification often identify services in the program's classes.

Some of these verbs are different descriptions of the same thing. For example, an alarm rings to remind you of something. It does so by displaying a message and playing a sound to get your attention. All of that could be collapsed into a single `ring` service in the `Alarm` class.

That still leaves setting the alarms, which sounds like it might be a service of the `AlarmClock` class, and running the program. This phrase is often a generic way of saying we should execute the program. In this case, however, we actually need a method that keeps the time for the clock. We'll name it `run`.

These services and the classes to which they are assigned are also shown in Figure 8-14.

Implementing Methods in `Alarm`

Now let's turn to implementing these methods, beginning with the `Alarm` class. We will defer the sound until later; our first version will "ring" the alarm by only printing a message.

KEY IDEA

Defer nonessential features until after the core features are working.

The constructor is passed the hour and minute that the alarm should ring and the message that should print. We'll use a `DateTime` object internally to represent the time the alarm should ring. The time and message must be remembered until they are needed by the `ring` method and are therefore saved in instance variables.

PATTERN

Has-a (Composition)

```
public class Alarm extends Object
{
  private DateTime when;
  private boolean hasRung = false;
  private String msg = "";

  /** Construct a new Alarm for today at the given time.
  *   @param hr        the hour the alarm should "ring"
  *   @param min       the minute of the hour that the alarm should "ring"
  *   @param msg       the message the alarm gives */
  public Alarm(int hr, int min, String msg)
  { super();
    this.when = new DateTime();
    this.when.setTime(hr, min, 0);
    this.msg = msg;
  }
}
```

The `ring` method is shown in the following code. It prints the time and the alarm's message on the console, using the `format` method in line 5 to format the alarm's time as a `String`. Two method calls at lines 3 and 4 determine how much information is presented.

```
1  /** Alert the user. */
2  public void ring()
3  { this.when.setFormatInclude(DateTime.TIME_ONLY);
4    this.when.setFormatLength(DateTime.SHORT);
5    String time = this.when.format();
6    System.out.println(time + ": " + this.msg);
7  }
```

Implementing Methods in `AlarmClock`

KEY IDEA

Asking and answering questions is a useful technique, even if you are programming by yourself.

The `AlarmClock` class has three fundamental things to do: keep the current time, ring the alarms at the correct times, and provide a way to set the alarms. We'll start with the `run` method, which keeps the current time. It will also call a helper method to ring the alarms, if appropriate. This method is not trivial, so we'll return to the expert-and-novice format of earlier chapters.

Expert What does `run` method need to do?

Novice Keep track of the current time. And if it's time for one of the alarms to ring, it needs to ring it.

Expert Is this something it does just once?

Novice Not really. As time passes, it will need to check again and again whether it is time to ring an alarm.

Expert So it sounds like a loop would be appropriate. What needs to be repeated inside the loop?

Novice It needs to figure out the current time and check if the alarms should be rung.

Expert So when should that loop stop?

Novice When there are no more alarms to ring.

Expert What's the negation of that condition? That tells us whether the loop should continue.

Novice Hey. It sounds like you're leading me through the four-step process for building a loop. Step 1 is to identify the actions that must be repeated to solve the problem; Step 2 is to identify the test that must be true when the loop stops and to negate it; Step 3 is to assemble the loop; and Step 4 is determining what comes before or after the loop to complete the solution.

LOOKING BACK

The four-step process for constructing a loop is discussed in Section 5.1.2.

Expert You're absolutely right. Now, what about negating the test in Step 2?

Novice The loop continues as long as there is at least one alarm left to ring.

As for Step 3, I'd like to start with pseudocode. It's easier than thinking in Java right away. Something like this, perhaps?

KEY IDEA

Pseudocode helps you think about the algorithm without distracting Java details.

```
while (number of alarms left > 0)
{ get the current time
  check alarms and ring if it's the right time
}
```

Expert Excellent. The fourth step was to think through what needs to come before or after the loop. What do you think?

Novice I don't think we need to do anything after the loop. Before the loop, we'll need to initialize some variables or something to control the loop.

Expert Yes. We could use an instance variable to count the number of alarms that have not been rung. When we set an alarm, we'll increment the counter; when we ring an alarm, we'll decrement it. Given that, can you code a solution in Java?

Novice I think so. I'm going to assume a helper method to check and ring the alarms for me. That will keep this method simpler.

KEY IDEA

Keep methods short. Use helper methods to reduce complexity.

```
public void run()
{ DateTime currTime = new DateTime();
  while (this.numAlarmsLeft > 0)
  { currTime = new DateTime();
    this.checkAndRingAlarms(currTime);
  }
}
```

Expert How would you evaluate your efforts so far?

Novice Pretty good. With the help of the four-step process for building loops and the pseudocode, I'm pretty confident `run` will do what it is supposed to do.

Expert I agree. I do have one suggestion, however. Let's insert a call to the `sleep` method inside the loop. Your loop probably runs thousands of times per second. We could slow it down with a `sleep` command, giving the computer more time to do other things. If we insert `Utilities.sleep(1000)` at the end of the loop, it will still check about once per second.

KEY IDEA

Think about testing from the beginning.

Novice Great idea. One thing is bothering me, though. Testing this method is going to be really hard because it runs in real time. If we set an alarm for 3:30 in the afternoon and it's only 10 in the morning now, we'll have to wait 5½ hours to see if the program works!

Expert That *is* a problem. Normally we want to test the same code that makes up the finished solution. Here, however, we may need to make a slight change to make testing easier.

Here's my suggestion: Let's add an instance variable to indicate whether or not we are testing. When we're testing, we'll calculate the current time slightly differently to make time pass more quickly. When the `run` method sleeps for one second, we'll add two seconds to the current time. That makes time pass twice as fast. If we want the virtual time to pass even more quickly, add four or even more seconds to the current time in each iteration of the loop.

If we're *not* testing, we'll continue to calculate the current time as you suggested earlier. Creating a new instance of `DateTime` will keep the time accurate because that constructor actually uses the computer's clock.

Novice If we use a parameter, the method calling `run` can decide how fast the time should pass. Then our new method would look like this:

```
public void run(int secPerSec)
{ DateTime currTime = new DateTime();

  while (this.numAlarmsLeft > 0)
  { if (this.TESTING)
    { currTime.addSeconds(secPerSec);
    } else
    { currTime = new DateTime();
    }

    this.checkAndRingAlarms(currTime);
    Utilities.sleep(1000); // sleep one second real time
  }
}
```

Expert Good. Now, what does your helper method, `checkAndRingAlarms`, need to do?

Novice It will check each alarm's time against the current time. If it's time for the alarm to ring, it will call its `ring` method. Or, in pseudocode (because I know you're going to ask):

```
if (alarm1's time matches current time)
{ ring alarm1
} else if (alarm2's time matches current time)
{ ring alarm2
}
```

We'll need a couple of more tests for the other alarms. I'm assuming the alarms are stored in four instance variables. Seems pretty simple to me.

Expert Actually, I think I see two problems. The first problem is when there is no alarm set. How can you check whether its time matches? If you tried, I think you would get a `NullPointerException`.

The second problem is that you are assuming that only one alarm becomes due at any given time. Remember the Cascading-`if` pattern? It says that only one of the groups of statements will be executed. If two alarms happen to be set for the same time, only the first will ring.

LOOKING BACK

The Cascading-`if` pattern was discussed in Section 5.3.3.

Novice So we could have four separate groups of statements, each one like this:

```
if (alarm is not null)
{ if (alarm's time matches current time)
  { ring the alarm
    decrement the number of alarms left to ring
  }
}
```

Expert Can you improve this? Is the nested `if` statement really necessary? Do you really need to repeat almost the same code four times?

Novice Aha. We can use short-circuit evaluation. If the first part of the "and" is `false`, Java won't even bother to check the second part. And we can put the whole thing in a method to avoid the code duplication. Like this:

LOOKING BACK

Short-circuit evaluation was discussed in Section 5.4.3.

```
private void checkOneAlarm(Alarm alarm, DateTime currTime)
{ if (alarm ! = null && alarm.isTimeToRing(currTime))
  { alarm.ring();
    this.numAlarmsLeft -= 1;
  }
}
```

Expert Good. I see you'll need to add a method, `isTimeToRing`, to the `Alarm` class. I like the way you're asking that class to figure out the answer for you. It's the one with the needed data. Asking `Alarm` for the answer seems better than asking it for its time and then doing the computation yourself.

KEY IDEA

Put methods in the same class as the data they use.

With this helper method, the `checkAndRingAlarms` helper method becomes:

```
private void checkAndRingAlarms(DateTime currTime)
{ this.checkOneAlarm(this.alarm1, currTime);
  this.checkOneAlarm(this.alarm2, currTime);
  this.checkOneAlarm(this.alarm3, currTime);
  this.checkOneAlarm(this.alarm4, currTime);
}
```

The last big step is to set the alarms. Ideas?

Novice We already know we'll have four instance variables. I think we need to just check each one in turn to see if it's `null`. If it is, we can save the alarm in that variable. A cascading-`if` should work. Of course, we also need to construct the `Alarm` itself.

```
public void setAlarm(int hr, int min, String msg)
{ Alarm theAlarm = new Alarm(hr, min, msg);
  if (this.alarm1 == null)
  { this.alarm1 = theAlarm;
  } else if (this.alarm2 == null)
  { this.alarm2 = theAlarm;
  } else if (this.alarm3 == null)
  { this.alarm3 = theAlarm;
  } else if (this.alarm4 == null)
  { this.alarm4 = theAlarm;
  }
}
```

Expert Looks good. But aren't you forgetting something? We made an assumption earlier that we had a count of the number of alarms yet to ring. This seems like the place to include it.

Novice Oops. Add the following to the end of the method:

```
this.numAlarmsLeft++;
```

Expert One more detail to consider for `setAlarm`. What happens if we try to set five alarms?

Novice Right now, absolutely nothing happens. The cascading-`if` statement doesn't have any tests that match and there is no `else` clause. I think the user should know about the error, so I'll add a warning in an `else` clause, as follows:

```
  ...
  } else if (this.alarm4 == null)
  { this.alarm4 = theAlarm;
  } else
  { System.out.println("Too many alarms.");
  }
```

Expert This is a fine solution for now, but throwing an exception would be better. I'm sure you'll learn how soon.

Excellent job. I think we're about done!

All these ideas come together in Listing 8-6 and Listing 8-7.

The `isTimeToRing` method in the `Alarm` class is mentioned in the dialogue but not discussed thoroughly. In this application, we dare not compare two times for equality to see if the alarm should ring because it's possible that the time might be skipped over—particularly given the time acceleration that we built into the `run` method. Instead, we need to check if the time for the alarm has passed and the alarm has not yet been rung. This requires an extra instance variable at line 10 in the `Alarm` class that is checked in the `isTimeToRing` method (line 28) and changed in the `ring` method (line 37).

FIND THE CODE

ch08/alarmClock/

PATTERN

Has-a (Composition)

Listing 8-6: *The* `Alarm` *class*

```
1  import becker.util.DateTime;
2  import becker.util.Utilities;
3
4  /** An Alarm represents a time when someone or something needs to be interrupted.
5   *
6   * @author Byron Weber Becker */
7  public class Alarm extends Object
8  {
9    private DateTime when;
10   private boolean hasRung = false;
11   private String msg = "";
12
13   /** Construct a new Alarm for today at the given time.
14    * @param hr       the hour the alarm should "ring"
15    * @param min      the minute of the hour that the alarm should "ring"
16    * @param msg      the message the alarm gives */
17   public Alarm(int hr, int min, String msg)
18   { super();
19     this.when = new DateTime();
20     this.when.setTime(min, hr, 0); // Deliberate bug
21     this.msg = msg;
22   }
23
24   /** Is it time for this alarm to ring?
25    * @param currTime the current time, as determined by the calling clock
26    * @return true if time for the alarm; false otherwise. */
27   public boolean isTimeToRing(DateTime currTime)
28   { return !this.hasRung && this.when.isBefore(currTime);
29   }
```

Listing 8-6: *The* `Alarm` *class* (continued)

```

  /** Alert the user. */
  public void ring()
  { this.when.setFormatInclude(DateTime.TIME_ONLY);
    this.when.setFormatLength(DateTime.SHORT);
    String time = this.when.format();
    System.out.println(time + ":" + this.msg);
    this.hasRung = true;
  }
}
```

FIND THE CODE

ch08/alarmClock/

Listing 8-7: *The* `AlarmClock` *class*

PATTERN

Has-a (Composition)

```
import becker.util.DateTime;
import becker.util.Utilities;

/** Maintain a set of up to four alarms. Keep time and ring alarms at the appropriate times.
*
*  @author Byron Weber Becker */
public class AlarmClock extends Object
{
  // Allow up to four alarms.
  private Alarm alarm1 = null;
  private Alarm alarm2 = null;
  private Alarm alarm3 = null;
  private Alarm alarm4 = null;

  // Count the alarms left to be rung.
  private int numAlarmsLeft = 0;
  // Make time pass more quickly when testing.
  private final boolean TESTING;

  /** Construct a new alarm clock.
  *  @param test When true, the run method makes time pass more quickly for testing. */
  public AlarmClock(boolean test)
  { super();
    this.TESTING = test;
  }

  /** Run the clock for one day, ringing any alarms at the appropriate times.
  *  @param secPerSec The speed with which the clock should run (for testing purposes).
```

Listing 8-7: *The* `AlarmClock` *class* (continued)

```
   * Each second of real time advances this clock the given number of seconds. With
   * a value of 3600 one "day" takes about 24 seconds of elapsed time. */
   public void run(int secPerSec)
   { DateTime currTime = new DateTime();

     while (this.numAlarmsLeft > 0)
     { if (this.TESTING)
       { currTime.addSeconds(secPerSec);
       } else
       { currTime = new DateTime();
       }

       this.checkAndRingAlarms(currTime);
       Utilities.sleep(1000); // sleep one second real time
     }
   }

   // Check each alarm. Ring it if it's time.
   private void checkAndRingAlarms(DateTime currTime)
   { this.checkOneAlarm(this.alarm1, currTime);
     this.checkOneAlarm(this.alarm2, currTime);
     this.checkOneAlarm(this.alarm3, currTime);
     this.checkOneAlarm(this.alarm4, currTime);
   }

   // Check one alarm. Ring it if it's time.
   private void checkOneAlarm(Alarm alarm, DateTime currTime)
   { if (alarm != null && alarm.isTimeToRing(currTime))
     { alarm.ring();
       this.numAlarmsLeft1-=1;
     }
   }

   /** Set an alarm to ring at the given time today. A maximum of four alarms may be set.
   * @param hr      The hour the alarm should ring.
   * @param min     The minute of the hour the alarm should ring.
   * @param msg     Why the alarm is being set */
   public void setAlarm(int hr, int min, String msg)
   { Alarm theAlarm = new Alarm(hr, min, msg);
     if (this.alarm1 == null)
     { this.alarm1 = theAlarm;
     } else if (this.alarm2 == null)
     { this.alarm2 = theAlarm;
```

Listing 8-7: *The* `AlarmClock` *class* (continued)

```
    } else if (this.alarm3 == null)
    { this.alarm3 = theAlarm;
    } else if (this.alarm4 == null)
    { this.alarm4 = theAlarm;
    } else
    { System.out.println("Too many alarms.");
    }

    this.numAlarmsLeft++;
  }

  // For testing
  public static void main(String[] args)
  { AlarmClock clock = new AlarmClock(true);

    clock.setAlarm(10, 30, "Coffee break");
    clock.setAlarm(11, 00, "Call Amy");
    clock.setAlarm(17, 30, "Turn off the computer and get a life!");

    clock.run(3600);
  }
}
```

8.3.3 Step 3: Solving the Problem

The hard part is over. The last step in the methodology is to solve the problem using the methods we created for the various classes. For the alarm clock problem, we can use a `main` method that constructs an `AlarmClock` object, sets alarms, and then calls the `run` method. A sample is shown in Listing 8-8.

FIND THE CODE

ch08/alarmClock/

Listing 8-8: *A* `main` *method to run the alarm clock program*

```
import becker.util.DateTime;

/** Run the alarm clock with today's alarms.
 *
 *  @author Byron Weber Becker */
public class AlarmClockMain extends Object
{
  public static void main(String[] args)
```

Listing 8-8: *A* `main` *method to run the alarm clock program* (continued)

```
   { AlarmClock clock = new AlarmClock(false);

      clock.setAlarm(10, 30, "Coffee break");
      clock.setAlarm(11, 00, "Call Amy");
      clock.setAlarm(17, 30, "Turn off the computer and get a life!");

      clock.run(1);
   }
}
```

8.4 Introducing Exceptions

In writing the `setAlarm` method in the `AlarmClock` class (lines 66–81 of Listing 8-7) we noted an error that could occur. An `AlarmClock` object can only store four alarms. If someone tries to add a fifth alarm, he or she should be warned that the maximum has been exceeded. We added a warning `print` statement to address this issue; we can do better.

8.4.1 Throwing Exceptions

Java provides **exceptions** for handling exceptional circumstances—like adding too many alarms to an alarm clock. An `Exception` is an object that, when it is thrown, interrupts the program's normal flow of control. **Throwing an exception** immediately stops the currently executing method, and if nothing is done to intervene, the program will stop with an error message displayed on the console.

There are various subclasses of `Exception` that are more specific about the exceptional circumstance. For example, adding a fifth alarm when our alarm clock can only handle four is attempting to put the object into an illegal state. In such a circumstance, the `IllegalStateException` is applicable.

The original `setAlarm` method used a cascading-`if` statement that concluded with the following code:

```
74      } else if (this.alarm4 == null)
75      { this.alarm4 = theAlarm;
76      } else
77      { System.out.println("Too many alarms.");
78      }
```

Replacing the print statement in line 77 with the following line will throw an `IllegalStateException`.

```
throw new IllegalStateException("Too many alarms.");
```

The constructor's argument is a string describing in more detail what caused the problem. The result of throwing this exception is shown in Figure 8-15.

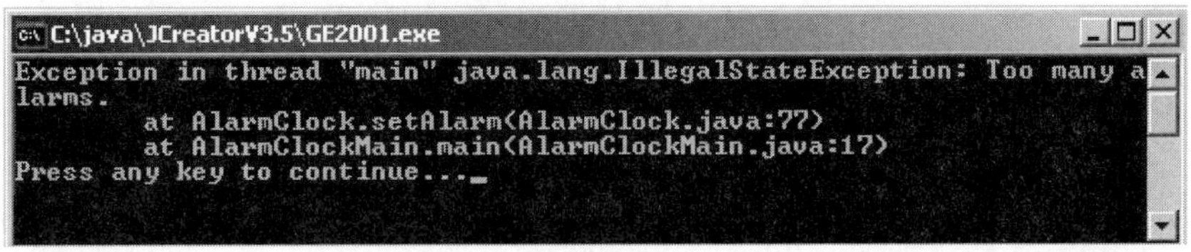

(figure 8-15)

Exception message printed after attempting to add a fifth alarm

```
C:\java\JCreatorV3.5\GE2001.exe
Exception in thread "main" java.lang.IllegalStateException: Too many a
larms.
        at AlarmClock.setAlarm(AlarmClock.java:77)
        at AlarmClockMain.main(AlarmClockMain.java:17)
Press any key to continue..._
```

One of the most common exceptions to throw is `IllegalArgumentException`. A good defensive programming strategy is to check the arguments passed to your methods to ensure that they are appropriate. For example, the `setAlarm` method is passed an hour and a minute. The following check, and a similar one for minutes, would be appropriate:

```
if (hr < 0 || hr > 23)
{ throw new IllegalArgumentException(
                    "Hour = " + hr + "; should be 0–23, inclusive.");
}
```

These checks are especially important in constructors where the arguments are often used to initialize instance variables.

8.4.2 Reading a Stack Trace

The information printed when an exception is thrown is very useful for debugging. For example, one run of the alarm clock program produced the exception message shown in Figure 8-16.

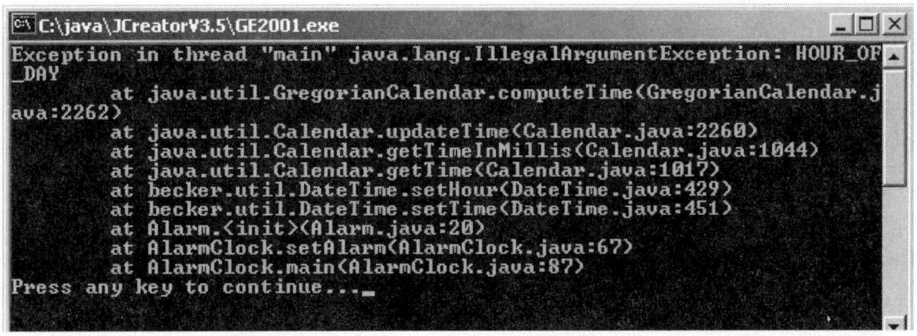

(figure 8-16)

Stack trace printed as part of an exception message

```
C:\java\JCreatorV3.5\GE2001.exe
Exception in thread "main" java.lang.IllegalArgumentException: HOUR_OF
_DAY
        at java.util.GregorianCalendar.computeTime(GregorianCalendar.j
ava:2262)
        at java.util.Calendar.updateTime(Calendar.java:2260)
        at java.util.Calendar.getTimeInMillis(Calendar.java:1044)
        at java.util.Calendar.getTime(Calendar.java:1017)
        at becker.util.DateTime.setHour(DateTime.java:429)
        at becker.util.DateTime.setTime(DateTime.java:451)
        at Alarm.<init>(Alarm.java:20)
        at AlarmClock.setAlarm(AlarmClock.java:67)
        at AlarmClock.main(AlarmClock.java:87)
Press any key to continue..._
```

The first item of useful information is the name of the exception, `IllegalArgumentException`. The string passed to the exception when it was thrown is "`HOUR_OF_DAY`". Its relevance isn't known yet.

The nine lines following it, each beginning with "at," make up a **stack trace**. A stack trace follows the execution from the exception back to `main`, listing all of the methods that have not yet completed executing. Each line has the following form:

```
at «packageName».«className».«methodName»(«fileName»:«line»)
```

The alarm clock program's classes are not in a package, so that part is blank for the last three lines.

The last line of the stack trace tells us that the `main` method in the `AlarmClock` class called a method at line 87. The method it called is shown on the line above it, `setAlarm`. If we look at line 87 in Listing 8-7, we can verify that `main` calls the `setAlarm` method.

The second-to-last line of the stack trace tells us that `setAlarm` called a method at line 67 in `AlarmClock.java`. The third-to-last line tells us that method was `Alarm.<init>`. This refers to the initialization that occurs when an instance of `Alarm` is constructed, including the initialization of instance variables. In this case, it occurred at line 20 in `Alarm.java`. That line calls the `setTime` method in the `DateTime` class. The rest of the method calls shown in the stack trace are for code in libraries we used.

It's usually most fruitful to debug our code beginning with the line closest to the exception—that is, `Alarm.java` at line 20. It reads as follows:

```
20      this.when.setTime(min, hr, 0);
```

The variable `this.when` is an instance of `DateTime`. Because the exception was `IllegalArgumentException`, we can guess that something was wrong with the arguments passed to the method. In this case, the order looks wrong and a quick check of the documentation confirms that the order of `min` and `hr` is reversed.

8.4.3 Handling Exceptions

Java has two types of exception—checked and unchecked. **Checked exceptions** are exceptions from which the program may be able to recover; in addition, programmers are required to include code to check for them. **Unchecked exceptions** should be thrown only when they result from a program bug. Programmers are not required to check for them. `IllegalArgumentException` and `IllegalStateException` are two examples of unchecked exceptions. Unchecked exceptions include `Error`, `RuntimeException`, and their subclasses. All other exceptions are checked.

LOOKING AHEAD

We will need to construct a URL to make `Alarm` play a sound.

`MalformedURLException` is an example of a checked exception. It might arise from a user typing a Uniform Resource Locator (URL) into the address bar of a Web browser, as shown in Figure 8-17. In this browser, a dialog box is shown stating that "htt is not a registered protocol" (it should be "http" rather "htt").

(figure 8-17)

Address bar of a typical Web browser

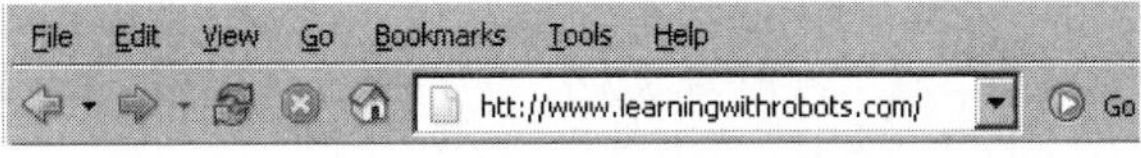

In a Java program, such an error would likely be discovered when it constructs a `URL` object. The `URL` constructor takes a string, such as the one typed by the user in the previous figure. If an error is found, the `URL` constructor throws a `MalformedURLException`. This fact is included in the online documentation.

Programmers can check for an exception and handle it with code derived from the following template:

```
try
{ «statements that may throw an exception»
} catch («ExceptionType1» «name1»)
{ «statements to handle exceptions of type ExceptionType1»
} catch («ExceptionType2» «name2»)
{ «statements to handle exceptions of type ExceptionType2»
...
} catch («ExceptionTypeN» «nameN»)
{ «statements to handle exceptions of type ExceptionTypeN»
} finally
{ «statements that are always executed»
}
```

The `try` block contains the statements that the program must try to execute and that may throw an exception. There is a `catch` block for each exception to handle. The `catch` blocks are formatted and executed similar to a cascading-`if` statement. When an exception is thrown, Java starts with the first `catch` block and works its way downward. It executes the statements in the first `catch` block where *«ExceptionType»* matches the exception thrown or is a superclass of the thrown exception.

For example, the mixture of pseudocode and Java in Listing 8-9 shows how to handle the `MalformedURLException` thrown by the `URL` constructor.

Listing 8-9: *A mixture of pseudocode and Java showing how an exception can be caught*

```
private void loadPage()
{ String urlString = get the url typed by the user
  try
  { URL url = new URL(urlString);      // can throw MalformedURLException
    use url to load the page           // can throw IOException
  } catch (MalformedURLException ex)
  { display a dialog box describing the error and asking the user to try again
  } catch (IOException ex)
  { display a dialog box describing the error
  }
}
```

If the `URL` constructor in this example throws an exception, the statements following it in the `try` block (using the URL) are *not* executed. When an exception is thrown, execution resumes with the nearest `catch` block.

KEY IDEA

An exception skips over code between the line throwing it and a matching `catch` *statement.*

Because `malformedURLexception` extends `IOException`, the order of the `catch` clauses is important. If `IOException` is listed first, it will handle both kinds of exceptions. When listing multiple `catch` clauses, always list the subclasses (most specific exceptions) first and the superclasses (most general exceptions) last.

The names in the `catch`'s parentheses are much like a parameter variable declaration. In the previous example, `ex` is a variable that can be used within the `catch` clause. Recall that an exception is an object, and `ex` can be used to access its methods. For example, the `getMessage` method returns the string that was passed to the exception's constructor. The `printStackTrace` method prints the stack trace. It is often followed with the statement `System.exit(1)`, which causes the program to terminate immediately. Without the call to `exit`, the program would resume after the `try-catch` statement.

The `finally` clause shown in the template is optional. If included, the code it contains will always be executed if any of the code in the `try` block is executed. The `finally` clause is executed even if an exception is thrown, whether or not it is handled in a `catch` clause. It's also executed if a `return`, `break`, or `continue` statement is executed within the `try` block to end it early.

KEY IDEA

Code in the `finally` *clause is always executed if code in the* `try` *block has executed.*

8.4.4 Propogating Exceptions

Methods often can't handle the exceptions thrown by the methods they call. They could catch the exceptions, but can't do anything constructive to respond to the error. In these cases, the exceptions should be propogated up the call stack. This is exactly what happened in Figure 8-16. The `computeTime` method threw an exception. It's caller, `updateTime`, couldn't handle it constructively and so allowed it to propogate to its caller, `getTimeInMillis`. Likewise, this method could not handle the exeception constructively and allowed it to propogate to its caller. This pattern continued a number of times.

When a checked exception is allowed to propogate like this, the method must declare that fact with the `throws` keyword. For example, suppose the `loadPage` method in Listing 8-9 is not an appropriate place to display a dialog box. The method can be rewritten as follows:

```
private void loadPage()
                  throws MalformedURLException, IOException
{ String urlString = get the url typed by the user
  URL url = new URL(urlString);    // can throw MalformedURLException
  use url to load the page         // can throw IOException
}
```

The `throws` clause alerts everyone who might use this method that it can throw the listed exceptions. The clause is required for checked exceptions. If it is omitted, the compiler will issue an error message with the following format:

```
«className»:«lineNum»: unreported exception «exceptionName»;
must be caught or declared to be thrown
```

The reference to "must be caught" means to include the code in a `try-catch` statement. The alternative, "declared to be thrown," means to change the method signature to include the keyword `throws`, as shown earlier.

8.4.5 Enhancing the Alarm Clock with Sound (optional)

We can use our new expertise with exceptions to add sound to the alarm clock program. One way that Java works with sound is via the `AudioClip` class. An `AudioClip` can be loaded from a file using the .wav, .au, or .midi formats (but not .mp3, unfortunately). There may be appropriate sound files already on your computer, or you can create your own with a program such as Audacity, a free sound editor found at *http://audacity.sourceforge.net/*.

The location of the sound file is specified with a URL and can be either on the Web or on your disk.

Listing 8-10 shows the additions to the `Alarm` class to accommodate sound. Four changes are required:

- Lines 3 and 4 import the `Applet`, `AudioClip`, `URL`, and `MalformedURLException` classes.
- Line 8 declares a class variable, `sound`. It's a class variable so that all the `Alarm` instances can share the same sound.

- Lines 13–24 load the sound from a location on the Web. A `URL` is required, which may throw a `MalformedURLException`,1 and so a `try-catch` statement is required. If the exception is thrown, lines 21–22 print a stack trace to aid debugging and exit the program. Because the sound is shared among all instances of `Alarm`, it only needs to be loaded once. The `if` statement at line 14 prevents it from loading more than once.
- Line 31 actually plays the sound. An `AudioClip` has three methods: `play` to play a sound, `stop` to stop a sound currently playing, and `loop` to play a sound repeatedly. Sounds play in their own thread. Line 31 starts that thread, but then execution of the program continues while the sound plays.

The part of this code most likely to cause a problem is specifying the URL for the sound file. If the form of the URL is correct but there is no sound file actually at that location, nothing will notify you; the program just won't play a sound. The best way to avoid this problem is to first locate the file using a Web browser. Then cut and paste the URL from the browser's address bar to the program.

The sound file may also be loaded from your disk drive using a URL similar to the following:

```
URL url = new URL("file:///D:/Robots/examples/ch08/alarmSound/ringin.wav");
```

FIND THE CODE

ch08/alarmSound/

Listing 8-10: *Modifying the `Alarm` class to play a sound*

```
1  import becker.util.DateTime;
2  import becker.util.Utilities;
3  import java.applet.*;
4  import java.net.*;
5
6  public class Alarm extends Object
7  { // Same as Listing 8-6.
8    private static AudioClip sound = null;
9
10   public Alarm(int hr, int min, String msg)
11   { // Same as Listing 8-6.
12
13     // Load the sound if it hasn't already been loaded.
14     if (Alarm.sound == null)
15     { try
16       { URL url = new URL(
17               "http://www.learningwithrobots.com/downloads/WakeupEverybody.wav");
18         Alarm.sound = Applet.newAudioClip(url);
19       }
20       catch (MalformedURLException ex)
21       { ex.printStackTrace();
```

Listing 8-10: *Modifying the* `Alarm` *class to play a sound* (continued)

```
         System.exit(1);
      }
    }
  }

  public void ring()
  { // Same as Listing 8-6.

    // Play the sound.
    Alarm.sound.play();
  }
}
```

8.5 Java's Collection Classes

Programs often need to have collections of similar objects. The alarm clock program we developed in the previous section is a prime example. Even with a collection of only four alarms, code such as `setAlarm` and `checkAndRingAlarms` got tedious. Furthermore, why should there be only four alarms? Why not 40 or 400 or even 4 million?

Four million alarms seems excessive, but other programs could easily have a collection of 4 million or more objects. Consider an inventory program for a large chain of stores, for example. When our collections of similar objects grow beyond four or five, we need better techniques than we used in `AlarmClock`.

Fortunately, Java provides a set of classes for maintaining collections of objects. These classes are used when objects in a collection need to be treated in a similar way: a collection of `Alarm` objects that need to be checked and perhaps rung, a collection of `Student` objects that need to be enrolled in a course, or a collection of `Image` objects that need to display on a computer monitor. The objects maintained by these collections are usually called the **elements** of the collection.

Java has three kinds of collections:

- A **list** is an ordered collection of elements, perhaps with duplicates. Because the list is ordered, you can ask for the element in position 5, for example.
- A **set** is an unordered collection of unique elements; duplicates are not allowed.
- A **map** is an unordered collection of associated **keys** and **values**. A key is used to find the associated value in the collection. For example, your student number is a key that is often used to look up an associated value, such as your address or grades.

Collection objects cannot hold primitive types, only objects. We'll discuss a way around that limitation in Section 8.5.4.

KEY IDEA

Collections hold objects, not primitives.

These collection classes are sophisticated, and covering all the details would require several chapters. Therefore, we will focus on constructing the objects; adding and removing elements, plus a few other useful methods; and processing all the elements (for example, checking all the `Alarm` objects to see if one should be rung). We'll look at one example of each kind of collection. We'll look at a list class first in some detail. We will go faster when we examine sets and maps because much of what we learn with lists will also apply to them.

The approach taken in this textbook assumes that you are using Java 5.0 or higher. Previous versions of Java have these classes, but they are more difficult to use without the advances made in Java 5.0

KEY IDEA

This section assumes you are using Java 5.0 or higher.

8.5.1 A List Class: `ArrayList`

A list is probably the most natural collection class to use for our `AlarmClock` program. It can hold any kind of object (sets and maps have some restrictions) and allows us to easily process all of the elements or to get just one.

There are two distinct ways to write a list class—ArrayList and `LinkedList`. Both are in the `java.util` package, meaning that you'll need to import from that package if you want to use the classes. `ArrayList` is the one we'll study here. By the end of Chapter 10, you will be able to write a simple version of `ArrayList`. By the end of your second computer science course, you should be able to write your own version of `LinkedList`.

Lists such as `ArrayList` keep its elements in order. It makes sense to speak of the first element or the last element. Like a `String`, an individual element is identified by its index—a number greater than or equal to zero and less than the number of elements in the list. The number of elements in the list can be obtained with the `size` query.

KEY IDEA

The `size` query returns the number of elements in the list.

Construction

The type of a collection specifies the collection's class and the class of object it holds. For example, one type that could hold a collection of `Alarm` objects is `ArrayList<Alarm>`. The type of objects held in the collection is placed between angle brackets. This type can be used to declare and initialize a variable, as follows:

```
ArrayList<Alarm> alarms = new ArrayList<Alarm>();
```

KEY IDEA

The type of the collection includes the type of objects to be stored in it.

A list of Robot objects and a list of Person objects would be created similarly:

```
ArrayList<Robot> workers = new ArrayList<Robot>();
ArrayList<Person> friends = new ArrayList<Person>();
```

Of course, if we're declaring instance variables, we would include the keyword private at the beginning of each line.

KEY IDEA

A collection allows you to access many objects using only one variable.

In the AlarmClock class shown in Listing 8-7, the declaration of the four Alarm instance variables in lines 10–13 can be replaced with the following line:

```
private ArrayList<Alarm> alarms = new ArrayList<Alarm>();
```

Furthermore, we are no longer limited to just four alarms.

FIND THE CODE

ch08/alarmsWithLists/

Adding Elements

The power of using a collection class becomes evident in the setAlarm method. In Listing 8-7, we devote lines 68–78 to assigning an alarm to one of the four instance variables—11 lines. Even so, we're limited to only four alarms. For each additional alarm, we need to add an instance variable and two more lines in the setAlarm method.

Using an ArrayList to store the alarms reduces lines 68–78 to a single line:

```
this.alarms.add(theAlarm);
```

Furthermore, we can now have an almost unlimited number of alarms.

The add method just shown adds the new alarm to the end of the list. An overloaded version of add allows you to state the index in the list where the alarm should be added. Like Strings, an ArrayList numbers the positions in its list starting with 0. Therefore, the following line adds a new alarm in the third position:

```
this.alarms.add(2, theAlarm);
```

The alarms at indices 0 and 1 come before it. Objects at indices 2 and larger are moved over by one position to make room for the new object. Figure 8-18 illustrates inserting a new Alarm for 11:00 at index 2.

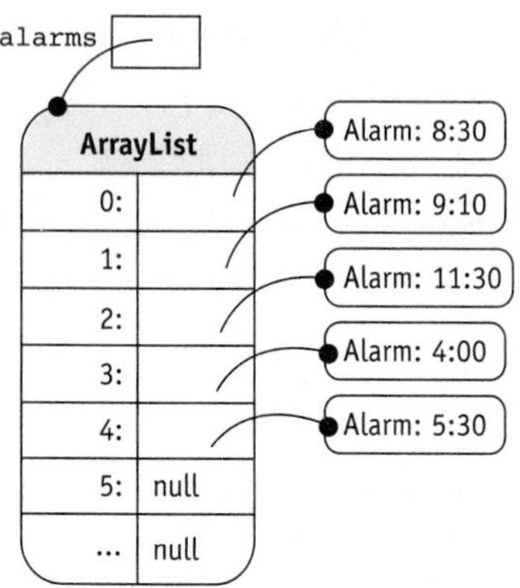

Before inserting an `Alarm` at `index` 2

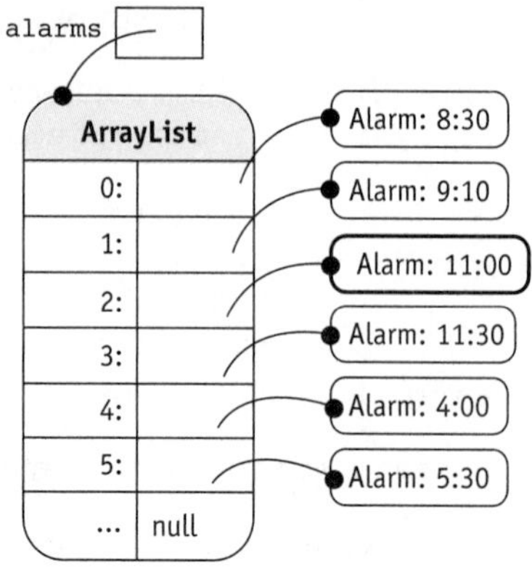

After inserting an `Alarm` at `index` 2

(figure 8-18)

Inserting an `Alarm` into an `ArrayList` at index 2

The index for add must be in the range `0..size()`. Positions can't be skipped when adding objects. For example, you can't add an object at index 2 before there is data at indices 0 and 1. Doing so results in an `IndexOutOfBoundsException`.

Getting, Setting, and Removing Elements

A single element of the collection can be accessed using the `get` method and specifying the object's index. For example, to get a reference to the third alarm (which is at index 2 because numbering starts at 0), write the following statements:

```
Alarm anAlarm = this.alarms.get(2);
anAlarm.ring();                  // do something with the alarm
```

As with any other method that returns a reference, you aren't required to assign the reference to a variable before calling a method. We could condense the previous two statements to a single line:

```
this.alarms.get(2).ring();
```

An element can be replaced using the `set` method. Its parameters are the index of the element to replace and the object to put there. For example, Figure 8-19 illustrates the change made by the following code fragment:

```
Alarm oldAlarm = null;
Alarm newAlarm = new Alarm(11, 15, "Meeting with Mohamed");
oldAlarm = this.alarms.set(2, newAlarm);
```

(figure 8-19)

Effects of the `set` *method*

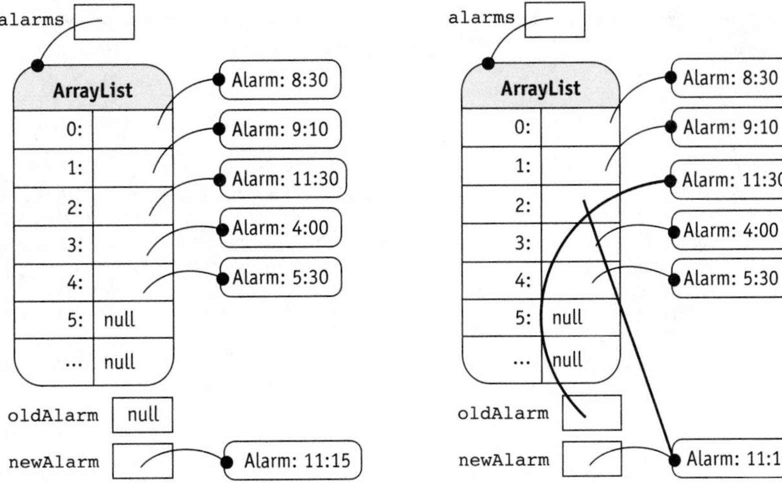

Notice that the element at index 2 now refers to the new alarm. The `set` method returns a reference to the element that is replaced, which is assigned to `oldAlarm`.

An element can be removed from the `ArrayList` with the `remove` method. Its only argument is the index of the element to remove. After removing the element, any elements in subsequent positions are moved up to occupy the now open position—the opposite of what `add` does. Like `set`, `remove` returns a reference to the removed element.

Other Useful Methods

There are many other methods in the `ArrayList` class and its superclasses. Table 8-1 lists the name and purpose of some of the most useful methods. `E` represents the type of elements stored in this particular collection.

The `contains` and `indexOf` methods depend on the element's class overriding the equals method to test for equivalence. As noted in Section 8.2.4, we don't have the tools to do this yet for the classes we write. Provided classes such as `String`, `DateTime`, and others should meet this requirement.

(table 8-1)

Some of the most useful methods in the `ArrayList` class. `E` is the type of the elements

Method	Purpose
`boolean add(E elem)`	Add the specified element to the end of this list. Return `true`.
`void add(int index, E elem)`	Insert the specified element at the specified index in this list. `0 ≤ index < size()`.
`void clear()`	Remove all of the elements from this list.
`boolean contains(Object elem)`	Return `true` if this list contains the specified element.
`E get(int index)`	Return the element at the specified index. `0 ≤ index < size()`.
`int indexOf(Object elem)`	Search for the first element in this list that is equal to `elem`, and return its index or `-1` if there is no such element in this list.
`boolean isEmpty()`	Return `true` if this list contains no elements.
`E remove(int index)`	Remove and return the element at the given index. `0 ≤ index < size()`.
`E set(int index, E elem)`	Replace the element at the given position in this list with `elem`. Return the old element. `0 ≤ index < size()`.
`int size()`	Return the number of elements in this list.

Processing All Elements

The last detail needed to replace the four `Alarm` variables with a list is checking each alarm to see if it's time to ring it. In Listing 8-7, we did this in lines 47–52. Each line calls a helper method to check one of the alarms. That means 4 alarms, 4 lines of code; 400 alarms, 400 lines of code.

There are three distinct ways[3] to process all of the elements in an `ArrayList`. We've already seen the basic tools for one of them: the `get` and `size` methods. We can use them in a `for` loop to get each element in turn:

PATTERN

Process All Elements

```
private void checkAndRingAlarms(DateTime currTime)
{ for (int index = 0; index < this.alarms.size(); index++)
  { Alarm anAlarm = this.alarms.get(index);
    this.checkOneAlarm(anAlarm, currTime);
  }
}
```

[3] The third way uses iterators, a topic we won't be covering in this textbook.

These six lines of code completely replace `checkAndRingAlarms` in lines 47–52 of Listing 8-7. Furthermore, this code will work for almost[4] any number of alarms—from zero on up.

A loop to process all of the elements in a collection is so common that Java 5.0 introduced a special version of the `for` loop just to make these situations easier. It is sometimes called a **foreach** loop—the body of the loop executes once for each element in the collection.

Using a *foreach* loop to process each alarm results in the following method:

PATTERN

Process All Elements

```
private void checkAndRingAlarms(DateTime currTime)
{ for(Alarm anAlarm : this.alarms)
  { this.checkOneAlarm(anAlarm, currTime);
  }
}
```

A template for the *foreach* loop is as follows:

```
for(«elementType» «varName» : «collection»)
{
}
```

The statement includes the keyword `for`, but instead of specifying a loop index, the `for each` loop declares a variable, *`«varName»`*, of the same type as the objects contained in *`«collection»`*. The variable name is followed with a colon and the collection that we want to process. *`«varName»`* can only be used within the body of the loop.

A version of `AlarmClock` that uses an `ArrayList` is shown in Listing 8-11. Note that changes are shown in bold. Documentation is identical to Listing 8-7, so it is omitted.

FIND THE CODE

ch08/alarmsWithLists/

Listing 8-11: *The* `AlarmClock` *class implemented with an* `ArrayList`

```
import becker.util.DateTime;
import becker.util.Utilities;
import java.util.ArrayList;

public class AlarmClock extends Object
{
  // A list of alarms.
  private ArrayList<Alarm> alarms = new ArrayList<Alarm>();

  private int numAlarmsLeft = 0;
```

[4] We don't say `ArrayList` will handle any number because eventually your computer would run out of memory to store them all.

Listing 8-11: *The* `AlarmClock` *class implemented with an* `ArrayList` (continued)

```
  private final boolean TESTING;

  public AlarmClock(boolean test)
  { // Same as Listing 8-7.
  }

  public void run(int secPerSec)
  { // Same as Listing 8-7.
  }

  private void checkAndRingAlarms(DateTime currTime)
  { for(Alarm anAlarm : this.alarms)
    { this.checkOneAlarm(anAlarm, currTime);
    }
  }

  private void checkOneAlarm(Alarm alarm, DateTime currTime)
  { // Same as Listing 8-7.
  }

  public void setAlarm(int hr, int min, String msg)
  { Alarm theAlarm = new Alarm(hr, min, msg);
    this.alarms.add(theAlarm);
    this.numAlarmsLeft++;
  }

  public static void main(String[] args)
  { // Same as Listing 8-7.
  }
}
```

Class Diagrams

Someone drawing a class diagram for `AlarmClock`, as shown in Listing 8-11, would probably draw a diagram as shown in Figure 8-20a. However, collection classes like `ArrayList` appear so often in Java programs and their function is so well known that most programmers prefer to draw the abbreviated class diagram shown in Figure 8-20b.

(figure 8-20)

Class diagrams

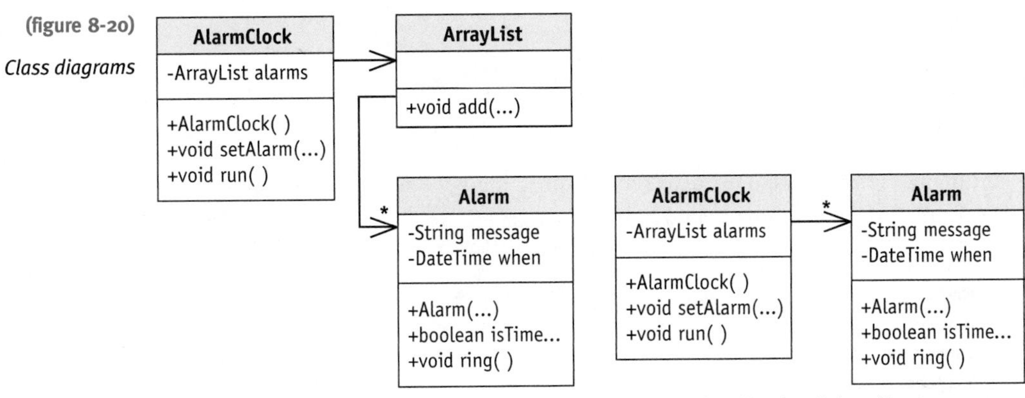

a. Full class diagram

b. Abbreviated class diagram

8.5.2 A Set Class: `HashSet`

Like a list, a set also manages a collection of objects. There are two important differences:

- A set does not allow duplicate elements. Sets ignore attempts to add an element that is already in the set.
- The elements are not ordered. None of the methods in `HashSet` take an index as an argument.

KEY IDEA

Sets do not allow duplicates.

These restrictions don't affect the `AlarmClock` class—each alarm is unique and individual alarms are not important; they are all processed as a group. In fact, changing `ArrayList` to `HashSet` in line 8 of Listing 8-11 is all that is needed to convert that program to use a set.

LOOKING AHEAD

Processing files is a major topic of Chapter 9.

So how might we exploit the specific properties of a set? We could use it, for example, to count the number of unique strings in a file. About two dozen lines of code are enough to discover that William Shakespeare's play *Hamlet* contains 7,467 unique "words." (Words is quoted because the program doesn't remove punctuation or numbers, meaning that "merry" and "merry?" are considered different words.)

Construction

We'll use an instance of the `HashSet` class to count the words. An instance of `HashSet` is constructed just like `ArrayList`—specify the type of the elements you want it to manage in angle brackets. In this case, we'll store our words as strings.

```
HashSet<String> words = new HashSet<String>();
```

Useful Methods

Words can be added to this set with the add method. If the word is already there, it will be ignored.

To add many words, we should read them from a file—the topic of Section 9.1. Until then, we can add some words from *Hamlet* manually:

```
words.add("to");
words.add("be");
words.add("or");
words.add("not");
words.add("to");
words.add("be");
```

FIND THE CODE

ch08/collections/

The size method returns the number of elements in the set. Given the previous six calls to add, size would return 4.

The word "not" could be removed with the statement words.remove("not"). In general, an object is removed from the set by passing the object to the remove method.

The contains method will return true if the set contains the given object and false otherwise. Other useful methods are summarized in Table 8-2.

Method	Purpose
boolean add(E elem)	Add the specified element to this set. Return true if the element was already present.
void clear()	Remove all of the elements from this set.
boolean contains(Object elem)	Return true if this set contains the specified element.
boolean isEmpty()	Return true if this set contains no elements.
boolean remove(Object elem)	Remove the specified element from this set, if present. Return true if the element was present.
int size()	Return the number of elements in this set.

(table 8-2)

Some of the most useful methods in the HashSet *class (*E *is the type of the elements)*

Processing All Elements

We can print all of the words in the set using a for each loop, just as we processed all of the elements in the ArrayList earlier.

KEY IDEA

A set's for each *loop works the same way as for a list.*

```
for (String w : words)
{ System.out.print(w + "  ");
}
```

PATTERN
Process All Elements

Executing this loop after adding the first six words of Hamlet's speech would yield "to," "be," "or," and "not." The order in which they are printed is *not* specified.

Limitations

`HashSet` uses a technique known as **hashing**, in which elements are stored in an order defined by the element's `hashCode` method. The hash code is carefully constructed to make operations such as `contains` and `remove` faster than for an `ArrayList`. When the elements are printed, however, they appear in an order that seems random.

`hashCode` is inherited from the `Object` class. As defined there, no two objects are considered equal or equivalent. If two elements in your set should be considered equivalent (for example, two different date objects both representing the same date), the `equals` and `hashCode` methods must both be overridden. Unfortunately, overriding `hashCode` is beyond the scope of this textbook. However, you should have no problem using `HashSet` if you either use it with a set of unique objects or use it with provided classes, such as `String` or `DateTime`.

8.5.3 A Map Class: TreeMap

KEY IDEA
A map associates a key with a value. Use the key to look up the value.

A map is a collection of associated keys and values. A key is used to find the associated value in the collection. For example, we could associate the names of our friends (the keys) with their phone numbers (the values), as shown in Figure 8-21.

(figure 8-21)
Key-value pairs

Key	Value
Sue	578-3948
Fazila	886-4957
Jo	1-604-329-1023
Don	578-3948
Rama	886-9521

With these associations between keys and values, we can ask questions such as "What's the phone number for Don?" We use the key, "Don," to look up the associated value, "578-3948."

KEY IDEA
The keys in any given map must be unique.

Notice that all the keys are unique; that's a fundamental requirement of a map. If we have two friends named "Don" we must distinguish between them, perhaps by adding initials or last names. However, the associated values do not need to be unique. In this example, Don and Sue both appear in the mapping even though they have the same phone number.

Java provides two classes implementing a map, `TreeMap` and `HashMap`. Each one has different advantages and disadvantages. `HashMaps` have the advantage of being somewhat faster but require a correct implementation of the `hashCode` method. On the other hand, `TreeMaps` keep the keys in sorted order but require a way to order the elements. We'll use a `TreeMap` to build a simple phone book.

Construction

When declaring and constructing a `TreeMap` object, the types for both the keys and the values must be specified. For our simple phone book, we'll use `Strings` for both the keys and the values:

```
TreeMap<String, String> phoneBook =
                              new TreeMap<String, String>();
```

Although this example happens to use strings for both keys and values, that need not be the case. The types of the keys and values are often different and must be a reference type—not a primitive type like `int`, `double`, or `char`.

How can you figure out that `TreeMap` needs two types to define it but that `ArrayList` and `HashSet` require only one? Look at the class documentation. Figure 8-22 shows the beginning of the online documentation for `TreeMap`, which includes `TreeMap<K, V>` in large type. The two capital letters between the angle brackets indicate that two types are needed when a `TreeMap` is constructed. Finding out that `K` stands for the type of the key and `V` stands for the type of the value is, unfortunately, not as easy to figure out from the documentation.

There is one restriction on the type of the key. Because `TreeMap` keeps the keys in sorted order, it needs a way to compare them. It relies on the key's class to implement the `Comparable` interface. The keys are then known to have a `compareTo` method. `String` and `DateTime` both implement the interface and can be used as keys.

You can tell if a class implements `Comparable` by looking at the "All Implemented Interfaces" line in the documentation. You can see an example of this line in Figure 8-22. Also, if you look at the documentation for `Comparable`, it will list the classes in the Java library that implement it.

LOOKING AHEAD

Writing your own classes that implement the `Comparable` *interface will be discussed in Section 12.5.1.*

(figure 8-22)

Part of the online documentation for `TreeMap`

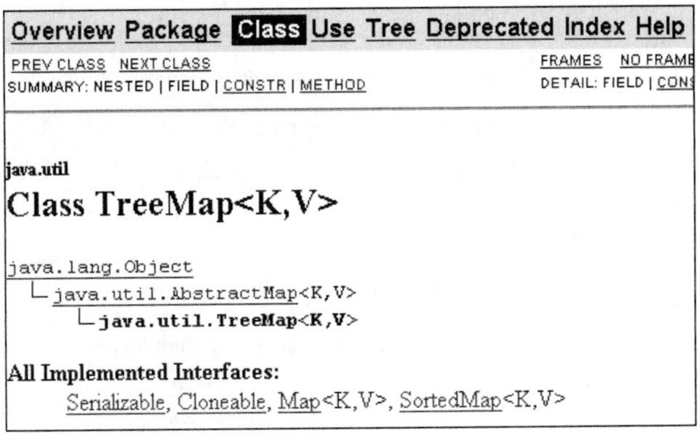

Overview Package Class Use Tree Deprecated Index Help

PREV CLASS NEXT CLASS FRAMES NO FRAME
SUMMARY: NESTED | FIELD | CONSTR | METHOD DETAIL: FIELD | CONS

java.util

Class TreeMap<K,V>

java.lang.Object
└ java.util.AbstractMap<K,V>
 └ **java.util.TreeMap<K,V>**

All Implemented Interfaces:
Serializable, Cloneable, Map<K,V>, SortedMap<K,V>

Useful Methods

Pairs are added to a map with the `put` method. It takes a key and a value as arguments:

```
phoneBook.put("Sue", "578-3948");
phoneBook.put("Fazila", "886-4957");
```

If the key already exists in the map, the value associated with that key will be replaced by the new value.

A value can be retrieved with the `get` method. The key of the desired value is passed as an argument. For example, after executing the following line:

```
String number = phoneBook.get("Sue");
```

the variable `number` will contain "578-3948" (assuming the associations shown in Figure 8-21). It's similar to accessing an element in a list except that instead of specifying the element's index, you specify the element's key.

The `remove` method takes a key as its only argument and removes both the key and its associated value.

Like a list and a set, a map has `isEmpty`, `clear`, and `size` methods. Instead of `contains`, it has two methods: `containsKey` and `containsValue`, which both return a Boolean result. These methods are summarized in Table 8-3.

Method	Purpose
`void clear()`	Remove all of the key-value pairs from this mapping.
`boolean containsKey (Object elem)`	Return `true` if this mapping contains the specified key.
`boolean containsValue (Object elem)`	Return `true` if this mapping contains the specified value.
`V get(Object key)`	Return the value associated with the specified key.
`boolean isEmpty()`	Return `true` if this mapping contains no elements.
`Set<K> keySet()`	Return a set containing the keys in this mapping.
`V put(K key, V value)`	Associate the specified key with the specified value in this mapping. Return the value previously associated with the key or `null` if there wasn't one.
`V remove(Object key)`	Remove and return the value associated with the specified key, if it exists. Return `null` if there was no mapping for the key.
`int size()`	Return the number of key-value pairs in this mapping.

(table 8-3)

Some of the most useful methods in the `TreeMap` *class (*`K` *is the type of the keys;* `V` *is the type of the values)*

Processing All Elements

Processing all the elements in a map is more complicated than a list or a set because each element is a pair of objects rather than just one thing.

One approach is to use the `keySet` method to get all of the keys in the map as a set. We can then loop through all of the keys using the `for each` loop. As part of the processing, we can also get the associated value, as shown in the following example:

```
// print the phoneBook
for (String key : phoneBook.keySet())
{ System.out.println(key + "=" + phoneBook.get(key));
}
```

PATTERN

Process All Elements

Completed Program

The completed telephone book program is shown in Listing 8-12. It uses a `Scanner` object in 27 and 30 to obtain a name from the program's user. Using `Scanner` effectively is one of the primary topics of the next chapter.

FIND THE CODE

ch08/collections/

Listing 8-12: *An electronic telephone book*

```
import java.util.*;

/** An electronic  telephone book.
 *
 *  @author Byron Weber Becker */
public class MapExample extends Object
{
  public static void main(String[] args)
  { // Create the mapping between names and phone numbers.
    TreeMap<String, String> phoneBook =
                                new TreeMap<String, String>();

    // Insert the phone numbers.
    phoneBook.put("Sue", "578-3948");
    phoneBook.put("Fazila", "886-4957");
    phoneBook.put("Jo", "1-604-329-1023");
    phoneBook.put("Don", "578-3948");
    phoneBook.put("Rama", "886-9521");

    // Print the phonebook.
    for (String k : phoneBook.keySet())
    { System.out.println(k + "=" + phoneBook.get(k));
    }

    // Repeatedly ask the user for a name until "done" is entered.
    // Scanner is discussed in detail in Chapter 9.
    Scanner in = new Scanner(System.in);
    while (true)
    { System.out.print("Enter a name or 'done': ");
      String name = in.next();

      if (name.equalsIgnoreCase("done"))
      { break;    // Break out of the loop.
      }

      System.out.println(name + ": " + phoneBook.get(name));
    }
  }
}
```

8.5.4 Wrapper Classes

What if we want to store integers or characters or some other primitive type in one of the collection classes? For example, we might need a set of the prime numbers (integers that can only be divided evenly by 1 and itself). If we write

```
HashSet<int> primeNumbers = new HashSet<int>();
```

the Java compiler will give us a compile-time error, perhaps with the cryptic message "unexpected type." The problem is that the compiler is expecting a reference type—the name of a class—between the angle brackets. `int`, of course, is a primitive type.

We can get around this by using a **wrapper class**. It "wraps" a primitive value in a class. A simplified wrapper class for `int` is as follows:

```
public class IntWrapper extends Object
{ private int value;

  public IntWrapper(int aValue)
  { super();
    this.value = aValue;
  }

  public int intValue()
  { return this.value;
  }
}
```

Fortunately, Java provides a wrapper class for each of the primitive types: `Integer`, `Double`, `Boolean`, `Character`, and so on. These are in the `java.lang` package, which is automatically imported into every class.

We can use these built-in wrapper classes to construct a set of integers:

```
HashSet<Integer> primes = new HashSet<Integer>();
```

The Java compiler will automatically convert between an `int` and an instance of `Integer` when using `primes`. For example, consider the program in Listing 8-13. In lines 12–17, the `add` method takes an `int`, not an instance of `Integer`. The `contains` method in line 25 is the same. Before Java 5.0 the programmer needed to manually include code to convert between primitives and wrapper objects.

KEY IDEA

Java 5.0 automatically converts between primitive values and wrapper classes.

FIND THE CODE

ch08/collections/

Listing 8-13: *A program to help classify prime numbers*

```
import java.util.*;

/** Help the user find out if a number is prime.
 *
 * @author Byron Weber Becker */
public class WrapperExample extends Object
{
  public static void main(String[] args)
  { HashSet<Integer> primes = new HashSet<Integer>();

    // The prime numbers we know.
    primes.add(2);
    primes.add(3);
    primes.add(5);
    primes.add(7);
    primes.add(11);
    primes.add(13);

    // Help the user classify numbers.
    // Scanner is discussed in detail in Chapter 9.
    Scanner in = new Scanner(System.in);
    System.out.print("Enter a number: ");
    int num = in.nextInt();

    if (primes.contains(num))
    { System.out.println(num + " is prime.");
    } else if (num <= 13)
    { System.out.println(num + " is not prime.");
    } else
    { System.out.println(
             num + " might be prime; it's too big for me to know.");
    }
  }
}
```

8.6 GUIs and Collaborating Classes

Programs with graphical user interfaces almost always use collaborating classes in two ways. Collaborating classes makes these programs easier to understand, write, debug, and maintain.

8.6.1 Using Libraries of Components

First, GUIs are constructed from a library of components. You've already used a number of these: `JFrame`, `JPanel`, `JComponent`, `JButton`, and so on. `JFrame` typically collaborates with `JPanel` to organize a number of components to display. `JPanel` collaborates with one or more components such as `JButton` to display information in the right format.

For example, consider the program written in Section 6.7. It displays three temperatures using a custom thermometer component. The class diagram in Figure 8-23 shows that the `JFrame` has-a `JPanel` to help organize the components it displays. The `JPanel` has-a `Thermometer` to actually display a temperature. In fact, the `JPanel` has a number of `Thermometer` objects. Finally, the `Thermometer` class is-a `JComponent`. The two classes collaborate to provide a standard set of services with the customized appearance provided by `paintComponent`.

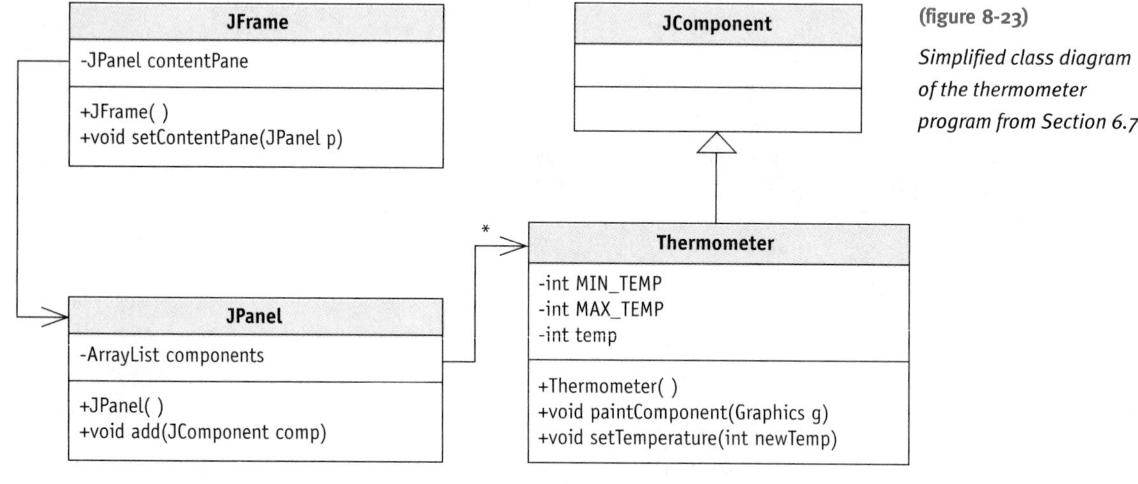

(figure 8-23)

Simplified class diagram of the thermometer program from Section 6.7

The collaboration between these classes allows each to have a specific focus. Focused classes are easier to understand, write, debug, and maintain.

8.6.2 Introducing the Model-View-Controller Pattern

Collaborating classes are also used with modern graphical user interfaces via the Model-View-Controller pattern. This pattern splits a program into three collaborating classes or groups of classes.

- The **model** is responsible for modeling the current problem. For example, the `AlarmClock` class we wrote earlier models the problem of keeping the current time and determining when to ring the alarms, but has little to do with displaying anything to the user.

- The **view** shows relevant information in the model to the user. In an alarm clock program, the view is the class (or group of classes) that show the user what time it is and when the alarms are due to ring. This is information that the view obtains from the model.
- The **controller** is responsible for gathering input from the user and using it to modify the model, for example, by changing the current time or the time when an alarm is due to ring. When the controller changes the model, the view should also change to show the new information.

The view and the controller work together closely and are known as the user interface.

The relationships between these three groups of classes are shown in Figure 8-24. The eye represents the user observing the model via the view. The mouse represents the user changing the model via the controller. The arrow between the controller and the view indicates that the controller may call methods in the view, but the view has no need to interact with the controller. The two arrows from the user interface to the model indicate that both the view and the controller will have reason to call methods in the model. The last arrow is dotted to indicate that the model will call methods in the user interface, but in a limited and controlled way.

(figure 8-24)

The view and controller interact with the user and the model

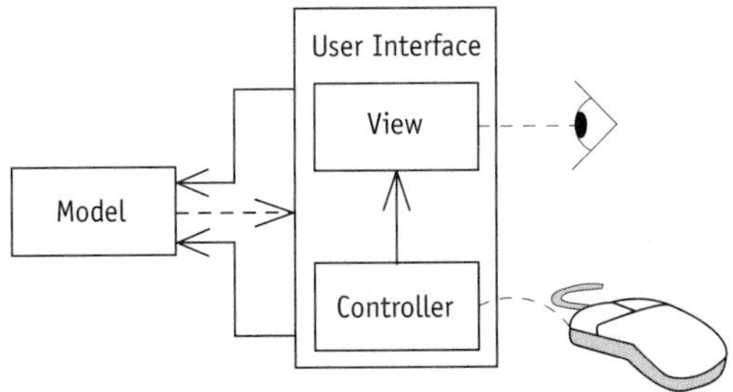

The Model-View-Controller pattern will be explored fully in Chapter 13, Graphical User Interfaces.

8.7 Patterns

8.7.1 The Has-a (Composition) Pattern

Name: Has-a (Composition)

Context: A class is getting overly complex.

Solution: Identify one or more subsets of methods and instance variables that form a cohesive concept. Make each subset into a separate helper class that the original class can use to solve the overall problem. The original class will likely have one or more instance variables referring to instances of the helper classes. A general pattern is shown in the following code:

```
public class «className»...
{ private «helperClassName» «var1»;

  public «className»(...)
  { // initialize the helper class
    this.«var1» = ...
  }

  ... «methodName»(...)
  { // use the helper class
    ... this.«var1».«methodName»...
  }
}
```

This pattern results in the class diagram shown in Figure 8-25.

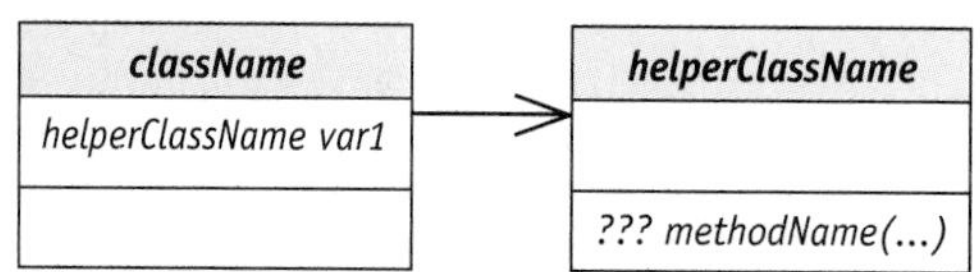

(figure 8-25)

Class diagram resulting from Has-a (composition) pattern

Consequences: The individual classes will become smaller and more focused on a particular task, making them easier to write, test, debug, and modify.

Related Pattern: The Has-a pattern is a special case of the Instance Variable pattern, where the instance variable is an object reference.

8.7.2 The Equivalence Test Pattern

Name: Equivalence Test

Context: A method is required to test whether two objects are equivalent to each other in value.

Solution: Write a method, `isEquivalent`, that takes one of the objects as an argument and tests all the relevant fields for equivalence. In general,

```
public class «className» ...
{ private «primitiveType» «relevantField1»
  ...
```

```
    private «referenceType» «relevantField2»
    ...

    public boolean isEquivalent(«className» other)
    { return other != null &&
            this.«relevantField1» == other.«relevantField1» &&
            ...
            this.«relevantField2».isEquivalent(
                                         other.«relevantField2») &&
            ...;
    }
}
```

where == is used for primitive fields and either `isEquivalent` or `equals` is used for objects.

Consequences: The method will determine whether two objects are equivalent by testing all the relevant fields for equivalence. Using `isEquivalent` may give unexpected results with methods such as `contains` in Java's collection classes. Those classes assume that `equals` has been properly overridden, but that requires concepts first discussed in Chapter 12.

Related Patterns:

- The Equivalence Test pattern is a specialization of the Predicate pattern.
- The Equals pattern (Section 12.7.3) is a better choice than this pattern, once the details of implementing `equals` have been mastered.

8.7.3 The Throw an Exception Pattern

Name: Throw an Exception

Context: Your method detects an exceptional event that is most appropriately handled by the method's client.

Solution: Create an exception object to report details of the exceptional event and use Java's `throw` statement, as follows:

```
if («testForErrorCondition»)
{ throw new «exceptionName»(«stringDescription»);
}
```

Consequences: Clients of the called method are informed of the exceptional event and may be able to recover if the exception is handled. In the case of a checked exception such as `FileNotFoundException`, clients must either handle the exception or declare that they throw it.

Related Pattern: Thrown exceptions may be caught and handled with the Catch an Exception pattern.

8.7.4 The Catch an Exception Pattern

Name: Catch an Exception

Context: You are calling a method that can throw an exception. You want to handle the exception to protect the program's users from the consequences of the problem.

Solution: Catch the exception using a `try-catch` statement and the following template:

```
try
{ «statements that may throw an exception»
} catch («exception_1 e»)
{ «statements to handle excepton_1»
} catch («exception_2 e»)
{ «statements to handle excepton_2»
}
```

More `catch` clauses can also be added.

Consequences: Exceptions that are thrown by statements within the `try` clause are handled in the matching `catch` clause, if one exists. If there is no matching `catch` clause, the exception is propagated to the caller. The `catch` clauses are evaluated in order, with the result that the most specific exceptions should appear first and the most general exceptions later.

Related Pattern: Exceptions are thrown with the Throw an Exception pattern.

8.7.5 The Process All Elements Pattern

Name: Process All Elements

Context: The same operation must be performed to all the objects in a collection.

Solution: Store all of the relevant objects in an `ArrayList`, `HashSet`, `TreeMap`, or similar collection object. Use one of the following forms to retrieve all of the objects one at a time to perform the required operation.

The exact form of the pattern depends on the type of collection. For a list, the following code may be used.

```
for (int i = 0; i < «collection».size(); i++)
{ «elementType» element = «collection».get(i);
  «statements to process element»
}
```

The following form, available in Java 5.0 and later, is applicable to both lists and sets:

```
for («elementType» element : «collection»)
{ «statements to process element»
}
```

If the collection is an instance of a mapping, such as `TreeMap`, a slight variant of the preceding template is required:

```
for («keyType» key : «collection».getKeySet())
{ «valueType» value = «collection».get(key);
  «statements to process key and value»
}
```

Consequences: Using a collection to handle multiple objects of the same type can make lots of code much simpler, especially code that processes each of the elements in turn.

Related Patterns:

- The Process All Elements pattern is related to the Process File pattern (Section 9.9.3) and will be recast using arrays in Section 10.8.1.
- Processing all the characters in a `String` is similar to this pattern, although the `for each` loop is not applicable in that setting.

8.8 Summary and Concept Map

Structuring programs so that classes work together to solve a problem is a great idea. By delegating work to other classes, each class can be simpler and more focused on one particular idea. This makes the program easier to understand, write, debug, and maintain.

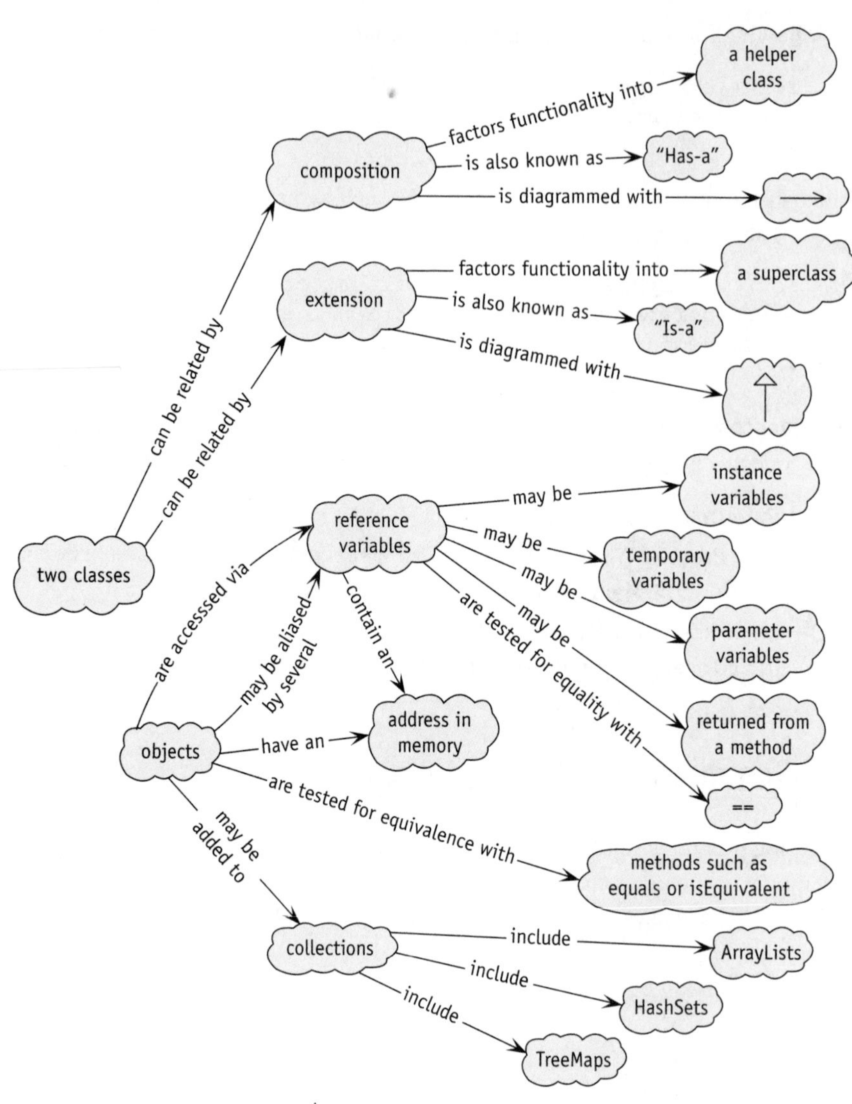

8.9 Problem Set

Written Exercises

8.1 A book has a title, an author, and a call number. A library patron has a name and an ID number, and may or may not have a book checked out.

a. Draw a class diagram for `Patron` where only a single book may be checked out at any given time. Include the methods necessary to check out a book, and print which book (if any) the patron has.

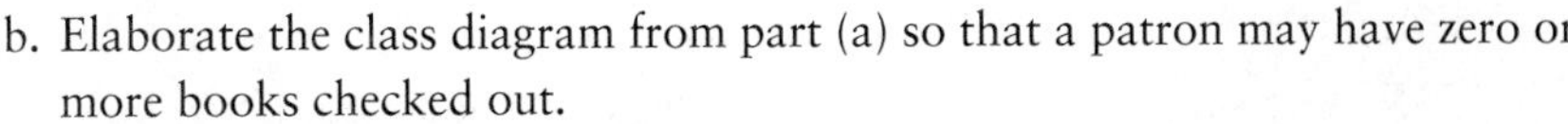

b. Elaborate the class diagram from part (a) so that a patron may have zero or more books checked out.

c. Draw a class diagram including a `Library` object. A library, of course, has many patrons and many books. Include the methods required to check out a book to a patron, given the patron's ID number and the book's call number. Also include the methods required to list which books a patron has, given the patron's ID number.

8.2 Consider the class diagram shown in Figure 8-26. It shows one possible relationship between a bank's client and the client's account. Each client has a personal identification number (PIN) to use in accessing his account. The methods requiring a PIN do nothing if the PIN doesn't match the one stored for the client.

(figure 8-26)

Partial class diagram for a bank

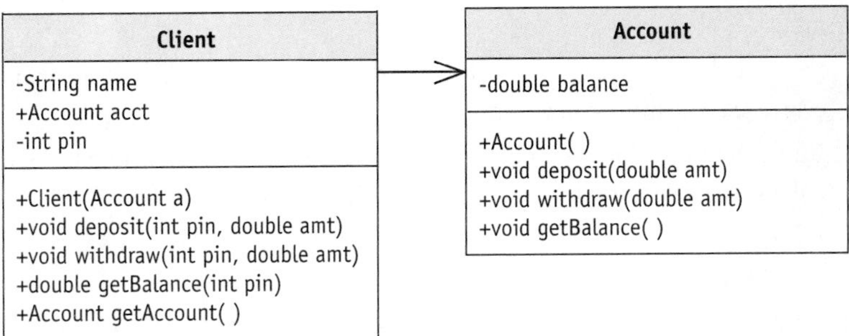

Suppose you are a programmer working on the `Bank` class, which contains references to objects representing all of the bank's clients. Explain three ways in which you could transfer money from one client's account to your account without knowing the client's PIN. In each case, explain how this security hole could be closed.

Assume the programmer who implemented `Client` and `Account` knows nothing of the dangers of using aliases.

Programming Exercises

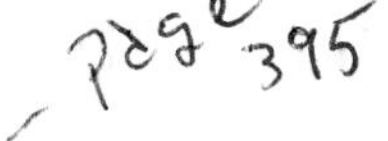

8.3 Consider the program in Listing 8-2. According to the surrounding text, it was used to find that Luke was 5,009 days old on the day that paragraph was written. Modify the program to print the date the paragraph was written.

8.4 Consider a `FuelBot` class. It extends `Robot` and uses a `FuelTank`. Each time the robot moves, it will use 0.4 liters of fuel from the tank. The tank holds 3 liters of fuel when it is full. If the robot comes to an intersection with a `Thing` on it, refill its tank. If the robot ever runs out of fuel, it breaks.

a. Draw a class diagram that includes the `Robot`, `FuelBot`, and `FuelTank` classes. Include variables and methods.

b. Implement `FuelBot`. Write a `main` method to test your class.

c. Make a simple game by overriding the `keyTyped` method to allow the user to control the robot (see Listing 7-5). Scatter gas stations around the city. Put a `Thing` with a different color at a random location to serve as the goal. Can the robot reach it before running out of fuel? Use the robot's `setLabel` command to display the amount of fuel remaining as a percentage.

8.5 A normal playing card has a rank (one of Ace, 2, 3, 4, ..., 10, Jack, Queen, King) and a suit (one of Diamonds, Clubs, Hearts, or Spades). Players in a card game usually have a "hand" consisting of several cards. For a game, a player will want to know the value of his or her hand. The value is calculated by summing the rank of each card, where Ace is 1, Jack is 11, Queen is 12, and King is 13. The number cards have their number as their value. There is one exception: the Ace of the trump suit is valued at 14. The trump suit is specified when the hand is created.

a. Draw a class diagram of the `Hand` and `Card` classes. Assume that a hand consists of at most four cards.

b. Implement `Hand` and `Card`. Write a `main` method to test the hand's value calculation. Assume the hand consists of at most four cards.

c. Draw a class diagram of the `Hand` and `Card` classes. Use an `ArrayList` or `HashSet`.

d. Implement `Hand` and `Card`. Write a `main` method to test the hand's value calculation. Don't make any assumptions about the number of cards in a hand.

8.6 In a simplified version of the game of Monopoly, a player may have between 0 and 4 properties. Each property has a name, a purchase price, and a rent. The purchase price is typically between $60 and $400, and the rent is typically between 10 percent and 15 percent of the purchase price. A player needs to calculate the total of the purchase price of its properties, return whether it owns a specified property, and return the rent for a property. Properties are identified to these methods by their names.

a. Draw a class diagram showing the `Player` and `Property` classes.

b. Implement the classes without using a collection class. Include a `main` method in `Player` to test the class.

c. Implement the classes, removing the restriction of owning no more than four properties. Include a `main` method in `Player` to test the class.

8.7 The `Person` class in Listing 8-3 uses a `String` to store the person's mother and father. Why not use an instance of `Person`? After all, mothers and fathers are persons.

Revise the class using this idea. Provide a second `Person` constructor for when parents aren't known; it sets `mother` and `father` to `null`. Include a `toString` method in `Person` that returns the person's name.

Write a `main` method that creates objects for seven people—you, your parents, and your grandparents. Make up any data you don't know. Print the results of the `toString` method for each of the seven `Person` objects.

a. Replace `toString` with a method that prints "[«*name*»: m = «*name*» f = «*name*»]", where each «*name*» is filled in with the appropriate name. If either the mother or the father is `null`, print "unknown" for the name.

b. Modify the `toString` method from part (a). Instead of printing the name of the mother and father, call that person's `toString` method. As before, if the mother or father is `null`, print "unknown."

Programming Projects

LOOKING BACK

Dotted lines between classes mean a class uses another class but doesn't hold an instance variable to it. See Section 8.2.2.

8.8 Implement a program to run at a checkout counter in a store. The `main` method will create the `CheckOut` object and then give it a number of `Items` to check out. The `CheckOut` object will be able to produce an itemized receipt. (*Hint*: You can use an `ArrayList` or a `String` to build the receipt as items are sold.) A partial class diagram is shown in Figure 8-27.

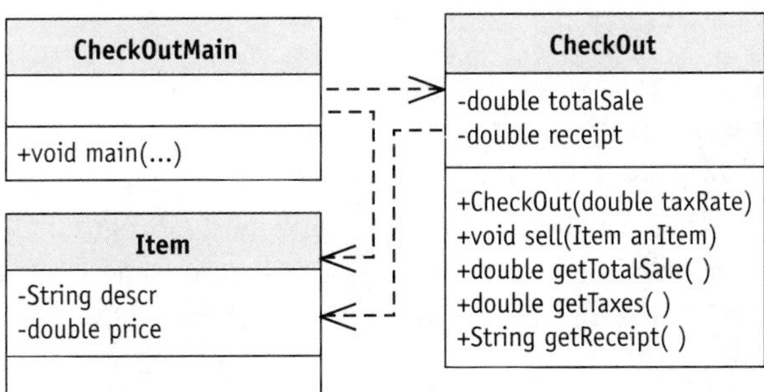

(figure 8-27)

Partial class diagram for checking out items at a store

8.9 A class diagram for another store's checkout counter is shown in Figure 8-28. Write a program where the `main` method creates a `CheckOut` object and a `Customer` object, complete with a number of `Items` to buy. Call the `checkout` method to generate an itemized receipt. Print the receipt.

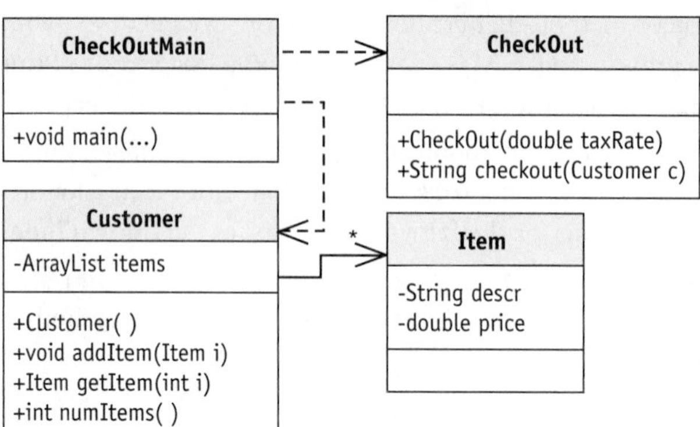

(figure 8-28)

Another partial class diagram for checking out items at a store

8.10 A checkbook has an opening balance and zero or more checks. Each check has a check number, the name of the person or company who can cash it, an amount, and a memo. A checkbook should be able to return information about a check, given its check number. It should also be able to give the current balance.

a. Would you implement this program using a list, set, or map? Why?

b. Without prejudicing your answer to part (a), draw a class diagram assuming the program uses a map.

c. Implement the classes as shown in part (b). Include a `main` method in the `Checkbook` class to test it.

8.11 Modify the prime number program in Listing 8-13 to include all the prime numbers less than 10,000. Obviously, you want the program to calculate these values. The most straightforward approach is to consider every integer between 2 and 10,000. If the integer is prime, add it to the set. How do you test if the integer *i* is prime? Divide *i* by every number between 2 and *i*-1. If the remainder is 0 for any of them, *i* is *not* prime. *The* `%` operator yields the remainder of an integer division.

An equivalent test that is more efficient is to only divide by the prime numbers less than *i*—that is, the numbers that are already in your set of prime numbers. Use this more efficient approach to calculate the prime numbers.

8.12 Write a main method that repeatedly asks the user for the URL of a sound file, downloads it, and plays it. You will need to use the `newAudioClip` method in the `java.applet.Applet` class along with the `java.applet.AudioClip` and `java.net.URL` classes, among others. Unfortunately, these classes won't play `.mp3` files. There is a `.wav` file you may test your program with at `www.learningwithrobots.com/downloads/WakeupEverybody.wav`. It's a large file but only plays for a few seconds.

The sample solution is less than 30 lines of code. You will need to handle at least one checked exception.

Chapter 9 Input and Output

After studying this chapter, you should be able to:

- Use the `Scanner` class to read information from files and the `PrintWriter` class to write information to files
- Locate files using absolute and relative paths
- Use the `Scanner` class to obtain information from the user
- Prompt users for information and check it for errors
- Give users more control over programs by using command interpreters
- Put commonly used classes in a package
- Use a dialog box to obtain a filename from the user
- Display an image stored in a file

Computers excel at managing large amounts of data. The data might consist of credit card transactions at your bank, student records at your school, the card catalog at your local library, or a song on your computer. Such data is stored in a file on a hard drive or similar device.

In this chapter, we will learn how to work with files: How to open a file, process the data, and close the file.

These same techniques form the basis for interacting with the program's user via text. The program displays text to the user; the user types text to the program. Learning these basic techniques still has value, even in an age of graphical user interfaces. Writing a graphical user interface is difficult and, for many programs, simply isn't worth the trouble. Text interfaces are often sufficient.

9.1 Basic File Input and Output

Each time you visit a Web page with your browser, the Web server responsible for delivering that page records what it does in a log. On a busy Web server, this log can grow to include millions of records. On the computer hosting my personal home page, one week of log entries during a quiet time of year resulted in more than 360,000 records. A **record** refers to one entry within the file consisting of several related pieces of information. Each piece of information in a record is called a **field**. For example, a typical record[1] in the server's log contains the information shown in Table 9-1. This particular record shows that someone at the University of Massachusetts looked at a graphic on my Web page on August 19, 2005.

KEY IDEA

Files are often organized using records.

Field Contents	Meaning
128.119.246.74	The **IP address**, or Internet Protocol address, of the computer requesting the Web page.
vinci5.cs.umass.edu	The **host name** of the computer requesting the Web page. The host name and the IP address are largely interchangeable. One is easier for computers; the other is easier for people.
2005/8/19@11:24:14	The date and time the Web page was served.
GET	The command that came from the browser requesting the page. Other commands include POST (used for pages with forms) and PUT (used for uploading data).
/~bwbecker/mandel/ Gods_Eye_Heart.GIF	The specific file that was requested. In this case, it isn't a Web page at all but a graphic that is part of a Web page. Once you know the name of the Web server (www.cs.uwaterloo.ca), you can reconstruct the requested URL and look at it with a browser (*www.cs.uwaterloo.ca/~bwbecker/mandel/Gods_Eye_Heart.GIF*).
200	The completion code. A code that begins with 2 indicates that the request completed normally.
135215	The size of the requested file. If the server encountered an error, the size is replaced with a dash (-).

(table 9-1)

Information from a typical record in a Web server's log

In this chapter, we will write a series of programs that can be used to explore a Web server's log. If you have a personal home page, you may want to obtain a log to see what you can learn about who is accessing your page and how frequently your page is requested.

[1] The format of the record has been adjusted slightly. The program that does so is included with the examples for this chapter in the directory `formatLog`. The changes consist of removing several uninteresting fields, looking up the IP address to obtain the host name, and reformatting the date.

When I used these programs to explore the server log for my personal home page, I was surprised by how many times my page was accessed—612 times in one week! A little further investigation revealed that at least 140 of these were generated by search engines building their databases. I noticed that a professor at my alma mater accessed my Web page, presumably to find my e-mail address (I received an e-mail from him later that week). I was also surprised at the number of international hits (including Finland, South Africa, Australia, Israel, Singapore, Bosnia/Herzegovina, Netherlands, and Mexico). It was interesting to speculate how these visitors found my home page and what kind of information they were seeking.

9.1.1 Reading from a File

The program in Listing 9-1 provides a first look at a program that processes a file, which involves three important steps:

- Lines 13–21 locate the file on the disk drive and construct a `Scanner` object to obtain the information it contains. This process is called **opening** a file.
- Lines 24–29 process the file one record at a time, printing selected records. It uses two methods in the `Scanner` class, `hasNextLine` and `nextLine`. Obtaining data from a file is called **reading** a file. The information obtained from the file is called the program's **input**.
- Line 32 **closes** the file when it is no longer being used.

These three steps will be explored in detail in the following sections.

FIND THE CODE

ch09/processLines/

PATTERN

Open File for Input

Listing 9-1: *A program to read a Web server's log and print records containing a given string*

```
1  import java.io.File;
2  import java.io.FileNotFoundException;
3  import java.util.Scanner;
4
5  /** Read a Web server's log record by record. Print those records that contain the
6   *  substring "bwbecker".
7   *
8   *  @author Byron Weber Becker */
9  public class ReadServerLog
10 {
11   public static void main(String[] args)
12   { // Open the file.
13     Scanner in = null;
14     try
15     { File file = new File("server_log.txt");
16       in = new Scanner(file);
17     } catch (FileNotFoundException ex)
```

Listing 9-1: *A program to read a Web server's log and print records containing a given string* (continued)

```
18       { System.out.println(ex.getMessage());
19         System.out.println("in " + System.getProperty("user.dir"));
20         System.exit(1);
21       }
22
23       // Read and process each record.
24       while (in.hasNextLine())
25       { String record = in.nextLine();
26         if (record.indexOf("bwbecker") >= 0)       // author's Web pages
27         { System.out.println(record);
28         }
29       }
30
31       // Close the file.
32       in.close();
33     }
34  }
```

PATTERN

Process File

Opening a File

Conceptually, opening a file is simple. All we want to do is execute the following two lines:

```
File file = new File("server_log.txt");
Scanner in = new Scanner(file);
```

The first line creates a `File` object that describes where the program should look for the file named `server_log.txt`. The second line creates an object used to access the file at that location.

If only it were that simple. In reality, things can go wrong. The most common problem, and the only one that throws a checked exception, is when the file is not at the expected location. The programmer may have misspelled the name as `serverlog.txt`, the file may have been moved, the program may be running in an unexpected location, or the file may not have been created yet. In any of these cases, the `Scanner` constructor will throw a `FileNotFoundException`. Handling this exception expands the two lines we need to execute into nine lines in Listing 9-1.

LOOKING BACK

Exceptions were discussed in Section 8.4.

First, we need to introduce a `try-catch` statement around the `Scanner` constructor call to handle the `FileNotFoundException`. We will need the `Scanner` object outside of the `try-catch` statement, and so it is declared in line 13.

KEY IDEA

The working directory is useful information when a file is not found.

Second, it is wise to handle the exception by giving the user as much information as possible about where the program was looking for the missing file. This is done by getting and printing the **working directory** in line 19. The working directory is the directory (directories are also called folders) from which a program begins looking for a file. The working directory is set when the program begins execution. The working directory can be obtained with the query `System.getProperty("user.dir")`.

This code results in a message similar to the one shown in Figure 9-1. The message says the system started looking for the file with a disk drive labeled `D:`. That drive has a directory named `Robots`. Inside `Robots` is a directory named `examples`, which contains a directory named `ch09`. Inside `ch09` is `processLines`. That is the directory where the program expected to find the file named `server_log.txt`.

For the time being, we'll assume that in such circumstances you will simply move the file to the directory where the system expects to find it. Later, we will learn how to open files in other locations.

(figure 9-1)

Example of the message printed when a file is not found

```
C:\java\JCREAT~1.5\GE2001.exe
server_log.txt (The system cannot find the file specified)
in D:\Robots\examples\ch09\processLines
Press any key to continue...
```

Processing a File

Lines 24–29 in Listing 9-1 are responsible for processing the data in the file. Many files, including the server log, are organized as one record per line of text, as shown in Figure 9-2. The requested filenames are shortened so that each record fits on one line.

(figure 9-2)

Four records from the `server_log.txt` *file*

```
131.107.0.106 tide536.microsoft.com 2005/8/19@11:24:13 GET /~zqu/...enu.jpg 301 354
128.119.246.74 vinci5.cs.umass.edu 2005/8/19@11:24:14 GET /~bwb...rt.GIF 200 135215
210.8.90.45 cam1.gw.connect.com.au 2005/8/19@11:24:16 GET /~hza...zed.jpg 200 54297
131.107.0.106 tide536.microsoft.com 2005/8/19@11:24:16 GET /~zqu/...enu.jpg 302 326
```

The `nextLine` method, used in line 25 of Listing 9-1, retrieves one line from the file. With each repetition of the loop, it obtains the next line. This continues as long as `hasNextLine` returns `true`. When the last line has been read, `hasNextLine` will return `false` and the loop will stop.

Finally, the `if` statement contained within the loop prints out only those lines that contain the string `bwbecker`—that is, it prints out the log records pertaining to the author's Web pages.

Closing a File

Files use significant resources. Closing the file with the `close` method (line 32) allows the system to free up those resources for other uses.

9.1.2 Writing to a File

The previous program simply displays selected records in the console window. If a large number of records are selected, the first records will scroll out of view long before the last records are displayed. An alternative is for the program to copy the selected records to their own file. The process of creating a file and placing records in it is called **writing** a file. The information written is called the program's **output**. The terms *input* and *output* are often used together and abbreviated as **I/O**.

KEY IDEA

Writing a file is the opposite of reading it.

The program in Listing 9-2 is the same as the previous program except that it writes the selected records to a file named `bwbecker.txt` instead of printing them on the console. As with reading, there are three steps to writing the file:

- The file is opened at line 18 by constructing an instance of `PrintWriter`. This object opens the file and provides methods for writing data to it. Like opening a file to read it, a `FileNotFoundException` can be thrown. Therefore, the constructor call is placed inside the `try-catch` statement but the variable, `out`, is declared earlier, in line 15.
- The selected records are written to the file, one record at a time, in line 29. The `PrintWriter` class provides the same methods as `System.out`, including `print`, `println`, and `printf`.
- Finally, the file is closed at line 36.

These changes are shown in bold.

FIND THE CODE

ch09/processLines/

Listing 9-2: *A program that writes matching records to a file*

```
 1 import java.io.File;
 2 import java.io.FileNotFoundException;
 3 import java.io.PrintWriter;
 4 import java.util.Scanner;
 5
 6 /** Read a Web server's access log record by record. Write those records that contain the
 7  *  substring "bwbecker" to a file.
 8  *
 9  *  @author Byron Weber Becker */
10 public class WriteMatchingLines
11 {
12   public static void main(String[] args)
```

Listing 9-2: *A program that writes matching records to a file* (continued)

```
13     { // Open the files.
14       Scanner in = null;
15       PrintWriter out = null;
16       try
17       { in = new Scanner(new File("server_log.txt"));
18         out = new PrintWriter("bwbecker.txt");
19       } catch (FileNotFoundException ex)
20       { System.out.println(ex.getMessage());
21         System.out.println("in " + System.getProperty("user.dir"));
22         System.exit(1);
23       }
24
25       // Read and process each record.
26       while (in.hasNextLine())
27       { String record = in.nextLine();
28         if (record.indexOf("bwbecker") > 0)
29         { out.println(record);
30         }
31
32       }
33
34       // Close the files.
35       in.close();
36       out.close();
37     }
38   }
```

PATTERN

Open File for Input
Open File for Output

PATTERN

Process File

KEY IDEA

Ensure that all data is written by calling `close` *before the program ends.*

Java does not always write information to the file immediately. By collecting information from several calls to `print` and `println` and writing them all at once, substantial gains in efficiency can be realized. This process is called **buffering**. Some information may not be written to the file at all if the program ends at the wrong time. To prevent this, you should always call the `close` method after you are done writing to the file. It is an error to call a print method after `close` has been called.

What happens if the preceding code is executed again and the file `bwbecker.txt` already exists? The existing file and all the information within it will be deleted, as a new file with the same name is created.

Sometimes you would rather append new data to the end of an existing file. In that case, an extra step is required. Replace line 18 with the following two lines:

```
FileWriter fw = new FileWriter("bwbecker.txt", true);
out = new PrintWriter(fw);
```

The first line constructs an object that opens the file so that new data will be appended to it. However, the `FileWriter`'s methods only write individual characters; we still want to be able to use the `print` methods in `PrintWriter`. Fortunately, the two classes can work together to provide this capability.

LOOKING AHEAD

Java's I/O classes are designed to work together. More details in Section 9.7.

If your program uses these two lines but the specified file does not exist, a new file will be created.

9.1.3 The Structure of Files

Consider the following records from the inventory file of a computer store. The four fields are quantity on hand, part identifier, description, and price.

```
10 002D9249 Computer  1595.99
5 293E993C Keyboard   24.99
12 0003922M Monitor   349.99
```

The two programs examined in this chapter so far read such files as lines of text. In fact, text has a richer structure.

A file is a sequence of characters. The characters that are displayed visibly on the screen include letters, numbers, and punctuation, such as `y`, `M`, `8`, and `?`. Each of these is represented in the computer using a unique value.

Some characters are less obvious, such as spaces. They are represented on the screen as empty space. In the computer, however, they are represented by a value, just as `M` and `y` are represented by a value. For clarity, we will often show a space as a single dot in the middle of the line (·). Most word processors have a similar feature to help users understand how a document is formatted.

KEY IDEA

Every character, even spaces, corresponds to a value.

Another less obvious character is the tab character. Like the space character, a tab is also displayed by blank space. The length of that blank space, however, depends on a number of factors. But no matter how long the space is, it is represented in the computer as a single value. For clarity, we will show a tab character with a small arrow: →.

Finally, the end of a line is also represented by a character. The exact value used depends on the computer's operating system, and some use a sequence of two characters. Fortunately, the `Scanner` and `PrintWriter` classes allow us to ignore this detail most of the time. We will refer to this character as the **newline character**. It is displayed on the screen by moving the **insertion point**—the point where the next character is displayed—to the left side of the screen and down one line. For clarity, we will show the newline character as a down and left arrow: ↵.

The space, tab, and newline characters are collectively known as **whitespace** because they appear as white space when printed on a white sheet of paper.

Finally, we will represent the end of the file[2] with □.

With these conventions, the three inventory records are shown as follows:

```
10·002D9249·Computer→1595.99↵
5·293E993C·Keyboard→24.99↵
12·0003922M·Monitor→349.99↵
□
```

KEY IDEA

Lines are divided into tokens separated by delimiters.

Lines of text are often divided into groups of characters called **tokens**. The characters that divide one token from the next are called **delimiters**. The most common delimiters are white space characters. Using white space as delimiters, the previous lines each contain four tokens. Dividing the line into tokens enables us to obtain the information it contains more flexibly.

Data Acquisition Methods

The `Scanner` class provides methods to read a file token by token as well as line by line. The `next` method will read the next token, returning it as a `String`. Calling the `next` method on the inventory records will return, in order, the strings `10`, `002D9249`, `Computer`, and so on.

Another method, `nextInt`, will attempt to read the next token and convert it to an integer before returning it. If the next token can't be converted to an integer, `nextInt` will throw an `InputMismatchException`. A third method, `nextDouble`, behaves similarly except that it attempts to convert the next token to a `double` value. These methods can be described as **data acquisition methods** because they are used to acquire data from the file.

A program fragment that reads the inventory records and prints a simple report is shown in Listing 9-3. It assumes a `Scanner` object named `in` has already been created.

FIND THE CODE

ch09/inventoryReport/

Listing 9-3: *A program fragment that reads the tokens in an inventory record*

```
// Open the file.
while (in.hasNextLine())
{ int quantity = in.nextInt();
  String partID = in.next();
  String description = in.next();
  double cost = in.nextDouble();
  in.nextLine();
```

[2] Actually, the end of the file is not a character in the same way that a space or newline is a character. Nevertheless, showing it as a character is a useful fiction.

Listing 9-3: *A program fragment that reads the tokens in an inventory record* (continued)

```
9      // Print in a different order, including a calculated value.
10     System.out.printf("%-15s%5d%8.2f%10.2f%n", description,
11                     quantity, cost, quantity * cost);
12  }
```

LOOKING BACK

The `printf` *method was discussed in Section 7.2.4.*

As this program reads the file, the `Scanner` object maintains a **cursor** that marks its position. The cursor divides the file into two parts: the part that has already been read, and the part that has not. The cursor is positioned just before the first character when the file is opened.

Table 9-2 traces part of the execution of the previous program. It shows the position of the cursor with a diamond (♦) in the column labeled "Input."

(table 9-2)

Tracing the partial execution of the program fragment in Listing 9-3

Statement	Input	quantity	partID	descr	cost
	`♦10·002D9249·Computer→1595.99↵`				
`2 while (in.hasNextLine())`					
	`♦10·002D9249·Computer→1595.99↵`				
`3 { int quantity = in.nextInt();`					
	`10♦·002D9249·Computer→1595.99↵`	10			
`4   String partNum = in.next();`					
	`10·002D9249♦·Computer→1595.99↵`	10	002D9249		
`5   String description = in.next();`					
	`10·002D9249·Computer♦→1595.99↵`	10	002D9249	Computer	
`6   double cost = in.nextDouble();`					
	`10·002D9249·Computer→1595.99♦↵`	10	002D9249	Computer	1595.99
`7   in.nextLine();`					
	`10·002D9249·Computer→1595.99↵` `♦5·293E993C·Keyboard→24.99↵`	10	002D9249	Computer	1595.99
`10  System.out.printf...` `2 while (in.hasNextLine())`					
	`10·002D9249·Computer→1595.99↵` `♦5·293E993C·Keyboard→24.99↵`	10	002D9249	Computer	1595.99

Statement	Input	quantity	partID	descr	cost
3 { int quantity = in.nextInt();					
	10·002D9249·Computer1→1595.99↵ 5♦·293E993C·Keyboard→24.99↵	5	002D9249	Computer	1595.99

(table 9-2) *continued*

Tracing the partial execution of the program fragment in Listing 9-3

Beginning at the top of Table 9-2, the `while` statement calls `hasNextLine` to determine whether additional text comes after the cursor. `hasNextLine` does not move the cursor.

When the `nextInt` method executes, it begins at the cursor and looks ahead at the following characters. It skips any leading delimiters such as spaces, and then examines the characters until the next delimiter character is found. In this example, these characters are `10`, which can be interpreted as an integer. The cursor is therefore moved just past the token, and the integer `10` is returned. If the characters cannot be interpreted as an integer, an exception is thrown and the cursor does not move.

The `Scanner` class contains methods to read and interpret the next token for many types. They all behave essentially the same as `nextInt`:

- Skip delimiting characters.
- Examine the characters up to the next delimiter.
- If the examined characters can be interpreted as the specified type, move the cursor beyond them and return the token as the specified type. If the characters cannot be interpreted as the specified type, throw a `InputMismatchException` and leave the cursor's position unchanged.

KEY IDEA

`nextLine` *does not skip leading white space. Other* `next` *methods do.*

The exception is the `nextLine` method. It does not skip leading white space and returns the rest of the line rather than a token.

The most commonly used data acquisition methods in the `Scanner` class are shown in Table 9-3. In this table, each method is followed by a description and examples.

(table 9-3)

Data acquisition methods in the `Scanner` *class*

Method	Description and Examples
`int nextInt()`	Examines the next token in the input, skipping any leading delimiters. If the token can be interpreted as an `int`, the cursor is moved past the token and the `int` value is returned. Otherwise, an `InputMismatchException` is thrown and the cursor is not moved. Examples: Initial Situation / Returns / Final Situation ABC♦··10·DEF↵ / 10 / ABC··10♦·DEF↵ ABC♦·-15↵ / -15 / ABC·-15♦↵ ABC♦·ten·DEF↵ / Exception / ABC♦·ten·DEF↵ ABC♦·↵10·DEF / 10 / ABC·↵10♦·DEF Please note that the last example contains a newline character ↵ in the middle of the line. A text editor would show this as two lines.
`double nextDouble()`	Like `nextInt`, but attempts to interpret the token as a `double`. Examples: Initial Situation / Returns / Final Situation ABC♦··10.5·DEF↵ / 10.5 / ABC··10.5♦·DEF↵ ABC♦·-1.5E3·DEF↵ / -1500.0 / ABC·-1.5E3♦·DEF↵ ABC♦·10·DEF↵ / 10.0 / ABC·10♦·DEF↵ ABC♦·ten·DEF↵ / Exception / ABC♦·ten·DEF↵
`boolean nextBoolean()`	Like `nextInt`, but attempts to interpret the token as a `boolean`. Examples: Initial Situation / Returns / Final Situation ABC♦··true·DEF↵ / true / ABC··true♦·DEF↵ ABC♦·FALSE↵ / false / ABC·FALSE♦↵ ABC♦·truest·DEF↵ / Exception / ABC♦·truest·DEF↵
`String next()`	Reads the next token and returns it as a `String`. Examples: Initial Situation / Returns / Final Situation ABC♦··xyz·DEF↵ / "xyz" / ABC··xyz♦·DEF↵ ABC♦·FALSE↵ / "FALSE" / ABC·FALSE♦↵ ABC♦·10·DEF↵ / "10" / ABC·10♦·DEF↵ ABC♦□ / Exception / ABC♦□ ABC♦↵··xyz·DEF / "xyz" / ABC↵··xyz♦·DEF
`String nextLine()`	Reads and returns as a `String` all the characters from the cursor up to the next newline character or the end of the file, whichever comes first. Moves the cursor past the characters that were read and the following newline, if there is one. `nextLine` does not skip leading delimiters. Examples: Initial Situation / Returns / Final Situation ABC♦··xyz·DEF↵ / "··xyz·DEF" / ABC··xyz·DEF↵♦ ABC♦··xyz·DEF□ / "··xyz·DEF" / ABC··xyz·DEF♦□ ABC♦□ / Exception / ABC♦□

KEY IDEA

Choose a method based on the desired return type.

Many tokens may be read with more than one method. For example, the token `10` can be read with `nextInt`, `nextDouble`, and `next`. It can also be read with `nextLine`, which may also include additional tokens. The difference is in the type returned. `nextInt` returns the token as an `int`, ready to be assigned to an integer variable. `next`, on the other hand, returns it as a `String`, which can be assigned to a variable of type `String` but not a variable of type `int`.

Data Availability Methods

KEY IDEA

`hasNextInt` is used to determine if calling `nextInt` will succeed.

In addition to the data access methods shown in Table 9-3, the `Scanner` class has data availability methods. `hasNextLine` is one of these methods. **Data availability methods** are used to determine whether data of a given type is available. Each of the data acquisition methods have a corresponding data availability method that can be used to determine if calling the data acquisition method will succeed.

These methods include `hasNext`, `hasNextInt`, `hasNextDouble`, `hasNextBoolean`, and `hasNextLine`. They all return `boolean` values.

For an example of using a data availability method, consider again the Web server log. Normally, the last token of the record is an integer specifying the size of the data served. However, if the server encounters an error and cannot serve the requested data, the log will contain a dash (-). If `nextInt` is called on such a record, an exception will be thrown.

Instead, use `hasNextInt` to determine if an integer is available. If it is, call `nextInt` to acquire it. If `hasNextInt` returns `false`, we can read the information another way. This is shown in Listing 9-4 in lines 10–15.

Listing 9-4: *A code fragment to read individual tokens in a Web server's log, accounting for either an integer size or a dash (–) in the last token*

```
1   while(in.hasNextLine())
2   { String ipAddress = in.next();
3     String hostName = in.next();
4     String when = in.next();
5     String cmd = in.next();
6     String url = in.next();
7     int completionCode = in.nextInt();
8
9     // Read the size of the served page. Set size to 0 if there was an error recorded.
10    int size = 0;
11    if (in.hasNextInt())
12    { size = in.nextInt();                         // Read the size.
13    } else
```

Listing 9-4: *A code fragment to read individual tokens in a Web server's log, accounting for either an integer size or a dash (–) in the last token* (continued)

```
14        { in.next();                                // Skip the dash.
15        }
16        in.nextLine();                              // Move cursor to next line.
17
18        // Process the data.
19    }
```

9.2 Representing Records as Objects

Reading one record can become complex, as Listing 9-4 indicates. The complexity only gets worse as the number of fields and the number of exceptions increase as in lines 11–15. All that code can obscure our understanding of the enclosing loop and the code processing the records.

An excellent way to address these issues is to write helper methods. An even better solution is to write a new class so that each record can be represented as an object. The helper methods go in that class.

KEY IDEA

Represent records as objects.

9.2.1 Reading Records as Objects

For an example of representing a record as an object, consider the `ServerRecord` class shown in Listing 9-5. The helper method to read the file is actually the constructor. It takes a `Scanner` object as a parameter and uses it to read the information for one server log record. The code opening the file, the loop reading multiple records, and the code closing the file are in another class (see Listing 9-6).

Instance variables in `ServerRecord` correspond to the fields in the record. Each field is stored in the appropriate variable when it is read.

Note that the date and time from the record is stored as a `DateTime` object. Furthermore, the `DateTime` class has a constructor taking a `Scanner` object as a parameter. This allows the `ServerRecord` constructor to quickly and easily delegate reading the date and time to the `DateTime` class in line 25.

This technique assumes that the constructor is called with the `Scanner`'s cursor positioned immediately before the record. When the constructor finishes executing, the cursor must be immediately after the record, ready for the next record to be read.

KEY IDEA

The constructor begins and ends with the cursor at the beginning of a record.

`ServerRecord` should also provide methods required to process the record. Examples might include methods to get the size of the served page, to determine if the URL contains a specified string, to determine if the hostname contains a specified string, or to get the date the page was served.

The `ServerRecord` class also includes a method named `write` that writes the record to a file in the same format in which it was read. This allows the program to read its own files. `write` takes a `PrintWriter` object as its parameter. As with the reading of the file, the responsibility for opening and closing the file rests with the calling code (see Listing 9-6).

FIND THE CODE

ch09/processRecords/

LOOKING AHEAD

A class like `ServerRecord` is an excellent candidate for a library. See Section 9.6.

PATTERN

Construct Record from File

Listing 9-5: *A class representing records in a Web server's log*

```
import java.util.Scanner;
import java.io.PrintWriter;
import becker.util.DateTime;

/** Represent one server log record.
 *
 *  @author Byron Weber Becker */
public class ServerRecord extends Object
{
  private String ipAddress;
  private String hostName;
  private DateTime when;
  private String cmd;
  private String url;
  private int completionCode;
  private int size = 0;
  private boolean error = true;      // Assume an error until proven otherwise.

  /** Construct an object representing one server record using information read from a file.
   *  @param in An open file, positioned at the beginning of the next record. */
  public ServerRecord(Scanner in)
  { super();
    this.ipAddress = in.next();
    this.hostName = in.next();
    this.when = new DateTime(in);
    this.cmd = in.next();
    this.url = in.next();
    this.completionCode = in.nextInt();
    if (in.hasNextInt())
    { this.size = in.nextInt();
      this.error = false;
    }

```

Listing 9-5: *A class representing records in a Web server's log* (continued)

```
      // Get ready to read the next record
      in.nextLine();
    }

    /** Write the record to a file in the same format it was read.
     * @param out An open output file. */
    public void write(PrintWriter out)
    { out.print(this.ipAddress + " " + this.hostName + " ");
      out.print(this.when.toString() + " " + this.cmd + " ");
      out.print(this.url + " " + this.completionCode + " ");
      if (this.error)
      { out.print("-");
      } else
      { out.print(this.size);
      }
      out.println();
    }

    // Some methods have been omitted.
}
```

Listing 9-6: *Client code to read server records and write selected records to a file*

FIND THE CODE

ch09/processRecords/

```
import java.io.*;
import java.net.*;
import java.util.Scanner;

/** Read a Web server's access log. Write selected records to a file.
 *
 *  @author Byron Weber Becker */
public class ReadServerRecords
{
  public static void main(String[] args)
  { // Open the files.
    Scanner in = null;
    PrintWriter out = null;
    try
    { in = new Scanner(new File("server_log.txt"));
      out = new PrintWriter("largeFiles.txt");
    } catch (FileNotFoundException ex)
```

PATTERN

Open File for Input
Open File for Output

Listing 9-6: *Client code to read server records and write selected records to a file* (continued)

```
    { System.out.println(ex.getMessage());
      System.out.println("in " + System.getProperty("user.dir"));
      System.exit(1);
    }

    // Read and process each record.
    while (in.hasNextLine())
    { ServerRecord sr = new ServerRecord(in);
      if (sr.getSize() >= 25000)
      { sr.write(out);
      }
    }

    // Close the files.
    in.close();
    out.close();
  }
}
```

PATTERN
Process File

9.2.2 File Formats

KEY IDEA
Every program using a file must agree on the file's format.

Many files are used by more than one program. For example, the Web server writes the log file while various reporting programs read it. These programs need to agree on how the file is organized: the order of the fields within the record, which delimiters are used to separate tokens, and so on. The organization of the file is known as the **file format**.

To better appreciate the effect the file format has on the program, let's consider again the simple file format for the computer store inventory file. Recall that it had four fields, as shown in the following example records:

```
10 002D9249 Computer  1595.99
5 293E993C Keyboard   24.99
12 0003922M Monitor   349.99
```

A constructor to read these records is quite simple:

FIND THE CODE
ch09/fileFormat/

PATTERN
Construct Record from File

```
public Inventory1(Scanner in)
{ super();
  this.quantity = in.nextInt();
  this.partID = in.next();
  this.description = in.next();
  this.price = in.nextDouble();
  in.nextLine();
}
```

However, this code assumes that each field consists of a single token. If the description were `LCD Monitor` instead of simply `Monitor`, this would not work because `in.next()` would read `LCD`. The call to `nextDouble()` would attempt to turn the string `Monitor` into a `double`, and fail.

The simplest way to handle this change is to change the file format. By putting single token fields such as quantity, price, and part identifier first, and putting the multiple token field (description) last, the description can be read using `nextLine`; in other words, order the record as shown in the following example:

KEY IDEA

Simple changes to the file format can make a big difference in the code that reads it.

```
12 0003922M 349.99 LCD Monitor
```

Code to read this file format can be found in `ch09/fileFormat/Inventory2.java`.

However, suppose that there is a second multiple token field, such as the name of the supplier. If we simply add it on to the end of the record, we have no reliable way of knowing where one field ends and the next begins unless we use a different delimiter that does not appear in either field, such as a colon (`:`). This is shown in the following record:

```
12 0003922M 349.99 LCD Monitor : ACME Computer Distributors
```

Such a record could be read with code such as the following. It reads the description a token at a time, building up the description until the delimiter is found. It then reads the last multiple token field with `nextLine`, trimming off any leading or trailing blanks.

FIND THE CODE

ch09/fileFormat/

```
public Inventory3(Scanner in)
{ // Code to read quantity, part identifier, and price is omitted
  this.description = "";
  String token = in.next();
  while (!token.equals(":"))
  { this.description += " " + token;
    token = in.next();
  }
  this.distributor = in.nextLine().trim();
}
```

The `Scanner` class takes this idea one step further by allowing us to specify the delimiters it uses. If we replace each white space delimiter with a colon, for example, then even multiword phrases are treated as a single token. Consider the following record:

```
12:M0003922:349.99:LCD Monitor:ACME Computer Distributors:
```

This record can be read by calling `in.useDelimiter(":")` immediately after opening the file. The `ServerRecord` constructor can now read each of the tokens with a single call, as follows:

FIND THE CODE

ch09/fileFormat/

```
public Inventory4(Scanner in)
{ this.quantity = in.nextInt();
  this.partID = in.next();
  this.price = in.nextDouble();
  this.description = in.next();
  this.distributor = in.next();
  in.nextLine();                    // Move to the next line of the file.
}
```

Because newline characters are no longer delimiters, the colon at the end of the record and the call to `nextLine` are required.

KEY IDEA

Design the file format to make your code easy to read, write, and understand.

There is one more file format variation that bears mentioning: Simply place each multiple token field like `description` and `distributor` on its own line. No law requires a record to use only one line. This simple idea of placing each multiple token field on its own line helps keep both the file and the code easy to read, write, and understand. To make the file easier to read, you may want to place a blank line between each pair of records.

9.3 Using the File Class

To open a file, a `File` object must be constructed and given the name of the file, such as `server_log.txt`. The resulting object can be passed to a `Scanner` constructor, but it can also be useful by itself. The sections that follow investigate valid filenames, explain how to specify file locations, and discuss the methods this class provides.

9.3.1 Filenames

You can't name a file anything you want because some characters are not allowed. The Windows operating system, for example, does not allow a filename to contain any of the following characters: \ / : * ? " < > |.

Filenames often have an **extension**, such as `.txt`. An extension is whatever follows the last period in the name, and is often used to identify the kind of information stored in the file. For example, a file with an extension of `.html` contains a Web page, whereas a file with an extension of `.jpg` means it contains a graphic.

9.3.2 Specifying File Locations

Modern computers use a hierarchical system for locating directories and files. The hierarchy is depicted as an upside-down tree with branches, as shown in Figure 9-3. Directories can contain either files (white) or other directories (green). For example, the directory `cs101` contains two other directories, `A09` and `A10`. The directory `A09` contains four files, including `ServerRecord.java`. `A09` also includes a directory, `logs`, which includes three additional files.

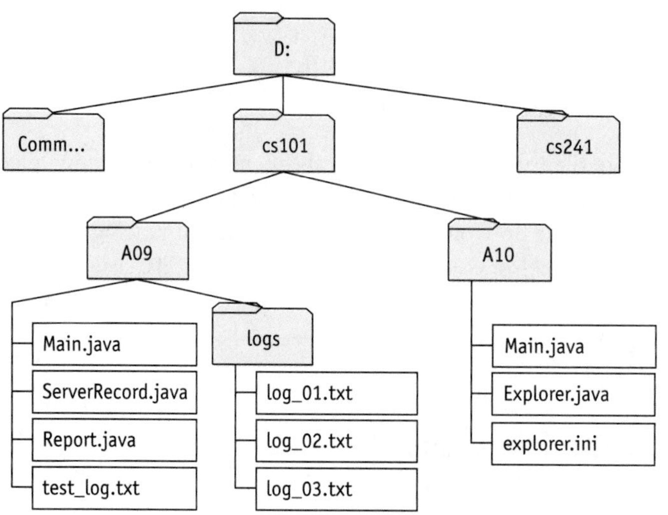

(figure 9-3)

Hierarchical file system in which folder icons represent directories and boxes represent files

An **absolute path** begins with the root of the tree (`D:`) and specifies all of the directories between it and the desired file. For example, the hierarchy shown in Figure 9-3 contains two files named `Main.java`. The following statement uses an absolute path to specify one of them:

```
File f = new File("D:/cs101/A09/Main.java");
```

The directories in the path are separated with a special character, typically / (Unix and Macintosh) or \ (Windows). Java will accept either, but / is easier because \ is Java's escape character for strings.

Files can also be specified with a **relative path** from the program's working directory. Suppose the current working directory is `A09`. A name without a prefix specifies a file in that directory—for example, `test_log.txt`. You can also name a file in a subdirectory of the working directory—for example, `logs/log_01.txt`. The special name `..` specifies the parent directory. The following statement uses a relative path to specify the initialization file in `A10`:

```
File init = new File("../A10/explorer.ini");
```

Relative paths are most useful when the program's location and the file's location are related. If the program moves to a new location (such as submitting it electronically to be marked), the file should also move. Absolute paths are more useful when the location of the file is independent of the location of the program using it.

Knowing your program's working directory is a key to using relative paths effectively. You can find it with the following statement:

```
System.out.println(System.getProperty("user.dir");
```

The `System` class maintains a map of keys and properties for the running program. The string "`user.dir`" is the key for the working directory property. Other keys include "`user.name`" (the user's account name); "`os.name`" (the computer's operating system); and "`line.separator`" (the character or sequence of characters separating lines in a file, represented earlier with ↵).

9.3.3 Manipulating Files

The `File` constructor can have either an absolute or a relative path as its argument. The resulting object represents a path to a file or a directory. The file or directory may or may not exist.

A `File` object can both answer a number of useful questions about the path it represents and perform a number of operations on the file system. Some of these operations are summarized in Table 9-4. Technically, a directory is a special kind of file. The online documentation often uses "file" to refer to either; Table 9-4 does the same.

(table 9-4)

Summary of methods in the `File` class

Method	Description
`boolean canRead()`	Determines whether this program has permission to read from the file.
`boolean canWrite()`	Determines whether this program has permission to write to the file.
`boolean delete()`	Deletes the file or directory. Directories must be empty before they can be deleted. Returns `true` if successful.
`boolean exists()`	Determines whether the file exists.
`String getAbsolutePath()`	Gets the absolute path for this file.
`File getParentFile()`	Gets a `File` object representing this file's parent directory. Returns `null` if this file doesn't have a parent.
`boolean isFile()`	Determines whether the path specifies a file.

(table 9-4) *continued*

Summary of methods in the `File` *class*

Method	Description
`boolean isDirectory()`	Determines whether the path specifies a directory.
`long length()`	Gets the number of characters in the file.
`boolean mkDir()`	Makes the directory represented by this `File`. Returns `true` if successful.

9.4 Interacting with Users

Without input from users, most programs are not worth writing. A word processor that always typed the same essay, regardless of what the user wanted to say, would be worthless. A game program that didn't react to the game player's decisions would be boring.

This section and the next will discuss how to interact with the user of your program to modify how the program behaves. As an example, we will modify the program in Listing 9-6, which currently processes a server log, printing only those records resulting from serving a file larger than or equal to 25,000 bytes. Our new program will ask the user which log file to process and the minimum served file size to report. In particular, we want to implement the following pseudocode:

```
String fileName = ask the user for the log file to open
int minSize = ask the user for the minimum served file size
open the log file named in fileName
while (log file has another line)
{ ServerRecord sr = new ServerRecord(log file);
  if (sr.getSize() >= minSize)
  { print the record
  }
}
close the log file
```

9.4.1 Reading from the Console

Fortunately, the techniques we learned to read from a file can also be used to read information from the console. We still use the `Scanner` class, but we construct the `Scanner` object slightly differently, as follows:

```
Scanner cin = new Scanner(System.in);
```

`System.in` is an object similar to `System.out`. `Scanner` uses it to read from the console. Unlike opening a file, we are not required to catch any exceptions.

Before we implement the pseudocode discussed earlier, consider the sample program shown in Listing 9-7. It illustrates the important elements of reading from the console. The result of running this program is shown in Figure 9-4.

FIND THE CODE

ch09/readConsole/

Listing 9-7: *A short program demonstrating reading from the console*

```
1  import java.util.Scanner;
2
3  public class ReadConsole
4  {
5     public static void main(String[] args)
6     { Scanner cin = new Scanner(System.in);
7
8        System.out.print("Enter an integer: ");
9        int a = cin.nextInt();
10       System.out.print("Enter an integer: ");
11       int b = cin.nextInt();
12
13       System.out.println(a + "*" + b + " = " + a * b);
14    }
15 }
```

The program begins by creating a new `Scanner` object used to read from the console. It's named `cin`, short for "console input."

KEY IDEA

Prompt the user when input is expected.

At lines 8 and 10, the program prints a **prompt** for the user. The prompt informs the user that input is expected. In Figure 9-4, the user responded to the first prompt with 3↵. That is, the user entered the digit 3 and the Enter key. The Enter key is the user's cue to the program that it should read the input and process it. The program waits to read the input until Enter is pressed. The online documentation uses the term **block**, which means to wait for input.

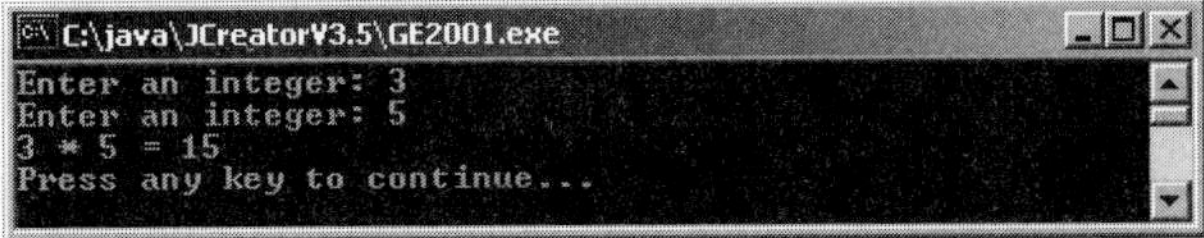

(figure 9-4)

Result of running the program shown in Listing 9-7

9.4.2 Checking Input for Errors

Unfortunately, if the user misreads the prompt and enters `three`↵, the program will throw an exception, as shown in Figure 9-5.

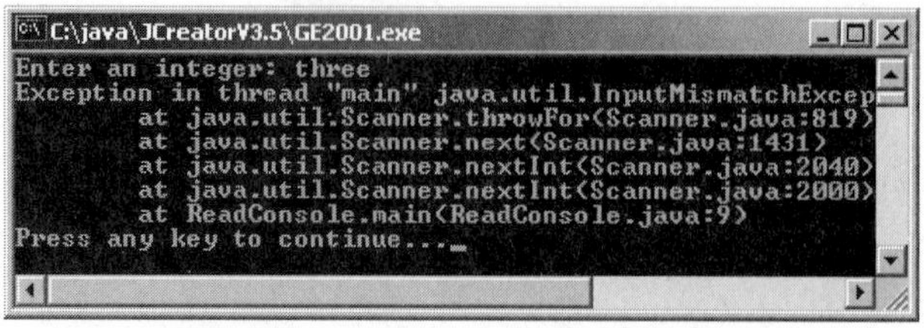

```
C:\java\JCreatorV3.5\GE2001.exe
Enter an integer: three
Exception in thread "main" java.util.InputMismatchExcep
        at java.util.Scanner.throwFor(Scanner.java:819)
        at java.util.Scanner.next(Scanner.java:1431)
        at java.util.Scanner.nextInt(Scanner.java:2040)
        at java.util.Scanner.nextInt(Scanner.java:2000)
        at ReadConsole.main(ReadConsole.java:9)
Press any key to continue..._
```

(figure 9-5)

Result of entering data with an inappropriate type

The program can be protected from such errors with the code shown in Listing 9-8. The loop in lines 9–19 verifies that the next token is an integer. If it is not, the program reads it and displays a helpful message. This action gives the user the opportunity to try again. When an integer is entered, it is read in line 12, and the loop ends with the `break` in line 14.

FIND THE CODE

ch09/readConsole/

Listing 9-8: *Rewriting Listing 9-7 to check for input errors*

```
1  import java.util.Scanner;
2
3  public class ReadConsoleChecked
4  {
5    public static void main(String[ ] args)
6    { Scanner cin = new Scanner(System.in);
7
8      int a = 0;
9      while (true)
10     { System.out.print("Enter an integer: ");
11       if (cin.hasNextInt())
12       { a = cin.nextInt();
13         cin.nextLine();                    // consume remaining input
14         break;
15       } else
16       { String next = cin.nextLine();      // consume the error
17         System.out.println(next + " is not an integer such as 10 or -3.");
18       }
19     }
20     // Repeat lines 8–19, but read the data entered into variable b.
33
34     System.out.println(a + " * " + b + " = " + a * b);
35   }
36 }
```

PATTERN

Error-Checked Input

The need to repeat essentially identical code to read the second integer suggests that a method should be written. Such a method does not rely on any instance variables and can therefore be a class method. In fact, a whole set of similar methods will be needed.

LOOKING BACK

Class methods were discussed in Section 7.5.2

We can place them in a class named `Prompt` and call them as shown in the following example:

```
int a = Prompt.forInt("Enter an integer: ");
```

KEY IDEA

The `Prompt` class must be used for all of the console input—or none of it.

Listing 9-9 shows the beginning of the class. Notice that line 9 declares a `static` (class) variable used to read from the console. One consequence of this decision is that *all* input from the console must be obtained with the methods in this class. Using more than one `Scanner` object to read from the same source (that is, `System.in`) will not work reliably.

LOOKING AHEAD

The problem set will ask you to add to this library.

Listing 9-9 also includes the methods `forInputFile` and `forInputScanner`. The first method uses the `File` class to verify that a string entered by the user specifies a file that exists and can be read by this program. The second method uses the first to open the specified file using `Scanner`. Putting this code in its own class has the following advantages:

- We can avoid writing it anew for each program that asks the user for a file or integer to process.
- We can put the `try-catch` statement here, rather than cluttering the main program with it.
- If the methods need enhancing or debugging, there is only one place that requires attention.

FIND THE CODE

ch09/userIO/

Listing 9-9: *A class providing error-checked reading of an integer and a filename*

```
1  import java.util.Scanner;
2  import java.io.*;
3
4  /** A set of useful static methods for interacting with a user via the console.
5  *
6  * @author Byron Weber Becker */
7  public class Prompt extends Object
8  {
9    private static final Scanner in = new Scanner(System.in);
10
11   /** Prompt the user to enter an integer.
12   * @param prompt The prompting message for the user.
13   * @return The integer entered by the user. */
14   public static int forInt(String prompt)
15   { while (true)
16     { System.out.print(prompt);
17       if (Prompt.in.hasNextInt())
18       { int answer = Prompt.in.nextInt();
19         Prompt.in.nextLine(); // consume remaining input
```

PATTERN

Error-Checked Input

Listing 9-9: *A class providing error-checked reading of an integer and a filename* (continued)

```
            return answer;
        } else
        { String input = Prompt.in.nextLine();
          System.out.println("Error: " + input
                + " not recognized as an integer such as '10' or '-3'.");
        }
      }
    }

    /** Prompt the user for a file to use as input.
     * @param prompt The prompting message for the user.
     * @return A File object representing a file that exists and is readable. */
    public static File forInputFile(String prompt)
    { while (true)
      { System.out.print(prompt);
        String name = in.nextLine().trim();
        File f = new File(name);
        if (!f.exists())
        { System.out.println("Error: " + name + " does not exist.");
        } else if (f.isDirectory())
        { System.out.println("Error: " + name + " is a directory.");
        } else if (!f.canRead())
        { System.out.println("Error: " + name + " is not readable.");
        } else
        { return f;
        }
      }
    }

    /** Prompt the user for a file to use as input.
     * @param prompt The prompting message for the user.
     * @return A Scanner object ready to read the file specified by the user. */
    public static Scanner forInputScanner(String prompt)
    { try
      { return new Scanner(Prompt.forInputFile(prompt));
      } catch (FileNotFoundException ex)
      { // Shouldn't happen, given the work we do in forInputFile.
        System.out.println(ex.getMessage());
        System.exit(1);
      }
      return null; // for the compiler
    }
  }
```

Using `Prompt`

The completed program for interacting with the user to ask for a specific Web server log file to process and the minimum size of returned page to print in a report is shown in Listing 9-10. Notice that it uses the `Prompt` class in lines 11 and 14.

FIND THE CODE

ch09/userIO/

Listing 9-10: *A program that processes a Web server log based on user input*

```
1  import java.util.Scanner;
2
3  /** List files in a user-specified Web server log that meet a minimum size criteria.
4   *  Report the number of files that are printed.
5   *
6   *  @author Byron Weber Becker */
7  public class ListFilesBySize
8  {
9    public static void main(String[] args)
10   { // Prompt for the file to process.
11     Scanner in = Prompt.forInputScanner("Web server log name: ");
12
13     // Get the minimum size from the user.
14     int minSize = Prompt.forInt("Minimum served file size: ");
15
16     // Process the files.
17     int count = 0;
18     while (in.hasNextLine())
19     { ServerRecord sr = new ServerRecord(in);
20       if (sr.getSize() >= minSize)
21       { System.out.println(sr.toString());
22         count++;
23       }
24     }
25
26     // Close the input file and report the count.
27     in.close();
28     System.out.println(count + " files served were at least "
29                              + minSize + " bytes.");
30   }
31 }
```

9.5 Command Interpreters

The techniques for interacting with users shown in the previous section are adequate if the user must always enter the same information in the same order each time the program is run. There are many programs, however, for which more flexibility is desired. One way to achieve more flexibility (without the work of implementing a graphical user interface) is to write a **command interpreter**. A command interpreter repeatedly waits for the user to enter a command, and then it executes the command.

9.5.1 Using a Command Interpreter

To illustrate the principles involved, we will write a program called `LogExplorer`, which will process a Web server log, selecting records that meet criteria set by the user. The user interface will allow the user to:

- Specify a string to find in the client host name field.
- Specify a minimum served file size.
- Specify whether each matching record is shown.
- Specify whether the number of matching records is shown.
- Display a help message.
- Process a specified file with the current settings.

Furthermore, the structure of the program will make it easy to add functionality. An example of running the program is shown in Figure 9-6. The prompt for a command is >. Information required by the command is entered on the same line. As you can see, commands are usually terse.

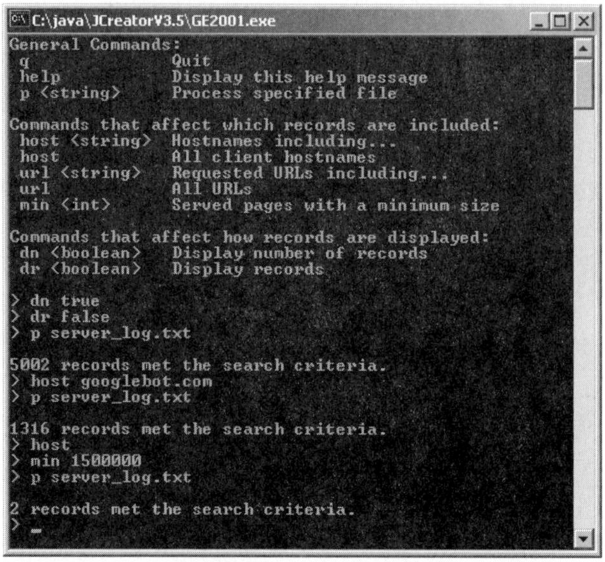

```
C:\java\JCreatorV3.5\GE2001.exe
General Commands:
 q               Quit
 help            Display this help message
 p <string>      Process specified file

Commands that affect which records are included:
 host <string>   Hostnames including...
 host            All client hostnames
 url <string>    Requested URLs including...
 url             All URLs
 min <int>       Served pages with a minimum size

Commands that affect how records are displayed:
 dn <boolean>    Display number of records
 dr <boolean>    Display records

> dn true
> dr false
> p server_log.txt

5002 records met the search criteria.
> host googlebot.com
> p server_log.txt

1316 records met the search criteria.
> host
> min 1500000
> p server_log.txt

2 records met the search criteria.
> _
```

(figure 9-6)

Running a program that uses a command interpreter

9.5.2 Implementing a Command Interpreter

The pseudocode for a command interpreter is as follows:

LOOKING AHEAD

A graphical user interface uses a similar loop, called an "event loop."

```
while (the quit command has not been received)
{ get a command
  execute the command
}
```

We get the command by prompting the user to enter a command and reading it from the console. Executing the command is done with a cascading-`if` statement, often in a separate method.

Unfortunately, a pair of commands like *host* and *host <string>* complicates matters. The problem lies with determining whether the user has entered a string following the *host* command. It would seem that calling `hasNext()` would easily resolve that question, but it doesn't—`Scanner` will keep looking up to the end of the "file" to see if there is a token present. But when scanning `System.in` (the console), there is no end of file. `Scanner` waits for whatever the user types in next (ignoring white space, including Enter). When the user does type something, `Scanner` returns `true`. `hasNextLine` has similar issues.

We can solve this problem by reading the input a line at a time—but then we have to find out what is on the line, as indicated by the following pseudocode:

PATTERN

Command Interpreter

```
while (the quit command has not been received)
{ System.out.print("> ");                    // Prompt for a command.
  String line = in.nextLine();
  get the command and argument (if there is one) out of the line
  execute the command
}
```

KEY IDEA

The `Scanner` class can also process strings.

Now there is the problem of extracting the information on the line to find the command (such as *host*, *min*, or *p*) and the argument (such as *googlebot.com* or *1500000*), if there is one. Fortunately, `Scanner` can scan strings in addition to files. For example, the following code will print "`host true googlebot.com`".

```
Scanner s = new Scanner("host googlebot.com");
System.out.print(s.next());
System.out.print(s.hasNext());
System.out.print(s.next());
```

The following code fragment will print "`host false`".

```
Scanner s = new Scanner("host");
System.out.print(s.next());
System.out.print(s.hasNext());
```

By creating a `Scanner` for each line we read, we can determine exactly what is on it. With this insight, we can structure the command interpreter as follows:

```
Scanner cin = new Scanner(System.in);
while (the quit command has not been received)
{ System.out.print("> ");
  String line = cin.nextLine();
  Scanner lineScanner = new Scanner(line);
  String cmd = lineScanner.next();
  if (cmd is "host" and line has another token)
  { remember given hostname for next search
  } else if (cmd is "host")
  { next search will be for all hosts
  } else if (cmd is "min" and line has an integer)
  { remember given minimum size for the next search
  } else if (cmd is "p" and line has another token)
  { process the given file with the settings given by previous commands
  ...
  } else
  { error message
  }
}
```

These ideas are implemented in the class shown in Listing 9-11. The command interpreter is at lines 23–31; it delegates the task of executing the commands to `executeCmd`, lines 35–59.

The heart of the actual application is the `processFile` method. It's overloaded, with one method taking a `String` parameter (the filename) and another taking a `Scanner` object. The first one handles the messy details of opening the file and then calls the second one, which actually does the work. It reads each record in the log, printing and counting those that match the criteria. The task of deciding which records match is delegated to `includeRecord`.

`LogExplorer` works as shown, but the design could be improved by separating the user interface from the rest of the program. Section 9.5.3 explains how.

FIND THE CODE

ch09/logExplorer/

Listing 9-11: *The `LogExplorer` program with an integrated command interpreter*

```
1 import java.io.*;
2 import java.util.Scanner;
3
4 /** Explore a Web server log by displaying/counting records meeting user-specified criteria.
5 *
6 * @author Byron Weber Becker */
7 public class LogExplorer extends Object
8 {
```

Listing 9-11: *The* `LogExplorer` *program with an integrated command interpreter* (continued)

```
// Search criteria
private String searchHost = "";          // String to find in hostname.
private int minSize = 0;                 // Minimum size of returned page.

private boolean done = false;            // Received quit command yet?
private boolean displayNum = true;       // Display # of matching records?
private boolean displayRec = true;       // Display each matching record?

/** Create a new explorer object; displays all log records by default. */
public LogExplorer()
{ super();
}

/** Interpret the commands entered by the user. */
public void cmdInterpreter()
{ this.displayHelp();
  Scanner cin = new Scanner(System.in);
  while (!this.done)
  { System.out.print("> ");
    String line = cin.nextLine();
    this.executeCmd(line);
  }
}

/** Execute one line entered by the user.
 *  @param cmdLine The one line of command and optional arguments to execute. */
private void executeCmd(String cmdLine)
{ Scanner line = new Scanner(cmdLine);
  if (line.hasNext())
  { String cmd = line.next();
    if (cmd.equals("host") && line.hasNext())
    { this.searchHost = line.next();
    } else if (cmd.equals("host"))
    { this.searchHost = "";
    } else if (cmd.equals("min") && line.hasNextInt())
    { this.minSize = line.nextInt();
    } else if (cmd.equals("p") && line.hasNext())
    { this.processFile(line.next());
    } else if (cmd.equals("q"))
    { this.done = true;
    } else if (cmd.equals("help"))
    { this.displayHelp();
    } else if (cmd.equals("dr") && line.hasNextBoolean())
```

PATTERN
Command Interpreter

Listing 9-11: *The* `LogExplorer` *program with an integrated command interpreter* (continued)

```
      { this.displayRec = line.nextBoolean();
      } else if (cmd.equals("dn") && line.hasNextBoolean())
      { this.displayNum = line.nextBoolean();
      } else
      { System.out.println("Command '" + line + "' not recognized.");
      }
    }
  }

  /** Process a log file via the specified Scanner object. Display and count each record that
  *  matches the criteria set previously.
  *  @param in A scanner for the input file to process. */
  private void processFile(Scanner in)
  { int count = 0;
    while (in.hasNextLine())
    { ServerRecord sr = new ServerRecord(in);
      if (this.includeRecord(sr))
      { if (this.displayRec)
        { this.displayRecord(sr);
        }
        count++;
      }
    }
    if (this.displayNum)
    { this.displayCount(count);
    }
  }

  /** Process the specified file.
  *  @param fName The name of the file to process. */
  private void processFile(String fName)
  { Scanner in = null;
    try
    { in = new Scanner(new File(fName));
      this.processFile(in);
      in.close();
    } catch (FileNotFoundException ex)
    {  System.err.println("Can't find file " +
          System.getProperty("user.dir") + "/" + fName + ".");
    }
  }

  /** Determine whether a record should be included in the report. Include records that meet
```

Listing 9-11: *The* `LogExplorer` *program with an integrated command interpreter* (continued)

```
     * ALL the specified criteria. If a criterion wasn't set (for example, no client host name was
     * specified), we need a way to ignore it, typically with an "or" condition. */
    private boolean includeRecord(ServerRecord sr)
    { return (this.searchHost.length() == 0 ||
                sr.hostnameContains(this.searchHost))
                && sr.getSize() >= this.minSize;
    }

    /** Display one record to the user.
     * @param sr The record to display. */
    private void displayRecord(ServerRecord sr)
    { System.out.printf("%-15s %s%n",
              sr.getIPAddress(), sr.getClientHostname());
      System.out.printf(" %5d%10d%5s %s%n",
              sr.getCompletionCode(), sr.getSize(),
              sr.getCommand(), sr.getURL());
    }

    /** Display the number of matching records.
     * @param count The number of matching records to display. */
    private void displayCount(int count)
    { System.out.println();
      System.out.println(count + " records met the search criteria.");
    }

    /** Display a help message. */
    private void displayHelp()
    { final String helpFmt = "%-14s %s%n";
      final PrintStream out = System.out;
      out.println("General Commands:");
      out.printf(helpFmt, "q", "Quit");
      out.printf(helpFmt, "help", "Display this help message");
      out.printf(helpFmt, "p <string>", "Process specified file");
      out.println();
      out.println("Commands that affect which records are included:");
      out.printf(helpFmt, "host <string>", "Hostnames including...");
      out.printf(helpFmt, "host", "All client hostnames");
      out.printf(helpFmt, "url <string>", "Requested URLs including...");
      out.printf(helpFmt, "url", "All URLs");
      out.printf(helpFmt, "min <int>", "Served pages with a minimum size");
      out.println();
      out.println("Commands that affect how records are displayed:");
      out.printf(helpFmt, "dn <boolean>", "Display number of records");
```

Listing 9-11: *The `LogExplorer` program with an integrated command interpreter* (continued)

```
138        out.printf(helpFmt, "dr <boolean>", "Display records");
139        out.println();
140    }
141 }
```

9.5.3 Separating the User Interface from the Model

The `LogExplorer` program shown in Listing 9-10 combines the code that solves the problem (the model) with the code that interacts with the user (the user interface, composed of a view and controller). By correctly separating these two aspects of the program, we can achieve the following benefits:

LOOKING BACK

Models, views, and controllers were discussed in Section 8.6.2.

- Separating these aspects makes the program easier to understand. In all but the simplest programs, it is easier to understand a program when each class has a specific focus. In this case, the model should focus on determining which records to display, and the user interface should focus on interacting with the user.
- Separating these aspects enables attaching different user interfaces to the model without changing the model. For example, an experienced user may use the program with a terse command interpreter that allows him to work quickly. An inexperienced user may use the program with a command interpreter that reads a command and then prompts for additional information. When a graphical user interface becomes available, the command interpreter can be replaced by it without changing the model.

Identifying Parts That Belong to the User Interface

We can begin by reviewing Listing 9-11 and identifying the parts that have to do with communicating with the user. They include the following:

- The `cmdInterpreter` method in lines 22–31
- The `executeCmd` method in lines 33–59
- The `displayRecord` method in lines 103–111
- The `displayCount` method in lines 113–118
- The `displayHelp` method in lines 120–140
- The `processFile` method's error message at lines 89–91
- The other `processFile` method's two `if` statements that determine whether each record or the total number of records is displayed to the user (lines 69 and 75)

➤ Three instance variables—`done`, `displayNum`, and `displayRec`—that control user interface functions (lines 13–15)

All of these elements will be moving to a new class named `CmdInterpreter`. With these parts gone, there won't be much left to the model (`LogExplorer`).

Setting Up Relationships between Classes

For these two classes to work together, `LogExplorer` will need to call the `displayRecord` and `displayCount` methods in `CmdInterpreter`. Similarly, the `CmdInterpreter` class will need to call methods such as `processFile` in the `LogExplorer` class. This implies that we need to set the classes up as shown in Figure 9-7.

(figure 9-7)

Structuring the `LogExplorer` *program*

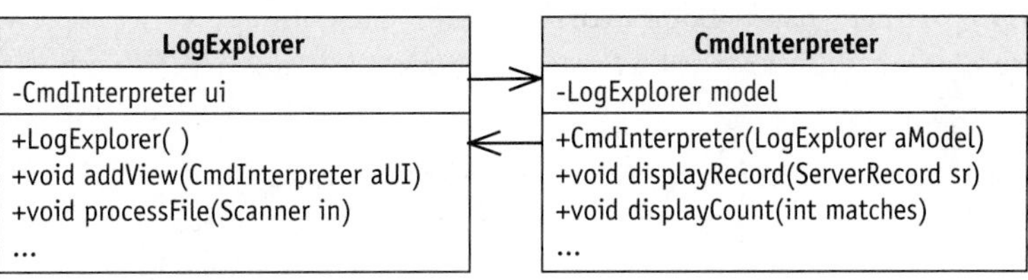

LOOKING BACK

Interfaces were discussed in Section 7.6.

However, implementing this class diagram will not allow us to change user interfaces, as we claimed earlier. With this implementation, the only user interface that can be used with `LogExplorer` is a class named `CmdInterpreter`. To fix this, we will define a Java interface declaring the methods `displayRecord` and `displayCount`. If `LogExplorer` uses this interface, then any user interface that implements it can be used with `LogExplorer`. Therefore, the high-level class diagram for the program will be the one shown in Figure 9-8.

(figure 9-8)

Structuring the `LogExplorer` *program with a Java interface*

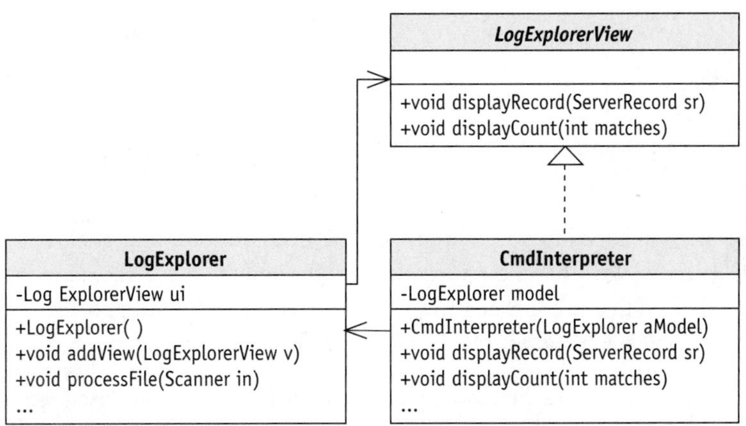

The program can be set up with these relationships using the following code fragments. The `main` method has the responsibility to create both the `LogExplorer` and the `CmdInterpreter` objects, as follows:

```
public static void main(String[] args)
{ LogExplorer explorer = new LogExplorer();
  CmdInterpreter cmd = new CmdInterpreter(explorer);

  cmd.cmdInterpreter();              // Run the command interpreter.
}
```

Notice that a reference to the `LogExplorer` object is passed to the `CmdInterpreter` constructor. This is used to set up the "`CmdInterpreter` has-a `LogExplorer`" relationship shown in Figure 9-8.

The "`LogExplorer` has-a `LogExplorerView`" relationship is set up when the `CmdInterpreter` constructor calls `LogExplorer`'s `addView` method with itself as the parameter, as follows:

```
 1 public class CmdInterpreter extends Object
 2                                implements LogExplorerView
 3 {
 4   private LogExplorer model;
 5
 6   public CmdInterpreter(LogExplorer aModel)
 7   { super();
 8     this.model = aModel;
 9     this.model.addView(this);
10   }
11 }
```

The `CmdInterpreter` class implements the `LogExplorerView` interface in line 2, as expected by the `LogExplorer` class.

Finishing Up

Just a little bit of cleanup remains to complete the reorganization of the `LogExplorer` program.

LOOKING AHEAD

Programming Project 9.10 asks you to complete the implementation.

First, the original user interface simply set the `searchHost` and `minSize` instance variables directly. Now that these variables and the code that sets them are in different classes, we'll need to add some methods to `LogExplorer` to give appropriate access to the variables. The methods, of course, are called from the user interface.

Second, the `processFile` method cannot remain `private`. The user interface will need to call it at the appropriate times.

Third, the original program determined inside the `processFile` method whether to display each matching record and whether to display the count of matching records. This, however, is more appropriately a function of the user interface. One way to handle this is for `processFile` to always call `displayRecord` and `displayCount`. These methods, in the user interface, can each include an `if` statement to determine whether they do anything.

9.6 Constructing a Library

In this chapter, the `ServerRecord` and `Prompt` classes have been used in several different programs. So far, this has been handled by simply making a copy of the class for each program that uses it. This, however, is not a good idea. Suppose the class needs to change because a bug is found, an enhancement is needed, or the file format is changed. In each of these cases, multiple copies of the class must be changed—an error-prone process that is a waste of time and energy.

KEY IDEA

Most programming languages have a way to make a library of reusable code. In Java, it's done with packages.

A better solution is to place reusable code—such as `ServerRecord` and `Prompt`—into a **library**. A library is a collection of resources that are meant to be used in many different programs. The concept of a library is implemented in Java with **packages**. A package is a collection of related classes that may contain subpackages. The classes in `becker.robots` constitute a library, as do the classes in `becker.util` and `java.awt`. A program accesses the classes in a package with the `import` statement.

Understanding how programs are compiled and run is important background for understanding how to use packages. Integrated development environments often hide these details, so we begin with a brief tour of compiling and running programs using a command line.

9.6.1 Compiling without an IDE

Most computers have a way to run programs from a command line. A simple program (one that uses only imports from the `java` and `javax` packages or no imports at all) can be compiled and run, as shown in Figure 9-9. The example is `ListFilesBySize`, taken from Listing 9-10 with two minor changes. First, the `ServerRecord` class has been modified to use a `String` instead of the `DateTime` class (to simplify the first example; it will be put back afterwards). Second, the program itself has been modified to print only the number of matching records to reduce the amount of output.

```
>cd d:/cs101/ch09/userIO/

>ls
ListFilesBySize.java  ServerRecord.java
Prompt.java           server_log.txt

>javac *.java

>ls
ListFilesBySize.class  ServerRecord.class
ListFilesBySize.java   ServerRecord.java
Prompt.class           server_log.txt
Prompt.java

>java -classpath d:/cs101/ch09/userIO/ ListFilesBySize
Server log to process: server_log.txt
Minimum file size: 1000000
5 files are at least 1000000 bytes.

>
```

(figure 9-9)

Compiling a program with no `import` *statements*

The five commands shown perform the following actions:

- `cd` changes into a new directory specified by the path `D:/cs101/ch09/userIO/`.
- `ls` lists the contents of the directory, showing the data file and the three `.java` files that make up the program.
- `javac` runs the Java compiler to translate the `.java` files into a form more easily understood by the computer. It puts the translation of each file into a file with the same name but replaces `.java` with `.class`. The `*.java` means any file in the working directory that ends with `.java`.
- `ls` lists the contents of the directory again. It shows the same files as before plus the newly created `.class` files.
- `java` runs the compiled program. It is told where to search for the program's `.class` files with `-classpath D:/cs101/ch09/userIO/`. The first part, `-classpath`, tells Java that the following path is the directory to search. The following three lines are the result of running the program.

A single dot (`.`) is an abbreviation for the current working directory. Therefore, a more succinct replacement for `-classpath D:/cs101/ch09/userIO/` is `-classpath .`.

With this background, we are now ready to return to understanding how to easily reuse classes by placing them in packages.

9.6.2 Creating and Using a Package

The `package` statement places a class into a named package. For example, the `Robot` class begins with the following statement:

```
package becker.robots;
```

Classes in the `becker.robots` package can be used by including the familiar statement `import becker.robots.*;`.

The package name should be unique. The recommended way to make it unique is to reverse your e-mail address. The author could use the reverse of `bwbecker@learningwithrobots.com`, as shown in the following package statement:

```
package com.learningwithrobots.bwbecker;
```

The `package` statement must be the first statement in the class, before any `import` statements or the `class` statement. However, comments may come before the `package` statement.

The `package` statement places constraints on the location of the file containing the source code. With the above `package` statement, the `ServerRecord` class must be located in the file `com/learningwithrobots/bwbecker/ServerRecord.java`. Notice that this path and name has three parts:

- The package name, but with the dots replaced with the directory separator character /
- The name of the class, `ServerRecord`
- The extension, `.java`

This is shown in Figure 9-10. Notice that the path beginning with `com/learn...` is not the entire path. We will need to tell the compiler about the first part, `D:/cs101/`.

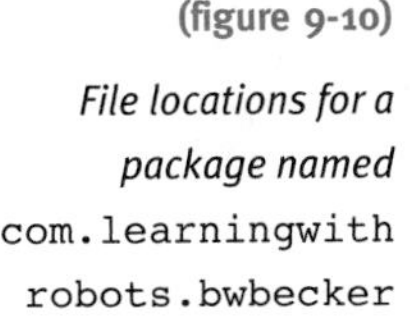

(figure 9-10)

File locations for a package named `com.learningwithrobots.bwbecker`

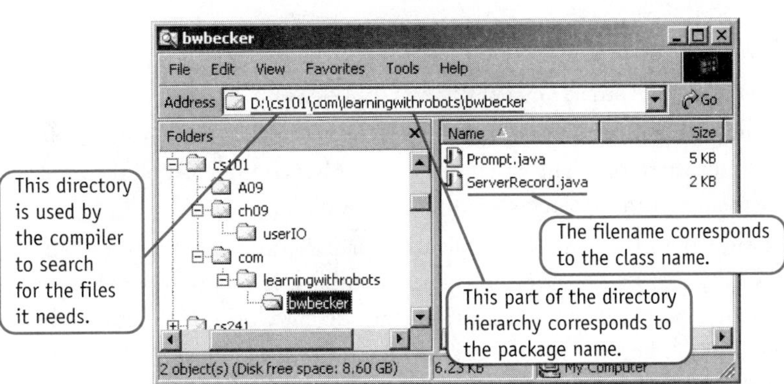

In summary, compared to the program compiled in Figure 9-9, we need to make the following changes:

- Add a `package` statement to `ServerRecord.java` and a similar one to `Prompt.java`.
- Move `ServerRecord.java` and `Prompt.java` to the locations specified by their new `package` statements. The location of `ServerRecord.java` is shown in Figure 9-10.
- Modify `ListFilesBySize.java` to `import` the classes in the new package.

We can compile the revised program as shown in Figure 9-11.

```
>cd d:/cs101/ch09/userIO/

>ls
ListFilesBySize.java  server_log.txt

>javac -sourcepath d:/cs101/ *.java

>ls
ListFilesBySize.class  server_log.txt
ListFilesBySize.java

>java -classpath "d:/cs101/;." ListFilesBySize
Server log to process: server_log.txt
Minimum file size: 1000000
5 files are at least 1000000 bytes.

>
```

(figure 9-11)

Compiling the `ListFilesBySize` *program using packages*

The five commands shown perform the following actions:

- `cd` changes to the directory containing our program.
- `ls` shows that the directory now contains only `ListFilesBySize`. The other files have been moved to the library to facilitate easy reuse by many programs.
- `javac` runs the Java compiler. The compiler is told where to search for the packages it needs with `-sourcepath D:/cs101/`. When the compiler attempts to import `com.learningwithrobots.bwbecker.ServerRecord`, it looks in `D:/cs101/com/learningwithrobots/bwbecker/`.
- `ls` shows that only the `.class` file for `ListFilesBySize` has been added to the current directory. The other files were also compiled, but their `.class` files were left with the corresponding `.java` files.
- `java` runs the program. Now, because our class files are in several different places, the `-classpath` option is more complex. It lists two paths, separated by a semicolon (`;`). The second path is the current working directory, abbreviated with "`.`". Because of the semicolon, the entire list must be placed in double quotes. The first path specifies where to start the search for classes in the `bwbecker` package. The second path specifies where to find `ListFilesBySize`.

The preceding explanation may seem complex, but it's worth it because we can now write many programs that use the `ServerRecord` and `Prompt` classes. No matter how many programs use them, we have only one copy of the `.java` files—that is, only one copy to enhance or debug. Furthermore, we can use them simply by specifying a source path and a class path to the compiler. For commonly used classes, these are big advantages.

9.6.3 Using `.jar` Files

You may remember that we simplified `ServerRecord` somewhat to avoid using the `DateTime` class. To address that issue, assume that `ServerRecord` once again imports and uses `becker.util.DateTime`.

The complication is that we don't have the source code to `DateTime` like we have for `ServerRecord`. The `.class` files for `DateTime`, the robot classes, and many others are all stored in a single file named `becker.jar`. Storing them all in a `.jar` file makes them easier to distribute to other people. The `.jar` extension means **Java Archive**.

The `javac` command will need those `.class` files to compile the program. We tell it where to look for them by adding the `-classpath` option. Likewise, the `java` command will need the classes to run the program. Therefore, we must add the `.jar` file to its classpath as well. All this is shown in Figure 9-12. The `.jar` file is in the directory `D:/cs101/`.

(figure 9-12)

Compiling with classes in a `.jar` file

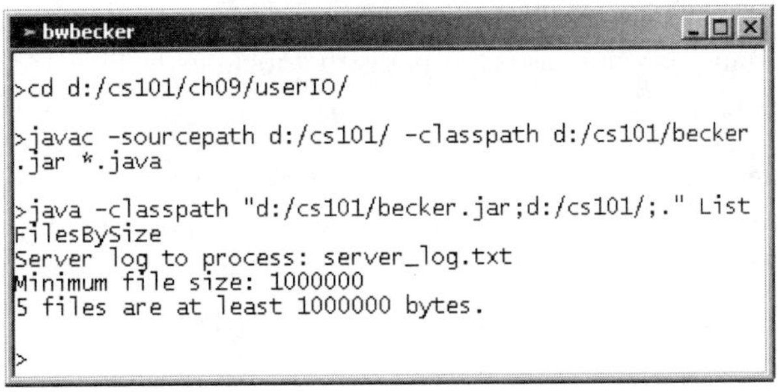

```
bwbecker
>cd d:/cs101/ch09/userIO/

>javac -sourcepath d:/cs101/ -classpath d:/cs101/becker
.jar *.java

>java -classpath "d:/cs101/becker.jar;d:/cs101/;." List
FilesBySize
Server log to process: server_log.txt
Minimum file size: 1000000
5 files are at least 1000000 bytes.

>
```

We may also want to put our own classes into a `.jar` file to make them easier to manage. This is done with a command named `jar`, as shown in Figure 9-13.

```
>cd d:/cs101/

>ls
A09  becker.jar  ch09  com

>jar -cf cs101Lib.jar com/learningwithrobots/bwbecker/*
.class

>ls
A09  becker.jar  ch09  com  cs101Lib.jar

>cd ch09/userIO/

>javac -classpath "d:/cs101/cs101Lib.jar;d:/cs101/becke
r.jar" *.java

>java -classpath "d:/cs101/cs101Lib.jar;d:/cs101/becker
.jar;." ListFilesBySize
Server log to process: server_log.txt
Minimum file size: 1000000
5 files are at least 1000000 bytes.

>
```

(figure 9-13)

Creating and using a `.jar` *file*

The crucial differences from what we've done before are as follows:

- `cd` changes to the directory we've been using for the source and class path for our package, `D:/cs101`.
- `jar` creates a new `.jar` file named `cs101Lib.jar`. The `.class` files to put into it are specified with the last part of the command, `*.class`. The asterisk (`*`) means to include every file ending in `.class`. In this situation, that would be `ServerRecord.class` and `Prompt.class`.
- `javac` and `java` now use class paths that include the new `.jar` file instead of `D:/cs101/`.

Fortunately, integrated development environments, which you probably use, know about source paths and class paths. Look for these terms among the IDE's settings; the documentation should explain how to include the path or `.jar` file for your personal library.

9.7 Streams (advanced)

Java's input and output library is based on the concept of **streams**. A stream is an ordered collection of information that moves from a **source** to a destination, or **sink**. It is similar to a stream of water flowing from a source (a spring or a lake) to a sink (the ocean).

Streams can be categorized using three questions:

- Is it an **input stream**, which carries information from a source to the program, or an **output stream**, which carries information from the program to a sink?

- Is it a **character stream**, which carries information in the form of 16-bit Unicode characters (usually human readable), or a **byte stream**, which carries binary information such as images or sounds in 8-bit bytes?
- Is it a **provider stream** that provides information from a source or to a sink, or is it a **processing stream** that processes or transforms information as it flows between a source and a sink?

Take `Scanner` as an example. `Scanner` is an input stream because the program uses it to get input from a source. It reads information as characters, either from a user or a file, and is thus a character stream. Finally, `Scanner` is a processing stream because it processes consecutive characters in the stream into higher-level constructs, such as an entire string or an integer. To do this, it makes use of an underlying provider stream. When we use `Scanner` to read from the console, for example, the provider stream is `System.in`.

`PrintWriter` is categorized much like `Scanner` except that it is an output stream that writes characters rather than bytes. It, too, is a processing stream because it processes higher-level constructs into the individual characters it writes out. Like `Scanner`, it uses an underlying provider stream to do the actual writing.

The philosophy of the Java I/O (input/output) library is that each class should do one thing well, and that each class should combine easily with other classes to obtain the strengths of both. Covering all the possibilities is beyond the scope of this textbook. Instead, we will provide an orientation and direct interested readers to other sources, such as the online Java Tutorial at *http://java.sun.com/docs/books/tutorial/index.html.*

9.7.1 Character Input Streams

The core class for character input is `Reader`. It's core method is `read`, which reads one or more characters from the source. `Reader` is extended to form four provider streams, corresponding to four different kinds of sources:

- `FileReader`: reads characters from a file
- `StringReader`: reads characters from a `String`; ultimately, this allows you to use `next`, `nextInt`, and similar methods in `Scanner` to read information from a `String` as easily as you can from a file.
- `CharArrayReader`: similar to `StringReader`
- `PipedReader`: reads characters that are produced by another thread in the program

Using these provider streams directly is not very easy. All they really provide is the ability to read a sequence of characters. A number of processing streams are provided to help form those characters into useful information. To use a processing stream, you must first construct a provider stream for it to use. Then, pass the provider stream to the processing stream's constructor. For example, BufferedReader is a processing stream that has a method to read an entire line of characters at once. It could be used like this:

```
// Construct a buffered reader that processes input from a file
FileReader fileIn = new FileReader("phoneBook.txt");
BufferedReader buffIn = new BufferedReader(fileIn);

// Read and process each line of characters in the file.
String line = buffIn.readLine();
while (line != null)
{ // process the line here
  line = buffIn.readLine();
}
buffIn.close();
```

The processing streams that work with character input streams include:

- BufferedReader: reads an entire line of characters at once
- LineNumberReader: reads an entire line at once and provides a count of the lines read so far
- PushbackReader: allows a program to read some characters, examine them, and then push them back on the stream to be read again at a later time
- Scanner: divides the input stream into tokens and provides conversion of each token into appropriate types, such as int

Scanner is the most sophisticated of the processing streams. As we have already seen, it provides many methods to convert the raw stream of characters into useful information. It also has some convenience constructors to make it easier to use. For example, one constructor takes a string as an argument and automatically uses it to construct a StringReader to use as the source. Another constructor takes a File object as an argument and automatically constructs a FileReader to use as the source.

9.7.2 Character Output Streams

There are many similarities between character input streams and character output streams. Just as Reader is the core class for input, Writer is the core class for output, providing a write method to write one or more characters to the sink. It is extended four times, each class corresponding to four different kinds of sinks. The four subclasses are FileWriter, StringWriter, CharArrayWriter, and PipedWriter. A FileWriter writes characters to a file, of course. A StringWriter appends the characters to a string.

Only two interesting processing streams are associated with character output streams. One is BufferedWriter, which collects a large number of characters and then writes them all at once using its provider stream. BufferedWriter is typically combined with a `FileWriter` because writing only one character at a time to a file is tremendously inefficient.

The other interesting processing stream is `PrintWriter`, which has already been discussed. It adds methods such as `print`, `println`, and `printf` to convert types such as `int` and `double` into individual characters.

9.7.3 Byte Streams

The structure of the byte input streams is similar to character input streams. A core class, `InputStream`, is extended four times to provide bytes from files, string buffers, byte arrays, and pipes. A similar set of classes provide processing streams to buffer the stream, count the lines, and push back information previously read.

Similarly, the byte output streams mirror the character output streams. The core class, `OutputStream`, is extended to write bytes to files, byte arrays, and pipes. `BufferedOutputStream` and `PrintStream` are analogous to `BufferedWriter` and `PrintWriter`.

9.8 GUI: File Choosers and Images

Files are used with graphical user interfaces in a number of ways. One is to ask the user for a filename with an easy-to-use dialog box, as shown in Figure 9-14. Another is to read an image from a file and paint it on the screen. The image could have been created with a separate editor or taken with a camera.

(figure 9-14)

Dialog box displayed by `JFileChooser` *to choose a file*

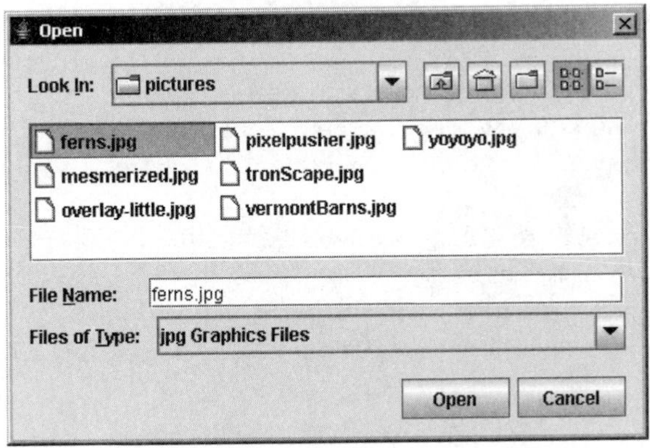

9.8.1 Using `JFileChooser`

Using a professional dialog box to obtain a filename from a user is easy, thanks to the libraries that come with Java. The test program in Listing 9-12 displays a dialog box like the one shown in Figure 9-14.

In lines 13–14, the dialog box is created and shown to the user. The method `showOpenDialog` is meant for opening existing files. Another method, `showSaveDialog`, is for saving a file. The difference is the text placed on the buttons and the title bar.

The user's action is returned as an integer from `showOpenDialog`, and could be `APPROVE_OPTION` (the user chose a file), `CANCEL_OPTION` (the user cancelled the dialog without choosing a file), or `ERROR_OPTION` (an error occurred). If the user chooses a file, the full path and filename can be obtained with the code shown in line 19. Of course, your program should open and use the file instead of only printing the name on the console.

FIND THE CODE

ch09/fileChooser/

Listing 9-12: *A program demonstrating the use of* `JFileChooser`

```
1  import javax.swing.JFileChooser;
2  import java.io.File;
3
4  /** A program testing the operation of JFileChooser.
5   *
6   *  @author Byron Weber Becker */
7  public class Main extends Object
8  {
9     public static void main(String[ ] args)
10    { System.out.println("Ready to get a filename.");
11
12       // construct the dialog and show it to the user
13       JFileChooser chooser = new JFileChooser();
14       int result = chooser.showOpenDialog(null);
15
16       if (result == JFileChooser.APPROVE_OPTION)
17       { // Open the file and use it
18          System.out.println("You chose '" +
19                chooser.getSelectedFile().getPath());
20       }
21    }
22 }
```

Typically your program will be interested only certain kinds of files. For example, the next section shows how to display certain kinds of images on the screen. These images are normally stored in files that end with an extension of either `.gif` or `.jpg`. With the help of the `FileExtensionFilter` class, shown in Listing 9-13, `JFileChooser` will show only the relevant classes. Use it by adding the following lines between lines 13 and 14 in Listing 9-12:

```
chooser.addChoosableFileFilter(
          new FileExtensionFilter(".jpg", "jpg Graphics Files"));
chooser.addChoosableFileFilter(
          new FileExtensionFilter(".gif", "gif Graphics Files"));
```

`FileExtensionFilter` works by overriding the `accept` method in its superclass. `JFileChooser` calls this method once for each file or directory in the current directory. If `accept` returns `true`, the file or directory is displayed so the user can choose it.

FIND THE CODE

ch09/fileChooser/

Listing 9-13: *A filter used by* `JFileChooser` *to show only files with the specified extension*

```
import javax.swing.filechooser.FileFilter;
import java.io.File;

/** A class used to filter out some files so that JFileChooser only shows files with a
 * specified extension.
 *
 * @author Byron Weber Becker */
public class FileExtensionFilter extends FileFilter
{
  private String ext;
  private String descr;

  /** Accept files ending with the given extension.
   * @param extension The extension to accept (e.g., ".jpg")
   * @param description A description of the file accepted */
  public FileExtensionFilter(String extension,
                             String description)
  { super();
    this.ext = extension.toLowerCase();
    this.descr = description;
  }

  /** Decide whether or not the given file should be displayed. In our case, include
   * directories as well as files with a name ending in the specified extension.
   * @param f A description of one file.
   * @return True if the file should be displayed to the user; false otherwise. */
```

Listing 9-13: *A filter used by* `JFileChooser` *to show only files with the specified extension* (continued)

```
    public boolean accept(File f)
    { return f.isDirectory() ||
                  f.getName().toLowerCase().endsWith(this.ext);
    }

    /** Return the description of the files accepted.
     *  @return A description of the files this filter accepts.*/
    public String getDescription()
    { return this.descr;
    }
}
```

9.8.2 Displaying Images from a File

The program in Listing 9-12 can be easily modified to display an image from a file. The program currently prints the name of the file selected by the user (see lines 18–19). The new program will replace lines 18–19 with the following code to create a component that displays an image it reads from a file, and then shows that component in a frame. Notice that the filename is obtained from the chooser and passed to `ImageComponent`'s constructor.

```
// Create a component to display an image
ImageComponent imageComp = new
      ImageComponent(chooser.getSelectedFile().getPath());

// Display the image component in a frame
JFrame f = new JFrame("Image");
f.setContentPane(imageComp);
f.setSize(500, 500);
f.setDefaultCloseOperation(JFrame.EXIT_ON_CLOSE);
f.setVisible(true);
```

LOOKING BACK

This code uses the Display a Frame pattern. See Section 1.7.5.

The source code for `ImageComponent` is more interesting and is shown in Listing 9-14. It is passed the name of the image file via the parameter in the constructor. A class from the Java library, `ImageIcon`, is used to read the image from the file. Supported types of images include `.gif`, `.jpg`, and `.png`. Once the image is loaded, the preferred size for the component is set to the image's size. If the preferred size is not set, the `JFrame` will make it so small that it can't be seen.

As with previous extensions of `JComponent`, the `paintComponent` method is overridden to do the painting. In the past, the `Graphics` parameter, `g`, has been used to call such methods as `drawRect` and `fillOval`. Here, it is used in line 24 to paint the image read from the file. The second and third parameters give the desired location of the upper-left corner of the image. The zero values shown here put the image in the upper-left corner of the component.

`drawImage` is overloaded. Another version includes two more parameters to specify the painted image's width and height. This is useful if you want to scale the image. It is also possible to use `drawImage` to draw a background image and then add details on top with calls to `drawRect` and similar methods.

FIND THE CODE

ch09/displayImage/

Listing 9-14: *A new kind of component that displays an image from a file*

```
import java.awt.*;
import javax.swing.*;

/** A component that paints an image stored in a file.
 *
 * @author Byron Weber Becker */
public class ImageComponent extends JComponent
{
  private ImageIcon image;

  /** Construct the new component.
   * @param fileName The file where the image is stored. */
  public ImageComponent(String fileName)
  { super();
    this.image = new ImageIcon(fileName);
    this.setPreferredSize(new Dimension(
                         this.image.getIconWidth(),
                         this.image.getIconHeight()));
  }

  /** Paint this component, including its image. */
  public void paintComponent(Graphics g)
  { super.paintComponent(g);
    g.drawImage(this.image.getImage(), 0, 0, null);
  }
}
```

9.9 Patterns

9.9.1 The Open File for Input Pattern

Name: Open File for Input

Context: You need to read information stored in a file.

Solution: Open the file and use `Scanner` to obtain the individual tokens within the file. The following template applies:

```
Scanner «in» = null;
try
{ «in» = new Scanner(new File(«fileName»));
} catch (FileNotFoundException ex)
{ System.out.println(ex.getMessage());
  System.out.println("in " + System.getProperty("user.dir"));
  System.exit(-1);
}
«statements to read file»
«in».close();
```

Consequences: The file is opened for reading. If the file does not exist, an exception is thrown and the program stops.

Related Patterns:

- The Open File for Output pattern is used to write information to a file.
- The Process File pattern depends on this pattern to open the file.

9.9.2 The Open File for Output Pattern

This pattern is almost identical to Open File for Input.

9.9.3 The Process File Pattern

Name: Process File

Context: You need to process all of the records in a data file, one after another.

Solution: Use an instance of `Scanner` to provide the records, one at a time. A `while` loop that tests for the end of the file controls the processing.

```
Scanner in = this.openFile(«fileName»);
while (in.hasNextLine())
{ «read one record»
  «process one record»
}

in.close();
```

A record is often represented by an instance of a class. Reading it is often best done in a constructor or factory method belonging to that class.

LOOKING AHEAD

A factory method is simply a `static` *method that creates and returns an object. Listing 12-11 contains an example.*

Consequences: The file is read from beginning to end. If it must be processed again, the file must be reopened to reset the file cursor back to the beginning of the file.

Related Patterns:

- This pattern uses the Open File for Input pattern to open the file. In the above template, the pattern would be implemented in the `openFile` method.
- The action of processing one record is often delegated using the Construct Record from File pattern.

9.9.4 The Construct Record from File Pattern

Writing this pattern is an exercise for the student in Written Exercise 9.2.

9.9.5 The Error-Checked Input Pattern

Name: Error-Checked Input

Context: Input from the user is required. Because the user may enter erroneous data, error checking is appropriate.

Solution: The pattern to use depends on the amount of error checking required. If only the correct type of data (integer, double, and so on) matters, then a simpler pattern will suffice. In the following, *«hasNext»* is a method such as `hasNextInt` or `hasNextDouble` in the `Scanner` class, and *«next»* is the corresponding method to get the next value, such as `nextInt` or `nextDouble`.

```
Scanner in = new Scanner(System.in);
...
System.out.print(«initialPrompt»);
while (!in.«hasNext»())        // type might be Int or Double or ...
{ in.nextLine();               // skip offending input
  System.out.print(«errorPrompt»);
}
«type» «varName» = in.«next»();
```

If the value entered matters as well, then a more complex pattern is appropriate:

```
Scanner in = new Scanner(System.in);
...
«type» answer = «initialValue»;    // will contain the answer
boolean ok = false;
System.out.print(«prompt»);
while (!ok)
{ if (in.«hasNext»())
  { answer = in.«next»();
    if («testForCorrectValues»)
    { ok = true;
    } else
    { System.out.print(«incorrectValueErrorPrompt»);
    }
  } else
  { System.out.print(«incorrectTypeErrorPrompt»);
    in.nextLine();
 }
}
```

Consequences: The user will be repeatedly prompted until a correct value is input. There is no provision for the user to cancel the operation or otherwise break out of the loop. Due to the amount of code, this pattern is best contained in a method.

Related Pattern: This pattern may be used by the Command Interpreter pattern.

9.9.6 The Command Interpreter Pattern

Name: Command Interpreter

Context: You are writing a program in which the user can give commands from a prompt. You need to interpret the commands and execute code corresponding to each one.

Solution: Implement a command interpreter with the following pseudocode.

```
show initial instructions
while (the user is not done)
{ display current program state or prompt
  get a command from the user
  interpret and execute the command
}
```

Getting the command from the user is often as simple as getting one word or token using `Scanner`. The step to interpret and execute the command is usually performed with a cascading-`if` statement. A helper method should be used if more than one or two lines of code are needed to execute the command.

Consequences: By using a cascading-`if` statement, the task of interpreting and executing the commands is given a regular structure. This makes it easier to understand the program and to extend it with new commands.

Related Pattern: The Error-Checked Input pattern is an important part of making the command interpreter respond appropriately to user errors.

9.10 Summary and Concept Map

Programs may read information from either the user (via the console) or a file. Reading is typically done with an instance of `Scanner`, which has a variety of methods to acquire data and convert it to an appropriate type. Another set of methods can determine if data of a specified type is available.

Programs may also write information to either the console, using `System.out`, or a file, using `PrintWriter`. The location of a file is specified by a path and filename. Paths may be either relative to the current working directory or absolute.

It is usually appropriate to represent a record in a file with a class, delegating the input and output to methods in the class. If several programs use the same file, it is appropriate to put the class into a package to make reuse easy.

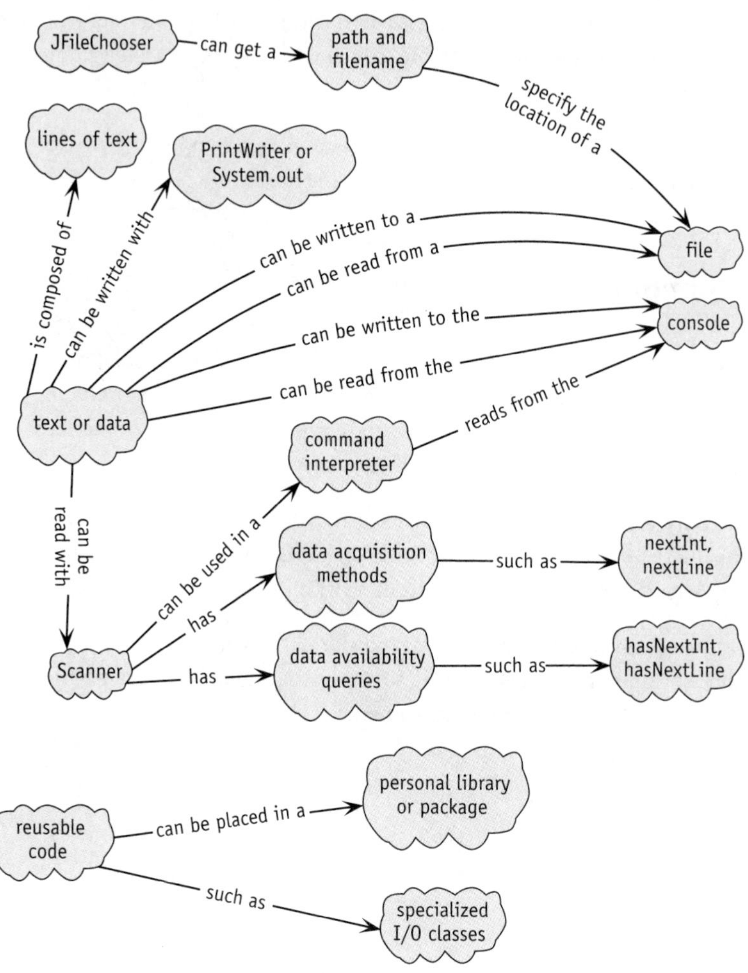

Problem Set

Written Exercises

9.1 Review Listing 9-4. Explain why the `else`-clause in lines 13–15 could be removed with no change in the function of the program.

9.2 Write the Construct Record from File pattern. See Section 9.2.1 for background and examples.

9.3 Describe how to modify the command interpreter in Listing 9-11 to allow the user to enter either a word or a single character for each command. For example, to set the minimum file size, the user can enter `m`, `M`, `min`, or even `MiN` followed by the desired size.

9.4 Consider writing a simple telephone book program, which will keep names and telephone numbers of friends and businesses you call frequently in a file. The program itself should repeatedly prompt for a name, displaying all of the matching names and their associated telephone numbers.

a. Develop two different file formats for your program. Describe both, indicating which one you consider the better design and why.

b. Write pseudocode for the program. Include prompting, opening and closing files, and the search algorithm.

c. Suppose the specification is modified so that the program prints only the first name it finds, if it finds one at all. Consider the following pseudocode and describe the bug(s) in each algorithm.

```
while (true)
{ read the next record
  if (at the end of the file)
  { print message
    exit the loop
  }
  if (found the name)
  { print message
    exit the loop
  }
}
```

```
while (not at end of file)
{ read the next record
  if (found the name)
  { print message
    exit the loop
  }
}
if (at end of file)
{ print not found message
}
```

Programming Exercises

9.5 The package `becker.xtras.hangman` includes classes implementing the game of Hangman. Figure 7-13 has an image of the user interface. Extend `SampleHangman` and override the `newGame()` method to open a file, choose a random phrase, and then call the other `newGame` method with the chosen phrase. Create a file with the phrases. Create a `main` method, as shown in the package overview, to run your program.

9.6 Write a program that reads a text file and writes it to a new file, performing one of the following transformations. (*Note:* Other than the described transformation, the two files should be identical.)

a. Write the new file entirely in uppercase letters.

b. Double space the new file.

c. Make an identical copy of the file except for a statement at the end telling how many characters, words (tokens), and lines it contains. For the purpose of counting characters, ignore newline characters.

d. Reverse the characters in each line of the file. If the first line of input is "It was a dark and stormy night." the first line of output should be ".thgin ymrots dna krad a saw tI".

e. Put a prefix such as > at the beginning of each line of output.

f. Output only those lines that contain a given string.

g. Output the first *n* lines of the input file.

Programming Projects

9.7 Write a calculator that accepts input like the one shown in Figure 9-15. The program has a variable that stores the calculation as performed so far. When a line begins with a number, that number goes in to the variable. An operation such as + or * is remembered so that the next number can be combined appropriately with the number currently stored in the variable. An equal sign causes the current value of the variable to be printed. A line that starts with an operator such as / continues to use the number in the variable from previous operations. In addition to the operators shown, implement subtraction.

(figure 9-15)

Calculator program

9.8 Write your own version of the `Prompt` class (see Listing 9-9).

a. Implement the `forInt`, `forInputFile`, and `forInputScanner` shown in Listing 9-9.

b. Implement `forBoolean`, `forDouble`, and `forToken`. Each take a prompt as a parameter and return a `boolean`, `double`, or single `String` token, respectively.

c. Implement `forInt` with three parameters: a prompt, a minimum value, and a maximum value. The method returns an integer value between the minimum and the maximum, inclusive. The method invocation `forInt("Enter your choice", 1, 5)` should produce the prompt "`Enter your choice [1..5]: `". Entering text that is outside of this range or is not an integer should produce a prompt explaining the error.

d. Implement `forInt` with two parameters: a prompt and a default value. The method returns the integer value entered by the user, or the default value if the user only hits Enter. Of course, if the user enters something else, an appropriate error message is displayed and the user is given another opportunity. The method invocation `forInt("Enter your choice", 0)` should produce the prompt "`Enter your choice (0): `". (*Hint*: To detect only Enter, you will need to read the response using `nextLine`, removing leading and trailing blanks with the `trim` method in `String`. If the result is not empty, you will need to determine if it contains an integer. Check the constructors in `Scanner` for ideas.)

e. Implement `forString` with two parameters: a prompt and a list of valid values. The method returns the entered string, but only if the response appears in the list of valid values. If it does not, print the list of valid values and ask the user to try again. (*Hint*: The list of valid values could be either a string with appropriate delimiters—such as "`|exit|stop|go|`"—or one of the collection classes discussed in Section 8.5.)

f. Put the `Prompt` class in an appropriately named package for easy reuse. In a different directory, create a simple program that uses at least one of the methods from your package. Run it.

9.9 Write a class named `HangmanTextUI` that can be used to play a text-based version of Hangman. Your program will have a similar structure to the `LogExplorer` program described in Section 9.5. You may use the `SampleHangman` class in `becker.xtras.hangman` to implement the actual game.

9.10 Complete the reorganization of the model and user interface for the `LogExplorer` program as described in Section 9.5.3.

a. Complete the class diagram shown in Figure 9-8.

b. If necessary, download the files for `/ch09/logExplorer2/` and complete the program it contains. It includes the original `LogExplorer` class plus the `LogExplorerView` Java interface and a graphical user interface. The `main` method will ask you which interface you would like to use.

Modifying the program as described will allow you to choose between the command interpreter and the graphical user interface when the program runs. The graphical user interface does not require any changes as long as the methods named `setSearchHost` and `setMinSize` are provided in `LogExplorer`.

9.11 Implement all the parts of Programming Exercise 9.6, providing a command interpreter to specify which transformation should be performed. Commands to the command interpreter should be of the following form:

```
reverse <in> [<out>]
prefix <str> <in> [<out>]
first <int> <in> [<out>]
```

`<in>` is the name of an input file. `<out>` is the name of an output file. Placing `<out>` in square brackets means that entering an output file is optional, in which case output is displayed on the screen. `<str>` and `<int>` indicate that a string or an integer is expected, respectively.

9.12 Write a program to display a slide show on the computer's display by combining the programs in Section 9.8. Modify the `ImageComponent` class shown in Listing 9-14 to include the method `setImage(String fileName)`. When called, the component should read the image from the named file and display it. Recall the function of `repaint`, as discussed in Section 6.7.2. Set the preferred size of the component to 500 x 500 instead of basing it on a specific image.

a. Use `JFileChooser` to obtain a file named by the user. Each record in the file will contain an image filename and the number of seconds to display the image. The image files are assumed to be in the same directory as the file listing them (which may be different from the program's working directory).

b. Use `JFileChooser` to obtain the list of images to show. `JFileChooser` can allow the user to select several files at the same time by holding down the Shift or Control keys while selecting files. To enable this behavior, the programmer must call the chooser's `setMultiSelectionEnabled` method before the chooser is shown. The list of files chosen can be retrieved with the following statement:

```
List<File> fNames = Arrays.asList(
                               chooser.getSelectedFiles());
```

Use a *foreach* loop, as discussed in Section 8.5.1, to access each file. Use `Thread.sleep` to pause for two seconds between each image.

9.13 A cipher transforms text to conceal its meaning. One of the simplest ciphers is the Caesar cipher, which replaces each letter in the message with the letter n positions away in the alphabet, where n remains constant. For example, when $n = 3$, `A` is replaced with `D`, `B` with `E`, `C` with `F`, and so on. Letters at the end of the alphabet will wrap around to be replaced with letters at the beginning of the alphabet. See Figure 9-16.

(figure 9-16)

Caesar cipher

Using $n = 3$ to encode the message `MEET AT DAWN` results in the encoded message `PHHW DW GDZQ`. One can do this in a program by placing the letters in a string. For each letter in the message, find its position, p, in the string and write the letter at $(p + n)$ % 26 to the output file. Any character not in the string is written as itself. For example, period (`.`) will appear identically in both the input and the output.

a. Write a program implementing the Caesar cipher described above except that the string includes all the letters present on your keyboard. Your program should ask the user for an offset, an input file, and an output file. When your program is complete, encode a message with $n = 5$. You should be able to decode the message by running the program again with $n = -5$. Be careful with the `%` operator, however. If the first operand is negative, the answer will be negative as well.

b. The Caesar cipher is easy to break because there are so few combinations to try. One could easily write a program to simply try each value of n. A better approach asks the user for a key, for example `SMOKESTACK`, and a value of n. Insert the letters in the key into a string, ignoring duplicates. Then add all the remaining characters to encode in order, skipping any that are already present. For example, with the key `SMOKESTACK`, one would have the following string: `SMOKETACBDFGHIJLNPQRUVWXYZ`. Now encode the message as with the Caesar cipher. Of course, this is more effective if the string contains lowercase letters, digits, punctuation, and so on. It is also more effective if the key contains some of these characters as well. Write a program implementing this encoding scheme. Verify that you can use the same program to decode the message.

c. The keyed cipher in part (b) is still relatively easy to break using letter frequencies. Assuming the coded message is written in English, the characters that appear most often in the coded message are likely to be the most frequently occurring English letters: `E`, `T`, `A`, `R`, and `N`.

One way around this is use a key again. Suppose the key is `CIPHER` and the message to encode is `MEET AT DAWN`. The first letter of the message, `M`, is encoded as `O` using an offset of 2 because there are two letters between the beginning of the alphabet and `C`, the first letter of the key. See Figure 9-17.

(figure 9-17)
First step of using a key

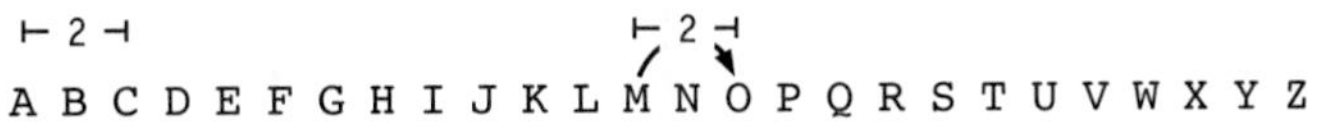

```
|- 2 -|                 |- 2 -|
A B C D E F G H I J K L M N O P Q R S T U V W X Y Z
```

Similarly, the second letter of the message, `E`, is encoded using the second letter of the key to determine the offset. The offset is 8 because there are 8 letters between the beginning of the alphabet and `I`. Therefore `E` is encoded as `M`. See Figure 9-18.

(figure 9-18)
Second step of using a key

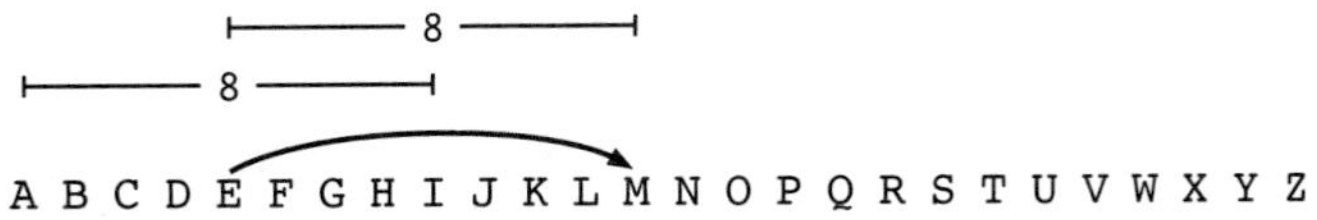

```
        |------ 8 ------|
|------ 8 ------|
A B C D E F G H I J K L M N O P Q R S T U V W X Y Z
```

Notice, however, that the second `E` in `MEET` is encoded differently than the first one. That's because the third letter of the key is `P`. Therefore, an offset of 15 is used instead of an offset of `8`, encoding `E` as `T`. See Figure 9-19.

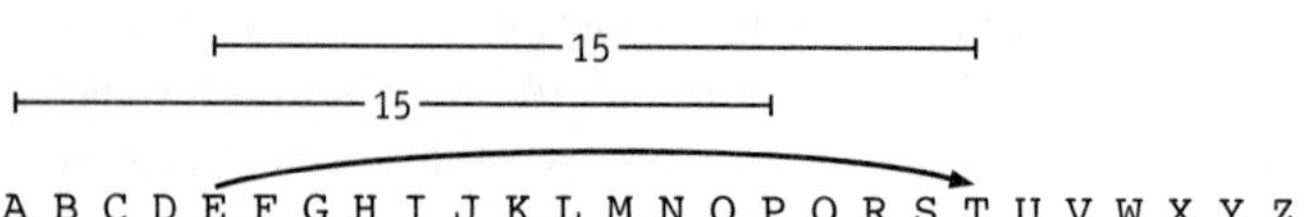

(figure 9-19)

Using an offset of 15 to encode `E` *as* `T`

When the end of the key is reached, simply wrap around to the beginning to encode the next letter of the message. Implement this improved algorithm in the class `Cipher3.java`.

Chapter 10 Arrays

Chapter Objectives

After studying this chapter, you should be able to:

- Store data in an array, access a single element, process all elements, search for a particular element, and put the elements in order.
- Declare, allocate, and initialize an array.
- Handle changing numbers of elements in an array, including inserting a new element and deleting an old one.
- Enlarge or shrink the size of an array.
- Manipulate data stored in a multi-dimensional array.

We often work with lists in our daily lives: grocery lists, to-do lists, lists of books needed for a particular course, the invitation list for our next party, and so on. To be useful, computers must also work with lists: a list of the `Thing` objects in a `City`, a list of concert tickets, or a list of bank accounts, to identify just a few.

There are several ways to implement lists in Java. One of the most fundamental approaches is with an array, a kind of variable. Once a list is stored in the array we can do many things: tick off the third item in our to-do list, print the entire list of books for a course, search our list of invitations to verify that it includes James Gosling, or sort the list alphabetically.

In Section 8.5, we studied classes in the Java library that are similar to arrays in that they store a collection of objects. Some of these, such as `ArrayList`, are thinly disguised arrays. Others, such as `HashMap`, provide more sophisticated ways to find objects in the collection. But underneath it all, many of these classes use an array.

10.1 Using Arrays

Big Brothers/Big Sisters is a charitable association that matches men and women with boys and girls between the ages of 6 and 16 who could benefit from an older friend and role model. In many cases the boys and girls are missing a parent due to death or divorce and don't have many positive role models in their lives.

KEY IDEA

See www.bbbsc.ca or www.bbbsa.org for more information on Big Brothers/ Big Sisters.

Obviously, an association like Big Brothers/Big Sisters keeps lists. One of the most crucial is the list of "bigs" (the adults) and "littles" (the girls and boys) participating in the association. In this chapter we will consider a computer program that maintains a list of `Person` objects (see Figure 10-1). We will learn how to print the entire list of people or just the people that meet certain qualifications, such as being a six-year-old girl. We will learn how to search the list for a specific person and learn to find the person that meets a maximum or minimum criterion (such as the oldest or youngest). Of course, all these techniques will apply to lists of other kinds of objects as well.

KEY IDEA

There are many algorithms that work with lists of things.

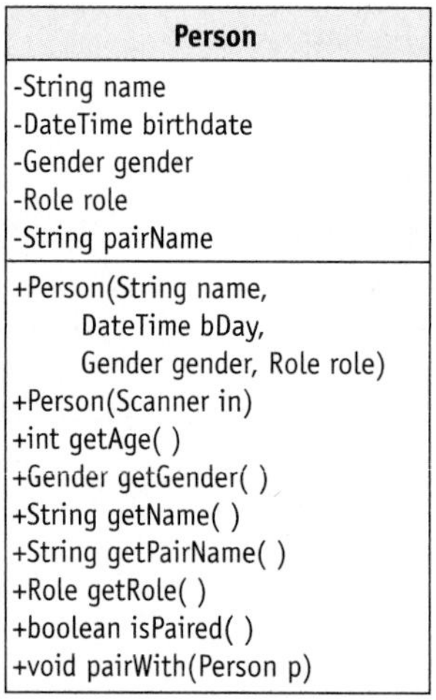

Person
-String name -DateTime birthdate -Gender gender -Role role -String pairName
+Person(String name, DateTime bDay, Gender gender, Role role) +Person(Scanner in) +int getAge( ) +Gender getGender( ) +String getName( ) +String getPairName( ) +Role getRole( ) +boolean isPaired( ) +void pairWith(Person p)

(figure 10-1)

Class diagram for `Person`

The simplified version of `Person`, shown in Figure 10-1, uses two enumerations: `Gender` and `Role`. The first enumeration provides the values `MALE` and `FEMALE`; the `Role` enumeration provides the values `BIG` to represent an adult participant and `LITTLE` to represent a young person. The `pairWith` command will pair this person with the person, `p`, specified as a parameter. It does this by setting the `pairName` appropriately in both objects.

LOOKING BACK

Enumerations are new in Java 1.5 and are discussed in Section 7.3.4.

Throughout this section, we will assume that we have an array named `persons` containing a list of `Person` objects. In Section 10.2, we will learn how to create such a variable and fill it with data.

10.1.1 Visualizing an Array

LOOKING BACK

Object diagrams were first discussed in Chapter 1. References were discussed in Section 8.2.

An object diagram for an array will require showing many `Person` objects. The diagram will become quite large if we use our usual format for each `Person` object (see Figure 10-2). To avoid this problem, we will abbreviate each person object in the diagram as shown in Figure 10-3.

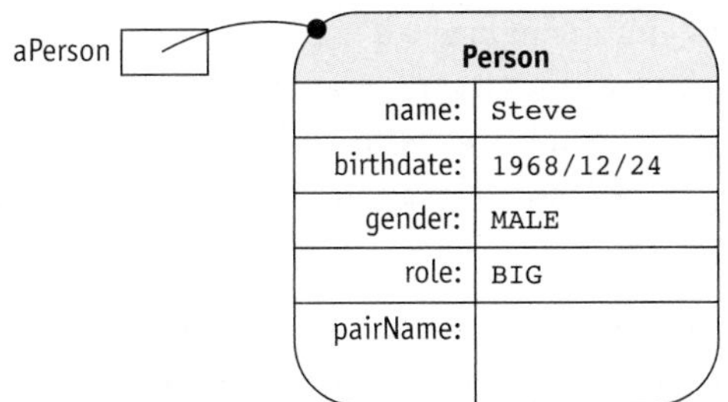

(figure 10-2)

Object diagram showing a variable referring to a `Person` *object*

aPerson

Steve, 1968/12/24, M, B

(figure 10-3)

Abbreviated object diagram

In both diagrams, the box labeled `aPerson` is a variable that refers to an object—the round-cornered box labeled `Person`.

So, what does an array look like? Figure 10-4 shows a visualization of an array of `Person` objects. The reference variable `persons` refers to an array object. The array object refers to many `Person` objects. Each reference, called an **element** of the array, is numbered beginning with zero. This number is called the **index**.

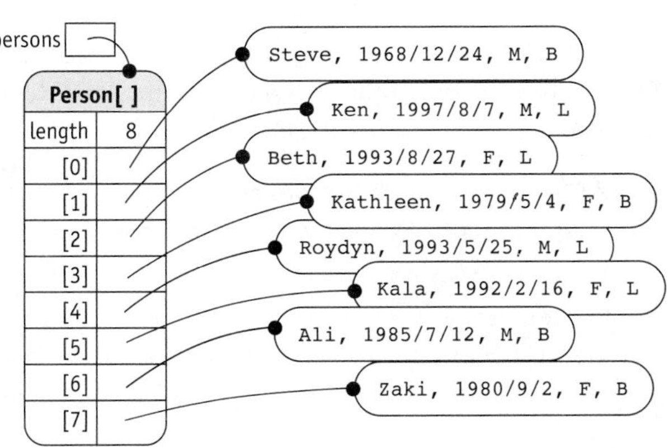

(figure 10-4)

Visualizing an array of `Person` *objects*

Notice that an array is illustrated almost exactly like other kinds of objects. Similarities include a variable, such as `persons`, that refers to the array object just as the variable `karel` referred to a `Robot` object in earlier chapters. An array object contains a public final instance variable named `length`, but has no methods. `length` stores the number of elements in the array.

The crucial difference between arrays and objects is that the array has instance variables that are accessed with square brackets and a number instead of a name. This is illustrated in Figure 10-4 with variables named `[0]`, `[1]`, and so on. The numbering always starts at zero. This language rule often causes beginning programmers grief because most people naturally begin numbering with one. Furthermore, the indices run from zero to one less than the number stored in `length`. For example, in Figure 10-4, `length` is `8` but the indices run from `0` to `7`.

KEY IDEA

Elements in an array are numbered beginning with zero.

The fact that the elements in the array are numbered gives them an order. It makes sense to speak of the first element (the element numbered `0`), the second element, and the last element.

KEY IDEA

Each element has an index giving its position in the array.

10.1.2 Accessing One Array Element

Accessing a specific element in an array is as easy as accessing a normal variable—except that the index of the desired element must also be specified. If we had a simple variable named `aPerson` we could print the name with the following line of code:

```
System.out.println(aPerson.getName());
```

Printing the name of the first person in our array is almost as easy. Instead of only naming the variable, we name the array and the position of the element we want:

```
System.out.println(persons[0].getName());
```

The index of the desired element is given by appending square brackets to the name of the array. The index appears between the brackets. You may use the result in exactly the same ways that you use a variable of the same type.

KEY IDEA

Arrays are indexed with square brackets and an integer expression.

Here is another code fragment that shows the `persons` array in use. In each case, `persons` is followed by the index of a specific element in the array.

```
// Check if Kathleen (see Figure 10-4) is a "Big"
if (persons[3].getRole() == Role.BIG)
{ System.out.println(persons[3].getName() + " is a Big.");
}
```

KEY IDEA

An element in an array can be assigned to another variable.

It is also possible to assign a reference from the array to a regular variable. For example, the previous code fragment could have been written like this:

```
1 Person kathy;
2 // Check if Kathleen (see Figure 10-4) is a "Big"
3 kathy = persons[3];
4 if (kathy.getRole() == Role.BIG)
5 { System.out.println(kathy.getName() + " is a Big.");
6 }
```

The effect of the reference assignment in line 3 is just like assigning references between non-array variables and is traced in Figure 10-5. Assigning a reference from an array to an appropriately named temporary variable can make code much more understandable.

(figure 10-5)

Tracing a reference assignment using an array and a non-array variable

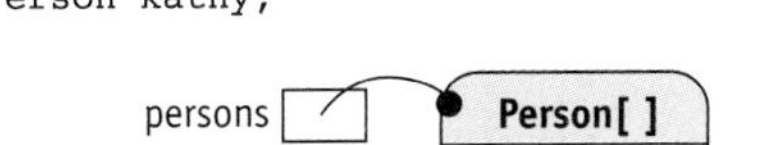

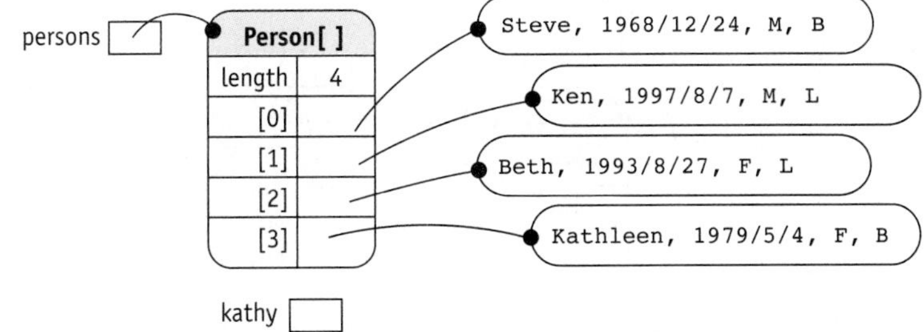


```
kathy = persons[3];
```

persons

Person[ ]

length 4

[0]

[1]

[2]

[3]

Steve, 1968/12/24, M, B

Ken, 1997/8/7, M, L

Beth, 1993/8/27, F, L

Kathleen, 1979/5/4, F, B

kathy

References stored in an array may also be passed as arguments. For example, Kathleen and Beth could be paired as Big and Little Sisters with the following sequence of statements:

```
// Pair Kathleen and Beth
Person kathy = persons[3];
Person beth = persons[2];
kathy.pairWith(beth);
```

However, because elements of an array can be used just like a regular variable, we could also pair Kathleen and Beth this way:

```
// Pair Kathleen and Beth
persons[3].pairWith(persons[2]);
```

KEY IDEA

The golden rule for arrays: Do unto an array element as you would do unto a variable of the same type.

Finally, we can also assign a reference to an array element. For example, suppose Kathleen is replaced by her friend Claire. The following code constructs an object to represent Claire and then replaces the reference to Kathleen's object with a reference to Claire's object.

```
Person c = new Person("Claire", new DateTime(1981,4,14),
                                Gender.FEMALE, Role.BIG);
persons[3] = c;
```

This code fragment is traced in Figure 10-6.

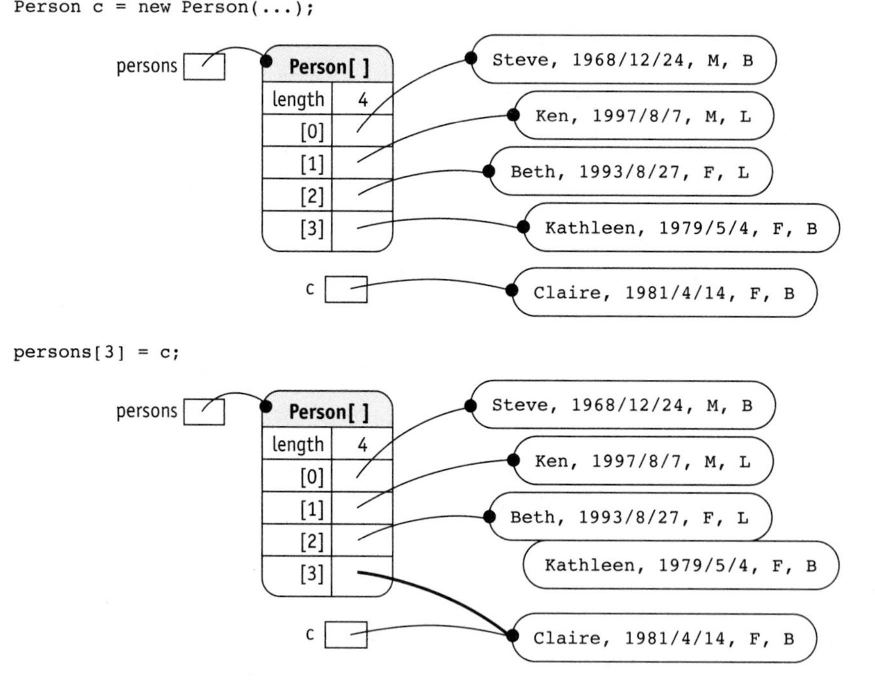

(figure 10-6)

Tracing the assignment of a reference into an array element

The object modeling Kathleen will be garbage collected unless another variable is referencing it.

LOOKING BACK

When an object has no references to it, the resources it uses are recycled. See Section 8.2.3.

10.1.3 Swapping Array Elements

We can easily exchange, or swap, two elements in an array. For example, suppose we wanted to switch the places of Ken and Beth within the array. A temporary variable is needed to store a reference to one of the elements while the swap is taking place. A method to perform a swap follows. It takes two arguments, the indices of the two elements to swap. Note that we are now assuming that `persons` is an instance variable.

FIND THE CODE

ch10/bbbs/

```
class BigBroBigSis extends Object
{ ... persons ...

  /** Swap the person object at index a with the object at index b. */
  public void swap(int a, int b)
  { Person temp = this.persons[a];
    this.persons[a] = this.persons[b];
    this.persons[b] = temp;
  }
}
```

After the `swap` method finishes executing, the temporary variable `temp` will cease to exist. The object it referenced, however, is still referenced by one element in the array and will not be garbage collected.

Figure 10-7 traces the execution of `swap(1, 2)`.

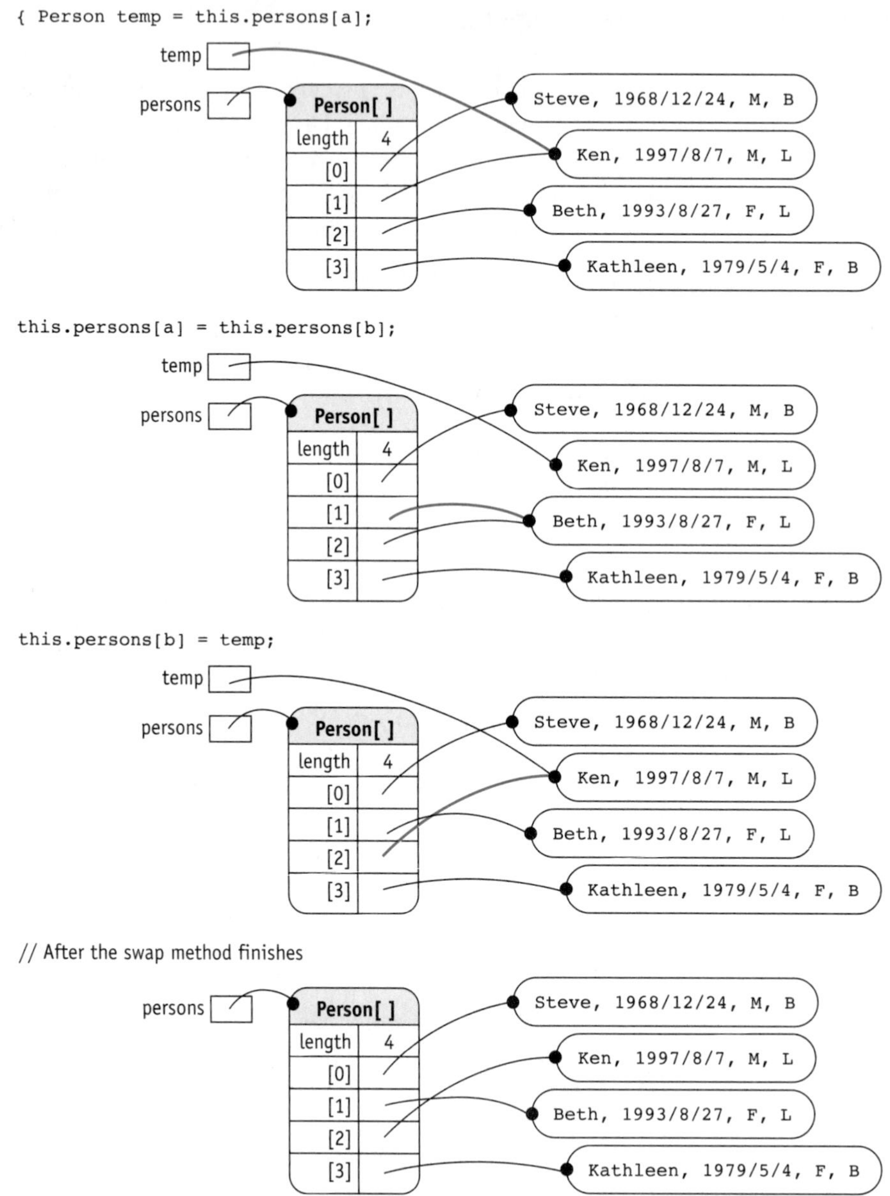

(figure 10-7)

Tracing `swap(1, 2)`; *the parameter* `a` *has the value* `1` *and* `b` *has the value* `2`

10.1.4 Processing All the Elements in an Array

Accessing an element of an array using a number may not seem particularly helpful. We could, after all, simply declare many variables that just have a number in each name:

```
Person person00;
Person person01;
Person person02;
```

But consider printing the name of each person in the list. Without an array, we would need statements for each named variable:

```
System.out.println(person00.getName());
System.out.println(person01.getName());
System.out.println(person02.getName());
    ...
```

If the list contained 1,000 people, the method to print their names would have about 1,000 lines. What a pain!

KEY IDEA

Arrays may be indexed with variables.

Fortunately, an array's index may be a variable—or any other expression that evaluates to an integer. This is where the power of arrays really becomes apparent. By putting the `println` statement inside a loop that increments a variable index, we can print the entire array with only three lines of code—no matter how many elements are in it.

PATTERN

Process All Elements

```
// Print the the name of every person in the array.
for (int i = 0; i < this.persons.length; i++)
{ System.out.println(this.persons[i].getName());
}
```

KEY IDEA

The number of elements in an array can be found with `.length`.

KEY IDEA

The last index is one less than the length of the array.

One item of note in this code fragment is the test in the `for` loop. The length of an array can always be found with the array's public final instance variable, `length`. If the array is as illustrated in Figure 10-4, `this.persons.length` will return `8`, the number of elements in the array. The index, `i`, takes values starting with `0` and ending with `7`, one less than the array's length. The length of the array is `8` but the index of the last element is one less, `7`. This is surely one of the most confusing aspects of arrays for beginning programmers.

So far we have encountered three different mechanisms to find the number of elements in a collection. Arrays use the public instance variable, `length`. The number of characters in a string is found with a method, `length()`. Finally, Java's collection classes such as `ArrayList` and `HashMap` also use a method to find the number of elements, but it has a different name, `size()`.

Another task that uses a loop to access each element in turn is to calculate the average age of the people in the array. For this task, we will use a variable to accumulate the ages while we loop through the array. After we have added all the ages, we'll divide by the length of the array to find the average age.

```
/** Calculate the average age of persons in the array. */
public double calcAverageAge()
{ int sumAges = 0;
  for (int i = 0; i < this.persons.length; i++)
  { Person p = this.persons[i];
    sumAges = sumAges + p.getAge();
  }
  return (double)sumAges/this.persons.length;
}
```

FIND THE CODE

ch10/bbbs/

The variable sumAges has the role of a gatherer: It gathers all the individual ages together. That value is then used to find the average age.

The loop controlling the index, i, is exactly the same in calcAverageAge as it was in the example to print all the names. This looping idiom—starting the index at 0 and incrementing by one as long as it is less than the length of the array—is extremely common when using arrays. Using it should become an automatic response for every programmer confronted with processing all the elements in an array.

Using the *foreach* Loop

You may remember that processing each element was also a common activity when using the collection classes, such as ArrayList and HashSet. In that situation, we used the *foreach* loop introduced with Java 1.5. The *foreach* loop also works with arrays. The following loop is equivalent to the one used in calcAverageAge, shown earlier.

```
for (Person p : this.persons)
{ sumAges = sumAges + p.getAge();
}
```

PATTERN

Process All Elements

The *foreach* loop is a generalized loop designed for use with unordered data structures such as maps and trees, for which asking for element *n* makes no sense. Hence, a *foreach* loop has no index. Instead, one element from the collection is provided for each iteration of the loop until all of the elements have been processed.

Programmers should be familiar with both looping styles. To emphasize this, we'll alternate between the two.

10.1.5 Processing Matching Elements

The method just written, calcAverageAge(), does not seem nearly as useful as a method to find the average age of only the littles or only the bigs. In the previous example, we added the age of every element in the array. To find the average age of only the littles, we want to include the ages only if the person is, in fact, a little. This logic is shown in the following pseudocode:

PATTERN

Process Matching Elements

```
for each person in the array
{ if (the person is a little)
  { include this person in the average
  }
}
return average
```

By adding the `if` statement inside the loop, we restrict its effects to only those elements that match the test. We process the matching elements. Notice that this pattern is very similar to the Process All Elements pattern.

This pseudocode translates to Java as follows:

FIND THE CODE

ch10/bbbs/

```
/** Find the average age of the "littles". */
public double getAverageLittleAge()
{ int sumAges = 0;
  int numLittles = 0;
  for (Person p : this.persons)
  { if (p.getRole() == Role.LITTLE)
    { sumAges = sumAges + p.getAge();
      numLittles = numLittles + 1;
    }
  }
  return (double) sumAges/numLittles;
}
```

LOOKING AHEAD

We'll learn how to generalize these methods with interfaces and polymorphism in Chapter 12.

Of course, by changing the test in the `if` statement, we change which objects we process. By changing the body of the `if` statement, we change how they are processed. For example, the following code fragment prints all the "bigs" who have not been paired with a "little."

```
// Print the names of unpaired "bigs"
for (int i = 0; i < this.persons.length; i++)
{ Person p = this.persons[i];
  if (p.getRole() == Person.BIG && !p.isPaired())
  { System.out.println(p.getName());
  }
}
```

10.1.6 Searching for a Specified Element

In one of our first examples we paired Beth, the person at index 2, with Kathleen, the person at index 3. But when we've decided to pair Beth and Kathleen, how do we find their positions in the array? We search for them.

Searching involves using some identifying information—such as a name, telephone number, or government identification number—and finding the corresponding object in the array. The identifying information is often called a key. If each key is unique, then at most one object in the array will match the key. Government identification numbers usually identify a unique person. On the other hand, names and telephone numbers may match several different people. In that case, a search generally returns the first object that matches.

In most cases we don't know that our search will be successful. It might be that no object matches the key. Therefore, we need a way to indicate failure. This is usually done by returning a special value such as `null` or `-1`. We can use `null` when the search method returns the object that was found and `-1` when the search method returns the array index where the object was found. We use `null` and `-1` for this role because `null` is never a legal reference to an object and `-1` is never a legal array index.

The easiest way to write a search method is a variation of the Process Matching Elements pattern—except that the "processing" is to exit the loop and return the answer. Suppose we are looking for a person using their name as a key. The logic is shown in the following pseudocode:

```
for each person in the array
{ if (the person's name matches the key)
  { exit the loop and return the person
  }
}
return null
```

PATTERN
Linear Search

We can exit the loop when we find the right person with the `return` statement. If we examine all of the people in the array and do not find one matching the key, the code will exit the loop at the bottom and return `null`, indicating the search failed.

In Java, this can be implemented as the method shown in Listing 10-1.

FIND THE CODE
ch10/bbbs/

PATTERN
Linear Search

Listing 10-1: *Searching an array*

```
/** Search for the first person object matching the given name.
 *  @param name The name of the person to find (the key).
 *  @return The first matching person object; null if there is none. */
public Person search(String name)
{ for (int i = 0; i < this.persons.length; i++)
  { Person p = this.persons[i];
    if (p.getName().equalsIgnoreCase(name))
    { return p;       // Success. Exit the loop and return the person found.
    }
  }
  return null;        // Failure.
}
```

The search method can also be written without the temporary variable p, as follows:

```
public Person search(String name)
{ for (int i = 0; i < this.persons.length; i++)
  { if (this.persons[i].getName().equalsIgnoreCase(name))
    { return this.persons[i];                    // Search succeeded.
    }
  }
  return null;                                   // Search failed.
}
```

LOOKING BACK

The Prompt *class was discussed in Section 9.4.2.*

We can use the search method to pair Kathleen and Beth as follows:

```
String bigName = Prompt.forString("Big's Name: ");
Person big = this.search(bigName);
String littleName = Prompt.forString("Little's Name: ");
Person little = this.search(littleName);
big.pairWith(little);                   // Dangerous code!
```

KEY IDEA

Always confirm a search was successful before proceeding.

The last line is marked as dangerous code because one or both of the searches may have failed, in which case big or little will contain the value null. Then a NullPointerException will be generated when the last line executes. The outcome of a search should *always* be verified and failure handled. The following is better code because it checks that the searches were successful.

```
String bigName = Prompt.forString("Big's Name: ");
Person big = this.search(bigName);
while (big == null)
{ System.out.println(bigName + " not found.");
  bigName = Prompt.forString("Big's Name: ");
  big = this.search(bigName);
}

// Repeat the above to find the little.

big.pairWith(little);    // Safe because both big and little have been found.
```

Another Approach to Searching

Many people think it is a bad idea to exit a loop early. They think that a line such as the following is like a contract between the programmer and the reader.

```
for (int i = 0; i < this.persons.length; i++)
```

The contract says this code will execute one time for every person in the array. Returning from the middle of the loop, like the search in Listing 10-1, breaks the contract.

A search algorithm that respects this view uses a `while` loop, which does not imply that every element in the array will be visited. The core idea is to repeatedly increment an index variable so that elements of the array are examined in turn. This is Step 1 of the Four-Step Process for constructing a `while` loop. The loop stops (Step 2) when either the end of the array is reached or the desired element is found, which ever comes first. Therefore, the loop continues as long as we have *not* reached the end of the array and we have not found the desired element. The loop is assembled (Step 3) with the results of Steps 1 and 2. Finally, after the loop (Step 4), we need to determine the answer and return it.

LOOKING BACK

The Four-Step Process for constructing a loop is discussed in Section 5.1.2.

The logic is shown in the following pseudocode:

```
while (not at the end of the array and matching object not found)
{ increment index to examine the next object
}
if (at the end of the array)
{ the search failed; return null
} else
{ the search succeeded; return the object
}
```

PATTERN

Linear Search

Making this pseudocode concrete to search for a person results in Listing 10-2.

FIND THE CODE

ch10/bbbs/

Listing 10-2: *Another approach to searching an array*

```
/** Search for the first person object matching the given name.
 *  @param name The name of the person to find (the key). */
public Person searchAlt(String name)
{ int i = 0;
  while (i < this.persons.length &&
          !this.persons[i].getName().equalsIgnoreCase(name))
  { i++;
  }

  if (i == this.persons.length)
  { return null;                   // Failure: got to the end without finding it.
  } else
  { return this.persons[i];   // Success.
  }
}
```

10.1.7 Finding an Extreme Element

An extreme element has the most of something or the least of something. It might be the person with the most age (oldest person) or the least age (youngest person). In other contexts, extreme elements might be the employee with the highest salary, the robot with the most things, the stock with the highest price/earnings ratio, or the name appearing first in dictionary ordering.

The strategy is to step through the array using the Process All Elements pattern. As we go, we'll remember the element that best meets the criteria so far. For each new element we examine, we'll ask if it meets the criteria better than the one we're remembering. If it does, remember it instead. Expressed in pseudocode, this algorithm is:

PATTERN

Find an Extreme

```
remember the first element as the best seen so far
for each remaining element in the array
{ if (the current element is better than the best seen so far)
  { remember the current element as the best seen so far
  }
}
```

Listing 10-3 applies this algorithm to the problem of finding the oldest person in the array. It begins, in line 3, by remembering the first person in the array (at index 0) as the oldest we've seen so far. This must be true, because we haven't looked at anyone else.

In line 5, we start looking at the rest of the people in the array. Lines 6–8 check if the current person matches the criteria better than `oldestSoFar`. If it does, the old value of `oldestSoFar` is replaced with `currentPerson`. When the loop ends, `oldestSoFar` will contain the oldest person in the entire list.

FIND THE CODE

ch10/bbbs/

Listing 10-3: *An example of finding an extreme element: the oldest person in the array*

```
1  /** Find oldest person in the list. (Assumes there is at least one person in the array.) */
2  public Person findOldestPerson()
3  { Person oldestSoFar = this.persons[0];
4
5    for (Person currentPerson : this.persons)
6    { if (currentPerson.getAge() > oldestSoFar.getAge())
7      { oldestSoFar = currentPerson;
8      }
9    }
10   return oldestSoFar;
11 }
```

What happens if two elements in the array meet the criteria equally well? What if two people have the same age? The algorithm given here will return the first one found and ignore anyone occurring later in the array who happens to be the same age. Changing the > in line 6 to >= results in finding the oldest person who appears last.

LOOKING AHEAD

Problem 10.4 makes the algorithm more accurate. In Section 10.3, we will learn how to return an array of people who all meet the same criteria.

Listing 10-3 returns the extreme element. Sometimes it is desirable to return the index of that element instead. Implementing such a method requires replacing the ***foreach*** loop with a regular `for` loop which makes the index explicit.

Java allows an empty array (an array with length zero), as shown in Figure 10-8.

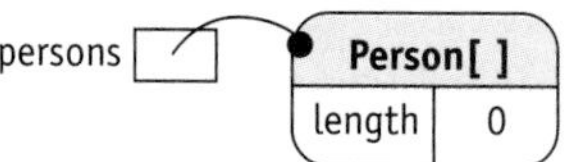

(figure 10-8)

Empty array

The code in Listing 10-3 will fail on such an array with an `ArrayIndexOutOfBoundsException` at line 3. Programmers should always be aware of such a possibility and decide how to handle it. Options include the following:

- Document that calling the method with an empty array is an error. Check for that situation and throw an exception, if required.
- Document the value the method will return if the array is empty. This would typically be `null` if the method returns the extreme element and `-1` if it returns the index of the extreme element. Of course, a check must be made for empty arrays so the correct value can be returned.

10.1.8 Sorting an Array

Collections of things are often easier to work with if they are sorted. Card players usually sort the collection of playing cards in their hands. A collection of words in a dictionary is usually sorted in alphabetical order, as are names in a telephone book. A collection of banking transactions are sorted by date on the bank statement.

Different algorithms can sort an array. Many of these algorithms have been given names: Insertion Sort, Selection Sort, QuickSort, HeapSort, ShellSort, MergeSort, and so on. Selection Sort is one of the easiest sorting algorithms to master. It builds on three patterns we have already seen: Process All Elements, Find an Extreme, and Swap Two Elements.

These sorting algorithms vary widely in their efficiency and in their ease of implementation. Insertion Sort and Selection Sort are easy to implement but slow to execute. QuickSort, HeapSort, ShellSort, and MergeSort are all much, much faster for large arrays but are more difficult to implement. They are typically included in a second year Computer Science course.

Understanding Selection Sort

Diagrams help us understand how a sort works. For simplicity, our diagrams will use an array of letters; when the array is sorted, the letters will be in alphabetical order.

The core idea of Selection Sort is to divide the array into two parts, as shown in Figure 10-9: the part that is already sorted (shown with a dark background) and the part that isn't (shown with a white background).

(figure 10-9)

Dividing an array into two parts

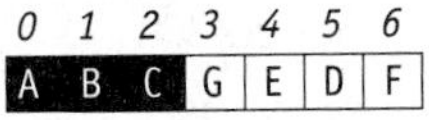

0	1	2	3	4	5	6
A	B	C	G	E	D	F

At each step in the algorithm, we extend the sorted portion of the array by one element. The next element to add to the sorted portion is the smallest element in the unsorted portion of the array, D. It goes in the position currently occupied by G. These two elements are highlighted in Figure 10-10.

(figure 10-10)

Extending the array

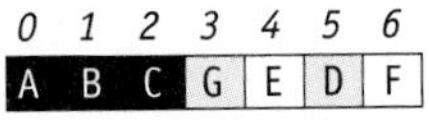

0	1	2	3	4	5	6
A	B	C	G	E	D	F

The last part of this step is to swap these two elements, thus extending the sorted portion of the array by one element. See Figure 10-11.

(figure 10-11)

Swapping the two elements; extending the sorted part of the array

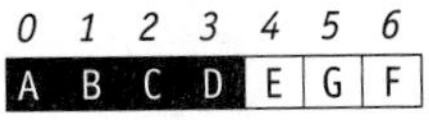

0	1	2	3	4	5	6
A	B	C	D	E	G	F

These two actions—finding the element that belongs in the next position and swapping it with the one already there—are performed repeatedly until the entire array is sorted. The algorithm begins with the sorted portion of the array being empty and the unsorted portion consuming the entire array. Figure 10-12 shows the entire sorting operation on a small array.

	0	1	2	3	4	5	6
The initial, unsorted array.	F	E	A	G	B	D	C
Find the element that belongs at index 0.	F	E	A	G	B	D	C
Swap elements at 0 and 2, extending sorted part.	A	E	F	G	B	D	C
Find the element that belongs at index 1.	A	E	F	G	B	D	C
Swap elements at 1 and 4, extending sorted part.	A	B	F	G	E	D	C
Find the element that belongs at index 2.	A	B	F	G	E	D	C
Swap elements at 2 and 6, extending sorted part.	A	B	C	G	E	D	F
Find the element that belongs at index 3.	A	B	C	G	E	D	F
Swap elements at 3 and 5, extending sorted part.	A	B	C	D	E	G	F
Find the element that belongs at index 4.	A	B	C	D	E	G	F
Swap elements at 4 and 4, extending sorted part.	A	B	C	D	E	G	F
Find the element that belongs at index 5.	A	B	C	D	E	G	F
Swap elements at 5 and 6, extending sorted part.	A	B	C	D	E	F	G

(figure 10-12)

Sorting an array of letters into alphabetical order

Two points in this example are worth elaboration. First, notice that when the element in the next to last position (index 5) is swapped into position, the last element (index 6) is automatically placed correctly as well. A moment's thought will explain why: When all the elements but the last are in their correct places, the last one must also be in its correct place because there is no where else for it to be.

Second, when it was time to look for the element to place at index 4, the element just happened to already be there. In this case, we would not need to perform the swapping step. We will anyway, however, because the "cure" of testing for this condition for every position in the array is worse than the "disease" of performing the swap every once in a while.

Coding Selection Sort

Based on this example, we see that two actions are repeated: Find the element that belongs in the next position and swap it with the one already there. These actions are performed for each position in the array, in ascending order, except for the last one. These observations yield the following pseudocode:

```
for each position in the array except the last
{ find the element that should go in this position
  swap that element with the element currently there
}
```

PATTERN

Selection Sort

In this case the *foreach* loop is inappropriate because we will *not* be examining every element in the array and because we need the index of the current element.

We can use this algorithm to sort our list of persons, but first we need to decide on the order we want. Sorted by age? Sorted by name in alphabetical order? Something else?

In the first example, we will sort the array by name. To do so, we'll use the `compareTo` method in the `String` class. If we have two `String` variables, `s1` and `s2`, then `s1.compareTo(s2)` returns `0` if the two strings are equal, a negative number if `s1` comes before `s2` in dictionary order, and a positive number if `s1` comes after `s2`.

Listing 10-4 shows the Selection Sort algorithm coded in Java. Let's look briefly at the patterns it uses.

First, the `sort` method uses a very slight variation of the Process All Elements pattern. The difference is that it processes all the elements except the last one. As noted earlier, by the time all the other elements are in their place, the last one must be in its place as well.

Second, the helper method uses a variation of the Find an Extreme pattern. It differs from the pattern in Section 10.1.7 in two ways:

- It finds the extreme in only the unsorted part of the array. We pass the index of the first element it should consider as an argument.
- We are concerned with the position of the extreme element, not the element itself. So our most-wanted holder variable in `findExtreme`, `indexBestSoFar`, stores the index of the best `Person` object seen so far rather than a reference to the object.

Third, the `swap` helper method is exactly as we saw before.

FIND THE CODE

ch10/bbbs/

PATTERN

Selection Sort

Listing 10-4: *Implementing Selection Sort to sort an array of* `Person` *objects by name*

```
public class BBBS extends Object
{ ... persons ...                    // an array of Person objects

   /** Sort the list of persons in alphabetical order by name. */
   public void sort()
   { for (int firstUnsorted = 0;
              firstUnsorted < this.persons.length-1;
              firstUnsorted++)
     { int extremeIndex = this.findExtreme(firstUnsorted);
       this.swap(firstUnsorted, extremeIndex);
     }
   }

   /** Find the extreme element in the unsorted portion of the array.
    * @param indexToStart The smallest index in the unsorted portion of the array.
    * @return The index of the extreme element. */
   private int findExtreme(int indexToStart)
   { int indexBestSoFar = indexToStart;
     String nameBestSoFar =
             this.persons[indexBestSoFar].getName();
```

Listing 10-4: *Implementing Selection Sort to sort an array of* `Person` *objects by name* (continued)

```
      for (int i=indexToStart+1; i<this.persons.length; i++)
      { String currPersonName = this.persons[i].getName();
        if (currPersonName.compareTo(nameBestSoFar) < 0)
        { indexBestSoFar = i;
          nameBestSoFar = this.persons[i].getName();
        }
      }
      return indexBestSoFar;
    }

    /** Swap the elements at indices a and b. */
    private void swap(int a, int b)
    { Person temp = this.persons[a];
      this.persons[a] = this.persons[b];
      this.persons[b] = temp;
    }
}
```

Sorting without Helper Methods (optional)

Sorting is performed so frequently that a great deal of effort has been spent to make the operation as fast as possible. The greatest gains in efficiency have been made by employing different algorithms. QuickSort and HeapSort are among the best, but are beyond the scope of this book.

Selection Sort can be made faster by eliminating the helper methods. Normally, eliminating helper methods just to speed up an algorithm is *not* a good idea. In this case, however, it may be justified because the algorithm is still relatively understandable. Listing 10-5 implements `sortByAge` as a single method. The age comparison is somewhat simpler than comparing names and so some temporary variables have been eliminated as well.

LOOKING AHEAD

This code will be made more flexible and reusable in Listing 12.18 in Section 12.5.

FIND THE CODE

ch10/bbbs/

Listing 10-5: *Implementing Selection Sort in a single method to sort an array of* `Person` *objects by age*

```
public class BigBroBigSis extends Object
{ ... persons ...              // An array of Person objects.

   /** Sort the persons array in increasing order by age. */
   public void sortByAge()
   { for (int firstUnsorted=0;
```

Listing 10-5: *Implementing Selection Sort in a single method to sort an array of* `Person` *objects by age* (continued)

PATTERN
Selection Sort

```
          firstUnsorted<this.persons.length-1;
          firstUnsorted++)
      { // Find the index of the youngest unsorted person.
        int extremeIndex = firstUnsorted;
        for (int i = firstUnsorted + 1;
                 i < this.persons.length; i++)
        { if (this.persons[i].getAge() <
                this.persons[extremeIndex].getAge())
          { extremeIndex = i;
          }
        }

        // Swap the youngest unsorted person with the person at firstUnsorted.
        Person temp = this.persons[extremeIndex];
        this.persons[extremeIndex] =
                                    this.persons[firstUnsorted];
        this.persons[firstUnsorted] = temp;
      }
    }
}
```

Sorting with the Java Library

Sorting an array is a very common activity and so it's natural that the Java library provides support for it via the `java.util.Arrays` class. It provides methods to sort arrays of all of the primitive types as well as arrays of objects.

The ordering of the primitive types is defined naturally by their values. Not so with arrays of objects. When sorting an array of `Person` objects, for example, how does the library sort know whether to sort by age or name or some other criteria?

The library sorts use two different approaches, both of which are explained in Chapter 12. One approach depends on the objects being sorted implementing the `Comparable` interface. This interface specifies a single method, `compareTo`, that compares two objects and returns a number indicating which should come first. Classes that implement this interface include `String`, `DateTime`, `File`, and enumerated types such as `Direction`. Sorting a list of strings, for example, can be accomplished with the code in Listing 10-6.

The vast majority of the code, lines 11–19 and 25–28, is concerned with reading the strings from the user and printing out the sorted list. The actual sorting is accomplished by a single line of code calling a method in the Java library (line 22).

Listing 10-6: *Sorting strings read from the console*

FIND THE CODE

ch10/librarySort/

```
import java.util.Arrays;
import java.util.Scanner;

/** Sort the strings read from a file.
 *
 * @author Byron Weber Becker */
public class Sort
{
  public static void main(String[ ] args)
  { // Get the strings from the user.
    Scanner in = new Scanner(System.in);
    System.out.print("How many strings: ");
    int num = in.nextInt();
    in.nextLine();

    String[ ] strings = new String[num];
    for (int i = 0; i < num; i++)
    { strings[i] = in.nextLine();
    }

    // Sort the strings.
    Arrays.sort(strings);

    // Display the sorted list of strings.
    System.out.println("The sorted strings:");
    for (int i = 0; i < strings.length; i++)
    { System.out.println(strings[i]);
    }
  }
}
```

The second approach to ordering objects is to pass the sort method the list to sort and an object implementing the `Comparator` interface. This is the most flexible approach and is discussed in Chapter 12.

10.1.9 Comparing Arrays and Files

Some beginning programmers have a hard time distinguishing an array from a file. After all, both store an ordered collection of objects. Both often use algorithms that process all of the objects in the collection.

So what's the difference? The core difference is that a file stores the objects on a disk drive or a related device. An array is stored in the computer's memory.

One consequence is that accessing an array is much faster than accessing a file. The disk drive holding your file has moving parts; waiting for them to move makes accessing a file slow. Memory, on the other hand, stores the array by arranging electrons in its chips. Manipulating electrons is *much* faster.

Files are linear structures. When a file is stored on the disk, all the information is placed into one long line. It's processed by reading the first item of information from the line, then the second, and so on. It's possible to read an item from the middle of the line, but you have to know exactly where to start in considerable detail. You need to know not just that you want the 132nd item, but the exact length of the 131 items that come before it.

Arrays, on the other hand, support **random access** naturally. If you want the 132nd item, use `131` as the index into the array (because arrays are indexed starting at `0`). Random access makes sorting an array easy but sorting a file difficult.

So why do we use files at all? Why not store everything in an array? Because storing information on a disk drive is *much* cheaper and because disk drives retain the information even when the power is off; memory does not.

Arrays and files are complementary. We often store information in files while we aren't working on it. When we begin to use the information, we use a program that loads the information from the file into an array. After we're done, usually as one of the last things a program does, the information is written from the array back to the disk where it waits until the next time we use it.

10.2 Creating an Array

So far we have assumed that the `BBBS` class contains an instance variable that is an array of `Person` objects. In this section, we'll see how to create such an array.

KEY IDEA

Creating an array has three steps: declaration, allocation, and initialization.

Briefly, creating an array has three steps: declaring the variable, allocating the memory, and initializing each element in the array to a desired value. In some ways, creating an array is like hosting a dinner party. The declaration states your intent to have an array—like sending out invitations to your dinner party. When you allocate memory you decide how many elements your array will have—like counting up the responses to your invitation and setting that many dinner places at the table. Finally, initialization puts a value in each element of the array—like seating one of your guests at each place around your table. These three steps are illustrated in Figure 10-13.

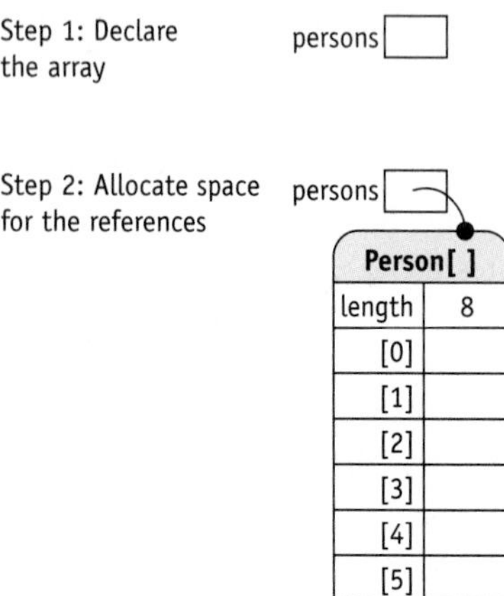

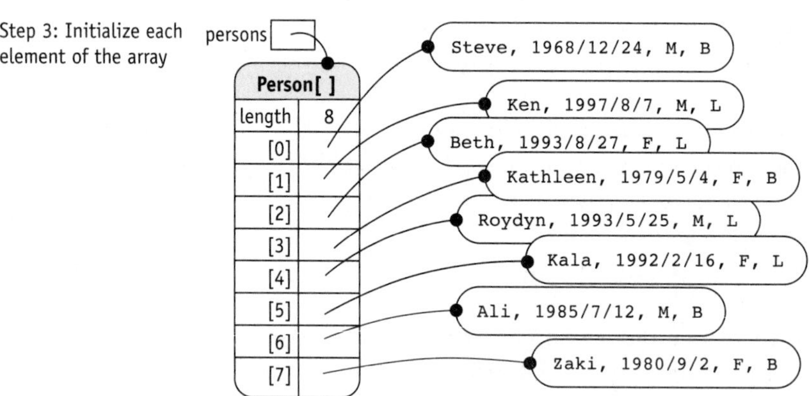

(figure 10-13)

Three steps in preparing an array for use

10.2.1 Declaration

Declaring an array is like declaring any other reference variable. A type such as `Person` or `Robot` is required, followed by the name of the variable. If the array is an instance variable, then an access modifier such as `private` is appropriate.

The only trick is knowing the type. The type for an array of `Person` objects is `Person[]` and the type for an array of `Robot` objects is `Robot[]`. Simply add a set of square brackets after the type of elements the array will hold. You might think of the brackets as making the type plural. A variable of type `Person` holds one person. A variable of type `Person[]` holds many persons.

KEY IDEA

The type of an array is the same as the type of each element, but with `[]` appended.

With this background, we can replace the following code:

```
public class BBBS extends Object
{ ... persons ...                    // An array of Person objects.
```

shown in the listings in Section 10.1 with the complete declaration:

```
public class BBBS extends Object
{ private Person[] persons;          // An array of Person objects.
```

The `persons` array can only hold `Person` objects.

LOOKING AHEAD

In Chapter 12, we will see that the `persons` array can also hold subclasses of `Person`.

10.2.2 Allocation

The declaration of an array does not create the array, but only a place to hold a reference to an array. See Step 1 in Figure 10-13. We also need to allocate the array object itself, similar to constructing any other kind of object. See Step 2 in Figure 10-13.

KEY IDEA

Use the `new` keyword to set aside space for a specific number of elements.

The following code fragment constructs an array object, allocating space for eight elements. It uses the `new` keyword followed by the type of the elements the array will store. In square brackets is the number of elements the array will be able to hold.

```
this.persons = new Person[8];
```

Of course, including a different number in place of the `8` would allocate space for a different number of elements. The `8` in this example can also be replaced with any expression that evaluates to an integer, including a simple variable or a complex calculation. This calculation may, for example, be based on information obtained from a user, as shown in the following code fragment:

```
public class BBBS extends Object
{ private Person[] persons;
  ...

  private void createArray()
  { Scanner in = new Scanner(System.in);
    System.out.print("How many persons: ";
    int numPersons = in.nextInt();

    this.persons = new Person[numPersons];
    ...
  }
}
```

KEY IDEA

An array may be declared and allocated in one statement when you know how many elements it will hold.

The programmer often knows how many elements will be in the array when the program is written. In this case, the declaration and the allocation may be combined:

```
private Person[] persons = new Person[100];
```

10.2.3 Initialization

The final step in creating an array is to initialize each element, as illustrated in Step 3 of Figure 10-13. The simplest approach is to call an appropriate constructor for each element in the array. For example, a small array of `Person` objects could be initialized like this:

```
this.persons[0] = new Person("Steve", "1968/12/24",
                          Gender.MALE, Role.BIG);
this.persons[1] = new Person("Ken", "1997/8/7",
                          Gender.MALE, Role.LITTLE);
this.persons[2] = new Person("Beth", "1993/8/27",
                          Gender.FEMALE, Role.LITTLE);
```

This approach works, but is impractical for a large number of elements. Array initialization is often performed by reading information from a file and constructing an object for each of the file's records.

The main problem is knowing how many records are in the file. This information is needed to allocate the correct number of elements for the array.

One approach is to simply count the records. The file is opened and the records are read, counting each one. When the end of the file is reached, it is closed and then opened again. The array is allocated using the count just obtained. The entire file is then read a second time, storing each object in the array.

LOOKING AHEAD

Reading objects from a file was discussed in Section 9.2.1.

Listing 10-7 shows the constructor to the `BBBS` class in lines 14–36. The initialization of the array takes place in the constructor. The relevant points are:

- The array is declared at line 10.
- In lines 18–24, the file is opened, every record is read and counted, and then the file is closed.
- In line 27, the array is allocated using the count of the records in the file.
- In lines 30–33, the file is again opened and the records read. This time, however, the objects created with the data are stored in the array at line 32. The file is closed again in line 34 after all of the records have been read.

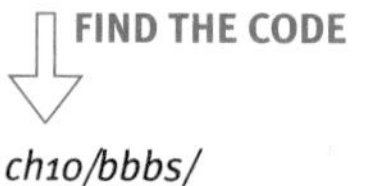

ch10/bbbs/

Listing 10-7: *Initializing an array from a file*

```
1  import java.util.Scanner;
2
3  /** A list of the "bigs" and "littles" associated with a Big Brother/Big Sister program.
4   *  "Bigs" are the Big Brothers and Big Sisters; "littles" are the Little Brothers and Sisters
5   *  they are (potentially) paired with.
6
7   *  @author Byron Weber Becker */
```

Listing 10-7: *Initializing an array from a file* (continued)

```
public class BigBroBigSis extends Object
{
   private Person[] persons;                    // the list of bigs and littles

   /** Construct a new object by reading all the bigs and littles from a file.
    *  @param fileName the name of the file storing the information for bigs and littles */
   public BigBroBigSis(String fileName)
   { super();

      // Count the number of Persons in the file.
      int count = 0;
      Scanner in = this.openFile(fileName);
      while (in.hasNextLine())
      { Person p = new Person(in);
        count++;
      }
      in.close();

      // Allocate an array to hold each object we read.
      this.persons = new Person[count];

      // Read the data, storing a reference to each object in the array.
      in = this.openFile(fileName);
      for (int i = 0; i < count; i++)
      { this.persons[i] = new Person(in);
      }
      in.close();

   }
   ...
}
```

One disadvantage of reading the file twice is inefficiency. Reading from a file is inherently slow and it would be more efficient to avoid reading the entire file twice.

Another approach is to store the number of records as the first item in the file, as shown in Figure 10-14. The constructor can simply read this data item and allocate the array. The records can then be read and stored into the array the first time the file is read.

```
5
Kenneth A Parsons
1997/8/7 M L
Beth A Reyburn
1993/8/27 F L
Kathleen A Waller
1979/5/4 F B
Roydyn A. Clayton
1993/5/25 M L
Christopher Aaron Fairles
1981/2/2 M B
```

(figure 10-14)

File with the number of records stored as the first data item

A disadvantage of this approach is that the number of records must be kept accurate. This may be hard to guarantee if the file is edited directly by users. However, it is not difficult if the file is always created by a program.

LOOKING AHEAD

An array that appears to grow can also solve this problem. See Section 10.4.

Listing 10-8 shows a constructor using this approach. It could be substituted for the constructor shown in Listing 10-7, provided the data file were changed to include the number of records in the file.

Listing 10-8: *Initializing an array when the data file contains the number of records*

```
public BigBroBigSis(String fileName)
{ super();
  Scanner in = this.openFile(fileName);

  // Get the number of records in the file.
  int count = in.readInt();
  in.nextLine();

  // Allocate an array to hold each record we read.
  this.persons = new Person[count];

  // Read the data, storing a reference to each object in the array.
  for (int i = 0; i < count; i++)
  { this.persons[i] = new Person(in);
  }
  in.close();
}
```

Array Initializers (optional)

Java provides a handy shortcut to initialize an array if you know its contents when you write the program. Essentially, you place the array elements in a comma-separated list between curly braces, as shown in the following example:

```
bbbs.persons = new Person[]
  { new Person("Byron", "1961/3/21",
        Gender.MALE, Role.BIG),
    new Person("Ann", "1960/12/3",
        Gender.FEMALE, Role.BIG),
    new Person("Luke", "1990/10/1",
        Gender.MALE, Role.LITTLE),
    new Person("Joel", "1994/2/28",
        Gender.MALE, Role.LITTLE)
  };
```

Java will automatically create an array of the right length to hold all the elements listed. In fact, if you try to specify the size yourself, the compiler will give you an error.

10.3 Passing and Returning Arrays

Like other reference variables, references to arrays can be passed to a method via parameters and returned from a method using the `return` keyword.

LOOKING AHEAD

Problem 12.13 generalizes this method with interfaces and polymorphism.

One common activity that demonstrates both passing and returning arrays is to extract a subset from a larger array. For example, return an array of `Person` objects that contains only "bigs" who are female. To make the method more versatile, we'll pass the desired gender and role as arguments. The method's signature is as follows:

```
public Person[] extractSubset(Gender g, Role r)
```

The return type of `Person[]` indicates that the method will return a reference to an array of `Person` objects.

To solve this problem, we need to create an appropriately sized array—which means figuring out the size of the subset. Then we need to fill the array. In pseudocode, we can state our tasks as follows:

size = count number of items in the subset
subset = a new array to store size Person objects
fill subset with the appropriate objects
return subset

The first step, counting the size of the subset, is an application of the Process Matching Elements pattern in which the process performed is simply counting. Its signature and method documentation are as follows; implementing it is Problem 10.7.

PATTERN

Process Matching Elements

```
/** Count the number of persons matching the given gender and role.
 * @param g    The gender of persons to be included in the subset.
 * @param r    The role of the persons to be included in the subset. */
private int countSubset(Gender g, Role r)
```

The second step, allocating a temporary array, illustrates that declaring and allocating an array within a method is both possible and useful. As always, the access modifier, such as `private`, is omitted when declaring a temporary variable.

```
Person[] subset = new Person[size];
```

The third step, filling the `subset` array, is the tricky one. We'll pass the method the gender and role of the `Person` objects desired, as well as a reference to the temporary array. The method's signature will be:

```
private void fillSubset(Person[] ss, Gender g, Role r)
```

Again, notice the type `Person[]`. The parameter variable `ss` will refer to an array of `Person` objects. Like other references passed as parameters, `ss` will contain an alias to `subset`; both references refer to the same array and both can be used to access and change the contents of the array. The reference itself cannot be changed, but the thing it refers to can be changed.

LOOKING AHEAD

Aliases were discussed in Section 8.2.2.

Inside the method, we'll repeatedly find the next person object with the appropriate gender and role, copying a reference to it into the next available space in the temporary array. This will require two index variables, one to keep track of where we are in the `persons` array and the other to track our position in the `subset` array.

Figure 10-15 shows the situation immediately after the first `Person` object has been inserted into the subset. The index variable `ssPos` ("subset position") gives the index of the next available position in the `subset` array. The variable `arrPos` ("array position") gives the index of the next `Person` object to consider. The colored arrows show `Person` objects that have yet to be copied.

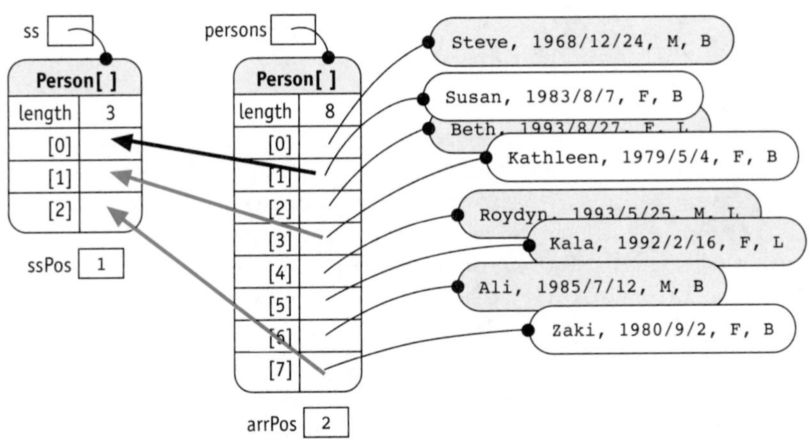

(figure 10-15)

Filling the `subset` *array, immediately after the first* `Person` *object reference has been copied to the* `subset` *array*

The code for the helper method is shown in lines 27–38 of Listing 10-9. Notice that `ssPos` is only incremented when a new element is added to the subset (line 34) but that `arrPos` is incremented each time a new `Person` object is considered (line 36).

The final step in the `extractSubset` method is to return a reference to the `subset` array (line 13).

FIND THE CODE

ch10/bbbs/

Listing 10-9: *Completed code for the* `extractSubset` *method*

```
1  public class BigBroBigSis extends Object
2  { private Person[ ] persons;      // The list of bigs and littles.
3
4    ...
5
6    /** Extract a subset of all the persons who have the given gender and role.
7     * @param g        The gender of all members of the subset.
8     * @param r        The role of all members of the subset. */
9    public Person[ ] extractSubset(Gender g, Role r)
10   { int ssSize = this.countSubset(g, r);
11     Person[ ] subset = new Person[ssSize];
12     this.fillSubset(subset, g, r);
13     return subset;
14   }
15
16   /** Count the number of persons matching the given gender and role.
17    * @param g        The gender of persons to be counted.
18    * @param r        The role of the persons to be counted. */
19   private int countSubset(Gender g, Role r)
20   {        // to be completed as an exercise
21   }
```

Listing 10-9: *Completed code for the* `extractSubset` *method* (continued)

```

  /** Fill the subset array with Person objects matching the given gender and role.
   * @param subset   The array to fill with elements belonging to the subset.
   * @param g        The gender of persons to be included in the subset.
   * @param r        The role of the persons to be included in the subset. */
  private void fillSubset(Person[] ss, Gender g, Role r)
  { int ssPos = 0;     // position within the subset
    int arrPos = 0;    // position within the array
    while (ssPos < ss.length)
    { Person p = this.persons[arrPos];
      if (p.getGender() == g && p.getRole() == r)
      { ss[ssPos] = p;
        ssPos++;
      }
      arrPos++;
    }
  }
}
```

Client code using the `BBBS` class could use the `extractSubset` method as follows:

```
Person[] femaleBigs = bbbs.extractSubset(Gender.FEMALE,
                                          Role.BIG);
System.out.println("Female Bigs:");
for (Person p : femaleBigs)
{ System.out.println(p.getName());
}
```

Passing and returning arrays of information are useful techniques. For example, the Big Brother/Big Sister project might have a reporting subsystem that could use such techniques extensively. Imagine a suite of subset extraction methods that each return a subset of a passed array. They could be put together in endless combinations. We could have, for example, a query like this, in which each `extract` method takes a criterion and an array as arguments:

```
Person[] ss = this.extract(Gender.MALE,
                 this.extract(Role.LITTLE,
                    this.extract(Interests.SPORTS,
                       this.persons)));
this.print(ss);
```

10.4 Dynamic Arrays

So far, the number of elements stored in our arrays has been fixed. We've neither added elements nor removed them. To be truly useful, this must change. For example, in the Big Brother/Big Sister program, we need a method to add a new person to the `persons` array:

```
/** Add another person to the array of Person objects.
* @param p The Person object to add. */
public void add(Person p)
```

To implement `add`, we must figure out how to "create" additional space in the array. In this section, we'll explore two approaches to this problem, and ultimately conclude that the best solution uses features of both.

10.4.1 Partially Filled Arrays

KEY IDEA

Allocate extra space for the array. Use the first elements to store data. Keep the number of elements in use in another variable.

The first approach uses a simple idea: Create an array with room to grow, if necessary. This separates the notion of the size of the array (the number of elements it currently stores) from the length of the array (the maximum number of elements it can store). This requires an auxiliary variable that we usually name `size`. Such an array is usually only partly filled, so we'll call it a **partially filled array**.

We will adopt a convention that indices in the range `0..size-1` will hold the valid elements while indices `size..length-1` will be "empty." This is illustrated in Figure 10-16.

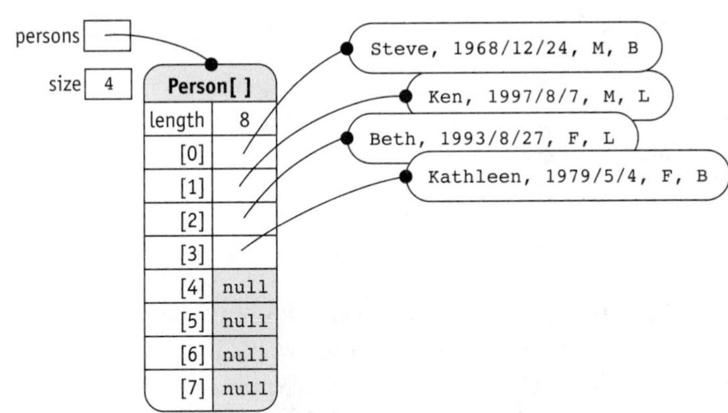

(figure 10-16)

Partially filled array with four elements

The auxiliary variable, `size`, can be interpreted two ways. First, it can be interpreted as the number of elements in the array that store valid data. This interpretation is useful for the Process All Elements and related patterns. For example, to print all the names in the partially filled `persons` array, we write

KEY IDEA

`size` says how many elements have valid data.

```
for (int i = 0; i < this.size; i++)
{ Person p = this.persons[i];
  System.out.println(p.getName());
}
```

Notice the use of `this.size` rather than `this.persons.length` to control the loop. If the array is as shown in Figure 10-16, using `length` would result in a `NullPointerException` when the name for `persons[4]` is printed because `p` would be `null`.

The other Process All Elements idiom, using the ***foreach*** loop, will not work with partially filled arrays. Writing `for (Person p : this.persons)` is the same as writing `for (int i = 0; i < this.persons.length; i++)`.

KEY IDEA

The foreach loop doesn't work for partially filled arrays.

The second interpretation of `size` is as the first element of the "empty" portion of the array. This interpretation is the natural one for the `add` method because it tells us where to put the new element.

KEY IDEA

`size` also says where the next element should be added.

```
public void add(Person p)
{ this.persons[this.size] = p;
  this.size++;
}
```

After a new element is added, the auxiliary variable must be incremented.

Of course, if the array is already full (`size` has the same value as `persons.length`), the `add` method will fail with an `ArrayIndexOutOfBoundsException`. We will investigate a solution to this problem shortly.

Inserting into a Sorted Array

If the array is already sorted and you want to keep it sorted, simply adding the new element to the end isn't good enough. One approach would be to add to the end and then sort the entire array, but that is inefficient. A much better approach is to move elements larger than the new element down in the array. The new element can then be inserted in the resulting "hole." These steps are shown in Figure 10-17.

LOOKING AHEAD

Implementing this algorithm is Problem 10.8.

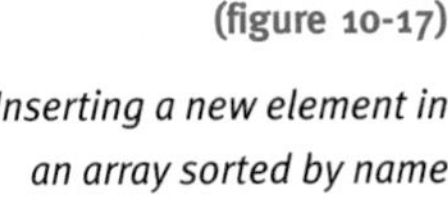

(figure 10-17)
Inserting a new element in an array sorted by name

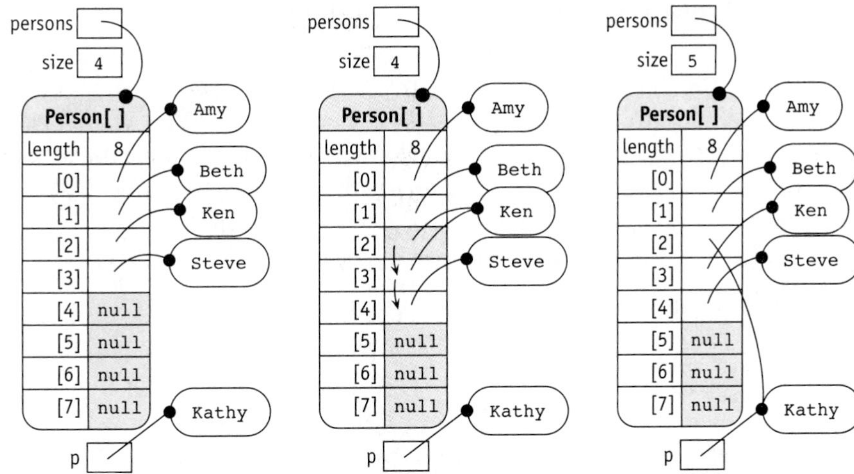

The original array containing four `Person` objects

Move references at the end of the array down by one to make room for the new element

Insert the new element and increment the auxiliary variable, `size`

Deletion

When deleting an element, we need to fill the "hole" left by the deleted element so that all the valid array elements are kept at the beginning of the partially filled array and all the unused space at the end. We'll use the following algorithm:

> d = *find the index of the element to delete*
> *fill* d *with another element from the array*
> *decrement* size, *the auxiliary variable*
> *assign* null *to the element at* size

The first step may be trivial if we are given the index of the element to delete. In other situations, we may need to search for the element to find the index.

The second step varies, depending on whether a sorted order must be maintained. If the array is unsorted, use the last element of the array to replace the element being deleted. In a sorted array, the elements with indices larger than `d` all need to be moved up one position in the array.

The third step recognizes that there is now one less element in the array.

LOOKING AHEAD

Written Exercise 10.1 asks you to explain why this step is optional.

The last step is not strictly necessary, however it is a good idea to assign `null` to the element for two reasons. First, it can make debugging easier because accidentally accessing an element in the unused portion of the partially filled array will generate a `NullPointerException`, quickly informing us that we made a mistake. Second, it may free an object for garbage collection, thereby reducing the memory required by our program.

Problems with Partially Filled Arrays

Unfortunately, partially filled arrays pose two significant problems. First, a partially filled array solves the problem of adding elements to an array, but only up to a point. There is still a limit. If the array is initially allocated to hold 500 elements, we can't insert 501. The last one just won't fit. Using the algorithms discussed earlier will result in an `ArrayIndexOutOfBoundsException`. If this abrupt ending to the program isn't desired, a check with a friendlier message can be made:

```
public void add(Person p)
{ if (this.size < this.persons.length)
  { this.persons[this.size] = p;
    this.size++;
  } else
  { // error message
  }
}
```

One way of addressing the first problem is to allocate arrays with more space than we think we'll ever use. Unfortunately, this leads to the second problem with partially filled arrays—wasting lots of memory. In addition, history is filled with programmers who dramatically misjudged how much data would be poured into their programs. For example, a program written to handle people associated with the local chapter of Big Brothers/Big Sisters might be deployed nationally and suddenly need to deal with *much* more information.

In spite of these two problems, partially filled arrays are a great solution where the amount of data can be reliably estimated.

10.4.2 Resizing Arrays

A second approach to the problem of adding and deleting elements in an array is to "change" the size of the array. Once an array is allocated, its size can't be changed, but we can allocate a new array with a different size and then copy the elements from the old array to the new array. After updating the array's reference to point to the new array, it appears as though the array has simply grown. The new element can then be added. These four steps are shown in Figure 10-18.

KEY IDEA

Arrays can't change size, but we can make it appear as if they do.

(figure 10-18)

Reallocating an array

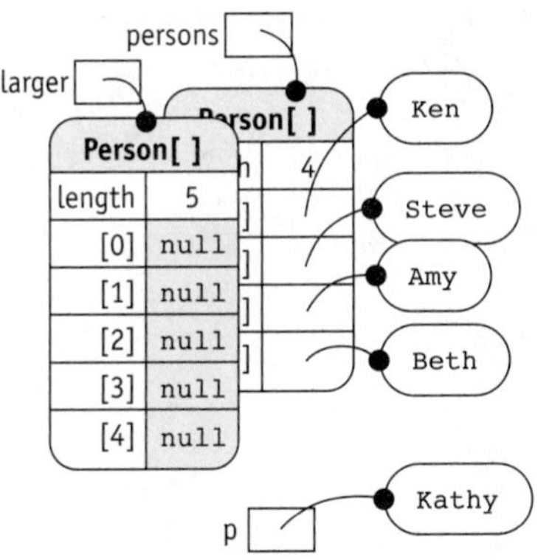

Step 1: Allocate a new, larger array

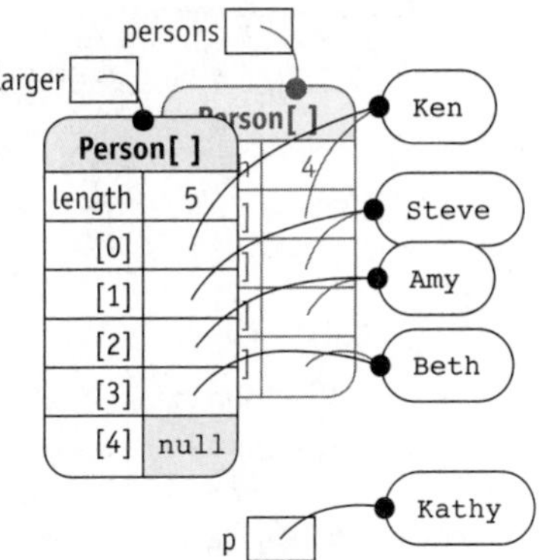

Step 2: Copy the contents to the larger array

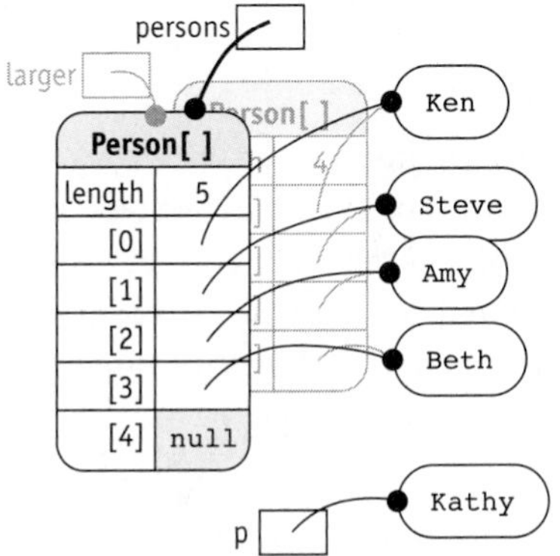

Step 3: Reassign the array reference

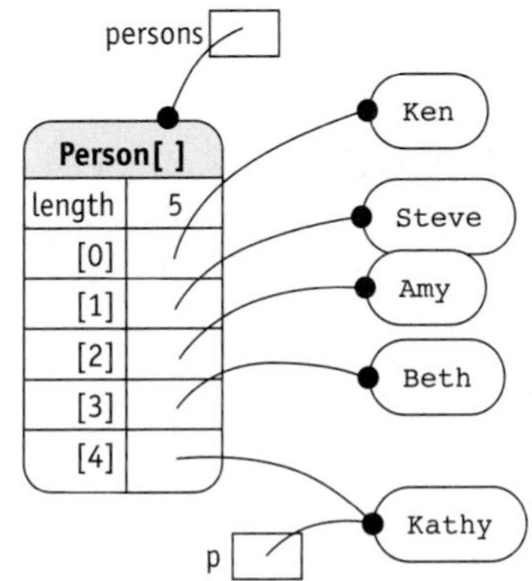

Step 4: Add the new element

The code to add a person to an unordered array is shown in Listing 10-10.

Listing 10-10: *Adding a* `Person` *object to an unordered array*

```
public class BBBS extends Object
{ private Person[] persons;

   ...

   /** Add a new person to the persons array.
    *  @param p          The new person to add. */
   public void add(Person p)
   { // Step 1: Allocate a larger array.
      Person[] larger = new Person[this.persons.length + 1];

```

Listing 10-10: *Adding a* `Person` *object to an unordered array* (continued)

```
      // Step 2: Copy elements from the old array to the new, larger array.
      for (int i = 0; i < this.persons.length; i++)
      { this.larger[i] = this.persons[i];
      }

      // Step 3: Reassign the array reference.
      this.persons = larger;

      // Step 4: Add the new element.
      this.persons[this.persons.length-1] = p;
   }
}
```

There is, however, a big disadvantage to this approach. Inserting many elements is very time consuming because so much copying is required. For example, one test[1] produced the data shown in Figure 10-19. The first column shows the number of insertions. The second column shows the time, in seconds, required to make the insertions into an array that grows by one with each insertion. The last column shows the number of seconds required to insert the same data into a partially filled array.

a) Time to insert into an array

Insertions	Grow	PFA
10,000	0.4	0.000
20,000	1.8	0.000
30,000	6.1	0.000
40,000	14.2	0.015
50,000	28.4	0.015
60,000	46.8	0.015
70,000	78.3	0.015
80,000	123.3	0.015
90,000	179.8	0.015
100,000	239.2	0.015
110,000	304.4	0.015
120,000	389.6	0.015
130,000	476.8	0.015
140,000	623.7	0.015
150,000	779.8	0.015

b) Graphing the time to insert data into an array that grows

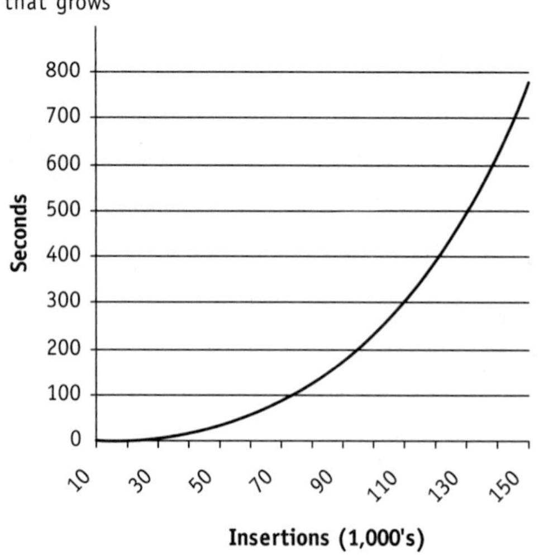

(figure 10-19)

Inserting elements in an array

[1] Using the code in `examples/ch10/growArrayTest` on a machine with a 2.8GHz Pentium 4 CPU and 1G of RAM running Windows XP and Java 5.

The test clearly shows that the more insertions there are, the worse the problem is. For example, the time taken to insert the first 10,000 items is less than half a second. Inserting the last 10,000 items, however, requires more than three minutes. Meanwhile, inserting 150,000 items into a partially filled array is so fast the computer's clock isn't accurate enough to time it and on the graph it can't be distinguished from the *x* axis.

10.4.3 Combining Approaches

The disadvantages of a partially filled array are an upper limit on the number of insertions and wasted space if some program executions use lots of data but most do not. On the other hand, expanding the array with each insertion solves those two problems, but introduces a performance problem.

KEY IDEA

Expandable, partially filled arrays give the best of both approaches.

Combining the two approaches addresses all three issues. The strategy is to use a partially filled array. When it gets full, allocate a larger array. However, don't increase the array by only one element. Instead, double the size of the array. That typically wastes some space, but not more than a factor of two. If that's too much, the array could be increased by 25% each time it is enlarged.

The same test as shown in Figure 10-19 takes only 0.047 seconds to insert 150,000 items—a little worse than a partially filled array that is initially allocated to hold 150,000 items, but not nearly as bad as growing the array by one each time.

The `ArrayList` class in the Java library uses exactly this approach. It is simply a partially filled array that can grow when it gets full, wrapped in a class.

Listing 10-11 shows an `add` method for a partially filled array that is doubled whenever it becomes full. Note that this same method can be used in the constructor, eliminating the need to count the number of items in the file (compare Listing 10-11 with Listing 10-7).

FIND THE CODE

ch10/ bbbsPartiallyFilled/

Listing 10-11: *Initializing and adding to an expandable, partially filled array*

```
public class BigBroBigSis extends Object
{
  private Person[] persons = new Person[1];   // List of bigs and littles.
  private int size;                           // Actual number of persons.

  /** Construct a new object by reading all the bigs and littles from a file.
  *  @param fileName The name of the file storing the information for bigs and littles. */
  public BigBroBigSis(String fileName)
  { super();

```

Listing 10-11: *Initializing and adding to an expandable, partially filled array* (continued)

```
    // Read the data, adding each person to the array
    Scanner in = this.openFile(fileName);
    while (in.hasNextLine())
    { this.add(new Person(in));
    }
    in.close();
  }

  /** Add a person to the the list of persons. */
  public void add(Person p)
  { if (this.persons.length == this.size)
    { // The array is full -- grow it.
      Person[] larger = new Person[this.size * 2];
      for (int i = 0; i < this.size; i++)
      { larger[i] = this.persons[i];
      }
      this.persons = larger;
    }
    this.persons[this.size] = p;
    this.size++;
  }
}
```

10.5 Arrays of Primitive Types

So far we have only discussed arrays of objects. Java also allows arrays of primitive types such as integers, Booleans, and doubles. Arrays of primitives and arrays of objects share many similarities. For example, declaring and allocating an array of four doubles bears a striking resemblance to declaring and allocating an array of four `Person` objects:

```
Person[] persons = new Person[4];
double[] interests = new double[4];
```

In these examples, each element in `persons` is automatically initialized to `null` and each element in `interests` is automatically initialized to `0.0`.

10.5.1 Using an Array of `double`

The `Person` class used in the Big Brother/Big Sister program defines four variables to store potential interests of the participants: the extent to which they like sports, crafts, games, and the outdoors. A value of `0.0` indicates they don't have an interest in it at all whereas a value of `1.0` indicates a very high interest. Before two people are paired, their compatibility is determined with the `getCompatibility` query:

```
public double getCompatibility(Person p)
{ return (this.likesCrafts * p.likesCrafts
      + this.likesGames * p.likesGames
      + this.likesOutdoors * p.likesOutdoors
      + this.likesSports * p.likesSports)
      /4.0;
}
```

Suppose it was determined that these four interests need to be supplemented with an additional 16, for a total of 20 different interests. Using separate variables for each one would be tedious; an array is a much better choice. Using an array, the `Person` class is written as shown in Listing 10-12.

Listing 10-12: *Using an array of* `doubles` *to represent interests*

```
public class Person extends Object
{ ...
  private static final int NUM_INTERESTS = 20;
  private double[] interests = new double[NUM_INTERESTS];
  ...

  public Person(Scanner in)
  { ...
    // Read this person's interests from the file.
    for (int i = 0; i < Person.NUM_INTERESTS; i++)
    { this.interests[i] = in.nextDouble();
    }
    ...
  }

  /** How compatible is this person with person p? A score of 0.0 means not at all
   *  compatible; 1.0 means extremely compatible. */
  public double getCompatibility(Person p)
  { double compat = 0.0;
    for (int i = 0; i < Person.NUM_INTERESTS; i++)
    { compat = compat + this.interests[i] * p.interests[i];
    }
    return compat / Person.NUM_INTERESTS;
  }
}
```

10.5.2 Meaningful Indices

So far the indices of our arrays have been just positions. They haven't had any meaning attached to them, though it is sometimes useful to do just that. Suppose, for example, that we wanted to know the distribution of ages of the people participating in the Big Brother/Big Sister program. That is, we want to know how many people are 10 years old, how many are 11, and so on. We'll assume no one is over 200 years old.

To solve this problem we can allocate an array named `ageCounters` with 200 elements. Each element will be a counter for a particular year. Which year? The year corresponding to the index. Thus, `ageCounters[10]` will be the number of 10 year-olds and `ageCounters[25]` will be the number of 25 year-olds. We'll have a counter for everyone between 0 and 199 years old, inclusive.

The method shown in Listing 10-13, when added to the `BigBroBigSis` class, will return a filled array giving the number of participants for each age. It could be used like this:

```
int[] ages = bbbs.getAgeCounts();
for (int i = 0; i < ages.length; i++)
{ if (ages[i] > 0)
  { System.out.println ("There are " + ages[i] +
                        " participants that are " + i + " years old.");
  }
}
```

FIND THE CODE

ch10/ bbbsPartiallyFilled/

Listing 10-13: *A method to count the participants in each age group*

```
public class BigBroBigSis extends Object
{ private Person[] persons;
  private int size = 0;

  ...

  /** Find the number of participants in each age group.
   * @return A filled array where a[i] is the number of people i years old. */
  public int[] getAgeCounts()
  { int[] ageCounters = new int[200];
    for (int i = 0; i < this.size; i++)
    { int age = this.persons[i].getAge();
      ageCounters[age]++;
    }
    return ageCounters;
  }
}
```

In the last example, the indices naturally matched ages because both ranges start at 0. Sometimes that isn't the case. Consider a slight modification of this problem: Count the number of coins in a collection by the year they were minted. Assume the oldest coin was minted in 1850.

This problem could be solved by allocating an array with 1850 unused elements. A better approach is to offset the indices by 1850, as shown in Listing 10-14. The crucial lines are 5, 16, and 22. In line 5, the constants `EARLIEST` and `LATEST` are used to calculate the actual number of elements or counters that are needed. This avoids the unused elements at the beginning of the array. In line 16, the year entered by the user is reduced by the appropriate amount so that it can be used as an index into the array. In line 22, the reverse is done to map the index to the appropriate year.

Listing 10-14: *Offsetting an index to start at zero*

```
1  /** Count the number of coins minted in each year. */
2  public static void main(String[] args)
3  { int EARLIEST = 1850;
4    int LATEST = 2008;
5    int[] ages = new int[LATEST - EARLIEST + 1];
6
7    // Count the coins.
8    Scanner in = new Scanner(System.in);
9    while (true)
10   { System.out.print("Enter a mint year or -1 to exit: ");
11     int yr = in.nextInt();
12     if (yr == -1)
13     { break;
14     }
15
16     ages[yr - EARLIEST]++;
17   }
18
19   // Print out the number of coins for each year.
20   for (int i = 0; i < ages.length; i++)
21   { System.out.println(ages[i] +
22                         " coins minted in " + (i + EARLIEST));
23   }
24 }
```

10.6 Multi-Dimensional Arrays

Sometimes an array with more than one dimension is useful. For example, consider a two-dimensional (2D) array recording the money given to Big Brothers/Big Sisters by month and source. Figure 10-20 shows the source of the money across the top in categories such as United Way and government grants. Down the left side are the months. At the intersection of each row and column is the amount of money received in a particular category in a particular month. For example, the cell in the column labeled "Individual Donations" and in the row labeled "Apr" indicates that $4,833 were received in April from individual donations.

	United Way	Corporate Donations	Individual Donations	Fundraising	Govt. Grants
Jan	0	3,000	6,915	0	15,500
Feb	0	2,125	4,606	0	5,500
Mar	0	2,000	5,448	0	5,500
Apr	0	3,000	4,833	13,983	15,500
May	20,569	2,000	6,091	0	5,500
Jun	0	8,000	4,867	0	5,500
Jul	0	3,000	4,196	0	15,500
Aug	0	2,550	4,736	0	5,500
Sep	0	2,000	4,305	0	5,500
Oct	0	3,000	5,286	32,254	15,500
Nov	0	2,000	6,834	0	5,500
Dec	9,351	2,000	7,459	0	5,500

(figure 10-20)

Two-dimensional array recording income by source and month

Java uses one pair of brackets for each dimension of an array. The one-dimensional arrays we used earlier in the chapter use one pair of brackets; the two-dimensional array shown in Figure 10-20 uses two. Of course, a three-dimensional array uses three pairs. The pattern continues for as many dimensions as you need.

```
int[][] income = new int[12][5]
```

The declaration on the left side of the equal sign specifies a 2D array where each cell stores an integer. The allocation on the right side specifies that the array has 12 rows and five columns.

KEY IDEA

The first pair of brackets is for the rows; the second pair of brackets is for the columns.

Figure 10-20 is actually a bit misleading, for the following reasons:

- Column names like "Corporate Donations" and row names like "May" are not directly associated with an array. The array itself is declared to store only integers. It cannot store strings as column or row labels.

- Rows and columns must be accessed using integer indices.
- The variable name, `income`, actually refers to memory that holds the array; it isn't the array itself.

A more accurate picture of the array is shown in Figure 10-21 which takes all this into account.

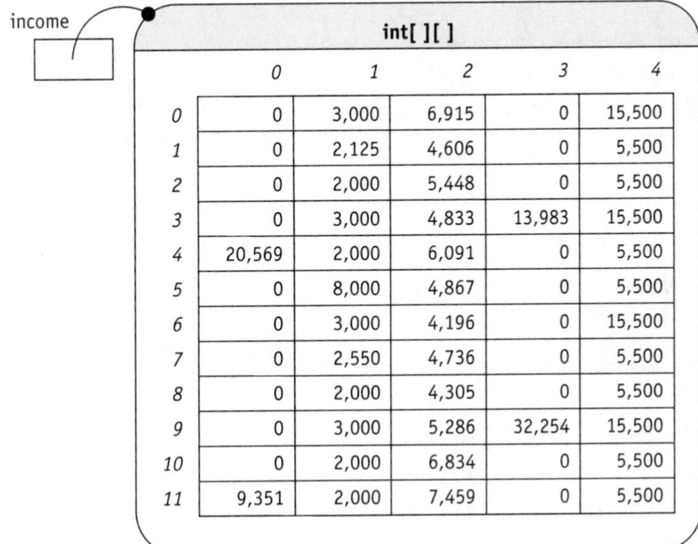

	0	1	2	3	4
0	0	3,000	6,915	0	15,500
1	0	2,125	4,606	0	5,500
2	0	2,000	5,448	0	5,500
3	0	3,000	4,833	13,983	15,500
4	20,569	2,000	6,091	0	5,500
5	0	8,000	4,867	0	5,500
6	0	3,000	4,196	0	15,500
7	0	2,550	4,736	0	5,500
8	0	2,000	4,305	0	5,500
9	0	3,000	5,286	32,254	15,500
10	0	2,000	6,834	0	5,500
11	9,351	2,000	7,459	0	5,500

(figure 10-21)

More accurate visualization of a two-dimensional array

10.6.1 2D Array Algorithms

Most algorithms that process a 2D array use two nested loops. The outside loop generally specifies which row to access and the inside loop generally specifies the column. A number of the following algorithms will display this general pattern. We say that such an algorithm accesses the array in **row-major order**. Some algorithms access the array in **column-major order**—the columns are indexed by the outer loop.

Printing Every Element

For example, to print the `income` array we could use a method like the one shown in Listing 10-15.

Listing 10-15: *Printing a 2D array*

```
1  public class BBBSIncome extends Object
2  { // income by month (row) and source (column)
3    private int[][] income;
4
5    ...
6
7    /** Print the income chart. */
8    public void printIncomeChart()
9    { for (int r = 0; r < this.income.length; r++)
10     { for (int c = 0; c < this.income[r].length; c++)
11       { System.out.print(this.income[r][c] + "\t");
12       }
13       System.out.println();
14     }
15   }
16 }
```

FIND THE CODE

ch10/income/

The inside loop, lines 10–12, prints one entire row each time it executes. The row it prints is specified by the outer loop, row `r`. After the row is printed, line 13 ends the current line of text and begins a new line. This process of printing a row is repeated for each row specified by the outer loop.

Notice that the number of rows is found in line 9 with `this.income.length` while the number of columns in a particular row is found in line 10 with `this.income[r].length`. They differ because in Java a 2D array can be ragged—each row may have its own length. We will see an example of this in Section 10.6.3.

KEY IDEA

It's possible to find the number of rows in a 2D array, as well as the number of columns in each row.

Sum Every Element

The same nested looping pattern can be used to find the total income, from all sources, for the entire year:

```
/** Calculate the total income for the year. */
public int getTotalIncome()
{ int total = 0;
  for (int r = 0; r < this.income.length; r++)
  { for (int c = 0; c < this.income[r].length; c++)
    { total = total + this.income[r][c];
    }
  }
  return total;
}
```

Every time you need to examine every cell in a 2D array, you will likely use this nested looping pattern.

Summing a Column

To find the total of the individual donations in one year, we need to sum column 2 in the `income` array. This task requires a single loop because it is working in a single dimension—moving down the column. Passing the column index as a parameter makes the method more flexible:

```
/** Calculate the total income for a given category for the year.
*  @param columnNum           The index of the column containing the desired category. */
public int getTotalByCategory(int columnNum)
{ int total = 0;
  for (int r = 0; r < this.income.length; r++)
  { total = total + this.income[r][columnNum];
  }
  return total;
}
```

10.6.2 Allocating and Initializing a 2D Array

As with a one-dimensional array, the declaration and allocation of the array can be split. This means that determining the size of an array can be delayed until the program is actually executing. For example, the array could be initialized from a file where the first two numbers indicate the number of rows and columns, respectively.

The first five rows of such a data file are shown in Figure 10-22. The constructor shown in Listing 10-16 shows how the array is allocated and then initialized using this data. The size of the array is determined in lines 11 and 12. The array itself is allocated using those sizes in line 16. Finally, the data is read and stored in the array using the by now familiar double loop in lines 19-24. The calls to `nextLine` in lines 13 and 23 are not strictly necessary because `nextInt` will read across line boundaries; however, using `nextLine` shows where line endings are expected in the file and adds to the clarity of the code.

(figure 10-22)

Sample data file

```
12 5
0      3000    6915    0        15500
0      2125    4606    0        5500
0      2000    5448    0        5500
0      3000    4833    13983    15500
...
```

Listing 10-16: *Allocating and initializing a 2D array from a file*

FIND THE CODE

ch10/income/

```
public class BBBSIncome extends Object
{
   // Income by month (row) and source (column).
   private int[][] income;

   /** Read the income data from a file.
    * @param in      The open file containing the data. */
   public BBBSIncome(Scanner in)
   { super();
      // Get the size of the array.
      int rows = in.nextInt();
      int cols = in.nextInt();
      in.nextLine();

      // Allocate the array.
      this.income = new int[rows][cols];

      // Fill the array.
      for (int r = 0; r < this.income.length; r++)
      { for (int c = 0; c < this.income[r].length; c++)
         { this.income[r][c] = in.nextInt();
         }
         in.nextLine();
      }
   }
}
```

10.6.3 Arrays of Arrays

The picture we've used so far of a 2D array having rows and columns is adequate in most circumstances (see Figure 10-21). However, it doesn't match reality and sometimes knowing all the details is useful.

In reality, a 2D array is an array of arrays, as illustrated in Figure 10-23. The variable `income` actually refers to a one-dimensional array with 12 elements. Each element in that 1D array refers to an array with five elements—a "row" of the 2D array.

We can now understand accessing the number of rows and columns in an array. When we write `this.income.length`, it returns the length of the array holding the rows—the number of rows in the 2D array. When we write `this.income[r].length`, it returns the length of the array stored in `income[r]`—the length of row `r`, or the number of columns in that row.

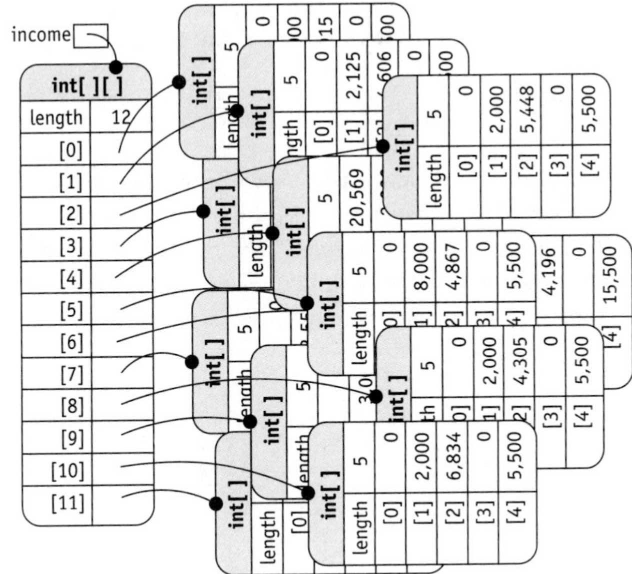

(figure 10-23)

Viewing a 2D array as an array of arrays

Sometimes, viewing a 2D array this way can work to our advantage in writing a program, too. For example, suppose you want to swap row `r` and row `s` in the array `income`. Rather than swap each element in row `r` with the corresponding element in row `s`, we can write:

```
int[] temp = income[r];
income[r] = income[s];
income[s] = temp;
```

The first line declares a temporary variable to store a 1D array. Then the rows are swapped by swapping their references. There is no equivalent way to swap columns.

Another way in which the array of arrays viewpoint can make a difference in our code is a method that takes an entire row as a parameter. For example, we might already have a simple utility method to sum a 1D array:

```
private int sum(int[] a)
{ int sum = 0;
  for (int i = 0; i < a.length; i++)
  { sum = sum + a[i];
  }
  return sum;
}
```

We can find the sum of the entire income array by passing sum a row at a time:

```
public int getTotalIncome()
{ int total = 0;
  for (int r = 0; r < this.income.length; r++)
  { total = total + this.sum(this.income[r]);
  }
  return total;
}
```

A final use of the array-of-arrays view is when rows of the array have different lengths. For example, Blaise Pascal explored the many properties of a pattern of numbers that has come to be known as "Pascal's Triangle." The first five rows of the triangle are shown in Figure 10-24. The first and last element of each row is 1. The elements in between are the sum of two elements from the row before it.

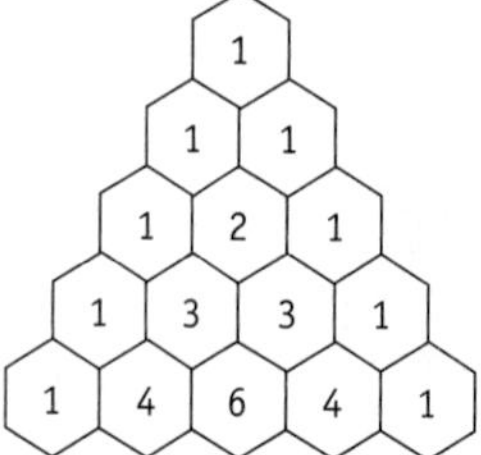

(figure 10-24)

Pascal's Triangle

A 2D array to store the first 10 rows of Pascal's Triangle can be declared and allocated with the following statement:

```
int[][] pascal = new int[10][];
```

Notice that the last pair of brackets is empty. This causes Java to allocate only one dimension of the array. We can now allocate the rest of the array—with each row having the appropriate length—with the following loop. It first allocates a 1D array the correct length and then inserts it into the pascal array.

```
for (int r = 0; r < pascal.length; r++)
{ pascal[r] = new int[r+1];

  // the array must still be initialized with the correct values!
}
```

LOOKING AHEAD

See Problem 10.12.

This solution provides two interesting elements: First, because each row is just the right length, no space is wasted. Second, the array can still be printed with our standard nested loop, as follows:

```
for (int r = 0; r < pascal.length; r++)
{ for (int c = 0; c < pascal[r].length; c++)
  { System.out.print(pascal[r][c] + "\t");
  }
  System.out.println();
}
```

10.7 GUI: Animation

There are several ways to perform animation in a graphical user interface. We've already seen a primitive animation in the Thermometer example in Section 6.7.3. In that example, the line representing the mercury in the thermometer was drawn several times, each time a little longer than before.

In Chapter 9, we saw how to display a single image from a file. In this section, we'll combine that capability with arrays to display a simple animation. The principle of this animation approach is to store a sequence of images in an array. The image displayed is switched from one image to the next quickly enough that it fools the eye into thinking there is smooth motion. Our example will use the six images shown in Figure 10-25. When shown repeatedly in quick succession, the eyes appear to roll. The images themselves were created with a graphics program that can create `.gif` files.

(figure 10-25)

Six images used in an animation

Listing 10-17 and Listing 10-18 work together to show two happy face images, one with the eyes rolling clockwise and the other with the eyes rolling counterclockwise. One goes through the array forward as it displays the images; the other goes through the array backward as it displays the images.

The main method for the program is shown in Listing 10-17 and follows our standard pattern: Create the components we need (two instances of a custom component named `AnimateImage`), put them in an instance of `JPanel`, and then put the panel in an instance of `JFrame`.

Lines 25-28 start two threads, one for each animation. Just like threads allowed robots in Section 3.5.2 to move independently and simultaneously, these threads allow each animation to run independently of the other.

FIND THE CODE

ch10/animation/

Listing 10-17: *The* `main` *method for an animation*

```
1  import javax.swing.*;
2
3  /** Create an animated image.
4   *
5   * @author Byron Weber Becker */
6  public class Main extends Object
7  {
8    public static void main(String[] args)
9    { // Create two animated components.
10     AnimateImage anim1 = new AnimateImage("img", 6, ".gif", 1);
11     AnimateImage anim2 = new AnimateImage("img", 6, ".gif", -1);
12
13     // Put the components in a panel and then in a frame.
14     JPanel contents = new JPanel();
15     contents.add(anim1);
16     contents.add(anim2);
17
18     JFrame f = new JFrame("Animations");
19     f.setContentPane(contents);
20     f.pack();
21     f.setDefaultCloseOperation(JFrame.EXIT_ON_CLOSE);
22     f.setVisible(true);
23
24     // Run each animation in its own thread.
25     Thread t1 = new Thread(anim1);
26     t1.start();
27     Thread t2 = new Thread(anim2);
28     t2.start();
29   }
30 }
```

The component that actually does the animation is shown in Listing 10-18. Its key features are the following:

- An array to store the images comprising the animation is declared (line 10) and initialized with the images (lines 28–31).
- An instance variable, `currentImage`, holds the array index of the image currently being displayed.

- A method overriding `paintComponent` paints the image indexed by `currentImage` on the screen.
- A `run` method is required to implement the interface `Runnable`. When the thread is started in the `main` method, this is the method that runs. It loops forever. With each iteration, it advances `currentImage` to be either the next image or the previous image, depending on the value stored in the instance variable `direction`. After requesting that the system repaint the component by calling `repaint`, the method sleeps for 0.10 seconds to give the user time to see the new image.

FIND THE CODE

ch10/animation/

Listing 10-18: *A component that shows images in sequence to produce an animation*

```
import javax.swing.*;
import java.awt.*;

/** Instances of AnimateImage show a sequence of images to produce an animation.
 *
 * @author Byron Weber Becker */
public class AnimateImage extends JComponent
                implements Runnable
{
  private ImageIcon[] images;
  private int currentImage = 0;
  private int direction;

  /** Construct a new animation component, loading all the images. Images are read from
   * files whose names have three parts: a root string, a sequence number, and an extension.
   *
   * @param fileNameRoot    The root of the image filenames.
   * @param numImages       The number of images in the animation.
   * @param extension       The extension used for the images (e.g., .gif)
   * @param dir             1 to animate going forward through the array; -1 to animate
   *                        going backward through the array. */
  public AnimateImage(String fileNameRoot, int numImages,
                      String extension, int dir)
  { super();
    this.images = new ImageIcon[numImages];
    this.direction = dir;

    for (int i=0; i<numImages; i++)
    { String fileName = fileNameRoot + i + extension;
      this.images[i] = new ImageIcon(fileName);
    }

```

Listing 10-18: *A component that shows images in sequence to produce an animation* (continued)

```
      this.setPreferredSize(new Dimension(
              this.images[0].getIconWidth(),
              this.images[0].getIconHeight()));
   }

   /** Paint the current image on the screen. */
   public void paintComponent(Graphics g)
   { super.paintComponent(g);
      Image img = this.images[this.currentImage].getImage();
      g.drawImage(img, 0, 0, null);
   }

   /** Run the animation. */
   public void run()
   { while (true)
      { // Select the next image and call for the system to repaint the component.
         // If this.dir is negative, the remainder operator doesn't work as desired. Add
         // this.images.length to compensate.
         this.currentImage = (this.currentImage + this.direction
               + this.images.length) % this.images.length;
         this.repaint();
         try
         { Thread.sleep(100);       // Use the sleep method in the Java library.
         } catch (InterruptedException ex)
         {// ignore
         }
      }
   }
}
```

10.8 Patterns

Many patterns involve arrays. They include initialization and changing the size of an array, as well as many algorithms. This section contains only a sampling of what could be considered patterns in this chapter.

10.8.1 The Process All Elements Pattern

Name: Process All Elements

Context: You have a collection of values stored in an array and need to perform the same operation on all of them.

Solution: Use a `for` loop to process each element of the array, one element with each iteration of the loop. The following code template applies:

```
for («elementType» «elementName» : «arrayName»)
{ «statements to process element»
}
```

For example, to print the names of all the elements in the `persons` array:

```
for (Person p : this.persons)
{ System.out.println(p.getName());
}
```

Consequences: Each element in the array is processed by the statements inside the loop. If the array happens to be partially filled, the preceding form will cause a null pointer exception. Then the alternate form, which uses an explicit index and an auxiliary variable, should be used.

Related Patterns: The Process Matching Elements, Find an Extreme, Selection Sort, and many other patterns are specializations of the Process All Elements pattern.

10.8.2 The Linear Search Pattern

Name: Linear Search

Context: You have an ordered collection and are interested in objects in the collection that satisfy a particular property. You want to do one of the following tasks:

- determine whether an element satisfying the property exists in the collection
- determine the position of the first or last element in the collection that satisfies the property
- retrieve the first or last element in the collection that satisfies the property

Solution: Write a method that takes the criteria that identify the desired element as one or more parameters. Use the Process All Elements pattern to test each element of the array against the criteria. An element satisfying them can be saved and returned after the loop, or more efficiently, returned as soon as it is found. The following code template uses the early return approach and assumes a partially filled array.

```
public «typeOfElement» «methodName»(«type» «criteria»)
{ for (int i = 0; i < «auxVar»; i++)
  { «typeOfElement» «elem» = «arrayName»[i];
    if («elem» satisfies «criteria»)
    { return «elem»;
    }
  }
  return «failureValue»;
}
```

This basic pattern has many variations. Some of the differences are whether the array is partially filled, whether the element is guaranteed to be found, and whether you want to know whether such an element exists, its position, or the element itself.

Many people prefer to use a `while` loop instead of a `for` loop. In that case, use the following variant of the pattern. The `while` loop depends on short circuit evaluation to stop the loop when the element is not found. For this to work, the test for the index being in bounds must be first.

```
public «typeOfElement» «methodName»(«type» «criteria»)
{ int i = 0;
  while (i < «auxVar» &&
           !(«arrayName»[i] satisfies «criteria»))
  { i++;
  }

  if (i == «auxVar»)  { return «failureValue»;    }
  else                { return «arrayName»[i];    }
}
```

Consequences: The desired element is either found and returned, or a designated *«failureValue»* is returned. If the array contains objects, the *«failureValue»* is `null`. If the array contains primitive values, the failure value must be chosen carefully to avoid all valid values that could be stored in the array. If no such value exists, another technique must be used such as setting an instance variable as an error flag, returning an object that contains the primitive value or is `null`, or throwing an exception.

Related Patterns: Some variations of this pattern are similar to the Process All Elements pattern.

10.9 Summary and Concept Map

This chapter has focused on arrays, a fundamental programming structure for storing multiple values using a single name, with individual values referenced using an integer index. Arrays are closely related to collection classes such as `ArrayList`. An array should be used when efficiency matters or when more precise control over the size of the array is desired.

Many important algorithms apply to collections that are stored in an array. Examples include Process All Elements, Find an Extreme, Search, and Sort.

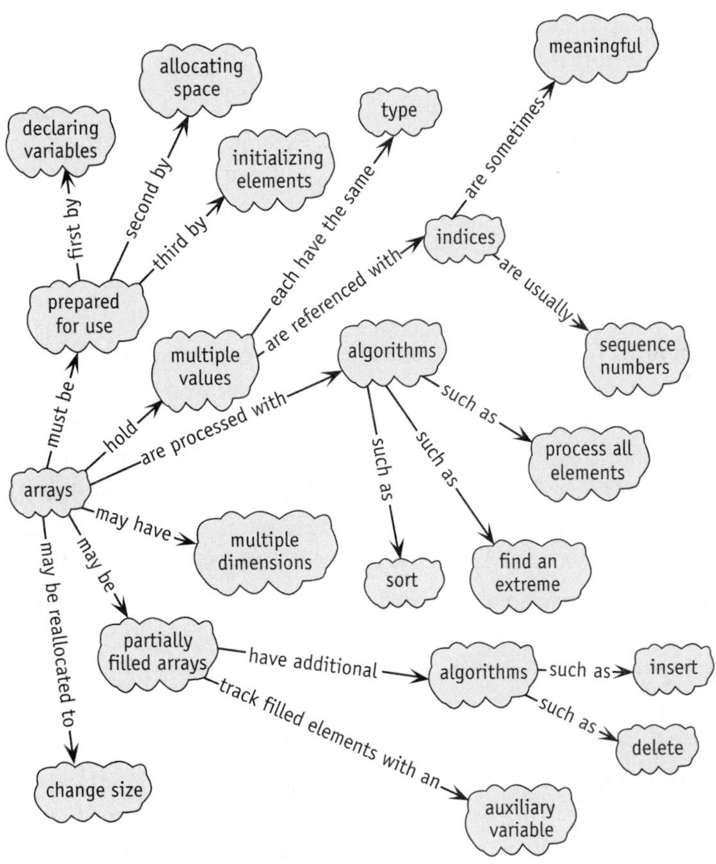

10.10 Problem Set

Written Exercises

10.1 In Section 10.4.1, it was noted that assigning `null` to an unused element after a deletion from a partially filled array is not strictly necessary. Explain why a program should work as implemented without that step. Drawing pictures may help.

10.2 Consider the code shown in Section 10.6.3 that swaps two rows of a 2D array.

a. Draw four diagrams, each one similar to Figure 10-23, that trace the three lines of code. Assume the array has five rows with three columns each and that `r` is one and `s` is three.

b. Write pseudocode for a method that swaps two rows by swapping individual elements rather than entire rows.

10.3 Write patterns, in the same style as Section 10.8, for the following:

a. Declaring, allocating, and initializing a filled array where the initial values are read from a file

b. Finding an extreme element

c. Deleting an element from a specified index in an unsorted, partially filled array

d. Inserting an elëment into a sorted, partially filled array

e. Enlarging a partially filled array

Programming Exercises

10.4 In Section 10.1.7, we found the oldest person by comparing the ages of everyone in the array. This, however, is accurate only to the nearest year. On 364 days of the year, a person born April 1, 1987 and another born April 2, 1987 will be the same number of years old—yet one is clearly older than the other. Rewrite the `findOldestPerson` method to compare their birth dates rather than their ages. With this modification, two people must be born on exactly the same day and year to be considered equally old. You will need to add a method to the `Person` class.

10.5 Write a method named `split`. This method is passed a `Scanner` object. It reads all of the tokens up to the end of the file, returning them as a filled array of strings (no blanks or nulls). Do not use the `split` method in the `String` class nor any of the collection classes.

10.6 The package `becker.xtras.hangman` includes classes implementing the game of Hangman. Figure 7-13 has an image of the user interface. Extend `SampleHangman`. Your new constructor should read a file of phrases that you create and store them in an array. Override the `newGame()` method to choose a random phrase from the array and then call the other `newGame` method with the chosen phrase. Create a `main` method, as shown in the package overview, to run your program.

10.7 Complete the `countSubset` helper method discussed in Section 10.3.

10.8 Write a method named `add` that adds a new `Person` object into a sorted, partially filled array. You may find Figure 10-17 helpful for this.

10.9 Implement a method with the signature `void delete(int d)` that deletes the element at index `d` from a partially filled array.

a. Assume the partially filled array is unsorted.

b. Assume the array is sorted.

10.10 Write a program that reads a series of daily high temperatures from a file. Print out the number of days that each high was achieved. If you normally think of temperatures in degrees Celsius, assume the temperatures fall between -40° and 50°. If you normally think in Fahrenheit, assume they fall between -40° and 110°.

10.11 Write methods in the `BBBSIncome` class to:

a. Find the month with the largest income in a given category.

b. Find the category with the largest income for a given month.

c. Find the month with the largest total income from all sources.

10.12 Review Pascal's Triangle and the code after Figure 10-24 to allocate an array for it.

a. Draw an object diagram, similar to Figure 10-23, showing Pascal's Triangle as an array of arrays.

b. Complete the initialization code. Print the triangle using the algorithm in Listing 10-15 to verify the correctness of your code.

c. Write a method, `printFormatted`, that prints an array representing Pascal's Triangle with appropriate spacing. Your output will be spaced similarly to Figure 10-24, but will not display the background grid. You may find the `printf` method useful; see Section 7.2.4.

d. Write a method, `rowsSumToPowers`. It verifies that the sum of the numbers in each row is 2^n, where n is the row number. That is, the sum of row 0 is 2^0 (or 1) and the sum of row 1 is 2^1 (or 2). Use the `pow` method in the `Math` class to calculate 2^n.

e. Write a method, `naturalNumbers`. It should verify that the elements next to the end of each row except the first, when taken in sequence, are the natural numbers. For example, the 2nd element in row 1 is 1. The second element in row 2 is 2, and the second element in row 3 is 3. The same is true for the element next to the end of each row. Return `true` if the property holds; `false` otherwise.

Programming Projects

10.13 Write a program implementing a robot bucket brigade. The bucket brigade consists of some number of `RobotSE`s positioned on consecutive intersections. There are a number of `Thing` objects (buckets) on the same intersection as the first robot in the brigade. When the program executes, the first robot will pick up one `Thing` and move it to the next robot's intersection, put it down, and return to its original position. The next robot will then move the `Thing` one more position down the line, and so on. When the brigade is finished, all the `Thing`s will be at the other end of the line of robots, one intersection beyond the last robot.

10.14 Implement a class named `SortTest`. It asks the user for an array size, a filename, and a sorting algorithm. It then allocates an array of strings the given length and fills it by reading tokens from the file. If the file doesn't have enough tokens, close it and begin reading again from the beginning. When the array is filled, sort it using either Selection Sort or the sort method implemented in `java.util.Arrays` (an implementation of MergeSort). Use the program to construct a graph for each algorithm comparing the number of tokens on the x axis with the time to sort on the y axis. What conclusions can you draw about the performance of the two algorithms? (*Hint*: A good source for tokens is a book such as *Moby Dick*, available from *www.gutenberg.org*.)

10.15 The user interface for graphing mathematical functions presented in Problem 7.14 is also capable of graphing polynomial functions. Polynomials have n terms added together. Each term has the form $a_i x^i$, where a_i is called the coefficient. The overall form of a polynomial is $a_n x^n + a_{n-1} x^{n-1} + \ldots + a_0 x^0$. Write a class named `PolyFunc` that extends `Object` and implements `IPolynomialFunction`. Write another class, `Main`, that includes a `main` method to run the program.

a. Use `PolyFunc` to graph $a_4x^4 + a_3x^3 + a_2x^2 + a_1x + a_0$, using a_4=0.5, a_3= -0.75, a_2=0.1, a_1=0.0, and a_0=-1.0.

b. Without changing `PolyFunc` in any way, graph $a_6x^6 + a_5x^5 + a_4x^4 + a_3x^3 + a_2x^2 + a_1x + a_0$ (You may, however, change your `main` method.) Choose your own coefficients.

10.16 Explore the documentation for `becker.xtras.imageTransformation`. This package provides a graphical user interface for a program to transform images by rotating, cropping, brightening, darkening, stretching, and so on. See Figure 10-26. The actual transformations are provided by a class implementing the `ITransformations` interface.

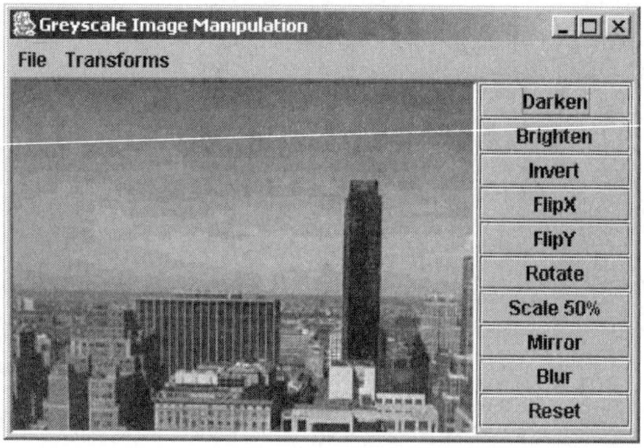

(figure 10-26)

Image transformation graphical user interface

Write a class named `Transformer` that implements `ITransformations` and provides a reset function to reset the image to the original image that was provided as a parameter to `setPixels`. (*Hint*: Assigning references will not be enough. You need to actually copy the array.) Add code to implement the following transformations:

a. "Darken" divides the intensity of each pixel by two.

b. "Brighten" multiplies the intensity of each pixel by two; pixels that have a resulting value larger than `255` are set to `255`.

c. "Invert" makes the light pixels dark and the dark pixels light.

d. "FlipX" turns the picture upside down.

e. "FlipY" reverses the left and right sides of the image.

f. "FlipDiag" reverses the lower left and upper right corners.

g. "Rotate" turns the image ¼ turn to the left (be careful that you don't inadvertently implement "FlipDiag").

h. "Scale50" removes every other row and every other column from the image, making the result .25 times the size of the original.

i. "Mirror" makes an image that is twice as wide as the original image, where the left half contains the original and the right side contains a mirror image.

j. "Blur" sets each pixel to the average of its neighbors.

10.17 Explore the documentation for the package `becker.xtras.jotto`. A graphical user interface, as shown in Figure 10-27, is provided in the package.

(figure 10-27)

Jotto's graphical user interface

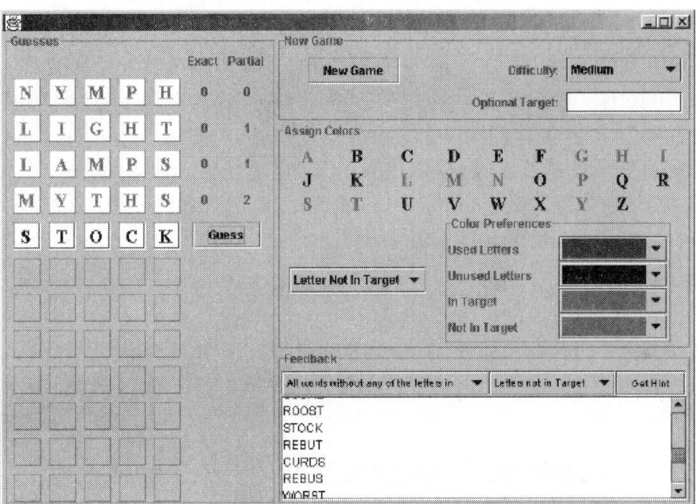

a. Write a `main` method, as described in the package overview, so that you can play a game of Jotto using the supplied `SampleWordList` and `SampleGuessEvaluator` classes together with the supplied user interface.

b. Write a class named `WordList` that implements the interface `IWordList`. Modify your `main` method to run the program using your new class. Implement it using a completely filled array.

c. Write a class named `WordList` that implements the interface `IWordList`. Modify your `main` method to run the program using your new class. Implement it using a partially filled array that includes an `addWord` method which enlarges the array as required.

d. Write a class named `HintContainsLetter` that extends `Hint` and contains the code shown in the documentation for the `Hint` class. Modify your `main` method so you can play the game and use your new hint mechanism.

e. Write a class named `HintExcludesLetter`. It will be similar to the class written in part (d) except that `isOK` will return true when the specified word does *not* contain the given character.

f. Write a class named `HintContainsLetters`. It will extend `Hint` and its `isOK` method will return true if the specified word contains all of the letters obtained with the `getLetters` method in the `IHintData` object passed as a parameter.

g. Write a class named `HintExcludesLetters`. It will extend `Hint` and its `isOK` method will return true if the specified word does not contain any of the letters obtained with the `getLetters` method in the `IHintData` object passed as a parameter.

h. Write a class named `HintContains3Letters`. It will extend `Hint` and its `isOK` method will return true when the specified word contains at least 3 of the letters obtained with the `getLetters` method in the `IHintData` object passed as a parameter.

i. Generalize the class described in part (h) so that the number of letters can be specified when the object is constructed. Name the class `HintContainsNLetters`.

10.18 Explore the documentation for the package `becker.xtras.marks`. Write a class named `Marks` that implements the interface `IMarks`. Write another class named `Main` that contains a `main` method as shown in the documentation. The result should appear similar to Figure 10-28.

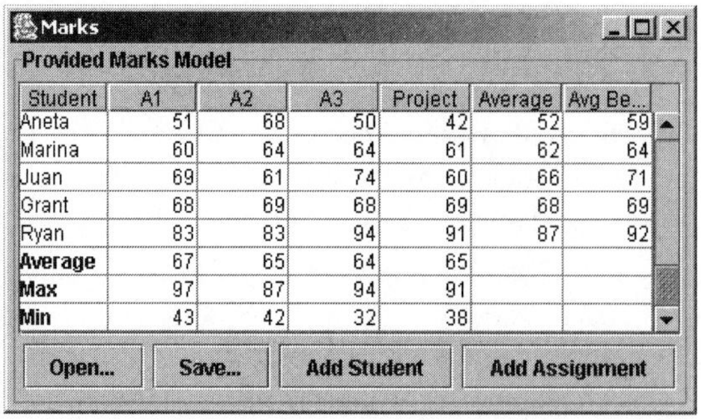

Marks

Provided Marks Model

Student	A1	A2	A3	Project	Average	Avg Be...
Aneta	51	68	50	42	52	59
Marina	60	64	64	61	62	64
Juan	69	61	74	60	66	71
Grant	68	69	68	69	68	69
Ryan	83	83	94	91	87	92
Average	67	65	64	65		
Max	97	87	94	91		
Min	43	42	32	38		

Open... Save... Add Student Add Assignment

(figure 10-28)

Graphical user interface for a spreadsheet storing marks or grades

10.19 Consider Table 10-1. It gives distances between pairs of cities, similar to the charts found in some road atlases. Write a class, `Distances`, that has an instance variable referring to a 2D array storing the distances. Initialize the array from a file.

(table 10-1)

Distances in kilometers between cities in southern Ontario

	Kitchener	London	Stratford	Toronto
Kitchener	0	110	45	107
London	110	0	61	194
Stratford	45	61	0	149
Toronto	107	194	149	0

Add the following methods:

a. `displayFarthestPair` finds and prints the pair of cities that is farthest apart.

b. `displayClosestPair` finds and prints the pair of distinct cities that are closest together.

c. `isSymmetrical` verifies that the table is symmetrical; that is, it returns `true` if the distance from X to Y is the same as from Y to X for each pair of cities, and if the distance from X to X is 0.

d. `getDistance` returns the distance between two cities, given their names. (*Hint*: You'll need to add a 1D array of `Strings` to store the city names. Finding "Stratford" at index *i* indicates that *i* should be used as the index in the row or column of the 2D array of distances. You may need to adjust the format of your input file to include the city names.)

e. `getTripDistance` returns the total distance for a trip when given an array of city names. The order of the names in the array corresponds to the order the cities are visited on the trip.

10.20 Notice that less than half of the data in the distance chart shown in Table 10-1 is actually needed. The upper half of the chart isn't needed because the array is symmetrical. Write a program that reads data from a file such as

```
4
110
45     61
107  194     149
```

where the first line gives the number of cities and the remaining lines give the distances between cities X and Y where the index of city X is less than the index of city Y. Note that this data corresponds to the lower left corner of Table 10-1.

a. Write a constructor that reads this data but constructs a full 2D array, the same as Problem 10.19.

b. Write a constructor that reads this data into a 2D array where each row is only long enough to store the required data.

c. Add methods that perform the same calculations as a, b, d, and e in Problem 10.19.

Chapter 11

Building Quality Software

Chapter Objectives

After studying this chapter, you should be able to:

- Identify characteristics of quality software, both from the users' and programmers' perspectives
- Follow a development process that promotes quality as you develop your programs
- Avoid common pitfalls in designing object-oriented programs
- Include defensive programming measures to make errors more likely to expose themselves so they can be fixed
- Explain characteristics of quality user interfaces and describe an iterative methodology for developing them

Suppose your rich uncle offered you a choice of two automobiles. One is known for its high performance, luxurious leather interior, and precision workmanship. The other is underpowered, needs frequent repair, and will probably have visible body rust before it's five years old. Both are free, no strings attached. Which would you take?

Most of us have a highly developed sense of quality. It's sometimes hard to define exactly what quality is, but given a choice, we prefer the higher quality option.

This chapter begins by describing what to look for in high-quality software. The rest of the chapter describes how to improve the quality of the software we write.

cover on Nov 26th

11.1 Defining Quality Software

The dictionary defines quality as "the degree of excellence of a thing." In the automobile example in the introduction, quality was described in terms of performance, interior finishing, workmanship, reliability, and susceptibility to rust. In an article of clothing, the relevant characteristics might include the strength, wrinkle resistance, and color fastness of the fabric, as well as the perceived style of the garment.

Sometimes we can take measurements that correspond very well to quality. For example, an automobile's top speed or time to accelerate from 0 to 60 miles per hour are easily measured and indicate the car's performance pretty well. Similarly, the number of threads per inch is easily measured and often corresponds to the quality of a garment's fabric. The quality of other characteristics such as an automobile's reliability or the style of a garment is more subjective and must be measured less directly. For example, one could survey car owners for the number of repairs they have required over the last 5 years or survey shoppers on their reactions to a garment.

In the remainder of this section we'll examine characteristics that are important to "the degree of excellence" or quality of software.

11.1.1 Quality from a User's Perspective

The user of a program judges its quality based on many characteristics. Three of the most important, however, are correctness, usability, and reliability.

A program is **correct** if it meets its specifications. A payroll program that ignores overtime or withholds too much tax would not be correct. A Web browser that only displays the first five paragraphs of a Web page cannot be considered correct. However, a program can be missing your favorite feature and still be correct. The key is whether it meets its specification—whether it does what it is supposed to do—correctly. It's a fact of life, however, that all but the simplest programs will be less than 100% correct.

The **usability** of a program is determined by the effort required to learn, operate, prepare input, and interpret output when compared to the alternatives. A more usable program is a higher quality program. But usability is subjective and must take the user into account. A beginning digital photographer may want a very simple program to crop photos and touch up "red-eye." The "ease-of-use" of this program would be nothing but frustration to a professional photographer that also wants to manipulate the color balance or merge parts of one image into another.

A third characteristic of quality programs is **reliability**. A program is reliable if it does not crash, does not lose or corrupt data, and is consistent in how it works. Obviously, an unreliable program is not a quality program.

11.1.2 Quality from a Programmer's Perspective

It may seem strange, at first, to consider quality from any other perspective than the user. However, when buying a new car, your mechanic may tell you to avoid certain models because they are difficult to repair. From the mechanic's perspective, the models differ in quality. New home buyers often have the home inspected by someone trained to look beneath the paint. The inspector determines whether the foundation is sound or whether shortcuts were taken in insulating the windows. From the inspector's perspective, two homes that look the same may have different levels of quality.

Similarly, two programs may look exactly the same to the user but have radically different quality levels to programmers. From their perspective, a quality program makes their life easier because it is understandable, testable, and maintainable.

Understandable Programs

A program is understandable if it is easy to determine how the program works. Choosing descriptive variable and method names is one of the easiest ways to increase the understandability of a program. Appropriate comments describing each class and method, as well as explanatory comments for more difficult code, also play a large role in the understandability of a program.

Understandability is important because most programs are read by many people over many years. A program in an insurance company may be written and debugged by a team of programmers over several months. Understandability helps the team work together. Several months later, another programmer may read the code to correct bugs. Five years later, the program may need extensive modifications to accommodate a new product offered by the company and two years after that it may again need modification to accommodate a change to the business practice of the company. In each of these situations, the programmer's life is improved by working with understandable code.

Most professional programs last much longer than those written by students learning to program. A typical student program is written in a few hours or at most a few weeks. After it is handed in, someone reads it, assigns a grade, and the program's useful life is over. With such short lifespans and so few people involved, program understandability has less importance—although it never hurts to ensure that the person assigning the grade can understand what you've written!

Understandability becomes more important as the size of the program grows. A typical student program may contain between twenty and several hundred lines of code. At this scale, programmers can keep most of the important details for the entire program in mind or can easily remind themselves if they forget. Not so for commercial programs that may involve between several thousand and several million lines of code. In such programs, understandability is vital to successfully writing or fixing the program.

Testable Programs

Programmers need to test their code. It's a simple fact of a programmer's life. Designing software that is easy to test makes this part of programming easier and more enjoyable, and improves the program's quality from the programmer's perspective.

It is also likely to improve the program's quality from the user's perspective. Recall that correctness is a major factor. A testable program is more likely to be tested, and is therefore more likely to be correct.

A testable program has classes with a single, well-defined purpose. Methods have a single purpose and few dependencies on other parts of the code. A testable program has an infrastructure for testing, allowing it to be easily tested whenever it is modified using the techniques discussed in Section 7.1.

Maintainable Programs

As noted earlier, a typical program is often changed over its lifetime to accommodate new requirements. A high-quality program is maintainable if it is easy to find and correct bugs, easy to adapt to new requirements, and easy to improve its overall quality in a process called **refactoring**. Refactoring modifies the code to improve its quality but doesn't actually change what the program does.

The maintainability of a program is strongly influenced by how understandable and testable it is. Carefully designed programs are more maintainable. Later in this chapter we will investigate a number of design guidelines such as writing appropriately parameterized methods, avoiding duplicated code, and using private instance variables.

11.2 Using a Development Process

How do we build high-quality software? It doesn't just happen! We need some discipline and a **development process**—a set of steps that help us know what to do next.

Many development processes have been proposed over the years. The one we will use is illustrated in Figure 11-1. It combines the best of the older, plan-first development processes with the newer, object-oriented and agile development processes.

Program development begins with defining the requirements. Upon completing each stage, development proceeds to the next stage as shown by the heavier arrows. At each stage, perhaps with the exception of implementing scenarios, lots of interaction with users should be expected.

KEY IDEA

User involvement is vital to a successful project.

In the following sections we'll examine each of the major stages shown in Figure 11-1 and illustrate the process with a case study.

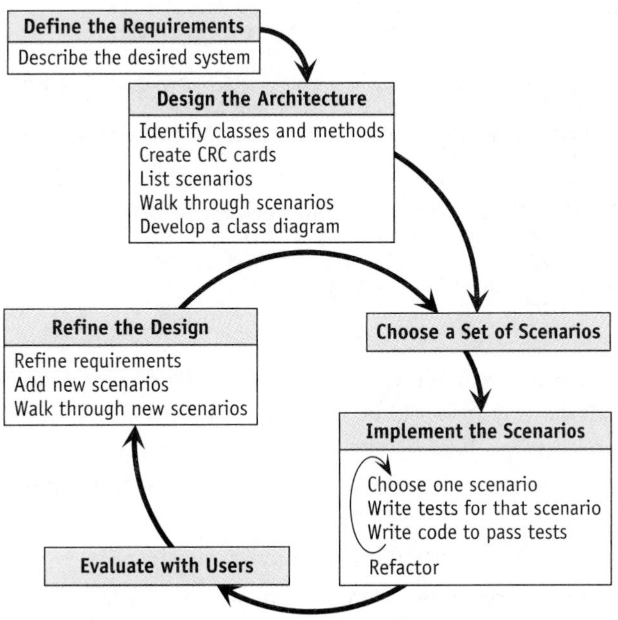

(figure 11-1)

Software development process

11.2.1 Defining Requirements

The first stage of the development process is defining the **requirements**, also known as the **specification**. The requirements are a written statement of what the program is supposed to do. Depending on the complexity of the problem, it could be several paragraphs or many pages.

Requirements often start with a single person's idea, but are usually developed by talking with people who are expected to use the program. Questions might include:

- How do you currently do the job (without the program)?
- What are the good parts and the bad parts of your current approach?
- What capabilities would you like to have that you don't have now?

Eventually, the answers to these questions are written down. They might result in a document that contains information similar to the paragraphs shown in Figure 11-2. We will use it as a running example for the remainder of this section.

```
The video store system is used to rent videos to the store's customers.

The system has a list of videos and a list of customers. Each video has a unique
identifying number, title, and genre. The system must be able to add new customers and
videos to these lists, as well as remove inactive customers and videos no longer in
circulation.

Customers are charged a rental fee of $.99 for videos released more than one year ago
and $2.99 for new releases, plus any accumulated late fees, when they rent a video.
Customers are assessed late fees if a video is returned past its due date. Customers
have a rental history to help resolve late fee disputes.
```

(figure 11-2)

Requirements for a video store system

Requirements are seldom complete. This is a fact of life that programmers must deal with, rather than the way it should be. Incomplete requirements mean that programmers typically need to go back to the users with questions about what the system should do. Some of the issues these requirements should address, but don't, include the following:

- Can the store have multiple copies of the same video?
- Can a customer rent more than one video at one time?
- Are there additional fees such as taxes?
- Will other pricing strategies be offered? For example, three videos for three nights at a reduced rate?
- What kind of reports are required?
- What are the possible genres?
- Does this program run on a single computer or many? (Running on many computers with coordinated data is much beyond the scope of this book.)

For this example, we will assume the store can have multiple copies of a video and that customers can rent more than one video at a time. We will ignore the other issues for now.

11.2.2 Designing the Architecture

The second stage of the software development process is designing the program's architecture. The **architecture** refers to how the most important classes interact with each other. Crucial decisions here have consequences throughout the life of the program, so it's important to get it right. Designing the architecture consists of five tasks, as shown in Figure 11-1. The five tasks are as follows:

KEY IDEA

Defining the architecture includes some of the most important and far-reaching decisions of the project.

- Identify the most important classes and methods for the program using an analysis of the nouns and verbs in the requirements.
- Summarize the responsibilities and collaborators for each class on index cards.
- List scenarios in which the software will be used.
- Walk through the scenarios using the index cards to further develop the responsibilities and collaborators.

- Develop a class diagram based on the responsibilities and collaborators listed on the index cards.

These five tasks are elaborated in the sections that follow.

Identify Classes and Methods

In Section 8.3 we introduced an object-based design strategy, reproduced in Figure 11-3. The methodology uses nouns and noun phrases in the requirements to help identify objects and classes, and verbs and verb phrases to help identify methods. Recall that a noun is a word indicating a person, place, thing, or idea, while a verb is a word expressing an action or a state of being.

(figure 11-3)

Object-based design methodology (reproduced from Figure 8-13)

1. Read the description of what the program is supposed to do, highlighting the nouns and noun phrases. These are the objects your program must declare. If there are any objects that cannot be directly represented using existing types, define classes to represent such objects.
2. Highlight the verbs and verb phrases in the description. These are the services. If a service is not predefined:
   a. Define a method to perform the service.
   b. Store it in the class responsible for providing the service.
3. Apply the services from Step 2 to the objects from Step 1 in a way that solves the problem.

Applying this methodology is easier if the specification is rewritten using simpler sentences. All sentences have a **subject** and a **predicate**. The subject is a noun or noun phrase and provides the answer of who or what did the action. The predicate contains a verb and explains the action or condition of the subject.

The rewritten specification should use a verb in the active voice. Such a sentence has a subject that does something or is in a state of being. The alternative is a passive voice where the subject receives the action. "Customers are charged a rental fee of $.99 ..." is passive. "Customers pay a rental fee of $.99 ..." is active.

The rewritten specification should also remove connecting words like "and" in the predicates, wherever possible. This will introduce some verbal redundancy. For example, "The system has a list of videos and a list of customers" will turn into two sentences: "The system has a list of videos" and "The system has a list of customers." Such rewriting must be done carefully to ensure that the meaning is unchanged.

The result of rewriting the requirements in Figure 11-2 is shown in Figure 11-4. The verb is underlined in each case.

The system rents videos to customers.
The system has a list of videos.
The system has a list of customers.
Each video has a unique identifying number.
Each video has a title.
Each video has a genre.
The system adds new customers (to its list of customers).
The system adds new videos (to its list of videos).
The system removes inactive customers (from its list of customers).
The system removes videos (from its list of videos).
Customers pay a rental fee of $.99 for releases more than one year old.
Customers pay a rental fee of $2.99 for new releases.
Customers pay a late fee after a video has been returned late.
Customers have a rental history to help resolve late fee disputes.

(figure 11-4)

Requirements rewritten using the active voice and simpler sentences

With the requirements in this form, we can more easily use the nouns and verbs to identify classes and methods, as suggested by the methodology in Figure 11-3. The following guidelines are relevant:

- Nouns in the sentence's subject are almost always relevant classes.
- Some nouns will represent instance variables in a class. Examples from Figure 11-4 include "unique identifying number" and "title." Nouns that can be represented using existing types such as `int` and `String` or occur with a verb such as *has* are particularly likely to be instance variables rather than new classes.
- Look at nouns in the predicate as well. For example, "rental history" looks like it might be a class we need to write.
- Name classes with singular nouns. If we need many videos or customers, we will construct many `Video` or `Customer` objects.
- Don't let adjectives fool you. They describe or modify a noun, but rarely represent a new class. For example, we do not need one class for customers and another class for inactive customers ("inactive" is the adjective).
- Sometimes synonyms or abbreviations are given for the same thing—for example, "video store system" and "system." Choose just one name to represent all of these different ways of saying the same thing.
- Class names are important. Take enough time to find just the right words to describe the objects they represent. In this case, `Video`, `Customer`, and `RentalHistory` are fairly obvious choices. "The system" needs more work. `VideoStore` is one reasonable choice to encompass the whole "system."

The predicates in the rewritten requirements represent the **responsibilities** of each class. Responsibilities come in two flavors: information the class must know or derive, and actions the class must be able to carry out. The first kind of responsibility is often represented by possessive verbs such as have, has, or keeps. The second kind is often represented by active verbs such as add, remove, rent, or charge.

Create CRC Cards

KEY IDEA

CRC cards list a class's responsibilities and collaborators.

CRC cards are a handy way to record the classes and responsibilities identified in the previous step. CRC stands for Classes, Responsibilities, and Collaborators. The cards are usually made from 4 x 6 inch index cards and are divided into three areas, as shown in Figure 11-5.

(figure 11-5)

Sample CRC card

VideoStore	
rent videos to customers	video
has a list of videos	customer
has a list of customers	
add and remove videos	
add and remove customers	
charge customers for videos	
assess late fees	

The top area of the CRC card contains the name of the class. Below the class name, the responsibilities are listed on the left side. The right side contains a list of the **collaborators**. The collaborators section is a recognition that classes usually do not act alone. They collaborate with other classes to do their work. For example, to rent a video, the `VideoStore` class will likely need to work with instances of the `Video` and `Customer` classes. Hence, both classes are listed to the right. A collaborator is only listed once even though it may be involved with several responsibilities.

It's important to use real index cards rather than making these lists on a computer because in one of the following steps we will distribute the CRC cards to people in a group. The size is also important. These cards are meant to represent an overview of the class. If we can't express it in the space on one card, we are using too much detail. That's why the closely related actions of adding and removing customers are compressed into a single responsibility in Figure 11-5.

These CRC cards represent the classes likely to play the most important roles within the program. As such, they form the foundation of the program's architecture.

However, we now set the CRC cards aside while we develop scenarios. The scenarios will eventually be used with the cards to further develop their responsibilities and collaborations.

Develop Scenarios

A **scenario** is a specific task that a user might want to do with the program. Scenarios are also known as **use cases**. We will use scenarios to simulate the program to gain a better understanding of what classes are needed, the services they need to support, and how the classes interact with each other.

Scenarios for the video store system might include:

- A program is started.
- A new customer is added.
- An existing customer rents a video.
- An existing customer rents three videos.
- A new customer rents a video.
- A video is returned on time.
- An overdue video is returned.
- A customer returns an overdue video and wants to pay the late fee without renting another video.
- A customer would like a list of all the drama videos released in the last two years that he or she has not already rented.
- A report is prepared of all customers with videos more than one week overdue.
- A video has been lost and must be removed from the system.

A complex system could have hundreds or even thousands of scenarios. List as many as you can think of.

Walk Through Several Scenarios

CRC cards and scenarios are brought together in a **walk-through**. A walk-through proceeds through one scenario in an orderly fashion to develop the tasks that each class must perform. A walk-through works best with a group of people in which each person is assigned one of the CRC cards. That person gives voice to the class's responsibilities as the group walks through the scenario. If a group of people is not available, the process can be simulated by just one person.

A walk-through is an active process that is best illustrated by examining a transcript. The "speaking parts" are people holding their assigned CRC card. We'll identify them in the transcript by the classes named on their cards. The first scenario is an existing customer, Ashley Wong, renting the video *Star Wars: A New Hope*.

`VideoStore:` "Well, I already have a responsibility to 'rent videos to customers,' so I guess I'll start this one. I'd better find Ashley in my list of customers."

KEY IDEA

Responsibilities are often added during a walk-through.

`Customer:` "That sounds like a new responsibility. You'd better write it down on your card." (`VideoStore` adds ***find customer*** to her card.)

`VideoStore:` "I have a list of customer objects. `Customer`, what kind of information do I need to find one of you in the list?"

KEY IDEA

Defining responsibilities often identifies required instance variables.

`Customer:` "I don't have any responsibilities related to that. I guess I could have a name or an ID number. I'll write that down on my card." (`Customer` adds ***has info like name and ID*** to his card.) "I could also have a responsibility to determine if a given name or ID matches me." (`Customer` adds ***determine if given name or ID matches me.***)

`VideoStore:` "So I need to have a way to get a customer name or an ID from the user. I can also see that eventually I'm going to need information to identify a video, too. But I've already got a long list of responsibilities from the noun/verb analysis!"

`Video:` "What if we had a user interface (`UI`) class to collect that kind of information? That would off-load some of that responsibility from you."

`VideoStore:` "Great idea!"

KEY IDEA

New CRC cards are often added during a walk-through.

`VideoStore` adds `UI` as a collaborator. Someone makes a new CRC card for `UI` and adds the responsibilities ***accept customer ID or name*** and ***accept video ID*** as responsibilities. `VideoStore` is added as a collaborator.

`VideoStore:` "OK. So now I can get a customer number from the `UI` and collaborate with `Customer` to find the specific customer. I can do the same with `Video` to find the video. So `Video`, you already have the responsibility to ***have info like ID, title, and genre*** from our noun/verb analysis. You'd better do like `Customer` did and add ***determine if given ID matches me***. I'll also add the responsibility ***find a video***.

"Now I've got a `Video` and a `Customer` and I'm supposed to rent one to the other. I'd really like to give that responsibility to someone else. `Video`, can you rent yourself to the `Customer`?"

`Video:` "I suppose so. But I recall that the `Customer` class has responsibilities for having a rental history and paying rental fees. I think it would make more sense for him to have that responsibility."

`Customer:` "Yeah, I can do that. I'll add ***rent video*** as a responsibility. To rent a video, I need to find out if the video is a new release or not. `Video`, can you answer that question for me?"

`Video:` "You really want that information so you know how much to charge, right? I think it would be better if you just asked me that question directly rather than whether I'm a new release."

`Customer:` "You're right!"

`Video` adds ***get rental fee*** to its responsibilities.

`Customer:` I also need to add the video to the rental history. So I'll add the responsibility ***add video to rental history*** and add `RentalHistory` as a collaborator.

`RentalHistory:` "That makes me think that I'm just a list of some other kind of object. I think "rental history" is really just an `ArrayList` in the `Customer` class. I propose renaming myself to just `Rental`. Then I would have the responsibility of having information about one rental—mainly the video, the date rented, and the due date."

The `RentalHistory` card is thrown away and a new one named `Rental` is created. The responsibility to ***have info like video, date rented, date due*** is added. `RentalHistory` collaborates with `Video`. The collaborator on the `Customer` card is changed from `RentalHistory` to just `Rental`.

We'll stop our transcript here. To finish this scenario the participants need to decide how to charge the customer for the rental and perhaps for accumulated late charges.

After finishing this scenario, the group should walk through additional scenarios. It's good to do several radically different scenarios early to verify that the evolving architecture can handle them. The architecture often changes quite a bit while walking through the first several scenarios, but then settles down to a stable design. Eventually scenarios will not result in new CRC cards or collaborations and will produce only a few new responsibilities. At that point, the walk-through process can stop.

KEY IDEA

Walk through several scenarios.

A walk-through blurs the distinction between objects and classes. In practice, it doesn't matter. The same person can represent all the instances of one class and generally doesn't need to keep track of them as distinct objects.

Beginners often skip walking through scenarios, perhaps because they feel embarrassed by the role playing this process demands. Don't! A walk-through is a *very* effective way to understand how the system will work and to come to a common agreement on the design.

Develop a Class Diagram

The final step in designing the architecture is to develop a class diagram from the CRC cards. "Knowing" responsibilities often turn into instance variables. The other responsibilities turn into methods. Collaborations turn into associations between classes. The CRC cards developed so far for the video store yield the class diagram shown in Figure 11-6.

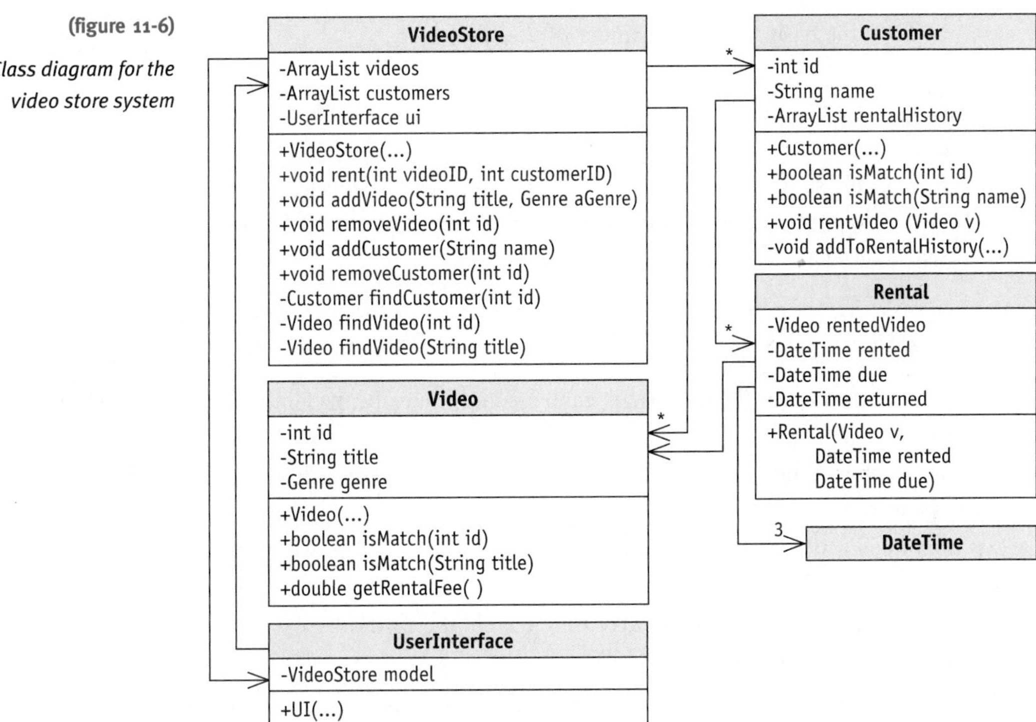

(figure 11-6)

Class diagram for the video store system

11.2.3 Iterative Development

The main body of the development methodology, shown in Figure 11-1, consists of four repeated steps called the **development cycle**:

- Choose a set of scenarios to implement.
- Implement those scenarios.
- Evaluate the resulting system with users.
- Refine the design based on user evaluation, perhaps by adding new requirements or scenarios or revising the existing ones.

In a large project, the development team will repeat this development cycle many times. With each iteration, they have a program that is closer to the finished product, and with adequate feedback from users, refined into a product that actually meets their needs.

Choose a Set of Scenarios

The development cycle begins with choosing a subset of the scenarios to implement. The choice should be made with the users. Which scenarios will they find most useful? Which scenarios are required for the most basic functionality? For example, we need to add videos and customers before we can rent videos. So we might choose adding videos and customers as the first scenarios to implement.

These scenarios form the basis for the remainder of the cycle.

Implement the Chosen Scenarios

The implementation phase is when the code is actually written. As illustrated by the development methodology diagram in Figure 11-1, implementation itself is iterative within the larger iterative process.

Each implementation iteration begins with choosing one scenario—for example, adding a video. This scenario is represented in the class diagram by the `addVideo` method.

Next, write tests to determine if the scenario is implemented correctly. Recall that a test involves five steps:

- Decide which method you want to test. In this case, `addVideo` will be our primary concern.
- Set up a known situation. For example, a brand new `VideoStore` object that has zero videos.
- Determine the expected results of executing the chosen method.
- Execute the code you want to test.
- Verify the results. For example, verify that calling `addVideo` causes the `VideoStore` object to have one more video than before. Verifying that the video can also be retrieved is another good test.

LOOKING BACK

Testing was first discussed in Section 7.1.

Testing a command such as `addVideo` also requires queries to determine the current state of the `VideoStore` class.

These suggestions result in tests such as those shown in Listing 11-1.

Listing 11-1: *Tests for the* `VideoStore` *class*

```
public class VideoStore extends Object
{ // Methods omitted.

   public static void main(String[] args)
   {
      System.out.println("Testing adding a video...");
      VideoStore vs = new VideoStore();
      Test.ckEquals("no videos", 0, vs.getNumVideos());
      vs.addVideo("Star Wars: A New Hope", Genre.SCI_FI);
      Test.ckEquals("one video", 1, vs.getNumVideos());

      // test finding by name
      Video v1 = vs.findVideo("Star Wars: A New Hope");
      Test.ckEquals("found video", true,
                    v1.isMatch("Star Wars: A New Hope"));

      // test finding by id
      Video v2 = vs.findVideo(v1.getID());
      Test.ckEquals("found video", true,
                    v2.isMatch("Star Wars: A New Hope"));

      // test not found condition
      Video v3 = vs.findVideo("Gone with the Wind");
      Test.ckIsNull("not found", v3);
   }
}
```

Another set of tests should be written in the `Video` class. Among them, tests for `isMatch` and tests to verify that each instance of `Video` is assigned a unique identification number.

KEY IDEA

Some programmers use the mantra "Test a little, code a little; test a little, code a little...."

After writing the tests, implement the methods required so that the tests pass. This means actually compiling the program (and fixing the compile-time errors) and running it (and fixing any bugs the tests expose).

When the scenario passes its tests, choose another scenario and repeat the process. Keep choosing new scenarios, writing tests, and writing code until all the scenarios for this development cycle are implemented.

Finally, reexamine the program in light of the new code that has been added. There may be areas that are overly complex or where code is duplicated. Take the time to simplify it (**refactor**) before moving on.

Evaluate with Users

After the scenarios for this development cycle have been implemented, evaluate the resulting program with users. Does it do what they expect? Are there ways to improve how they interact with the program? Does it spark new ideas for how the program can be used to do their jobs more efficiently?

Users' needs change over time. In fact, introducing the program itself changes users and their needs. It could be that what they thought was needed when the project began is very different now—and the project must adapt to that new reality.

Refine the Design

The evaluation step may require refining the design. Perhaps the requirements themselves need to be refined. Perhaps a key scenario needs to be changed with a new walk-through, or it is realized that some scenarios won't actually be needed, or (more likely) that some scenarios need to be added.

After refining the design, repeat the development cycle again, beginning with choosing a new set of scenarios to develop.

Advantages of the Iterative Approach

The iterative approach to implementation has a number of advantages, especially compared to an older approach known as the **waterfall model**. It was named the waterfall model because the results of each stage of development fell into the next, much like a series of waterfalls. The waterfall model is illustrated in Figure 11-7.

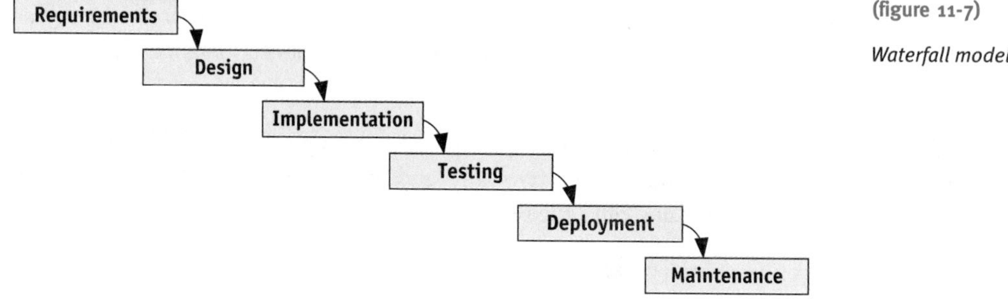

(figure 11-7)

Waterfall model

The iterative approach offers at least six specific advantages (in no particular order):

- In the iterative approach, bugs are produced, identified, and fixed in small groups. In the waterfall model, many bugs are produced all at once during the implementation phase, and then must be found and fixed all at once during the testing phase. This is considerably harder because one bug can interfere with finding and fixing another.

- The program is always close to working with the iterative approach. If a deadline is looming (you need to hand in the assignment or your customer wants to see how the program is coming along), you have all the completed scenarios to show. Using the waterfall model, it may be that a lot of work has been done but nothing can actually be demonstrated because the debugging is incomplete.
- The iterative approach does a better job of maintaining programmer morale. Each small victory of seeing another test pass boosts morale, but a long debugging process in the waterfall model saps morale.
- Choosing one scenario to implement and writing tests for it gives programmers many specific goals to focus their programming efforts. It also provides an objective means to determine when the goals have been met.
- As the program changes over time, the tests generated in the iterative approach are useful for verifying that everything that used to work still works.
- Frequent user evaluation helps keep the project on track with the real, changing needs of the users.

11.3 Designing Classes and Methods

In Section 11.2 we discussed a development process for discovering and implementing classes. In this section we will explore some concrete rules or heuristics for classes and methods that increase the understandability, testability, and maintainability of a program. We will look at a pair of classes that illustrate a number of *very* poor design decisions. We will examine the consequences of those decisions and what better decisions could have been made.

The program we will examine is the beginnings of an e-mail client such as *Thunderbird*, *Eudora*, or *Outlook*. The program doesn't have any code to actually send or receive e-mail, but the core classes to store messages and manipulate them in a mailbox exist. A provided graphical user interface allows new messages to be created, and existing messages to be saved to a file, replied to, or deleted.

Our examination will concentrate on just two classes: `Mailbox` and `Message`. The `Message` class models a single message that has been either sent or received. It has instance variables to store the sender, recipient, date, subject, and the body of the message. The `Mailbox` class stores and manipulates a number of `Message` objects. It has an instance variable, `msgs`, that is a partially filled array of `Message` objects. It also has methods such as `sendMessage`, `replyToMessage`, and `deleteMessage`.

The program uses two instances of `Mailbox`, one for the "in box" (received messages) and another for the "out box" (sent messages).

The code for these two classes is shown in Listings 11-2 and 11-3. A class diagram for the program is shown in Figure 11-8. You should take some time to examine these classes and try to understand what they do and how they work. Remember, the code has many poor design decisions. This is *not* code to emulate! Many of these poor choices are shown in annotations within the listing.

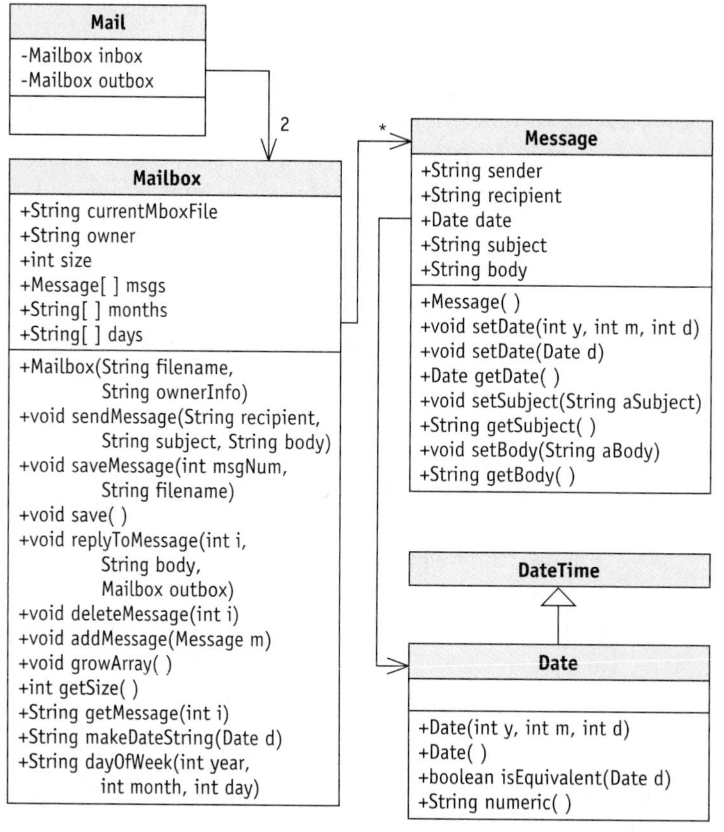

(figure 11-8)

Class diagram for the e-mail program

FIND THE CODE

ch11/email/

Listing 11-2: *A very poor implementation of the* `Mailbox` *class for an e-mail program*

```
import java.util.Scanner;
import java.io.*;
import becker.util.*;

/** A mailbox holds messages for an e-mail program.
 *
 *  @author Jack Rehder, Byron Weber Becker */
public class Mailbox extends Object
```

Listing 11-2: *A very poor implementation of the* `Mailbox` *class for an e-mail program* (continued)

```
{
  public String currentMboxFile = "";
  public String owner; // who's mailbox is this?

  public int size = 0; // number of messages
  public Message[] msgs = new Message[5];

  public static final String[] months = {"Jan", "Feb", "Mar",
    "Apr", "May", "Jun", "Jul", "Aug", "Sep", "Oct", "Nov", "Dec"};
  public static final String[] days = {"Sunday", "Monday",
    "Tuesday", "Wednesday", "Thursday", "Friday", "Saturday"};

  public Mailbox(String filename, String ownerInfo)
                                 throws FileNotFoundException
  { super();
    this.owner = ownerInfo;

    this.currentMboxFile = filename;
    Scanner in = new Scanner(new File(filename));

    while (in.hasNextLine())
    { Message msg = new Message();  // start a new message
      in.next();                    // skip From: tag
      msg.sender = in.nextLine().trim();
      in.next();                    // skip To: tag
      msg.recipient = in.nextLine().trim();
      in.next();                    // skip Date: tag
      msg.setDate(in.nextInt(),
                  in.nextInt(), in.nextInt());
      in.next();                    // skip Subject: tag
      msg.setSubject(in.nextLine().trim());

      String body = "";
      while (true)
      { String line = in.nextLine();
        if (line.equals("EOM"))
        { break;
        }
        body = body + line + "\n";
      }
      msg.setBody(body);
      this.addMessage(msg);
    }
```

public instance variables

Instance variables that have little to do with the class's core purpose.

Many set methods leave data in `Message` objects unprotected.

Code to read a message belongs in the `Message` class.

Nested loops are hard to understand.

Listing 11-2: *A very poor implementation of the* `Mailbox` *class for an e-mail program* (continued)

```
      in.close();
   }

   public void sendMessage(String recipient,
                           String subject, String body)
   { Message m = new Message();
     m.recipient = recipient;
     m.setSubject(subject);
     m.date = new Date();
     m.setBody(body);
     m.sender = this.owner;

     this.addMessage(m);

     PrintWriter out = this.openOutputFile("outbox.txt");
     out.println("From: " + m.sender + "\nTo: " + m.recipient
         + "\nDate: " + m.getDate().numeric() + "\nSubject: "
         + m.getSubject() + "\n" + m.getBody());
     out.close();
   }

   public void saveMessage(int msgNum, String filename)
   { PrintWriter out = this.openOutputFile(filename);
     out.println("From: " + this.msgs[msgNum].sender + "\nTo: "
         + this.msgs[msgNum].recipient + "\nDate: "
         + this.msgs[msgNum].getDate().numeric() + "\nSubject: "
         + this.msgs[msgNum].getSubject() + "\n"
         + this.msgs[msgNum].getBody());
     out.close();
   }

   public void save()
   { PrintWriter out =
               this.openOutputFile(this.currentMboxFile);

     for (int i = 0; i < this.size; i++)
     { Message m = this.msgs[i];
       out.print("From: " + m.sender + "\nTo: " + m.recipient
           + "\nDate: " + m.getDate().numeric() + "\nSubject: "
           + m.getSubject() + "\n"+ m.getBody() + "EOM\n");
     }
     out.close();
   }
```

Constructor apparently does nothing.

Public instance variables leave data unprotected.

This code is repeated five times (look for the other four times).

Listing 11-2: *A very poor implementation of the* `Mailbox` *class for an e-mail program* (continued)

```
  public void replyToMessage(int i, String body,
                             Mailbox outBox)
  { Message reply = new Message();

    reply.setDate(new Date());
    String sender = this.msgs[i].recipient;
    reply.sender = sender;
    String recipient = this.msgs[i].sender;
    reply.recipient = recipient;
    String subject = this.msgs[i].getSubject();
    reply.setSubject("Re: " + subject);
    Date d = this.msgs[i].getDate();

    String who = this.msgs[i].sender;
    String BEGIN = "**On " + d.numeric() + ","
        + who.substring(0, who.indexOf('<')).trim()
        + " wrote:\n";
    String END = "**end original message**\n\n";

    String origMsg = this.msgs[i].getBody();
    String replyBody = BEGIN + origMsg + END + body;
    reply.setBody(replyBody);

    PrintWriter out = this.openOutputFile("outbox.txt");
    out.println("From: " + reply.sender + "\nTo: "
                         + reply.recipient
        + "\nDate: " + reply.getDate().numeric() + "\nSubject: "
        + reply.getSubject() + "\n" + reply.getBody());
    out.close();
    outBox.addMessage(reply);
  }

  public void deleteMessage(int n)
  { for (int i = n; i < this.size - 1; i++)
    { this.msgs[i] = this.msgs[i + 1];
    }
    this.size--;
  }

  public void addMessage(Message m)
  { if (this.size == this.msgs.length)
```

This method is too long and complex. Much of the code belongs elsewhere.

More repeated code.

No documentation.

Listing 11-2: *A very poor implementation of the* `Mailbox` *class for an e-mail program* (continued)

```
    { this.growArray();
    }
    this.msgs[this.size] = m;
    this.size++;
  }

  public void growArray()
  { Message[] temp = new Message[this.msgs.length * 2];
    for (int i = 0; i < this.msgs.length; i++)
    { temp[i] = this.msgs[i];
    }
    this.msgs = temp;
  }

  public int getSize()
  { return this.size;
  }

  public String getMessage(int i)
  { return "From: " + this.msgs[i].sender
                  + "\nTo: " + this.msgs[i].recipient
                  + "\nDate: " + this.msgs[i].getDate().numeric()
                  + "\nSubject: " + this.msgs[i].getSubject() + "\n"
                  + this.msgs[i].getBody();
  }

  public String makeDateString(Date d)
  { if (d.isEquivalent(new Date()))
    { return "Today";
    }

    int month = d.getMonth();
    int year = d.getYear();
    int day = d.getDay();

    String wkDay = this.dayOfWeek(year, month, day);
    return wkDay + "," + months[month-1] + "" + day + "" + year;
  }

  public String dayOfWeek(int year, int month, int day)
  { int a = (int) Math.floor((14 - month) / 12);
    int y = year - a;
    int m = month + 12 * a - 2;
```

Many methods that should be `private` are `public`.

This kind of processing belongs in the `Message` class.

These methods have little to do with the core purpose of the class and should be elsewhere.

Listing 11-2: *A very poor implementation of the* `Mailbox` *class for an e-mail program* (continued)

```
    int d = (day + y + (int)Math.floor(y / 4)
        - (int)Math.floor(y/100) + (int)Math.floor(y/400)
        + (int) Math.floor((31 * m)/12)) % 7;

    return this.days[d];
  }

  public PrintWriter openOutputFile(String filename)
  { try
    { return new PrintWriter(filename);
    }
    catch (Exception ex)
    { ex.printStackTrace();
      System.exit(1);
    }
    return null;
  }
}
```

No attempt to handle the error.

FIND THE CODE

ch11/email/

Listing 11-3: *A very poor implementation of the* `Message` *class for an e-mail program*

```
/** Store one message in the mail program.
 *
 * @author Jack Rehder; Byron Weber Becker */
public class Message extends Object
{
  public String sender;
  public String recipient;
  public Date date;
  public String subject;
  public String body = "";

  public Message()
  {}

  public void setDate(int y, int m, int d)
  { this.date = new Date(y, m, d);
  }

  public void setDate(Date d)
```

`public` instance variables are open to abuse.

Constructor doesn't initialize instance variables.

Set methods required to overcome inadequacies in the constructor.

This class should provide services for its clients other than simply storing information.

Listing 11-3: *A very poor implementation of the* `Message` *class for an e-mail program* (continued)

```
   { this.date = d;
   }

   public Date getDate()
   { return this.date;
   }

   public void setSubject(String aSubject)
   { this.subject = aSubject;
   }

   public String getSubject()
   { return this.subject;
   }

   public void setBody(String aBody)
   { this.body = aBody;
   }

   public String getBody()
   { return this.body;
   }
}
```

11.3.1 Rules of Thumb for Writing Quality Code

In this section we will discuss a number of rules of thumb for writing quality code. In Section 11.3.2 we will put them into a larger framework.

Document Classes and Methods

You probably noticed that the `Mailbox` and `Message` classes have almost no documentation. If you read the code for comprehension, you probably wished that it had more documentation to help you understand it.

Documentation, or the lack of it, obviously affects how easily a class or method can be understood. That, in turn, affects how easily the code can be maintained and, to some extent, tested.

KEY IDEA

Document what the method should do, then write the code.

Writing documentation is one of a programmer's more dreaded jobs, but it definitely pays dividends later when someone needs to read and understand the code. An acceptable practice is to write the documentation and code in parallel, while both are still fresh in your mind. Don't write more code until the code you have is documented. However, many people agree that the best practice is to write the documentation *before* writing the code. Writing the documentation first can often help clarify in your mind what the code is supposed to do, making the code easier to write and more likely to be correct.

Avoid Nested Loops

The `Mailbox` constructor contains a loop within a loop. Such structures are difficult for programmers to understand. Simplify them by putting the inner loop into an appropriately named helper method. Naming the task helps you clarify the responsibilities of both the outer loop and the inner loop.

Keep Methods Short

Research published by psychologist George A. Miller in 1956 shows that people can only store and process a limited amount of information in short term, or working, memory. The limit is often given as seven chunks of information, plus or minus two.

This research supports writing short methods. Methods are more likely to be written and understood correctly if they have fewer chunks of information. The most appropriate way to write such methods is using stepwise refinement, as discussed in Chapter 3.

The `Mailbox` class has at least two methods that are too long: the constructor and `replyToMessage`. Instead of a constructor that is 32 lines long, consider one that uses a helper method to read one message:

```
public Mailbox(String filename, String ownerInfo)
               throws FileNotFoundException
{ super();
  this.owner = ownerInfo;

  this.currentMboxFile = filename;
  Scanner in = new Scanner(new File(filename));

  while (in.hasNextLine())
  { Message msg = this.readOneMessage(in);
    this.addMessage(msg);
  }
  in.close();
}
```

In this version, all the details of reading a message, lines 30–49 in Listing 11-2, are collapsed into `readOneMessage`. That method might be further refined using two more helper methods, `readHeader` and `readBody`.

Using helper methods provides at least three benefits. First, each helper method gives the code it contains a name. A well-chosen name helps identify what the code does, making the helper method easier to understand. Second, the name summarizes the code, making the client that calls it easier to read and understand. Third, helper methods make testing easier. The code in each helper method can often be tested separately, which is easier than testing the same code written as a single method.

Make Helper Methods Private

Methods that do not need to be called from outside their containing class should be declared `private`. For example, there is no reason to call `readOneMessage` from outside the `Mailbox` class. The same is true for `growArray` and probably for `makeDateString` and `dayOfWeek`.

Making these methods `private` offers two advantages. First, it prevents programmers from using them inappropriately, either maliciously or by mistake. For example, a programmer may think it is his responsibility to call `growArray` before adding a message to the mailbox. Doing so could slow the program dramatically and could waste a huge amount of memory. Taking active steps to prevent such problems can make the program as a whole more bug free.

Second, when a bug does occur, appropriate use of accessibility helps track it down by elimination. If a problem occurs within a private method, we know with absolute certainty that it was called from within the same class. With non-private methods, we might be surprised to find that it was called from some place completely unexpected.

Put Duplicated Code in a Helper Method

The code in Listing 11-2 has five places where essentially the same code is repeated. Take a moment to find them. The code itself isn't exactly the same, but the results are.

The repeated code assembles an e-mail message into a string to be saved or displayed in the user interface and occurs in lines 67–69, 75–79, 89–91, 120–123, and 156–160. This is undesirable for a number of reasons:

- It makes the class longer, with more code for programmers to read and understand.
- If a change to the way messages are represented is required, there are five copies of the code that need to change.

- If a bug is found, parallel changes must be made in five places. It will be easy to overlook at least one of them—maybe all except for one!
- All of the repeated code must be tested. That's a silly waste of time and energy if the code is essentially the same.

The solution is to make a helper method that can be called from many places in the program rather than duplicating the code itself. In fact, it may appear that `getMessage` is precisely the helper method we need:

```
155   public String getMessage(int i)
156   { return "From: " + this.msgs[i].sender
157                     + "\nTo: " + this.msgs[i].recipient
158                     + "\nDate: " + this.msgs[i].getDate().numeric()
159                     + "\nSubject: " + this.msgs[i].getSubject()
160                     + "\n" + this.msgs[i].getBody();
161   }
```

This method can be used to replace code in `saveMessage` (lines 75–79) and `save` (lines 89–91), but is much more difficult for `sendMessage` (lines 67–69) and `replyToMessage` (lines 120–123). Passing an index as the argument works for the first two methods, but the last two work with `Message` objects that are not yet in an array and thus can't be accessed with an index.

LOOKING AHEAD

Later, we consider the question "Which class should contain the helper method?" It will lead to an even better solution.

One solution is writing a helper method, `formatMessage`, with a `Message` object as a parameter. Then `getMessage`, above, can be written as follows:

```
155   public String getMessage(int i)
156   { return this.formatMessage(this.msgs[i]);
161   }
```

and lines 89–91 can be rewritten as follows:

```
89       out.print(this.formatMessage(m) + "EOM\n");
```

In addition to reducing wasted time and energy, putting duplicate code into a method gives you an added abstraction to work with. If you've already used the same code several times, chances are good that it represents a higher-level idea, or abstraction, within your code. Putting it in a method increases the chances that you'll recognize when it is appropriate to use it, and makes using it trivial—just call the method.

Make Instance Variables Private

`Mailbox` and `Message` both have many public instance variables. This is unfortunate for several reasons. First, it makes the classes more difficult to change. For example, the `Message` class uses `Strings` to store the sender and receiver. They both have two distinct parts, the real name and the e-mail address in angle brackets, as in the following example:

```
Byron Weber Becker <bwbecker@email.com>
```

It may be decided later that it would be better to define a class named `Contact` for this information. Instances could store the real name in one field and the e-mail address in another. Other information might be added such as nicknames, telephone numbers, or mailing addresses.

If the instance variables were private, making this change would be straightforward. We would have to find all the places inside the `Message` class that accessed either `sender` or `recipient` and change them to use the new `Contact` class. However, if the instance variables are public our search must expand beyond the containing class to include the entire program. In fact, it is possible for many programs to use a given class—and any of them might need changing if they used the instance variable instead of an appropriate method.

A second reason to keep instance variables private is to prevent misuse, either accidentally or maliciously. For example, a programmer writing the user interface may need to know the number of messages in an instance of `Mailbox`. He might write `this.mBox.msgs.length`, failing to realize that `msgs` is a partially filled array and that the number of messages does not correspond to the space in the array. Or perhaps you wrote the `Mailbox` class and the programmer working on the user interface has either a grudge against you or a really wacky sense of humor and adds the following in an obscure part of the user interface code:

```
if (Math.random() < 0.01)
{ this.mBox.size--;
}
```

The effect of this insertion is that one message is lost from the mailbox 1% of the times the above code executes. It seems like a bug in the `Mailbox` class, but who would think to look in a completely unrelated part of the user interface? You could spend a lot of time tracking down this "bug" and face a lot of pressure from management while you're doing it! The best policy is to simply avoid the issue by making instance variables private.

Write Powerful Constructors

The previous advice to make instance variables private is largely circumvented if instance variables have `set` methods. Public `get` and `set` methods allow a client to change a private instance variable just as if it were public.

KEY IDEA

A constructor should return an object that is ready to use.

In the Message class, the only reason to have set methods is to give the instance variables their initial values—the constructor's job. By the time the constructor has finished executing, the object should be ready to use. All the instance variables should have meaningful initial values. Because all of the values are available at once in a well-written constructor, more stringent checking for inconsistent data can be performed.

In the case of the Message class, two constructors might be appropriate. The first would be used in the Mailbox constructor to read one message from a file. It would take a single argument, an open Scanner object. The second could be used by the replyToMessage and sendMessage methods to construct an object from the constituent pieces.

Powerful constructors make the Message class more understandable because it eliminates the need for many set methods. Many bugs arise from variables being given incorrect values. By minimizing the places where new values are given, bugs are made less likely and those that do exist are easier to find.

Powerful constructors also eliminate the problem of incompletely initialized objects. With an appropriate constructor it is impossible for a programmer to overlook setting an instance variable. This might occur, for example, when a new instance variable is added to the class. In the current program all the places where an instance is constructed must be found and modified. This is a much easier maintenance task if all the initialization is done in the constructors.

Keep Data and Processing Together

The largest change, and the biggest benefit, to the Mailbox and Message classes comes from keeping data and processing together. The major clues that these classes don't keep them together are:

- Message is a "container" class. It contains information, but doesn't have any methods that actually process that information.
- Mailbox gets many individual pieces of data from instances of Message and then processes them in some way.

KEY IDEA

The class with the data should do the processing.

A better approach is to have the class with the data do the processing. For example, the formatMessage helper method we described earlier really belongs in the Message class, not the Mailbox class. By moving it, you can avoid passing an argument and use the instance variables directly instead of using the get methods.

A more dramatic example comes from moving much of replyToMessage to the Message class. Because much of the information for a reply comes from the original message, it makes sense to keep the data and processing together by asking the message to construct the reply. Using this approach, the replyToMessage method in Mailbox could become only three lines of code, as shown in Listing 11-4.

Listing 11-4: *The* `replyToMessage` *method, written assuming a* `constructReply` *method exists in the* `Message` *class*

```
/** Reply to the given message with the given body.
 * @param i          the index of the message to reply to
 * @param body       the body of the reply
 * @param outBox     the mailbox instance collecting sent mail. */
public void replyToMessage(int i, String body,
                           Mailbox outBox)
{ Message reply = this.msgs[i].constructReply(body);
  outBox.addMessage(reply);
  reply.save(Mailbox.SEND_BOX);
}
```

This code also strongly hints that a message should save itself to a file rather than expecting the `Mailbox` class to do it. After all, the message is where the data that requires saving is located.

It should be obvious that understanding and maintaining `replyToMessage` has become much easier with this change. It is true that programmers may need to find three additional methods (`constructReply`, `addMessage`, and `save`) and understand them. On the other hand, each of these methods has a clear focus that is clearly indicated by its name. That may be enough to allow the programmer to avoid needing to understand their details. If the programmer does need to understand them, the fact that they are focused on a single task and have a clear name will make understanding them much easier.

Write Immutable Classes

A class is **mutable** if its instances can be changed after they are constructed. A class is **immutable** if instances can not be changed after construction. An example of an immutable class is `String`. There are no methods to change a string once it has been created, only methods that create a new string that is similar to the old one in some way. For example, the `name.toUppercase()` method does *not* change the string `name`; it creates a new string like `name` except that lowercase characters are converted to uppercase.

Immutable classes are simple. Their objects have only a single state—the state in which they were created. If the state is correct when it's created, it will be correct for all time without any further work by you or the programmers using the class. References to immutable classes can be shared freely because there is no way to change the object's state. Mutable classes, on the other hand, can have objects in a wide variety of states that change over time. That makes them harder to use and understand than immutable classes.

Classes that represent a value, like `Date` or `String`, should almost always be made immutable. All other classes should be made as immutable as possible. It obviously isn't possible to make `Mailbox` immutable because messages need to be added and deleted from it. But `Message` can be made immutable. Once created, there is no reason to change a message.

There are a few simple rules to make a class immutable:

- Don't provide methods that modify the object.
- Make all the instance variables private. This prevents anyone from changing them directly.
- Make sure that you don't allow aliases to mutable components. For example, instances of `Message` have references to a `Date` object. Because a `getDate` method is provided, the designer of `Message` must ensure that either `Date` is immutable or that `getDate` makes a copy of the date object to return. Another option is to provide queries such as `getYear` to answer questions about the mutable component. It's also important the other way. If a client passes a reference to a mutable object, make a copy of that object before storing it in an instance variable.

LOOKING BACK

This issue is discussed in more detail beginning in Section 8.2.

If you want to really go the extra mile for your immutable classes, you need to follow two more rules:

- Use the `final` keyword for instance variables. For example, `private final String subject` in the `Message` class emphasizes that `subject`'s value should not change after the first assignment. This is enforced by the compiler.
- Use the `final` keyword for the class as a whole. For example, `public final class Message` prevents someone from overriding the methods in the `Message` class and changing their behaviors.

The `DateTime` class is mutable, even though it represents a value and should be immutable according to the criteria given earlier. Suppose you wanted an immutable `Date` class. Extending `DateTime` doesn't work because methods like `addDays` would still be available via inheritance. But `DateTime` has a lot of functionality that would be good to reuse.

The solution is for the `Date` class to have an instance of `DateTime` as a private instance variable. It can then provide exactly the methods it requires and omit the problematic ones. For example, see Listing 11-5. Of course, nothing prevents you from adding new methods to the class as well.

Listing 11-5: *Making an immutable class using a mutable class*

```
public final class Date extends Object
{
  private final DateTime myDate;

  public Date(int year, int month, int day)
  { super();
    this.myDate = new DateTime(year, month, day);
  }

  // For internal use only. Assumes that the caller does NOT keep a reference to d.
  private Date(DateTime d)
  { super();
    this.myDate = d;
  }

  public int getYear()  {  return this.myDate.getYear();  }
  public int getMonth() {  return this.myDate.getMonth(); }

  // Return a new date, adding the given number of days.
  public Date addDays(int howMany)
  { DateTime copy = new DateTime(this.myDate);
    copy.addDays(howMany);
    return new Date(copy);
  }
  // etc.
}
```

Delegate Work to Helper Classes

A class should represent a single abstraction. The `Message` class should model an e-mail message and the `Mailbox` class should be focused only on managing a group of messages. Mixing in peripheral concepts makes a class harder to understand, test, and maintain. However, in Listing 11-2, the `Mailbox` class does just that.

The problem is that, in addition to its core responsibility of managing messages, the `Mailbox` class also has responsibilities for formatting dates. The major clues are instance variables storing the names of days and months along with methods to turn a date into a formatted string and calculate the day of the week.

Particularly in a program where a `Date` class already exists, these instance variables and methods should be moved there. In general, a class should delegate work to "helper classes" using the "has-a" or containment relationship discussed in Section 8.1.3 so that each class remains focused on a single idea.

Limiting each class to one cohesive set of responsibilities makes the class easier to understand. It's easier to test one set of responsibilities than to test two or more that are intertwined in the same class. Finally, if changes need to be made, it's easier to figure out where and actually make the changes in well-focused classes.

11.3.2 Managing Complexity

Many of these coding heuristics relate to four features that have been long recognized as crucial to quality code. These four features have stood the test of time, across many different programming languages and development methodologies. They seem to be invariant. Defined in terms of Java, they are:

- **Encapsulation**—Grouping data and related services into a class.
- **Cohesion**—The extent to which each class models a single, well-defined abstraction and each method implements a single, well-defined task.
- **Information hiding**—Hiding and protecting the details of a class's operation from others.
- **Coupling**—The extent to which interactions and dependencies between classes are minimized.

KEY IDEA

Managing complexity is one of the hardest parts of writing software.

Each of these relates to a fundamental problem in constructing software: managing complexity. Most programs have a huge number of details, each affecting the overall correctness of the system. Managing them so that a change to one detail does not create a problem with another is difficult!

Let's define **detail**, for the moment, as either a method or an instance variable, and define **interaction** as a method calling another method or accessing an instance variable.

We can get an idea of the complexity of a program by making a diagram with circles representing details and lines representing interactions. For example, consider a class with one instance variable and three methods. Two methods access the instance variable and one method calls the third as a helper method. The complexity diagram would appear as shown in Figure 11-9. The instance variable is shown with crossed lines within it.

(figure 11-9)

Complexity diagram for a very simple class

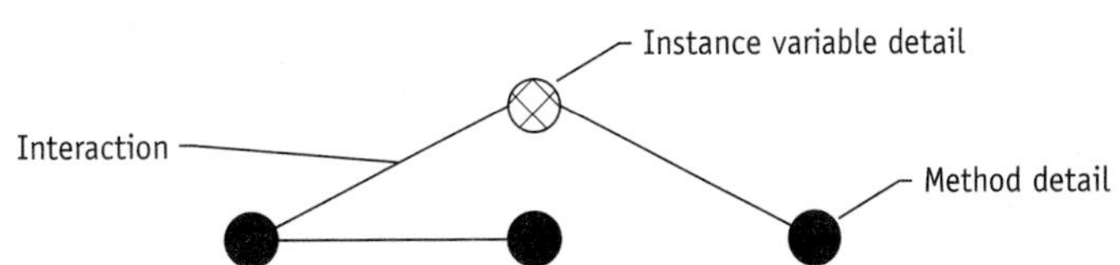

Figure 11-10 shows a diagram for a considerably more complex program. We will use it to show how the ideas of encapsulation, cohesion, information hiding, and coupling can help us manage complexity.

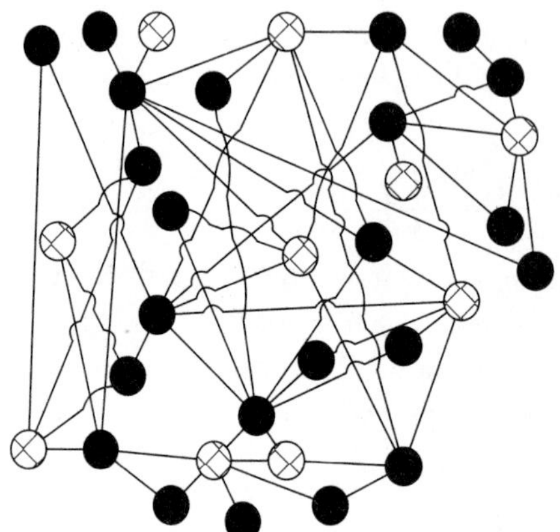

(figure 11-10)

Unconstrained interactions between details

The best solution to date for managing complexity is to impose voluntary constraints on how we write programs so that some interactions can't happen, and to organize the other interactions so that they are easier to think about. Encapsulation, cohesion, information hiding, and coupling all have a role to play in managing complexity through voluntary constraints.

KEY IDEA

Java allows us to write poorly designed programs. As programmers, we must choose to write excellent programs.

Encapsulation

Think of a class as a capsule—something that encapsulates or encloses a number of related instance variables and methods (details). By putting them into the same capsule, we clearly indicate that they belong together.

Encapsulation is illustrated in Figure 11-11. It's the same as Figure 11-10 except that details have been grouped and encapsulated using ovals. Encapsulation makes it easier to see how interactions are organized because now they fall into two groups.

(figure 11-11)

Classes that are encapsulated, but do meet the ideal for cohesion, information hiding, or coupling

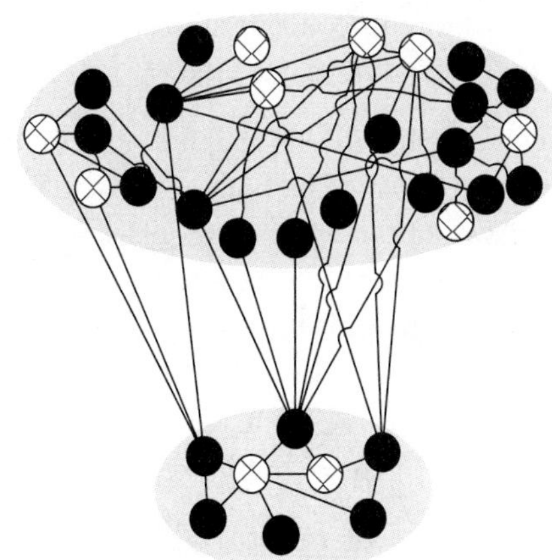

KEY IDEA

Encapsulation divides interactions into those within a class and those between classes.

The first group are interactions between details within the same class. Of all the possible interactions in our program, encapsulation focuses our attention on a group that works together using closely related details. These details, and the interactions between them, are the primary concern of the programmer or small group of programmers responsible for implementing and maintaining the class.

The second group of interactions are the primary concern of programmers using the class—the interactions between details in different classes. Of all the possible interactions within a program, encapsulation helps these programmers focus on the most relevant ones. By grouping interactions inside classes and between classes, we help manage complexity.

Java's class mechanism provides a natural way to group details. Unfortunately, Java does not force them to be grouped—that requires good design decisions on our part. The heuristics noted earlier that support encapsulation include the following:

- ➤ Keep Data and Processing Together
- ➤ Delegate Work to Helper Classes

Cohesion

Cohesion emphasizes the "relatedness" of the details that we encapsulate. We should not encapsulate just any details that happen to interact. We should make sure those details represent a cohesive whole. In concrete terms, a class should model a single, well-defined entity. A method should have one, and only one, task.

In the mail program presented earlier in this chapter, one could imagine the `Message` class containing instance variables and methods related to both dates and contacts (senders and receivers). This would represent "low cohesion." The ideal is "high cohesion" in which details related to dates are split into their own class, as are the details related to contacts. This kind of change is illustrated in Figure 11-12.

KEY IDEA

In a highly cohesive program, each class is focused on one abstraction.

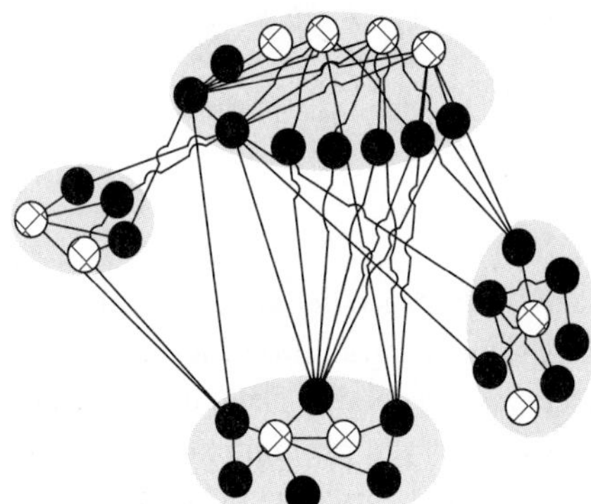

(figure 11-12)

Encapsulated, cohesive classes that do not yet meet the ideal for information hiding and coupling

Cohesive classes and methods make it easier for us to understand them. It's easier to focus on just one abstraction or one task than to understand two or more that are mixed together.

Heuristics related to cohesion include:

- Delegate Work to Helper Classes
- Keep Methods Short
- Put Duplicated Code in a Helper Method

Information Hiding

Encapsulation groups details of a program together in a class so that a programmer can focus primarily on them. Information hiding says which of those details are important to programmers using the class and hides the rest behind the capsule wall, as shown in Figure 11-13. Note the dark wall around each oval and that public details have moved to straddle the capsule wall.

(figure 11-13)

Information hiding emphasizes some details and hides the rest from view

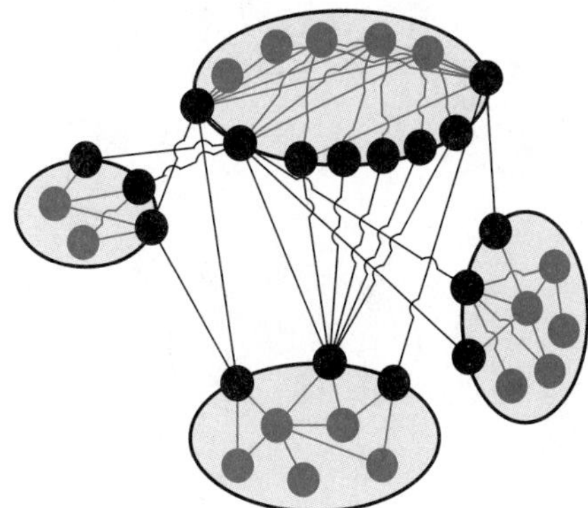

Information hiding distinguishes *what* a class can do from *how* it does it. The parts that are left exposed (declared `public`) are always methods. Their names and documentation indicate what can be done with the class. The details of the instance variables required and the helper methods used are all hidden inside the class.

KEY IDEA

Information hiding removes many possible interactions from a programmer's consideration.

For programmers who want to use a class, information hiding eliminates many possible interactions from their consideration and helps manage the complexity.

Another advantage, as noted before, is that hiding details allows us to change how the class operates without affecting the code that uses the class. As long as the public methods continue to behave as before, the details of just *how* they work can change to accommodate better approaches.

Information hiding also allows us to limit our testing to only the public parts. If they are tested thoroughly, we can be more relaxed about testing internal details.

Heuristics that are related to information hiding include:

- Make Instance Variables Private
- Make Helper Methods Private
- Write Powerful Constructors
- Keep Data and Processing Together

Coupling

Ideally, we would like to be able to understand or change one class with only minimal knowledge or changes of other classes. When this is true, we say the classes are "weakly coupled." See Figure 11-14.

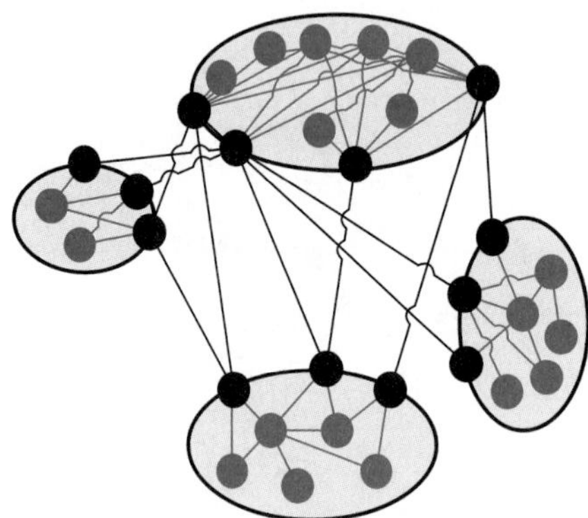

(figure 11-14)

Weakly coupled classes have few dependencies on each other

Information hiding already reduces the coupling between classes by forcing the classes to interact only through public methods. We can go one step further, however, and ask ourselves whether we have the right public methods.

For example, the `Message` class in Listing 11-3 has public instance variables but no methods that really do anything, resulting in strong coupling. The `Mailbox` class is forced to interact often with the `Message` class in order to do its work.

Simply hiding the instance variables and making public accessor methods would not improve the coupling, however. The `Mailbox` class would still need many interactions with the `Message` class. The coupling between these two classes improved dramatically, however, when we wrote higher-level methods like `constructReply` and `save`, substantially reducing the dependency on accessor methods like `getSubject`.

KEY IDEA

Weakly coupled classes use powerful methods to minimize dependencies between classes.

Heuristics that affect coupling include:

- Keep Data and Processing Together
- Make Instance Variables Private
- Write Powerful Constructors
- Write Immutable Classes

Working together, the heuristics in Section 11.3.1 and the overall goals of encapsulation, high cohesion, information hiding, and weak coupling yield classes and programs that are easier to understand, easier to test, and easier to change. All of these are attributes contributing to quality code, from a programmer's perspective.

11.4 Programming Defensively

The quality of software generally increases with the disciplined use of a development methodology. Quality also increases dramatically through good design. But even with these efforts, users may still enter erroneous input, a necessary file may still be accidentally deleted, or a program bug may still bring the program to an abrupt halt. Quality software will proactively attempt to detect and, if possible, handle such errors. This section discusses important techniques for doing so, including exceptions, design by contract, and assertions.

11.4.1 Exceptions

We learned about exceptions in Section 8.4. We learned that exceptions are thrown when an exceptional circumstance arises. The exception interrupts the program's normal flow of control and if nothing is done to intervene, the program will stop with an error message displayed on the console. Programmers can intervene in this process with the `try-catch` statement. Statements that may throw an exception are placed in the `try` clause. A series of `catch` clauses after it can include code to handle exceptions that are thrown.

Using exceptions effectively is an important part of writing quality software for a number of reasons. First, exceptions provide a uniform approach to reporting and handling errors. Languages that do not support exceptions force programmers to adopt ad hoc methods for reporting errors using an instance variable to signal that an error occurred or returning an error code from a method. Figuring out a variety of error reporting methods takes time and increases the probability of mistakes being made.

When using ad hoc methods to report errors, programmers often do not bother to check the error indicators, resulting in software that sometimes fails. Forcing programmers to confront possible errors and decide how to handle them is the second advantage of exceptions. For example, Java forces the programmer to think about how to handle a FileNotFoundException. The programmer could decide to simply report the error and stop, ask the user to enter the filename again, or read an alternate file—but the error can't simply be ignored with the hope that it won't happen.

Third, exceptions separate error-handling code from the code for normal processing. This separation makes the logic for both the normal processing and handling errors easier to understand.

Fourth, an exception's stack trace provides valuable information for programmers when debugging a program.

Many beginning programmers dread exceptions because they are often the first sign of an unwelcome debugging session. This is the wrong attitude. Instead, exceptions should be welcomed as a programmer's friends. They tell us as soon as possible, with helpful debugging information, what went wrong. Finding a bug that is exposed right away, with helpful information, is much easier than debugging in languages without exceptions. In those languages, an error may go undetected until much later in the program's execution. When it is finally noticed, finding its cause may be very difficult.

11.4.2 Design by Contract

One excellent use for exceptions is to inform programmers when a method has been called with inappropriate arguments. For example, consider the deleteMessage method in the e-mail program. It takes a single argument, the number of the message to delete. This number is really the index into the partially filled array of messages and must be between 0 and this.getSize()-1, inclusive. If the message number is outside of this range, it represents a bug and an exception, typically IllegalArgumentException, should be thrown:

```
public void deleteMessage(int msgNum)
{ if (msgNum < 0 || msgNum > this.getSize()-1)
  { throw new IllegalArgumentException("msgNum = " + msgNum
                          + "; must be 0.." + (this.getSize()-1));
  }

  // existing code to delete the message
}
```

The requirement that msgNum be between 0 and this.getSize()-1 is called a **precondition**. More generally, a precondition is anything that must be true when the method is called for it to execute correctly. It is the responsibility of the method's client to ensure that the preconditions are met. Checking the preconditions inside the method is simply a favor to those using the method: the method fails quickly with an appropriate exception that helps them find their bugs more easily. But it is a favor that should

KEY IDEA

Verifying preconditions is a huge favor to those using the method—which usually includes the programmer who wrote it.

always be extended. Consider what might happen if an invalid argument slips through and is used in a method:

- The method might fail in the middle of its processing with a confusing exception.
- The method might complete normally but compute a wrong result that affects the correctness of the program.
- The method might complete normally but leave the object in an invalid state, causing an error later in the program in an unrelated part of the code.

All of these results are undesirable and easily prevented by checking parameters for validity.

If the method's client has met the preconditions, the method is obligated to meet its **postconditions**. A postcondition is what should be true after the method executes. If the preconditions have not been met, the postconditions likely won't be met either.

The postcondition for `deleteMessage` is that the given message, `n`, has been removed from the list and all the remaining messages are renumbered to fill the "hole."

Both pre- and postconditions should be documented. Unfortunately, the standard JavaDoc tool does not support them explicitly. It does have a `@throws` tag which can be used instead. An appropriate comment for `deleteMessage` might be

```
/** Delete message number n from this mailbox, renumbering all messages from
 *   n+1..this.getSize()-1 to have numbers n...this.getSize()-2. The renumbering
 *   preserves the order of the messages.
 *   @param n    The number of the message to delete
 *   @throws IllegalArgumentException if n is outside the range 0..this.getSize()-1 */
```

The word after `@throws` is expected to be the name of an exception class.

Pre- and postconditions are often viewed as contracts between the client and the method and using them consistently is called **design by contract** [1]. The core idea of this phrase is that each interaction between a client and a method is bound by a **contract**. The contract specifies what the client and the server can each expect of the other.

The contract between a client and method is similar to the contracts we encounter in everyday life. For example, a cell phone provider may have a contract that says if you (the client) pay $20.00 per month, they (the server) will provide up to 500 minutes of cell phone service per month. If you sign the contract and live up to your responsibilities of paying $20.00 per month, they are obligated to provide the service. If they don't, you could take them to court and sue for breach of contract. On the other hand,

[1] This phrase was trademarked by Bertrand Meyer, the developer of the Eiffel programming language. Eiffel makes extensive use of the ideas behind "Design by Contract."

if you don't pay the $20.00, they are under no obligation to provide the cell phone service. They might, but they certainly don't have to.

11.4.3 Assertions

An **assertion** is something the programmer believes will always be true at a certain point in the code. Starting with Java 1.4, the keyword `assert` is available to test assertions. It is followed by a Boolean test that should be true at that point in the program. For example, in the e-mail program, `growArray` should only be called if the partially filled array of messages is full. Thus, `growArray` should have an assertion:

```
private void growArray()
{ assert this.size == this.msgs.length;
  ...
```

If the assertion fails, the program behaves as if an exception named `AssertionError` were thrown. If the behavior is the same, what advantages do assertions have over using an exception? There are two advantages. First, assertions are easier and faster to write because they combine the test with implicitly creating and throwing the exception object.

Second, assertions can be turned off easily. Some assertions might slow the program down unacceptably. For example, some searching techniques require the array being searched to be sorted. Checking that precondition takes longer than doing the actual search. Such a precondition can be used during development and debugging, but then turned off so they have no effect on the program when deployed to users. To turn assertion checking on, execute the program using the following command line:

```
java -enableassertions «ClassName»
```

If you use an IDE, find the place where command line arguments are set and add `-enableassertions`.

It may seem natural to use `assert` to check preconditions as well. Throwing a specified exception, however, is a better solution in this case because it can document the error more accurately in terms the method's user can understand.

11.5 GUIs: Quality Interfaces

Just as the notion of quality applies to programs as a whole, it also applies to the user interface in particular. This has been driven home to me personally in a program I use to access information about students. For example:

- The information I need 90% of the time is buried in four levels of menus. Most of those menus have a single selection.

- The information I most often need is at the top of the screen but to search for another student I need to scroll through several pages of text to reach the "New Search" button.
- The program presents a substantial amount of unimportant information. The useful information is harder to use because of the clutter.

As you can tell, I am not a happy user!

11.5.1 Iterative User Interface Design

Like developing a program, developing a user interface should follow a development process. It shouldn't be surprising that excellent user interfaces are rarely achieved on the first try, so iteration is important. A simplified approach is shown in Figure 11-15.

(figure 11-15)

Iterative user interface design and evaluation process

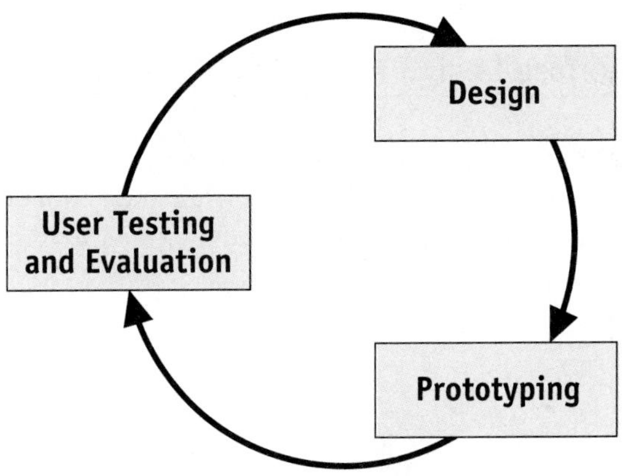

Prototyping refers to making a model of the completed design. It may be a **low-fidelity prototype** drawn on paper index cards or a **high-fidelity prototype** that actually performs many of the operations of the finished program—or anywhere between these two extremes.

In the user evaluation and testing phase, users work with the prototype to evaluate it. Evaluation often involves the **five E's**:

- **Effective**—The completeness and accuracy with which users achieve their goals.
- **Efficient**—The speed and accuracy with which users can complete their tasks.
- **Engaging**—The degree to which the tone and style of the interface makes the product pleasant or satisfying to use.

- **Error tolerant**—How well the design prevents errors or helps with recovery from those that do occur.
- **Easy to learn**—How well the product supports both initial orientation and deepening understanding of its capabilities.

Ideally, each of the five E's is objectively measured and compared to a stated goal. For example, effectiveness might be measured by having a group of users complete a prescribed set of tasks, measuring their error rate. Efficiency might be measured by counting keystrokes and mouse clicks on a set of realistic tasks. Whether the user interface is engaging might be measured with user interviews or questionnaires. Counting the "false starts" users make would be one way to measure whether the user interface is easy to learn.

Obviously, evaluation of a user interface requires users. Having the developers act like users is not good enough—they know too much about the application and how it works.

11.5.2 User Interface Design Principles

Just as the principles of encapsulation, cohesion, information hiding, and coupling have emerged as being important to quality software, a number of design principles are important to quality user interfaces. Well-designed user interfaces are:

- Controlled by the user
- Responsive
- Understandable
- Forgiving

Controlled by the User

Modern user interfaces should give the user as much control over the process as is consistent with the user's knowledge and skill level. Whenever possible, allow the user to choose the ordering of tasks and subtasks. Allow the user to choose between using the keyboard or a mouse. Assume that the user will be interrupted and need to come back to the task later. Allow the user to customize the interface to suit his own preferences.

Responsive

Users need constant feedback to tell them how the system has interpreted their commands. To understand why, put on a blindfold and attempt to send an e-mail message. How far can you get (without specialized tools to give you feedback)?

Feedback happens in many ways: echoing characters typed by the user, highlighting buttons to show they have been "activated" but can still be aborted, disabling controls that are not appropriate in the current context, providing progress bars during long-running tasks, and so on.

Another side of a responsive system is that the feedback comes fast enough to keep the user working at full speed, whenever possible.

Understandable

A quality user interface will be as understandable as possible.

Consistency is one way to keep a user interface understandable. Users will be able to transfer what they have learned in one part of the application to another, and probably even from one application to another. Examples of consistency include using the same language to describe the same concepts, organizing the controls on dialog boxes in the same way, using the same kinds of controls to achieve distinct but similar tasks, and so on. A set of design guidelines helps achieve consistency, as does using a standard library of user interface controls (such as `javax.swing`).

Structuring information and controls also helps promote understandability. For example, the print dialog box shown in Figure 11-16 has information grouped into three areas: Printer, Print Range, and Copies. All of the information in the Printer area is about the physical printer—which one to use, its type, whether it's ready, and so on. Many psychology studies have shown that such structure makes it easier for users to find, organize, and use the information presented to them.

(figure 11-16)

Print dialog box showing structured information and controls

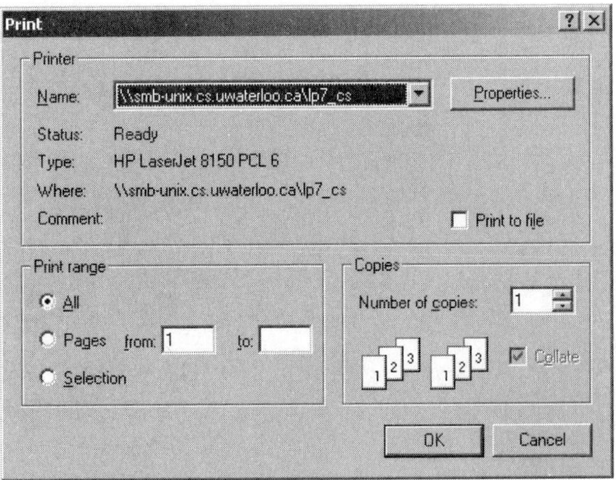

Finally, make use of the fact that people recognize information much more easily than they recall it. For example, the drop-down list of printer names contains two names not shown in Figure 11-16, `\\smb-unix.cs-uwaterloo.ca\ljp_dc3109` and `Splash G620 DocuColor 12PM`. Recognizing which of these three printers is desired is much easier than recalling 35 or more characters and typing them into a text field.

Forgiving

Finally, a quality user interface should be forgiving of user mistakes. Ideally, the interface should prevent as many mistakes as possible by, for example, disabling commands that are not applicable in the current context. But users will still make mistakes due to fatigue, distraction, uncertainty, and so on. The user interface should make it easy to correct these mistakes. It might do this by allowing the user to undo commands, or by allowing users to correct their input and reissue commands.

11.6 Summary and Concept Map

Quality software is a pleasure to work with, both as a user and as a programmer. Quality is generally increased by using an iterative development methodology and paying particular attention to the design. The concepts of encapsulation, cohesion, information hiding, and coupling all play a significant role in maintaining the internal quality of software. Similar kinds of principles apply to user interface design as well. Finally, proactively detecting and reporting bugs and exceptional events via exception objects also increases the quality of the software we write.

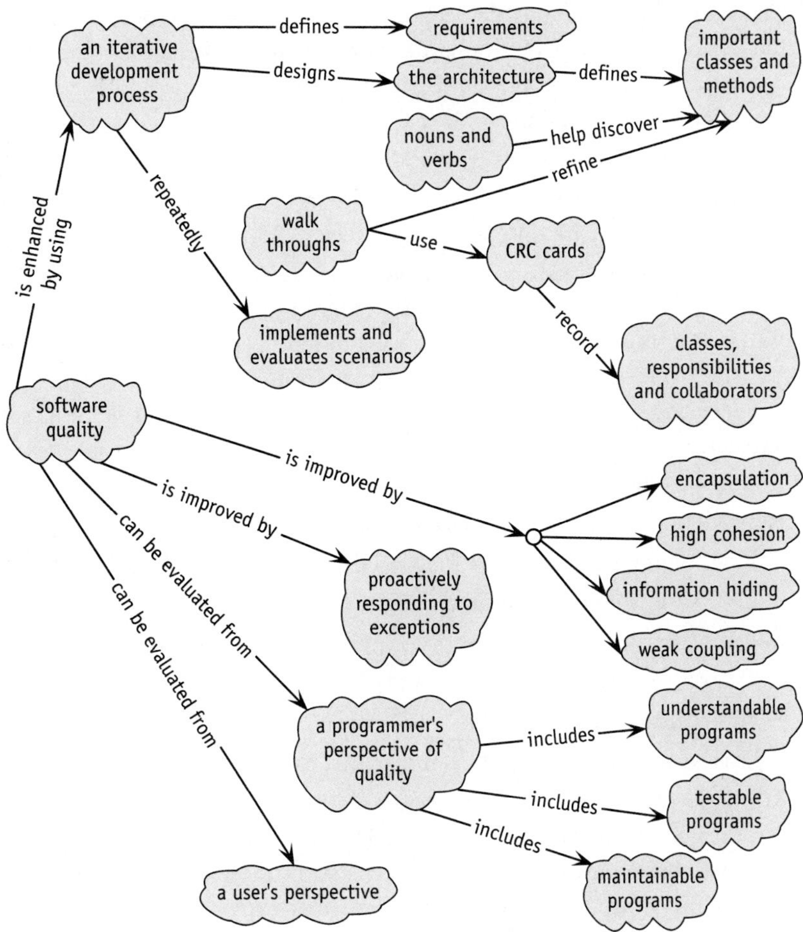

11.7 Problem Set

Written Exercises

11.1 Make CRC cards based on the transcript in Section 11.2.2. For each subproblem, a–d, hand in updated CRC cards and a transcript of the walk-through.

a. Finish walking through the scenario of renting one video. For example, how does the system's user know how much to charge the customer?

b. Walk through adding a new customer.

c. Walk through the scenario of returning a video on time.

d. Walk through producing a report of all customers with videos more than one week late.

11.2 The alarm clock case study in Section 8.3 uses the `newAudioClip` method in the `Applet` class to load a sound file from the disk drive. If the sound file does not exist or is in the wrong format, the `newAudioClip` method doesn't do anything at all. Is this a good idea? Defend your answer.

11.3 Is the `Video` class shown in Figure 11-6 immutable? Why or why not?

11.4 Explain why the `Customer` class, as shown in Figure 11-6, is mutable. Is this class a good candidate for an immutable class? Why?

11.5 Expand the list of scenarios for the video store given in Section 11.2.1. (*Hint*: It would be fruitful to imagine the program having just been installed in a store. What must be done before it can be used to rent a video?) Now consider the iterative nature of the software development process, as shown in Figure 11-1. Organize the scenarios into three groups: the set to implement first, the set to implement next, and the set to implement last. Give a brief rationale describing why you grouped the scenarios as you did.

11.6 For each of the following requirements documents, hand in the following:

a. Rewritten requirements (see Figure 11-4)

b CRC cards that result from the rewritten requirements

c. List of scenarios

d. Transcript of walking through one scenario

e. CRC cards as refined by the walk-through

f. Class diagram constructed from the CRC cards

Requirements Document 1: The concert hall's ticketing system is used to sell concert tickets to concert hall patrons. The system has a list of patrons who have previously purchased tickets as well as a list of upcoming concerts. It also has a map of the concert hall showing how many rows of seats there are and how many seats are in each row.

Users must be able to add new patrons, add newly scheduled concerts, and sell tickets to a particular concert to patrons. Patrons may request of block of adjacent seats in the same row.

The hall's manager will want periodic reports of how many tickets have been sold for each upcoming concert as well as patrons who have purchased tickets to more than four concerts in the last 18 months.

Requirements Document 2: A program is required to synchronize the files in two directories. This is useful, for example, to synchronize a person's laptop computer with files on their primary desktop computer.

Each file has a name and a modification date (the date and time when it was last changed). Each directory has a list of files it contains.

Input to the program are the paths to the two directories to synchronize. The program also has a list of the files that existed the last time the directories were synchronized. Let's refer to the two directories as A and B and to the list as L.

For each file *f* in directory A, the program will copy *f* to B if it does not appear in either B or L (it's a newly created file). It will delete *f* from A if *f* appears in L but not in B (it was previously deleted from B). It will copy *f* to B if it appears in B and L, and the modification date of *f* is newer than the modification date of the copy in B and the copy in B is older than L (it was changed in A but not B). It will ask the user what to do if *f* and the corresponding copy in B are both newer than L.

Similar processing also occurs for each file in B.

After both directories have been processed, they should both have exactly the same files. Write the list of those files out to use the next time the directories are synchronized.

Requirements Document 3: The game of Adventure has a series of rooms in a cave. Each room has a passage to at least one other room. Rooms may also have treasures such as lamps, keys, gold, and so on. Each treasure has an associated weight and value. A player moves between rooms with commands such as "north," "west," and "down." Each room is described when the player enters it.

A player can pick up treasures (but the player has a limit to how much he can carry—it can't carry all of the treasures). The player can also put down treasures it has previously picked up.

The game is over when the player enters the "quit" command. If the value of the player's accumulated treasures is high enough, the player is added to the game's top ten players list.

(For more information on the original adventure game, search the Web for "Colossal Cave Adventure.")

Requirements Document 4: An online auction service has a list of items for sale. Each item has a description, a seller, a current bid, and an auction close date. Buyers may search the list for items with descriptions that contain the search terms they enter. If buyers see an item they want to buy, they may bid on the item, provided the auction close date has not passed and their bid is higher than all previous bids for the item.

Once per day, the system notifies buyers and sellers of auctions that closed that day.

11.7 This chapter mentions the term *refactor* but does not describe it extensively. Research this term on the Web and write a short essay on what the term means. Some sites give concrete refactoring patterns. Describe two or three of these patterns and how they can improve code quality.

Programming Exercises

11.8 Listing 11-4 shows how `replyToMessage` could be written if there was a `constructReply` method in the `Message` class. Write `constructReply`.

Programming Projects

11.9 Find the code to the e-mail program shown in Listings 11-2 and 11-3. Rewrite the program using the heuristics in Section 11.3 and adding exceptions where appropriate. You should not need to modify `MailUI.java`, but other classes may need changing and new classes may be added. The user of your rewritten program should not be able to detect any differences between it and the original. Only the programmers working with it will know how much the quality has improved.

11.10 Consider the video store program discussed in Section 11.2.

a. Write code so that the tests given in Listing 11-1 will pass.

b. Walk through the scenario of adding a customer. Develop tests for this scenario and implement the code required to pass the tests. Assume that a user interface gathers the required information about the customer and provides it to your code.

c. Walk through the scenario of renting a video to an existing customer. Develop tests and implement the code to pass the tests. Assume that a user interface gathers a customer identification number and a video identification number and provides them to your code.

Chapter 12 Polymorphism

Chapter Objectives

After studying this chapter, you should be able to:

- Write a polymorphic program using inheritance
- Write a polymorphic program using an interface
- Build an inheritance hierarchy
- Use the Strategy and Factory Method patterns to make your programs more flexible
- Override standard methods in the `Object` class

In science fiction movies, an alien sometimes morphs from one shape to another, as the need arises. Someone shaped like a man may reshape himself into a hawk or a panther or even a liquid. Later, after using the advantages the new shape gives him, he changes back into his original shape.

Morph is a Greek word that means "shape." The prefix *poly* means "many." Thus, *polymorph* means "many shapes." The movie alien is truly polymorphic. However, even though he has many outward shapes, the core of his being remains unchanged.

Java is also polymorphic. A class representing a core idea can morph in different ways via its subclasses. After studying inheritance in Chapter 2, this may sound like nothing new. However, in that chapter, we usually added new methods to a subclass. In this chapter, we will focus much more on overriding methods from the superclass. The power of this technique will become evident when we are free from knowing whether we're using the superclass or one of its subclasses.

We will also find similar benefits in using interfaces.

12.1 Introduction to Polymorphism

Java provides two ways to implement polymorphism. One uses inheritance and the other uses interfaces. Both depend on having two or more classes that either extend the same class or implement the same interface. We will return to the robot world to illustrate the core ideas and then move to other examples.

KEY IDEA

Polymorphism can be implemented with inheritance or interfaces.

12.1.1 Dancing Robots

Let's define two rather fanciful robots that dance, one to the left and one to the right, as they move to the next intersection. The arrows in Figure 12-1 show the paths they take as they move from their initial position (shown in black) to their final position (shown in white). `LeftDancer` is labeled with an "L" and `RightDancer` is labeled with an "R".

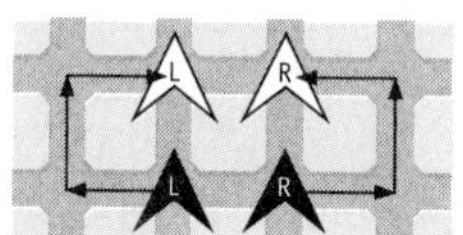

(figure 12-1)

Paths that dancing robots take as they move to the next intersection

The code implementing `LeftDancer` is shown in Listing 12-1. `RightDancer` is similar.

FIND THE CODE

ch12/dancers/

Listing 12-1: *A robot that dances to the left as it moves forward*

```
import becker.robots.*;

/** LeftDancers dance to the left as they move forward.
 *
 * @author Byron Weber Becker */
public class LeftDancer extends RobotSE
{
  public LeftDancer(City c, int str, int ave, Direction dir)
  { super(c, str, ave, dir);
    this.setLabel("L");
  }

  /** Dance to the left. */
  public void move()
  { this.turnLeft();
    super.move();
    this.turnRight();
```

Listing 12-1: *A robot that dances to the left as it moves forward* (continued)

```
18        super.move();
19        this.turnRight();
20        super.move();
21        this.turnLeft();
22    }
23 }
```

Method Resolution Review

How Java determines which method to execute is called method resolution. This concept was first discussed in Section 2.6.2, but it is worth reviewing because it is important to understand how these classes work.

When a method is invoked, say `karel.move()`, Java looks for the `move` method beginning with the object's class. If the object was originally created with the phrase `new LeftDancer(...)`, Java will look for the `move` method beginning with the `LeftDancer` class. That class has a `move` method, so it's executed.

On the other hand, suppose that the `turnLeft` method was invoked. Once again, the search for the method begins with the object's class, `LeftDancer`. That class, however, doesn't have a `turnLeft` method. The search continues in its superclass, `RobotSE`. It doesn't have a `turnLeft` method either and so the search continues in its superclass. `Robot` has a `turnLeft` method; that's the method that is executed. The search for the method to execute starts with the object's actual class and proceeds up the inheritance hierarchy until it is found. If no such method exists, that fact is determined when the program is compiled and an error message is issued.

LOOKING AHEAD

What would happen if line 16 was `this.move()`*? See Written Exercise 12.1.*

When the statement uses `super` to call the method, the search starts at a different place—the superclass of the class containing the method. Thus, the statement `super.move()` at lines 16, 18, and 20 in Listing 12-1 begins to search for `move` in the `RobotSE` class, executing the first `move` method found as it moves up the inheritance hierarchy. In this case, it executes the `move` method in the `Robot` class, resulting in the familiar movement from one intersection to another.

12.1.2 Polymorphism via Inheritance

So far we haven't seen anything new. `LeftDancer` could have been an assignment in Chapter 2. So where is the polymorphism? It's in how these classes are *used*.

Let's use these classes in a way that appears silly at first: Let's assign a `LeftDancer` to a `RobotSE` reference variable, as follows:

```
RobotSE karel = new LeftDancer(...);
```

Java allows this kind of assignment, as long as the reference on the right is a subclass of the reference on the left. It would not work to assign a `LeftDancer` to a `City` variable or even to a `RightDancer` variable because neither is a superclass of `LeftDancer`.

If we can do this, we can also put several `LeftDancers` and `RightDancers` into a single array. Imagine a chorus line of dancing robots, as implemented in Listing 12-2. The core feature is an array that contains *all* the robots, no matter what their type.

FIND THE CODE

ch12/dancers/

PATTERN

Polymorphic Call

Listing 12-2: *An array filled with different kinds of robots*

```
import becker.robots.*;

/** Run a chorus line of dancing robots.
 *
 * @author Byron Weber Becker */
public class DanceHall
{
   public static void main(String[] args)
   { City stage = new City();
      RobotSE[] chorusline = new RobotSE[5];

      // Initialize the array.
      chorusline[0] = new LeftDancer(
                              stage, 1, 0, Direction.EAST);
      chorusline[1] = new RightDancer(
                              stage, 2, 0, Direction.EAST);
      chorusline[2] = new LeftDancer(
                              stage, 3, 0, Direction.EAST);
      chorusline[3] = new RightDancer(
                              stage, 4, 0, Direction.EAST);
      chorusline[4] = new RobotSE(
                              stage, 5, 0, Direction.EAST);

      for (int i = 0; i < chorusline.length; i++)
      { chorusline[i].move();
      }
   }
}
```

For now, remember that all of the objects in the array have a move method. We can tell each of the robots to move with the loop in lines 24–26. But how do these robots move? Do they move like instances of RobotSE because the array is declared that way, or do they each move like the LeftDancer, RightDancer, or RobotSE that they really are?

KEY IDEA

Polymorphism uses a subclass as if it were a superclass, relying on the subclass to override methods appropriately.

The answer is that each object executes the move method in its own class. That is, a LeftDancer moves to the left because that's how that kind of robot was defined to move. RightDancers move to the right, as their move method says they should. The lone RobotSE at the end of the line moves as any other instance of RobotSE would move.

This is polymorphism in action: the statement chorusline[i].move() tells a robot to move, but this particular statement does not need to know or care what kind of robot it is. For example, it doesn't need to tell the LeftDancers to move to the left. It just tells each robot to move and that robot moves in the way it is defined to move. This is like a choreographer telling a dance troupe to "begin on the count of three: one, two, three." All the dancers begin dancing their parts without individual instruction from the choreographer.

KEY IDEA

Polymorphic programs have key identifying features.

A class diagram for what we have just done is typical of polymorphic programs and is shown in Figure 12-2. The characteristic feature is a superclass (RobotSE) that is extended with at least two subclasses. Another class—DanceHall in this case—uses instances of the subclasses as if they were the superclass.

(figure 12-2)

Class diagram for a polymorphic robot program

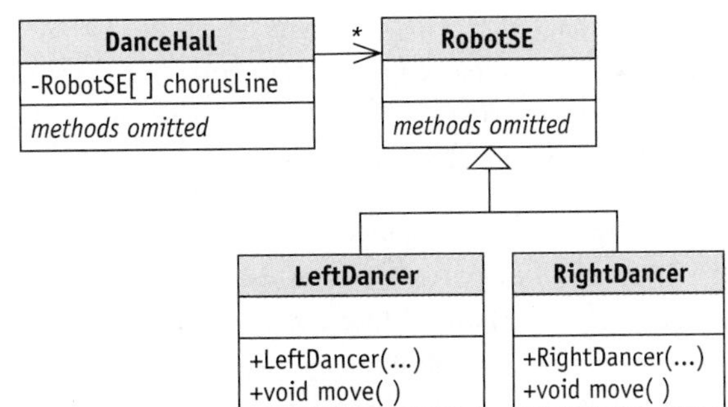

Adding a New Method

Consider adding a pirouette method to both LeftDancer and RightDancer. When a dancer pirouettes, she turns completely around. A LeftDancer turns to the left, as follows, whereas a RightDancer turns to the right.

```
public class LeftDancer extends RobotSE
```

```
{ // Constructor and move method omitted.

  /** Turn completely around. */
  public void pirouette()
  { this.turnLeft();
    this.turnLeft();
    this.turnLeft();
    this.turnLeft();
  }
}
```

FIND THE CODE

ch12/dancers2/

With this change, can we tell the dancers in `chorusline` to pirouette?

```
1 RobotSE[] chorusline = new RobotSE[5];
2 // Initialization of chorusline is omitted.
3 for (int i = 0; i < chorusline.length; i++)
4 { chorusline[i].pirouette();
5 }
```

We cannot. This code will not even compile because line 1 declares that each element of `chorusline` will refer to a `RobotSE` object or one of its subclasses. Most kinds of robots do not have a `pirouette` method and so the compiler assumes the worst—that in line 4, `chorusline[i]` refers to an ordinary robot that lacks a `pirouette` method.

The rule is this: The type of the reference variable determines the names of the methods that can be called; the type of the actual object determines which code is executed. In this example, `chorusline[i]` is the reference variable and its type is `RobotSE`. Therefore, the only methods you can call are methods that appear in the `RobotSE` class. On the other hand, when you call one of those methods (like `chorusline[i].move()`), the type of the actual object (for example, `LeftDancer`) is what determines how the robot moves.

KEY IDEA

The reference's type determines which methods can be called; the object's type determines which code is executed.

To include the `pirouette` method in a dancer's repertoire, we need to add a new class, as shown in Figure 12-3. The `Dancer` class extends `RobotSE` and adds a `pirouette` method. The `DanceHall` class is changed to use an array of `Dancer` objects rather than `RobotSE`. This implies that the single `RobotSE` object shown at line 17 of Listing 12-2 can no longer be included in the array because it is not a subclass of `Dancer`.

(figure 12-3)

Using an abstract class; abstract classes and methods are labeled in italics

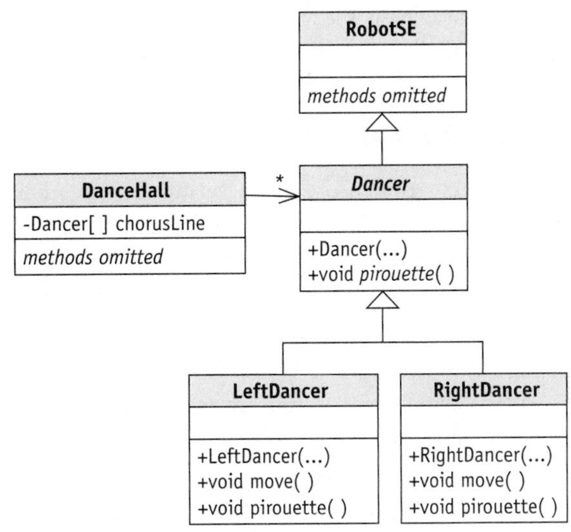

Abstract Classes

When we write the code for the `Dancer` class, should `pirouette` turn to the left like a `LeftDancer` or turn to the right like a `RightDancer`? No matter which choice we make, it will be wrong for at least one of the subclasses.

The best option is to make `pirouette` an **abstract method**. Such a method includes only the access modifier, return type, and signature (method name and parameter list). The method body is replaced with a semicolon. For example:

```
/** Turn this dancer around 360 degrees in its preferred direction. */
public abstract void pirouette();
```

KEY IDEA

An abstract method enables polymorphism even when implementation details are not known.

The purpose of an abstract method is to declare a name that can be used polymorphically, even though it does not declare how the method will be implemented.

Abstract methods must be overridden in a subclass to supply a method body. For example, `pirouette` is overridden in `LeftDancer` with a method that turns to the left; in `RightDancer`, it is overridden with a method that turns to the right.

A class that declares or inherits a method without a body is called an **abstract class** and must be declared with the keyword `abstract`, as follows:

```
public abstract class Dancer extends RobotSE
```

An abstract class such as `Dancer` can be extended by another class, *`X`*, even though *`X`* does not supply a body for `pirouette`. However, *`X`* must also be declared abstract.

An abstract class cannot be used to instantiate an object.

When an abstract method or class is shown in a class diagram, its name will be in italics, as shown in Figure 12-3.

KEY IDEA

Names of abstract methods and classes are shown in italics in class diagrams.

12.1.3 Examples of Polymorphism

Let's take a brief break from robots to examine a number of other examples where polymorphism may be appropriate. All of these cases have the same basic structure as the `DanceHall` example shown in Figure 12-2. In Figure 12-4, we give the participating classes more general names so that in the examples that follow, we can identify how the classes interact. We will use the names as follows:

- The client class uses the services of another class. In the previous example, `DanceHall` is the client that uses the services (`move`) of another class—it just happens to use them polymorphically.
- The abstract class is used to declare variables in the client. It also lists the methods that can be used by the client. In Figure 12-2, `RobotSE` is the abstract class; in Figure 12-3, it's `Dancer`. (The class that defines the names used polymorphically is called "abstract" even though it might not use the `abstract` keyword.)
- A concrete class implements the methods named in the abstract class. In the previous example, `LeftDancer` and `RightDancer` are both concrete classes.

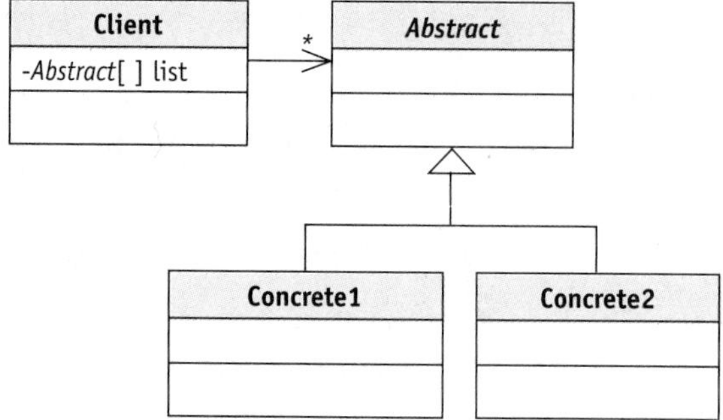

(figure 12-4)

Common pattern for inheritance-based polymorphism

Example: Bank Accounts

A `Bank` class (the client) has many `Accounts` (the abstract class). The `Account` class has both an instance variable to maintain the account's balance and methods to deposit money, withdraw money, and transfer money to another account. It also has methods to get the balance and to charge a service fee at the end of the month. See Figure 12-5.

(figure 12-5)

Class diagram for a bank

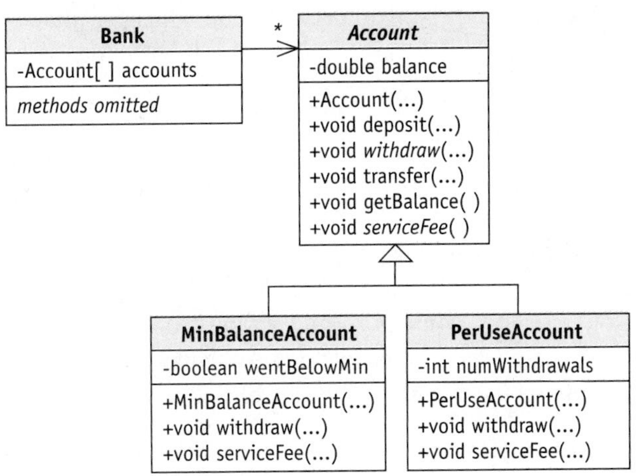

However, each account is really an instance of `MinBalanceAccount` or `PerUseAccount`, both concrete classes. A `MinBalanceAccount` is a kind of account that is free as long as the customer maintains a minimum balance of $1,000. The `withdraw` method is overridden to set an instance variable if the balance ever goes below the minimum. The service fee method is also overridden to charge (or not charge) the service fee.

Similarly, `PerUseAccount` overrides the `withdraw` method to count the number of withdrawals. It also overrides the `serviceFee` method to charge the appropriate fee based on the number of withdrawals.

PATTERN

Polymorphic Call

With this design, the `Bank` class can process every transaction in the same way. It doesn't need to know or care what kind of account the customer has because each account will handle the transaction in a manner that is appropriate for that account.

Example: Drawing Program

A drawing program constructs a drawing out of different kinds of shapes: ovals, rectangles, lines, polygons, characters, and so on. In this case, `Drawing` would be the client class. It has an array of `Shape` objects. `Shape` is the abstract class. It's most crucial method is `draw`.

Classes like `Oval`, `Rectangle`, and `Line` are the concrete classes that extend `Shape`. Each of them override the `draw` method to draw the appropriate shape: an `Oval` draws an oval, a `Rectangle` draws a rectangle, and a `Line` draws a line.

With this design, the Drawing class can draw the entire image with a simple for loop, which tells each Shape object in its array to draw itself, as follows:

```
for (int i = 0; i < this.numShapes; i++)
{ this.shapes[i].draw(...);
}
```

PATTERN
Polymorphic Call

Example: Computer-Game Strategies

Computer versions of chess, Monopoly, and various card games have two or more players. Sometimes the players are people and sometimes the computer controls the extra players. Sometimes the computer has several skill levels.

Each Player object must have a strategy for generating its next move. There might be several ways to do this: ask a human for the next move, find the first legal move, generate a random move, or invoke some sophisticated "artificial intelligence."

The idea of polymorphism is useful here. Player is the client class. Rather than an array, it has a single instance variable holding a MoveStrategy object. This class is the abstract class shown in Figure 12-4. Its most important method is getNextMove. MoveStrategy is extended by several concrete classes: AskUserStrategy, FirstLegalStrategy, RandomStrategy, and AIStrategy. They each override getNextMove to get the next move for the player in their own particular way (see Figure 12-6).

PATTERN
Strategy

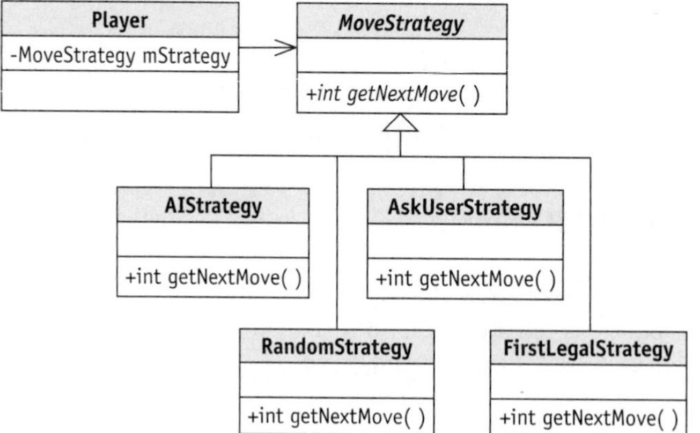

(figure 12-6)
Class diagram of a Player class that uses a polymorphic move strategy

When the game program is set up this way, a Player object can ask for its next move without knowing or caring which particular strategy is being used to generate the move. The strategy can even be changed mid-game by simply assigning a new subclass of MoveStrategy to the Player object's instance variable.

12.1.4 Polymorphism via Interfaces

In a polymorphic program, the client says *what* it wants done (move) but not *how*. How the task is accomplished is determined by the details of the concrete classes.

When polymorphism is achieved via inheritance, the abstract class and the superclass are the same. That combination constrains both what can be done and how it can be implemented. The superclass already contains the methods that can be called, limiting what can be done by the client. The fact that the concrete classes extend the abstract class means that they are not free to extend another class, thus limiting how tasks are accomplished.

KEY IDEA

Java interfaces separate what an object can do from how it can be implemented.

Java interfaces provide another way to implement polymorphism that cleanly separates what can be done from how it can be implemented. Recall from Section 7.6 that interfaces list method signatures and return types, but do not provide the method bodies. For example, the following is an interface for classes that can move:

```
public interface IMove
{
   /** Move this object. */
   public void move();
}
```

We can use this interface with `LeftDancer` and `RightDancer` by including the `implements` keyword and the interface name in the class declaration, as follows:

```
public class LeftDancer extends RobotSE implements IMove
{  // Constructor omitted.
   public void move()
   {  // Same as the move method in Listing 12-1.
   }
}
```

The `implements` clause causes the compiler to verify that `LeftDancer`, or one of its superclasses, implements all of the methods listed in the `IMove` interface.

`DanceHall`, the client class, can use the interface to declare the array of dancers, as follows:

```
IMove[] chorusline = new IMove[5];
chorusLine[0] = new LeftDancer(stage, 1, 0, Direction.EAST);
```

However, an instance of `RobotSE` cannot be inserted into the array because it does not implement `IMove`.

It may seem that we haven't gained anything by introducing `IMove`. But imagine a parade of robots where a `LeftDancer` and a `RightDancer` are carrying a banner. We want the banner to float above everything in the city and display the text "Robot

Parade". The banner should move as the robots move. Figure 12-7 shows two screen captures of such a program.

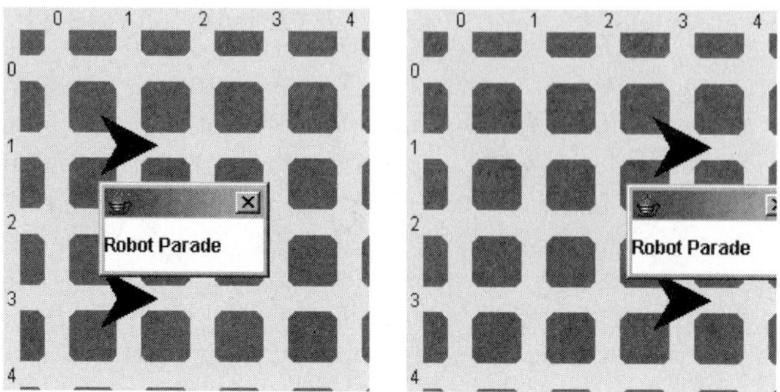

(figure 12-7)

Before and after moving robots and their banner

A class implementing such a banner is shown in Listing 12-3. It displays a small window that floats above all other windows. It has a `move` method to move it a given distance. It extends `JDialog` but also implements the `IMove` interface and can therefore be put in the same array as the robots that carry it, as follows:

PATTERN

Polymorphic Call

```
public static void main(String[] args)
{ City c = new City();

  IMove[] movers = new IMove[3];

  movers[0] = new LeftDancer(c, 1, 1, Direction.EAST);
  movers[1] = new RightDancer(c, 3, 1, Direction.EAST);
  movers[2] = new Banner(80, 165, 40, "Robot Parade");

  for (int numMoves = 0; numMoves < 2; numMoves++)
  { for (int i = 0; i < movers.length; i++)
    { movers[i].move();
    }
  }
}
```

For both the banner and the robots, the client can say *what* to do (`move`), but the details of *how* they move are very different. This is the essence of polymorphism, but using an interface instead of extending a class.

FIND THE CODE

ch12/iMove/

Listing 12-3: *A banner that floats above a city and everything in it*

```
import javax.swing.*;

/** A "banner" that passes over a robot city.
 *
```

Listing 12-3: *A banner that floats above a city and everything in it* (continued)

```
 * @author Byron Weber Becker */
public class Banner extends JDialog implements IMove
{ private int x;
  private int y;
  private int deltaX;

  /** Display a message in a floating window.
   * @param initX      The initial x position of the banner.
   * @param initY      The initial y position of the banner.
   * @param moveX      The distance to move.
   * @param msg        The msg to display. */
  public Banner(int initX, int initY, int moveX, String msg)
  { super();
    this.deltaX = moveX;
    this.x = initX;
    this.y = initY;
    this.setSize(20, 60);
    this.setLocation(this.x, this.y);
    this.setAlwaysOnTop(true);
    this.setContentPane(new JLabel(msg));
    this.setVisible(true);
  }

  /** Move the banner. */
  public void move()
  { this.x += this.deltaX;
    this.setLocation(this.x, this.y);
  }
}
```

12.1.5 The Substitution Principle

A key to understanding polymorphism is the **substitution principle**, introduced by Barbara Liskov. It says that an object of one type, *A*, can substitute for an object of another type, *B*, if *A* can be used any place that *B* can be used.

For example, consider an automobile rental agency that has vans, sports cars, and sedans. If a customer calls a week ahead to reserve an automobile, the agency can substitute a van if that's what is most available. A van is a kind of automobile and can do everything an automobile can do. On the other hand, if the customer called to reserve a van, the agency cannot substitute a sports car. Maybe the customer specifically needs the extra passenger space provided by the van.

In Java, a subclass can always be used anywhere the superclass can be used. A `LeftDancer` (the subclass) can always be substituted for a `Dancer` (the superclass)—just like a van (the subclass) can be substituted for an automobile (the superclass). Why? Inheritance guarantees that a `LeftDancer` has all of the methods that a `RobotSE` has.

KEY IDEA

A subclass that does things differently can be substituted for the superclass.

Similarly, a class such as `Banner` can be substituted for its interface because the compiler guarantees that every method named in the interface will be implemented in the concrete class.

KEY IDEA

Classes can be substituted for the interfaces they implement.

A polymorphic program exploits the fact that even though a concrete class may be substituted for the abstract class, they do not necessarily act the same way. The key feature of a polymorphic program is setting up the classes so that some operations can be performed without knowing the actual types of the objects being used.

12.1.6 Choosing between Interfaces and Inheritance

We've seen that a polymorphic program can be written using either interfaces or inheritance. On what basis do we choose one approach over the other?

The simple rule is to use an interface unless there is some commonality between all the concrete classes that can be implemented in a superclass.

KEY IDEA

Use interfaces for polymorphism unless there is a reason to use inheritance.

In the first example, `LeftDancer` and `RightDancer` have many common details that are implemented in `RobotSE` and its superclasses. These include the ability to move the usual way, turn left or right, and display itself in the city. In the second example, there are no such commonalities. The robots and the banner are implemented completely differently with different superclasses—and thus an interface was appropriate.

In Chapter 11 we talked about loose coupling being a good design decision. That is, classes should depend on each other as little as possible. Modern object-oriented design makes extensive use of interfaces to cleanly separate what classes do from how they do them. That is, a client that uses interfaces is less dependent than one that doesn't. If another concrete class becomes available that implements the interface, it can be substituted with no change to the client. That's loose coupling!

12.2 Case Study: Invoices

In Sections 8.3 and 11.2.2 we studied a simple design methodology to help us start writing an object-oriented program. We now extend that methodology for the last time to incorporate polymorphism. The changes from Section 8.3 are shown in italics in Figure 12-8.

(figure 12-8)

Object-oriented design methodology

1. Read the description of what the program is supposed to do, highlighting the nouns and noun phrases. These are the objects your program must declare.
   a. If there are any objects that cannot be directly represented using existing types, define classes to represent such objects.
   b. *If two or more classes have common attributes and pass the 'is-a' test, consolidate those attributes into a superclass, and extend the superclass to define the classes.*
2. Highlight the verbs and verb phrases in the description. These are the services. If a service is not predefined:
   a. Define a method to perform the service.
   b. Place it in the class responsible for providing the service.
   c. *Where necessary, override methods in subclasses.*
   d. *If a class is responsible for a service but cannot implement it, declare an abstract method.*
3. Apply the services from Step 2 to the objects from Step 1 in a way that solves the problem.

In this section, we'll see how this methodology works by applying it to an invoicing application. The problem statement (or specification) and a sample invoice are shown in Figure 12-9.

Print an invoice to request payment for items provided to a customer by the company. The invoice shows the customer's name and address, and the total invoice amount.

In addition to the above, add one line item for each group of identical items sold. Each line item shows the quantity of items sold, a description, the unit cost, and the total amount charged for items in the group.

The company provides three kinds of items:

Goods (like computers or software): calculate the amount charged as the quantity times the unit cost.
Services (such as providing an Internet connection or a service contract on a computer): calculate the amount charged as the quantity (number of connections or contracts) times the unit cost per month times the number of months.
Consulting: calculate the amount charged as the hourly rate times the time spent.

A sample invoice is shown below. Notice that some of the variation between different kinds of items is shown in the description.

Computers To You
1 Byte Way
Waterloo, Ontario N2G 3H4

Byron Weber Becker
122 Nomad Street
Waterloo, Ontario N2L 3G1

Qty	Description	Unit Cost	Amount
3	Desktop computers	$1,750.00	$5,250.00
1	Premium office suite	$750.00	$750.00
3	Computer service contracts (12 months)	$5.95	$214.20
1	Consulting re: printer installation (0.75 hrs)	$75.00	$56.25
1	Consulting re: LAN wiring (5.00 hrs)	$75.00	$375.00
		Total:	$ 6,645.45

(figure 12-9)

Problem statement for a simple invoicing application

12.2.1 Step 1: Identifying Objects and Classes

Step 1 in the object-oriented design methodology (Figure 12-8) tells us to highlight the nouns and noun phrases. Recall that a noun is a word that can refer to a person, place, or thing and is often the subject or object of a verb. The nouns and noun phrases in the problem statement are listed in Figure 12-10 in the left column.

(figure 12-10)

Nouns and noun phrases from the problem statement

Nouns and Noun Phrases	Types	Class Names
invoice		`Invoice`
~~payment for items provided~~		
customer		`Customer`
company		`Company`
customer's name	`String`	
customer's address		`Address`
total invoice amount	`double`	
line item		`LineItem`
~~group of identical items sold~~		
quantity of items sold	`int`	
description of items sold	`String`	
unit cost of items sold	`double`	
total amount charged for items in the group	`double`	
items		`Item`
goods		`Good`
amount charged	`double`	
services		`Service`
unit cost per month	`double`	
number of months	`int`	
consulting		`Consulting`
hourly rate	`double`	
time spent	`double`	

Some of the nouns are not relevant and can be eliminated. For example, "payment for items provided" is in a clause explaining the purpose of the system and represents something the customer does in response to receiving an invoice. Similarly, "group of identical items sold" seems to define the term "line item." These two noun phrases are crossed out in the list.

Some nouns in the list duplicate each other. For example, two entries in the table talk about "unit cost." Furthermore, the sample invoice shows the hourly rate for consulting in the unit cost column. They can probably all be combined into the single term "unit cost."

Some of these nouns can be represented with existing types such as integers and strings. These are noted in the middle column. Other nouns will require that we define a class, as suggested by Step 1a of Figure 12-8. Suggested class names are shown in the right column.

Class Relationships

LOOKING BACK

"Is-a" and "Has-a" are two ways of relating classes. They were discussed in Section 8.1.3.

We've identified a number of potential classes in Figure 12-10. How are they related to each other? If we use the "is-a" and "has-a" tests, the sentence "An invoice has a customer" makes much more sense than "An invoice is a customer." Similarly, "A customer has an address" and "An invoice has a line item" make more sense than saying "A customer is an address" or "An invoice is a line item."

Examining the specification's three paragraphs related to the three kinds of items indicates that `Goods` have amounts charged, quantities, and unit costs. `Services`, on the other hand, have amounts charged, quantities, unit costs per month, and the number of months. Finally, `Consulting` objects have hourly rates and time spent. We see that these classes definitely have some common attributes; therefore, Step 1b of Figure 12-8 (which suggests forming a superclass) may apply. The phrase "three kinds of items" suggests that we might name the superclass `Item` and already hints that inheritance may be appropriate.

The remaining question is whether these classes pass the "is-a" test. Recall that the "is-a" test consists of forming a sentence using "is-a" or "is a kind of" with the two classes in question. For example, "A `Service` is a kind of `Item`" or "A `Consulting` is a kind of `Item`."

These sentences don't sound quite right. The problem might be that the inheritance relationship isn't correct. However, the specification explicitly says that there are "three kinds of items: goods, services, and consulting."

Perhaps the problem with these sentences is the names we've chosen. "Service" and "consulting" refer to what the company provided to the customer. In programming the invoicing system, we are really concerned with what goes on the invoice to represent the goods and the consulting. That is, we're most concerned with the line items. The sample invoice shown in Figure 12-9 has five line items. The first line item is for three computers, the second line item is for an office suite, the third is for service contracts, and the last two line items are for consulting.

KEY IDEA

Choose appropriate names for classes.

The three "kinds of items" the specification refers to are three kinds of line items. If we name them `GoodsLineItem`, `ServicesLineItem`, and `ConsultingLineItem`, then an is-a statement like "A `GoodsLineItem` is a kind of `LineItem`" makes sense. We can conclude that inheritance is appropriate.

These relationships are shown in Figure 12-11. Observe the striking resemblance to the common pattern for polymorphism shown in Figure 12-4.

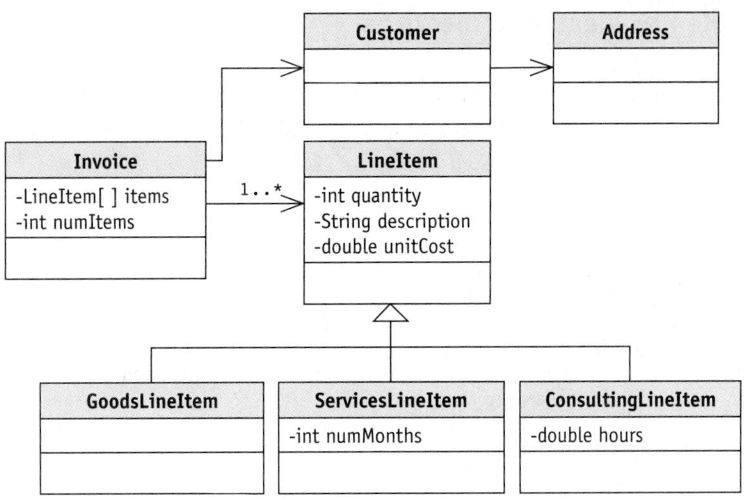

(figure 12-11)

Initial class diagram for the invoicing system

Assigning Attributes

Some of the nouns and noun phrases will correspond to attributes in these classes. An initial assignment is also shown in Figure 12-11. The `Customer` and `Address` classes are not relevant to the main topics of this chapter and are omitted from the rest of the discussion.

We know from the specification's second paragraph that each line item shows a quantity, description, unit cost, and amount. These seem like good attributes to add to the `LineItem` class. Before we do that, however, we should check two things. First, is it better to compute the value or store it in an attribute? The amount seems like a value that is better computed by a method than stored in an attribute, especially given the extensive explanations about how to calculate it from other values.

KEY IDEA

If an attribute is in a superclass, it should be applicable to all the subclasses.

Second, before placing these attributes in the `LineItem` class we should ask whether they apply to all of `LineItem`'s subclasses. A quick glance at the sample invoice shows that each kind of line item shows all the values. Therefore we conclude that quantity, description, and unit cost can go into `LineItem`.

KEY IDEA

Some attributes do *not belong in the superclass.*

The time spent consulting and the number of months a service is provided are obviously unique to `ConsultingLineItem` and `ServicesLineItem`, respectively.

The remaining attributes all seem to be variations of attributes we have already discussed.

12.2.2 Step 2: Identifying Services

Step 2 of the object-oriented design methodology in Figure 12-8 is to identify potential services by considering the verbs in the specification. The verbs, with slight transformations to show context, are shown in Figure 12-12.

```
print an invoice
~~request payment for items~~
~~provide items to a customer~~
show customer name, address, total amount billed
add a line item
show line item info (quantity, description, unit cost, total amount)
calculate the amount charged for goods
calculate the amount charged for services
calculate the amount charged for consulting
```

(figure 12-12)

Verbs from the problem's specification

As with nouns, some of the verb phrases may not belong. For example, "request payment" describes the purpose of the invoice and "provide items to a customer" is something the company does. Neither are things that this computer system should do. Both are crossed off the list.

Assigning Methods to Classes

Printing an invoice is an activity of the `Invoice` class and is assigned there, as is adding a line item. Showing the quantity, description, unit cost, and amount are associated with all line item objects, so we will assign these to the `LineItem` class. They are most likely to be used by the `print` method to get the associated values, so we'll name them `getX rather` than `showX` (where *X* is replaced with a name).

Each line item must calculate the amount to charge for the goods, services, or consulting it represents. On the other hand, we also know that these values are all calculated differently, strongly suggesting that `calcAmount` should be an abstract method in `LineItem`. This allows it to be called polymorphically, but defers the decision of how to calculate the amount to the appropriate subclasses.

The sample invoice shows that the description is displayed differently for each kind of line item. A `ConsultingLineItem` displays the number of hours and a `ServicesLineItem` displays the number of months. This seems similar to `calcAmount`, suggesting another abstract method. However, we also need an accessor method in `LineItem` for `description`, suggesting an accessor method that is overridden as needed in the subclasses.

Figure 12-13 shows the class diagram with these assignments made.

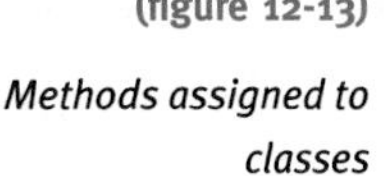

(figure 12-13)

Methods assigned to classes

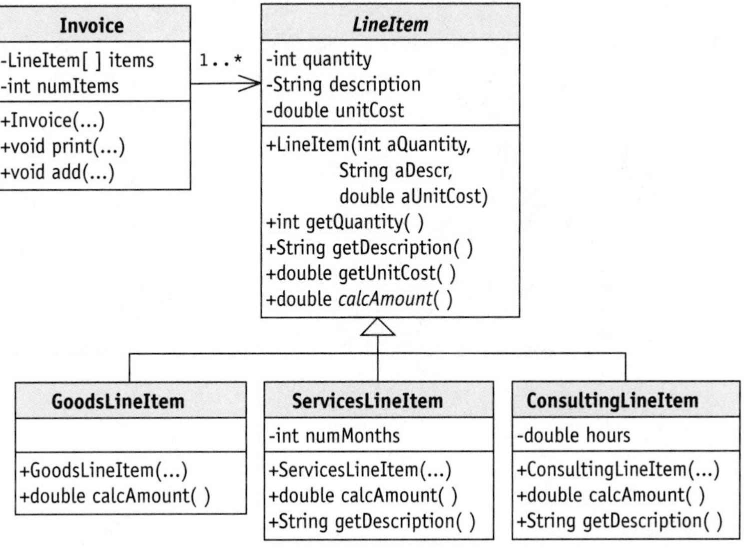

Implementing Methods

Relevant portions of the `LineItem` class are shown in Listing 12-4. There is nothing unusual about it except for the abstract method to calculate the line item's amount (line 23) and the resulting `abstract` keyword applied to the class (line 4).

FIND THE CODE

ch12/invoice/

Listing 12-4: *The* `LineItem` *class with an abstract method*

```
1  /** A line item is one kind of thing provided by the company for the customer.
2   *
3   * @author Byron Weber Becker */
4  public abstract class LineItem extends Object
5  {
6    private int quantity;
7    private String description;
8    private double unitCost;
9
10   /** Construct a new line item.
11    * @param aQuantity     The number of things provided to the customer.
12    * @param aDescr        A description of the things provided.
13    * @param aunitCost     The cost of each of the things. */
14   public LineItem(int aQuantity, String aDescr,
15                   double aUnitCost)
16   { super();
17     this.quantity = aQuantity;
18     this.description = aDescr;
```

Listing 12-4: *The* `LineItem` *class with an abstract method* (continued)

```
      this.unitCost = aUnitCost;
   }

   /** Calculate the total amount owing due to this line item. */
   public abstract double calcAmount();

   // Accessor methods omitted.
}
```

The interesting methods in `ServicesLineItem` are implemented as shown in Listing 12-5. Invoicing for services requires knowing the number of months the service is provided, resulting in the instance variable `numMonths` in line 6. A value to initialize `numMonths` is passed as an argument to the constructor, also with values to initialize the superclass. It is common for a subclass' constructor to have more parameters than the superclass. It uses some of them to initialize its own instance variables, and passes the rest of them to the superclass.

This class provides a body for `calcAmount` (lines 20–23). Because the quantity and unit cost of the service contracts are stored in `LineItem`, accessor methods are used to get their values.

The `getDescription` method is overridden to add the number of months to the description.

FIND THE CODE

ch12/invoice/

Listing 12-5: *Implementing the interesting methods in the* `ServicesLineItem` *class*

```
 1 /** Invoice the customer for 1 or more identical service contracts.
 2  *
 3  * @author Byron Weber Becker */
 4 public class ServicesLineItem extends LineItem
 5 {
 6    private int numMonths;
 7
 8    /** Construct a new line item for services provided.
 9     * @param aQuantity      The number of service contracts provided to the customer.
10     * @param aDescr         A description of the services provided.
11     * @param aMthlyCost     The monthly cost of each service contract.
12     * @param aNumMonths     The number of months the service contract lasts. */
13    public ServicesLineItem(int aQuantity, String aDescr,
14                            double aMthlyCost, int aNumMonths)
15    { super(aQuantity, aDescr, aMthlyCost);
```

Listing 12-5: *Implementing the interesting methods in the* `ServicesLineItem` *class* (continued)

```
      this.numMonths = aNumMonths;
   }

   /** Calculate the total amount owing due to this line item. */
   public double calcAmount()
   { return this.getQuantity() * this.getUnitCost()
                               * this.numMonths;
   }

   /** Get the description of the services represented by this line item. */
   public String getDescription()
   { return super.getDescription() +
                  " (" + this.numMonths + " months)";
   }
}
```

12.2.3 Step 3: Solving the Problem

The last step in the object-oriented design methodology shown in Figure 12-8 is to "apply the services from Step 2 to the objects from Step 1 in a way that solves the problem." We won't solve the entire problem here. We will focus on the `print` method in `Invoice` to show how it uses polymorphism and the inheritance hierarchy we've built. We'll also briefly discuss how to read invoices from a file.

Printing Invoices

The following pseudocode for `print` follows directly from the sample invoice shown in Figure 12-9.

PATTERN
Polymorphic Call

```
print the company's address
print the customer's address
print column headers
totalAmountBilled = 0
for each line item
{ print the quantity, description, unit cost and amount
  totalAmountBilled = totalAmountBilled + amount
}
print totalAmountBilled
```

This code is polymorphic because it does not need to know or care what kind of line item object is in the array of line items. Thanks to polymorphism, the `print` method can simply call the `calcAmount` and `getDescription` methods and they will return a value appropriate to their actual type.

However, we should recall the lessons learned in Chapter 11. The code inside the loop separates the processing (printing a line item) from the data (information stored in the line item). A better design would keep the data and processing together by placing a `print` method in the `LineItem` class. The `print` method in the `Invoice` class calls `LineItem`'s `print` polymorphically, as shown in Listing 12-6.

FIND THE CODE

ch12/invoice/

Listing 12-6: *The simplified* `print` *method in the* `Invoice` *class*

```
public class Invoice extends Object
{
  private LineItem[] items = new LineItem[1];
  private int numItems = 0;
  // Constructors, methods, and some instance variables omitted.

  public void print(PrintWriter out)
  { this.printCompanyAddress(out);
    this.printCustomerAddress(out);
    this.printColumnHeaders(out);

    double totalAmountBilled = 0.0;
    for (int i = 0; i < this.numItems; i++)
    { LineItem item = this.items[i];
      item.print(out);                     // polymorphism
      double amt = item.calcAmount();      // polymorphism
      totalAmountBilled = totalAmountBilled + amt;
    }

    this.printTotal(out, totalAmountBilled);
  }
}
```

The `print` method itself is shown in Listing 12-7.

FIND THE CODE

ch12/invoice/

Listing 12-7: *A method to print one* `LineItem`

```
public abstract class LineItem extends Object
{
  private static final NumberFormat money =
          NumberFormat.getCurrencyInstance();
  // Some instance variables, constructors, and methods omitted.

```

Listing 12-7: *A method to print one* `LineItem` (continued)

```
7      /** Print this line item to the specified file. */
8      public void print(PrintWriter out)
9      { out.printf("%3d %-50s%10s%10s%n",
10              this.getQuantity(),
11              this.getDescription(),
12              this.money.format(this.unitCost),
13              this.money.format(this.calcAmount()));
14     }
15 }
```

KEY IDEA

Polymorphism can also occur when an overridden method is called from a superclass.

Polymorphism is at work in this example in two ways. The first is calling `print` polymorphically from the `Invoice` class. The second is that each use of the keyword `this` inside `LineItem`'s `print` method refers to one of the three concrete classes. Therefore, `this.getDescription()` will search for the method `getDescription` beginning with the concrete class, one of `GoodsLineItem`, `ServicesLineItem`, or `ConsultingLineItem`. If `getDescription` was overridden, the more specialized version will be called. Furthermore, when `calcAmount` is called in line 13, the version in this line item's concrete class will be called. This is polymorphism because the client, `LineItem`, doesn't need to know or care what kind of line item it is. Because it is calling methods that may be overridden, this method has a lot in common with the Template Method pattern studied in Section 3.5.3.

Reading an Invoice from a File

Reading an invoice from a file is trickier than the examples covered in Chapter 9 because of polymorphism. The file must contain all the information needed to reconstruct the different kinds of line items. This has two implications. First, the file must indicate which of the various subclasses of `LineItem` to construct; second, the file must store more data for some line items than for others.

KEY IDEA

Include data in the file that says what kind of subclass to construct.

One possible file format is shown in the example in Figure 12-14. It contains customer information followed by the line items. Each line item uses two or more lines. The first line in each group is a string indicating which class to construct. The remaining lines in the group contain the data used to initialize the objects.

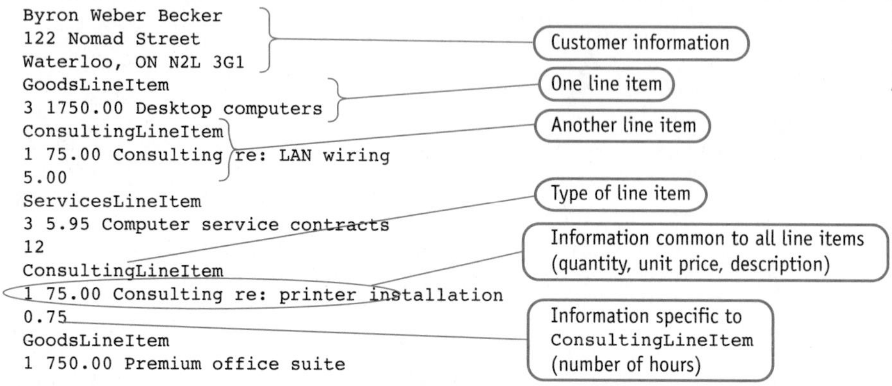

```
Byron Weber Becker
122 Nomad Street
Waterloo, ON N2L 3G1
GoodsLineItem
3 1750.00 Desktop computers
ConsultingLineItem
1 75.00 Consulting re: LAN wiring
5.00
ServicesLineItem
3 5.95 Computer service contracts
12
ConsultingLineItem
1 75.00 Consulting re: printer installation
0.75
GoodsLineItem
1 750.00 Premium office suite
```

Customer information

One line item

Another line item

Type of line item

Information common to all line items (quantity, unit price, description)

Information specific to ConsultingLineItem (number of hours)

(figure 12-14)

One possible file format for storing line items

An `Invoice` constructor that reads this file is shown in Listing 12-8. It repeatedly reads a line identifying the type of line item required (line 13). The cascading-`if` statement in lines 14–22 calls the appropriate constructor based on the name that was read. By the time control returns to line 12, all of the data for that line item has been read, and the program is ready to read the name of the next subclass.

FIND THE CODE

ch12/invoice/

Listing 12-8: *A constructor for the* `Invoice` *class*

```
1  public class Invoice extends Object
2  {
3    private LineItem[] items = new LineItem[1];
4    private int numItems = 0;
5    // Some constructors, methods, and instance variables omitted.
6
7    /** Read an invoice from a file. */
8    public Invoice(Scanner in)
9    { this.customer = new Customer(in);
10
11     // Read and construct the line items, putting them in the array.
12     while (in.hasNextLine())
13     { String subclass = in.nextLine();
14       if (subclass.equals("GoodsLineItem"))
15       { this.addLineItem(new GoodsLineItem(in));
16       } else if (subclass.equals("ServicesLineItem"))
17       { this.addLineItem(new ServicesLineItem(in));
18       } else if (subclass.equals("ConsultingLineItem"))
19       { this.addLineItem(new ConsultingLineItem(in));
20       } else
21       { throw new Error("Unknown subclass: " + subclass + ".");
22       }
23     }
24   }
```

Listing 12-8: *A constructor for the* `Invoice` *class* (continued)

```
  /** Add one line item to items array. Enlarge the array, if necessary. */
  public void addLineItem(LineItem item)
  { // Remainder of method omitted.
  }
}
```

KEY IDEA

Each class reads the data it needs to initialize itself.

The remaining task is to write the constructors needed to read a line item. A total of four are required: one for `LineItem` and one for each of the subclasses. The `LineItem` constructor will be called using `super` in each of the subclass constructors. After it has read the information it requires, reading will resume in the subclass constructor. It reads any remaining information to initialize its own instance variables. Listing 12-9 shows the relevant code for `LineItem`, and Listing 12-10 shows the relevant code for `ConsultingLineItem`.

FIND THE CODE

ch12/invoice/

Listing 12-9: *A constructor to read information for one* `LineItem` *object from a file*

```
public abstract class LineItem extends Object
{ private int quantity;
  private double unitCost;
  private String description;

  public LineItem(Scanner in)
  { super();                    // Read only the data stored in this class.
    this.quantity = in.nextInt();
    this.unitCost = in.nextDouble();
    this.description = in.nextLine();
  }

  // Remainder of class omitted.
}
```

Listing 12-10: *A constructor showing how to use a constructor in the superclass*

FIND THE CODE

ch12/invoice/

```
public class ConsultingLineItem extends LineItem
{ private double hours;

  public ConsultingLineItem(Scanner in)
  { super(in);        // Superclass reads what it needs from the file, leaving the
                      // file cursor just before the number of consulting hours.
    this.hours = in.nextDouble();
    in.nextLine();
  }

  // Remainder of class omitted.
}
```

Using a Factory Method

The approach shown in the preceding listings works. Its disadvantage is the complexity in the `Invoice` constructor that has little to do with invoices and much to do with line items.

A better approach is to move the complexity of determining which subclass to construct and the actual construction into a static method named `read` in the `LineItem` class. That method can determine which kind of line item is next in the file, construct one, and return it. `read` must be a method and not a constructor because a method can return a subclass of `LineItem`—something a constructor can't do.

KEY IDEA

A static method can return the required subclass of `LineItem`.

The `read` method, shown in Listing 12-11, is very similar to lines 13–22 in Listing 12-8. It must be `static` so that it can be called without an instance of an object.

Listing 12-11: *A factory method*

FIND THE CODE

ch12/invoice/

```
public abstract class LineItem extends Object
{ // Instance variables, constructors, and most methods omitted.

  public static LineItem read(Scanner in)
  { String subclass = in.nextLine();
    if (subclass.equals("GoodsLineItem"))
    { return new GoodsLineItem(in);
    } else if (subclass.equals("ServicesLineItem"))
    { return new ServicesLineItem(in);
    } else if (subclass.equals("ConsultingLineItem"))
```

PATTERN

Factory Method

Listing 12-11: *A factory method* (continued)

```
      { return new ConsultingLineItem(in);
      } else
      { throw new Error("Unknown subclass: " + subclass + ".");
      }
   }
}
```

This simplifies the constructor in `Invoice`, as shown in Listing 12-12.

Listing 12-12: *Reading line items using a factory method*

```
public Invoice(Scanner in)
{ this.customer = new Customer(in);

      // Read and construct the line items, putting them in the array.
      while (in.hasNextLine())
   { this.addLineItem(LineItem.read(in));
   }
}
```

12.3 Polymorphism without Arrays

So far most of our examples of polymorphism have used an array. For example, consider the following statement:

```
double amt = this.items[i].calcAmount();
```

It calls `calcAmount` polymorphically because the array might hold a `GoodsLineItem` or a `ConsultingLineItem`—and this code fragment doesn't need to know or care.

Arrays, however, are *not* a requirement for using polymorphism. In Listing 12-7 we called `this.getDescription()` and the correct subclass of `LineItem` returned the answer.

In fact, the potential for polymorphism exists any time you have a reference to an object. What are some other examples?

KEY IDEA

Polymorphism is a possibility any time you have a reference to an object.

A method may return a reference that is used polymorphically. For example, `Invoice` might have a method to return the most expensive line item, for printing in a report. The report's method could use it this way:

```
LineItem expensive = anInvoice.getMostExpensiveLineItem();
double cost = expensive.calcAmount();
```

The call to `calcAmount` is polymorphic because this code does not need to know what kind of `LineItem` it's dealing with. In fact, this code could be written without using the variable `expensive`:

```
double cost =
  anInvoice.getMostExpensiveLineItem().calcAmount();
```

A reference can also be passed to a parameter, allowing for polymorphism within a method. For example, suppose we had a method with the signature `void gatherStatistics(LineItem item)`. Inside the method, it can call any of the methods declared by `LineItem` without knowing whether it's really a `GoodsLineItem`, a `ServicesLineItem`, or a `ConsultingLineItem`.

An instance variable can also hold an object reference that is used polymorphically.

12.4 Overriding Methods in `object`

With a new understanding of inheritance and polymorphism, we are now in a better position to understand some of the methods in the class `Object`. There are three that we need to discuss: `toString`, `equals`, and `clone`.

12.4.1 `toString`

Overriding `toString` was discussed in Section 7.3.3. There isn't much to add here except to note that we now know in more detail how Java chooses which `toString` method to execute—and that when `toString` is called, thanks to polymorphism, the caller doesn't need to know or care which subclass of `Object` calculates the answer.

12.4.2 equals

LOOKING BACK

The `DateTime` class in the `becker` library includes the notion of time. We're ignoring that here.

Section 8.2.4 discussed comparing objects for equivalence. The example was to check whether two dates "mean" the same thing. We discovered that comparing them with `==` was not the right thing to do. To check for equivalence, a method is required. At that point we wrote the following method:

```
public class DateTime extends Object
{ private int year;
  private int month;
  private int day;

  // Other methods omitted.

  /** Return true if this date represents the same date as other. */
  public boolean isEquivalent(DateTime other)
  { return other != null && this.year == other.year &&
          this.month == other.month && this.day == other.day;
  }
}
```

This method is fine except that the designers of Java provide a method in the `Object` class for this purpose: `boolean equals(Object other)`. Their intent is that we override `equals` with the correct implementation for classes we write.

We can't simply change "`isEquivalent`" to "`equals`" in the preceding code because that would produce two different method signatures—the `equals` method in the `Object` class takes an `Object` as its argument whereas the `equals` method in `DateTime` takes a `DateTime` object as its argument. This provides overloading but not overriding, and makes a difference as well. Suppose we have two objects:

```
Object d1 = new DateTime(2008, 1, 1);
DateTime d2 = new DateTime(2008, 1, 1);
```

`d2.equals(d1)` calls the method with the signature `equals(Object other)` (returning `false`) while `d2.equals(d2)` calls the method with the signature `equals(DateTime other)` (returning `true`).

KEY IDEA

Use the right signature to override `equals`. Overloading isn't good enough.

To override `equals` correctly, we must use the same signature as defined in `Object`: `public boolean equals(Object other)`.

In the `isEquivalent` method, we know that the object passed via the parameter is a `DateTime` object. With `equals`, any object at all may be passed. We first need to verify that `other` is an instance of the right type, `DateTime`. Fortunately, Java provides a Boolean operator for that purpose. If `x` is a reference variable and `T` is the name of a class or interface, then `x instanceof T` returns `true` if `x` is a non-`null` reference that can call all of the methods specified in T. The type of x might be T, a subclass of T, or a class that implements the interface T.

We can use instanceof as a key part of our equals method, as follows:

KEY IDEA

instanceof *is used to verify the type of an object.*

```
if (!(other instanceof DateTime))
{ // other isn't a DateTime object, so it can't possibly be equal to this DateTime object.
  return false;
}
```

However, if other is an instance of DateTime, we need to access its fields or methods to compare the dates. Because other is declared as an Object, we can't just call other.getYear(). We need to first assign it to a DateTime reference, but Java will not allow us to simply perform the following assignment because it can't verify at compile time that other will refer to a DateTime object.

```
DateTime dt = other;      // will not compile
```

We can tell the compiler to make an exception with a **cast**. A cast is our assurance to the compiler that we believe other will, in fact, refer to a DateTime object when the code executes. The compiler doesn't completely trust us, however. It will verify at runtime that other can substitute for an object of the specified type. If it cannot, a ClassCastException will be thrown.

The syntax for casting an object is like that for casting a primitive type, as in the following:

```
DateTime dt = (DateTime)other;
```

The meaning, however, is different. When casting a primitive type, the value is actually changed. For example, int i = (int)3.99999 assigns i the value 3. When an object reference is cast, the type of the object doesn't change; it's the program's interpretation of the object that changes. Instead of interpreting it as an instance of Object, the program now interprets it as an instance of what it really is, DateTime.

KEY IDEA

Casting an object reference changes the program's interpretation of the object.

After casting other to dt, we can perform the comparisons as in isEquivalent. Recall that this code is inside the DateTime class, so we can access instance variables via dt as well as via this:

```
return this.year == dt.year && this.month == dt.month
        && this.day == dt.day;
```

Lastly, an object is compared to itself surprisingly often. This test can be performed very efficiently with == and is often included before any of the other tests discussed here.

The complete equals method is as follows:

PATTERN

Equals

```
public boolean equals(Object other)
{ if (this == other)
    return true;          // other is exactly the same object as this.

  if (!(other instanceof DateTime))
    return false;         // other is not an instance of DateTime (or a subclass).

  // Compare the relevant fields for equality.
  DateTime dt = (DateTime)other;
  return this.year == dt.year && this.month == dt.month
        && this.day == dt.day;
}
```

KEY IDEA

Many classes should not override equals.

When should equals be overridden? Classes that represent a value such as Integer, DateTime, or Color should have their own equals method. Classes where an object is only equal to itself should not. Examples include Student (two students may have the same name, but they are not equal to each other) or BankAccount (my account shouldn't be "equal" to your account, even if the balances happen to be the same).

Finally, a warning. Whenever equals is overridden, a method named hashCode should also be overridden, but that's beyond the scope of this book. If you use your class with a class from the Java libraries that includes the word "Hash", watch out! You may get strange results if you override equals but not hashCode.

12.4.3 clone (advanced)

Sometimes an exact copy of an object is required. Suppose, for example, that a back order in our invoicing system begins by requesting a duplicate of a line item. The Java system provides a convention for providing this service based on the clone method that all classes inherit from the Object class.

The clone method has the following goals:

- x.clone() != x (the object returned by cloning x is not the original object).
- x.clone().equals(x) (the cloned object is equal to the original object).
- x.clone().getClass() == x.getClass() (the clone and the original have the same run-time class; one is not a subclass of the other).

Using Clone

Suppose that someone has already implemented `clone` for the `LineItem` class. We could then use it to create a duplicate line item object like this:

```
LineItem duplicate = (LineItem)aLineItem.clone();
```

The cast to a `LineItem` is required because the `clone` method is declared to return an `Object`.

Polymorphism comes into play here because `clone` may be overridden in the subclasses of `LineItem`, but we don't need to know or care. The correct method will be called for the actual run-time type of `aLineItem`.

Implementing Clone

The `clone` method in the `object` class implements the following pseudocode:

```
newObject = a new object with the same run-time class as this
for(each instance variable in this)
{ copy the variable's value to newObject
}
return newObject;
```

The `clone` method in `Object` returns an object with the same run-time type as the original object and the same values for all its instance variables.

It may sound like the existing `clone` method is all that's required. Unfortunately, that's not the case. It's dangerous to call `clone` unless issues have been thought about carefully for subclasses (more on these issues will follow). To help ensure that `clone` cannot be called without thinking these issues through, Java's designers have done two things. First, `clone` is protected, meaning it can only be called by a subclass. Therefore, the only way to effectively use `clone` is to override the method and declare it public.

Second, the `clone` method implemented in `Object` checks to make sure that the class implements the `Cloneable` interface. If it doesn't, `clone` throws the `CloneNotSupportedException`. Either that exception must be caught or your `clone` method must declare that it also throws the exception. It's worth noting that this is an unusual use of an interface; it affects the behavior of an existing method rather than guaranteeing the presence of methods. Many programmers believe that this design is a serious mistake. Nevertheless, `clone` is used widely enough that it's worth understanding how it works.

Taking these things into account, an appropriate implementation of `clone` in the `LineItem` class would be as shown in Listing 12-13. Implemented this way, it will also work for the subclasses of `LineItem` discussed earlier in the chapter.

FIND THE CODE

ch12/invoice/

Listing 12-13: *An implementation of* `clone` *in the* `LineItem` *class*

```
public abstract class LineItem extends Object
                              implements Cloneable
{
  // Instance variables, constructors, and methods omitted.

  /** Make a duplicate copy of this object. */
  public Object clone()
  { try
    { return super.clone();
    } catch (CloneNotSupportedException e)
    { // CloneNotSupportedException should never be thrown because we have
      // implemented Cloneable. Error is an unchecked exception.
      throw new Error("Should never happen.");
    }
  }
}
```

Dangers: Shallow Copies vs. Deep Copies

It seems like the `clone` method in the `Object` class does everything required. Why is it so thoroughly protected? The `clone` method in `Object` simply copies the value in each instance variable from the original object to the new object. For primitive types like integers, characters, and immutable classes like `String`, this works very well. For reference types, it often does not.

LOOKING BACK

The value in a reference variable is the address of an object, not the object itself. See Section 8.2.1.

Consider cloning an `Invoice` object. The `items` instance variable refers to an array. The value it stores is a reference to the array, not the array itself. If we call `clone` to clone the invoice, it will copy this array reference but it won't make a copy of the array itself. Both invoices then refer to the same array of line items. If a line item is deleted from the copy of the invoice, it would also be deleted from the original invoice. However, the original's `numItems` variable would *not* be updated, probably leading to nasty results.

Figure 12-15 shows what it is known as a **shallow copy**. That's where only the values in the instance variables are copied from one object to the other. Cloning an invoice should make a **deep copy**. A deep copy also clones objects that the object references. The result of a deep copy is shown in Figure 12-16.

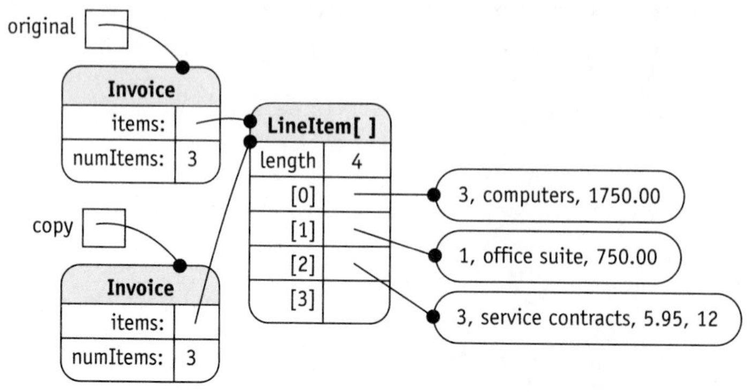

(figure 12-15)

Shallow copy of an `Invoice` *object*

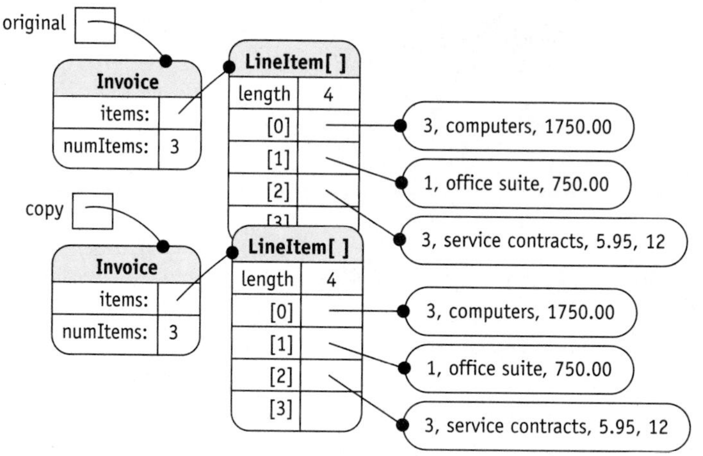

(figure 12-16)

Deep copy of an `Invoice` *object*

For a deep copy, we need to create a new array and clone each element in the old array. The `clone` method in Listing 12-14 shows how.

FIND THE CODE

ch12/invoice/

Listing 12-14: *A clone method that does a deep copy of* `Invoice`

```
public class Invoice extends Object implements Cloneable
{ private LineItem[] items = new LineItem[5];
  private int numItems = 0;

  // Constructors and methods omitted.

  /** Make a copy of this invoice. */
  public Object clone()
  { try
    { Invoice copy = (Invoice)super.clone();
```

Listing 12-14: *A clone method that does a deep copy of* `Invoice` (continued)

```
         // Do a deep copy of the array of line items.
         copy.items = new LineItem[this.numItems];
         for (int i = 0; i < this.numItems; i++)
         { copy.items[i] = (LineItem)this.items[i].clone();
         }
         return copy;
      } catch (CloneNotSupportedException e)
      { throw new Error("Should never happen.");
      }
   }
}
```

KEY IDEA

Immutable objects can't change and thus don't need to be cloned.

Sometimes a deep copy is not needed, even though references are being used. If the reference is to an immutable object such as `String`, a shallow copy is sufficient. Immutable objects can't change after they are constructed, so there is no danger in having the clone and the original object share the same strings—or any other immutable object.

12.5 Increasing Flexibility with Interfaces

Using interfaces appropriately can allow for more flexible use of the code we write. Flexible code can be used in more situations, often enabling us to avoid writing new code. As an example, we'll explore how the sorting method developed in Section 10.1.8 can be refactored for use in many situations. To make the example concrete, we'll sort instances of `LineItem` in a variety of ways. In our first example, we will consider how to sort `LineItem` by description.

The original sorting method is reproduced in Listing 12-15. The statements shown in bold must change to sort `LineItem` objects. The required changes fall into three categories:

- The documentation, which is very specific to the original project
- The references to a specific array to sort
- The condition used to sort the array

Listing 12-15: *The sorting algorithm from the Big Brother/Big Sister project. Required changes to sort line items are shown in bold*

```
public class BBBS extends Object
{ ... persons ...              // an array of Person objects

   /** Sort the persons array in increasing order by age. */
```

Listing 12-15: *The sorting algorithm from the Big Brother/Big Sister project. Required changes to sort line items are shown in bold.* (continued)

```
   public void sortByAge()
   { for (int firstUnsorted=0;
          firstUnsorted < this.persons.length - 1;
          firstUnsorted++)
     { // Find the index of the youngest unsorted person.
       int extremeIndex = firstUnsorted;
       for (int i = firstUnsorted + 1;
             i < this.persons.length; i++)
       { if (this.persons[i].getAge() <
             this.persons[extremeIndex].getAge())
         { extremeIndex = i;
         }
       }

       // Swap the youngest unsorted person with the person at firstUnsorted.
       Person temp = this.persons[extremeIndex];
       this.persons[extremeIndex] =
             this.persons[firstUnsorted];
       this.persons[firstUnsorted] = temp;
     }
   }
}
```

Of the three categories of change identified earlier, the first two are easy. Generalizing the documentation is trivial, and the problems with the names can be handled with appropriate parameters. Once we use parameters, all reliance on instance variables is removed, and the `sort` method can be made a class (`static`) method in a utilities class. The first set of changes is shown in Listing 12-16. The only part left is to figure out how to replace the pseudocode in line 10, which will influence the type of array passed as an argument in line 4 and the type of temporary variable in line 16.

Listing 12-16: *Making* `sort` *more reusable with parameters*

```
1 public class Utilities extends Object
2 {
3    /** Sort an array of objects. */
4    public static void sort(????[] a)
5    { for (int firstUnsorted = 0; firstUnsorted < a.length-1;
6             firstUnsorted++)
```

Listing 12-16: *Making* `sort` *more reusable with parameters* (continued)

```
7         { // Find the index of extreme ("smallest") unsorted element.
8           int extremeIndex = firstUnsorted;
9           for (int i = firstUnsorted + 1; i < a.length; i++)
10          { if (a[i] is less than a[extremeIndex])
11            { extremeIndex = i;
12            }
13          }
14
15          // Swap the extreme unsorted element with the element at firstUnsorted.
16          ???? temp = a[extremeIndex];
17          a[extremeIndex] = a[firstUnsorted];
18          a[firstUnsorted] = temp;
19        }
20      }
21  }
```

12.5.1 Using an Interface

Line 10 of Listing 12-16 requires comparing two elements in the array to determine which is "less" than the other, or which one should occur first in sorted order.

It would be really nice if the `Object` class had an `isLessThan` method similar to the `equals` method. If it did, we could pass an array of `Objects` in line 4 and replace the pseudocode in line 10 with:

```
if (a[i].isLessThan(a[extremeIndex]))
```

and the `sort` method would be done. It would depend, of course, on subclasses of `Object` overriding `isLessThan` appropriately. Unfortunately, `Object` does not provide such a method.

Another approach is to define `isLessThan` in the `LineItem` class and declare `sort` to take an array of `LineItem` objects as its parameter. This works, but only allows `sort` to sort `LineItems` and subclasses of `LineItem`. It would be preferable to have a solution that is much more general.

KEY IDEA

Implementing an interface gives the class an additional type.

An excellent solution is to use an interface. This allows a class such as `LineItem` to have an extra type—the type of the interface. Java already provides such an interface, `Comparable`. It's included in the package `java.lang`, which is automatically imported into every class. The interface is defined as shown in Listing 12-17.

Listing 12-17: *The* `Comparable` *interface from the Java library*

```
public interface Comparable
{ /** Compare this object with the specified object for order. Return a negative number
     * if this object is less than the specified object, a positive number if this object is greater,
     * and 0 if this object is equal to the specified object.
     * @param o The object to be compared. */
  public int compareTo(Object o);
}
```

To use this interface, we need to make the three changes to the `sort` method shown in Listing 12-16:

- In line 4, declare the array parameter variable using `Comparable`: `public static void sort(Comparable[] a)`.
- Declare the type of the temporary variable used to swap elements in line 16 using `Comparable`.
- Change line 10 to `{ if (a[i].compareTo(a[extremeIndex]) < 0)`.

Finally, in any class that we want to sort with this method, we need to implement `Comparable`. To sort the line items by description, we would change `LineItem` as follows:

```
 1 public abstract class LineItem extends Object
 2                              implements Comparable
 3 { private String description;
 4
 5   // Other instance variables, constructors, and methods omitted.
 6
 7   public int compareTo(Object o)
 8   { LineItem item = (LineItem)o;
 9     return this.description.compareTo(item.description);
10   }
11 }
```

The class declaration in lines 1 and 2 includes the phrase `implements Comparable`. The only method it specifies is declared in lines 7–10. Notice that in line 8, the object is cast to a `LineItem`. This is necessary to gain access to the instance variables required to do the comparison. This cast also works for subclasses of `LineItem` but will fail if o is something else, like a `Robot`. In that case, Java will throw a `ClassCastException` to indicate an error. The documentation in the `Comparable` interface says that this is what *should* happen when two objects can't be compared to each other.

KEY IDEA

Interfaces are another way to exploit polymorphism in a program.

What do sorting and interfaces have to do with polymorphism? Thanks to polymorphism, the `sort` method can call the `compareTo` method without knowing or caring which class actually implemented it. The `sort` method doesn't care whether the `compareTo` method is comparing descriptions or unit costs or the total cost of the line item.

Sorting in the Java Library

KEY IDEA

Use Java's sort instead of writing your own.

The Java library includes a sort method very similar to the one we have written except that it is much faster, particularly on large arrays. It's in the `java.util.Arrays` class and has the following signature:

```
public void sort(Object[] a)
```

If you want to sort a partially filled array, you can use a companion method with the following signature:

```
public void sort(Object[] a, int fromIndex, int toIndex)
```

These two methods have arrays of objects as parameters rather than arrays of `Comparable` like our `sort` method. How does that work?

The documentation states that all of the elements must implement `Comparable` and that `compareTo` must not throw an exception for any pair of elements. If these conditions are violated, `sort` will throw a `ClassCastException`. We can make our version of `sort` behave the same way by making two changes to Listing 12-16. First, change the type of the parameter in line 4 from `Comparable[]` to `Object[]`. Second, include a cast inside the loop that calls `compareTo`, as follows:

```
9       for (int i = firstUnsorted + 1; i < a.length; i++)
10      { if (((Comparable)a[i]).compareTo(a[extremeIndex]) < 0)
11        { extremeIndex = i;
12        }
13      }
```

Mixin Interfaces

A **mixin** is a type that supplements the "primary type" of a class. It provides some behavior that is mixed in with the normal behavior of the primary type. `Comparable` is one such mixin that allows comparing objects and thus sorting them.

Other mixin interfaces include the following:

- `IMove`: The interface we use in Section 12.1.4 to move dancing robots and the banner they carry (a subclass of `JDialog`) is a mixin interface.
- `Runnable`: It is used just for fun in Section 3.5.2 to allow several robots to move simultaneously.

- `Observer`: An interface used when one object wants to "observe" what happens in another. We'll use a variation of this when we write graphical user interfaces in Chapter 13.
- `Paintable`: The class we used in Section 6.1 to ensure that `SimpleBots` could be painted on the screen could just as easily have been a mixin interface.

You may want to define your own interface to use as a mixin when an application needs to process similarly a number of classes that don't have a natural common superclass.

12.5.2 Using the Strategy Pattern

Implementing the `Comparable` interface in `LineItem` is fine if you want to sort the line items in only one way. But suppose you are writing a report program for the marketing department. They want line items from all the invoices gathered into a single report, sorted by total amount. We can't redefine the `compareTo` method just for them, so what do we do?

The **Strategy pattern** uses objects that define a family of interchangeable algorithms. For sorting, we'll use a strategy object that defines the comparison algorithm. When we want a different sort order, we pass a different strategy object (defining a different algorithm) to the `sort` method. This is facilitated with the `Comparator` interface, as shown in Figure 12-17. Notice that the `sort` method in `Utilities` takes an instance of `Comparator` as an argument.

PATTERN

Strategy

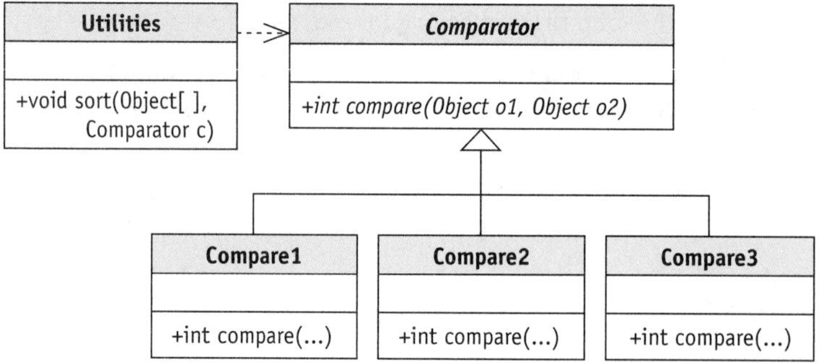

(figure 12-17)

Using strategy objects to define the sort order

A Strategy Object Using `Comparator`

The `Comparator` interface is defined in the `java.util` package and is quite similar to `Comparable`. They both define a method that compares two objects and returns an integer whose sign indicates which object is smaller. A key difference is that a `Comparator` is passed both objects as parameters rather than comparing one object to

KEY IDEA

Many different objects can implement `Comparator`*, each comparing objects in its own way.*

itself. A more minor difference is that `Comparator`'s method is named `compare` rather than `compareTo`. The `Comparator` interface is declared as follows:

```
public interface Comparator
{ /** Compare obj1 and obj2 for order. Return a negative number if obj1 is less than
   * obj2, a positive number if obj1 is greater than obj2, and 0 if they are equal.
   * @param obj1 One object to be compared.
   * @param obj2 The other object to be compared. */
  public int compare(Object obj1, Object obj2);
}
```

The following class defines a strategy object that can compare line items when sorting the marketing department's report. Notice that it includes the phrase `implements Comparator` in line 3. Lines 7–9 are formatted differently than we have seen before to save space.

```
1  /** Compare two line items using the value calculated by calcAmount. */
2  public class LineItemAmountComparator extends Object
3                                implements Comparator
4  { public int compare(Object obj1, Object obj2)
5    { double amt1 = ((LineItem)obj1).calcAmount();
6      double amt2 = ((LineItem)obj2).calcAmount();
7      if (amt1 < amt2)              { return -1;}
8      else if (amt1 > amt2)         { return 1; }
9      else                          { return 0; }
10   }
11 }
```

The `sort` method also needs to take an instance of `Comparator` as a parameter. This is shown in Listing 12-18. The method is just like the previous version of `sort` except for lines 4 and 11. In line 4, there is a new parameter to pass the strategy object implementing the comparison algorithm. In line 10, it's used to compare two line items.

With these changes, we can use `sort` to sort an array of *any* kind of object in any order we want, as long as we can provide a comparison strategy object. That's a lot of flexibility!

KEY IDEA

Use `java.util.Arrays` *rather than writing your own sort method.*

PATTERN

Strategy

In practice, however, we would not write our own `sort` routine. We would only write the `Comparator` and use it with the `sort` method in `java.util.Arrays`.

Listing 12-18: *A* `sort` *method that uses a comparator method*

```
1 public class Utilities extends Object
2 {
3   /** Sort a partially-filled array of objects. */
4   public static void sort(Object[] a, Comparator c)
5   { for (int firstUnsorted = 0; firstUnsorted < a.length-1;
```

Listing 12-18: *A sort method that uses a comparator method* (continued)

```
          firstUnsorted++)
    { // Find the index of extreme ("smallest") unsorted element.
      int extremeIndex = firstUnsorted;
      for (int i = firstUnsorted + 1; i < a.length; i++)
      { if (c.compare(a[i], a[extremeIndex]) < 0)
        { extremeIndex = i;
        }
      }

      // Swap the extreme unsorted element with the element at firstUnsorted.
      Object temp = a[extremeIndex];
      a[extremeIndex] = a[firstUnsorted];
      a[firstUnsorted] = temp;
    }
  }
}
```

Sorting with Multiple Keys

Suppose the marketing department wanted a report with all line items sorted first by description, and if the descriptions happen to be the same, then in descending order by total amount of the line item. The description is called the **primary key**. It is the most important determinant of the order. If two objects have different primary keys, then those keys alone are used to determine the order. However, if the primary keys are equal, then the **secondary key** is used to determine the order. In this case, total amount is the secondary key.

Following is a comparator that implements the described ordering:

```
class LineItemDescrTotalComparator extends Object
                              implements Comparator
{ public int compare(Object obj1, Object obj2)
  { LineItem li1 = (LineItem)obj1;
    LineItem li2 = (LineItem)obj2;

    // Compare using the primary key (description).
    int result = li1.getDescription().compareTo(
                              li2.getDescription());
    if (result == 0)          // Primary key is the same; use secondary key.
    { double amt1 = li1.calcAmount();
      double amt2 = li2.calcAmount();
      if (amt1 < amt2)
```

```
14          { result = 1;            // Descending order.
15          } else if (amt1 > amt2)
16          { result = -1;
17          }
18        }
19        return result;
20      }
21  }
```

KEY IDEA

Sort in descending order by reversing the signs of the returned values.

Notice the `if` statement for the secondary key in lines 13–17. Normally we return a negative number when the first argument is less than the second. Here we return positive 1, and –1 when the first argument is larger. Reversing these two values sorts the objects in descending order. Larger amounts are interpreted as "smaller" by this comparator.

Anonymous Classes (advanced)

Small strategy objects such as `Comparator` are so common that Java's designers included a shortcut for defining them quickly and easily. This shortcut is called an **anonymous class**. An anonymous class has the following properties:

- The class doesn't have a name (that's why it's called anonymous).
- It combines declaring a class and instantiating one (and only one) object.
- An anonymous class is defined at the same place the object it defines is needed. This can, if the class is small, improve the understandability of your code.

The following is an example of an anonymous class that sorts line items by description using a sort method from the Java library. To use this code, you must import `java.util.Arrays` and `java.util.Comparator`.

```
private void sortLineItems()
{ // An anonymous class to compare line items by description.
  Comparator c = new Comparator()
  {
    public int compare(Object obj1, Object obj2)
    { LineItem li1 = (LineItem)obj1;
      LineItem li2 = (LineItem)obj2;

      return li1.getDescription().compareTo(
                li2.getDescription());
    }
  };

  Arrays.sort(this.items, c);
}
```

The anonymous class appears in lines 3–12. Line 3 looks like any other object instantiation except that the semicolon is missing from the end of the line and `Comparator` is an interface rather than a class. `Comparator` can be replaced by the interface the anonymous class is to implement or the class it is to extend.

The body of the anonymous class appears between the "constructor" and the semicolon terminating the assignment statement. In the previous code, the body appears in lines 4–12.

Because the anonymous class has no name, it can't have a constructor, only methods. It may have instance variables, but they are uncommon and must always be initialized in their declaration because there is no constructor.

An anonymous class can be used to create exactly one object. This one is assigned to the variable `c`. This variable isn't required. In fact, experienced programmers will often replace the variable `c` in line 14 with the code between the equals in line 3 and the semicolon in line 12. However, this practice makes the code more difficult to read.

Applications of Strategy Objects

Strategy objects are widely used for more than sorting. They often have a single method but could have more. Here are a few uses:

- The Java library has a number of static sorting methods in the `java.util.Arrays` class that take a `Comparator` strategy object.
- Strategy objects are used to arrange components in graphical user interfaces. We'll discuss this more in Section 12.6.
- Many games use strategy objects to define different approaches for choosing the next move.
- Several classes within the `becker.robots` package, including `Robot`, include methods—such as `examineThings`—that take a strategy object as an argument. The method returns references to objects the robot may want to "examine." The strategy object determines which objects should be examined.

One particular use for strategy objects is handling objects that change behavior over time. For example, an employee might move from hourly compensation to a salary and perhaps to being compensated by contract over her tenure with a company. Using an inheritance-based approach would require replacing an `HourlyEmployee` object with a `SalariedEmployee` object, for example, as the employee is compensated differently.

Representing this kind of variation with subclasses creates problems as soon as there is more than one kind of variation. Suppose that mode of work (telecommute vs. office) is also represented with subclasses. Now we need `HourlyTelecommutingEmployee`, `SalariedTelecommutingEmployee`, `ContractTelecommutingEmployee`, plus three more for office employees. This quickly becomes unmanageable. Using strategy objects to represent how employees are paid and how they work is a much better solution. When their compensation method or their mode of work changes, simply replace the strategy object stored in their `Employee` object.

12.5.3 Flexibility in Choosing Implementations

Java interfaces allow several implementations to be used the same way. This can allow you to more easily change our minds later. For example, Java provides a set of classes for storing collections of objects, similar to arrays. Two of these classes are `ArrayList` and `LinkedList`. The two classes have many methods in common: `add`, `remove`, `contains`, and so on. They also implement the same interface, `List`.

Why provide two classes that apparently do exactly the same thing? The answer is that they are implemented differently and have different speed characteristics, as summarized in Table 12-1.

(table 12-1)

Speed characteristics of `ArrayList` *and* `LinkedList`

Operation	ArrayList	LinkedList
Add an object near the beginning of the list	slow	fast
Add an object near the end of the list	fast	fast
Remove from near the beginning of the list	slow	fast
Remove from near the end of the list	fast	slow
Get an object at a specified position	fast	slow
Set an object at a specified position	fast	slow
Determine if the list contains a specified object	slow	slow
Determine the size of the list	fast	fast

If your application adds and removes objects infrequently but uses `get` a lot, then `ArrayList` looks like a good choice. On the other hand, if `get` is infrequent but there are many additions and deletions, `LinkedList` seems better.

KEY IDEA

Interfaces make it easier to change which class is used.

Sound complicated? Afraid you might make the wrong choice and you'll want to change your mind later? Then use the `List` interface to declare your variables. This can isolate the decision of which class to use to a single point—which constructor to call when the list is first created. If you change your mind, there is only one place to change, and the entire program can take advantage of your new approach.

For example, an inventory program might include a method to remove the items just sold from the items in stock, as sketched in the code fragment shown in Listing 12-19. Note that `List` is used throughout, leaving lots of flexibility to use either `ArrayList`, `LinkedList`, or some other implementation of the `List` interface as the actual class.

Listing 12-19: *A class using interfaces to promote flexibility*

FIND THE CODE

ch12/inventory/

```
1 public class Inventory extends Object
2 { private List<Item> inventory = new ArrayList<Item>();
3   private List<Item> reorder = new LinkedList<Item>();
4   ...
5
6   /**Remove the specified items from the current inventory. Update the list of items
7    * to reorder.
8    * @itemsSold The items that have been sold and need to be removed from inventory. */
9   public void removeInventory(List<Item> itemsSold)
10  { for (Item item : itemsSold)
11    {
12      // Remove the item from the inventory.
13      this.inventory.remove(item);
14
15      // If it's the last one and not already on the reorder list, add it
16      if (!this.inventory.contains(item) &&
17                  !this.reorder.contains(item))
18      { this.reorder.add(item);
19      }
20    }
21  }
22 }
```

By using `List` to declare variables in lines 2, 3, and 9, the programmer has left lots of flexibility to change the actual classes being used. For example, the `ArrayList` in line 2 could be changed to a `LinkedList` with no further changes in the rest of the program.

12.6 GUI: Layout Managers

PATTERN

Strategy

Most graphical user interfaces allow users to interact with many components (buttons, text boxes, sliders, and so on). The issue to be addressed in this section is how Java arranges the components in a panel, both initially and as the user resizes the frame displaying the panel. The task of arranging the components on the panel is called **layout**. Java uses strategy objects called **layout managers** to determine how to arrange the components. By using strategy objects, `JPanel` can display the same set of components in many different arrangements.

12.6.1 The `FlowLayout` Strategy

The default layout strategy for a `JPanel` is an instance of `FlowLayout`. It adds components to the current row until there is no more room. It then starts a new row. The length of a row is determined by the width of the `JPanel`. Wider panels will have more components on a row.

The left image in Figure 12-18 shows four components organized with a `FlowLayout` strategy. The components are displayed left to right, top to bottom, in the same order they were added. The right image shows how those same components are reorganized when the frame is narrower.

(figure 12-18)

The `FlowLayout` *strategy*

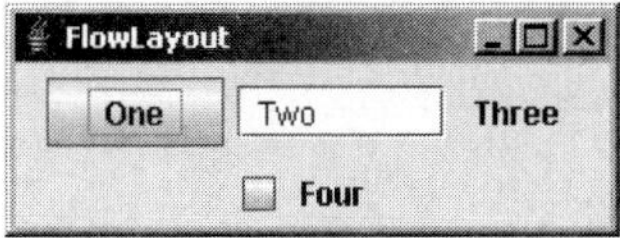

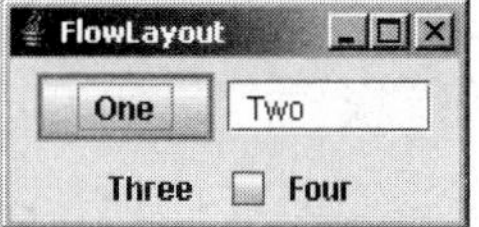

A `FlowLayout` object centers rows by default. It can also be set to align them on either the left or right side of the panel.

Each component has a preferred size, which is respected by `FlowLayout`. As we'll soon see, some layout managers ignore such size information.

12.6.2 The `GridLayout` Strategy

The strategy implemented by a `GridLayout` object is to place all of the components into a grid, as shown in Figure 12-19. Each component is made the same size as all the others, completely ignoring their preferred sizes. The number of rows and columns is set when the strategy object is created.

(figure 12-19)

The `GridLayout` *strategy*

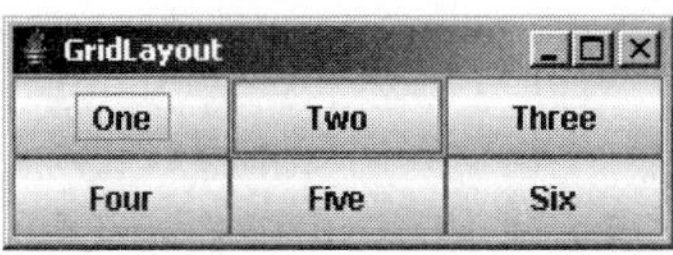

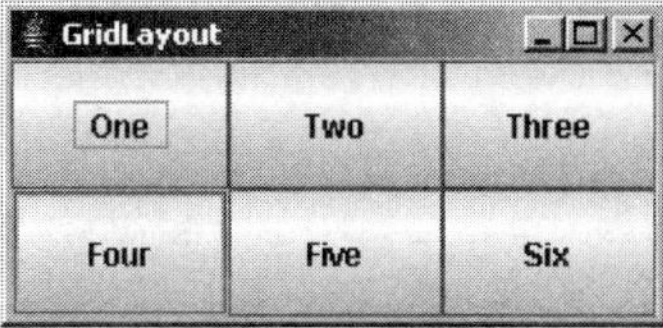

Setting a `JPanel`'s layout strategy is done with its `setLayout` method, as shown in lines 17–18 of Listing 12-20. This listing is already showing the program structure we will adopt for our graphical user interfaces. A group of components is combined by extending `JPanel`. Laying out the components is a distinct task that is delegated to a private helper method called `layoutView`.

Listing 12-21 displays an instance of this panel in a frame.

FIND THE CODE

ch12/layoutManagers/

Listing 12-20: *A* `JPanel` *extended to show a group of buttons, organized with a grid strategy*

```
import java.awt.*;
import javax.swing.*;

public class DemoGridLayout extends JPanel
{
  private JButton one = new JButton("One");
  private JButton two = new JButton("Two");
  // Instance variables for the last four buttons are omitted.

  public DemoGridLayout()
  { super();
    this.layoutView();
  }

  private void layoutView()
  { // Set the layout strategy to a grid with 2 rows and 3 columns.
    GridLayout strategy = new GridLayout(2, 3);
    this.setLayout(strategy);

    // Add the components.
    this.add(this.one);
    this.add(this.two);
    // Code to add the last four buttons is omitted.
  }
}
```

PATTERN

Strategy

FIND THE CODE

ch12/layoutManagers/

Listing 12-21: *A* `main` *method that displays a custom* `JPanel` *in a frame*

```
import javax.swing.*;

public class GridLayoutMain
{
  public static void main(String[] args)
  { JPanel p = new DemoGridLayout();

    JFrame f = new JFrame("GridLayout");
    f.setContentPane(p);
    f.setDefaultCloseOperation(JFrame.EXIT_ON_CLOSE);
    f.pack();              // Base frame size on preferred size of components.
    f.setVisible(true);
  }
}
```

12.6.3 The `BorderLayout` Strategy

The `BorderLayout` strategy lays out up to five objects in a panel, as shown in Figure 12-20. No matter what size the panel is, the north and south areas cover the entire width. Their heights are determined by the preferred heights of the components they hold. The east and west areas expand or contract to occupy the remaining height of the panel. Their widths are determined by the preferred sizes of the components they hold. Finally, the center area expands or contracts to occupy the remaining space.

(figure 12-20)

The `BorderLayout` *strategy*

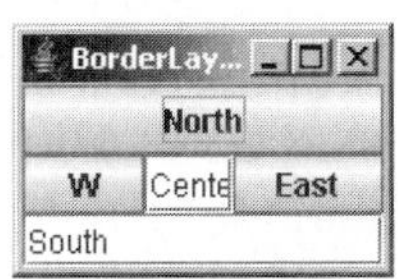

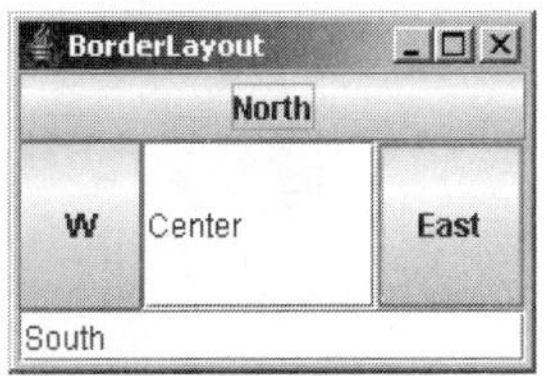

Areas that do not have a component will not take any space. For example, if the button was left out of the east area in Figure 12-20, the center area would simply expand to fill it.

The layout managers we've seen previously arrange the components according to the order in which they are added to the panel. `BorderLayout` handles positioning with a **constraint**, which is specified when the component is added. The constraint says where the component should be placed.

Listing 12-20 could be modified to use a `BorderLayout` strategy by changing line 17 to:

```
17      BorderLayout strategy = new BorderLayout();
```

and changing the lines that add the components to use the required constraints.

```
21      this.add(this.one, BorderLayout.EAST);
22      this.add(this.two, BorderLayout.NORTH);
```

12.6.4 Other Layout Strategies

The `BoxLayout` strategy arranges components in a horizontal row or a vertical column. It tries to respect the preferred sizes of components. However, if a component does not have a maximum size, it will grow or shrink to fill available space. Text fields and text areas, for example, do not have a maximum size unless you set one.

Like `GridLayout`, `GridBagLayout` uses a grid. However, its cells can vary in size, and a component can take up more than one cell in the grid. To accomplish all this, it uses a fairly complex constraint, called `GridBagConstraints`.

Another constraint-based layout strategy is `SpringLayout`. It works by specifying how the edges of each component relate to other components or to the edges of the enclosing panel.

12.6.5 Nesting Layout Strategies

A single layout strategy is usually not enough for a complex graphical user interface. Consider Figure 12-21, for example. None of the simpler layout strategies we've covered can handle this by themselves. `GridBagLayout` and `SpringLayout` could do it, but using them would involve a tremendous amount of work in setting all the constraints.

(figure 12-21)
A complex layout task

An excellent solution is based on the fact that `JPanel` is also a component. It can be added to another `JPanel` that is organized by its own layout strategy object. The user interface in Figure 12-21 is organized with four `JPanel` objects, as shown in Figure 12-22.

LOOKING AHEAD

Programming Exercise 12.12 asks you to finish implementing `HangmanView`.

(figure 12-22)
Laying out a complex user interface using nested panels, each with its own layout strategy

The four `JPanel` objects are as follows:

- `controls` is organized by a `GridLayout` and holds the `Forfeit` and `New Game` buttons.
- `letters` is also organized by a `GridLayout` and holds 26 buttons, one for each letter of the alphabet.
- `buttons` is organized by a `BoxLayout` and holds two `JPanel` components, `controls` and `letters`.
- `hangman` is organized by a `BorderLayout`. The center area holds the graphic showing the gallows. The south area holds a `JLabel` displaying the letters guessed so far. The east area holds the `buttons` panel (which holds `letters` and `controls`). The north and west area of the `BorderLayout` are empty and shrink to take no space.

This interface can be implemented with code similar to that shown in Listing 12-22.

FIND THE CODE

ch12/hangman/

PATTERN

Strategy

Listing 12-22: *Implementing nesting layout managers*

```
import becker.xtras.hangman.*;
import javax.swing.*;
import java.awt.*;

/** Layout the view for the game of hangman.
 *
 * @author Byron Weber Becker */
public class HangmanView extends JPanel
{ // Constructor omitted.

   /** Layout the view in a JPanel managed by BorderLayout. */
   private void layoutView()
   { JPanel hangman = this;        // Use same name as previous discussion
     hangman.setLayout(new BorderLayout());

     // South
     JLabel phrase = new JLabel("GO FLY A KITE");
     hangman.add(phrase, BorderLayout.SOUTH);

     // Center
     JComponent gallows = new GallowsView(
                                new SampleHangman());
     hangman.add(gallows, BorderLayout.CENTER);

     // East -- letters and controls
     JPanel buttons = this.buttonsPanel();
```

Listing 12-22: *Implementing nesting layout managers* (continued)

```
      hangman.add(buttons, BorderLayout.EAST);
   }

   /** Layout and return a subpanel with all the buttons. */
   private JPanel buttonsPanel()
   { // A JPanel holding 26 buttons, one for each letter of the alphabet.
      JPanel letters = new JPanel();
      letters.setLayout(new GridLayout(13, 2));
      for (char ch = 'A'; ch <= 'Z'; ch++)
      { letters.add(new JButton("" + ch));
      }

      // A JPanel holding the Forfeit and New Game buttons is omitted.

      return letters;
   }
}
```

12.7 Patterns

12.7.1 The Polymorphic Call Pattern

Name: Polymorphic Call

Context: You are writing a program that handles several variations of the same general idea (for example, several kinds of bank accounts). Each kind of thing has similar behaviors, but the details may differ.

Solution: Use a polymorphic method call so that the actual object being used determines which method is called. The most basic form of the pattern is identical to the Command Invocation pattern from Chapter 1 except for how the *«objReference»* is given its value. For example,

```
«varTypeName» «objReference» = «instance of objTypeName»;
...
«objReference».«serviceName»(«parameterList»);
```

where *«objTypeName»* is a subclass of *«varTypeName»* or *«objTypeName»* is a class that implements the interface *«varTypeName»*.

There are many variations. For example, *«objReference»* could be a simple instance variable, an array, a parameter, or a value returned from a method.

Consequences: *«varTypeName»* determines the names of the methods that can be called using *«objReference»*, but *«objTypeName»* determines the code that is actually executed.

Related Pattern: This pattern is a variation of the Command Invocation pattern.

12.7.2 The Strategy Pattern

Name: Strategy

Context: The way an object behaves may change over time or from application to application. Examples include how an employee is compensated as the nature of his or her employment changes, how a game chooses its move as the player adjusts preferences, or how a `JPanel` lays out the components it contains.

Solution: Identify the methods that may need to be executed differently, depending on the strategy. Define these methods in a superclass or an interface. Write several subclasses that implement the behavior required at specific phases in a program's life.

For example, in a game, a player object needs to make its next move depending on the preferences of the user. The `Player` class could be defined as follows, where `MoveStrategy` is either the superclass of several different strategy classes or an interface that is implemented by several strategy classes.

```
public class Player extends ...
{ private MoveStrategy moveStrategy =
            new DefaultMoveStrategy();
  ...
  public void setMoveStrategy(MoveStrategy aStrategy)
  { this.moveStrategy = aStrategy;
  }

  public Move getMove(...)
  { return this.moveStrategy.getMove(...);
  }
}
```

Consequences: The behavior of a class can be easily changed as the program proceeds simply by supplying a different strategy object.

Related Patterns:

- This pattern is a specialization of the Has-a (Composition) pattern.
- The Polymorphic Call pattern is used to call the methods in the strategy object.

12.7.3 The Equals Pattern

Name: Equals

Context: Objects must be compared for equivalency with each other. Comparisons may be done using such library code as `ArrayList` or `HashSet`, and so a standard approach must be used.

Solution: Override the `equals` method in the `Object` class. It is designated to take any instance of `Object` (including subclasses) as its argument, so care must be taken to ensure that the two objects can be compared. The following general template may be used:

```
public class «className» ...
{ private «primitiveType» «primitiveField1»
  ...
  private «primitiveType» «primitiveFieldN»
  private «referenceType» «referenceField1»
  ...
  private «referenceType» «referenceFieldN»

  public boolean equals(Object other)
  { if (this == other)
      return true;

    if (!(other instanceof «className»))
      return false;

    «className» o = («className»)other;
    return
       this.«primitiveField1» == o.«primitiveField1» &&
       ...
       this.«primitiveFieldN» == o.«primitiveFieldN» &&
       this.«referenceField1».equals(o.«referenceField1») &&
       ...
       this.«referenceFieldN».equals(o.«referenceFieldN»);
  }
}
```

where == is used for primitive fields and `equals` is used for object references. It may be that only a subset of the object fields are used to determine equality.

Consequences: The `equals` method can be used to check any object for equivalence with any other object.

Related Pattern: This pattern should be used in place of the Equivalence Test pattern.

12.7.4 The Factory Method Pattern

Name: Factory Method

Context: A specific subclass should be instantiated depending on various factors, such as the information found in a file or values obtained from a user. The logic for deciding which specific subclass to create should be localized in one place in the program.

Solution: Write a method that determines which subclass to instantiate and then returns it. In general,

```
public static «superClassName» «factoryMethodName»(...)
{ «superClassName» instance = null;
  if («testForSubclass1»)
  { instance = new «subclassName1»(...);
  } else if («testForSubclass2»)
  { instance = new «subclassName2»(...);
  } else ...

  return instance;
}
```

Consequences: A specific subclass is chosen to be instantiated and then returned for use.

Related Pattern: None.

12.8 Summary and Concept Map

Polymorphism is a programming technique in which a variable declared with a superclass or an interface, *X*, is actually assigned an instance of a different class, *Y*. *Y* must be either a subclass of *X* or a class implementing interface *X*.

The program typically calls a method defined by *X* but the behavior is determined by the object's actual class, *Y*. This allows:

- a collection of objects to be handled uniformly but still have individual differences
- the behavior of an object to be easily changed by changing a strategy object
- an alternative implementation to be used with a minimum number of changes to the client code

Polymorphism plays a significant role in the implementation and execution of methods inherited from the `Object` class, including `toString`, `equals`, and `clone`. The strategy pattern is used extensively in laying out graphical user interfaces.

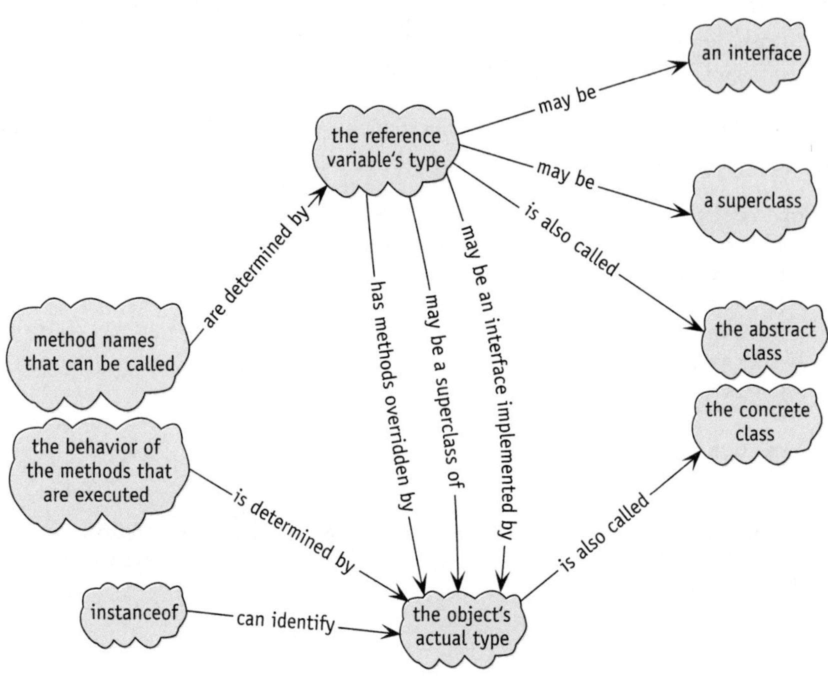

12.9 Problem Set

Written Exercises

12.1 The `move` method in the `LeftDancer` class (see Listing 12-1) contains the statement `super.move()` (lines 16, 18, and 20). What would happen if one of those statements were `this.move()`?

12.2 Polymorphism is like a ship's commanding officer yelling, "Battle stations!" Each member of the crew knows exactly what he should do in response to that order—and does it. The commander doesn't need to give each crew member individual instructions. Think of three more real-life analogies for polymorphism.

12.3 Write `comparator` classes that can be used to sort an array of:

a. `Robot` objects in ascending order by distance from the origin

b. `LineItem` objects in descending order by unit cost

c. `Person` objects (see Section 10.1) by role. Persons with the same role should be ordered by gender, while persons with the same role and gender should be ordered by decreasing age. (*Hint*: Use `compareTo` to compare enumerations.)

12.4 Draw a class diagram for the drawing program example in Section 12.1.3.

12.5 Study the documentation for the specified class. Draw a partial class diagram of it and its subclasses, showing the most important overridden methods and additional features of each subclass.

a. `becker.robots.Sim`

b. `java.text.Format`

c. `java.awt.Component` (This is the root of a huge hierarchy. Stop when your diagram includes about 10 classes, some of which are at least sub-subclasses of `Component`.)

d. `java.io.Reader` (Include a brief description of the functionality each subclass adds.)

12.6 Read the documentation for the `Box` class. What combination of classes does it replace? Describe what "struts" and "glue" are and how they might be used.

Programming Exercises

12.7 In the dancing robots example, it appears the fundamental difference between a `LeftDancer` and a `RightDancer` is not in how they move but in their favored direction to turn. Refactor the dancing robots example shown in Figure 12-3 so that `move` and `pirouette` are completely defined in the abstract class in terms of `turn` and `antiTurn`. These last two methods are abstract and must be overridden in both `LeftDancer` and `RightDancer`.

12.8 Investigate the documentation for `becker.robots.IPredicate`. For each of the following, write the predicate and a simple robot test program.

a. Write a predicate to identify a `Streetlight` that is on. Use it to turn off several streetlights.

b. The `City` class has a method named `setThingCountPredicate`. If `showThingCounts` is set to `true`, the number of things on each intersection that meet the predicate's criteria will be shown. The default counts the number of things that can be moved by a robot. Change it to show the total of all things, except robots.

c. Extend `Robot` to include a query, `northIsBlocked`, which returns `true` if the north exit to the intersection is blocked by a `Thing` such as a `Wall`. The query will use `isBesideThing` and a predicate that you write. The robot should not turn while executing this query.

d. Extend `Robot` to include a query, `dirIsBlocked(int dir)`. It is similar to `northIsBlocked` in part (c), but is not restricted to a single direction. The predicate will need an instance variable to remember the direction. The robot should not turn while executing this query.

12.9 Consider a family of robots that all have a `doMyThing` method. When a baby robot does its thing, it moves in a random direction with a random speed. Parent robots do their thing by moving and automatically picking up all the things found on their new intersection. Grandparent robots do their thing by moving at one-third the speed of a normal robot.

a. Implement the robot family by extending `RobotSE` three times. Write a `main` method containing an array of family members. Also scatter a number of `Thing` objects around. Make each robot do its thing 10 times. (*Hint*: You will need to introduce an abstract class.)

b. Implement the robot family by writing `FamilyMemberBot`. It extends `RobotSE` to use an instance of `IMoveStrategy`. Write the interface `IMoveStrategy` and three classes that implement it. Write a `main` method containing an array of `FamilyMemberBots`. Also scatter a number of `Thing` objects around. Make each robot do its thing five times. Change each robot to use a different move strategy, and then move each robot five more times. (*Hint*: The method in `IMoveStrategy` will take an instance of `FamilyMemberBot`, named `bot`, as a parameter and could contain method calls like `bot.move()`).

12.10 Some courses assign letter grades, whereas other courses assign a percentage between 0 and 100. Still others assign a pass/fail grade.

Write an interface named `Grade`. The `toPercent` method returns the grade as an integer percentage between 0 and 100 percent. The `toString` method prints the grade in its "native" format (a percentage, a letter grade, or either "Pass" or "Fail"). The `isPass` method returns `true` for a passing grade, `false` otherwise. The `includeInAverage` returns `true` for letter and numeric grades, but `false` for pass/fail grades.

Write three classes that implement `Grade`: `LetterGrade`, `PercentageGrade`, and `PassFailGrade`. Write a `main` method that fills an array with grades. For each grade, print on one line the native format, "Pass" or "Fail" (as appropriate), and the percentage (if it can be included in an average). After the list of grades, print the average grade as a percentage.

Use your school's mapping between letter grades and numeric grades, if it has one. Otherwise, make up something like `A+` is 95%, `A` is 90%, etc.

12.11 Write a main method that displays a JPanel inside a JFrame to arrange components as follows.

a. Use a GridLayout to arrange JCheckBox and JSlider components as shown in Figure 12-23a.

b. Use a combination of BorderLayout, BoxLayout, and FlowLayout to arrange JRadioButton, JButton, and JTextArea components as shown in Figure 12-23b. The text field will have no size unless you specify the rows and columns when it is created.

c. Approximate (b) as closely as you can using only BoxLayout and FlowLayout. You may find calling setAlignmentY(0.0F) on one of the panels useful.

d. Approximate (b) as closely as you can using only GridBagLayout and FlowLayout. You will need to read the GridBagConstraints class documentation carefully.

(figure 12-23)

Possible layouts

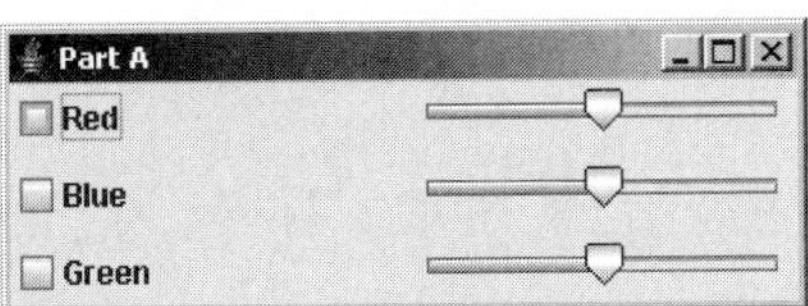

a) One layout

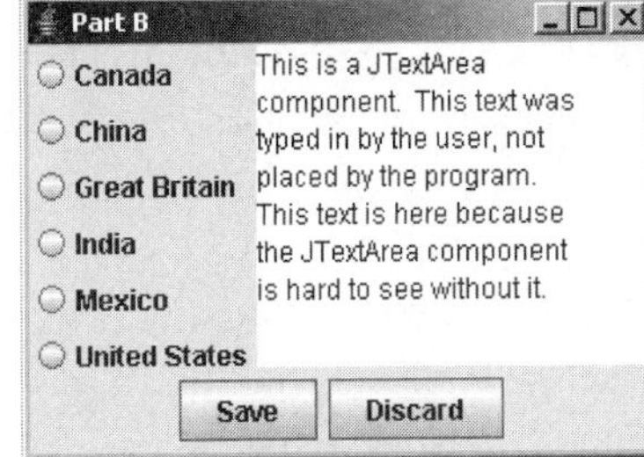

b) Another layout

12.12 Finish the program in Listing 12-22 so that it also displays Forfeit and New Game buttons, as shown in Figure 12-21. Include a main method that displays HangmanView in a JFrame. You won't be able to play a game with your program, but it should look good.

For an additional challenge, read about the Box class and figure out how to use it to replace a JPanel organized with a BoxLayout strategy.

12.13 In Section 10.1.5, we discussed various operations on those elements of an array that satisfy a specified property. For example, calculate the average age of everyone who is a "Little" or print all the people who are "Bigs."

Download the Big Brother/Big Sister example from Chapter 10 (ch10/bbbs/). Add an interface, IInclude, which has a single method, boolean include(Person p). Add the following methods to BigBroBigSis.java:

a. int countSatisfy(IInclude include) counts those persons who satisfy include.

b. `double averageAge(IInclude include)` finds the average age of all those people who satisfy `include`.

c. `void list(IInclude include, PrintWriter out)` lists to the specified file all those people who satisfy `include`.

d. `Person[] subset(IInclude include)` returns a filled array of all those people who satisfy `include`.

Write a `main` method to test your methods using an instance of `IInclude` that specifies female "Bigs."

Programming Projects

12.14 Implement a simple bank application. The bank will have many accounts, each with an account number and a balance. A command interpreter will allow customers to enter one of the following commands:

- `d xxx yyy` (deposits the amount `xxx` to account number `yyy`).
- `w xxx yyy` (withdraws the amount `xxx` from account `yyy`).
- `t xxx yyy zzz` (withdraws the amount `xxx` from account `yyy` and deposits the same amount in account `zzz`).
- `b yyy` (displays the balance of account `yyy`).

The bank has two kinds of accounts. A `PerUseAccount` charges a set fee of $0.50 for each withdrawal. A `MinBalanceAccount` charges a fee of $1.00 for each withdrawal if the balance is less than $1,000. If the balance is $1,000 or more, no fee is charged.

a. Implement the banking system *without* using polymorphism or inheritance. Write a brief document outlining in point form what would have to be done to add a new kind of bank account to the system.

b. Implement the banking system using an inheritance hierarchy for the account classes. Take advantage of polymorphism but minimize the use of casting. Write a brief document outlining in point form what would have to be done to add a new kind of bank account to the system.

12.15 Implement a simple guessing game in which the user chooses a number that the program will try to guess. After each guess, the user will answer with either `H` (the guess was too high), `L` (the guess was too low), or `C` (the guess was correct). Allow the user to easily change the guessing strategy used by the program at the beginning of each game. Strategies should include at least two of the following:

a. Guess a random number.

b. Guess a number that is one larger than the previous guess. The first guess should be the smallest legal number for the game.

c. Guess the smallest legal number. As long as the user responds with `L`, guess a number that is 10 larger than the previous guess. When the user says it's too large, start guessing a number that is one less than the previous guess.

d. Based on the user's answers, keep track of the upper and lower limits on the number that could have been chosen by the user. Each guess should be the average of these two values. After each guess, update the upper and lower limits. (This brief description describes how most people search a physical phonebook: start in the middle and successively eliminate half of the remaining entries.)

12.16 Extend `JComponent` to paint shapes on itself. The shapes that it paints and their locations will depend on which shapes are added to a list the component maintains. Your shapes should form an inheritance hierarchy with `Shape` at the root. `Shape` should extend `Object`.

a. Demonstrate your program with a `main` method that adds a number of rectangles, circles, lines, and stars to your subclass of `JComponent`.

b. Implement two additional shapes of your choice beyond those required in (a).

c. Enhance your program so that it will paint the shapes it reads from a file.

12.17 Implement a simplified game of Monopoly that has an inheritance hierarchy of `BoardSquare` objects. Subclasses must include `Property`, `Railroad`, `Go`, and `IncomeTax`. You will also need a `Player` class and a command interpreter to play the game.

Think carefully about whether the `Player` object should react according to the kind of square it landed on or whether the `BoardSquare` objects should react to `Players` landing on or crossing them.

a. Implement the game with two instances of `Player` that always ask a user for what to do.

b. Implement the game to allow between two and six players, each of which uses a `move` strategy object to determine how it plays. Provide at least three different strategies: one that asks the user, another that always buys a property if it can, and a third that only buys a property if it has at least $500. Give the user a choice of strategies for each player when the game begins.

12.18 ACME Inc. has a standing order for 50 widgets each week from XYZ Inc. The agreement is that ACME sends the widgets each Friday and XYZ will send a check to pay for them that same day. If both live up to their agreement, they both profit. On the other hand, XYZ might send a fraudulent check, hoping to receive goods for free; or ACME might not send the goods, hoping to receive unearned payment.

We'll say either company "cooperates" if it abides by its side of the agreement. If it does not, we'll say the company "defects." The payoff can then be represented with Table 12-2.

ACME's Action	XYZ's Action	Value to ACME	Value to XYZ
Cooperate	Cooperate	3	3
Cooperate	Defect	-2	5
Defect	Cooperate	5	-2
Defect	Defect	0	0

(table 12-2)
Company actions

If both companies want to maximize their profit, what should their strategies be? Cooperate all of the time? Cooperate most of the time but defect occasionally? Cooperate as much as the other company cooperates?

First, develop three strategies that implement the following interface. They might be as simple as always cooperating, cooperating with the same probability that the other player has cooperated in the past, repeating the other player's last decision, or always defecting.

```
public interface ICommerceStrategy
{ public static final int DEFECT = 0;
  public static final int COOPERATE = 1;

  /** Decide whether to cooperate with the other player, given the other's history of
   *   cooperating with this player.
   *   @param other          The decisions made by the other player in previous turns. Each
   *                         element of the array is one of {DEFECT, COOPERATE}.
   *   @param numTurns   The number of turns made (other is partially filled).
   *   @return one of {DEFECT, COOPERATE} */
  public int getDecision(int[] other, int numTurns);
}
```

Second, develop a program that plays each strategy against all the other strategies, including a copy of itself. Print the cumulative score for each strategy to determine the best one. Assume that the players do not know how many turns there will be. (Does it change your strategy if you know this is your last turn?)

Chapter 13 Graphical User Interfaces

Chapter Objectives

After studying this chapter, you should be able to:

- Write a graphical user interface using existing Java components
- Implement interfaces using the Model-View-Controller pattern
- Structure a graphical user interface using multiple views
- Write new components for use in graphical user interfaces

A graphical user interface (GUI) often gives us the first glimpse of a new program. The information it displays indicates the program's purpose, whereas a quick review of the interface's controls and menus gives us a feel for what the program can do.

Graphical user interfaces operate in a fundamentally different way from text-based interfaces. In a text-based interface, the program is in control, demanding information when it suits the program rather than the user. With a graphical user interface, the user has much more control; users can perform operations in their preferred order rather than according to the program's demands. Naturally, this difference requires structuring the program in a different way.

This chapter pulls together the graphical user interface thread running through each chapter and adds new material, enabling us to design and build graphical user interfaces for our programs.

13.1 Overview

Building the graphical user interface (GUI) for a program can be one of the more rewarding parts of programming. Finally, we begin to *see* the results of our labor and are able to manipulate our program directly. The user interface is also a place where we can use aesthetic skills and sensibilities.

On the other hand, creating GUIs can involve a lot of time and frustration. Developing them will call upon every skill we've learned so far: extending existing classes, writing methods, using collaborating classes and instance variables, using Java interfaces, and so on. However, following a concrete set of steps will make the job easier. Watch for patterns that occur repeatedly. Master those patterns, and you'll be able to write GUIs like a professional.

We will proceed by developing a variant of the game of Nim. The requirements are specified in Figure 13-1.

A game of Nim begins with a pile of tokens. Two players take turns removing one, two, or three tokens from the pile. The last player to remove a token wins the game. The players will be designated "red" and "black." The first one to move will be chosen randomly. The initial size of the pile is between ten and twenty tokens and is set randomly.

An example of one possible user interface is shown on the right.

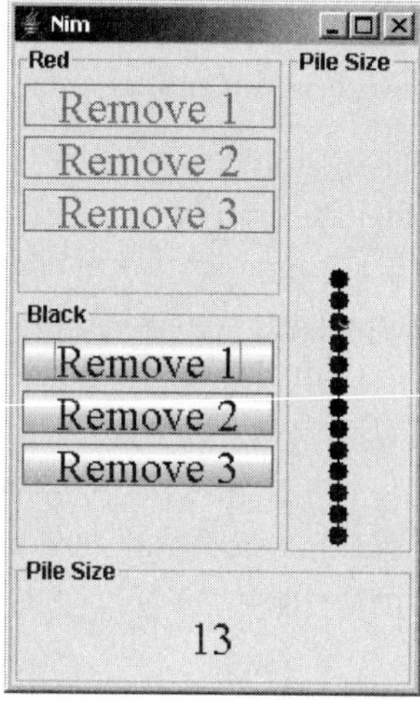

(figure 13-1)

Requirements for the game of Nim

13.1.1 Models, Views, and Controllers

Recall from Chapter 8 that graphical user interfaces are usually structured using the Model-View-Controller pattern. Figure 13-2, reproduced here from Section 8.6.2, shows the core ideas.

(figure 13-2)

View and controller interact with the user and the model

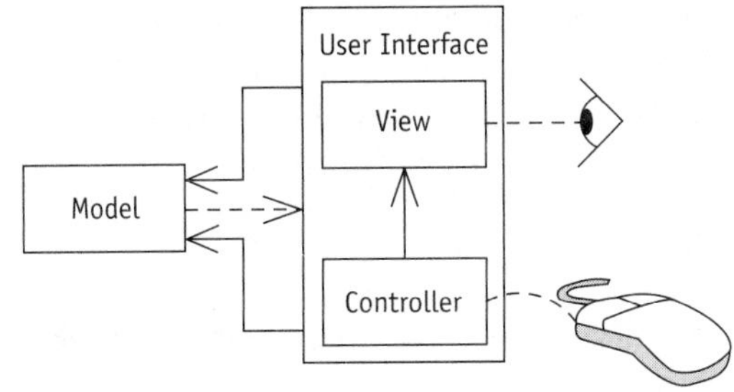

The model is the part of the program that represents the problem at hand. In our game of Nim, it's the model that will keep track of how many tokens remain on the pile, whose turn it is to move next, and who (if anyone) has won the game. The model also enforces rules. For example, it will not allow a player to take more than three tokens.

KEY IDEA

The model maintains relevant information, the view displays it, and the controller requests changes to it.

The user interface is composed of the view and the controller. The user, represented by the eye and the mouse, uses the view to obtain information from the model. It's the view, for example, that displays the current size of the pile and whose turn it is. The user interacts with the controller to change the model. In the case of Nim, the controller is used to remove some tokens or to start a new game.

The arrow between the controller and the view indicates that the controller will need to call methods in the view. The lack of an arrow going the other way indicates that the view will generally not need to call the controller's methods. The two arrows between the user interface and the model indicate that both the view and the controller will have reason to call the model's methods—the view to obtain information to display and the controller to tell the model how the user wants it to change. The dotted arrow from the model to the user interface indicates that the model will be very restrictive in how it calls methods in the interface. Essentially, it will call only a single method to tell the view that it has changed and that the view needs to update the display.

The interaction of the controller, model, and view may seem complicated at first. However, it follows a standard pattern, which includes the following typical steps, performed in the following order:

- The user manipulates the user interface—for example, enters text in a component.
- The user interface component notifies its controller by calling a method that we write.
- The controller calls a mutator method in the model, perhaps supplying additional information such as text that was entered in the component.
- Inside the mutator method, the model changes its state, as appropriate. Then it calls the view's `update` method, informing the view that it needs to update the information it displays.
- Inside the `update` method, the view calls accessor methods in the model to gather the information it needs to display. It then displays that information.

Our first graphical user interface will use a single view and controller. We will learn in Section 13.5, however, that using multiple views and controllers can actually make an interface easier to build. We will plan for that possibility from the beginning.

KEY IDEA

Interfaces usually have more than one view.

13.1.2 Using a Pattern

Models, views, and controllers make up a pattern that occurs repeatedly. The steps for using this pattern are shown in Figure 13-3. You'll find that many of the steps are familiar from previous chapters in the book. None of this is truly new material; it just puts together what we have already learned in a specific way, resulting in a graphical user interface.

PATTERN

Model-View-Controller

(figure 13-3)

Steps for building a graphical user interface

<table>
<tr><td colspan="2">Set up the Model and View

1. Write three nearly empty classes:
a. The model, implementing <code>becker.util.IModel</code>.
b. The view, extending <code>JPanel</code> and implementing <code>becker.util.IView</code>. The constructor takes an instance of the model as an argument.
c. A class containing a <code>main</code> method to run the program.
2. In <code>main</code>, create instances of the model and the view. Display the view in a frame.</td></tr>
<tr><td>Build and Test the Model

1. Design, implement, and test the model. In particular,
a. add commands used by the controllers to change the model
b. add queries used by the views to obtain the information to display
2. Call <code>updateAllViews</code> just before exiting any method that changes the model's state.</td><td>Build the View and Controllers

1. Design the interface.
2. Construct the required components and lay them out in the view.
3. Write <code>updateView</code> to update the information displayed by the view to reflect the model.
4. Write appropriate controllers for each of the components that update the model. Register the controllers.</td></tr>
</table>

We will elaborate on these steps in each of the next three subsections.

13.2 Setting up the Model and View

The first step sets up the basic architecture for the Model-View-Controller pattern. This is where the connections between the classes are established, and by the end of this step, we will have a program that we can run, even though it won't do anything more than show us an empty frame. The class diagram of the resulting program is shown in Figure 13-4.

(figure 13-4)

Partial class diagram for `Nim`

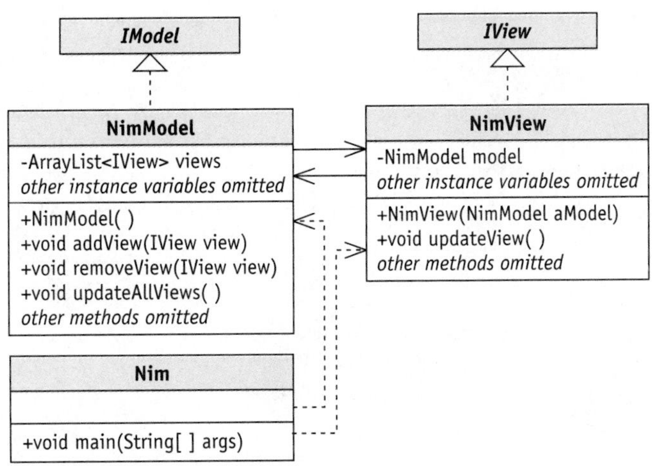

13.2.1 The Model's Infrastructure

The model's primary purpose is to model the problem, in our case the game of Nim. It must also inform the views each time the model changes (and therefore the view needs to change the information it displays). It is this update function that we are focusing on now.

LOOKING BACK

`ArrayList`*s were discussed in Section 8.5.1, interfaces in Section 7.6.*

It's possible that a model may have several views, and we will provide for that possibility right away by keeping a list of views that we need to inform of changes. These requirements are embodied in the `IModel` interface. It specifies that a model needs to be able to add a view, remove a view, and update all views. The model will only need to call one method in the views, `updateView`. It expects each view to implement the `IView` interface.

KEY IDEA

The `IModel` *interface specifies methods needed in the model to manage views.*

A class with this infrastructure is shown in Listing 13-1. Every model will start out just like this except that the name of the class, the constructor, and the class documentation will change to reflect the program's purpose.

FIND THE CODE

ch13/nim Infrastructure/

Listing 13-1: *The model's class with infrastructure to inform views of changes*

```
import becker.util.IModel;
import becker.util.IView;
import java.util.ArrayList;

/** A class implementing a version of Nim. There is a (virtual) pile of tokens. Two
 *  players take turns removing 1, 2, or 3 tokens. The player who takes the last token
 *  wins the game.
 *
 *  @author Byron Weber Becker */
public class NimModel extends Object implements IModel
```

Listing 13-1: *The model's class with infrastructure to inform views of changes* (continued)

```
{ private ArrayList<IView> views = new ArrayList<IView>();

  /** Construct a new instance of the game of Nim. */
  public NimModel()
  { super();
  }

  /** Add a view to display information about this model.
   * @param view The view to add. */
  public void addView(IView view)
  { this.views.add(view);
  }

  /** Remove a view that has been displaying information about this model.
   * @param view The view to remove. */
  public void removeView(IView view)
  { this.views.remove(view);
  }

  /** Inform all the views currently displaying information about this model that the
   * model has changed and their display may need changing too. */
  public void updateAllViews()
  { for (IView view : this.views)
    { view.updateView();
    }
  }
}
```

Of course, more must be added to `NimModel`. In particular, it does nothing yet to model the game of Nim. But when one of the players takes some tokens from the pile, for example, we now have the infrastructure in place to inform all of the views that they need to update the information they are showing the players.

Using `AbstractModel`

These three methods are always required to implement a model. Instead of writing them each time we create a model class, we can put them in their own class. Our model can simply extend that class.

Such a class, AbstractModel, is in the becker.util package. Its code is almost exactly like the code in Listing 13-1 except for the name of the class. NimModel is then implemented as follows:

```
import becker.util.AbstractModel;

public class NimModel extends AbstractModel
{
  public NimModel()
  { super();
  }

  // Other methods will be added here to implement the model.
}
```

AbstractModel implements IModel, implying that NimModel also implements that interface. The clause implements IModel does not need to be repeated.

The Java library has a class named Observable that is very similar to AbstractModel. It is designed to work with an interface named Observer that is very similar to IView. Why don't we use them instead? There are two reasons.

First, the update method in Observable is more complex than we need.

Second, and more importantly, the Java library doesn't have an interface corresponding to IModel. Therefore, the model must always extend Observable. Sometimes this isn't a problem (as with NimModel), but other times the model must extend another class. In those situations, the missing interface is required, and these classes can't be used.

At the time of this writing, Java library contains 6,558 classes. A number of those classes define their own versions of Observer and Observable, as we have done. It's interesting to note that none of the classes use Observer and Observable.

13.2.2 The View's Infrastructure

KEY IDEA

A component is nothing more than an object designed for user interfaces. Buttons, scroll bars, and text fields are all examples of components.

Each view will be a subclass of JPanel[1] that contains the user interface components required to interact with the model. For now, however, we will provide only the infrastructure for updating the view. That consists of implementing the IView interface, which specifies the updateView method called by the model in updateAllViews. This is all shown in Listing 13-2.

[1] This is true most of the time. It's convenient for menus to extend JMenuBar and toolbars to extend JToolBar.

The view is passed an instance of the model when it is constructed. The model is saved in an instance variable, and the view adds itself to the model's list of views. Finally, the view must update the information it displays by calling `updateView` in line 16.

FIND THE CODE

ch13/nim Infrastructure/

Listing 13-2: *The view's class set up to receive notification of changes in the model*

```
1  import javax.swing.JPanel;
2  import becker.util.IView;
3
4  /** Provide a view of the game of Nim to a user.
5   *
6   *  @author Byron Weber Becker */
7  public class NimView extends JPanel implements IView
8  { private NimModel model;
9
10    /** Construct the view.
11     *  @param aModel The model we will be displaying. */
12    public NimView(NimModel aModel)
13    { super();
14      this.model = aModel;
15      this.model.addView(this);
16      this.updateView();
17    }
18
19    /** Called by the model when it changes. Update the information this view displays. */
20    public void updateView()
21    {
22    }
23 }
```

13.2.3 The `main` Method

The last step in setting up the infrastructure is to write the `main` method. It constructs an instance of the model and an instance of the view. It then displays the view in an appropriately sized frame. This is shown in Listing 13-3.

FIND THE CODE

ch13/nim Infrastructure/

Listing 13-3: *The* `main` *method for running the program*

```
import javax.swing.JFrame;

/** Run the game of Nim. There is a (virtual) pile of tokens. Two players take turns
 *   removing 1, 2, or 3 tokens. The player who takes the last token wins the game.
 *
 *   @author Byron Weber Becker */
public class Nim
{
  public static void main(String[] args)
  { NimModel model = new NimModel();
    NimView view = new NimView(model);

    JFrame f = new JFrame("Nim");
    f.setSize(250, 200);
    f.setDefaultCloseOperation(JFrame.EXIT_ON_CLOSE);
    f.setContentPane(view);
    f.setVisible(true);
  }
}
```

13.3 Building and Testing the Model

Figure 13-3 describes the steps for building a user interface. It suggests that the model requires commands to change its state and queries for the views to use in updating the display. If we keep this in mind while using the development process discussed in Chapter 11, we will discover that the model for Nim needs the following methods:

- `removeTokens`, a command to remove one, two, or three tokens from the pile
- `getPileSize`, a query returning the current size of the pile
- `getWhoseTurn`, a query returning whose turn it is
- `getWinner`, a query returning which player, if any, has won the game

The requirements in Figure 13-1 specify that the first player and the initial size of the pile are chosen randomly. The default constructor will do that, but since randomness makes the class hard to test, we'll also add a private constructor, allowing our test harness to easily specify the pile size and first player.

LOOKING BACK

Enumerations were discussed in Section 7.3.4.

Representing the two players is a perfect job for an enumeration type. We will use three values: one for the red player, one for the black player, and one for nobody. The last one might be used, for example, as the answer to the query of who has won the game (if the game isn't over yet, nobody has won).

The `Player` enumeration is shown in Listing 13-4, and the `NimModel` class is shown in Listing 13-5. In `NimModel`, the only method (other than the constructors) that changes the model's state is `removeTokens`. After it has made its changes, it calls `updateAllViews` at line 96 to inform the views that they should update the information they display.

KEY IDEA

Call `updateAllViews` *before returning from a method that changes the model.*

FIND THE CODE

ch13/nimOneView/

Listing 13-4: *The* `Player` *enumeration type*

```
/** The players in the game of Nim, plus NOBODY to indicate situations where
 *   neither player is applicable (for example, when no one has won the game yet).
 *
 *   @author Byron Weber Becker */
public enum Player
{ RED, BLACK, NOBODY
}
```

FIND THE CODE

ch13/nimOneView/

Listing 13-5: *The completed* `NimModel` *class*

```
1  import becker.util.AbstractModel;
2  import becker.util.Test;
3
4  /** A class implementing a version of Nim. There is a (virtual) pile of tokens. Two
5   *   players take turns removing 1, 2, or 3 tokens. The player who takes the last token
6   *   wins the game.
7   *
8   *   @author Byron Weber Becker */
9  public class NimModel extends AbstractModel
10 { // Extending AbstractModel is an easy way to implement the IModel interface.
11
12    // Limit randomly generated pile sizes and how many tokens can be removed at once.
13    public static final int MIN_PILESIZE = 10;
14    public static final int MAX_PILESIZE = 20;
15    public static final int MAX_REMOVE = 3;
16
17    private int pileSize;
18    private Player whoseTurn;
19    private Player winner = Player.NOBODY;
20
21    /** Construct a new instance of the game of Nim. */
22    public NimModel()
23    { // Call the other constructor to do the initialization.
24      this(NimModel.random(MIN_PILESIZE, MAX_PILESIZE),
25           NimModel.chooseRandomPlayer());
26    }
```

Listing 13-5: *The completed* `NimModel` *class* (continued)

```

/** We need a way to create a nonrandom game for testing purposes. */
private NimModel(int pileSize, Player next)
{ super();
  this.pileSize = pileSize;
  this.whoseTurn = next;
}

/** Generate a random number between two bounds. */
private static int random(int lower, int upper)
{ return (int)(Math.random()*(upper-lower+1)) + lower;
}

/** Choose a player at random.
* @return Player.RED or Player.BLACK with 50% probability for each */
private static Player chooseRandomPlayer()
{ if (Math.random() < 0.5)
  { return Player.RED;
  } else
  { return Player.BLACK;
  }
}

/** Get the current size of the pile.
* @return the current size of the pile */
public int getPileSize()
{ return this.pileSize;
}

/** Get the next player to move.
* @return Either Player.RED or Player.BLACK if the game has not yet been won,
* or Player.NOBODY if the game has been won. */
public Player getWhoseTurn()
{ return this.whoseTurn;
}

/** Get the winner of the game.
* @return Either Player.RED or Player.BLACK if the game has already been won;
* Player.NOBODY if the game is still in progress. */
public Player getWinner()
{ return this.winner;
}
```

Listing 13-5: *The completed* `NimModel` *class* (continued)

```

/** Is the game over?
 *  @return true if the game is over; false otherwise. */
private boolean gameOver()
{ return this.pileSize == 0;
}

/** Remove one, two, or three tokens from the pile. Ignore any attempts to take
 *  too many or too few tokens. Otherwise, remove howMany tokens from the pile
 *  and update whose turn is next.
 *  @param howMany How many tokens to remove.
 *  @throws IllegalStateException if the game has already been won */
public void removeTokens(int howMany)
{ if (this.gameOver())
  { throw new IllegalStateException(
                                   "The game has already been won.");
  }

  if (this.isLegalMove(howMany))
  { this.pileSize = this.pileSize - howMany;
    if (this.gameOver())
    { this.winner = this.whoseTurn;
      this.whoseTurn = Player.NOBODY;
    } else
    { this.whoseTurn =
                 NimModel.otherPlayer(this.whoseTurn);
    }
    this.updateAllViews();
  }
}

// Is howMany a legal number of tokens to take?
private boolean isLegalMove(int howMany)
{ return howMany >= 1 && howMany <= MAX_REMOVE &&
         howMany <= this.pileSize;
}

// Return the other player.
private static Player otherPlayer(Player who)
{ if (who == Player.RED)
  { return Player.BLACK;
  } else if (who == Player.BLACK)
  { return Player.RED;
```

Listing 13-5: *The completed* `NimModel` *class* (continued)

```
      } else
      { throw new IllegalArgumentException();
      }
   }

   // The addView, removeView, and updateAllViews methods could be included
   // here. That isn't necessary in this case because NimModel extends AbstractModel.

   /** Test the class. */
   public static void main(String[ ] args)
   { System.out.println("Testing NimModel");
     NimModel nim = new NimModel(10, Player.RED);
     Test.ckEquals("pile size", 10, nim.getPileSize());
     Test.ckEquals("winner", Player.NOBODY, nim.getWinner());
     Test.ckEquals("next", Player.RED, nim.getWhoseTurn());

     /** ------ find the code to see complete test suite ------*/
   }
}
```

13.4 Building the View and Controllers

The view, of course, is what displays information from the model to the user. It is the visible part of the user interface. The controllers are what make the interface interactive. They listen for the user manipulating controls such as buttons or menus and then make appropriate calls to the commands in the model.

13.4.1 Designing the Interface

KEY IDEA

The program shown in Figure 13-5 contains lots of code to help get you started using components.

Java comes with many user interface components including buttons, text fields, menus, sliders, and labels. Some of these are shown in Figure 13-5. Designing an interface includes deciding which of these components are most appropriate both to display the model and to accept input from the user, and how to best arrange them on the screen. For now, while we're learning the basics, we will restrict ourselves to labels for displaying information and text fields to accept input from the user. In Section 13.7, we will explore other components.

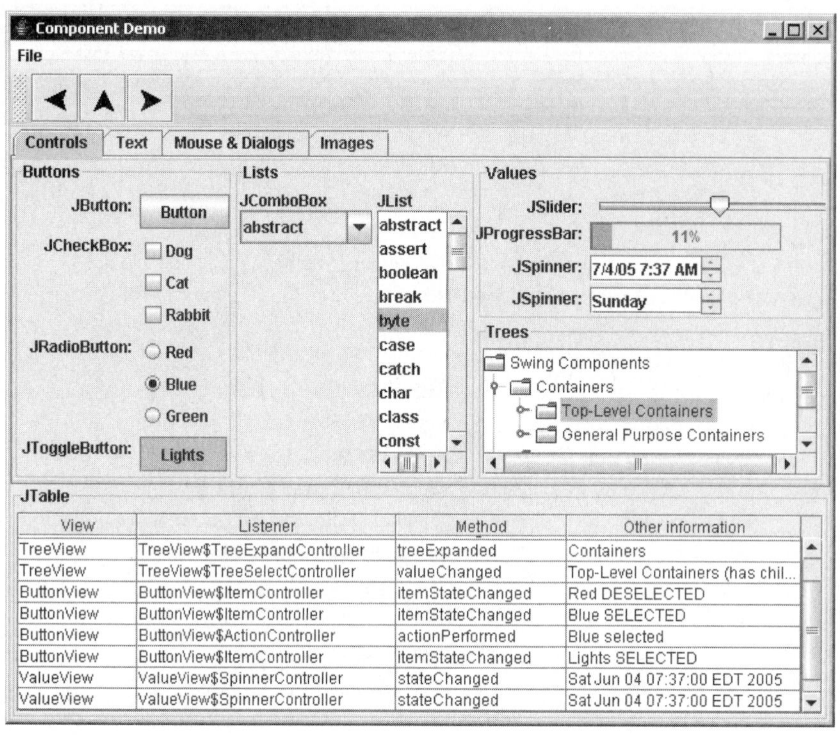

(figure 13-5)

Application demonstrating many of the components available for constructing views

FIND THE CODE

ch13/component Demo/

Our first view will appear as shown in Figure 13-6. It shows the end of the game after Red has won. The text areas (one has "2" in it, the other has "3") are enabled when it's the appropriate player's turn and disabled when it isn't. When the game is over, both are disabled, as shown here.

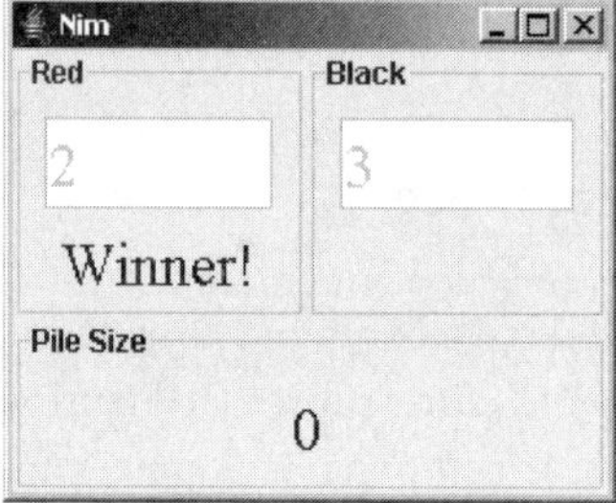

(figure 13-6)

First view for the game of Nim

13.4.2 Laying Out the Components

The components for any view can be divided into those that require ongoing access and those that don't. In this view, the following five components require ongoing access either to change the information they display or to obtain changes made by the user.

- Two `JTextFields` to accept input from the players
- One `JLabel` showing the pile's current size
- Two `JLabels` announcing the winner (they are not visible until there is a winner, and even then only one is shown)

KEY IDEA

References to components requiring ongoing access are stored in instance variables.

References to these objects will be stored in instance variables.

```
// Get how many tokens to remove.
private JTextField redRemoves = new JTextField(5);
private JTextField blackRemoves = new JTextField(5);

// Info to display.
private JLabel pileSize = new JLabel();
private JLabel redWins = new JLabel("Winner!");
private JLabel blackWins = new JLabel("Winner!");
```

LOOKING BACK

Layout managers were discussed in Section 12.6.

The components that do not require ongoing access include several `JPanel` objects used to organize the components and the borders around them. Instance variables storing references to these components are not required.

These components are laid out using four nested `JPanels`, as shown in Figure 13-7.

(figure 13-7)

`NimView` *uses nested* `JPanels` *to lay out the components*

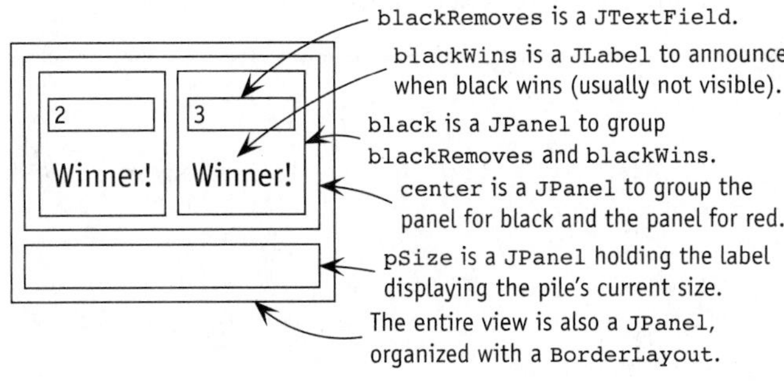

The task of laying out the components occurs when the view is constructed and is usually complex enough to merit a helper method called from the constructor. We'll call the helper method `layoutView`, as shown in Listing 13-6. The method carries out the following tasks:

- The first `JPanel`, named `red`, is defined in lines 12–15. It contains a `JTextField` to accept information from the red player and a label to announce if red is the winner. The `JPanel` itself is wrapped with a border to label it in line 15.
- The second `JPanel`, `black`, is just like `red` except that it contains components for the black player.
- The third `JPanel`, `pSize`, contains the label used to display the size of the pile. It, too, has a border to label it.
- The fourth `JPanel`, `center`, is not directly visible in the user interface. It exists solely to group the `red` and `black` `JPanels` into a single component that can be placed as a whole.

Finally, recall that `NimView` is itself a `JPanel` that can have its own layout manager. It is set in line 36 to be a `BorderLayout`. Only two of the layout's five areas are used, the center and the south side. The center section grows and shrinks as its container is resized. That's where we put the `center` panel containing `red` and `black`. The south area contains `pSize`.

Adding the `layoutView` method to `NimView`, as shown in Listing 13-6, and running the program results in something that looks much like Figure 13-6. The pile size won't be displayed and both players will be declared winners. To display that information correctly we need to update the view with information from the model.

FIND THE CODE

ch13/nimOneView/

Listing 13-6: *A helper method to lay out the view for Nim*

```
1  public class NimView extends JPanel implements IView
2  { // Instance variables omitted.
3
4    public NimView(NimModel aModel)
5    { // Details omitted.
6      this.layoutView();
7    }
8
9    // Layout the view.
10   private void layoutView()
11   { // A panel for the red player.
12     JPanel red = new JPanel();
13     red.add(this.redRemoves);
14     red.add(this.redWins);
```

Listing 13-6: *A helper method to lay out the view for Nim* (continued)

```
        red.setBorder(BorderFactory.createTitledBorder("Red"));

        // A panel for the black player.
        JPanel black = new JPanel();
        black.add(this.blackRemoves);
        black.add(this.blackWins);
        black.setBorder(BorderFactory.createTitledBorder("Black"));

        // Pile size information.
        JPanel pSize = new JPanel();
        pSize.add(this.pileSize);
        pSize.setBorder(
              BorderFactory.createTitledBorder("Pile Size"));

        // Group the red and black panels.
        JPanel center = new JPanel();
        center.setLayout(new GridLayout(1, 2));
        center.add(red);
        center.add(black);

        // Lay out the pieces in this view.
        this.setLayout(new BorderLayout());
        this.add(center, BorderLayout.CENTER);
        this.add(pSize, BorderLayout.SOUTH);
    }
}
```

13.4.3 Updating the View

KEY IDEA

The `updateView` method is responsible for updating the view with the latest information from the model.

The `updateView` method was already added when we set up the model and view architecture, but it doesn't do anything yet. It is called by the model each time the model changes so that it can update the view's components with current information.

For the moment, we want `updateView` to perform three basic tasks:

- Display the correct pile size.
- Enable the `JTextField` for the red player when it is the red player's turn and disable it otherwise, with similar behavior for the black player's text field. When a component is disabled, the players can't use it, thus forcing each player to take his or her turn at the right time.

- Make `redWins` visible when the red player wins the game and invisible when it hasn't, with similar behavior for `blackWins`.

Recall that the constructor received a reference to the model as a parameter. This reference was stored in an instance variable named, appropriately, `model`. We will use it to retrieve the necessary information from the model to carry out these tasks.

Updating the Size of the Pile

The component to display the size of the pile is a `JLabel`. It has a method, `setText`, which takes a string and causes the label to display it. Thus, we can update the pile size display with the following statement:

```
this.pileSize.setText("" + this.model.getPileSize());
```

The result from `getPileSize` is an `int`. "Adding" it to the empty string forces Java to convert it to a string, which is what `setText` requires.

If you run the program now, the user interface should show the pile size.

Updating the Text Fields

`redRemoves` is the name of the text field used by the red player to say how many tokens to remove. To enable or disable it, we'll use the `setEnabled` method, passing `true` to enable the component and `false` to disable it. We want the text field enabled when the following Boolean expression is `true`:

```
this.model.getWhoseTurn() == Player.RED
```

If this expression is `false` (it's not red's turn), the component should be disabled. Thus,

```
this.redRemoves.setEnabled(
                this.model.getWhoseTurn() == Player.RED);
```

enables `redRemoves` when it's the red player's turn and disables it otherwise. Recall that when the game is over, `getWhoseTurn` returns `Player.NOBODY`, resulting in both text fields being disabled.

Updating the Winners

When the game is over, we want either `redWins` or `blackWins` to become visible. If the game isn't over, we want both to be invisible. Every component has a method named `setVisible` that makes the component visible when passed the value `true` and invisible when passed the value `false`. We can again use a simple Boolean expression to pass the correct value:

```
this.redWins.setVisible(
            this.model.getWinner() == Player.RED);
```

LOOKING AHEAD

We will refine `updateView` *in Section 13.4.5.*

A similar statement for `blackWins` completes the method. Like `getWhoseTurn`, `getWinner` can also return `Player.NOBODY`.

The entire method is shown in Listing 13-7. If you run the program with this method completed, the user interface should display the initial pile size, one of the text fields should be enabled (indicating who removes the first tokens), and neither player should have their "Winner!" label showing. However, the game still can't be played because the components will not yet respond to the users.

FIND THE CODE

ch13/nimOneView/

Listing 13-7: *Updating the view with current information from the model*

```
public class NimView extends JPanel implements IView
{ private NimModel model;
  private JTextField redRemoves = new JTextField(5);
  // Other instance variables, constructor, and methods omitted.

  /** Called by the model when it changes. Update the information this view displays. */
  public void updateView()
  { // Update the size of the pile.
    this.pileSize.setText("" + this.model.getPileSize());

    // Enable and disable the text fields for each player.
    this.redRemoves.setEnabled(
            this.model.getWhoseTurn() == Player.RED);
    this.blackRemoves.setEnabled(
            this.model.getWhoseTurn() == Player.BLACK);

    // Proclaim the winner, if there is one.
    this.redWins.setVisible(
            this.model.getWinner() == Player.RED);
    this.blackWins.setVisible(
            this.model.getWinner() == Player.BLACK);
  }
}
```

13.4.4 Writing and Registering Controllers

The fundamental job of a controller is to detect when a user is manipulating a component and to respond in a way appropriate for the specific program. To best understand how this happens, we need to delve into a simplified version of a component. All of the Java components work similarly.

Understanding Events

For concreteness, let's consider `JTextField`. A simplified version appears in Listing 13-8. The key feature is the `handleEvent` method. It detects various kinds of **events** caused by the user, such as pressing the Enter key or using the Tab key to move either into or out of the text field. Listing 13-8 uses pseudocode for detecting these actions because we don't really need to know how they are accomplished. Thanks to encapsulation and information hiding, we can use the class without knowing those intimate details.

What is important is that when one of these events occurs, two things happen. First, the component constructs an **event object** describing the event and containing such information as when the event occurred, if any keys were pressed at the time, and which component created it.

Second, the component calls a specific method, passing the event object as an argument. This method is one that we write as part of our controller. It's in this method that we have an opportunity to take actions specific to our program, such as calling the `removeTokens` method in the model.

Listing 13-8: *A simplified version of* `JTextField`

```
public class JTextField extends ...
{ private ActionListener actionListener;
  private FocusListener focusListener;

  public void addActionListener(ActionListener aListener)
  { this.actionListener = aListener;
  }

  public void addFocusListener(FocusListener fListener)
  { this.focusListener = fListener;
  }

  private void handleEvent()
  { if (user pressed the "Enter" key)
```

Listing 13-8: *A simplified version of* `JTextField` (continued)

```
15        { construct an object, event, describing what happened
16          this.actionListener.actionPerformed(event);
17        } else if (user tabbed out of this text field)
18        { construct an object, event, describing what happened
19          this.focusListener.focusLost(event);
20        } else if (user tabbed into this text field)
21        { construct an object, event, describing what happened
22          this.focusListener.focusGained(event);
23        } else
24          ...
25    }
26  }
```

KEY IDEA

In Java, controllers implement methods defined in interfaces with names ending in `Listener`.

Obviously, the method called has a name. That means that our controller must have a method with the same name. Ensuring that it does is a perfect job for a Java interface. The names `ActionListener` and `FocusListener` at lines 2, 3, 5, and 9 in Listing 13-8 are, in fact, the names of Java interfaces. Our controllers will always implement at least one interface whose name ends with `Listener`.

KEY IDEA

In Java, we use listener interfaces to implement controllers.

There are, unfortunately, two competing terminologies. "Controller" is a well-established name for the part of a user interface that interprets events and calls the appropriate commands in the model. Java uses the term **listener** for a class that is called when an event occurs. Most of the time the two terms mean the same thing.

Implementing a Controller

When the user presses the Enter key inside a `JTextField` component, the component calls a method named `actionPerformed`. This method is defined in the `ActionListener` interface (and is, in fact, the only method defined there). It takes a single argument of type `ActionEvent`. Therefore, the skeleton for our controller class will be:

```
import java.awt.event.ActionListener;
import java.awt.event.ActionEvent;

public class RemovesController extends Object
                    implements ActionListener
{
  public void actionPerformed(ActionEvent e)
  {
  }
}
```

Inside `actionPerformed`, we need to obtain the value the user typed into the text field and then call the model with that value. One approach is to have instance variables storing references to the text field and the model for the game. Then `actionPerformed` can be written as

```
public void actionPerformed(ActionEvent e)
{ String enteredText = this.textfield.getText();
  int remove = convert enteredText to an integer;
  this.model.removeTokens(remove);
}
```

LOOKING AHEAD

Implementing controllers can use a number of shortcuts. Some of them will be explored in Section 13.6, Controller Variations.

The conversion from a string to an integer can be done with `parseInt`, a static method in the `Integer` class. It will throw a `NumberFormatException` if the user enters text that is not a valid integer. If this exception is thrown, we'll recover in the `catch` clause by selecting the entered text and ignoring what was entered.

The full method is shown in lines 21–29 of Listing 13-9. The rest of the listing, lines 11–19, is simply declaring the instance variables needed and initializing them in a constructor.

FIND THE CODE

ch13/nimOneView/

Listing 13-9: *A controller for a text field*

```
1  import javax.swing.JTextField;
2  import java.awt.event.*;
3
4  /** A controller for the game of Nim that informs the model how many tokens a player
5   *  wants to remove.
6   *
7   *  @author Byron Weber Becker */
8  public class RemovesController extends Object
9                implements ActionListener
10 {
11   private NimModel model;
12   private JTextField textfield;
13
14   public RemovesController(NimModel aModel,
15                JTextField aTextfield)
16   { super();
17     this.model = aModel;
18     this.textfield = aTextfield;
19   }
20
21   public void actionPerformed(ActionEvent e)
22   { try
23     { int remove =
24                Integer.parseInt(this.textfield.getText());
25       this.model.removeTokens(remove);
```

Listing 13-9: *A controller for a text field* (continued)

```
      } catch (NumberFormatException ex)
      { this.textfield.selectAll();
      }
   }
}
```

Registering Controllers

The very last step to make this user interface interactive is to construct the controllers and register them with the text fields. Recall that the simplified version of `JTextField` shown in Listing 13-8 contained methods such as `addActionListener` and `addFocusListener`. They each took an instance of the similarly named interface and saved it in an instance variable. **Registering** our controller simply means calling the appropriate `addXxxListener` method for the relevant component, passing an instance of the controller as an argument.

KEY IDEA

A controller must be registered with a component.

We've only written one controller class, but we'll use one instance of it for the `redRemoves` text field and a second instance for the `blackRemoves` text field. A user interface often has several controllers, so it makes sense to have a helper method, `registerControllers`, just for constructing and registering controllers. It is called from the view's constructor.

The code in Listing 13-10 registers the red controller in two steps but combines the steps for the black controller.

Listing 13-10: *A method registering the controllers with the appropriate components*

```
public class NimView extends JPanel implements IView
{ // Instance variables omitted.

   public NimView()
   { // Some details omitted.
      this.registerControllers();
   }

   /** Register controllers for the components the user can manipulate. */
   private void registerControllers()
   { RemoveController redController =
            new RemoveController(this.model, this.redRemoves);
      this.redRemoves.addActionListener(redController);
```

Listing 13-10: *A method registering the controllers with the appropriate components* (continued)

```

    this.blackRemoves.addActionListener(
        new RemoveController(this.model, this.blackRemoves));
  }
}
```

If you run the program with these additions, you should be able to play a complete, legal game, as shown in Figure 13-8.

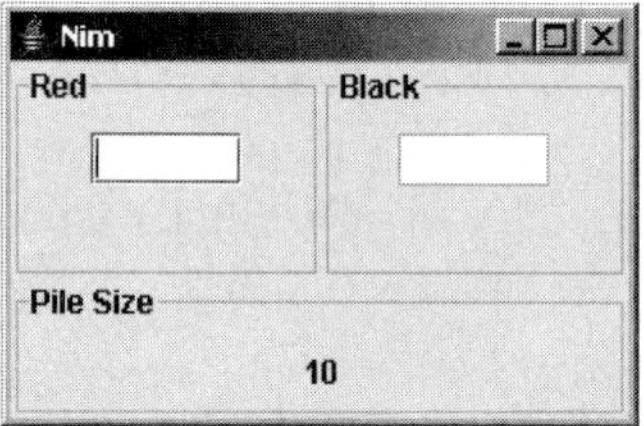

a) The game begins with a pile of 10. Red has the first turn.

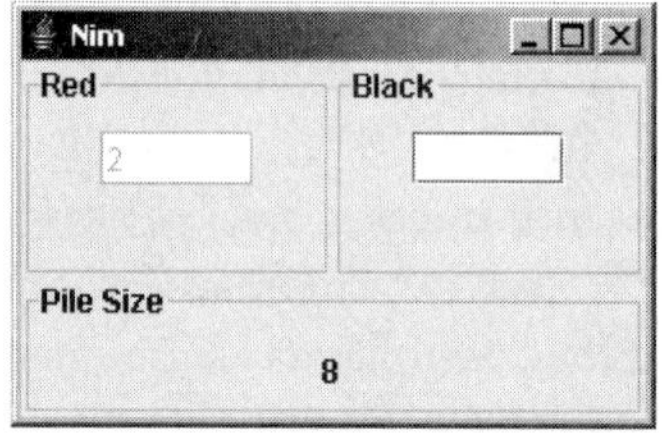

b) Red takes two tokens; now it's black's turn. The player must click in its text field before entering a value.

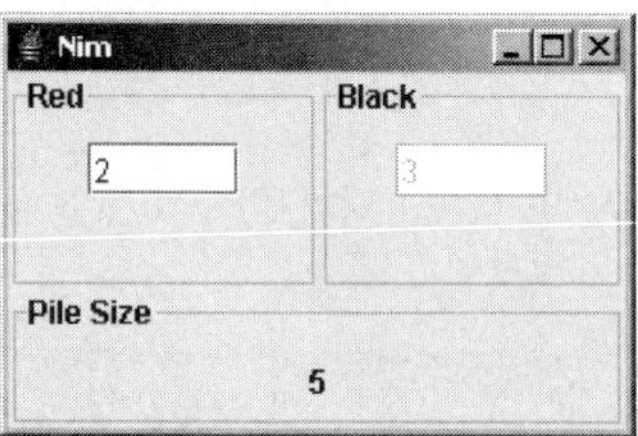

c) Black takes three tokens. It's red's turn. The "2" from red's previous turn still shows. Red does *not* need to click in its text field before entering a value but must delete the old value before entering a new one.

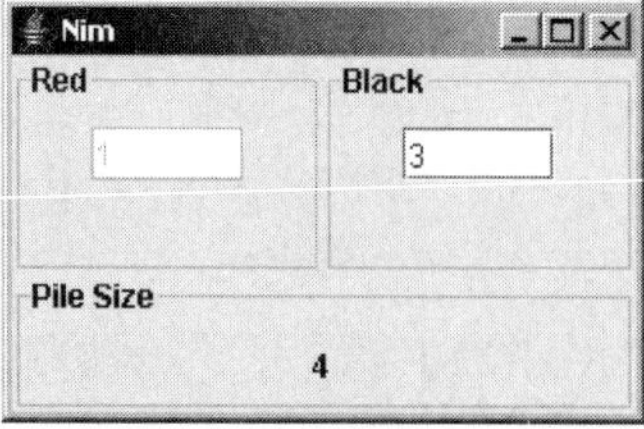

d) Red takes one token; now it's black's turn. The 3 from the previous turn still shows in the text field.

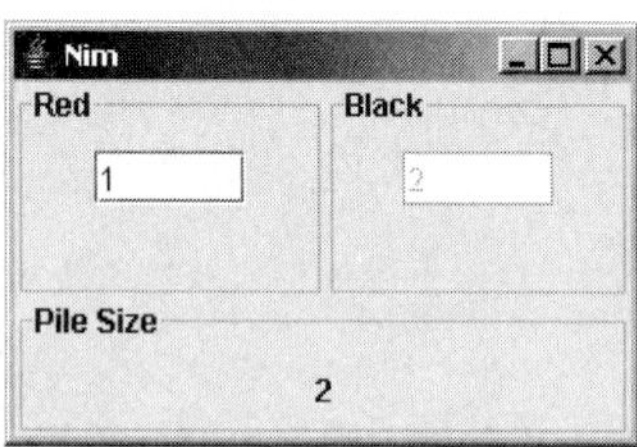

e) Black takes two tokens, setting up red for a win.

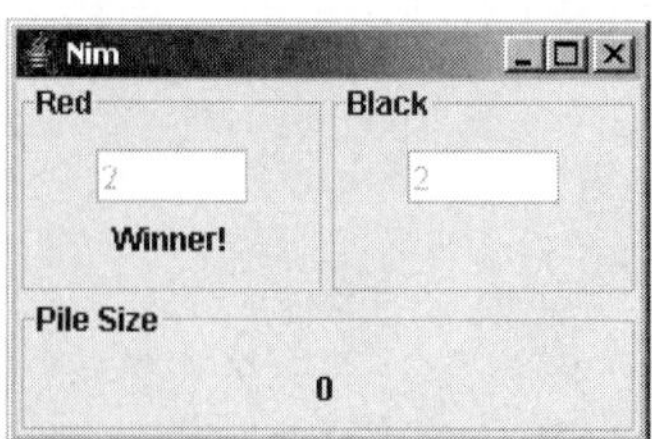

f) Red takes two tokens and is proclaimed the winner.

(figure 13-8)

User interface as it appears at each stage of a complete game

13.4.5 Refining the View

The program runs, as shown in Figure 13-8. However, there are three areas in which improvements could be made.

- The black user must click in its text field before entering a value. It would be nice if the player could simply type a new value.
- The value previously entered by a player remains in the text field and must be removed before entering a new value.
- Finally, the fonts used in the text fields and the `JLabels` are too small, given their importance in the user interface.

Focus

In any given user interface, one component at most will receive input from the user's keyboard. This component is said to have the **keyboard focus**. Usually a component will give some visible sign when it has the focus. A component that accepts text will show a flashing bar called the **insertion point**. A button that has the focus will often have a subtle box around its label.

Focus normally shifts from one component to the next in the order that they were added to their container. In the case of Nim, however, the component that should have the focus depends on whose turn it is. So, in the `updateView` method, we can update which component has the focus with the following code. This code also replaces the previously entered value with an empty string.

```
if (this.model.getWhoseTurn() == Player.RED)
{ this.redRemoves.requestFocusInWindow();
  this.redRemoves.setText("");
} else if (this.model.getWhoseTurn() == Player.BLACK)
{ this.blackRemoves.requestFocusInWindow();
  this.blackRemoves.setText("");
}
```

Another approach is to write a controller class implementing the `FocusListener` interface. It can detect when a component gains or loses focus. This is useful, for example, if action needs to be taken when a user moves into or out of a component using either the mouse or the keyboard.

Fonts

A larger font for the various components can be specified with the `setFont` method. Its argument is a `Font` object describing the desired font. The following code could be included in the `layoutView` method to change the font for the five components.

```
// Enlarge the fonts.
Font font = new Font("Serif", Font.PLAIN, 24);
this.redRemoves.setFont(font);
this.blackRemoves.setFont(font);
this.redWins.setFont(font);
this.blackWins.setFont(font);
this.pileSize.setFont(font);
```

The first argument to the `Font` constructor specifies to use a font with **serifs**. Such fonts have short lines at the ends of the main strokes of each letter. Common fonts that have serifs include Times New Roman, Bookman, and Palatino. The string "SansSerif" can be used to specify a font without serifs. Helvetica is a common sans serif font. The string "monospaced" indicates a font using a fixed width for each letter. An example is Courier.

You can also specify an actual font name like "Helvetica" as the first argument. However, you can't be sure that the font is actually installed on the computer unless you check. The program in Listing 13-11 will list all the names of all the fonts that are installed. Try it for yourself to see which fonts are installed on your computer.

FIND THE CODE

ch13/fonts/

Listing 13-11: *A program to list the names of fonts installed on a computer*

```
import java.awt.Font;
import java.awt.GraphicsEnvironment;

/** List the font names available on the current computer system.
 *
 * @author Byron Weber Becker */
public class ListFonts extends Object
{ public static void main(String[] args)
  { GraphicsEnvironment ge =
          GraphicsEnvironment.getLocalGraphicsEnvironment();
    Font[] names = ge.getAllFonts();

    for (Font f : names)
    { System.out.println(f.getName());
    }
  }
}
```

The second argument to the `Font` constructor is the style. There are three basic styles, defined as constants in the `Font` class: `PLAIN`, `ITALIC`, and `BOLD`. `ITALIC` makes the letters slant and `BOLD` makes the strokes thicker. A bold, italic font can also be specified by adding the `BOLD` and `ITALIC` constants together and passing the result to the constructor.

The third argument to the `Font` constructor is the font's size. The size is measured in **points**, where one point is 1/72 of an inch. Ten to 12 points is a comfortable size for reading; use 16 points or larger for labels and headlines.

This finishes our first view. The complete code is shown in Listing 13-12. Most components have many other ways to refine the way they look. Investigating them further falls outside the scope of this book. Exploring the documentation and method names for the component, as well as its superclasses, will often indicate what can be done.

FIND THE CODE

ch13/nimOneView/

Listing 13-12: *The completed code for the* `NimView` *class*

```
import javax.swing.JPanel;
import becker.util.IView;
import javax.swing.JTextField;
import javax.swing.JLabel;
import javax.swing.BorderFactory;
import java.awt.GridLayout;
import java.awt.BorderLayout;
import java.awt.Font;

/** Provide a view of the game of Nim to a user.
 *
 * @author Byron Weber Becker */
public class NimView extends JPanel implements IView
{ // The model implementing Nim's logic.
  private NimModel model;

  // Get how many tokens to remove.
  private JTextField redRemoves = new JTextField(5);
  private JTextField blackRemoves = new JTextField(5);

  // Info to display.
  private JLabel pileSize = new JLabel();
  private JLabel redWins = new JLabel("Winner!");
  private JLabel blackWins = new JLabel("Winner!");

  /** Construct the view.
   * @param aModel The model we will be displaying. */
  public NimView(NimModel aModel)
  { super();
    this.model = aModel;

    this.layoutView();
    this.registerControllers();

```

Listing 13-12: *The completed code for the* `NimView` *class* (continued)

```
    this.model.addView(this);
    this.updateView();
  }

  /** Called by the model when it changes. Update the information this view displays. */
  public void updateView()
  { this.pileSize.setText("" + this.model.getPileSize());

    this.redRemoves.setEnabled(
          this.model.getWhoseTurn() == Player.RED);
    this.blackRemoves.setEnabled(
          this.model.getWhoseTurn() == Player.BLACK);
    this.redWins.setVisible(
          this.model.getWinner() == Player.RED);
    this.blackWins.setVisible(
          this.model.getWinner() == Player.BLACK);

    if (this.model.getWhoseTurn() == Player.RED)
    { this.redRemoves.requestFocusInWindow();
      this.redRemoves.setText("");
    } else if (this.model.getWhoseTurn() == Player.BLACK)
    { this.blackRemoves.requestFocusInWindow();
      this.blackRemoves.setText("");
    }
  }

  /** Layout the view. */
  private void layoutView()
  { // A panel for the red player
    JPanel red = new JPanel();
    red.add(this.redRemoves);
    red.add(this.redWins);
    red.setBorder(BorderFactory.createTitledBorder("Red"));

    // A panel for the black player
    JPanel black = new JPanel();
    black.add(this.blackRemoves);
    black.add(this.blackWins);
    black.setBorder(BorderFactory.createTitledBorder("Black"));

    // Pilesize info.
    JPanel pSize = new JPanel();
```

Listing 13-12: *The completed code for the* `NimView` *class* (continued)

```
      pSize.add(this.pileSize);
      pSize.setBorder(
            BorderFactory.createTitledBorder("Pile Size"));

      // Group the red and black panels.
      JPanel center = new JPanel();
      center.setLayout(new GridLayout(1, 2));
      center.add(red);
      center.add(black);

      // Lay out the pieces in this view.
      this.setLayout(new BorderLayout());
      this.add(center, BorderLayout.CENTER);
      this.add(pSize, BorderLayout.SOUTH);

      // Enlarge the fonts.
      Font font = new Font("Serif", Font.PLAIN, 24);
      this.redRemoves.setFont(font);
      this.blackRemoves.setFont(font);
      this.redWins.setFont(font);
      this.blackWins.setFont(font);
      this.pileSize.setFont(font);
   }

   /** Register controllers for the components the user can manipulate. */
   private void registerControllers()
   { this.redRemoves.addActionListener(
         new RemovesController(this.model, this.redRemoves));
     this.blackRemoves.addActionListener(
       new RemovesController(this.model, this.blackRemoves));
   }
}
```

13.4.6 View Pattern

Views can be complex. However, they follow a common pattern, shown in Listing 13-13, which makes them much easier to understand and implement.

Listing 13-13: *A pattern template for a view*

```
import becker.util.IView;
import javax.swing.JPanel;
«list of other imports»

public class «viewName» extends JPanel implements IView
{ private «modelClassName» model;

  «component declarations»

  public «viewName»(«modelClassName» aModel)
  { super();
    this.model = aModel;
    this.layoutView();
    this.registerControllers();
    this.model.addView(this);
    this.updateView();
  }

  public void updateView()
  { «statements to update the components in the view»
  }

  private void layoutView()
  { «statements to lay out the components within the view»
  }

  private void registerControllers()
  { «statements to construct and register controllers»
  }
}
```

13.5 Using Multiple Views

Now let's implement a different user interface for the same game. Because the `NimModel` class exhibits very low coupling with its first view (calling only the `updateView` method via the `IView` interface), we will be able to replace the user interface without changing `NimModel` at all.

KEY IDEA

One of the strengths of the Model-View-Controller pattern is the low coupling between the various parts.

Our new interface is illustrated in Figure 13-9. Instead of typing in the number of tokens to remove, the user clicks the appropriate button. Like our previous interface, components are disabled when they don't apply. For example, the black player's buttons are shown disabled, and when there are only 2 tokens remaining on the pile, the "Remove 3 Tokens" button will be disabled for both players. Like our previous interface, "Winner!" is displayed for the winning player at the appropriate time.

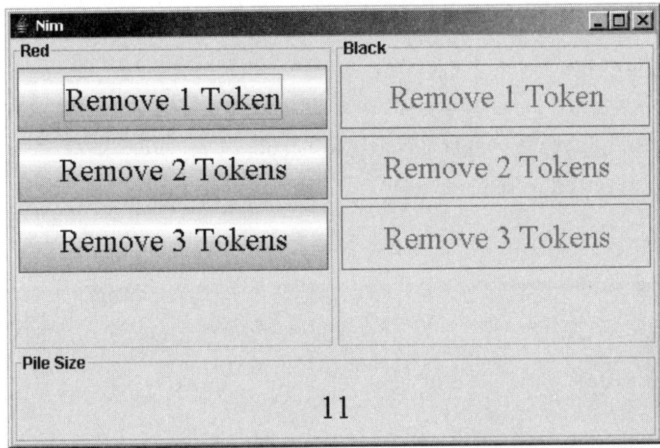

(figure 13-9)

Different user interface for Nim

We could write this user interface as one big view, as we did previously. However, this view has a total of nine components to manage, raising the overall complexity. Furthermore, the four components for the red player are managed almost exactly like those for the black player. This suggests that some good abstractions might simplify the problem.

KEY IDEA

A view can be partitioned into subviews.

Recall that we wrote the model anticipating multiple views. The model has a list of views, and each time the model's state changes, it goes through that list and tells each view to update itself. This allows us to decompose the overall view into a number of subviews. Each subview will add itself to the model's list of views and will have its `updateView` method called at the appropriate times.

This version of the interface will use three subviews: one for the red player, one for the black player, and one to display the pile size. `NimView` will still exist to organize the three subviews.

Dividing the view into several subviews has two distinct advantages. First, each view can focus on a smaller part of the overall job, allowing it to be simpler, easier to understand, easier to write, and easier to debug. Second, subviews can be easily changed or even replaced without fear of breaking the rest of the interface.

13.5.1 Implementing `NimView`

`NimView` is the overall view of the game. It is composed of the three subviews for the players and the pile size. `NimView` does not (directly) display information about the model nor does it (directly) update the model. Both of those tasks are delegated to the subviews. `NimView`'s only task is to organize the subviews in a panel.

In the following ways, it is a degenerate view:

- It doesn't need an instance variable storing a reference to the model.
- It doesn't have any controllers to construct or register.
- It doesn't need to register itself with the model.

As seen in Listing 13-14, all `NimView` does is instantiate and lay out the subviews.

FIND THE CODE

ch13/nimMultiView/

Listing 13-14: `NimView`, *a view consisting of three subviews*

```
import javax.swing.JPanel;
import javax.swing.BorderFactory;
import java.awt.GridLayout;
import java.awt.BorderLayout;

/** Provide a view of the game of Nim to a user.
 *
 *  @author Byron Weber Becker */
public class NimView extends JPanel
{
   /** Construct the view.
    *  @param aModel The model we will be displaying. */
   public NimView(NimModel aModel)
   { super();

      // Create the subviews.
      NimPlayerView red =
            new NimPlayerView(aModel, Player.RED);
      NimPlayerView black =
            new NimPlayerView(aModel, Player.BLACK);
      NimPileView pile = new NimPileView(aModel);

      // Put a title on each subview.
      red.setBorder(BorderFactory.createTitledBorder("Red"));
      black.setBorder(BorderFactory.createTitledBorder("Black"));
      pile.setBorder(BorderFactory.createTitledBorder("Pile Size"));

```

Listing 13-14: `NimView`, *a view consisting of three subviews* (continued)

```
        // Group the red and black views.
        JPanel center = new JPanel();
        center.setLayout(new GridLayout(2, 1));
        center.add(red);
        center.add(black);

        // Lay out the pieces in this view.
        this.setLayout(new BorderLayout());
        this.add(center, BorderLayout.CENTER);
        this.add(pile, BorderLayout.SOUTH);
    }
}
```

13.5.2 Implementing `NimPileView`

The `NimPileView` class, shown in Listing 13-15, is a simple view. It does not need to update the model, so there are no controllers. It only has a `JLabel` that is updated via the `updateView` method. `addView` is called at line 17 to add this view to the model's list of views.

FIND THE CODE

ch13/nimMultiView/

Listing 13-15: *The* `NimPileView` *class*

```
1  import becker.util.IView;
2  import javax.swing.*;
3  import java.awt.Font;
4
5  /** A view showing the current pile size for the game of Nim.
6   *
7   *  @author Byron Weber Becker */
8  public class NimPileView extends JPanel implements IView
9  { private NimModel model;
10   private JLabel pileSize = new JLabel();
11
12   /** Construct the view. */
13   public NimPileView(NimModel aModel)
14   { super();
15     this.model = aModel;
16     this.layoutView();
17     this.model.addView(this);
18     this.updateView();
```

Listing 13-15: *The* `NimPileView` *class* (continued)

```
    }

    /** Update the view. Called by the model when its state changes. */
    public void updateView()
    { this.pileSize.setText("" + this.model.getPileSize());
    }

    /** Layout the view. */
    private void layoutView()
    { this.pileSize.setFont(new Font("Serif", Font.PLAIN, 24));
      this.add(this.pileSize);
    }
}
```

13.5.3 Implementing `NimPlayerView`

`NimPlayerView` is a full-fledged view. It has its own components to lay out within itself. Those components are used to update the model, so they need to have controllers registered. The view also displays part of the state of the model—who's turn it is and who has won—and so it needs an `updateView` method and an instance variable to store a reference to the model.

We'll write `NimPlayerView` so that one instance of the class can be used for the red player and a second instance for the black player. To meet this goal, it must store the player it represents (lines 14 and 29 of Listing 13-16). The player is used in the `updateView` method (lines 45 and 48) to determine which buttons to enable and whether a winner should be declared.

The view has three buttons for user interaction. They all need to be added to the view, be enabled and disabled as appropriate, and have controllers registered. These tasks are all made easier by placing the buttons in an array (lines 16–20) and using loops (lines 43–46, 58–61, and 69–72).

FIND THE CODE

ch13/nimMultiView/

Listing 13-16: *The* `NimPlayerView` *class*

```
1 import becker.util.IView;
2 import javax.swing.JPanel;
3 import javax.swing.JButton;
4 import javax.swing.JLabel;
5 import javax.swing.SwingConstants;
```

Listing 13-16: *The* `NimPlayerView` *class* (continued)

```
import java.awt.Font;
import java.awt.GridLayout;

/** Provide a view of the game of Nim focused on one particular player to a user.
 *
 * @author Byron Weber Becker */
public class NimPlayerView extends JPanel implements IView
{ private NimModel model;
  private Player player;

  private JButton[] removeButtons = new JButton[] {
    new JButton("Remove 1 Token"),
    new JButton("Remove 2 Tokens"),
    new JButton("Remove 3 Tokens")
  };
  private JLabel winner = new JLabel("Winner!");

  /** Construct a view for one player.
   * @param aModel    The game's model.
   * @param player    The player for which this is the view. */
  public NimPlayerView(NimModel aModel, Player aPlayer)
  { super();
    this.model = aModel;
    this.player = aPlayer;

    this.layoutView();
    this.registerControllers();

    this.model.addView(this);
    this.updateView();
  }

  /** Update the view to reflect recent changes in the model's state. */
  public void updateView()
  { Player whoseTurn = this.model.getWhoseTurn();
    int pSize = this.model.getPileSize();
    // Enable buttons if it's my player's turn and there are enough tokens on the pile.
    for (int i = 0; i < this.removeButtons.length; i++)
    { this.removeButtons[i].setEnabled(
          whoseTurn == this.player && i + 1 <= pSize);
    }
    this.winner.setVisible(
          this.model.getWinner() == this.player);
```

Listing 13-16: *The* `NimPlayerView` *class* (continued)

```
49     }
50
51     /** Lay out the components for this view. */
52     private void layoutView()
53     { GridLayout grid = new GridLayout(4, 1, 5, 5);
54       this.setLayout(grid);
55
56       Font font = new Font("Serif", Font.PLAIN, 24);
57
58       for (JButton b : this.removeButtons)
59       { this.add(b);
60         b.setFont(font);
61       }
62
63       this.winner.setFont(font);
64       this.add(this.winner);
65     }
66
67     /** Register controllers for this view's components. */
68     private void registerControllers()
69     { for (int i = 0; i < this.removeButtons.length; i++)
70       { this.removeButtons[i].addActionListener(
71               new RemoveButtonController(this.model, i + 1));
72       }
73     }
74   }
```

Like `JTextField`, `JButton` objects use an `ActionListener`. When the button is clicked, it calls the `actionPerformed` method for all the listeners that have been added. Recall that it is inside the `actionPerformed` method that we specify the code to execute when the button is clicked. This is where we call the `removeTokens` method in the model.

In our previous controller the user typed the number of tokens to remove from the pile. We need a different way to find out how many tokens to remove. One approach is to have a separate controller object for each button. The controller has an instance variable that remembers how many tokens to remove. That instance variable is set, of course, when the controller is constructed. We can see this at line 71 of Listing 13-16, where a new controller is instantiated for each button.

The revised controller class is shown in Listing 13-17.

FIND THE CODE

ch13/nimMultiView/

Listing 13-17: *The controller for the* `JButtons` *used to remove tokens*

```
import java.awt.event.*;

/** A controller to remove tokens from the game of Nim.
 *
 * @author Byron Weber Becker */
public class RemoveButtonController extends Object
                 implements ActionListener
{
  private NimModel model;
  private int numRemove;

  /** Construct an instance of the cotroller.
   * @param aModel       The model this controls.
   * @param howMany      How many tokens to remove when the button is clicked. */
  public RemoveButtonController(NimModel aModel, int howMany)
  { super();
    this.model = aModel;
    this.numRemove = howMany;
  }

  /** Remove the right number of tokens from the model. */
  public void actionPerformed(ActionEvent evt)
  { this.model.removeTokens(this.numRemove);
  }
}
```

13.5.4 Sequence Diagrams

Removing a token involves six interacting classes. This is a level of complexity that we haven't seen before, but it is not uncommon. To keep things in perspective, it's important to think locally. For each method, we can ask, what is the job that this method has to do? What services does it need from other classes to do that job?

But a global perspective can help, too. Figure 13-10 is a **sequence diagram** that can help visualize the objects involved in removing a token and the sequence of actions taking place.

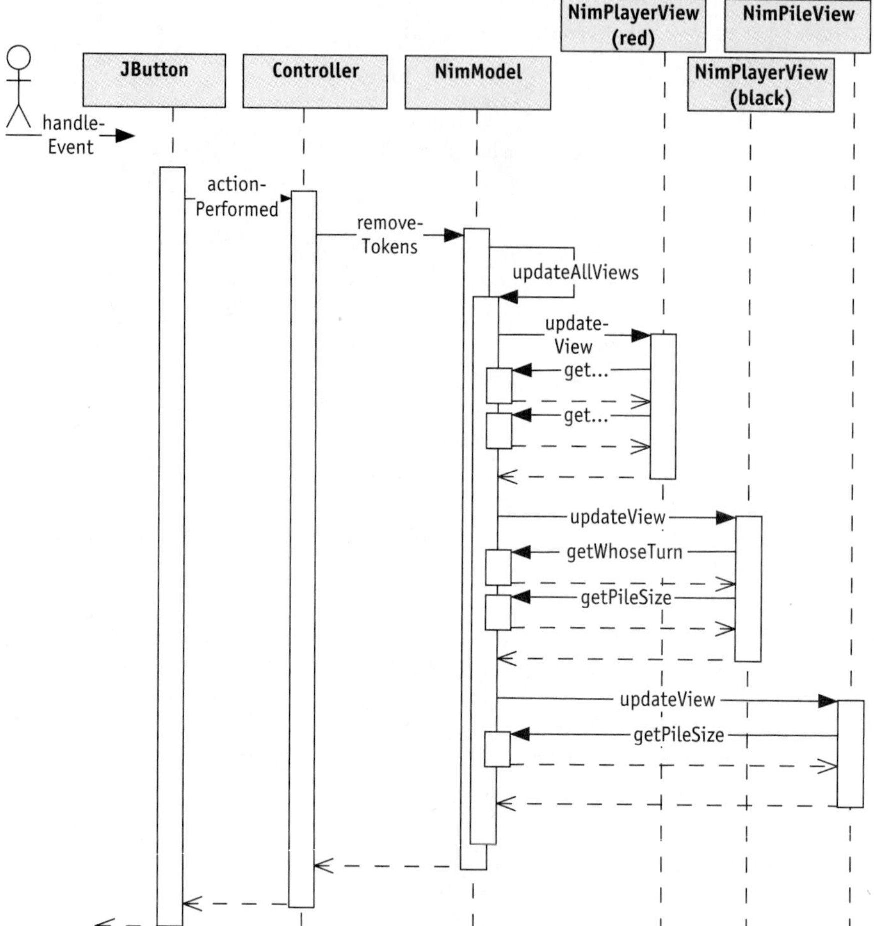

(figure 13-10)

Sequence diagram of the actions involved in removing tokens and updating the views

The six objects involved are shown at the top of the diagram, each with their class name. In the case of `NimPlayerView` there are two, so we distinguish between the instance for the red player and the instance for the black player. There are six `JButton` objects, but it isn't important to distinguish between them, so only one is shown.

The dashed line extending down from each object is its **lifeline**. In a complete sequence diagram, the lifeline would begin with the object's construction and end when the object is no longer needed. The boxes along the lifeline represent a method executing in that object. The solid arrows between the boxes represent one method calling another. A dashed arrow with an open arrowhead represents a method finishing execution and returning to its caller.

Putting all this together, the diagram begins in the upper-left corner with the `handleEvent` method in `JButton` being called, presumably because the user clicked the button. `handleEvent` calls the `actionPerformed` method in the controller. We can think of the `actionPerformed` method as executing for quite a while—all the time that it takes to call `removeTokens`, including the calls that `removeTokens` makes. This length of time is represented by the length of the box on the controller's lifeline.

On the lifeline for `NimModel`, we see that the longest box, corresponding to `removeTokens`, calls a helper method in the same class, `updateAllViews`. This helper method calls all the `updateView` methods in the views registered with `NimModel`. Each of these, of course, calls additional methods.

By the time execution returns to the `handleEvent` method in `JButton` at the bottom-left corner of the diagram, tokens have been removed from the model and all of the views have been updated accordingly.

13.6 Controller Variations

Three techniques are often used to simplify writing controllers. One nests the controller class inside the view's class. The second makes use of information passed in the event objects. The third is a shortcut often taken in sample code in other books and on the Internet.

13.6.1 Using Inner Classes

An **inner class** is a class that is nested inside another class.[2] Inner classes are most useful for defining small helper classes that are very specific to a particular task. By placing inner classes inside the class they are helping, we can make that relationship more explicit and keep the definition of the helper class very close to the class it is helping. Beyond this, the primary advantage of an inner class is that it can access the methods and instance variables of its enclosing class—even the private methods and instance variables.

KEY IDEA

An inner class can access instance variables and methods of its enclosing class.

Views are usually written with inner classes for the controllers.

Listing 13-18 shows the `NimPlayerView` (Listing 13-16) and `RemoveButtonController` (Listing 13-17) combined in a single file by making the controller an inner class.

[2] There are actually four varieties of inner classes. We will focus on member classes. The other three are nested top-level classes, local classes, and anonymous classes.

The first thing to notice about Listing 13-18 is that `RemoveButtonController` falls between the opening and closing braces of the `NimPlayerView` class. The actual order of instance variables, methods, and inner classes within the outer class doesn't matter to the compiler, but inner classes are generally placed at the end.

KEY IDEA

An inner class is placed inside another class, but outside of all methods.

FIND THE CODE

ch13/nimInnerClass/

Listing 13-18: *Using an inner class for a view's controller*

```
1  // Import classes needed by both view and controller.
2  public class NimPlayerView extends JPanel implements IView
3  { private NimModel model;
4
5     // Other instance variables, constructor, updateView, and layoutView are omitted.
6
7     private void registerControllers()
8     { for (int i = 0; i < this.removeButtons.length; i++)
9       { this.removeButtons[i].addActionListener(
10               new RemoveButtonController(i+1));
11      }
12    }
13
14    // Inner class for the controllers to remove tokens from the pile.
15    private class RemoveButtonController extends Object
16                   implements ActionListener
17    { private int numRemove;
18
19      public RemoveButtonController(int howMany)
20      { super();
21        this.numRemove = howMany;
22      }
23
24      public void actionPerformed(ActionEvent evt)
25      { NimPlayerView.this.model.removeTokens(this.numRemove);
26      }
27    }
28 }
```

Second, the inner class accesses the `model` instance variable from the outer class at line 25. The syntax for doing so is a little odd. We *cannot* write `this.model` because then we would be referring to an instance variable in the `RemoveButtonController` class. To access the outer class, first give the name of that class and then access the variable as usual. It is also possible to write the following and let the compiler figure it out:

```
model.removeTokens(this.numRemove);
```

For clarity, however, we will always write the longer version.

Third, because the inner class can access the model via the outer class, the `model` instance variable has disappeared along with code in the constructor to initialize it. The argument is also omitted when the constructor is called in line 10.

Each instance of the inner class is tied to a specific instance of the outer class. For example, the game creates two instances of `NimPlayerView`, one for the red player and one for the black player. Both of these objects create three controllers. The controllers created for red's instance of the view are forever tied to that instance. They will access the methods and instance variables in red's instance of the view and will never access those in black's instance.

13.6.2 Using Event Objects

The `actionPerformed` method is always passed an `ActionEvent` object which provides more details about the user's action. All of the methods in all of the listener interfaces have an event object as a parameter.

KEY IDEA

Use event objects to obtain more information about the event and the source that generated it.

One of the most useful items of information in an event object is the source of the event—that is, which component was manipulated by the user. Using that information, we can figure out how many tokens to remove without using an instance variable in the controller class. We'll simply compare the source to each `JButton` in the array. When we have a match, we'll know how many tokens to remove.

With this approach, the controller will have no instance variables at all. This has two implications. First, there are no instance variables to initialize, and we can let Java provide a default constructor for us.[3] Second, every instance is just like all the other instances, and we can use the same controller for all three buttons. Listing 13-19 shows how.

FIND THE CODE

ch13/nimInnerClass/

Listing 13-19: *A controller that uses the event object to avoid instance variables*

```
// Import classes needed by both view and controller.
public class NimPlayerView extends JPanel implements IView
{ private NimModel model;
  private JButton[] removeButtons = new JButton[]
  { new JButton("Remove 1 Token"),
    new JButton("Remove 2 Tokens"),
    new JButton("Remove 3 Tokens")
  };

  // Other instance variables, constructor, updateView, and layoutView are omitted.
```

[3] Omitting the parameterless or default constructor is an option for every class, but we have always included it, when applicable, for clarity. Controllers are usually so small and specialized, however, that we can omit them without loss of clarity.

Listing 13-19: *A controller that uses the event object to avoid instance variables* (continued)

```
11
12     /** Register controllers for this view's components. */
13     private void registerControllers()
14     { RemoveButtonController controller =
15             new RemoveButtonController();
16       for (int i = 0; i < this.removeButtons.length; i++)
17       { this.removeButtons[i].addActionListener(controller);
18       }
19     }
20
21     private class RemoveButtonController extends Object
22                implements ActionListener
23     { public void actionPerformed(ActionEvent evt)
24       { JButton src = (JButton)evt.getSource();
25         if (src == removeButtons[0])
26         { model.removeTokens(1);
27         } else if (src == removeButtons[1])
28         { model.removeTokens(2);
29         } else if (src == removeButtons[2])
30         { model.removeTokens(3);
31         } else
32         { assert false;          // Shouldn't happen!
33         }
34       }
35     }
36   }
```

Note in line 24 that the `getSource` method returns an `Object` which must be cast to an appropriate type. The source itself will often have useful information. For example, if it were a text field, we could get the text typed by the user.

The cascading-`if` structure in lines 25–33 is fine for a small number of components, but if the components are stored in an array, a loop can be more concise, as follows:

```
public void actionPerformed(ActionEvent evt)
{ JButton src = (JButton)evt.getSource();
  int i = 0;
  while (removeButtons[i] != src)
  { i++;
  }
  assert removeButtons[i] == src;
  model.removeTokens(i+1);
}
```

13.6.3 Integrating the Controller and View

KEY IDEA

This is not a recommended approach, but its use is widespread.

The controller and view can also be integrated into the same class without the use of an inner class. Many examples on the Web use this approach because it is quick and easy. It introduces a significant disadvantage, however, in that there is only one controller for all of the various components. With the previous techniques, you can easily write one controller for a `JButton` and a different controller for a `JTextField`. Each controller has its own `actionPerformed` method that is specific to a particular task. When the controller and view are integrated, a single `actionPerformed` method must handle both components. In terms of the software engineering principles studied in Section 11.3.2, such integration reduces the cohesion of the methods (recall that we want high cohesion). Nevertheless, the technique is shown here so that you can understand it if and when you see it.

The technique works by implementing the required interfaces in the view class itself. In Listing 13-20, the `ActionListener` interface is listed on the class header (lines 2–3) and its only method, `actionPerformed`, is implemented at lines 14–23 just like any other method. Note that there is no inner class. The "controller" is registered with the `JButton` objects in line 10. Instead of constructing a separate object, a reference to the view itself (that is, `this`) is passed to the button.

FIND THE CODE

ch13/nimIntegrated/

Listing 13-20: *A version of* `NimPlayerView` *that integrates the view and the controller*

```
1  // Import classes needed by both view and controller.
2  public class NimPlayerView extends JPanel
3                 implements IView, ActionListener
4  {
5    // Other instance variables, constructor, updateView, and layoutView are omitted.
6
7    /** Register controllers for this view's components. */
8    private void registerControllers()
9    { for (int i = 0; i < this.removeButtons.length; i++)
10     { this.removeButtons[i].addActionListener(this);
11     }
12   }
13
14   public void actionPerformed(ActionEvent evt)
15   { JButton src = (JButton)evt.getSource();
16
17     int i = 0;
18     while (removeButtons[i] != src)
19     { i++;
20     }
21     assert removeButtons[i] == src;
```

Listing 13-20: *A version of* `NimPlayerView` *that integrates the view and the controller* (continued)

```
        model.removeTokens(i+1);
    }
}
```

13.7 Other Components

So far, we have only worked with `JTextField` and `JButton` components. But there are many more components, too many to cover in a book such as this. So how can you learn to use them? Use the following strategies:

- Discover what components are available and might be applicable
- Identify the listeners used
- Skim the documentation
- Begin with sample code
- Work incrementally

In the following sections, we'll use these strategies to learn how to display a set of color names to use in Nim instead of "Red" and "Black".

13.7.1 Discover Available Components

There are several ways to discover available components. One is to look at "A Visual Index to the Swing Components," which can be found at *http://java.sun.com/docs/books/tutorial/uiswing/components/components.html.* It shows a sample of each component and has links to documentation where you can learn more. Figure 13-11 shows a part of the Web page that looks promising. It appears that at least two kinds of components can display lists of color names, as we would like to do.

Clicking the links labeled "Combo box" and "List" leads to pages titled "How to Use Combo Boxes" and "How to Use Lists." The first page refers to the component `JComboBox`, and the second page refers to `JList`.

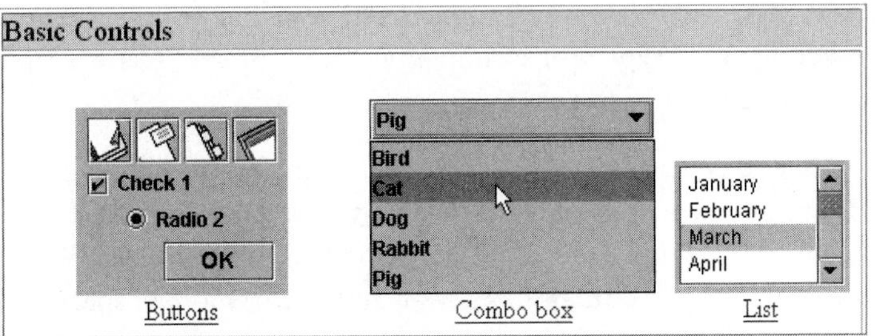

(figure 13-11)

Part of "A Visual Index to the Swing Components"

Another option is to find one of several demonstration programs available. One that comes with this textbook is shown in Figure 13-5. If you have downloaded the example code for the textbook, you'll find the code in the directory `ch13/componentDemo`. Running the program and playing with the components will show that `JSpinner` is also a possibility. In Figure 13-5, it displays "Sunday," but it also "spins" through the other days of the week. It could also spin through the color names we want to display.

Any of these options could work for us. Choosing between them is largely a matter of personal taste. For now, we'll choose `JList`.

13.7.2 Identify Listeners

When we identify the listeners for a component, we identify what kind of events it can tell us about and therefore what kind of controllers we can write. Every component may have the following six kinds of listeners:

- Component listeners listen for changes in the component's size, position, or visibility. Component listeners have methods like `componentHidden`, `componentResized`, and `componentMoved`.
- Focus listeners listen for the component gaining or losing the ability to receive keyboard input. Focus listeners have two methods, `focusGained` and `focusLost`.
- Key listeners listen for key press events. Such events are fired only by the component that has the keyboard focus. Key listeners have `keyPressed`, `keyReleased`, and `keyTyped` methods.
- Mouse listeners listen for mouse clicks and the mouse moving into and out of the component's drawing area. Mouse listeners have five methods, including `mouseEntered` and `mouseClicked`.
- Mouse motion listeners listen for changes in the cursor's position within the component. Such listeners have two methods, `mouseMoved` and `mouseDragged`.
- Mouse wheel listeners listen for mouse wheel movement over the component. They have a single method, `mouseWheelMoved`.

In addition to these six listeners, components have one or more additional listeners that vary by component type. For example, we have already seen that `JTextField` and `JButton` objects can have `ActionListeners`.

A complete table of components and listeners is maintained by the creators of Java at *http://java.sun.com/docs/books/tutorial/uiswing/events/eventsandcomponents.html.* This table is summarized in Figure 13-12. Looking at the list, we can tell that the `JList` component uses a `ListSelectionListener` and one or more unspecified listeners.

(figure 13-12)

Listeners used by some of Java's GUI components

Component	ActionListener	CaretListener	ChangeListener	DocumentListener	ItemListener	ListSelectionListener	WindowListener	Other
JButton	√		√		√			
JCheckBox	√		√		√			
JColorChooser			√					
JComboBox	√				√			
JDialog							√	
JEditorPane		√		√				√
JFileChooser	√							
JFormattedTextField	√	√		√				
JFrame							√	
JList						√		√
JMenu								√
JMenuItem	√		√		√			√
JPasswordField	√	√		√				
JPopupMenu								√
JProgressBar			√					
JRadioButton	√		√		√			
JSlider			√					
JSpinner			√					
JTabbedPane			√					
JTable						√		√
JTextArea		√		√				
JTextField	√	√		√				
JToggleButton	√		√		√			
JTree								√

Another approach is to look at the documentation for the component at *http://java.sun.com/j2se/1.5.0/docs/api/*. For example, find `JList` in the left side and click on it. Scroll down to the list of methods and look for methods named `addXxxxListener`, where the `Xxxx` can vary. `JList` has an `addListSelectionListener` method.

The documentation for `ListSelectionListener` says the interface specifies a single method, `valueChanged`. This is the method that our controller for `JList` will need to implement.

13.7.3 Skim the Documentation

There are two primary sources of information for working with Java's GUI components: the API documentation and the Java Tutorial.

Application Programming Interface (API) Documentation

KEY IDEA

The API documentation provides full details about each class.

One primary source of information is the **API**, or **application programming interface**, documentation. It is the class-by-class documentation found at *http://java.sun.com/j2se/1.5.0/docs/api/*. The documentation for each class gives an overview of the class, its inheritance hierarchy, a list of the constructors provided, and a list of the methods provided, including detailed descriptions of what they do.

The first time you use a component, skim this documentation looking for methods that sound useful. There may be lots of them—don't get overwhelmed. For `JList`, the documentation lists about 70 methods, plus the 344 methods it inherits from its superclasses.

What's important when getting started using a `JList`? Constructing the component, adding items to display in the list, adding a listener, and finding out which item on the list was selected. Skimming the documentation for methods that sound relevant yields the following:

- `JList()`: constructs an empty `JList`
- `JList(Object[] listData)`: constructs a `JList` that displays the elements in the specified array
- `addListSelectionListener`: adds a listener to the `JList`
- `getSelectedIndex`: returns the index of the first selected item; if nothing is selected, it returns -1
- `getSelectedIndicies`: returns an array of all the selected indices
- `getSelectedValue`: returns the first selected value

These methods answer most of our questions. We might have expected to find an "add item" method to add items to the list, but we didn't. Instead, it appears that we pass an array of items to display when the component is constructed. It also appears that several items can be selected at one time. We may want to make note of that for future reference.

The Java Tutorial

The *Java Tutorial* at *http://java.sun.com/docs/books/tutorial/* provides a wealth of practical examples for creating graphical user interfaces. Particularly relevant is the "Creating a GUI with JFC/Swing" chapter. It contains sections such as "Learning Swing by Example," "Using Swing Components," and "Writing Event Listeners." One subsection, at *http://java.sun.com/docs/books/tutorial/uiswing/components/componentlist.html*, contains a long list of topics with names like "How to Make Applets" and "How to Use Lists." The API documentation often provides direct links to these sections of the tutorial.

KEY IDEA

The Java Tutorial *contains lots of sample code.*

Clicking the "How to Use Lists" link opens a document that includes sample code and sections titled "Initializing a List," "Selecting Items in a List," and "Adding Items to and Removing Items from a List." All sound helpful!

13.7.4 Begin with Sample Code

Building on the discoveries of someone else is always easier than starting from scratch. When learning to use a new component, look for sample code using it. The *Java Tutorial* is a good place to look, particularly in the "How to..." sections referenced earlier.

Another source for sample code that matches the style presented in this textbook is the `componentDemo` program shown in Figure 13-5. If you run the program and click an element in the `JList`, an entry is added to the table at the bottom of the frame. The view column says "ListView." This is the name of the class containing the `JList`. The second column, "Listener," says "ListView$ListController." That's the name of the controller class that handled your mouse click—the `ListController` class that is an inner class within the `ListView` class.

Open the source for `ListView` and you'll find the code constructing the `JList`, laying it out within a view, and registering a controller, as well as the code for the controller itself. Much of this code can be cut and pasted directly into the program you're writing.

13.7.5 Work Incrementally

The last piece of advice is to work incrementally. Start with small goals for the component. Meet those goals and then move on to more ambitious goals. For example, you might begin by displaying the `JList` in a view. Listing 13-21 shows a minimal view with the goal of showing a `JList` with the names of some colors and detecting when one has been selected.

FIND THE CODE

ch13/usingJList/

Listing 13-21: *A simple view to display a list of colors and detect when one is selected*

```
import becker.util.IView;
import javax.swing.JPanel;
import javax.swing.JList;
import javax.swing.event.ListSelectionEvent;
import javax.swing.event.ListSelectionListener;

public class View extends JPanel implements IView
{ // private Object model;
  private JList list;

  public View(Object aModel)
  { super();
    // this.model = aModel;
    this.layoutView();
    this.registerControllers();
    // this.model.addView(this);
    this.updateView();
  }

  public void updateView()
  {// Statements to update the components in the view.
  }

  private void layoutView()
  { this.list = new JList(new String[] {"Red", "Green", "Blue",
          "Yellow", "Orange", "Pink", "Black"});
    this.add(this.list);
  }

  private void registerControllers()
  { this.list.addListSelectionListener(
          new ListController());
  }

  private class ListController extends Object
          implements ListSelectionListener
  { public void valueChanged(ListSelectionEvent evt)
    { System.out.println(
          "selected " + View.this.list.getSelectedValue());
    }
  }
}
```

Running a program that places this view in a frame appears as shown in Figure 13-13 and proves that we have made significant progress. The list shows the seven colors and it prints a message when one is selected. However, there are two problems. First, each time a color is selected, two copies of the message are printed by the controller. Second, the list has no scroll bars. If the window is made smaller than the list, part of the list simply disappears.

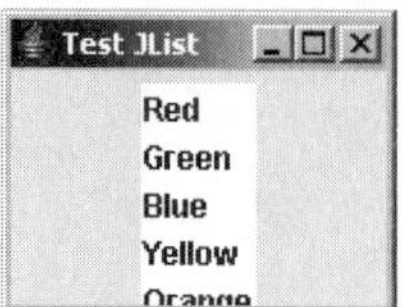

(figure 13-13)

Running the `JList` *test*

For the first problem, it seems like the `ListSelectionListener` documentation would be a good place to start. After all, the listener contains the code that is being called twice. However, that documentation provides no help.

If we look at the `ListSelectionEvent` documentation, we find a method named `getValueIsAdjusting`. Its description says "Returns `true` if this is one of multiple change events," which sounds promising. `JList` reports a list selection event both when the mouse is pressed and when it is released—as well as several more events in between if the user moves the mouse over different values in the list. Rewriting our controller's `valueChanged` method results in only one message being printed, the one selected when the mouse button is released:

```
public void valueChanged(ListSelectionEvent evt)
{ if (!evt.getValueIsAdjusting())
  { System.out.println(
        "selected " + View.this.list.getSelectedValue());
  }
}
```

The problem of the missing scroll bars can be solved by searching the `JList` class documentation for "scroll." That search finds the following:

> "`JList` doesn't support scrolling directly. To create a scrolling list you make the `JList` the viewport view of a `JScrollPane`. For example:
>
> ```
> JScrollPane scrollPane = new JScrollPane(dataList);
> ```
>
> where `dataList` is the instance of `JList` you want to display. The `JScrollPane` component is added to the view instead of the `JList`."

Working incrementally, we add equivalent code to the `layoutView` method in Listing 13-21 and run the program to see the results. Unfortunately, nothing has changed, and scroll bars still do not appear.

KEY IDEA

Component-size problems are often related to the layout manager.

It turns out that `JPanel`'s default layout manager, `FlowLayout`, allows the list to take up as much space as it requests. `JScrollPane` does not show the scroll bars until the available space is less than the requested space. `BorderLayout` is a layout manager that forces its components to fit within the available space. Using it to manage the view's layout results in the scroll bars appearing when the `JList` is small. The resulting code for `layoutView` is as follows:

```
private void layoutView()
{ this.setLayout(new BorderLayout());
  this.list = new JList(new String[] {"Red", "Green",
    "Blue", "Yellow", "Orange", "Pink", "Black"});
  JScrollPane scrollpane = new JScrollPane(this.list);
  this.add(scrollpane, BorderLayout.CENTER);
}
```

As shown here, it is unrealistic to expect to understand and use a complex class like `JList` on the first try. An excellent strategy is to work incrementally. Understand and implement the basics, make note of the remaining issues, and then solve them one at a time. Using this strategy, we are well on our way to making effective use of the `JList` component. Reasonable next steps include making calls to the model in response to user selections and, if required, learning how to add new values to the list while the program is running.

13.8 Graphical Views

Many components are available for Java programs, but sometimes none of them are quite right for a particular application. In those cases, you may need to make your own. We have, in fact, already done this. In Section 6.7, we wrote the `Thermometer` class, which displayed a temperature using an image of a thermometer.

In Section 13.8.1, we will implement a similar class to simply display a pile of tokens for the game of Nim. In Section 13.8.2, we will go a step further and add a listener for mouse events so that the user can utilize our new component to select the tokens to remove from the pile.

13.8.1 Painting a Component

Instances of our custom component, `PileComponent`, represent a pile of tokens as circles, drawn one on top of the other, as shown in Figure 13-14. Such a component that does its own painting usually extends the `JComponent` class (see Listing 13-22).

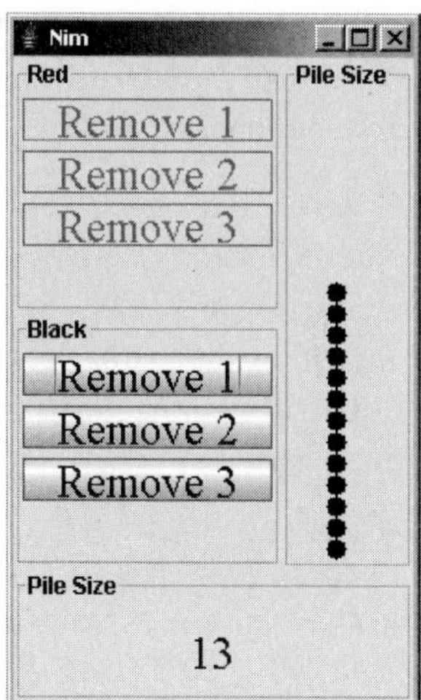

(figure 13-14)

Custom component representing a pile of tokens for Nim

Two crucial parts of the class are instance variables, used to either store or acquire the information required to do the painting (lines 4–5), and the `paintComponent` method (lines 27–40).

Two instance variables are required: `numTokens` stores the actual number of tokens to display; `maxTokens` stores the maximum number that could be displayed. The maximum is used to scale the circles appropriately; it is set with the constructor. `numTokens` is set using a mutator method, `setPileSize`, called from the `updateView` method in the view that contains the `PileComponent` object. When the pile size is changed, `this.repaint()` must be called. It tells the Java system that it should call `paintComponent` as soon as possible to redraw the pile.

LOOKING BACK

Repainting is explained in more detail in Section 6.7.2.

The `paintComponent` method begins by calculating useful values for painting (lines 29–32). The first two merely make temporary copies of the component's width and height to make them easier to use. The second two calculate the diameter of each token and where the left side will be painted.

Lines 35-39 use a loop to draw each of the tokens in the pile.

One other detail is setting the minimum and preferred size of the component in lines 12 and 13. Without these statements, the component's size will default to a barely visible 1 x 1 pixel square.

ch13/nimMultiView/

Listing 13-22: *A component that displays the size of a token pile graphically*

```
// Import statements omitted.
public class PileComponent extends JComponent
{
  private int numTokens = 0;
  private int maxTokens;

  /** Create a new component.
  *  @param max The maximum number of tokens that can be displayed. */
  public PileComponent(int max)
  { super();
    this.maxTokens = max;
    this.setMinimumSize(new Dimension(40, 60));
    this.setPreferredSize(new Dimension(60, 90));
  }

  /**  Reset the size of the pile.
  *  @param num The new pile size. 0 <= num <= maxTokens */
  public void setPileSize(int num)
  { if (num < 0 || num > this.maxTokens)
    { throw new IllegalArgumentException("too many/few tokens");
    }
    this.numTokens = num;
    this.repaint();
  }

  /** Paint the component. */
  public void paintComponent(Graphics g)
  { // Values to use in painting.
    int width = this.getWidth();
    int height = this.getHeight();
    int tokenDia = Math.min(width, height/this.maxTokens);
    int tokenLeft = width/2 - tokenDia;

    // Draw the tokens.
    g.setColor(Color.BLACK);
    for (int i = 0; i < this.numTokens; i++)
    { int top = height - (i + 1) * tokenDia;
      g.fillOval(tokenLeft, top, tokenDia, tokenDia);
    }
  }
}
```

13.8.2 Making a Graphical Component Interactive

We can make `PileComponent` interactive, enabling users to use the mouse to select a number of tokens by performing the following steps, also illustrated in Figure 13-15.

The steps are:

- Press the mouse button
- Drag the mouse over some of the tokens displayed by the component
- Release the mouse button

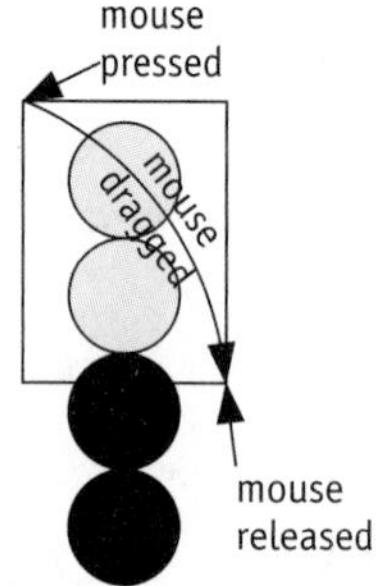

(figure 13-15)

Sequence of mouse actions triggering a selection

In general, implementing a custom component involves the five steps shown in Figure 13-16. The result is a component we can use in a view, complete with its own controllers—just like we use controllers with `JTextField` and `JButton` components.

1. Write a class that extends `JComponent`.
2. Declare instance variables to store the information required to paint the component appropriately. Override the `paintComponent` method to do the painting.
3. Write mutator methods to update the instance variables. Call the `repaint` method before exiting any method that changes the component's state.
4. Declare a list to store the component's listeners. Include methods to add and remove components from the list, and a `handleEvent` method to inform all listeners of a significant event.
5. Write and register listeners to detect and respond to the user's actions.

(figure 13-16)

Steps to implement an interactive component

You may notice similarities with what we have done before. For example, both a component and a model call a method when their state is changed (Step 3), and both have a list of objects to inform when something significant happens (Step 4).

KEY IDEA

A component has features in common with both models and views.

On the other hand, a component is also similar to a view. Both extend a kind of component (`JPanel` versus `JComponent` in Step 1), and both have listeners (Step 5), although in a view the listeners are called "controllers."

The first three steps in Figure 13-16 were already done in the earlier version of `PileComponent`. In the following subsections, we will discuss Steps 4 and 5 in more detail, referring to Listing 13-23, which contains the code for the completed component. This new, interactive version of `PileComponent` will be called `PileComponent2`.

Informing the Component's Listeners

When our component is used in a view, we will want to add controllers to it that update the model. They will implement an interface such as `ActionListener` or `ListSelectionListener`. Now, because we are writing the component, we can choose which listener interface to use. Of all the listeners listed in Figure 13-12, `ActionListener` seems the most appropriate.

Therefore, in lines 22–23 of Listing 13-23 we declare an `ArrayList` to store objects implementing `ActionListener`. In lines 45–48 we provide an `addActionListener` method, like the one provided in `JButton` and `JTextField`. A complete implementation would also provide a `removeActionListener` method.

LOOKING BACK

Listing 13-8 shows a simplified version of `JTextField`*. It also has a* `handleEvent` *method.*

In lines 101–108 we provide a private method named `handleEvent`, to be called when the component detects the user selecting some tokens. It constructs an `ActionEvent` object and then loops through all the registered controllers, calling their `actionPerformed` method and passing the event object.

Writing and Registering Listeners

The last step, and the most complicated one, is figuring out when to call the `handleEvent` method. To do so, we will write two inner classes implementing `MouseListener` and `MouseMotionListener`. The first listener[4] will be informed each time something happens to the mouse button. The second listener will be informed each time the mouse moves. Mouse-related events are split into two listeners because there are *many* motion events. If the component only cares about mouse clicks, we don't want to incur the overhead associated with mouse motion events.

[4] We use the term "listener" rather than "controller" because these classes will not be interacting with the program's model.

We need to detect the following three mouse events:

- When the mouse button is pressed, we will create a new rectangle that will bound the area (and tokens) selected.
- When the mouse is dragged, we will update the size of the bounding rectangle and repaint the component to show it.
- When the mouse button is released, we will update the size of the bounding rectangle one last time and then call the `handleEvent` method to inform all the registered controllers.

These three steps are performed in the `mousePressed`, `mouseDragged`, and `mouseReleased` methods, respectively, found in lines 121–125, 144–147, and 127–132 of Listing 13-23. All three use the `getPoint` method in the event object to find out where the mouse was when the event occurred.

Of course, the component should provide feedback on which tokens have been selected. This is accomplished in the `paintComponent` method. Lines 71–75 draw the bounding rectangle, and lines 82–84 determines if it surrounds the token currently being drawn. If it does, an instance variable is incremented, and the token's color is changed to yellow. An accessor method, `getNumSelected`, is provided to allow clients to get the number of selected tokens.

FIND THE CODE

ch13/nimMultiView/

Listing 13-23: *An interactive component that allows the user to select a number of tokens*

```
1  import javax.swing.JComponent;
2  import java.awt.Graphics;
3  import java.awt.Insets;
4  import java.awt.Dimension;
5  import java.awt.Point;
6  import java.awt.Color;
7  import java.awt.Rectangle;
8  import java.awt.event.MouseListener;
9  import java.awt.event.MouseMotionListener;
10 import java.awt.event.MouseEvent;
11 import java.awt.event.ActionListener;
12 import java.awt.event.ActionEvent;
13 import java.util.ArrayList;
14
15 /** A component that displays a pile of tokens and allows the user to select a number of
16  *  them. It informs registered listeners when tokens have been selected. Allows the
17  *  client to change the number of tokens in the pile.
18  *
19  *  @author Byron Weber Becker */
20 public class PileComponent2 extends JComponent
21 { // Store the controllers to inform when a selection takes place.
```

Listing 13-23: *An interactive component that allows the user to select a number of tokens* (continued)

```
   private ArrayList<ActionListener> actionListeners =
                  new ArrayList<ActionListener>();

   // Information for painting the component.
   private int numTokens = 0;
   private int maxTokens;

   private Rectangle selection = null;        // selected area
   private int numSelected = 0;               // # tokens in selected area

   /** Create a new component.
    *  @param maxTokens The maximum number of tokens that can be displayed. */
   public PileComponent2(int maxTokens)
   { super();
     this.maxTokens = maxTokens;
     this.setMinimumSize(new Dimension(40, 60));
     this.setPreferredSize(new Dimension(60, 90));

     // Add the mouse listener.
     this.addMouseListener(new MListener());
     this.addMouseMotionListener(new MMListener());
   }

   /** Add an action listener to this component's list of listeners. */
   public void addActionListener(ActionListener listener)
   { this.actionListeners.add(listener);
   }

   /** Set the size of the pile.
    *  @param num The new pile size. 0 <= num <= maxTokens */
   public void setPileSize(int num)
   { if (num < 0 || num > this.maxTokens)
     { throw new IllegalArgumentException("too many/few tokens");
     }
     this.numTokens = num;
     this.selection = null;
     this.numSelected = 0;
     this.repaint();
   }

   /** Paint the component. */
   public void paintComponent(Graphics g)
```

Listing 13-23: *An interactive component that allows the user to select a number of tokens* (continued)

```
{ //Values to use in painting.
  int width = this.getWidth();
  int height = this.getHeight();
  int tokenDia = Math.min(width, height/this.maxTokens);
  int tokenLeft = width/2 - tokenDia;

  // Draw the selection rectangle, if there is one.
  g.setColor(Color.BLACK);
  if (this.selection != null)
  { Rectangle sel = this.selection;
    g.drawRect(sel.x, sel.y, sel.width, sel.height);
  }

  // Draw the tokens. Detect which ones are selected. Count them
  // and color them differently.
  this.numSelected = 0;
  for (int i = 0; i < this.numTokens; i++)
  { int top = height - (i + 1) * tokenDia;
    if (this.selection != null &&
        this.selection.contains(tokenLeft + tokenDia / 2,
                                top + tokenDia / 2))
    { this.numSelected++;
      g.setColor(Color.YELLOW);
    } else
    { g.setColor(Color.BLACK);
    }

    g.fillOval(tokenLeft, top, tokenDia, tokenDia);
  }
}

/** Get the number of tokens currently selected.
*  @return the number of tokens currently selected */
public int getNumSelected()
{ return this.numSelected;
}

/** A helper method to inform all listeners that a selection has been made. */
private void handleEvent()
{ ActionEvent evt = new ActionEvent(
                    this, ActionEvent.ACTION_PERFORMED, "");
```

Listing 13-23: *An interactive component that allows the user to select a number of tokens* (continued)

```
    for (ActionListener al : this.actionListeners)
    { al.actionPerformed(evt);
    }
  }

  /** Adjust the selection's size. */
  private void adjustSelectionSize(Point mPos)
  { this.selection.setSize(mPos.x - this.selection.x,
                           mPos.y - this.selection.y);
    this.repaint();
  }

  /** Listen for mouse events within the pile. */
  private class MListener extends Object
                            implements MouseListener
  {
    /** A mousePressed event signals the beginning of a selection. */
    public void mousePressed(MouseEvent e)
    { PileComponent2.this.selection =
                          new Rectangle(e.getPoint());
    }

    /** A mouseReleased event signals the end of a selection. Finish up the
     * selection and inform the listeners. */
    public void mouseReleased(MouseEvent e)
    { PileComponent2.this.adjustSelectionSize(e.getPoint());
      PileComponent2.this.handleEvent();
    }

    // Required by MouseListener but not needed in this program.
    public void mouseClicked(MouseEvent e)   {}
    public void mouseEntered(MouseEvent e)   {}
    public void mouseExited(MouseEvent e)    {}
  }

  /** Listen for mouse events within the pile. */
  private class MMListener extends Object
                            implements MouseMotionListener
  {
```

Listing 13-23: *An interactive component that allows the user to select a number of tokens* (continued)

```
      /** The bounds of the selection's rectangle changed. Adjust it. */
      public void mouseDragged(MouseEvent e)
      { PileComponent2.this.adjustSelectionSize(e.getPoint());
      }

      // Required by MouseMotionListener but not needed in this program.
      public void mouseMoved(MouseEvent e)      {}
   }
}
```

13.9 Patterns

13.9.1 The Model-View-Controller Pattern

Name: Model-View-Controller

Context: A program requires a graphical user interface to interact with the user. You want to program it with the good software engineering principles of encapsulation, information hiding, high cohesion, and low coupling to facilitate future changes.

Solution: Organize the program into a model with one or more views and controllers. The model abstracts the problem the program is designed to solve. Each view displays some part of the model to the user, while controllers translate user actions in a view into method calls on the model.

The Model-View-Controller pattern requires three templates: one for the model, one for the combination of a view and a controller, and one for the main method. Listing 13-13 contains an excellent start on a template for views, but needs an inner class for a controller. Listing 13-1 and Listing 13-3 can be generalized for the model's template and the main method's template, respectively.

LOOKING AHEAD

Written Exercise 13.2 asks you to prepare these templates.

Consequences: Because the model depends only on objects implementing the `IView` interface, coupling is extremely low. The interface can be changed or even completely replaced, usually without changing the model.

Related Patterns:

- The Extended Class pattern is used by the views when they extend `JPanel`.
- The Has-a (Composition) pattern is used to relate the model to the views and the views to the model.
- The Process All Elements pattern is used to update all of the views with changes in the model.
- The Strategy pattern is used to lay out the view's components and to provide a controller (listener) that reacts appropriately to events in a particular component.

13.10 Summary and Concept Map

Graphical user interfaces use a library of objects, commonly called components, to interact with users. The program is organized into a model containing the abstractions related to the problem, views that display the model to the user, and controllers that interpret user actions to modify the model. One model may have several views, and each view may have several controllers.

It is also possible to create components to perform specific tasks for which no existing component is available.

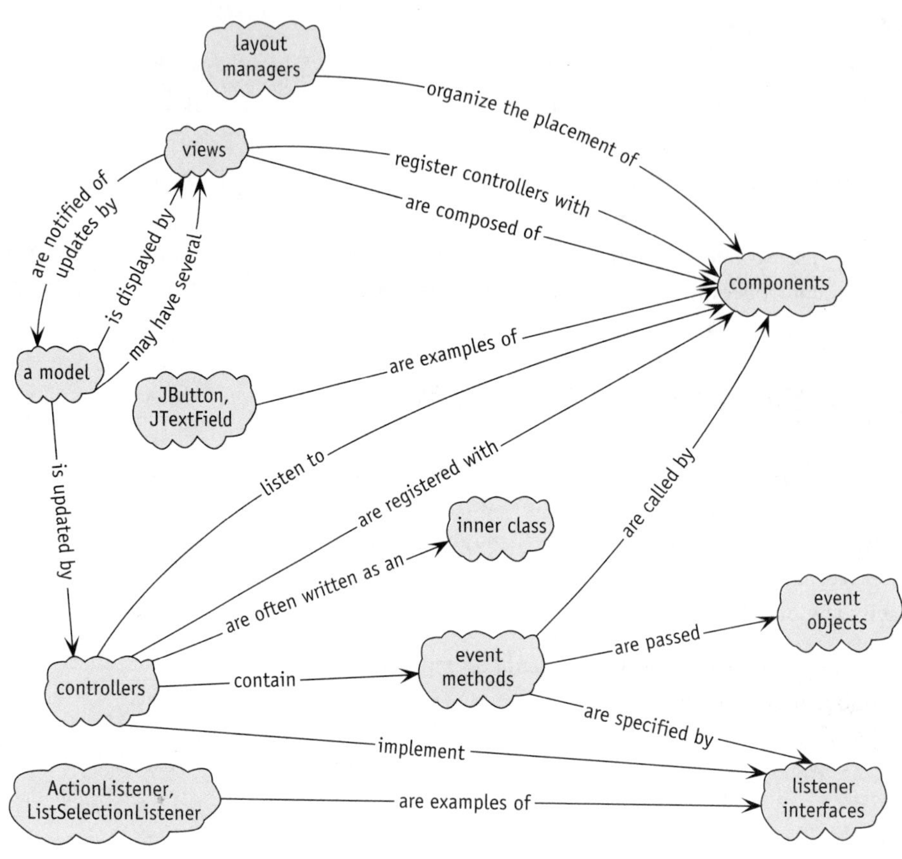

13.11 Problem Set

Written Exercises

13.1 Explain how using subviews (Section 13.5) is good software engineering. Refer specifically to the concepts of cohesion and coupling.

13.2 Write the three code templates required for the Model-View-Controller pattern. Listing 13-13 contains an excellent start on a template for views, but needs an inner class for a controller. Listing 13-1 and Listing 13-3 can be generalized for the model's template and the main method's template, respectively.

13.3 Prepare a class diagram showing the relationships between the classes in the Model-View-Controller pattern. Assume the controller has been written in a separate class, as shown in Listing 13-9, and implements an `ActionListener`.

13.4 List the signatures for all the methods required to implement a `WindowListener`.

13.5 The Java library contains two classes named `MouseAdapter` and `MouseMotionAdapter`. Discuss how they could be used to simplify the `PileComponent2` class shown in Listing 13-23.

13.6 The Java library contains an interface named `MouseInputListener`. Examine the documentation and discuss how it could be used in the `PileComponent2` class shown in Listing 13-23.

Programming Exercises

13.7 Find the code for the version of Nim with multiple views.

a. Add a new view whose function is to offer hints to the current player. (*Hint*: Assuming the rules where 1, 2, or 3 tokens may be removed, a player who leaves 1, 2, or 3 tokens for his or her opponent has made a serious mistake. Similarly, a player who leaves exactly four tokens is in a very strong position. Generalize these observations.)

b. Modify the `NimPlayerView` class to use a `JComboBox` for user input instead of `JButton` objects.

c. Modify the `NimPlayerView` class to use a `JSlider` for user input.

d. Add a new view whose function is to start a new game. The user should be able to specify who starts and how large the initial pile of tokens should be. The player should also be able to start a new game with the program choosing either or both of these values randomly.

e. Views do not actually need to belong to a graphical user interface. Write a class named `NimLogger` that implements `IView`. Modify the `Nim` program to use `NimLogger` to write the state of the game after each move to a file. (*Hint*: You should *not* extend `JPanel` or include any classes from the `javax.swing` or `java.awt` packages. Create the `NimLogger` object in the `main` method.)

f. Modify the model and the view so users may remove up to half of the remaining tokens in each turn. Start the game with a random pile of 20 to 30 tokens. The existing views with three buttons each are inappropriate. Design a new view.

g. Modify the `PileComponent2` class to show the tokens as a block, three tokens wide. The top row of the block may have less than three tokens.

h. The `PileComponent2` class shown in Listing 13-23 does not work when a user clicks and drags the mouse upward or leftward. The problem is that the width or the length of the selection rectangle becomes negative, resulting in an "empty" rectangle. Fix this problem.

i. The `PileComponent2` class shown in Listing 13-23 currently allows the user to select any number of visible tokens, even though the game only allows a maximum of three tokens to be removed. Fix the component so that the selection rectangle is not allowed to enclose more than three tokens.

13.8 Find the code displayed in Listing 13-21. Write a simple `main` method to display it in a frame. Observe that it is possible to select several items at once using the Shift or Control keys.

a. Modify the program to print all of the items that have been selected.

b. Modify the program so users can select only one item at a time.

c. The `JList` documentation includes sample code for a class named `MyCellRenderer`. Read the documentation, and then change the program so that each element of the list is displayed using the appropriate color.

Programming Projects

13.9 Write a program to assist users in calculating their target heart rate for an exercise program. You can find many formulas on the Web for calculating target heart rate. One is based on the user's age, resting heart rate, and targeted intensity: *intensity* * (220 – *age* – *restingHR*) + *restingHR*, where *intensity* is a percentage (typically 80 to 90%), *age* is the user's age in years, and *restingHR* is the user's resting heart rate in beats per minute. The model will have mutator methods for *intensity*, *age*, and *restingHR*, and accessor methods for those three plus the target heart rate.

Two possible views are shown in Figure 13-17.

a. Write the program's view using `JTextField` components.

b. Write the program's view using `JSlider` components.

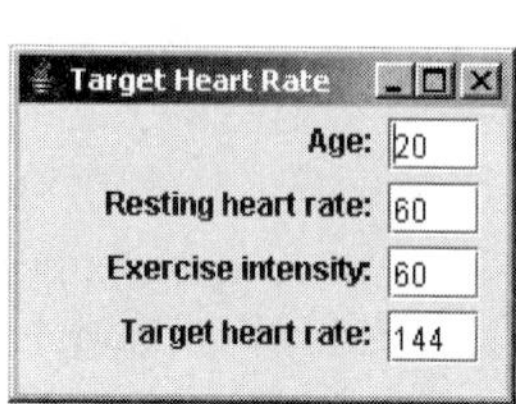

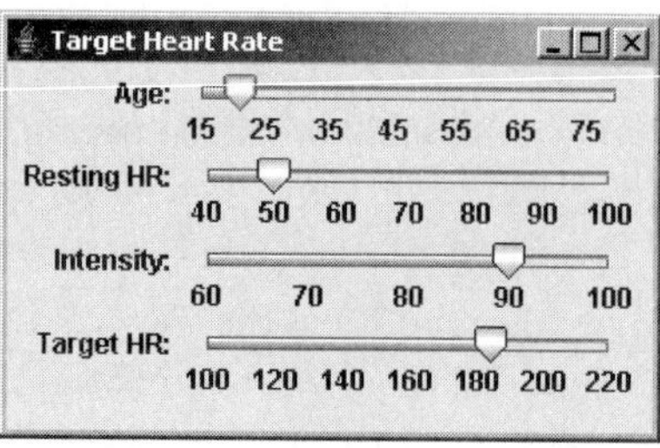

(figure 13-17)

Two possible views for a target heart rate calculator

13.10 Write a program that allows you to display font samples. A proposed user interface is shown in Figure 13-18. The model for this program will have methods such as `setFontName`, `setFontSize`, `setBold`, `setItalic`, and `getFont`. The components used in the interface include `JComboBox`, `JCheckBox`, `JTextArea`, and `becker.gui.FormLayout`.

(figure 13-18)

Two interfaces

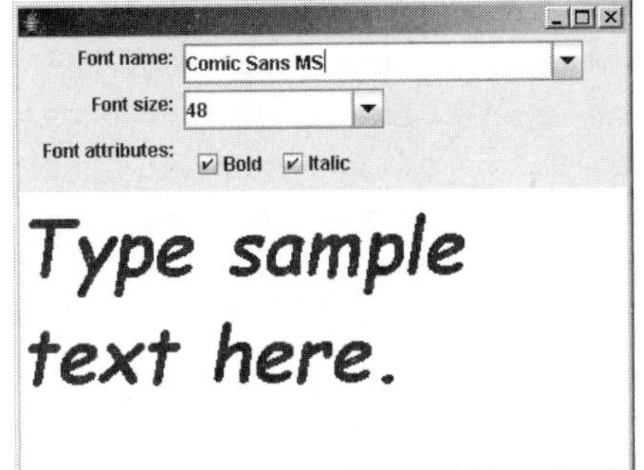

An interface for generating font samples

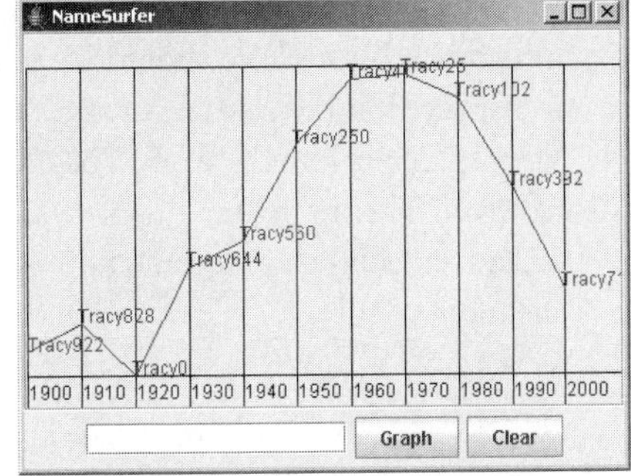

An interface for plotting the popularity of names through time

13.11 Explore the documentation for the `becker.xtras.nameSurfer` package.[5] In particular, see the package overview and Figure 13-18 for an example of the interface.

a. Write a model named `SurferModel`. Demonstrate your model, working with classes from the `nameSurfer` package to form a complete program.

b. Write a view named `SurferView`. Demonstrate your view, working with classes from the `nameSurfer` package to form a complete program. (*Hint*: You will need to implement a custom component to draw the graph.)

13.12 Implement a view to choose a color. Figure 13-19 has three `JSlider` components, one for each of the red, green, and blue parts of a color. Their values range between 0 and 255. Use an empty `JPanel` to display the current color as the sliders are moved by calling the panel's `setBackground` method.

Demonstrate your view with a simple program. The model will have two methods: `setColor` and `getColor`. `setColor` is called when the OK button is pressed, resulting in a second view being updated with the chosen color.

(figure 13-19)

Sample interfaces for a color chooser and a Web browser

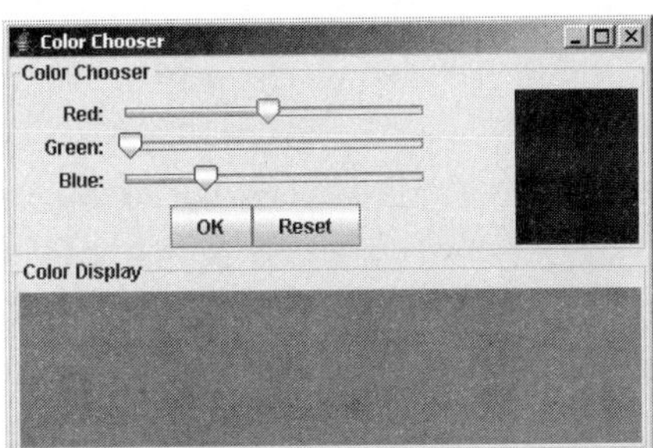

Simple color chooser

Simple Web browser

[5] The original idea for this problem is attributed to Nick Parlante at Stanford University.

13.13 Use the `JEditorPane` to implement a simple Web browser like the one shown in Figure 13-19. Users should be able to type a URL into a text field and have it displayed in the `JEditorPane`. Your browser should also correctly follow links to display a new page. The `JEditorPane` may not be editable for links to work. The model for the browser will be the current URL to display. Enhancements may require adding a history list and other features to the model.

a. Add scroll bars to the `JEditorPane` that show only if needed.

b. Add a toolbar with Forward, Back, and Home buttons.

c. Use a `JComboBox` for entering URLs. Add URLs the user has typed to the `JComboBox` for easier selection in the future.

13.14 Implement the game of Tic-Tac-Toe for two users (see Figure 13-20). Search the Web for the rules if you are unfamiliar with the game. Use a button for each of the nine squares to gather input from the users. Disable the buttons and change their labels as they are played. When the mouse is moved over an unplayed square, show either X or O, depending on whose turn it is. Announce the winner with a dialog box and start a new game.

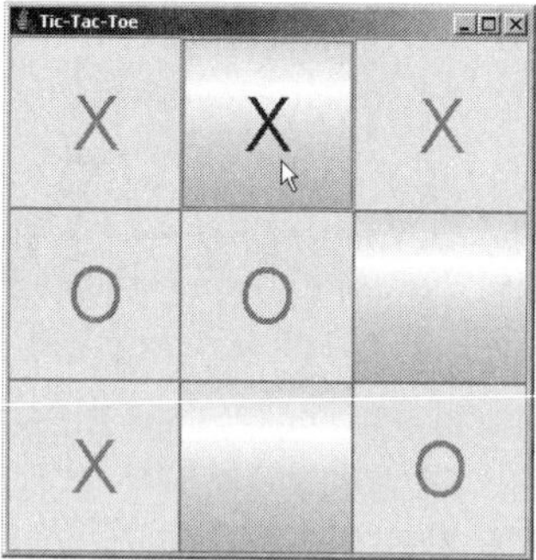

Tic-tac-toe game

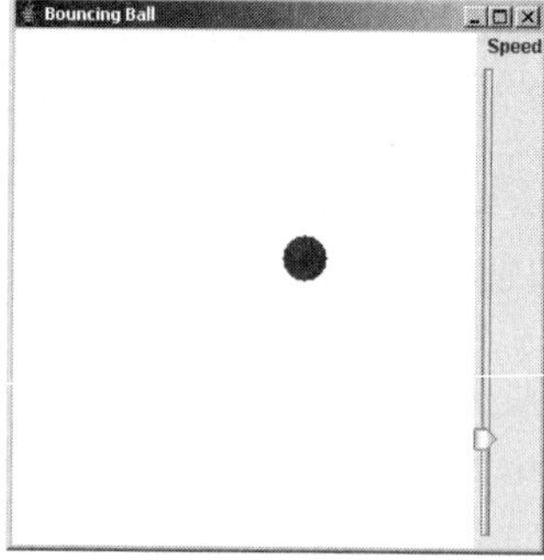

Animated bouncing ball

(figure 13-20)

Sample interfaces for a game and an animation

13.15 Write a program that displays a bouncing ball and allows for its speed to be changed and the size of the box it bounces in to be changed (see Figure 13-20). Note the following hints:

- Read the documentation for the `javax.swing.Timer` class. An appropriate delay is 1000/30. There are several classes named `Timer`; be sure to read the right one.
- Write a `BallModel` class with methods such as `getBallBounds` and `setBoxBounds`. The `java.awt.Rectangle` class is convenient for maintaining size and position information for both the ball and the box. The `BallModel` will also contain an instance of `Timer`, updating the position of the ball every time it "ticks."

- The `BallView` class should contain a custom component to draw the ball. It will need a controller implementing `ComponentListener` to resize the model's box when the component is resized.
- The `BallView` class should also contain an instance of `JSlider` to adjust the speed of the bouncing ball.

13.16 Implement a model for a right triangle. It will have two methods to set the base and the height but will calculate the length of the hypotenuse using the Pythagorean theorem ($a^2 + b^2 = c^2$). It will also have three methods to get the length of each side. The length of the base and the height must be between 1 and 100, inclusive. Figure 13-21 shows several different views of the model.

a. Implement a view using `JTextField` components.

b. Implement a view using `JSlider` components.

c. Implement a view using a `JButton` to increment the length of the base and another to decrement it. Do so similarly for the height.

d. Implement a view using `JSpinner` to adjust the base and height.

e. Implement a view using `JCombobox` or `JList` that allows the user to select one of several standard triangle sizes.

f. Implement a custom component that draws a picture of the triangle. Set the size of the triangle using one of the other views.

g. Implement a custom component that draws a picture of the triangle. Add a controller for the mouse that detects clicks on the triangle. When the triangle is clicked, paint "handles" to show that it is selected. Allow the user to change its size by dragging the handles.

h. Implement a view showing several of the preceding views other than (e). Be sure that they all display the same information about the triangle model.

(figure 13-21)

Several views of a triangle model

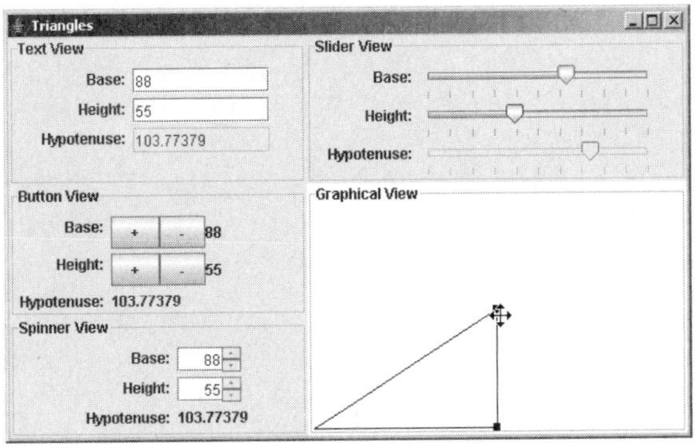

Epilogue

Congratulations! You've learned a lot about programming computers using this textbook. However, programming represents only a portion of what computer specialists do. If you choose to continue studying computer science, what do you have to look forward to? This epilogue gives a glimpse.

The topics discussed here are based on curricular recommendations by the Association for Computing Machinery and the Computer Society of the Institute for Electrical and Electronic Engineers, the two leading professional organizations for computing disciplines. These topics represent a widely accepted core of material that undergraduate computer science students should know.

Programming Fundamentals

Most of the material we have studied falls into the area of programming fundamentals. Future courses include further study of data structures and recursion. Data structures are used to organize data, arrays being one of the simplest. The `HashSet` and `TreeMap` classes are implementations of other data structures.

Recursion occurs when a method calls itself to solve a smaller instance of the same problem. It's a powerful technique that is often explored at the same time as recursive data structures, such as trees and lists.

Discrete Structures

Discrete structures are areas of mathematics that are particularly helpful to computing professionals, including the study of sets, logic, proof techniques, graphs, and trees. When we studied Boolean expressions, we were learning about logic.

Many problems in the real world, such as routing messages on the Internet, can be represented as a mathematical tree or graph (which is different from graphing data on a chart). Knowledge of discrete structures is often critical to solving such problems.

Algorithms and Complexity

When we explored enlarging arrays to hold more elements, we briefly touched on algorithms and complexity. We identified two different algorithms: one that enlarges the array by one element, and one that doubles the size of the array. However, their complexity—the amount of time each takes to do its job—was very different. Experimental results were given in Figure 10-19. It's also possible to approximate it mathematically.

Architecture and Organization

These topics address how the computer hardware is organized and how the very lowest levels of software interact with it. In Section 8.2.1 we discussed how the computer's memory is organized like a large array. Other topics within this area include how the CPU (central processing unit) works, how to connect devices such as keyboards and networks to the computer, and how your programs and data are represented within the computer.

Operating Systems

The operating system manages the computer's resources for its users and provides ways for programmers to access these resources. Perhaps one of the clearest ways we use the operating system is in performing input and output via the console or files. The operating system takes care of details like finding free space on the disk for our files, organizing the files into directories, and interacting with the electronics in the disk drive itself to read and write the data.

Modern operating systems appear to do many things concurrently. Our brief exploration of threads to run several robots concurrently (Section 3.5.2) introduce some of the techniques involved, but not their complexity.

Net-Centric Computing

Connecting computers over a network has fundamentally changed computing. The World Wide Web is only the most visible result of this shift. Programs running on one machine increasingly access services on other machines. These services might be as simple as reading a file or as complex as interfacing with the ordering systems of your company's suppliers.

Programming Languages

Java is one of many programming languages. As an object-oriented language, Java is similar to other object-oriented languages such as C++, C#, Smalltalk, Ada, and so on. On the other hand, it is quite different from functional languages such as Scheme and Lisp, or a scripting language such as Python. Each of these paradigms (object-oriented, functional, and scripting) has a different way of thinking about programming. Some problems that are hard to solve using one paradigm are much easier to solve using another.

Most computer scientists use only one or two languages from any given paradigm, but often switch between paradigms depending on the problem they are solving.

Human-Computer Interaction

Our work in building graphical user interfaces provides a good introduction to this area of study. Other topics in this area include how the psychology and physiology of people affect the design of interfaces, techniques for evaluating the quality of interfaces, and processes for designing interfaces.

A broader experience in implementing interfaces includes using a wider variety of components, including animation, and working with libraries for languages other than Java.

Graphics and Visual Computing

Graphics and visual computing is composed of four overlapping areas. First, computer graphics is the art and science of using computers to communicate using visual images. Such images will have an underlying model. Subareas of graphics include developing models to facilitate creating and viewing images, designing devices and techniques that facilitate human interaction with the model, finding techniques for converting the model to visual form, and storing images. Applications include everything from movie special effects to manipulating images taken with a digital camera.

Second, visualization displays information in a way that enhances human understanding of the information. Visualizing strands of DNA was one early use.

Third, virtual reality provides a 3D, computer-generated environment to enhance the interaction between a human and the environment. Applications include games, simulations, and remote handling of dangerous materials.

Lastly, computer vision seeks to understand the properties and structure of the 3D world using 2D images. A robot that can navigate around obstacles is a classic test for computer vision.

Intelligent Systems

This area is also called artificial intelligence (AI). It is concerned with designing autonomous agents that act rationally in interactions with their environment, other agents, and people. Robots are one application of such techniques.

Artificial intelligence also provides techniques for solving problems that are difficult or impractical to solve using exact methods. These include using heuristics to guide a search, representing a human expert's knowledge in a program to help non-experts, and exploring ways that programs can "learn" from experience.

Information Management

Managing information is critical to most uses of computers. The study of information management includes methods to capture, represent, organize, transform, and present information. It also includes algorithms for efficiently and effectively accessing and updating stored information. The most obvious application of these techniques is developing and deploying the database systems depended on by all but the smallest companies.

Social and Professional Issues

Computers are a tool that can be applied to the benefit or the detriment of society. Computing professionals must be able to ask serious questions about the impact of their work on their users and society as a whole, and have the intellectual tools to evaluate the proposed answers. This area of computer science interacts with philosophy, ethics, history, social studies, risk analysis, and similar fields.

Software Engineering

Software engineering is concerned with effectively and efficiently building software systems that satisfy standard requirements. The topics discussed in Chapter 11—using a development process, testing, evaluating software quality, and so on—are all activities crucial to software engineering.

Computational Science and Numerical Methods

Computers represent numbers with finite precision—for example, 1/10 cannot be represented exactly in a computer. This simple fact requires techniques to overcome the computer's limitations when it is used for applications such as modeling molecules, fluids, and drug interactions. Another area is concerned with performing calculations efficiently, often on the huge numbers of equations necessary to forecast weather.

Summary

Learning to program is only the tip of the iceberg known as computer science. Your new knowledge of programming can be a stepping stone to a successful career as a computing professional. However, whether or not you choose to pursue a computing career, your understanding of programming will help you use computers more effectively in almost any career you choose to pursue.

Appendix A Glossary

Most scientific disciplines have a specialized vocabulary, allowing experts in the field to communicate precisely with each other. Computer science is no different. Gathered here are all the specialized terms used in the text, together with brief definitions. Come here for a quick reminder of a term's definition.

Key Terms

absolute path—A sequence of directories separated by a special character and beginning with a known location that is used to specify the location of a file. *See also* relative path.

abstract class—A class that declares or inherits an abstract method. Such classes are declared using the `abstract` keyword and are often used to declare types in polymorphic programs.

abstract method—A method that does not have a body. Such methods must be declared with the `abstract` keyword.

Abstract Windowing Toolkit (AWT)—A collection of classes used to implement graphical user interfaces.

abstraction—A method of dealing with complexity that eliminates or hides irrelevant details and groups other sets of details into coherent, higher-level chunks.

access modifier—The keywords `public`, `private`, and `protected`. An access modifier controls which clients may have access to the method it modifies.

accessor method—A method that returns the value of an instance variable.

address—A numeric identifier for a particular memory location.

algorithm—A finite set of step-by-step instructions that specify a process.

alias—An alternate name or reference for an object. All of an object's aliases can be used to access the object.

and—A logical connector written in Java as `&&`. The result is `true` if and only if both operands are `true`.

anonymous class—A class without a name. It is used to declare and instantiate a single object at the point where the object is needed.

API—*See* application programming interface.

application programming interface (API)—The set of publicly available methods by which a program accesses the services offered by a class or package.

architecture—The manner in which the most important classes in a program relate to each other.

argument—A value that is copied to a corresponding parameter when a method or constructor is called.

assertion—A test that the programmer believes will always be `true` at a particular point in the code.

assignment statement—A statement that gives a new value to a variable on the left side of an equal sign (=).

attribute—An item of information encapsulated in a software object. *See also* instance variable.

avenue—A road on which robots may travel north or south. *See also* road, street.

AWT—*See* Abstract Window Toolkit.

blank final—An instance variable declared to be `final` but not given an initial value until the constructor is executed.

block—1. The statements contained between a matched pair of curly braces. 2. To wait for user input.

body—The statements controlled by the test in an `if` statement or a looping statement.

Boolean expression—An expression that evaluates to either `true` or `false`.

bottom factoring—To remove statements common to both clauses of an `if-else` statement and place them after the `if-else` statement.

bottom-up design—A design methodology that uses available resources to design a solution to a problem. *See also* top-down design.

bottom-up implementation—Implementing a program beginning with methods that perform relatively simple tasks and using them to build more complex methods. *See also* top-down implementation.

bounding box—The smallest rectangle that will enclose a shape drawn on a screen.

breakpoint—An identified place in the source code for a debugger to temporarily stop execution.

buffering—Collecting information until it can all be dealt with at once. Commonly used to improve performance in input and output operations.

bug—A defect in a program.

byte code—An encoding of a program that is more easily executed by a computer than source code. A Java compiler translates source code into byte code.

byte stream—An input or output stream that carries information encoded in binary and is generally not human readable. *See also* character stream, stream.

cascading-`if`—A sequence of `if-else` statements formatted to emphasize that at most, one of several clauses will be executed.

cast—Explicitly converting a value from one primitive type to another compatible type. Also used to assign an object reference to a variable with a more specific type.

character stream—An input or output stream that carries information encoded as characters and is generally human readable. *See also* byte stream, stream.

checked exception—An exception that is checked by the compiler to verify that it is either caught with a `try-catch` statement or declared to be thrown with a `throws` clause. *See also* exception, unchecked exception.

class—The source code that defines one or more objects that offer the same services and have the same attributes (but not necessarily the same attribute values).

class diagram—A graphical representation of one or more classes that show their attributes, services, and relationships with other classes.

class variable—A variable that is shared by all instances of a class. Also called a static variable. *See also* instance variable, parameter variable, temporary variable.

classpath—A list of one or more file paths where the Java system looks for the compiled classes used in a program.

client—An object that uses the services of another object, called the server.

close—To indicate that a program is finished using a file so that resources can be released.

closed for modification—The idea that a mature class should be extended rather than modified when changes or enhancements are needed. *See also* open for extension.

cohesion—The extent to which each class models a single, well-defined abstraction and each method implements a single, well-defined task.

collaborator—A class that works with another class to accomplish some task.

color chooser—A graphical user interface component designed to help a user choose a color.

column-major order—A 2D array algorithm that accesses the array such that the column changes more slowly than the row. *See also* row-major order.

command—A service that changes the state of an object or otherwise carries out some action. *See also* query, service.

command interpreter—A program that repeatedly accepts a textual command from a user and then interprets or executes the command.

comment—An annotation in the source code intended for human readers. Comments do not affect the execution of the program.

comment out code—To put code inside comments so that it is no longer executed when the program is run.

comparison operator—The operators used to compare the magnitude of two values: <, <=, ==, !=, >=, and >.

compile—To translate source code into a format more easily executed by a computer, such as byte code.

compiler—A computer program that compiles or translates source code into a format more easily executed by a computer.

compile-time error—A programming error that is found when the program is compiled. *See also* intent error, run-time error.

component—An object such as a button or text box that is designed to be used as part of a graphical user interface.

composition—A relationship between two classes in which one holds a reference to the other in an instance variable. *Also known as* has-a.

concatenation—Joining two strings to form a new string.

concept map—A diagram that uses labeled arrows to connect concepts, represented by a few words.

concrete class—A class that implements the abstract methods named in its superclasses or the methods named in an interface. *See also* abstract class.

console—A window used by a program to communicate with a person using printed characters on lines that appear one after another.

constant—A meaningful name given to a value that does not change.

constraint—An object limiting how a user interface component may be positioned.

constructor—A service provided by a class to construct or instantiate objects belonging to that class.

content pane—The part of a frame designed to display the components of a user interface.

contract—An agreement specifying what client and server objects can each expect from each other.

control characters—Character codes used to control a terminal or printer. Examples include the newline and tab characters.

controller—The part of the Model-View-Controller pattern responsible for gathering input from the user and using it to modify the model. *See also* model, view.

correct—A description of a program that meets its specification.

count-down loop—A loop controlled by a counter variable that is decremented until it reaches zero.

coupling—The extent to which the interactions between classes are minimized.

CRC card—A piece of paper recording the class name, responsibilities, and collaborators for one class during a program's walk-through. CRC is an abbreviation for Classes, Responsibilities, and Collaborators. *See also* walk-through.

cursor—A marker that divides a program's input into the part that has already been read and the part that has not yet been read. Also used to refer to an insertion point.

dangling `else`—A combination of `if` statements and an `else`-clause where it is unclear to which `if` statement the `else` clause belongs.

data acquisition methods—Methods used to obtain data from an input stream, such as the `Scanner` class. *See also* data availability methods.

data availability methods—Queries used to detect the kind of data available to be read from an input stream, such as the `Scanner` class. *See also* data acquisition methods.

debug—The process of removing bugs from a program.

debugger—A tool used to help debug programs by stopping the program's execution at designated points, executing the program one statement at a time, and showing the values of the program's variables.

declaration statement—A statement that introduces a new variable into a program.

deep copy—A copy of an object that also copies any objects to which it refers. *See also* shallow copy.

delimiter—A value such as a space or colon that separates other values or groups of values.

design by contract—A method for designing a program by consistently specifying the preconditions and postconditions of each method and invariants on classes as a whole.

detail—An informal term referring to an instance variable or a method.

development cycle—Steps that are repeated while implementing a program, including choosing scenarios, writing code to implement them, testing the result with users, and possibly updating the program's design. One part of a larger development process. *See also* development process.

development process—A process to direct the design and implementation of a program.

documentation comment—A comment designed to be extracted from the source code and used as reference material.

easy to learn—One of five criteria used to evaluate user interfaces. In particular, how well the program supports users learning to use it as well as those deepening their understanding of it. *See also* five Es.

effective—One of five criteria used to evaluate user interfaces. In particular, the completeness and accuracy with which users achieve their goals for using the program. *See also* five Es.

efficient—1. One of five criteria used to evaluate user interfaces. In particular, the speed and accuracy with which users complete tasks while using the program. *See also* five Es. 2. Solving a problem without wasting such resources as memory or time.

element—One item in a collection.

`else` clause—The part of an `if` statement that is executed if the Boolean expression is `false`.

encapsulation—Containing an object's attributes within itself, allowing access to them only via the object's public services.

engaging—One of five criteria used to evaluate user interfaces. In particular, the degree to which the program is pleasant or satisfying to use. *See also* five Es.

enumerated type—A reference type that has a programmer-defined set of values.

enumeration—*See* enumerated type.

equivalence—*See* object equality.

error tolerant—One of five criteria used to evaluate user interfaces. In particular, the degree to which the program prevents errors and facilitates recovery from those that do occur. *See also* five Es.

escape sequence—An alternative means of writing characters that are normally used for another purpose. For example, `\"` to include a double quote in a string.

evaluate—The process of calculating the value of an expression.

evaluation diagram—A diagram showing how an expression is evaluated.

event—An action in the user interface to which the program must respond.

event object—An object containing information about one event.

exception—A type of error message that includes information about how the program arrived at the point at which the error occurred. *See also* checked exception, unchecked exception.

exponent—The part of a number expressed in scientific notation that indicates how far and in which direction the decimal point should be shifted. *See also* mantissa, scientific notation.

expression—A combination of operators and operands that can be evaluated to produce a single value.

extend—To create a new class based on an existing class.

extension—The part of a file's name following the last period and used to indicate the kind of information contained in the file.

factory method—A method that creates and returns an object. Sometimes used as an alternative to a constructor.

field—One item of identifiable information in a record. *See also* record.

file—A place, usually on a disk drive, where information is stored.

file format—The design for how information is organized in a particular file.

final situation—A description of the desired state of a city and all that it contains, including robots, when a program ends. *See also* initial situation.

five Es—Five criteria used to evaluate the quality of user interfaces. *See also* easy to learn, effective, efficient, engaging, error tolerant.

floating point—A computer's internal representation of a number with a decimal point.

flow of control—One sequence of statements, each of which executes completely before the next begins. A program may have several flows of control, each of which is called a thread. *See also* thread.

flowchart—A diagram illustrating the different paths a program may take through a code fragment.

foreach—A variety of `for` loop that accesses each member of a collection one at a time.

format specifier—A code embedded in a format string specifying how one particular value should be formatted when output. *See also* format string.

format string—A string containing one or more format specifiers used to format output.

frame—A window appearing on a computer screen.

garbage—An object that does not have variables referencing it and therefore cannot be used.

garbage collection—The process of removing objects that can no longer be used by a program. *See also* garbage.

graphical user interface—A user interface with a visual representation that sends events to a program. The events are generated via user interaction with input devices such as a mouse or keyboard, and components drawn on the screen such as buttons or text boxes. *See also* event.

hang—A program behaving abnormally such that it does not respond to input and does not complete its execution.

has-a—*See* composition.

hashing—A technique for storing elements of a collection based on a hashcode. Used by some collection classes, such as `HashMap`.

helper method—A method that exists primarily to simplify another method.

high-fidelity prototype—A preliminary version of a program used for evaluation that may perform many of the functions expected in the final program. *See also* low-fidelity prototype, prototype.

host name—The name of a computer connected to the Internet.

identifier—A name for a part of a program, such as a class, a variable, or a method.

immutable—Immutable objects cannot be changed after they are created. *See also* mutable.

implicit parameter—A reference to the object used to call a method. May be accessed within the method with the keyword `this`.

index—The position of one element within an ordered collection, such as an array, a string, or an `ArrayList`.

infinite loop—A loop that lacks a way to affect the termination condition, resulting in its indefinite execution.

infinite recursion—A situation in which a method calls itself repeatedly with no provision for avoiding another call to itself.

information hiding—Hiding and protecting the details of a classes' operation from others.

inherit—To receive capabilities from another class because of a superclass-subclass relationship. The relationship between the classes is sometimes described with the term "is-a." *See also* extend.

inheritance hierarchy—The relationship of several classes that inherit from a common superclass. *See also* inherit.

initial value—The first value a variable is assigned.

initial situation—A description of the desired state of a city and all that it contains, including robots, when a program begins. *See also* final situation.

inner class—A class definition that is contained within the definition of another class, allowing it to access the outer classes' private methods and instance variables.

input—Information that is obtained from outside the program—for example, from the person running the program.

input stream—A stream that carries information from a source to a program. *See also* output stream, source, stream.

insertion point—The point on the console or in a user interface component where the next character typed by the user will appear.

instance—Each object is one instance of a class.

instance variable—A variable that is specific to an object. *See also* class variable, parameter variable, temporary variable.

instantiate—The act of constructing an instance of a class—that is, creating an object.

integer division—Division of an integer by another integer where any remainder or fractional part in the answer is discarded.

intent error—An error in which the program does not produce the desired results, even though it compiles correctly and does not generate run-time errors. *See also* compile-time error, run-time error.

interaction—An informal term referring to a method calling another method or using an instance variable. *See also* detail.

interface—A Java construct listing a set of methods. It is used to define a new type and also to specify that a class belongs to that type because it implements all of the methods listed by the interface.

invoke—To cause an object to perform a specific service.

I/O—An abbreviation for input and output.

IP address—The address of a computer on the Internet.

is-a—*See* inherit.

java archive (jar) file—A single file containing many compiled classes, making the classes easier to distribute.

javadoc comment—*See* documentation comment.

key—A value used to uniquely identify another value.

keyboard focus—A property of at most one component in a user interface, the component that will receive input from the keyboard.

keyword—The words defined by the language to have special meaning and that cannot be used as identifiers. Examples include `class`, `while`, and `int`. Also called a reserved word.

layout—The act of arranging components in a graphical user interface.

layout managers—An object that manages the layout of components in a graphical user interface.

left justified—Elements (typically lines of text) that are aligned vertically on the left side. *See also* right justified.

lexicographic order—Ordering strings by comparing their individual characters.

library—A collection of resources available to be used in many different programs. *See also* package.

lifeline—A part of a sequence diagram that shows the lifetime of an object.

lifetime—The time in which values are preserved in a variable before they are destroyed by either the object containing them being garbage-collected or the variable going out of scope.

list—An ordered collection of elements, perhaps with duplicates. *See also* map, set.

listener—An object registered with a component that responds to events generated by the component.

local variable—*See* temporary variable.

logic error—*See* intent error.

logical negation operator—The operator `!`. It negates the Boolean expression following it. *See also* negate.

loop—A statement that repeats the statements it controls. A `while` statement is a form of loop.

loop-and-a-half—A loop that must execute part of its body one more time than the rest of the body. Typically implemented with duplicate code before or after a `while` loop or with a `while-true` loop.

low-fidelity prototype—A model of a program used for evaluation purposes that only approximates the final design, perhaps using paper and pencil. *See also* high-fidelity prototype, prototype.

mantissa—The fractional portion of a number expressed in scientific notation. *See also* exponent, scientific notation.

map—An object storing a collection of objects, each identified by a key. *See also* key, list, set.

memory—Part of the computer hardware that stores information, such as variables and program instructions.

message—A client object sends a message to a server object to invoke one of its services.

method—The source code that implements a specific service.

method resolution—The process of determining the correct method to execute in response to a method call.

mixin—A type, defined by an interface, that supplements the primary type of a class.

model—1. A simplified description of a problem, usually in a formal notation such as mathematics or a computer program, that enables people to forecast the future, make decisions, or otherwise solve the problem. 2. The part of the Model-View-Controller pattern that models or abstracts a problem. 3. To create a simplified description of something to help us make decisions, predict future events, or maintain relevant information.

multi-line comment—A comment that may span multiple lines. It begins with `/*` and ends with `*/`. *See also* comment, documentation comment.

multiplicity—The notation on arrows in a class diagram indicating how many instances of a class are used by an object.

mutable—A mutable object can be changed after it has been created. *See also* immutable.

natural language—Language used in everyday speech.

negate—To make a Boolean expression return the opposite value.

nest—To place a control statement such as `if` or `while` within another control statement.

nested loop—A loop that occurs within another loop.

newline character—A character that divides two lines of text. It can be represented in a string with the character sequence '\n'.

null—A special value that can be assigned to any object reference, meaning it does not refer to any object.

object diagram—A diagram that shows one or more specific objects and the values of their attributes.

object equality—Tested with the `equals` method. Establishes whether two object references refer to objects that are equivalent. *See also* object identity.

object identity—Tested with ==. Establishes whether two object references refer to the same object. *See also* object equality.

object-oriented programming language—A computer programming language incorporating the ideas of encapsulation, inheritance, and polymorphism.

open—Preparing a file for input or output.

open for extension—A class that is written in such a way that it can be modified through inheritance. *See also* extend, inherit.

operand—The value, variable, or query on which an operation is to be done. *See also* operator.

operator—A symbol denoting an operation, such as addition or division, to be performed on its operands. *See also* operand.

or—A logical connector written in Java as `||`. The result is `true` if and only if at least one of the operands is `true`.

origin—The place from which measurement begins. In a robot city, the intersection of street 0 and avenue 0. On a computer screen, the upper-left corner.

output—Information that is produced by a program and displayed on a screen or written to a file.

output stream—A stream that carries information from a program to a sink or destination. *See also* input stream, sink, stream.

overload—Two or more methods with the same name but different signatures are overloaded. The Java system chooses which one to execute based on the actual parameters used when the method is called. *See also* signature.

override—Replacing a method in the class being extended with a new version of the method.

package—A group of classes, usually organized around a common purpose.

parameter variable—A type of variable used to communicate a value to a constructor or service to use in accomplishing its purpose. *See also* class variable, instance variable, temporary variable.

partially filled array—An array that uses the elements with indices 0..n-1 to store values, where $n \le s$, the size of the array. n is stored in an auxiliary variable.

picture element—A small dot displayed on a computer screen. Many picture elements compose the image displayed. Often abbreviated as "pixel."

pixel—*See* picture element.

point—A unit of measurement, used for fonts, equal to 1/72 of an inch.

polymorphism—Setting up two or more classes so that objects can be sent the same message but respond to the message differently—that is, in ways appropriate to the kind of object receiving the message.

postcondition—A statement of what should be true after a method executes. *See also* precondition.

precedence—A rule that determines which operations are done first when an expression is evaluated.

precision—The closeness of the approximation between a value stored in the computer and the actual value.

precondition—A situation that must be true when a method is called to ensure that it executes correctly. *See also* postcondition.

predicate—1. A query (method) that returns a value of either `true` or `false`. 2. The part of a sentence that contains a verb and explains the action or the condition of the subject. *See also* subject.

primary key—When sorting records, the primary key is the most important determinant of the order. *See also* secondary key.

primitive—The most basic available methods out of which more complex methods are built.

primitive type—A type whose values can be manipulated directly by the underlying hardware. In Java, they include `int`, `double`, and `boolean`. *See also* reference type.

processing stream—A stream that processes information as it flows from a source to a sink. *See also* provider stream, stream.

program—A detailed set of computer instructions designed to solve a problem.

prompt—An indication to the user that some action is required. A prompt is usually printed on the screen just before input is required from the user.

prototype—A preliminary version of a program used for evaluation or learning purposes. *See also* high-fidelity prototype, low-fidelity prototype.

provider stream—A stream that provides information from a source or to a sink. *See also* processing stream, sink, source, stream.

pseudocode—A blend of a natural language and a programming language, allowing people to think more rigorously about programs without worrying about programming language details.

query—A service or method that answers a question. *See also* command, method, service.

random access—A property of an information collection where every item can be accessed as easily and as fast as every other item.

range—The number of different values belonging to a type such as `int` or `double`.

read—Obtaining input from a file or other input stream.

record—A collection of information pertaining to one thing (for example, an employee) in a file that typically contains information about many of those things. *See also* field.

refactor—The process of modifying a program to improve its overall quality without changing its functionality.

reference—The information stored in a variable that refers or leads to a specific object.

reference type—A type whose values are defined by a class or an interface. *See also* primitive type.

reference variable—A variable that refers to an object or contains `null`.

register—Adding an object to a list of objects that should be notified when certain events occur.

relative path—A sequence of directories that gives a file location relative to the current working directory. *See also* absolute path, working directory.

reliability—A characteristic of quality programs in which the program does not crash, lose, or corrupt data, and is consistent in how it operates.

remainder operator—An operator that returns the remainder or part that is left after dividing one integer by another. *See also* integer division.

requirements—A written statement of what a program is supposed to do. *Also called* specifications.

reserved word—*See* keyword.

responsibility—The things a class must do to support the operation of the program. Identified during the design of the program.

return—The action of going back to the statement that called the currently executing method. If the method is a query, it also provides a value to the expression from which it was called.

return type—The type of the value returned by a query. Specified just before the method's name when it is declared.

right justified—Elements (typically lines of text) that are aligned vertically on the right side. *See also* left-justified.

road—A street or an avenue on which a robot may move between intersections. *See also* avenue, street.

row-major order—A 2D array algorithm that accesses the array such that the row changes more slowly than the column. *See also* column-major order.

run-time error—An error detected when a program executes or runs because it has executed an instruction in an illegal context. *See also* compile-time error, intent error.

scenario—A specific task that a user may want to perform with the program. *Also known as* use case.

scientific notation—A number expressed as the multiplication of a fractional number (the mantissa) and 10 raised to some power (the exponent). *See also* exponent, mantissa.

scope—That part of a program where an identifier is available for use.

search—The process of attempting to locate one value in a collection of values.

secondary key—When sorting records, the secondary key is used to determine the order of records that have equal primary keys. *See also* primary key.

self-documenting code—Code that is written to minimize the need for documentation. Well-chosen identifiers are the key tool used in writing self-documenting code.

semantics—The meaning of a statement. *See also* syntax.

sequence diagram—A diagram showing the sequence of activities among cooperating objects.

serif—Short lines at the end of each stroke of a printed letter.

server—An object that provides services to a client object. *See also* client.

service—An action that an object performs in response to a message. Services are subdivided into queries and commands. *See also* command, message, method, query.

set—An unordered collection of unique objects. *See also* list, map.

shallow copy—A copy of an object that does not copy any objects it references. *See also* deep copy.

short-circuit evaluation—Evaluating a Boolean expression so that sub-expressions that cannot affect the result are not evaluated.

side effect—A change in state caused by executing a method.

signature—The name of a method, together with an ordered list of all the types of its parameters.

simulate—*See* trace.

single-line comment—A comment extending from a double slash (//) until the end of the line. *See also* multiline comment, documentation comment.

sink—The destination for information flowing in a stream. *See also* source, stream.

software object—An abstraction in an object-oriented program used to model a real-world entity.

source—The origin of information that flows in a stream. *See also* sink, stream.

source code—The words and symbols written by programmers to instruct a computer what to do.

spaghetti code—A derisive description of source code written with undisciplined use of a `goto` construct (which Java does not have). *See also* structured programming.

special symbols—Symbols that have a special meaning in the Java language, including braces, parentheses, and the period and semicolon characters.

specification—*See* requirements.

stack trace—An ordered list of which methods called which methods, extending from the point an exception is thrown back to the `main` method.

state—The state of being of an object as defined by the contents of its attributes.

state change diagram—A diagram that shows how an object's state changes over time.

statement—An individual instruction in a programming language.

static variable—*See* class variable.

stepwise refinement—A method of writing programs where each method is defined in terms of helper methods, each of which implement one logical step in solving the problem. *Also known as* top-down design.

Strategy pattern—A pattern where one object uses another object that defines one algorithm from a family of algorithms, making it easy to change the behavior of the first object.

stream—An ordered collection of information that moves from a source to a destination or sink. *See also* byte stream, character stream, input stream, output stream, processing stream, provider stream.

street—A road on which robots may travel east or west. *See also* avenue, road.

structured programming—A programming discipline that restricts how flow of control can be shifted from one part of the program to another. *See also* spaghetti code.

stub—A method that has just enough code to compile, but not enough to actually do its job.

subclass—A class that receives part of its functionality from a superclass. *See also* extend, inherit, superclass.

subject—The part of a sentence that says who or what did the action. *See also* predicate.

substitution principle—A key principle underlying polymorphism where an object of one type, *A*, can substitute for an object of another type, *B*, if *A* can be used anyplace that *B* can be used. *See also* polymorphism.

superclass—A class that has been extended to create a subclass. *See also* extend, inherit, subclass.

Swing—A newer addition to the collection of classes available to write graphical user interfaces in Java. *See also* Abstract Window Toolkit.

syntax—The form of a statement. *See also* semantics.

tab stop—A predefined location where the insertion point will be located after a tab is inserted into text.

tag—A keyword such as `@param` or `@author` used to identify standardized information in documentation comments. *See also* documentation comment.

template method—A method implementing the common part of a problem that has several variations. The differences between the variations are expressed in helper methods contained in subclasses.

temporary variable—A variable defined within a method. The variable and the information it contains are discarded when the method finishes execution. *See also* class variable, instance variable, parameter variable.

test harness—A program used to test a method or class.

`then` clause—The statements that are executed when the test in an `if` statement is `true`.

thread—A sequence of statements that executes independently of other sequences of statements. The execution of two or more threads may be interleaved. *See also* flow of control.

throw—The action of interrupting the normal execution of a program with an exception.

token—A group of characters separated by delimiters. *See also* delimiter.

top factor—The process of removing redundant statements from the beginning of both clauses in an `if` statement.

top-down design—Designing a program or a method by dividing it into logical pieces that work together. These pieces are themselves designed using top-down design. This process continues until a piece is so simple that it can be solved without dividing it. *See also* stepwise refinement, top-down implementation.

top-down implementation—Implementing a method by writing it in terms of helper methods. Helper methods may also be defined in terms of other helper methods. Eventually, each helper method will be simple enough to implement using existing methods or without using helper methods. *See also* bottom-up implementation, top-down design.

trace—To execute a program without the aid of a computer, usually by recording state changes in a table. Also called simulate.

type—A designation of the valid values for a variable or parameter.

unchecked exception—An exception that the compiler does not require to be caught with a `try-catch` statement or declared to be thrown with a `throws` clause. Used for errors from which recovery should generally not be attempted. *See also* checked exception, exception.

Unicode—A character encoding standard that allows up to 65,536 different characters to be defined.

usability—A criteria of a program's quality from a user's perspective, determined by the effort required to learn, operate, prepare input, and interpret output when compared to the alternatives.

use case—*See* scenario.

validation—Determining if the intent of a program or program fragment is correct. *See also* verification.

value—One item of information stored in a map collection that is identified by a key. *See also* map.

variable—A named place where a program can store information. *See also* instance variable, parameter variable, temporary variable.

variable declaration—A programming language statement that introduces a variable in the source code and specifies its type.

verification—Determining if a program or program fragment correctly implements the intended functionality. *See also* validation.

view—The part of the Model-View-Controller pattern that displays relevant information from the model to the user. *See also* controller, model.

walk-through—The process of simulating the execution of a program using other people, each of which takes on the role of one or more classes.

wall—An element of a robot's environment that it cannot move through.

waterfall model—A development process in which the output of one phase is the input to another phase. The waterfall model does not explicitly include iteration. *See also* development process.

whitespace—Characters such as spaces and tabs that appear as white space when printed on paper.

working directory—An executing program's default directory. Files are read and written in the working directory unless their name includes an absolute or relative path.

wrapper class—A class whose only variable is a primitive, such as `int` or `double`. Such classes exist so that a primitive value can be treated as an object.

write—The process of placing information in a file. *See also* read.

Appendix B Precedence Rules

Precedence rules establish the order of operations when an expression is evaluated. For example, in 3 + 4 * 4, is the answer 19 or 28? It depends on whether you multiply or add first. Normal precedence rules dictate that multiplication is done before addition. Precedence can be overridden using parentheses. For example, (3 + 4) * 4 means that the addition should be performed before the multiplication, yielding 28.

Precedence of Java Operators

Table B-1 lists all of the Java operators in order from the highest precedence (operators that are used first) to the lowest (operators that are used last). Sometimes different operators have the same precedence. In this case, they are listed in indented groups. For example, all of the multiplicative operators (`*`, `/`, `%`) have the same precedence.

When two operators with the same precedence appear together, the operators are performed left to right. That is, 3 * 4 / 6 is the same as (3 * 4) / 6. The only exception is assignment. It is valid to write `a = b = c`, which means assign `c` to `b` and then assign `b` to `a`. This style is not used in this book.

Some of these operators are beyond the scope of an introductory text and are marked with an asterisk (*) on the right.

(table B-1) *Precedence of Java operators*

Operator	Syntax
Postfix operators	
Array access	«*arrayName*»[«*index*»]
Member access	«*object_or_class*».«*memberName*»
Parameter evaluation	«*methodName*»(«*parameterList*»)
Postfix increment	«*variable*»++
Postfix decrement	«*variable*»--
Unary operators	
Prefix increment	++«*variable*»
Prefix decrement	--«*variable*»
Unary plus	+«*expr*»

(table B-1) ***continued***

Precedence of Java operators

Operator	Syntax	
Unary minus	-«expr»	
Bitwise complement	~«expr»	*
Logical negation	!«expr»	
Creation and cast		
Object creation	new «className»	
Cast	(«type»)«expr»	
Multiplicative operators		
Multiplication	«expr» * «expr»	
Division	«expr» / «expr»	
Remainder	«expr» % «expr»	
Additive operators		
Addition	«expr» + «expr»	
Subtraction	«expr» - «expr»	
Bit shift operators		
Left shift (propagate sign)	«expr» << «expr»	*
Right shift (propagate sign)	«expr» >> «expr»	*
Right shift (propagate zero)	«expr» >>> «expr»	*
Relational operators		
Less than	«expr» < «expr»	
Less than or equal to	«expr» <= «expr»	
Greater than	«expr» > «expr»	
Greater than or equal to	«expr» >= «expr»	
Class membership	«object» instanceof «className»	
Equality operators		
Equals	«expr» == «expr»	
Not equals	«expr» != «expr»	
Bitwise AND operator	«expr» & «expr»	*
Bitwise exclusive OR operator	«expr» ^ «expr»	*
Bitwise inclusive OR operator	«expr» | «expr»	*
Logical AND operator	«expr» && «expr»	

(table B-1) *continued*

Precedence of Java operators

Operator	Syntax	
Logical OR operator	*«expr»* || *«expr»*	
Conditional	*«expr»* ? *«expr»* : *«expr»*	*
Assignment		
	«var» = *«expr»*	
	«var» += *«expr»*	
	«var» -= *«expr»*	
	«var» *= *«expr»*	
	«var» /= *«expr»*	
	«var» %= *«expr»*	
	«var» >>= *«expr»*	*
	«var» <<= *«expr»*	*
	«var» >>>= *«expr»*	*
	«var» &= *«expr»*	*
	«var» ^= *«expr»*	*
	«var» |= *«expr»*	*

Appendix C Variable Initialization Rules

Variables always have a value. Initialization guarantees that a variable has a known starting value. Without a known starting value, it is hard to have confidence in the correctness of any computations done with the variable. This brief appendix outlines the rules governing the initialization of instance variables, temporary variables, and parameter variables.

Instance and Class Variables

Instance and class variables are always given an initial value, either explicitly by the programmer or implicitly by the compiler. Implicit initializations by the compiler depend on the variable's type, as shown in Table C-1.

(table C-1) *Implicit variable initialization values*

Type	Implicit Initial Value
`byte, short, int, long`	`0`
`boolean`	`false`
`char`	`'\0000'`
`float`	`+0.0f`
`double`	`+0.0`
object reference (including `String`)	`null`

Temporary Variables

Temporary variables are *not* given an initial value by the compiler. The compiler attempts to verify that each temporary variable is initialized before it is used. If the compiler is unable to verify this property, it will issue a compile-time error.

Parameter Variables

Parameter variables are initialized by the corresponding actual parameter in the method's call.

Appendix D

Unicode Character Set

Fundamentally, computers simply store and manipulate numbers. Text can be processed because each character is assigned a number. The computer manipulates numbers but prints them as characters.

This appendix is about the assignment of characters to their numerical equivalents.

Understanding Encoding

Many children have played some sort of spy game that involved encoding secret messages. The encoding is usually something like this:

A	B	C	D	E	F	G	H	I	J	K	L	M	N	O	P	Q	R	S	T	U	V	W	X	Y	Z
J	H	Q	S	I	A	R	Z	X	B	D	N	C	O	W	M	T	P	F	U	Y	G	K	L	V	E

The message "GO TO THE HIDEOUT" is encoded by looking up "G" in the top row and writing down "R", the letter beneath it; then looking up "O" and writing down "W"; and so on. The entire encoded message would be "RW UW UZI ZXSIWYU". Someone receiving the coded message could perform the reverse operation to recover the original message.

The computer uses a similar encoding, except it matches letters with numbers:

A	B	C	D	E	F	G	H	I	J	K	L	M	N	O	P	...
65	66	67	68	69	70	71	72	73	74	75	76	77	78	79	80	...

When we type "GO TO THE HIDEOUT" into a program, the computer encodes it as 71 79 32 84 79 32 84 72 69 32 72 73 68 69 79 85 84. The spaces in the original message are encoded as 32. When it is time to print a message using, for example, `System.out.println`, the computer looks up the number 71 to discover it should display dots in the shape of "G".

Encoding Characters

A simple program that reads a line of text and displays the corresponding numeric encoding is shown in Listing D-1.

FIND THE CODE

appendices/charCodes/

Listing D-1: *A program to translate a line of text into the equivalent numeric codes*

```
import java.util.Scanner;

/** Translate characters into their integer equivalents.
 *
 * @author Byron Weber Becker */
public class CharacterCodes extends Object
{
  public static void main(String[ ] args)
  {
    System.out.println("Type a line of text to show the Unicode encoding.");
    System.out.println("Type \"quit\" to end.");

    Scanner in = new Scanner(System.in);
    while (true)
    { System.out.print("> ");
      String input = in.nextLine();

      if (input.equals("quit"))
      { break;
      }

      for (int i = 0; i < input.length(); i++)
      { char asChar = input.charAt(i);
        int asInt = input.charAt(i);
        System.out.println("" + asChar + "  (" + asInt + ")");
      }
    }

  }
}
```

The most common encodings correspond to the ASCII character set, one of the earliest standards. They represent the character encodings from the number 0 up to 127 and are shown in Table D-1.

(table D-1)

ASCII character set

decimal	char	decimal	char	decimal	char	decimal	char
0	NUL	32	Space	64	@	96	`
1	SOH	33	!	65	A	97	a
2	STX	34	"	66	B	98	b
3	ETX	35	#	67	C	99	c
4	EOT	36	$	68	D	100	d
5	ENQ	37	%	69	E	101	e
6	ACK	38	&	70	F	102	f
7	BEL	39	'	71	G	103	g
8	BS	40	(	72	H	104	h
9	TAB	41	)	73	I	105	i
10	LF	42	*	74	J	106	j
11	VT	43	+	75	K	107	k
12	FF	44	,	76	L	108	l
13	CR	45	-	77	M	109	m
14	SO	46	.	78	N	110	n
15	SI	47	/	79	O	111	o
16	DLE	48	0	80	P	112	p
17	DC1	49	1	81	Q	113	q
18	DC2	50	2	82	R	114	r
19	DC3	51	3	83	S	115	s
20	DC4	52	4	84	T	116	t
21	NAK	53	5	85	U	117	u
22	SYN	54	6	86	V	118	v
23	ETB	55	7	87	W	119	w
24	CAN	56	8	88	X	120	x
25	EM	57	9	89	Y	121	y
26	SUB	58	:	90	Z	122	z
27	ESC	59	;	91	[	123	{
28	FS	60	<	92	\	124	|
29	GS	61	=	93	]	125	}
30	RS	62	>	94	^	126	~
31	US	63	?	95	_	127	DEL

The first column of the table contains **control characters.** One of the main uses for these characters is to control some types of printers. If the character `CR` (carriage return) was sent to the printer, the print head would return to the beginning of the line. The `LF` character (line feed) moves the paper up one line.

Some of the control characters are still used and have escape sequences so they can be easily inserted into a string. These are shown in Table D-2.

(table D-2)

Escape sequences for selected control characters

Escape Sequence	Description	Escape Sequence	Description
`\n`	newline (`LF`)	`\r`	return (`CR`)
`\b`	backspace (`BS`)	`\\`	backslash
`\f`	form feed (`FF`)	`\'`	single quote
`\t`	tab (`TAB`)	`\"`	double quote

The last three exist so that we can insert the backslash, single quote, and double quote into strings. For example, if you really did want to print a backslash followed by the character `n`, you couldn't simply write:

```
System.out.println("\n");
```

because that would print a newline character. Instead, you would need to write

```
System.out.println("\\n");
```

The `\\` is interpreted as a single backslash character. The `n` is considered as just the letter `n`.

Appendix E Selected Robot Documentation

The `becker` library that accompanies this book includes many methods, particularly those related to robots and the cities they inhabit. Full documentation is available on the Web at *www.learningwithrobots.com/doc*. For the times that a computer isn't available, a briefer form of the documentation is printed below.

City

```
public class City extends java.lang.Object
```

A `City` contains intersections joined by streets and avenues. `Intersections` may contain `Things` such as `Walls`, `Streetlights`, and `Flashers`, as well as `Robots`.

Constructor Summary

```
City()
```

Construct a new `City` using the defaults stored in the `becker.robots.ini` file.

```
City(int numVisibleStreets, int numVisibleAvenues)
```

Construct a new `City` that displays streets 0 through `numVisibleStreets` – 1 and avenues 0 through `numVisibleAvenues` – 1.

```
City(int firstVisibleStreet, int firstVisibleAvenue,
     int numVisibleStreets, int numVisibleAvenues)
```

Construct a new `City` that displays streets `firstVisibleStreet` through `numVisibleStreets` – 1 and avenues `firstVisibleAvenue` through `numVisibleAvenues` – 1.

```
City(String fileName)
```

Construct a new `City` by reading information to construct it from a file.

```
City(java.util.Scanner in)
```

Construct a new `City` by reading information to construct it from a file.

Method Summary

`protected void customizeIntersection(Intersection intersection)`

Customize an `Intersection`, perhaps by adding `Things` to it.

`IIterate<Light> examineLights()`

Examine all the `Light` objects in this `City`, one at a time.

`IIterate<Robot> examineRobots()`

Examine all the `Robot` objects in this `City`, one at a time.

`IIterate<Thing> examineThings()`

Examine all the `Thing` objects in this `City`, one at a time.

`IIterate<Thing> examineThings(IPredicate aPredicate)`

Examine all the `Thing` objects in this `City` that match `aPredicate`, one at a time.

`protected Intersection getIntersection(int avenue, int street)`

Obtain a reference to a specified `Intersection` within this `City`.

`boolean isShowingThingCounts()`

Is this `City` showing the number of `Things` on each `Intersection`?

`protected void keyTyped(char key)`

This method is called when this `City`'s display has the focus and a key is typed.

`protected Intersection makeIntersection(int avenue, int street)`

Make an `Intersection` that will appear at the specified avenue and street.

`void save(String indent, java.io.PrintWriter out)`

Save a representation of this `City` to a file for later use.

`void setFrameTitle(String title)`

Set the title of the implicitly created frame, if there is one.

`void setSize(int width, int height)`

Set the size of the implicitly created frame, if there is one.

`void setThingCountPredicate(Predicate pred)`

Set the predicate for what kinds of `Things` to count when showing the number of `Things` on each `Intersection`.

`void showFrame(boolean show)`

Should this `City` be shown in a frame? The default is to show it.

`void showThingCounts(boolean show)`

Show the number of `Things` on each `Intersection`, counted according to the predicate set with the method `setThingCountPredicate`.

Direction

`public enum Direction`

Constants that define directions within a `City`.

Field Summary

```
public static int EAST
public static int NORTH
public static int WEST
public static int SOUTH
```

Method Summary

`Direction left()`

Which `Direction` is left of this `Direction`?

`Direction right()`

Which `Direction` is right of this `Direction`?

`Direction opposite()`

Which `Direction` is opposite of this `Direction`?

Flasher

`public class Flasher extends Light`

A `Flasher` is commonly used to mark construction hazards on streets and avenues. `Flashers` are small enough for a `Robot` to pick up and carry. They do not obstruct the movement of `Robots`. Like all `Lights`, they can be turned on and off. Unlike some kinds of `Lights`, when `Flashers` are "on," their lights cycle on and off. When `Flashers` are turned "off," their lights stay off.

Constructor Summary

`Flasher(City aCity, int aStreet, int anAvenue)`

Construct a new `Flasher`, initially turned off.

`Flasher(City aCity, int aStreet, int anAvenue, boolean isOn)`

Construct a new `Flasher`.

`Flasher(Robot heldBy)`

Construct a new `Flasher` held by a `Robot`.

Method Summary

`protected void save(String indent, java.io.PrintWriter out)`

Save a representation of this `Flasher` to an output stream.

`void turnOff()`

Turn the `Flasher` off.

`void turnOn()`

Turn the `Flasher` on so that it begins to flash.

Intersection

`public class Intersection extends Sim implements ILabel`

Karel the Robot lives in a city composed of intersections connected by roads. Roads that run north and south (up and down) are called "Avenues" and roads that run east and west are called "Streets."

`Intersections` may contain `Things` such as `Flashers`, `Walls`, and `Streetlights`. Some kinds of `Things` block `Robots` from entering or exiting an `Intersection`. It is possible to build `Things` that are one-way, blocking `Robots` from entering but not exiting (or vice versa) an `Intersection`.

Constructor Summary

`Intersection(City aCity, int aStreet, int anAvenue)`

Construct a new `Intersection`.

Method Summary

`protected void addSim(Sim theThing)`

Add a `Sim` to this `Intersection`.

`int countThings()`

Determine the number of `Things` currently on this `Intersection`.

`int countThings(IPredicate pred)`

Determine the number of `Things` currently on this `Intersection` that match the given predicate.

`protected boolean entryIsBlocked(Direction dir)`

Determine whether something on this `Intersection` blocks `Robots` from entering this `Intersection` from the given direction.

`IIterate<Light> examineLights(IPredicate aPredicate)`

Examine all the `Light` objects on this `Intersection` that match the given predicate, one at a time.

`IIterate<Robot> examineRobots(IPredicate aPredicate)`

Examine all the `Robot` objects on this `Intersection` that match the given predicate, one at a time.

`IIterate<Thing> examineThings(IPredicate aPredicate)`

Examine all the `Thing` objects on this `Intersection` that match the given predicate, one at a time.

`IIterate<Thing> examineThings()`

Examine all the `Thing` objects on this `Intersection`, one at a time.

`protected boolean exitIsBlocked(Direction dir)`

Determine whether something on this `Intersection` blocks `Robots` from exiting the `Intersection`.

`int getAvenue()`

Get the avenue intersecting this `Intersection`.

`protected Intersection getIntersection()`

Return a reference to this `Intersection`.

`String getLabel()`

Get the label for this `Intersection`.

`Intersection getNeighbor(Direction dir)`

Get the `Intersection` neighboring this one in the given direction.

`int getStreet()`

Get the street intersecting this `Intersection`.

`protected void removeSim(Sim s)`

Remove the given `Sim` (`Robot`, `Flasher`, `Streetlight`, `Wall`, and so on) from this `Intersection`.

`protected void save(String indent, java.io.PrintWriter out)`

Save a representation of this `Intersection` to an output stream.

`void setLabel(String aLabel)`

Set a label for this `Intersection`.

`String toString()`

Report the internal state of this `Intersection`.

IPredicate

`public interface IPredicate`

A predicate says whether something is true or false about a `Sim`. A class implementing the `IPredicate` interface does this via the `isOK` method, which returns `true` if some condition about a `Sim` is true, and `false` otherwise.

A typical use for a predicate is to find a certain kind of `Thing` for a `Robot` to examine—for example, a `Light`. To do this, define a class implementing `IPredicate` as follows:

```
public class ALightPred implements Predicate
{  //return true if the Sim passed is a Light, false otherwise
   public boolean isOK(Sim s)
   {  return s instanceof Light;
   }
}
```

In a subclass of `Robot`, invoke the `examineThings` method like this:

```
Light light = this.examineThing(new ALightPred()).next();
```

which will return a Light from the current Intersection, if there is one, and throw an exception if there is not. The isBesideThing method in the Robot class can be used to determine if the specified kind of Thing is available.

The IPredicate class also defines a number of useful predicates as constants. For example, to pick up a Thing that is a Flasher, one could write

```
karel.pickThing(IPredicate.aFlasher);
```

Field Summary

static IPredicate aFlasher

A predicate to test whether something is a Flasher.

static IPredicate aLight

A predicate to test whether something is a Light.

static IPredicate anyFlasher

A predicate to test whether something is a Flasher or a subclass of Flasher.

static IPredicate anyLight

A predicate to test whether something is a Light or a subclass of Light.

static IPredicate anyRobot

A predicate to test whether something is a Robot or a subclass of Robot.

static IPredicate anyStreetlight

A predicate to test whether something is a Streetlight or a subclass of Streetlight.

static IPredicate anyThing

A predicate to test whether something is a Thing or a subclass of Thing.

static Predicate anyWall

A predicate to test whether something is a Wall or a subclass of Wall.

static Predicate aRobot

A predicate to test whether something is a Robot.

static Predicate aStreetlight

A predicate to test whether something is a Streetlight.

`static Predicate aThing`

A predicate to test whether something is a `Thing`.

`static Predicate aWall`

A predicate to test whether something is a `Wall`.

`static Predicate canBeCarried`

A predicate to test whether the `Thing` is something that a `Robot` can carry.

Method Summary

`boolean isOK(Sim theSim)`

Returns `true` if a certain condition is true about `theSim`, `false` otherwise.

Light

`public abstract class Light extends Thing`

A `Light` is a kind of `Thing` that can be turned on to make it brighter and turned off to make it darker. Some `Lights` can be moved (`Flasher`) while others can't (`Streetlight`).

The `Light` class itself is abstract, meaning programmers cannot construct an instance of `Light`. It must be extended to create a class that can be instantiated. This class does define a common interface for all `Lights` so that any `Light` may be turned on or off without knowing what specific kind of `Light` it is (polymorphism).

Constructor Summary

`Light(City aCity, int aStreet, int anAvenue)`

Construct a new `Light` with the same default appearance as a `Thing`.

```
Light(City aCity, int aStreet, int anAvenue, Direction
   orientation, boolean canBeMoved, Icon anIcon)
```

Construct a new `Light`.

`Light(Robot heldBy)`

Construct a new `Light` held by a `Robot`.

Method Summary

`boolean isOn()`

Determine whether the `Light` is turned on.

`void turnOff()`

Turn the `Light` off.

`void turnOn()`

Turn the `Light` on.

Robot

`public class Robot extends Sim implements ILabel, IColor`

`Robots` exist on a rectangular grid of roads and can move, turn left ninety degrees, pick things up, carry things, and put things down. A `Robot` knows which avenue and street it is on and which direction it is facing. Its speed can be set and queried.

More advanced features include determining if it is safe to move forward, examining `Things` on the same `Intersection` as themselves, and determining if they are beside a specific kind of `Thing`. They can pick up and put down specific kinds of `Things` and determine how many `Things` they are carrying.

Constructor Summary

`Robot(City aCity, int aStreet, int anAvenue, Direction aDir)`

Construct a new `Robot` at the given location in the given `City` with nothing in its backpack.

`Robot(City c, int str, int ave, Direction aDir, int numThings)`

Construct a new `Robot` at the given location in the given `City` with the given number of `Things` in its backpack. Override `makeThing` to customize the kind of `Thing` added to the backpack.

Method Summary

`protected void breakRobot(String msg)`

This method is called when this `Robot` does something illegal such as trying to move through a `Wall` or picking up a nonexistent object. An exception is thrown that stops this `Robot`'s operation.

`boolean canPickThing()`

Determine whether this `Robot` is on the same `Intersection` as a `Thing` it can pick up.

`int countThingsInBackpack()`

How many `Thing` objects are in this `Robot`'s backpack?

`int countThingsInBackpack(IPredicate kindOfThing)`

How many of a specific kind of `Thing` are in this `Robot`'s backpack?

`IIterate<Light> examineLights()`

Examine all the `Light` objects that are on the same `Intersection` as this `Robot`, one at a time.

`IIterate<Robot> examineRobots()`

Examine all the `Robot` objects that are on the same `Intersection` as this `Robot`, one at a time.

`IIterate<Thing> examineThings(IPredicate aPredicate)`

Examine all the `Thing` objects that are on the same `Intersection` as this `Robot` and match the given predicate, one at a time.

`boolean frontIsClear()`

Can this `Robot` move forward to the next `Intersection` safely?

`int getAvenue()`

On which avenue is this `Robot`?

`Direction getDirection()`

Which `Direction` is this `Robot` facing?

`String getLabel()`

What is the string labeling this `Robot`?

`double getSpeed()`

How many moves and/or turns does this `Robot` complete in one second?

`int getStreet()`

On which street is this `Robot`?

`double getTransparency()`

Get this `Robot`'s transparency.

`boolean isBesideThing(IPredicate aPredicate)`

Determine whether this `Robot` is on the same `Intersection` as one or more instances of the specified kind of `Thing`.

`protected Thing makeThing(int nOf, int total)`

Make a new `Thing` to place in this `Robot`'s backpack. Override this method in a subclass to control what kind of `Thing` is made when a `Robot` is constructed with `Things` in its backpack.

`void move()`

Move this `Robot` from the `Intersection` it currently occupies to the next `Intersection` in the `Direction` it is currently facing, leaving it facing the same `Direction`.

`void pickThing()`

Attempt to pick up a movable `Thing` from the current `Intersection`.

`void pickThing(IPredicate kindOfThing)`

Attempt to pick up a particular kind of `Thing` from the `Intersection` this `Robot` currently occupies.

`void pickThing(Thing theThing)`

Attempt to pick up a particular `Thing` from the `Intersection` this `Robot` currently occupies.

`void putThing()`

Take something out of this `Robot`'s backpack and put it down on the `Intersection` this `Robot` currently occupies.

`void putThing(IPredicate kindOfThing)`

Attempt to take a particular kind of `Thing` out of this `Robot`'s backpack and put it down on the `Intersection` the `Robot` currently occupies.

`void putThing(Thing theThing)`

Attempt to put down a particular `Thing` on the `Intersection` this `Robot` currently occupies.

`protected void save(String indent, java.io.PrintWriter out)`

Save a representation of this `Robot` to an output stream.

`void setLabel(String theLabel)`

Set a label to identify this `Robot`.

`void setSpeed(double movesPerSecond)`

Set this `Robot`'s speed.

`void setTransparency(double trans)`

Set this `Robot`'s transparency.

`void turnLeft()`

Turn this `Robot` left by 90 degrees or one-quarter turn.

RobotRC

`public class RobotRC extends Robot`

A remote control robot, `RobotRC` for short, can be directed from a computer keyboard. The `City`'s view must have the keyboard focus when the program is running for the `Robot` to receive the instructions from the keyboard. When the `City`'s view has the focus, it will have a thin black outline. Shift the focus between the speed control and the start/stop button on the `City`'s view with the tab key.

Constructor Summary

`RobotRC(City aCity, int aStreet, int anAvenue, Direction aDir)`

Construct a new `RobotRC` with nothing in its backpack.

```
RobotRC(City aCity, int aStreet, int anAvenue, Direction aDir,
   int numThings)
```

Construct a new `RobotRC`.

Method Summary

`protected void keyTyped(char key)`

This method makes the robot respond to the user's key presses as shown in Table E-1. It may be overridden to make the robot respond differently.

(table E-1) *Keystroke responses*

Keys	Response
m, M	move
r, R	turn right
l, L	turn left
u, U	pick up a `Thing`
d, D	put down a `Thing`

RobotSE

`public class RobotSE extends Robot`

A new kind of `Robot` with extended capabilities, such as `turnAround` and `turnRight`.

Constructor Summary

`RobotSE(City aCity, int aStreet, int anAvenue, Direction aDir)`

Construct a new `RobotSE` with nothing in its backpack.

```
RobotSE(City aCity, int aStreet, int anAvenue, Direction aDir,
   int numThings)
```

Construct a new `RobotSE`.

Method Summary

`boolean isFacingEast()`

Determine whether this `Robot` is facing east.

`boolean isFacingNorth()`

Determine whether this `Robot` is facing north.

`boolean isFacingSouth()`

Determine whether this `Robot` is facing south.

`boolean isFacingWest()`

Determine whether this `Robot` is facing west.

`void move(int howFar)`

Move the given distance.

`void pickAllThings()`

Pick up all the `Things` that can be carried from the current `Intersection`.

`void pickAllThings(Predicate kindOfThing)`

Pick up all of the specified kind of `Things` from the current `Intersection`.

`void putAllThings()`

Put down all the `Things` in this `Robot`'s backpack on the current `Intersection`.

`void putAllThings(Predicate kindOfThing)`

Put down all of the specified kind of `Things` from the `Robot`'s backpack on the current `Intersection`.

`void turnAround()`

Turn this `Robot` around so it faces the opposite `Direction`.

`void turnLeft(int numTimes)`

Turn this `Robot` left the given number of times.

`void turnRight()`

Turn this `Robot` 90 degrees to the right.

`void turnRight(int numTimes)`

Turn this `Robot` right the given number of times.

Sim

`public abstract class Sim extends java.lang.Object`

A `Sim` is an element of a `City` that participates in the simulation, namely a `Thing` (such as `Walls` or `Lights`), a `Robot`, or an `Intersection`.

Since this class is abstract it cannot be instantiated; only subclasses may be instantiated. This class exists both to ensure that basic services required for the simulation are present and to provide common implementations for required several services.

Constructor Summary

`Sim(City aCity, int aStreet, int anAvenue, Direction orientation, Icon theIcon)`

Construct a new `Sim`.

Method Summary

`Icon getIcon()`

Return the icon used to display the visible characteristics of this `Sim`, based on the `Sim`'s current state.

`protected abstract Intersection getIntersection()`

Return the `Intersection` where this `Sim` is located.

`protected void keyTyped(char key)`

This method is called when a key is typed and keyboard input is directed to karel's world (the map, as opposed to a different window or the controls for karel's world).

`protected void notifyObservers()`

Notify any observers of this `Sim` (for instance, the user interface) that it has changed.

`protected void notifyObservers(java.lang.Object changeInfo)`

Notify any observers of this `Sim` (for instance, the user interface) that it has changed.

`void setIcon(Icon theIcon)`

Set the icon used to display this `Sim`.

Streetlight

`public class Streetlight extends Light`

A `Streetlight` is a kind of `Light` that lights an intersection. Like all `Lights`, it can be turned on and off. A `Streetlight` cannot be moved by a `Robot`.

Constructor Summary

`Streetlight(City city, int aStreet, int anAvenue, Direction corner)`

Construct a new `Streetlight`.

`Streetlight(City city, int aStreet, int anAvenue, Direction corner, boolean isOn)`

Construct a new `Streetlight`.

Method Summary

`protected void save(String indent, java.io.PrintWriter out)`

Save a representation of this `StreetLight` to an output stream.

`void turnOff()`

Turn the `Streetlight` off.

`void turnOn()`

Turn the `Streetlight` on.

Thing

`public class Thing extends Sim`

A `Thing` is something that can exist on an `Intersection`. All `Things` have a location (avenue and street). Some `Things` can be picked up and moved by a `Robot` (`Flashers`) while others cannot (`Streetlights`, `Walls`).

In addition to a location, all `Things` have an orientation, although it is common for the orientation to always have a default value. Examples where that is not the case include a `Wall` where the orientation determines which exit or entry into an `Intersection` is blocked, and a `Streetlight` where the orientation determines which corner of the `Intersection` it occupies.

Constructor Summary

`Thing(City city, int aStreet, int anAvenue)`

Construct a new `Thing` with a default appearance that can be carried.

`Thing(City aCity, int aStreet, int anAvenue, Direction orientation)`

Construct a new `Thing` with a default appearance that can be carried, in the given orientation.

`Thing(City aCity, int aStreet, int anAvenue, Direction orientation, boolean canBeMoved, Icon anIcon)`

Construct a new `Thing` with an appearance defined by `anIcon`.

`Thing(Robot heldBy)`

Construct a new `Thing` held by the given `Robot`.

Method Summary

`boolean blocksIntersectionEntry(Direction entryDir)`

Does this `Thing` block the entry of this `Intersection` from the given `Direction`?

`boolean blocksIntersectionExit(Direction exitDir)`

Does this `Thing` block the exit of this `Intersection` in the given `Direction`?

`boolean canBeCarried()`

Can this `Thing` be picked up, carried, and put down by a `Robot`?

`protected Intersection getIntersection()`

Return a reference to this `Thing`'s `Intersection`.

`protected void save(String indent, java.io.PrintWriter out)`

Save a representation of this `Thing` to an output stream.

`void setBlocksEntry(boolean north, boolean south, boolean east, boolean west)`

Set whether this `Thing` blocks a `Robot`'s entry from the given `Directions`.

`void setBlocksEntry(Direction aDir, boolean block)`

Set whether this `Thing` blocks a `Robot`'s entry from the given `Direction`.

`void setBlocksExit(boolean north, boolean south, boolean east, boolean west)`

Set whether this `Thing` blocks a `Robot`'s exit from the given `Directions`.

`void setBlocksExit(Direction aDir, boolean block)`

Set whether this `Thing` blocks a `Robot`'s exit from the given `Direction`.

`void setCanBeCarried(boolean canCarry)`

Set whether this `Thing` can be picked up and carried by a `Robot`.

Wall

```
public class Wall extends Thing
```

A `Wall` will block the movement of a `Robot` into or out of the `Intersection` that contains it, depending on the `Robot`'s direction of travel and the orientation of the `Wall`.

Constructor Summary

```
Wall(City city, int aStreet, int anAvenue, Direction orientation)
```

Construct a new `Wall`.

Method Summary

```
protected void save(String indent, java.io.PrintWriter out)
```

Save a representation of this `Wall` to an output stream.

Index

Note: page numbers in **boldface** type indicate key terms.

Special Characters

A

D

F

G

H

I

J

K

L

M

N

T

U

V

W

Z

Sun Microsystems, Inc. Binary Code License Agreement for the JAVA 2 PLATFORM STANDARD EDITION RUNTIME ENVIRONMENT 5.0

SUN MICROSYSTEMS, INC. ("SUN") IS WILLING TO LICENSE THE SOFTWARE IDENTIFIED BELOW TO YOU ONLY UPON THE CONDITION THAT YO ACCEPT ALL OF THE TERMS CONTAINED IN THIS BINARY CODE LICENSE AGREEMENT AND SUPPLEMENTAL LICENSE TERMS (COLLECTIVEL "AGREEMENT"). PLEASE READ THE AGREEMENT CAREFULLY. BY DOWNLOADING OR INSTALLING THIS SOFTWARE, YOU ACCEPT THE TERMS C THE AGREEMENT. INDICATE ACCEPTANCE BY SELECTING THE "ACCEPT" BUTTON AT THE BOTTOM OF THE AGREEMENT. IF YOU ARE NO WILLING TO BE BOUND BY ALL THE TERMS, SELECT THE "DECLINE" BUTTON AT THE BOTTOM OF THE AGREEMENT AND THE DOWNLOAD O INSTALL PROCESS WILL NOT CONTINUE.

1. **DEFINITIONS.** "Software" means the identified above in binary form, any other machine readable materials (including, but not limited to, libraries, source file header files, and data files), any updates or error corrections provided by Sun, and any user manuals, programming guides and other documentation provided to yc by Sun under this Agreement. "Programs" mean Java applets and applications intended to run on the Java 2 Platform Standard Edition (J2SE platform) platform c Java-enabled general purpose desktop computers and servers.
2. **LICENSE TO USE.** Subject to the terms and conditions of this Agreement, including, but not limited to the Java Technology Restrictions of the Supplement License Terms, Sun grants you a non-exclusive, non-transferable, limited license without license fees to reproduce and use internally Software complete and unmod fied for the sole purpose of running Programs. Additional licenses for developers and/or publishers are granted in the Supplemental License Terms.
3. **RESTRICTIONS.** Software is confidential and copyrighted. Title to Software and all associated intellectual property rights is retained by Sun and/or its licensor Unless enforcement is prohibited by applicable law, you may not modify, decompile, or reverse engineer Software. You acknowledge that Licensed Software is nc designed or intended for use in the design, construction, operation or maintenance of any nuclear facility. Sun Microsystems, Inc. disclaims any express or implie warranty of fitness for such uses. No right, title or interest in or to any trademark, service mark, logo or trade name of Sun or its licensors is granted under th Agreement. Additional restrictions for developers and/or publishers licenses are set forth in the Supplemental License Terms.
4. **LIMITED WARRANTY.** Sun warrants to you that for a period of ninety (90) days from the date of purchase, as evidenced by a copy of the receipt, the media o which Software is furnished (if any) will be free of defects in materials and workmanship under normal use. Except for the foregoing, Software is provided "AS IS" Your exclusive remedy and Sun's entire liability under this limited warranty will be at Sun's option to replace Software media or refund the fee paid for Softwar Any implied warranties on the Software are limited to 90 days. Some states do not allow limitations on duration of an implied warranty, so the above may not app to you. This limited warranty gives you specific legal rights. You may have others, which vary from state to state.
5. **DISCLAIMER OF WARRANTY.** UNLESS SPECIFIED IN THIS AGREEMENT, ALL EXPRESS OR IMPLIED CONDITIONS, REPRESENTATIONS AN WARRANTIES, INCLUDING ANY IMPLIED WARRANTY OF MERCHANTABILITY, FITNESS FOR A PARTICULAR PURPOSE OR NON-INFRINGEMEN ARE DISCLAIMED, EXCEPT TO THE EXTENT THAT THESE DISCLAIMERS ARE HELD TO BE LEGALLY INVALID.
6. **LIMITATION OF LIABILITY.** TO THE EXTENT NOT PROHIBITED BY LAW, IN NO EVENT WILL SUN OR ITS LICENSORS BE LIABLE FOR ANY LOS REVENUE, PROFIT OR DATA, OR FOR SPECIAL, INDIRECT, CONSEQUENTIAL, INCIDENTAL OR PUNITIVE DAMAGES, HOWEVER CAUSE REGARDLESS OF THE THEORY OF LIABILITY, ARISING OUT OF OR RELATED TO THE USE OF OR INABILITY TO USE SOFTWARE, EVEN IF SU HAS BEEN ADVISED OF THE POSSIBILITY OF SUCH DAMAGES. In no event will Sun's liability to you, whether in contract, tort (including negligence), or oth erwise, exceed the amount paid by you for Software under this Agreement. The foregoing limitations will apply even if the above stated warranty fails of its essenti purpose. Some states do not allow the exclusion of incidental or consequential damages, so some of the terms above may not be applicable to you.
7. **TERMINATION.** This Agreement is effective until terminated. You may terminate this Agreement at any time by destroying all copies of Software. This Agreemer will terminate immediately without notice from Sun if you fail to comply with any provision of this Agreement. Either party may terminate this Agreement immed ately should any Software become, or in either party's opinion be likely to become, the subject of a claim of infringement of any intellectual property right. Upo Termination, you must destroy all copies of Software.
8. **EXPORT REGULATIONS.** All Software and technical data dealivered under this Agreement are subject to US export control laws and may be subject to export o import regulations in other countries. You agree to comply strictly with all such laws and regulations and acknowledge that you have the responsibility to obtai such licenses to export, re-export, or import as may be required after delivery to you.
9. **TRADEMARKS AND LOGOS.** You acknowledge and agree as between you and Sun that Sun owns the SUN, SOLARIS, JAVA, JINI, FORTE, and iPLANE trademarks and all SUN, SOLARIS, JAVA, JINI, FORTE, and iPLANET-related trademarks, service marks, logos and other brand designations ("Sun Marks"), an you agree to comply with the Sun Trademark and Logo Usage Requirements currently located at http://www.sun.com/policies/trademarks. Any use you make of th Sun Marks inures to Sun's benefit.
10. **U.S. GOVERNMENT RESTRICTED RIGHTS.** If Software is being acquired by or on behalf of the U.S. Government or by a U.S. Government prime contractor o subcontractor (at any tier), then the Government's rights in Software and accompanying documentation will be only as set forth in this Agreement; this is in acco dance with 48 CFR 227.7201 through 227.7202-4 (for Department of Defense (DOD) acquisitions) and with 48 CFR 2.101 and 12.212 (for non-DOD acquisitions)
11. **GOVERNING LAW.** Any action related to this Agreement will be governed by California law and controlling U.S. federal law. No choice of law rules of an jurisdiction will apply.
12. **SEVERABILITY.** If any provision of this Agreement is held to be unenforceable, this Agreement will remain in effect with the provision omitted, unless omissio would frustrate the intent of the parties, in which case this Agreement will immediately terminate.
13. **INTEGRATION.** This Agreement is the entire agreement between you and Sun relating to its subject matter. It supersedes all prior or contemporaneous oral o written communications, proposals, representations and warranties and prevails over any conflicting or additional terms of any quote, order, acknowledgment, o other communication between the parties relating to its subject matter during the term of this Agreement. No modification of this Agreement will be binding, unles in writing and signed by an authorized representative of each party.

SUPPLEMENTAL LICENSE TERMS

These Supplemental License Terms add to or modify the terms of the Binary Code License Agreement. Capitalized terms not defined in these Supplemental Terms sha have the same meanings ascribed to them in the Binary Code License Agreement . These Supplemental Terms shall supersede any inconsistent or conflicting terms in th Binary Code License Agreement, or in any license contained within the Software.

A. **Software Internal Use and Development License Grant.** Subject to the terms and conditions of this Agreement and restrictions and exceptions set forth in the Softwar "README" file, including, but not limited to the Java Technology Restrictions of these Supplemental Terms, Sun grants you a non-exclusive, non-transferable, limite license without fees to reproduce internally and use internally the Software complete and unmodified for the purpose of designing, developing, and testing you Programs.

B. **License to Distribute Software.** Subject to the terms and conditions of this Agreement and restrictions and exceptions set forth in the Software README file, includ ing, but not limited to the Java Technology Restrictions of these Supplemental Terms, Sun grants you a non-exclusive, non-transferable, limited license without fee to reproduce and distribute the Software, provided that (i) you distribute the Software complete and unmodified and only bundled as part of, and for the sole pur pose of running, your Programs, (ii) the Programs add significant and primary functionality to the Software, (iii) you do not distribute additional software intende to replace any component(s) of the Software, (iv) you do not remove or alter any proprietary legends or notices contained in the Software, (v) you only distribute th Software subject to a license agreement that protects Sun's interests consistent with the terms contained in this Agreement, and (vi) you agree to defend and indem nify Sun and its licensors from and against any damages, costs, liabilities, settlement amounts and/or expenses (including attorneys' fees) incurred in connection wit any claim, lawsuit or action by any third party that arises or results from the use or distribution of any and all Programs and/or Software.

C. **Java Technology Restrictions.** You may not create, modify, or change the behavior of, or authorize your licensees to create, modify, or change the behavior of, classes interfaces, or subpackages that are in any way identified as "java", "javax", "sun" or similar convention as specified by Sun in any naming convention designation.

D. **Source Code.** Software may contain source code that, unless expressly licensed for other purposes, is provided solely for reference purposes pursuant to the terms o this Agreement. Source code may not be redistributed unless expressly provided for in this Agreement.

E. **Third Party Code.** Third Party Code. Additional copyright notices and license terms applicable to portions of the Software are set forth ir the THIRDPARTYLICENSEREADME.txt file. In addition to any terms and conditions of any third party opensource/freeware license identified in th THIRDPARTYLICENSEREADME.txt file, the disclaimer of warranty and limitation of liability provisions in paragraphs 5 and 6 of the Binary Code License Agreement shal apply to all Software in this distribution.

For inquiries please contact: Sun Microsystems, Inc., 4150 Network Circle, Santa Clara, California 95054, U.S.A.

(LFI#141623/Form ID#011801)